MICROSOFT® OFFICE 97 PROFESSIONAL

MICROSOFT® CERTIFIED BLUE RIBBON EDITION

Pamela R. Toliver

Yvonne Johnson

Philip A. Koneman
Colorado Christian University

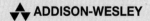
ADDISON-WESLEY

An imprint of Addison Wesley Longman, Inc.

Reading, Massachusetts • Menlo Park, California • New York • Harlow, England
Don Mills, Ontario • Sydney • Mexico City • Madrid • Amsterdam

Acquisitions Editor: Anita Devine
Editorial Assistant: Holly Rioux
Senior Marketing Manager: Tom Ziolkowski
Senior Marketing Coordinator: Deanna Storey
Production Supervision: Patty Mahtani and Diane Freed
Copyediting: Krista Hansing, Barb Terry, and Robin Drake
Technical Editing: Pauline Johnson and Emily Kim
Proofreader: Holly McLean-Aldis
Indexer: Irv Hershman
Composition and Art: Gillian Hall, The Aardvark Group
Cover Illustration: © Frederic Joos/SIS
Cover Designer: Anthony Saizon
Design Supervisor: Regina Hagen
Manufacturing: Sheila Spinney

Microsoft, Word, Excel, Access, and PowerPoint are registered trademarks of Microsoft Corporation.

0-201-43867-4 (Perfect bound)
0-201-43866-6 (Spiral)

Ordering from the SELECT System
For more information on ordering and pricing policies for the SELECT Lab Series and supplements, please contact your Addison Wesley Longman sales representative or fax 1-800-284-8292 or email: exam@awl.com. Questions? Email: is@awl.com

Addison-Wesley Publishing Company
One Jacob Way
Reading, MA 01867
http://hepg@awl.com/select

1 2 3 4 5 6 7 8 9 10-DOW-01009998

Microsoft Certified

Welcome to the *Microsoft® Certified Blue Ribbon Edition of Select: Office 97 Professional*. This project-based visual text is approved courseware for the Microsoft® Office User Specialist program. After completing the projects in this book, students will be prepared to take the Proficient level exams for Word 97 and Excel 97, and the Expert level exams for Access 97 and PowerPoint 97. Successful completion of these exams gives students marketable skills that they can use for summer jobs or after they graduate. The *Microsoft® Certified Blue Ribbon Edition of Select: Office 97 Professional* allows students to explore the essentials of software applications and learn the basic skills that are the foundation for business and academic success. Step-by-step exercises and full-color illustrations show students what to do, how to do it, and the exact result of their action.

We have updated the *Microsoft® Certified Blue Ribbon Edition of Select: Office 97 Professional* to include the latest versions of Office 97 software applications. New to the *Blue Ribbon Edition* is the Windows 95 Active Desktop with Windows 98, Internet Explorer 4.0, and many more review exercises and assignments.

QWIZ Assessment Software is a task-based test that simulates the Office 97 environment and tests students on measurable skills using the features of Office 97.

The Select Lab Series

Greater access to ideas and information is changing the way people work and learn. With Microsoft Office 97 software applications, you have greater integration capabilities and access to Internet resources than ever before. The *Select Lab Series* manuals help you take advantage of these valuable resources, with special assignments devoted to the Internet.

Dozens of proven and class-tested lab manuals are available within the *Select Lab Series*, from the latest operating systems and browsers to the most popular applications software for word processing, spreadsheets, databases, presentation graphics, and integrated packages to HTML and programming. The *Select Lab Series* also offers individually bound texts for each *Office 97* application. Knowing that you have specific needs for your lab course, we offer the quick and affordable TechSuite program. For your lab course, you can choose the combination of software lab manuals in *Brief*, *Standard*, or *Plus* Editions that best suits your classroom needs. Your choice of lab manuals will be sent to the bookstore, in a TechSuite box, allowing students to purchase all books in one convenient package at a significant discount.

In addition, your school may qualify for full Office 97 upgrades or licenses. Your Addison Wesley Longman representative will be happy to work with you and your bookstore manager to provide the most current menu of application software in addition to *Select Lab Series* offerings. Your representative will also outline the ordering process, and provide pricing, ISBNs, and delivery information. Call 1-800-447-2226 or visit our Web site at http://hepg.awl.com and click on ordering information.

Organization

The *Microsoft® Certified Blue Ribbon Edition of Select: Office 97 Professional* is organized into five parts: Overview of Windows 95, Outlook, Internet Explorer 4.0, and Windows 95 Active Desktop and Windows 98; Word 97; Excel 97; Access 97; and PowerPoint 97.

Before launching into the Office 97 applications, the *Microsoft® Certified Blue Ribbon Edition of Select: Office 97 Professional* familiarizes students with the operating system and Internet functionality with an Overview of Windows 95, Outlook, Internet Explorer and Windows 95 Active Desktop and Windows 98. Students learn the basics of starting Windows 95, using a mouse, using the basic features of Windows 95, organizing files, using Outlook for scheduling, recording tasks in the task list, sending e-mail, and using Internet Explorer 4.0. What's more, in case your computers are set up to run Windows 95 Active Desktop or Windows 98, we have included a new section that shows what the different desktops may look like, what makes them similar, and what differentiates them.

Each of the four *major* Office 97 applications is covered in-depth in five or six projects that teach beginning through intermediate skills. Each section begins with an Overview that introduces the basic concepts of the application and provides hands-on instructions to put students to work using the application immediately. As they work through the projects, students learn problem-solving techniques that provide practical, relevant, real-life business scenarios.

The *Microsoft® Certified Blue Ribbon Edition of Select: Office 97 Professional* provides several projects to help students learn how to use the integration capabilities in Office 97. In the Integration projects, students are introduced to the exciting possibilities of document creation using the data-sharing capabilities available with OLE (Object Linking and Embedding).

4

PROJECT

Viewing and Editing a Presentation

Most of the presentations you create are designed to provide powerful visuals to enhance oral presentations. Slides in a presentation can be formatted and shown on-screen by individuals or projected on an audiovisual screen or flat surface as you present a report to an audience.

Showing your presentations with style has a positive impact on your audience. The PowerPoint slide show feature enables you to show your presentation on a computer screen. Seeing your presentation "live" the first time can be quite satisfying—and exciting. In this project, you learn how to dress up your presentation for on-screen viewing and how to use Slide Sorter view to rearrange slides in the presentation.

Objectives

After completing this project, you will be able to:

➤ Present a slide show
➤ Use the slide show shortcut menu
➤ Rearrange slides in a presentation
➤ Add slide transitions
➤ Animate text
➤ Expand slides
➤ Hide slides and display hidden slides

PP-118

The Introduction sets up the real-world scenario that serves as the environment for learning.

Clearly defined and measurable **Objectives** give students direction and focus they need to learn new material.

The **Challenge** introduces the case, outlines the goal of the project, and shows the document, spreadsheet, database, or presentation to be created.

The **Solution** describes the plan for completing the project, which consists of tasks leading to the final product.

An illustration shows the outcome of the project.

The Setup tells the students exactly which settings should be chosen to match those in the illustrations.

Project 4: Viewing and Editing a Presentation   PP-119

The Challenge

Francesca Savoy has reviewed the presentation *The Willows* and has approved the design, graphics, and format of slides in the presentation. She now asks that the presentation be tweaked into its final form so that she can present it to the managers at their next meeting.

The Solution

To get the presentation *The Willows* into shape, you need to view the presentation as a slide show and then use Slide Sorter view to make final edits to the presentation. Figure 4.1 shows the final presentation in Slide Sorter view.

Figure 4.1

The Setup

You're switching to a different view for many of the activities in this section, and you're also going to be using the slide show feature in PowerPoint. As a result, you need to select some different settings to ensure that your screen will match the illustrations shown in this project.

When you switch to Slide Sorter view, make sure that the Standard and Slide Sorter toolbars display (As shown in Task 3, Step 1 of this project). If you don't see them, choose View, Toolbars, and then select them. Close the Common Tasks toolbar if it's open.

vi

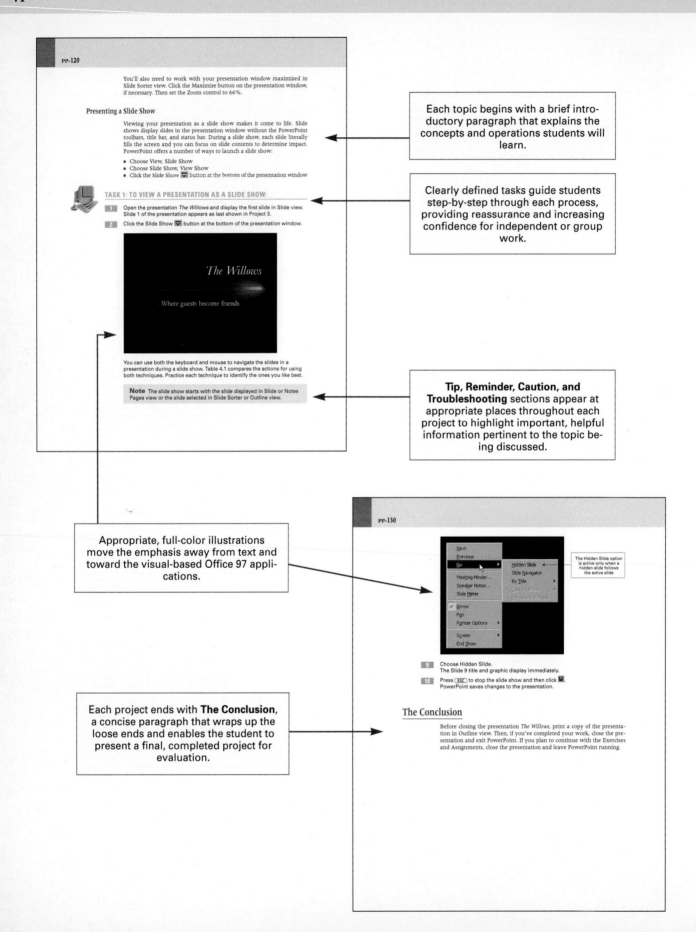

You'll also need to work with your presentation window maximized in Slide Sorter view. Click the Maximize button on the presentation window, if necessary. Then set the Zoom control to 66%.

Presenting a Slide Show

Viewing your presentation as a slide show makes it come to life. Slide shows display slides in the presentation window without the PowerPoint toolbars, title bar, and status bar. During a slide show, each slide literally fills the screen and you can focus on slide contents to determine impact. PowerPoint offers a number of ways to launch a slide show:

- Choose View, Slide Show
- Choose Slide Show, View Show
- Click the Slide Show button at the bottom of the presentation window

TASK 1: TO VIEW A PRESENTATION AS A SLIDE SHOW:

1. Open the presentation *The Willows* and display the first slide in Slide view. Slide 1 of the presentation appears as last shown in Project 3.
2. Click the Slide Show button at the bottom of the presentation window.

The Willows

Where guests become friends

You can use both the keyboard and mouse to navigate the slides in a presentation during a slide show. Table 4.1 compares the actions for using both techniques. Practice each technique to identify the ones you like best.

Note The slide show starts with the slide displayed in Slide or Notes Pages view or the slide selected in Slide Sorter or Outline view.

Each topic begins with a brief introductory paragraph that explains the concepts and operations students will learn.

Clearly defined tasks guide students step-by-step through each process, providing reassurance and increasing confidence for independent or group work.

Tip, Reminder, Caution, and Troubleshooting sections appear at appropriate places throughout each project to highlight important, helpful information pertinent to the topic being discussed.

Appropriate, full-color illustrations move the emphasis away from text and toward the visual-based Office 97 applications.

Next
Previous
Go
   Hidden Slide
   Slide Navigator
Meeting Minder...   By Title
Speaker Notes...   Custom Show
Slide Meter   Previously Viewed

✓ Arrow
Pen
Pointer Options
Screen
End Show

The Hidden Slide option is active only when a hidden slide follows the active slide

9. Choose Hidden Slide.
The Slide 9 title and graphic display immediately.

10. Press ESC to stop the slide show and then click
PowerPoint saves changes to the presentation.

The Conclusion

Before closing the presentation *The Willows*, print a copy of the presentation in Outline view. Then, if you've completed your work, close the presentation and exit PowerPoint. If you plan to continue with the Exercises and Assignments, close the presentation and leave PowerPoint running.

Each project ends with **The Conclusion**, a concise paragraph that wraps up the loose ends and enables the student to present a final, completed project for evaluation.

Summary and Exercises

Summary

- PowerPoint enables you to create blank presentations formatted with no special design as well as presentations formatted using special designs called templates. You can change the look of slides in a presentation by selecting a different template design.
- AutoLayout formats make creating slides with preformatted text easier.
- You can add, delete, format, and select presentation text using many of the same techniques used in other Windows-based programs.
- PowerPoint displays presentation slides using four different views: Slide view, Slide Sorter view, Notes Pages view, and Outline view. Each view is designed to help you accomplish specific tasks.
- Presentations normally contain numerous slides; you can add slides and move from slide to slide in a presentation using a variety of different mouse and keyboard techniques.
- You save, open, close, and print presentations using many of the same procedures used in other Windows applications; you can print a variety of different presentation materials by selecting the desired format from the Print dialog box.

Key Terms and Operations

Key Terms	Operations
AutoLayout	add slides to a presentation
handouts	create, save, open, and close a presentation
Outline view	move around a presentation
Notes Pages view	print slides and handouts
Slide Sorter view	switch presentation views
template	use templates to change the look of a presentation

Study Questions

Multiple Choice

1. To create a new, blank presentation,
   a. simply launch PowerPoint—a new presentation automatically appears.
   b. choose New Presentation from the PowerPoint dialog box.
   c. select Blank presentation from the PowerPoint dialog box and press Enter.
   d. select Template from the PowerPoint dialog box and press Enter.

2. Slides added to a presentation are formatted using
   a. an AutoLayout format.
   b. text and title boxes.
   c. blank slides that resemble blank pieces of paper.
   d. outlines.

3. New slide layouts contain
   a. fields.
   b. placeholders.
   c. tables.
   d. templates.

PP-46

A **Summary** in bulleted-list format further reinforces the Objectives and the material presented in the project.

Key terms are boldface and italicized throughout each project, and then listed for handy review in the summary section at the end of the project.

Study questions (Multiple Choice, Short Answer, and For Discussion) bring the content of the project into focus again and allow for independent or group review of the material learned.

PP-48

8. How do you apply a template?

9. How do you open a presentation when you launch PowerPoint?

10. How do you move from one placeholder on a slide to another without using the mouse?

For Discussion

1. What are the four options in the PowerPoint dialog box when you launch PowerPoint and what does each option enable you to do?

2. How do you identify the material you want to print, and what options should you check if you're using a black-and-white printer?

3. What are the advantages of formatting a presentation by using a template?

4. What kind of presentations could you create with PowerPoint for your other classes?

Review Exercises

1. Creating, saving, and adding slides and text to presentations
Ruth Lindsey, Manager of The Willows Shops, has been asked to display the diversity of gift items available in different shops at The Willows. She has developed the preliminary outline shown in Figure 1.6 and asks you to create a presentation using the outline.

1 **The Willows Shops** • Where Exploring Becomes an Adventure	5 **Live Oak Gifts**
2 **The Newsstand** • Newspapers • Magazines • Recent Publications • The Willows Post Office	6 **Creative Cutlery** • A Wide Assortment of Kitchen Wares
	7 **Cherry Street Market** • Home Grown Produce • Natural Flora from the Carolinas
3 **Sindy's Sun Closet** • Swimsuits • Bathing Accessories • Lotions • Towels • Flippers	8 **Victorian Tea Room** • Victorian gifts and clothing • Victorian High Tea Served Daily
	9 **Ken's Kids** • Children's games and toys • Children's clothing
4 **Weeping Willow Gallery** • Paintings • Sculpture • Iron Works • Local Artists	10 **Appalachian Crafts** • Treasures from the Hills • Displays of local artists

Figure 1.6

Using PowerPoint, create a new blank presentation named *The Willows Shops*. Follow these instructions to complete the presentation:

1. Launch PowerPoint and create a new blank presentation that contains a title slide.

Review Exercises present hands-on tasks for building on the skills acquired in the project.

Project 1: Building a Presentation PP-51

5. Apply a template to the presentation.

6. Redisplay Slide view and review each slide, making adjustments to slide text and format based on the template you applied.

7. Save changes to the presentation and print a copy of the presentation as black and white slides with six slides per page.

8. Print a copy of the presentation outline.

9. Close the presentation, saving changes, and exit PowerPoint.

Assignments

1. Creating, formatting, and saving a multi-slide presentation
The Willows area of South Carolina features a number of festivals and attractions. Create a presentation named *Festivals and Attractions* that contains the slides pictured in Figure 1.10.

Figure 1.10

Apply the Blush template and view the presentation in all four views. Save the presentation and print a copy of the presentation as black-and-white handouts with three slides per page. Close the presentation and exit PowerPoint when you have completed your work.

2. Finding templates on the Internet
Search the PowerPoint Internet site and locate additional templates that you can use to format presentations. (Go to Microsoft's home page at WWW.Microsoft.com and then click on Products.) Download a template and apply it to the Festivals and Attractions presentation created in the preceding assignment. Save the presentation as a presentation named *Reformatted Festivals* and print a copy of the title slide. Check with your instructor or lab assistant for special instructions for storing templates.

Assignments invoke critical thinking and integration of project skills.

Approach

The *Microsoft® Certified Blue Ribbon Edition of Select: Office 97 Professional* uses a document-centered approach to learning that focuses on *The Willows*; a running case study that helps students understand how the applications are used in a business setting. Each project begins with a list of measurable **Objectives**, a realistic case scenario called **The Challenge**, a well-defined plan called **The Solution**, and an illustration of the final product. **The Setup** enables students to verify that the settings on the computer match those needed for the project.

The project is arranged in carefully divided, highly visual objective-based tasks that foster confidence and self-reliance. Each project closes with a wrap-up of the project called **The Conclusion**, followed by summary questions, exercises, and assignments geared to reinforcing the information taught throughout the project.

Other Features

In addition to the document-centered, visual approach of each project, this book contains the following features:

- An **Overview** of both Windows 95 and each software application, to help students feel comfortable and confident in the working environment.
- A **Function Reference Guide** for each application. Functions are arranged alphabetically rather than by menu.
- **Keycaps** and **toolbar button icons** within each step so students can quickly perform the required action.
- A comprehensive, well-organized end-of-the-project **Summary** and **Exercises** section for reviewing, integrating, and applying new skills.
- Results of each step are illustrated or described so students know that they are on the right track throughout the project.

Student Supplements

QWIZ Assessment Software is a network-based skills assessment-testing program that measures student proficiency with Windows 95, Word 97, Excel 97, Access 97, and PowerPoint 97. Professors select the tasks to be tested and get student results immediately. The test is taken in a simulated software environment. On-screen instructions require students to perform tasks just as though they were using the actual application. The program automatically records responses, assesses student accuracy and reports the resulting score both in a printout or disk file as well as to the instructor's gradebook. The students receive immediate feedback from the program, including learning why a particular task was scored as incorrect and what part of the lab manual to review.

Instructor Supplements

Instructors get extra support for this text from supplemental materials, including the Instructor's Resource CD-ROM with screen shots, diagrams, and tables from the text, and files that correspond to key figures in the book that can be used as electronic slides. Screen-by-screen steps in a project can be displayed in class or reviewed by students in the computer lab. The Instructor's Resource CD-ROM also includes the entire Instructor's Manual in Microsoft Word format, and a Computerized Test Bank to create printed tests, network tests, and self-assessment quizzes for the Internet. Student data files and completed data files for Review Exercises and Assignments are also on the Instructor's Resource CD-ROM. All files from the Instructor's Resource CD-ROM can be downloaded from our instructor's password-protected Web site at http://hepg.awl.com/select/instructor.

The Computerized Test Bank allows you to view and edit test bank questions, create multiple versions of tests, easily search and arrange questions in order of preference, add or modify test bank questions, administer tests on a network, and convert your tests to HTML and then post to the Web for students' practice use.

The Instructor's Manual includes a Test Bank and Transparency Masters for each project in the student text, as well as Expanded Student Objectives, Answers to Study Questions, and Additional Assessment Techniques. The Test Bank contains two separate tests with answers, and consists of multiple choice, true/false, and fill-in questions referenced to pages in the student text. Transparency Masters illustrate key concepts and screen captures from the text.

Acknowledgments

When a *team* combines their knowledge and skills to produce a work designed to meet the needs of students and professors across the country, they take on an unenviable challenge. To **Anita Devine** for the steady editorial focus needed to make the *Microsoft Certified Blue Ribbon Edition* happen. To **Phil Koneman**, Series Consulting Editor, your suggestions and comments were invaluable. Thanks to **Emily Kim** and **Pauline Johnson** who were more than just technical editors, but who also made sure things worked the way we said they would. To those in production, especially to **Gillian Hall**, **Diane Freed**, and **Pat Mahtani**, your efforts have paid off in a highly user-friendly book. To **Tom Ziolkowski** and **Deanna Storey**, thanks for your strong marketing insights for this book. Many people helped form the cornerstone of the original work, and we would like to thank **Barb Terry**, **Robin Drake**, **Chuck Hutchinson**, **Martha Johnson**, **Robin Edwards**, and **Deborah Minyard**. And, finally, thanks to everyone at Addison Wesley Longman who has followed this project from start to finish.

Acknowledgments

Addison-Wesley Publishing Company would like to thank the following reviewers for their valuable contributions to the *SELECT Lab Series*.

James Agnew Northern Virginia Community College	**Joseph Aieta** Babson College	**Dr. Muzaffar Ali** Bellarmine College	**Tom Ashby** Oklahoma CC
Bob Barber Lane CC	**Robert Caruso** Santa Rosa Junior College	**Robert Chi** California State Long Beach	**Jill Davis** State University of New York at Stony Brook
Fredia Dillard Samford University	**Peter Drexel** Plymouth State College	**David Egle** University of Texas, Pan American	**Linda Ericksen** Lane Community College
Jonathan Frank Suffolk University	**Patrick Gilbert** University of Hawaii	**Maureen Greenbaum** Union County College	**Sally Ann Hanson** Mercer County CC
Sunil Hazari East Carolina University	**Gloria Henderson** Victor Valley College	**Bruce Herniter** University of Hartford	**Rick Homkes** Purdue University
Lisa Jackson Henderson CC	**Martha Johnson** (technical reviewer) Delta State University	**Cynthia Kachik** Santa Fe CC	**Bennett Kramer** Massasoit CC
Charles Lake Faulkner State Junior College	**Ron Leake** Johnson County CC	**Randy Marak** Hill College	**Charles Mattox, Jr.** St. Mary's University
Jim McCullough Porter and Chester Institute	**Gail Miles** Lenoir-Rhyne College	**Steve Moore** University of South Florida	**Anthony Nowakowski** Buffalo State College
Gloria Oman Portland State University	**John Passafiume** Clemson University	**Leonard Presby** William Paterson College	**Louis Pryor** Garland County CC
Michael Reilly University of Denver	**Dick Ricketts** Lane CC	**Dennis Santomauro** Kean College of New Jersey	**Pamela Schmidt** Oakton CC
Gary Schubert Alderson-Broaddus College	**T. Michael Smith** Austin CC	**Cynthia Thompson** Carl Sandburg College	**Marion Tucker** Northern Oklahoma College
JoAnn Weatherwax Saddleback College	**David Whitney** San Francisco State University	**James Wood** Tri-County Technical College	**Minnie Yen** University of Alaska, Anchorage
Allen Zilbert Long Island University			

Contents

PART III Excel 97

Overview of Windows 95, Outlook, Active Desktop, and Internet Explorer 4.0

Windows 95

Overview of Windows 95

Microsoft Windows 95 is an *operating system,* a special kind of computer program that performs three major functions. First, an operating system controls the actual *hardware* of the computer (the screen, the keyboard, the disk drives, and so on). Second, an operating system enables other software programs such as word processing or spreadsheet *applications* to run. Finally, an operating system determines how the user operates the computer and its programs or applications.

As an operating system, Windows 95 and all other programs written to run under it provide *graphics* (or pictures) called *icons* to carry out commands and run programs. For this reason, Windows 95 is referred to as a *Graphical User Interface* or GUI (pronounced *gooey*). You can use the keyboard or a device called a *mouse* to activate the icons.

This overview explains the basics of Windows 95 so that you can begin using your computer quickly and easily.

Objectives

After completing this project, you will be able to:

➤ **Launch Windows 95**

➤ **Identify the desktop elements**

➤ **Use a mouse**

➤ **Use the basic features of Windows 95**

➤ **Organize your computer**

➤ **Work with multiple programs**

➤ **Get help**

➤ **Exit Windows 95**

Launching Windows 95

Because Windows 95 is an operating system, it launches immediately when you turn on the computer. Depending on the way your computer is set up you may have to type your user name and password to log on—to get permission to begin using the program. After Windows 95 launches, the working environment, called the *desktop,* displays on the screen.

Identifying the Desktop Elements

Figure W.1 shows the Windows 95 desktop with several icons that represent the hardware and the software installed on the computer. *My Computer* enables you to organize your work. The *Recycle Bin* is a temporary storage area for files deleted from the hard disk. At the bottom of the desktop is the *Taskbar* for starting programs, accessing various areas of Windows 95, and switching among programs.

Figure W.1

> **Note** The desktop can be customized, so the desktop on the computer you're using will not look exactly like the one shown in the illustrations in this overview.

Using a Mouse

A pointing device is almost an indispensable tool for using Windows 95. Although you can use the keyboard to navigate and make selections, using a mouse is often more convenient and efficient.

When you move the mouse on your desk, a pointer moves on the screen. When the pointer is on the object you want to use, you can take one of the actions described in Table W.1 to give Windows 95 an instruction.

Table W.1   Mouse Actions

Action	Description
Point	Slide the mouse across a smooth surface (preferably a mouse pad) until the pointer on the screen is on the object.
Click	Press and release the left mouse button once.
Drag	Press and hold down the left mouse button while you move the mouse, and then release the mouse button to complete the action.
Right-click	Press and release the right mouse button once. Right-clicking usually displays a shortcut menu.
Double-click	Press and release the left mouse button twice in rapid succession.

TASK 1: TO PRACTICE USING THE MOUSE:

1 Point to the My Computer ⬚ icon, press and hold down the left mouse button, and then drag the mouse across the desk.
The icon moves.

2 Drag the My Computer icon back to its original location.

3 Right-click the icon.

Your shortcut menu may not match this menu

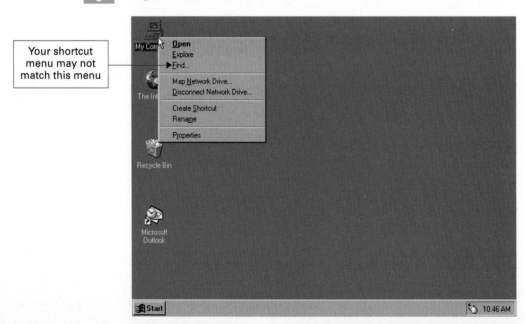

4 Click a blank space on the screen.
The shortcut menu closes.

5 Double-click the My Computer icon.

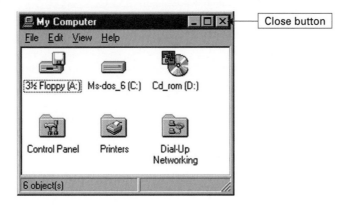

6 Click the Close ✖ button to close the My Computer window.

Using the Basic Features of Windows 95

The basic features of Windows 95 are menus, windows, menu bars, dialog boxes, and toolbars. These features are used in all programs that are written to run under Windows 95.

Using the Start Menu

Menus contain the commands you use to perform tasks. In Windows 95, you can use the Start menu shown in Figure W.2 to start programs and to access other Windows options.

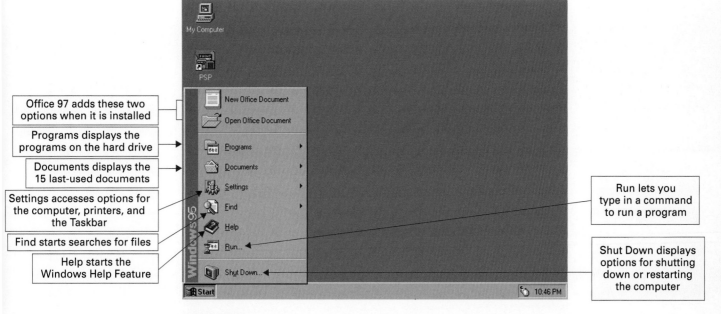

Figure W.2

TASK 2: TO USE THE START MENU TO LAUNCH A PROGRAM:

1 Click the Start button.
The triangles beside several of the menu options indicate that the options will display another menu.

2 Point to Programs and click the Windows Explorer icon on the cascading menu.
The Exploring window opens (see Figure W.3). You can use this feature of Windows 95 to manage files.

Using Windows

Clicking on the Windows Explorer icon opened a ***window,*** a Windows 95 feature that you saw earlier when you opened the My Computer window.

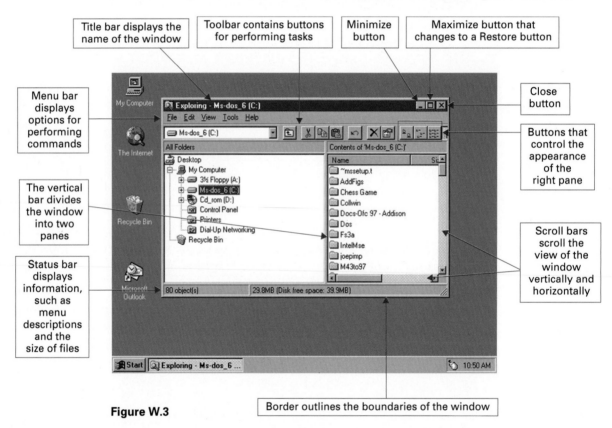

Title bar displays the name of the window

Toolbar contains buttons for performing tasks

Minimize button

Maximize button that changes to a Restore button

Menu bar displays options for performing commands

Close button

Buttons that control the appearance of the right pane

The vertical bar divides the window into two panes

Scroll bars scroll the view of the window vertically and horizontally

Status bar displays information, such as menu descriptions and the size of files

Border outlines the boundaries of the window

Figure W.3

Figure W.3 shows the common elements that most windows contain.

TASK 3: TO WORK WITH A WINDOW:

1 Click the Maximize button if it is displayed. If it is not displayed, click the Restore button, and then click the Maximize button.
The Maximize button changes to a Restore button.

2 Click the Minimize button.

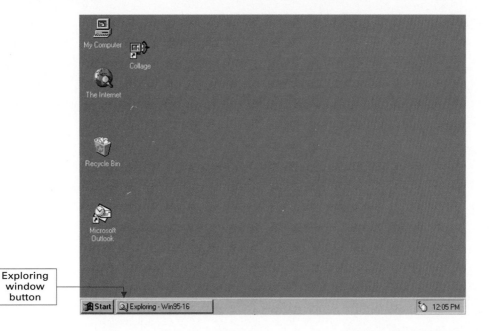

Exploring window button

Warning When you minimize a window, the program in the window is still running and therefore using computer memory. To exit a program that is running in a window, you must click the Close button, not the Minimize button.

3   Click the Exploring button on the Taskbar and then click 🔲.

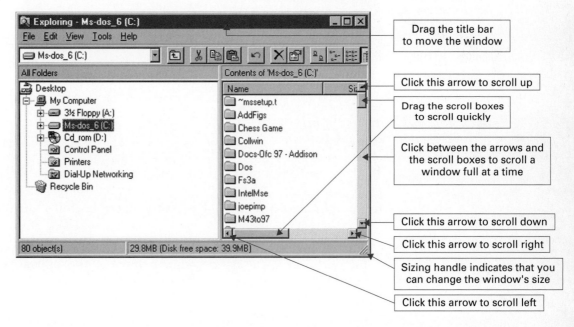

Drag the title bar to move the window

Click this arrow to scroll up

Drag the scroll boxes to scroll quickly

Click between the arrows and the scroll boxes to scroll a window full at a time

Click this arrow to scroll down

Click this arrow to scroll right

Sizing handle indicates that you can change the window's size

Click this arrow to scroll left

4   Point to the border of the Exploring window until the pointer changes to a double-headed black arrow, and then drag the border to make the window wider. (Be sure that all the buttons in the toolbar are visible.)

5   Practice scrolling.

6   When you are comfortable with your scrolling expertise, click 🔲.

Using Menu Bars and Toolbars

Menu bars and toolbars are generally located at the top of a window. You can select a menu option in a menu bar by clicking the option or by pressing (ALT) and then typing the underlined letter for the option. When you select an option, a drop-down menu appears. Figure W.4 shows a menu with many of the elements common to menus.

Note Because you can select menu commands in two ways, the steps with instructions to select a menu command will use the word choose instead of dictating the method of selection.

Check mark indicates that the menu option is active

The hot key for selecting the menu option if you are using the keyboard

Bullet indicates that the menu option is activated

Dimmed option indicates that the menu option is currently not appropriate and is therefore not available

Ellipsis indicates that a dialog box will display

Triangle indicates that a submenu will display

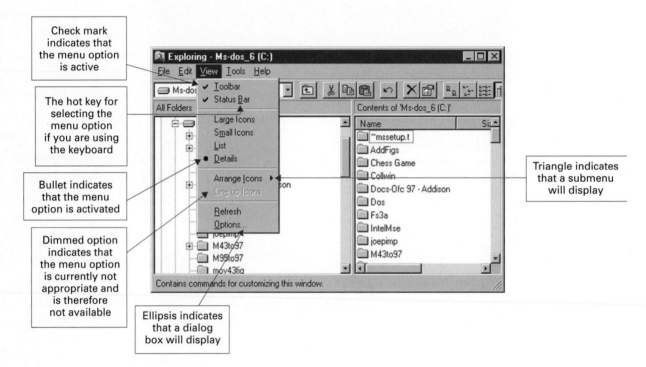

Figure W.4

Toolbars contain buttons that perform many of the same commands found on menus. To use a toolbar button, click the button; Windows 95 takes an immediate action, depending on the button's function.

Tip If you don't know what a button on the toolbar does, point to the button; a ToolTip, a brief description of the button, appears near the button.

TASK 4: TO USE MENUS AND TOOLBARS:

1. Choose View in the Exploring window.
The View menu shown in Figure W.4 displays.

2. Choose Large Icons.

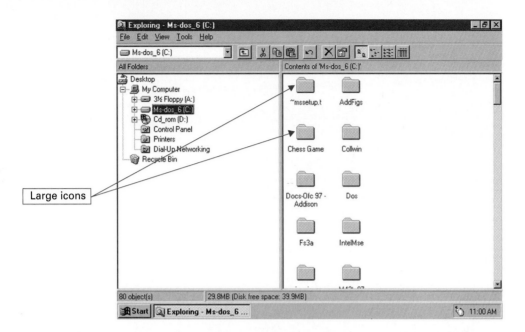

3   Click the Details ▦ button on the toolbar.

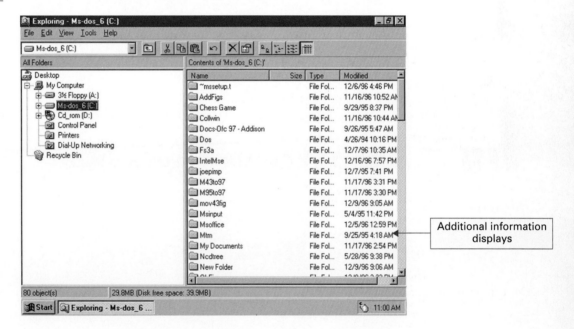

Using Dialog Boxes

When many options are available for a single task, Windows 95 conveniently groups the options in one place, called a *dialog box.* Some functions have so many options that Windows 95 divides them further into groups and places them on separate pages in the dialog box. Figures W.5 and W.6 show dialog boxes with different types of options. Throughout the remainder of this project, you practice using dialog boxes.

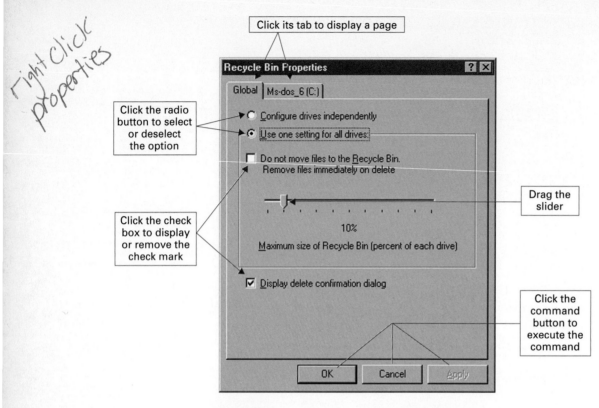

Figure W.5

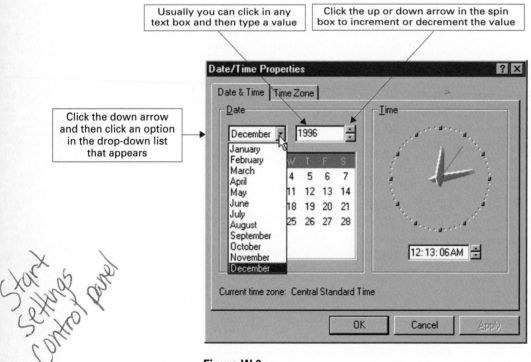

Figure W.6

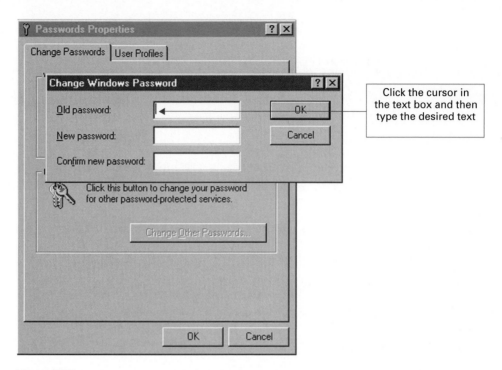

Figure W.7

Organizing Your Computer

A *disk drive* is designed to store the *files* you create (word processing documents, workbooks, databases, and so on). The computer you are using probably has at least two disk drives: a *hard disk drive* with a permanent disk and a *floppy disk drive* that uses a removable 5¼-inch or 3½-inch floppy disk (the floppy part of the disk is inside the protective covering). You also might have a *CD ROM drive.* If you are not sure what drives your computer has, you can find out by double-clicking the My Computer icon on the desktop. My Computer displays a window with icons for the elements installed on the computer.

Floppy drives are usually named with letters A or B. The hard drive is always C, and the CD ROM drive is D if there is only one hard drive.

> **Note** Before a computer can use a floppy disk, the disk must be formatted. Normally you format a disk only when it is new because formatting erases all files stored on a disk. If you need to format a new disk, place it in the floppy disk drive, right-click the floppy disk drive icon in Windows Explorer, click Format, click Full, and click Start. If you get a message that Windows cannot format the disk, go back to Windows Explorer, click on a different drive and then right-click the drive you want to format. After Windows 95 completes the formatting, click Close and then close the dialog box.

Creating Folders

The main directory (called the *root*) of any disk can hold only a limited number of files. Because you can have hundreds or thousands of files on a disk, you must create *folders* (also called *directories*) and store the files in the folders.

> **Tip** Do not store your data files in the same folders that contain program files. Create separate folders for data files.

TASK 5: TO CREATE A FOLDER ON DRIVE A:

1 Insert a formatted disk into drive A and click the drive A icon in the left pane, scrolling, if necessary.
The icon is highlighted.

2 Choose File, New, Folder.

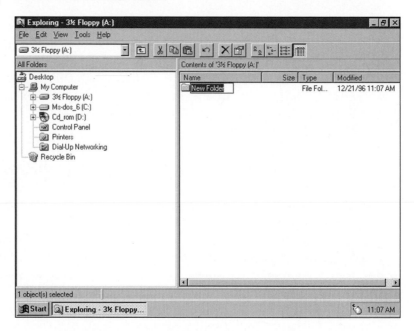

3 Type **Pictures** and press Enter.
The word Pictures replaces the words *New Folder*.

Copying and Renaming Files

One of the primary purposes of Windows Explorer is to enable users to manage files. Using Windows Explorer, you can easily copy files and rename them.

TASK 6: TO COPY FILES:

1 Click the plus beside drive C and then scroll if necessary and click the Windows folder.

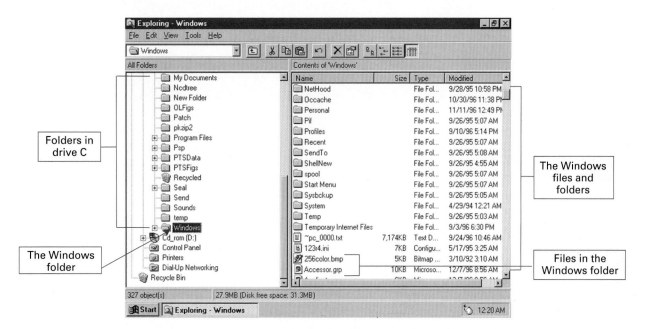

2   Scroll the right pane until you see files with a bmp extension and then click any bmp file. You don't need to select the files shown in the figure.

> **Note** If you don't see file extensions on your screen, choose View, Options, and click the View tab if necessary. Deselect Hide Ms-DOS file extensions for file types that are registered and then click OK.

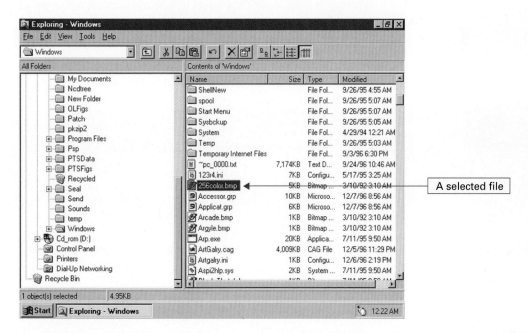

3   Press and hold down (CTRL) and then click another bmp file.
Both files are selected.

4   Click the Copy button in the toolbar.
The files are copied and held in a memory storage area referred to as the *Clipboard.*

5 Scroll if necessary and click drive A in the left pane; then click the Paste 🖺 button.

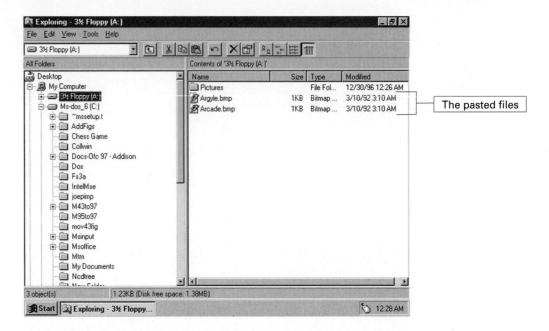

The pasted files

Note If you paste a file to the same location, Windows renames the file Copy of xxxxxxx.xxx (where xxxxxxx.xxx is the original file name).

Tip When copying files from the hard drive to a floppy drive, you also can right-click the files and choose Send to.

If you want to change the name of a file, you can rename it. When re-naming files, you should use the same extension.

TASK 7: TO RENAME A FILE:

1 Click one of the files you just copied to drive A.
The file is selected.

2 Click the name of the file.
The name is selected.

3 Type **Figure 1.bmp** and press (ENTER).
The file is renamed.

Moving Files

Occasionally you may want to reorganize the files and folders on a disk by moving them. The steps to move files are very similar to the steps for copying.

TASK 8: TO MOVE A FILE:

1 Click the plus beside the drive A icon.

The drive is expanded to show the folders →

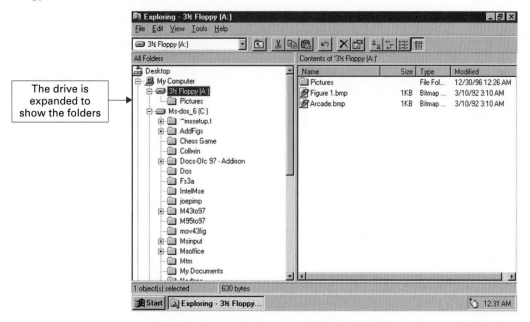

2 Point to Figure 1.bmp in the right pane and press the right mouse button while you drag the files to the Pictures folder in the left pane. (Be careful to release the mouse button only when the Pictures folder is selected.) A shortcut menu displays when you release the mouse button.

3 Click Move Here.
Windows 95 moves the file into the folder.

4 Click the Pictures folder in the left pane.

The opened Picture folder on drive A has Figure 1.bmp in it →

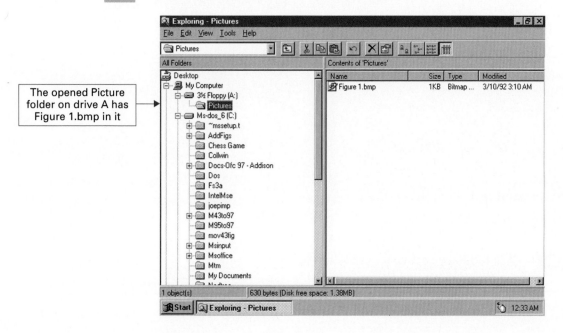

Deleting Files

When you delete a file on the hard disk, the file just moves into the Recycle Bin where it stays until it is deleted or restored. When you delete a file from a floppy disk, the file is removed and doesn't go into the Recycle Bin on the hard drive.

> **Tip** If you are deleting files in order to reclaim hard disk space, you must empty the Recycle Bin after you delete the files.

TASK 9: TO DELETE FILES:

1 Ensure that the icon for drive A is selected in the left pane and then click the bmp file in the right pane and press (DEL).

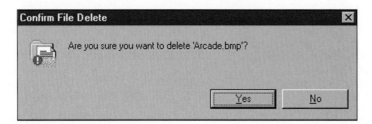

2 Click Yes to tell Windows 95 that you know what you're doing; you really do want to delete the file.
The file is deleted.

3 Select the Setup.bmp file in the Windows folder in drive C, write the name down, and then delete it.
The file is moved to the Recycle Bin.

> **Note** If you don't have a file named Setup.bmp, you can delete another file, but you should make a note of the filename so that you can restore the correct file in the next task.

Restoring Files

If you accidentally delete a file from the hard drive, you can restore it to its original location if the file is still in the Recycle Bin. (The Recycle Bin has a limited size. When the Recycle Bin fills up, older files are replaced by newer deleted files.)

TASK 10: TO RESTORE A FILE:

1 Click the Recycled folder in the left pane.

2   Click the name of the bmp file you deleted in the previous task. You did write the name down, didn't you? Just in case you didn't, it's Setup.bmp. The file is selected.

3   Click File and then click Restore.
Windows 95 restore the file to its original location.

4   Click ⊠.
The Windows Explorer closes.

Working with Multiple Programs

Windows 95's *multitasking* feature allows you to launch multiple programs and switch back and forth between them. Each open program is represented by a button on the Taskbar.

TASK 11: TO SWITCH BETWEEN WINDOWS:

1   Click Start and point to Programs.

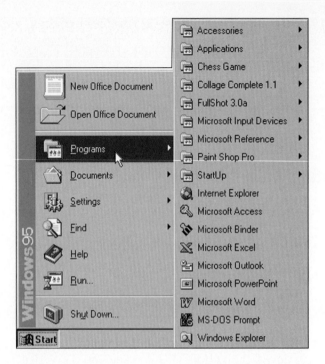

2 Point to Accessories and click Paint. (Maximize the window if necessary.)

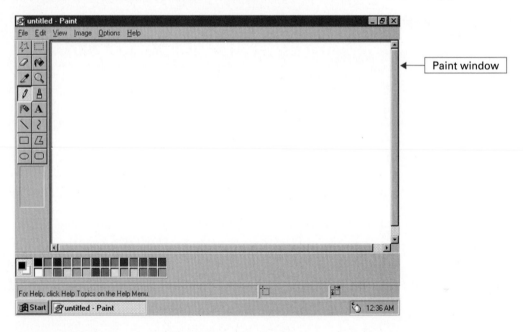

Paint window

3 Click Start, point to Programs, point to Accessories, and click WordPad. (Maximize the window if necessary.)

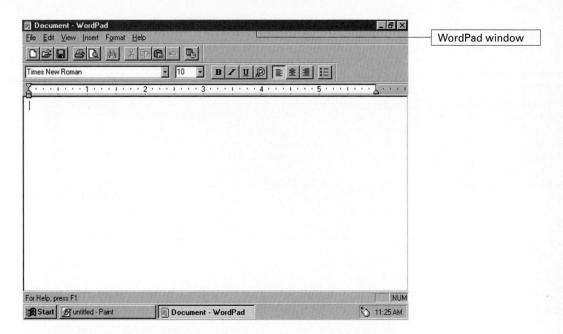

WordPad window

4   Type **What do you think of this graphic?** and press ENTER twice.

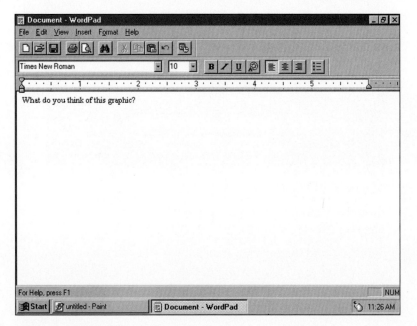

5   Click the Paint button in the Taskbar.
Windows switches to the Paint program.

6   Choose File, Open.

7 Click the down arrow to access the Look in drop-down list box and click drive A icon.

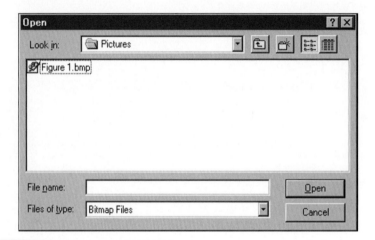

8 Double-click the Pictures folder.

9 Double-click the Figure 1.bmp file.
The Paint window opens with the graphic file in it.

10 Click Edit and then click Select All.

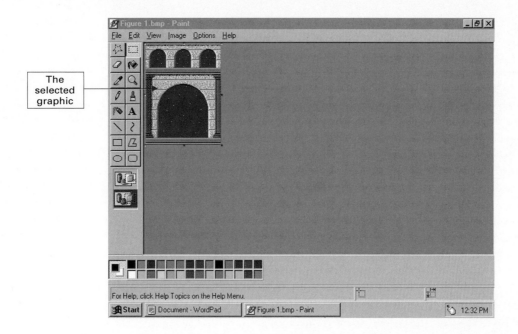

The
selected
graphic

Remember Your graphic may not match the illustration because you weren't told to copy a specific file.

11 Click Edit and then click Copy.
Windows 95 copies the image to the Clipboard memory area you used when you copied files.

12 Click the WordPad button in the Taskbar.
Windows switches to the WordPad program.

13 Click Edit and then click Paste.

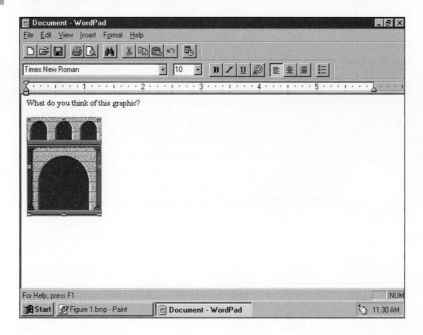

14 Click File, Save.

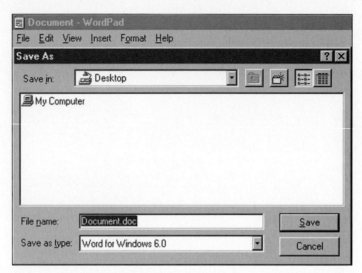

15 Type **a:\pictures\My File** in the File name text box and click Save. Windows 95 saves the file to the Pictures folder on drive A.

16 Click **X** in the WordPad window.
The WordPad program closes.

17 Click **X** in the Paint window.
The Paint window closes, and the Windows 95 desktop is visible again.

Getting Help

Windows 95 provides you with three methods of accessing help information: You can look up information in a table of contents; you can search for information in an index; or you can find a specific word or phrase in a database maintained by the Find feature.

Additionally, Windows 95 provides *context-sensitive help,* called *What's This?* for the topic you are working on. This type of help is generally found in dialog boxes.

After you learn to use Help in Windows 95, you can use help in any Windows program because all programs use the same help format.

TASK 12: TO USE HELP CONTENTS, INDEX, AND FIND:

1 Click the Start button on the Taskbar and click Help.

2   Click the Contents tab if a different page is displayed. The Contents page displays.

3   Double-click Tips and Tricks.

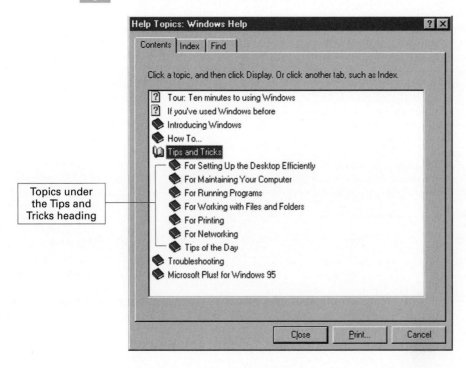

Topics under the Tips and Tricks heading

4   Double-click Tips of the Day.

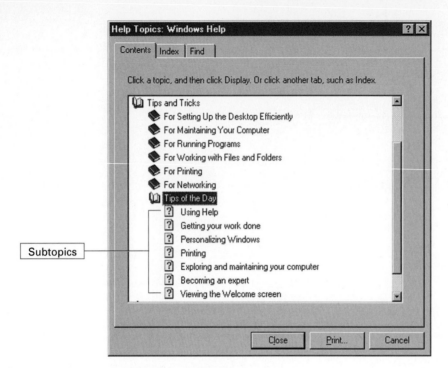

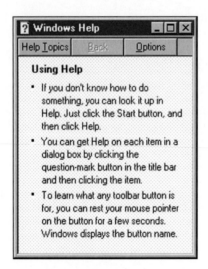

5 Double-click Using Help.

6 Read the information, click the Help Topics button, and then click the Index tab.

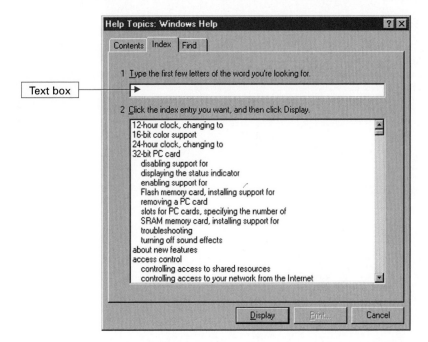

Text box

7   Type **shortcut** in the textbox.

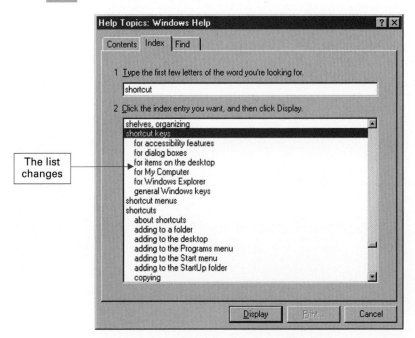

The list
changes

8   Double-click "shortcut menus" in the list.

9   Double-click "Using shortcut menus."

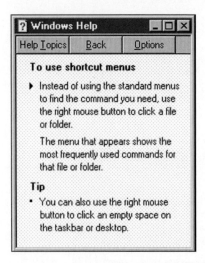

10   Read the information, click the Help Topics button, and then click the Find tab.

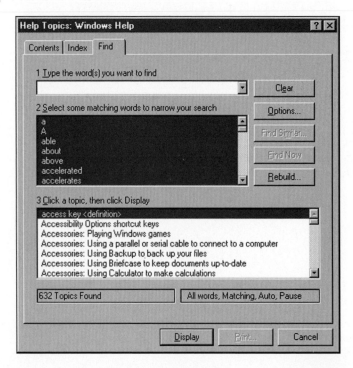

11   Click the What's This **?** button in the Help Topics title bar.
A question mark is attached to the mouse pointer.

12   Click the Options button.

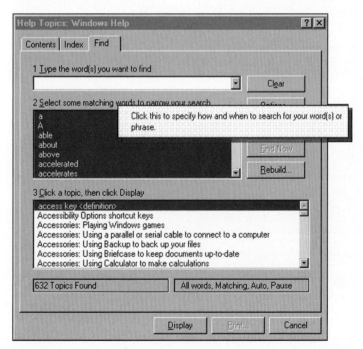

13   Read the pop-up message and then click it.
The message closes.

14   Type **printing help.** (If the list at the bottom of the screen doesn't change,
click the Find Now button.)

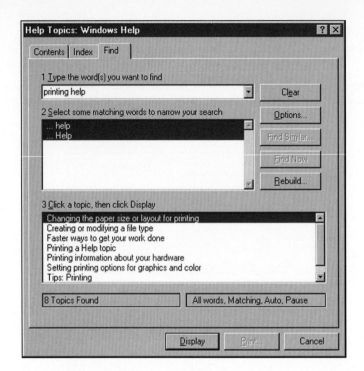

15 If necessary, scroll to "Printing a Help topic" in the list that displays and then double-click it.

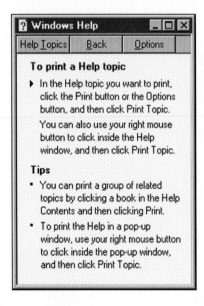

16 Click ⊠.
The Help dialog box closes.

Tip You can print any help article by right-clicking anywhere in the article and choosing Print Topic.

Exiting Windows 95

When you are ready to turn off the computer, you must exit Windows 95 first. You should never turn off the computer without following the proper exit procedure because Windows 95 has to do some utility tasks before it shuts down. Unlike most of us, Windows 95 likes to put everything away when it's finished. When you shut down improperly, you can cause serious problems in Windows 95.

TASK 13: TO EXIT WINDOWS 95:

1 Click the Start button and then click Shut Down.

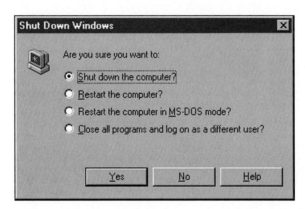

2 Click Shut down the computer? and then click Yes.

3 When the message "It's now safe to turn off your computer" appears, turn off the computer.

Outlook

Overview
of Outlook

Microsoft Outlook, a personal desktop organizer similar to Daytimer and Franklin Planner, is installed as an integral part of Microsoft Office 97. The features in Outlook help you track appointments, send and receive messages, maintain a list of "to do" tasks, monitor computer activities, and update business and personal contacts in an instant.

Objectives

After completing this project, you will be able to:

➤ **Identify Outlook features**

➤ **Launch Outlook**

➤ **Use the Outlook Bar**

➤ **Schedule appointments in the Calendar**

➤ **Record tasks in the Task List**

➤ **Track computer activities in the Journal**

➤ **Store contacts in the Contacts List**

➤ **Create, send, and receive e-mail**

➤ **Print from Outlook**

➤ **Exit Outlook**

Identifying Outlook Features

utlook comes with a number of features designed to keep you organized. You can keep Outlook open as you work in other applications and use it as a reference more easily. Table O.1 lists the features available in Outlook.

Table O.1:   Outlook Features

Use this feature	to do this:
Calendar	Schedule appointments and meetings.
Task List	Record things to do, prioritize the list, and check tasks off as they are completed.
Inbox	Keep track of messages you receive.
Journal	Monitor computer activities as they happen and create a timeline of events for projects.
Contacts	Record business and personal contacts on a Rolodex-type file for easy access.
Notes	Store notes during phone conversations and meetings using the mini-word processor or that lets you type electronic Post-It notes.
Deleted Items	Retrieve "thrown out" items from the wastebasket as long as it hasn't been emptied.
Outlook Bar	Access other features by clicking the feature icon located on the Outlook screen.

Launching Outlook

The typical installation of Microsoft Office 97 creates a desktop shortcut to Outlook for easy access. Double-click the Microsoft Outlook shortcut icon to launch the program.

TASK 1: TO LAUNCH MICROSOFT OUTLOOK:

1 Turn on the computer and launch Windows 95.

2 Double-click the desktop Microsoft Outlook shortcut icon.

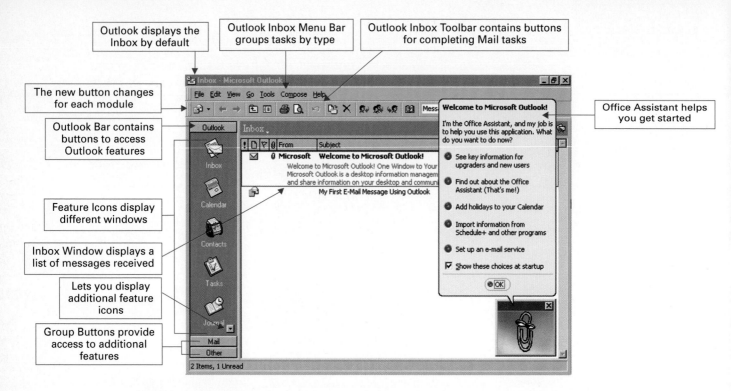

Outlook displays the Inbox by default

Outlook Inbox Menu Bar groups tasks by type

Outlook Inbox Toolbar contains buttons for completing Mail tasks

The new button changes for each module

Outlook Bar contains buttons to access Outlook features

Feature Icons display different windows

Inbox Window displays a list of messages received

Lets you display additional feature icons

Group Buttons provide access to additional features

Office Assistant helps you get started

3   Review the information the Office Assistant provides and then click OK.

Using the Outlook Bar

The Outlook Bar groups Outlook features into three different categories: Outlook, Mail, and Other. Category names appear on buttons on the Outlook Bar. When you click a category button, icons representing features within the category appear. When you click the icons on the Outlook Bar, the Outlook window changes, sometimes dividing into multiple window panes.

TASK 2: TO ACCESS OUTLOOK FEATURES:

1   Click the Outlook group button at the top of the Outlook Bar.
The Outlook default icons appear.

2 Click the Mail group button at the bottom of the Outlook Bar.

Displays feature buttons for the Mail group

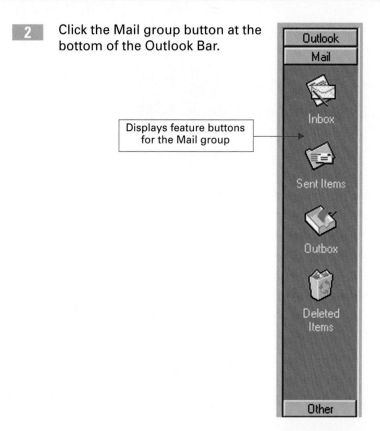

3 Click the Other group button at the bottom of the Outlook Bar.

Displays other feature buttons

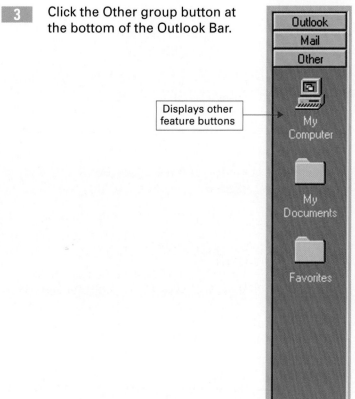

4 Click the Outlook group button on the Outlook Bar.
The Outlook Bar displays the buttons for accessing the Outlook features.

5 Click the scroll down button at the bottom of the Outlook Bar to display additional features.

Scroll up button redisplays original feature buttons

> **Note** Scroll buttons disappear when you reach the top or bottom of the Outlook Bar. If a scroll button isn't available, the first or last icon is on-screen.

6 Click the up scroll button at the top of the Outlook Bar.
The original feature icons redisplay.

Scheduling Appointments in the Calendar

Whether you use the Calendar to keep track of appointments or assignments, recording entries in the Calendar is easy. You can enter appointments directly in the Calendar window or use the Appointment dialog box to enter the appointment and set options.

TASK 3: TO SCHEDULE APPOINTMENTS IN THE CALENDAR:

1 Click the Calendar 📖 icon on the Outlook Bar.

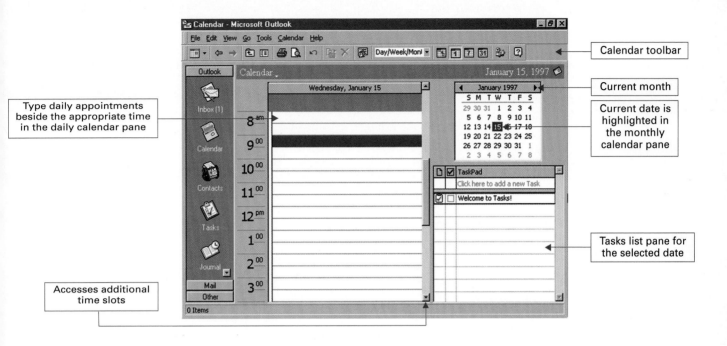

Calendar toolbar

Current month

Current date is highlighted in the monthly calendar pane

Tasks list pane for the selected date

Type daily appointments beside the appropriate time in the daily calendar pane

Accesses additional time slots

2   Double-click the 9:00 time slot on the Calendar appointment list.
The Appointment dialog box opens, offering more options than you have if you enter data directly into the Calendar window.

3   Enter the data indicated in the following Appointment dialog box, pressing
(TAB) to advance from field to field.

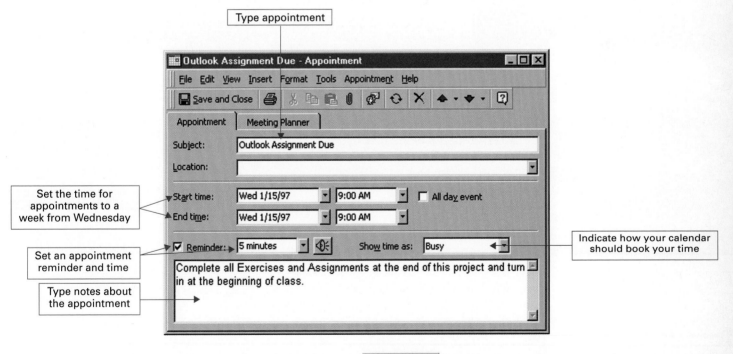

Type appointment

Set the time for appointments to a week from Wednesday

Set an appointment reminder and time

Type notes about the appointment

Indicate how your calendar should book your time

4   Click the toolbar Save and Close 🔲 Save and Close button.

Recording Tasks in the Task List

The Task List appears in a pane of the Calendar window for easy access. You can, however, display the Tasks in a full window. The procedures used to record entries in the Task List are the same regardless of which Task display you choose.

TASK 4: TO RECORD TASKS IN THE TASK LIST:

1 Click the Outlook Bar Tasks 📋 icon.

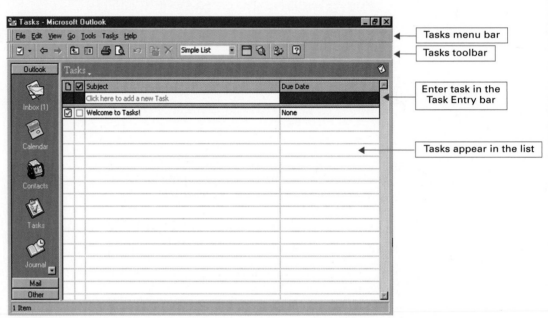

2 Click the instruction *Click here to add a new task* in the task entry bar.

3 Type **Pick up forms from career center** and press (ENTER).
The task appears in the task list.

4 Double-click the task entry bar.
The Tasks dialog box opens.

5 Type the data shown in the following Tasks dialog box, pressing (TAB) to advance from field to field.

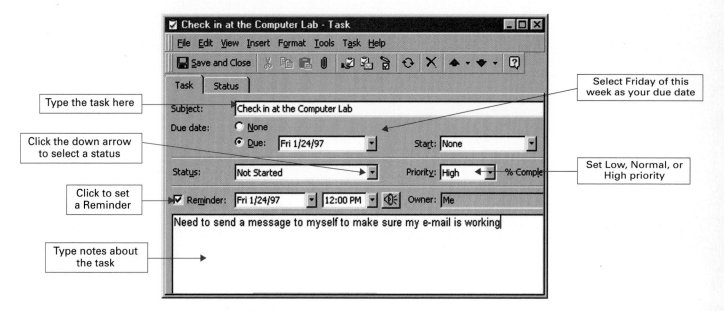

6 Click 🔲 Save and Close.

> **Tip** The text for overdue tasks is red. To quickly sort tasks by different columns, click the gray column heading button.

7 Double-click the line Welcome to Tasks! Information about the task displays in the notes area.

8 Click the Welcome to Tasks! window ❌ to close the task window.

9 Click the check box for the Pick up forms from career center task.

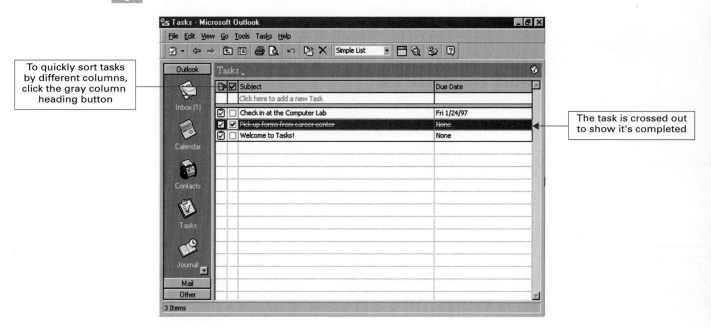

10   Click 📋 to view the Task list in the Calendar window.

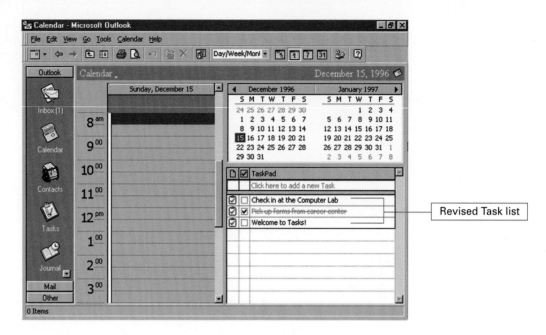

Revised Task list

Tracking Computer Activities in the Journal

The Journal feature in Outlook creates a timeline to record computer activities performed using Office 97 features and then groups journal entries by type to keep track of your activities. You also can use the Journal to manually record your thoughts, conversations, or notes.

TASK 5: TO DISPLAY JOURNAL ACTIVITIES AND RECORD ACTIVITIES MANUALLY:

1   Click the Outlook Bar Journal 📖 icon.

Journal menu

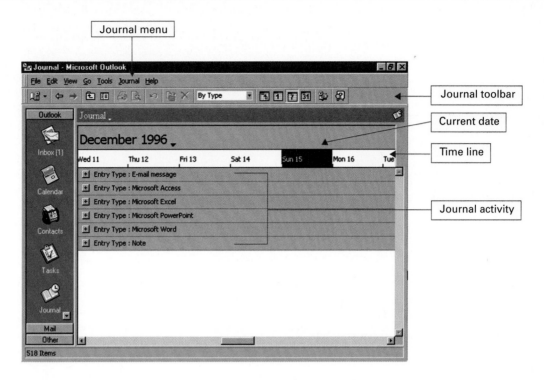

Journal toolbar

Current date

Time line

Journal activity

2 Click the plus ⊞ button to display grouped activities for each journal entry.

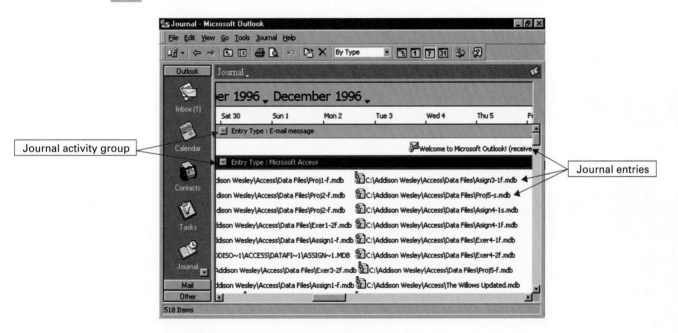

Journal activity group

Journal entries

3 Choose Journal, New Journal Entry.
The Journal dialog box opens.

4 Type the data shown in the following Journal dialog box, pressing ⌐TAB⌐ to advance from field to field.

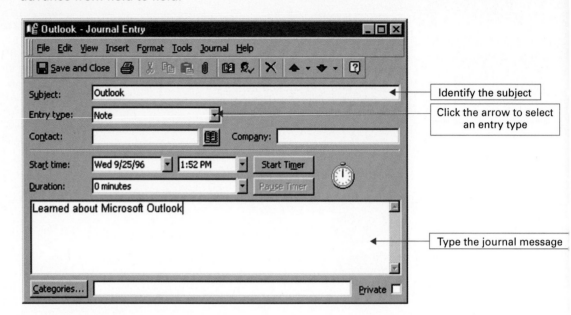

5 Click 🔲 Save and Close.

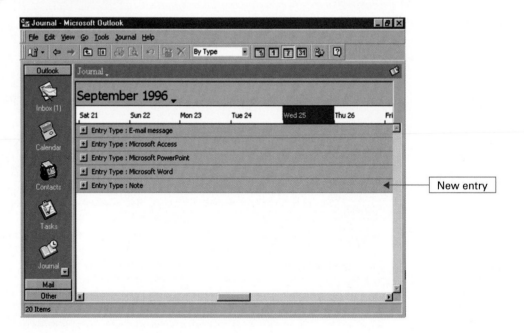

Storing Contacts in the Contacts List

The Contacts List stores names, addresses, phone numbers, company names, and so forth about your personal and/or business contacts. You can use information you store in the Contacts List in letters and databases. In addition, you can send messages called *e-mail*, directly to those people in the Contact List who have e-mail addresses that your system can access.

TASK 6: TO ADD CONTACTS TO THE CONTACT LIST:

1 Click the Outlook Bar Contacts 📖 icon.

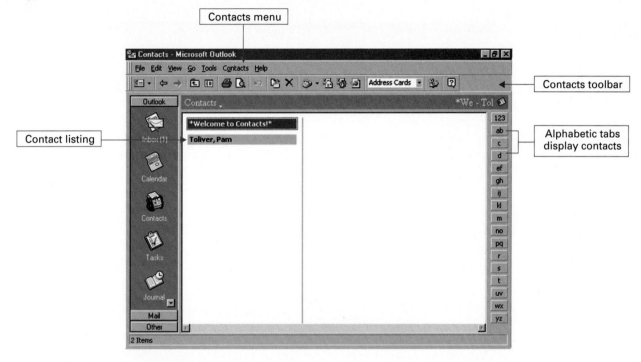

2 Double-click a blank area of the Contacts window.
The Contacts dialog box opens.

3 Type the data shown in the following Contact dialog box, pressing (TAB) to advance from field to field.

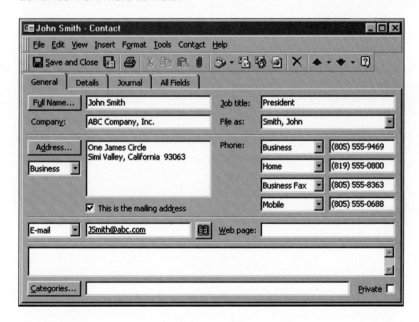

4 Click 🖫 Save and Close to save the contact.

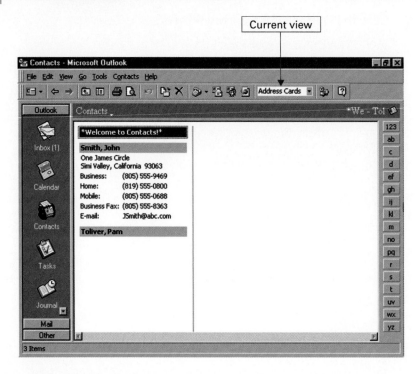

Current view

5 Click the drop-down list arrow beside the Current View area of the toolbar.

6 Click Detailed Address Cards.

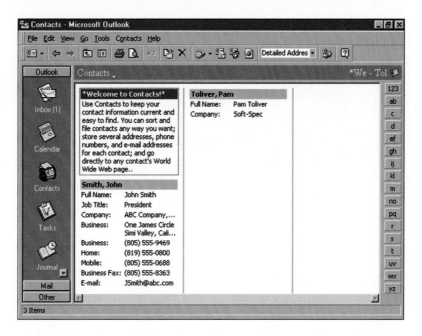

7 Select Address Cards from the Current View list to return the previous display.

8 Add your name, address, and e-mail address as a contact in the Contacts List.

Creating, Sending, and Receiving E-mail

Outlook comes equipped with an e-mail feature for communicating with people on a *local area network* (LAN) as well as with people on the *Internet,* the world-wide computer structure for sending information.

The Inbox stores messages you receive from others and automatically displays each time you launch Outlook to remind you to sign on or *log on* to the network and check for new messages. The Outbox stores messages you create until you log on to the network and send the messages.

TASK 7: TO USE THE OUTLOOK MAIL MESSAGE FEATURE:

1 Click the Inbox 🖾 icon in the Outlook Bar.
The Inbox window opens.

> **Troubleshooting** By default, the Inbox automatically appears each time you launch Outlook. If your settings are different and display another Outlook feature, click the Outlook Bar Inbox icon to display the Inbox.

2 Click the New Mail Message ⬚ icon on the Outlook toolbar.

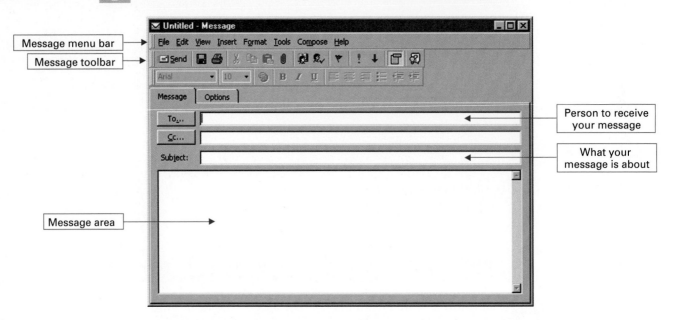

Message menu bar →

Message toolbar →

Message area →

Person to receive your message

What your message is about

Note If your system requires that you log on to the network to display a list of valid e-mail users, log on and type your password in the appropriate dialog box.

3 Click the To button to open the Select Names dialog box and either type or select your own e-mail address.

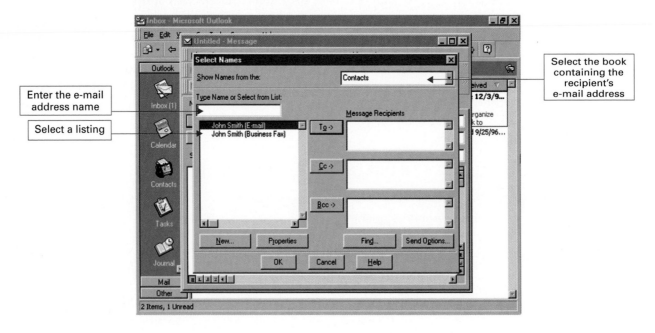

Enter the e-mail address name

Select a listing

Select the book containing the recipient's e-mail address

4   Type the subject **My First E-Mail Message Using Outlook** and the following text as your e-mail message. Then click the Send ⌐Send button to mail it.

This is my first message typed using the Outlook Mail feature that came with Microsoft Office 97. If I receive this message, I will know that I am actively connected to the campus e-mail system and am able to send messages.

If you are logged on to the e-mail system when you click Send, your message is sent immediately. If you aren't currently logged on to the e-mail system, your message is stored in the Outbox. When you exit Outlook, it reminds you that the Outbox has messages. You can choose Yes to log on and send messages before exiting Outlook or choose No to exit Outlook and keep the messages in the Outbox for later delivery.

Note The only reason to send a mail message to yourself is to test your e-mail delivery system, to have mail to read, or to determine approximately when messages you send are available to other recipients.

5   Choose Tools, Check for New Mail to log on to the e-mail system and access new mail sent to you since the last time you logged on.

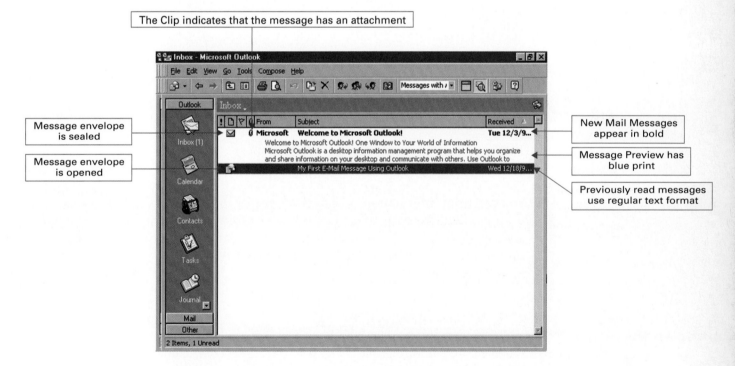

The Clip indicates that the message has an attachment

Message envelope is sealed

Message envelope is opened

New Mail Messages appear in bold

Message Preview has blue print

Previously read messages use regular text format

Note An *attachment* can be a file, a picture, or some other type of object that you can transmit electronically.

6 Double-click the message you received from yourself.
The full message appears in a window of its own. Use buttons on the toolbar to respond to the message, forward the message, or delete the message.

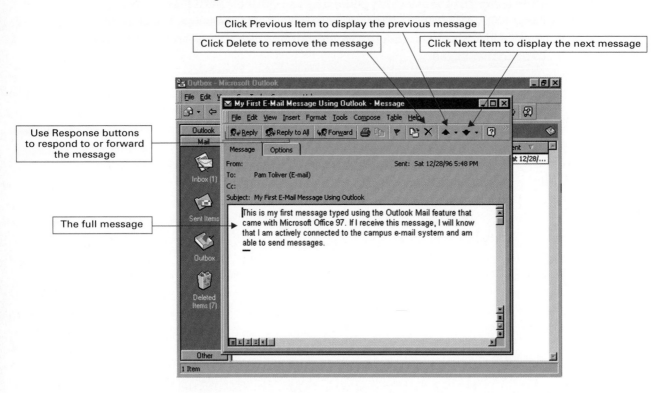

Click Previous Item to display the previous message

Click Delete to remove the message

Click Next Item to display the next message

Use Response buttons to respond to or forward the message

The full message

7 Click the message ☒ to close the message window.

Printing from Outlook

You can print information contained in any of the Outlook modules using a variety of different formats. Regardless of which module in Outlook you are using, you can print information using the same basic procedures. Features and styles displayed in the Print dialog box vary according to the module you have active when you print.

TASK 8: TO PRINT FROM OUTLOOK:

1 Display your Outlook Calendar, display the current week, and choose File, Print.

Displays a dialog box that shows paper size and orientation

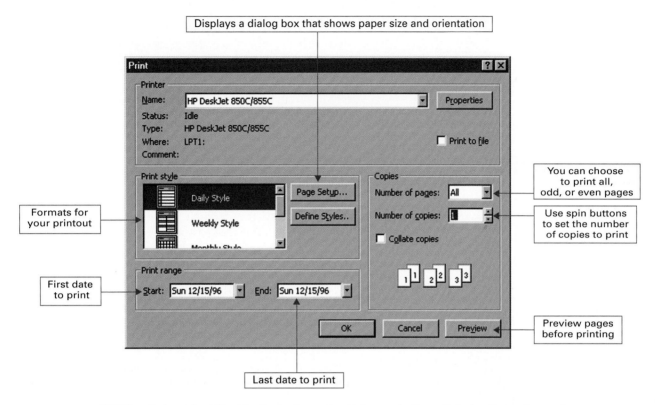

Formats for your printout

You can choose to print all, odd, or even pages

Use spin buttons to set the number of copies to print

First date to print

Preview pages before printing

Last date to print

2   Select the Weekly Style from the Print style list, click the Page Setup button, and ensure that your settings match these:

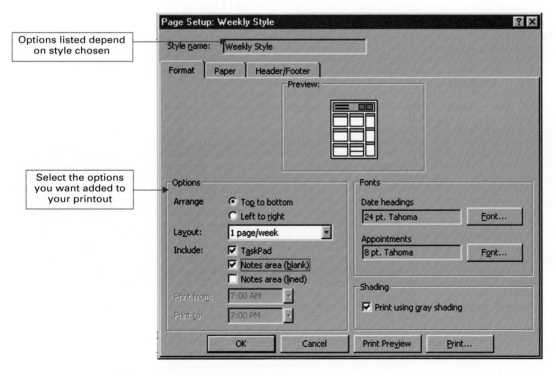

Options listed depend on style chosen

Select the options you want added to your printout

3   Click OK twice to print.

Exiting Outlook

Because Outlook is an application, you exit Outlook using the same techniques used to exit other applications designed for Windows 95.

TASK 9: TO EXIT OUTLOOK:

1   Click the Outlook application Close **X** button.

> **Note** The Microsoft Outlook message box shown below appears only when you have messages in your Outbox that haven't yet been delivered. If the Outbox contains no messages, Outlook closes automatically.

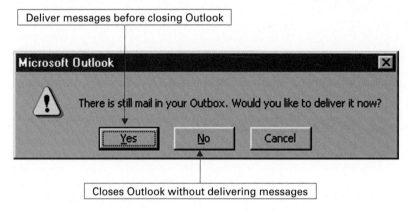

Deliver messages before closing Outlook

Closes Outlook without delivering messages

2   Click No if asked whether you want to deliver mail in the Outbox.

Summary and Exercises

Summary

- Microsoft Outlook is a personal desktop organizer designed after personal organizers such as Daytimer and Franklin Planner.
- Outlook combines a calendar, an address list, a task list, a journal, and an e-mail system into one efficient program.
- Microsoft Office 97 automatically creates a shortcut to access Outlook during a typical Office 97 installation; double click the shortcut icon on the desktop to launch Outlook.
- Because Outlook includes an e-mail program, you may be asked to provide log-on information when you launch Outlook.
- To use the e-mail feature of Outlook to communicate with others, you must have access to the Internet or be connected to a local area network.
- The Outlook Bar provides easy access to all features of Microsoft Outlook.
- The Print dialog box displays different options depending on the module of Outlook you have active when you print.

Key Terms and Operations

Key Terms	Operations
local area network (LAN)	Launch Microsoft Outlook
e-mail	Access Microsoft Outlook Features
log on	Record entries in the Outlook Calendar, Task List,
Internet	Contacts List, and Journal
Inbox	Send and receive e-mail
Outbox	Print from Outlook modules

Study Questions

Multiple Choice

1. You launch Microsoft Outlook by
   a. clicking the Outlook shortcut icon on the desktop.
   b. double-clicking the Outlook shortcut icon on the desktop.
   c. choosing Start, Control, Microsoft Outlook.
   d. pressing (ENTER).

2. To change from one Outlook feature to another,
   a. click the feature icon on the Outlook Bar.
   b. press (CTRL)+(F6).
   c. double click the feature on the Outlook toolbar.
   d. press (ENTER).

3. The Outlook feature designed to keep track of meetings is the
   a. Schedule.
   b. Journal.
   c. Calendar.
   d. Task List.

4. The Outlook feature designed to keep track of the things you need to do is the
   a. Calendar.
   b. Task List.
   c. Schedule.
   d. Journal.

5. The Outlook feature that tracks your computer activity is the
   a. Task List.
   b. Calendar.
   c. Journal.
   d. Schedule.

6. The Outlook feature that lists messages received is the
   a. e-mail.
   b. Inbox.
   c. Outbox.
   d. Trash Can.

7. The Outlook feature that stores messages you want to send is the
   a. e-mail.
   b. Inbox.
   c. Outbox.
   d. Trash Can.

8. The Outlook feature designed to store names and addresses of business associates is
   a. the Inbox.
   b. the Journal.
   c. the Calendar.
   d. Contacts.

9. To exit Outlook,
   a. click the application Close button.
   b. press ALT + F6.
   c. choose File, Close.
   d. press ENTER.

10. To schedule an appointment in the Calendar,
   a. Outlook must be running in the background.
   b. select the Calendar date and type the appointment.
   c. copy the appointment from the Journal.
   d. press ENTER

Short Answer

1. List the features in Microsoft Outlook.

2. What happens to messages you create and send when you aren't logged on to the e-mail system?

3. When viewing messages in the Inbox, how can you tell if a message has been read?

4. How are features arranged on the Outlook Bar?

5. In which Outlook Bar group does Outbox appear?

6. Which Outlook features can you use to record notes during a telephone conversation?

7. What computer activities does the Journal track?

8. How do you access a different month in the Calendar?

9. What is each section of the Calendar window called?

10. How do you access a blank form for adding contacts to the Contact List?

For Discussion

1. List and describe the features contained in Microsoft Outlook.

2. Describe the procedure for recording an entry in the Task List and how you would indicate that the task is complete.

3. Describe the Outlook feature you believe you would use most frequently and briefly tell how you would use the feature.

4. List your e-mail address and describe procedures for logging on to your local area network.

Review Exercises

1. Exploring Outlook
Launch Outlook and display Office Assistant. Ask the Office Assistant how to insert files to send with e-mail messages. After reviewing the information the Office Assistant displays, create an e-mail message to your instructor summarizing what you have discovered. Then print the message.

Ask the Office Assistant how to access the Outlook Web page. Then access the Outlook Web page and review some of the additional features available in Outlook. Look for some innovative ways others are using Outlook, if they are available. List the three most interesting features and try implementing them using Outlook on your computer. Type a summary of the features you discover in an e-mail message to your instructor, describe how the feature can benefit you in your work, and then print (but don't send) the message.

2. Scheduling Assignments
Launch Outlook and display the Outlook Calendar. Record the following items in your Outlook Calendar:
- All scheduled class assignments and tests for all classes
- Personal activities for the semester
- Important dates to remember
- Holidays
- Final Exam Week
- End of the Semester

Print a listing of each month's Calendar using the Monthly Style.

Create a list of tasks associated with the assignments and activities and record the tasks in the Tasks List.

Assignments

1. Adding Contacts to the Contacts List
Launch Outlook and display the Contacts screen. Create additional contact listings for the following:

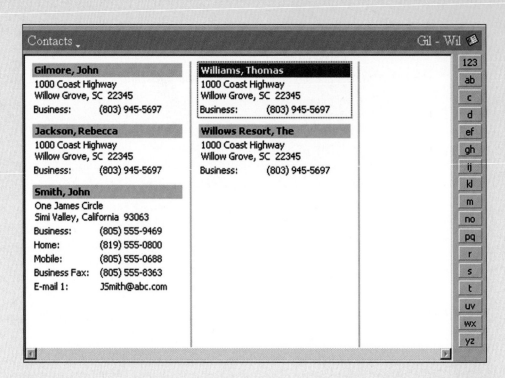

Your personal record will appear alphabetically among the contacts shown. The record for John Smith was added during the activities presented earlier in this overview. Print copies of the Contacts List in Small Booklet Style.

2. Using Office Assistant

Ask the Office Assistant how to set recurring appointments in the Calendar. Then use the information to set a recurring appointment for your Office 97 class. Print a copy of two months of classes using the monthly view format.

Print a list of tasks contained in the tasks list. Then mark completed tasks on your tasks list. Ask the Office Assistant how to prioritize tasks and then use the information to prioritize your tasks list. Prioritize incomplete tasks. Print a list of your revised tasks list.

Active Desktop and Windows 98 Preview

Active Desktop and Windows 98 Preview

If you are running Windows 95 and your desktop looks significantly different from the desktop pictures found in the Overview of Windows 95, you may have Internet Explorer 4.0 installed with the Active Desktop. The Active Desktop contains features such as Taskbar toolbars, Internet Explorer Channel bar, and a Web-designed desktop background—features also available in Windows 98.

Other Windows 98 features—such as memory managers and file allocation tables—operate behind the scenes to improve the efficiency of your computer. Like Windows 95, Windows 98 is an operating system. Windows 98, however, operates with increased memory management capabilities. As a result, unless your computer is an older computer running less than 166 MHz, you should notice smoother transition when you move between programs, increased speed when performing basic tasks, and fewer program errors.

Many of the basic Windows 95 features, such as toolbars, are updated with a new look in Windows 98 because of the Active Desktop enhancement and the integration of Internet Explorer 4.0. Other features—such as the title bar and the minimize, maximize, and close buttons—remain unchanged. You will find that both Windows 98 and the Windows 95 Active Desktop are intimately integrated with the Internet and the World Wide Web. With the Active Desktop features, these "worlds" are literally just a click away.

This Active Desktop overview provides a preview of what to expect with Windows 98. You'll find that, in most cases, the procedures for using Windows 95 Active Desktop/Windows 98 features are identical to the procedures for using Windows 95 features.

Objectives

After completing this project, you will be able to:

➤ **Identify elements of the Windows 95 Active Desktop**

➤ **Use desktop ToolTips**

➤ **Launch programs**

➤ **Customize the Windows 95 Active Desktop**

> **Edit the Start menu**
> **Restore the desktop to its original format**

Identifying Elements of the Windows 95 Active Desktop

Both Windows 95 and Windows 98 start automatically each time you power up your computer. The appearance of the Active Desktop is controlled by options you choose when you install Internet Explorer 4.0. When you install Windows 98 the Active Desktop is installed, and the Web Channels bar displays automatically on your computer. You can choose to view your desktop as a Web page and to view the Internet Explorer Channel bar to provide easy access to pre-defined Web sites. These features are identified in the Active Desktop displayed in Figure A.1. If these features were not selected when you installed Internet Explorer 4.0 or Windows 98 on your computer, you can display the features from the Active Desktop.

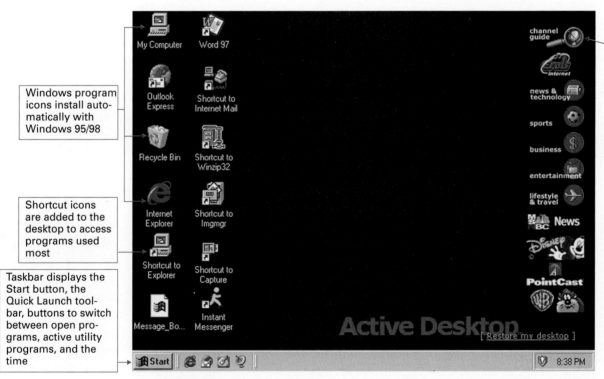

Internet Explorer Channel bar provides single-click access to popular Web sites.

Windows program icons install automatically with Windows 95/98

Shortcut icons are added to the desktop to access programs used most

Taskbar displays the Start button, the Quick Launch toolbar, buttons to switch between open programs, active utility programs, and the time

Figure A.1

Note Because the desktop can be customized, your desktop may not appear exactly as the one shown in the illustrations in this preview — even if you choose to display the Internet Explorer Channel bar and the desktop as a Web page.

Displaying the Internet Explorer Channel Bar

The Internet Explorer Channel bar appears in its own window when it is active. As a result, you can close the window by clicking the Close button that appears when you position the mouse pointer near the top edge of the Channel Guide button at the top of the Channel bar. Then use these procedures to restore the Internet Explorer Channel bar.

TASK 1: TO DISPLAY THE INTERNET EXPLORER CHANNEL BAR AFTER INSTALLATION:

1 Right-click a blank area of the Active Desktop and choose Active Desktop, as shown in the following figure.

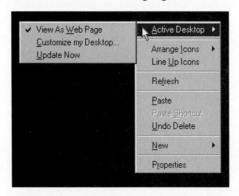

2 Choose Customize my Desktop.
The Display Properties dialog box opens.

3 Click the Web page of the dialog box, if necessary, as illustrated in the following figure.

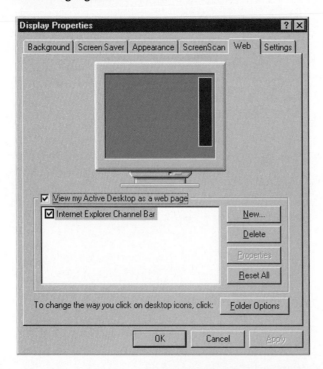

4 Check the View my Active Desktop as a web page check box, if necessary.

5 Check the Internet Explorer Channel Bar check box.
The Internet Explorer Channel bar shape appears in the preview monitor.

6 Choose Apply and then choose OK.

Displaying the Active Desktop Wallpaper

The default Active Desktop Web wallpaper displays a pre-formatted background. If your desktop is formatted with a different background, you can change the wallpaper to the Active Desktop Web wallpaper.

TASK 2: TO DISPLAY THE ACTIVE DESKTOP WALLPAPER AFTER INSTALLATION:

1 Right-click on a blank area on the Active Desktop and choose Properties.
The Display Properties dialog box opens.

2 Click the Background page tab, if necessary, to produce the screen shown in the following figure.

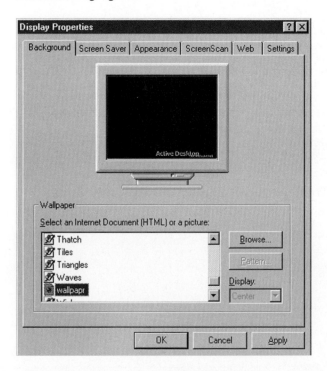

3 Select wallpapr from the Wallpaper list.
The preview monitor displays the Active Desktop Web wallpaper.

> **Note** The list of background designs varies depending on programs previously installed on your computer. If wallpapr is unavailable, select the background identified by your instructor.

4 Choose Apply and then choose OK.
The desktop is reformatted.

Using Desktop ToolTips

Other features that have been enhanced by the Active Desktop and Windows 98 include desktop ToolTips and shortcut menus. With the Active Desktop, simply pointing to an icon or desktop feature identifies the feature and, in some instances, displays explanatory information about the feature.

TASK 3: TO DISPLAY DESKTOP TOOLTIPS:

1 Click on a blank area of the Desktop to make it active.
The Desktop must be active before ToolTips appear.

2 Position the mouse pointer on the selected icon, as shown in the following figure.

The ToolTip explains how to use the My Computer program.

> **Note** The ToolTip appears different, depending on how the Active Desktop is installed on your computer. If it is installed using Internet Explorer 4.0 with Windows 95, it displays as shown in the figure. If the Active Desktop is installed with Windows 98, the information provided by the ToolTip will be different.

3 Point to the Start button.

4 Point to a button on the Internet Explorer Channel bar, as shown here.

5 Point to the Time at the right end of the Taskbar, as shown in this figure.

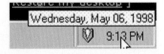

6   Point to an icon on the Quick Launch toolbar, as shown here.

Launching Programs

The same basic techniques used to launch programs in Windows 95 can be used to launch programs from the Active Desktop and Windows 98 Start menu and desktop shortcuts. The Active Desktop, however, enables you to use the Quick Launch toolbar located on the Taskbar to launch programs. In addition, you can change the setup of your desktop so that all program icons, shortcuts, and filenames act as hyperlinks. Clicking a filename, program icon, shortcut, or folder that is formatted as a hyperlink automatically opens the item. You'll also find that when Start menus contain more items than will fit on a cascading menu, the cascading menu displays an arrow at the top and/or bottom to indicate the presence of additional items.

TASK 4: TO LAUNCH PROGRAMS FROM THE ACTIVE DESKTOP:

1   Click the Outlook Express button on the Quick Launch toolbar, as shown here.

Title bars and title bar buttons are unchanged

Toolbars have a new look

The Internet Explorer icon has a new design

2 Choose Start, Programs, as the following figure indicates.

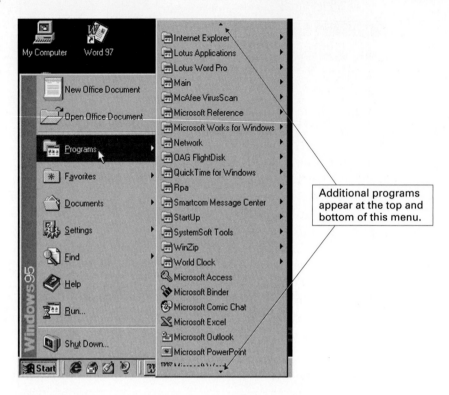

Additional programs appear at the top and bottom of this menu.

3 Click the arrow at the top or bottom of the cascading menu. Additional menu items scroll onscreen.

4 Double-click My Computer
The My Computer window opens.

5 Maximize the window and click once on the hard disk drive for your computer, as shown in the next figure.

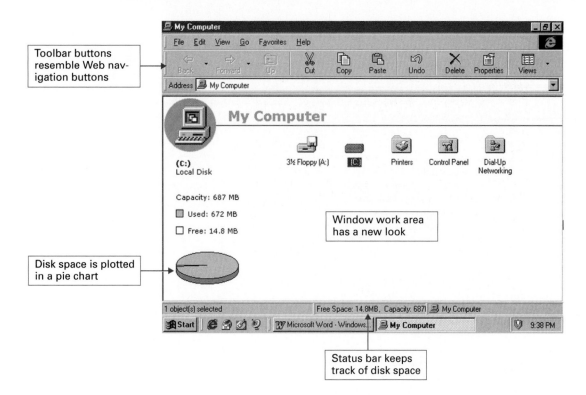

Toolbar buttons resemble Web navigation buttons

Window work area has a new look

Disk space is plotted in a pie chart

Status bar keeps track of disk space

6   Choose View, Folder Options to display the screen shown here.

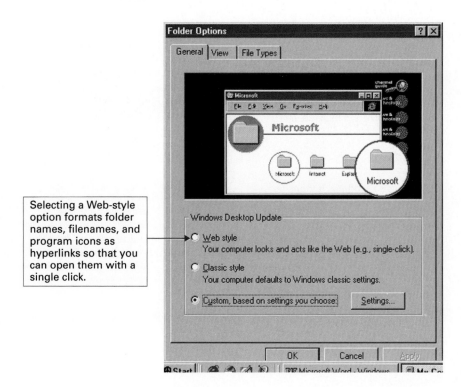

Selecting a Web-style option formats folder names, filenames, and program icons as hyperlinks so that you can open them with a single click.

7   Choose Cancel and close the My Computer window.

Customizing the Windows 95 Active Desktop

Windows 95 Active Desktop enables you to customize the Windows 95 environment for the way you work. You've already explored changing the Desktop background to the Web-style wallpaper. Now you'll move and size the Taskbar.

Sizing and Repositioning the Taskbar

The default position for the Taskbar is at the bottom of the desktop. The Taskbar can be expanded to provide more space for the features displayed and moved to a new location on the desktop.

TASK 5: TO MOVE AND SIZE THE TASKBAR:

1 Position the mouse pointer on the border between the desktop and the Taskbar.
The mouse pointer appears as a two-headed vertical arrow.

2 Drag the border toward the top of the desktop, as shown in this figure.

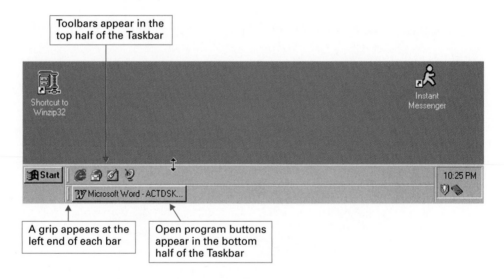

3 Drag the border of the Taskbar to its original size.

4 Position the mouse pointer on a blank area of the Taskbar.
The mouse pointer should be a white arrow.

5 Click and drag the Taskbar to the top of the desktop, and drop it.
The Taskbar appears at the top of the desktop.

6 Drag the Taskbar to the right or left side of the desktop, and drop it. The Taskbar appears as a vertical bar down the side of the desktop.

7 Return the Taskbar to its original position.

Displaying Additional Toolbars on the Taskbar

The Active Desktop provides four toolbars that you can display on the Taskbar. The Quick Launch toolbar is displayed by default. You can also display the Address, Links, and Web toolbars.

TASK 6: TO DISPLAY ADDITIONAL TOOLBARS:

1 Point to a blank area of the Taskbar, and right-click.
The Taskbar shortcut menu opens.

2 Choose Toolbars, as shown in this figure.

3 Choose Desktop, illustrated in this figure.

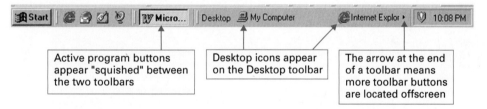

Active program buttons appear "squished" between the two toolbars

Desktop icons appear on the Desktop toolbar

The arrow at the end of a toolbar means more toolbar buttons are located offscreen

4 Right-click a blank area of the Taskbar, choose Toolbars, and choose Desktop to remove the toolbar.
The Desktop toolbar is removed from the Taskbar, and the Taskbar program buttons are restored.

Customizing Taskbar Toolbars

Each of the toolbars displayed on the Taskbar can be customized to contain the tools you use most. To remove tools from the toolbars, drag the button from the toolbar. To add a tool, drag a program item or feature onto the toolbar.

TASK 7: TO CUSTOMIZE THE QUICK LAUNCH TOOLBAR:

1 Click the Show Desktop ☑ button on the Quick Launch Toolbar.
All open programs minimize and the Active Desktop is visible.

2 Click and drag the Launch Internet Explorer Browser button from the Quick Launch Toolbar onto the desktop, and drop it.
The program button appears as a shortcut on the desktop, and the button no longer appears on the toolbar.

3 Select the Launch Internet Explorer Browser shortcut icon on the desktop, and drag and drop it in its original position on the Quick Launch toolbar.
The toolbar button appears on the toolbar, and the shortcut remains on the desktop.

4 Click the shortcut icon on the desktop, and press ⌐DEL⌐.
The Confirm File Deletion dialog box opens.

5 Choose Yes to confirm the deletion.

Floating and Restoring Toolbars

Toolbars take up valuable space on the Taskbar. When you have more programs active than will comfortably fit on the Taskbar, you can drag a toolbar to the desktop so that program buttons have more space.

TASK 8: TO MOVE AND RESTORE A TASKBAR TOOLBAR:

1 Position the mouse pointer on the Quick Launch toolbar grip.

> **Note** The mouse pointer appears as a horizontal mouse shape when you point to the grip.

2 Click and drag the toolbar from the Taskbar onto the desktop.
Your screen should look like the one in the following figure.

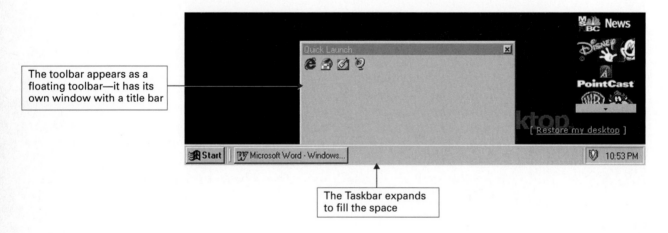

The toolbar appears as a floating toolbar—it has its own window with a title bar

The Taskbar expands to fill the space

3 Click and drag the Quick Launch title bar until the mouse pointer crosses the border of the Taskbar, as shown in this figure.

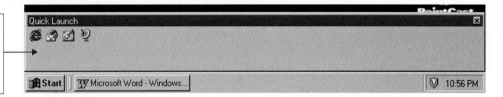

The toolbar stretches across the desktop just above the Taskbar after the mouse pointer crosses the Taskbar border—the toolbar will hop onto the Taskbar when you release the mouse button.

4 Release the mouse button.
The Quick Launch toolbar appears at the right side of the Taskbar.

5 Drag the grip beside the Start button to the right end of the Taskbar.
When the Taskbar grip is dragged past the Quick Launch toolbar, the toolbar assumes its original position.

6 Drag the toolbar and Taskbar grips until the Taskbar returns to normal.

Editing the Start Menu

The Active Desktop makes customizing the Start menu quick and easy. You can remove items from the Start menu to the desktop, or you can drag items from dialog boxes, the desktop, and folders and then place them on the Start menu.

Creating Shortcuts from the Start Menu

Dragging an item from the Start menu removes the item from the menu. To leave items on the Start menu and create shortcuts for the item on the desktop, you generally want to copy the Start menu item as you drag it to the desktop. You can drag Start menu items to the desktop or to an open dialog box or folder.

TASK 9: TO CREATE SHORTCUTS FROM THE START MENU:

1 Choose Start, Programs.
The Programs cascading menu opens.

2 Press and hold (CTRL), then click and drag the Windows Explorer icon and title to the desktop.

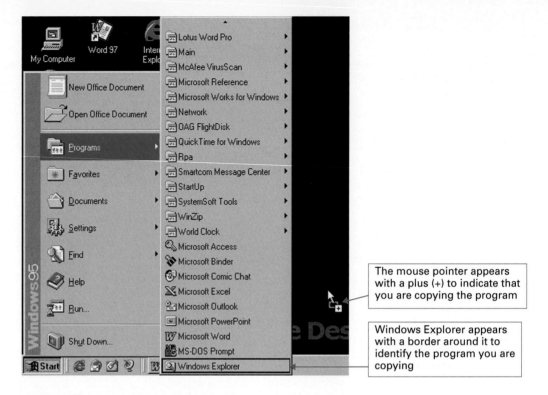

The mouse pointer appears with a plus (+) to indicate that you are copying the program

Windows Explorer appears with a border around it to identify the program you are copying

3 Drop the program on the desktop.
A Windows Explorer shortcut appears on the desktop.

4 Choose Start, Programs to ensure that the Windows Explorer icon remains on the menu.

Adding Items to the Start Menu

Adding items to the Start menu is as easy as copying shortcuts from the menu. Simply drag the item to the Start button and position the item on the menu in the desired position. It is important to keep the mouse button depressed from the time you start dragging the icon until it is properly positioned. You can also use the techniques presented here to reorganize items on the Start menu.

TASK 10: TO ADD ITEMS TO THE START MENU:

1 Drag the Windows Explorer Shortcut icon to the Start button.
The Start menu opens.

> **Troubleshooting** Do not release the mouse button until the item is properly positioned.

2 Drag the icon to the top of the Start menu, as shown in this figure.

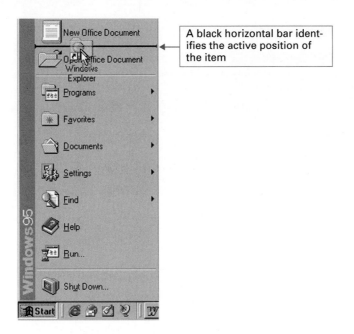

New Office Document

Open Office Document

Windows Explorer

Programs ▶

Favorites ▶

Documents ▶

Settings ▶

Find ▶

Help

Run...

Shut Down...

Start

A black horizontal bar identifies the active position of
the item

3 Release the mouse button when the item is appropriately positioned.

4 Choose Start and drag the Windows Explorer from the top of the menu to the desktop.

5 Select the Windows Explorer shortcut on the desktop, and press DEL.

Restoring the Desktop

Tasks in this preview have most likely left your desktop in a bit of a mess. You can restore the desktop to its original format using the desktop itself.

TASK 11: RESTORING THE DESKTOP:

1 Point to the Restore my desktop hyperlink on the Active Desktop, as shown in this figure.

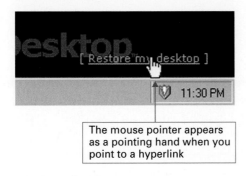

[Restore my desktop]

11:30 PM

The mouse pointer appears
as a pointing hand when you
point to a hyperlink

2   Click the hyperlink, illustrated in this figure.

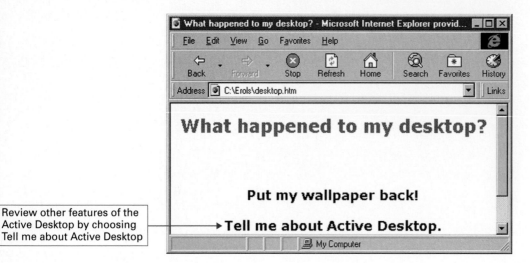

Review other features of the
Active Desktop by choosing
Tell me about Active Desktop

3   Choose Put my wallpaper back.
The dialog box shown in this figure appears.

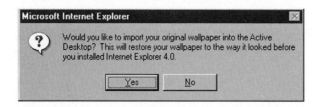

4   Choose Yes.
The original wallpaper forms the desktop background.

5   Close all open programs, if necessary, and shut down Windows 95.

Conclusion

While Windows 95 Active Desktop offers the capabilities you've worked with in this Project, Windows 98 Active Desktop enables users to add new and different objects to the Desktop. For example, with Windows 98 Active Desktop, you can add Java programs such as stock market tickers to the Desktop. In addition, you can subscribe to Web services and newsgroups and add shortcuts to these features to your Desktop. When Windows 98 is available and installed on your computer, explore Windows 98 and look for these features. Then identify other features and benefits Windows 98 has available.

Internet Explorer 4.0

Overview
of Internet
Explorer 4.0

Internet Explorer 4.0 is your "ride" on the information highway, taking you to places you want to go on the Internet and helping you obtain all sorts of information that you find there. This overview presents methods for using Internet Explorer 4.0 to access the basic resources on the Internet.

Objectives

After completing this project, you will be able to:

➤ **Identify the structure and purpose of the Internet**

➤ **Launch Internet Explorer 4.0**

➤ **Identify the Internet Explorer 4.0 screen elements**

➤ **Navigate the Internet**

➤ **Download a file via FTP**

➤ **Access resources with a Gopher**

➤ **Use channels**

➤ **Access newsgroups**

➤ **Create, send, and read e-mail**

➤ **Exit Internet Explorer 4.0**

Identifying the Structure and Purpose of the Internet

The Internet is a network of networks consisting of millions of computers, located all over the world, all using a common set of computer code called **Internet Protocol (IP)** to communicate. The Internet began with a network set up by the Department of Defense, called Advanced Research Projects Agency Network (ARPANET). Soon the National Science Foundation joined the Internet, and many universities followed. The Internet quickly established a culture of free exchange of information and ideas.

The latest addition to the Internet, the Commercial Internet Exchange (CIX) seeks to profit from the Internet. Many traditional Internet users resent the addition of the CIX because its commercial orientation is in direct opposition to the original tenets of the Internet.

The Internet is still expanding and improving. In 1997 two new initiatives were launched by the U.S. government, Next Generation Internet and Internet 2, to research, develop, and test advanced networking technologies that will revolutionize the Internet in the coming years.

> **Note** A network generally consists of many satellite computers, called clients, that are attached to a main computer, called the server. The server provides the client computers with storage space, programs, a post office, and so on.

It is amazing that an entity as large as the Internet can operate without "someone in charge." No one organization or company "owns and operates" the Internet; however, **InterNIC** does issue unique server identifiers (IP addresses) to companies and organizations that want to join the Internet. Additionally, InterNIC keeps a database of all IP addresses on the Internet and makes this information available.

> **Note** InterNIC is a collaborative project supported by the National Science Foundation for the purpose of registering and managing Internet domain names.

Connecting to the Internet

To connect to the Internet, you must be connected to a host computer. Many businesses, universities, colleges, and schools have host computers so that their employees, students, and staff can access the Internet. If you don't have access to a host computer but your computer has a modem, you can connect to the Internet through an **Internet Service Provider (ISP)**. Fees vary among ISPs — some charge a set fee for unlimited use, while others charge based on the amount of time spent online. If you find that you have become addicted to the Internet, spend most of your free time surfing, and are flunking out of school, you better look for an ISP that offers unlimited usage for a set fee.

Identifying Services on the Internet

A variety of services are available on the Internet. The most popular of these are described in Table I.1.

Table I.1: Services Available on the Internet

Service	Description
Electronic mail (e-mail)	Sends and receives electronic messages.
World Wide Web (WWW)	Provides information in a graphical format that can contain multimedia components such as sound and video. Hyperlinks link content on the WWW.
Newsgroups	Provides a bulletin board service for discussion groups.
File Transfer Protocol (FTP)	Information retrieval system that provides a means to upload and download files between computers.
Internet Relay Chat (IRC)	Provides a connection for online discussions in real time (that is, as they happen).
Gopher	Provides a menu system for locating resources on the Internet.
Telnet	Enables remote login to another computer or network.

You can connect to a site on the Internet if you know the address of the site. An address, also called a ***Uniform Resource Locator (URL)***, uses the following syntax: **protocol://domain_name/path/filename**

Table I.2 explains each part of the syntax.

Here is an example of a World Wide Web URL:

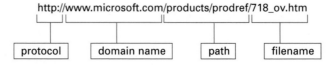

Table I.2:   Syntax of the URL

Syntax	Description
Protocol	Identifies the protocol used by the server. The World Wide Web uses HTTP protocol; File Transfer servers use FTP protocol; and gopher servers use GOPHER protocol.
Domain_name	Identifies the name assigned to the server. The name is issued by InterNIC, an organization that regulates IP addresses. The name itself must follow a specific syntax. Typical domain names are www.microsoft.com, uiuc.edu, www.novell.com, www.netscape.com, and so on. Every domain name represents a specific IP address which can be used instead of the domain name to access the Internet site. Domain names are easier to remember than IP addresses. For example, the IP address for www.microsoft.com is 207.68.156.52.
Path	Identifies the folders where the file is stored. The path may contain several folder names separated by slashes. This part of the syntax isn't used if the site is a home page (the first page of a site) on the World Wide Web.
Filename	Identifies the name of the file. This part of the syntax also isn't used if the site is a home page.

Launching Internet Explorer 4.0

Internet Explorer 4.0 is a program designed for the Windows 95/Windows NT platform. It is classified as a Web browser program because its interface is designed specifically for accessing the graphical features (pictures, icons, buttons, and so on) of the *World Wide Web*. Internet Explorer 4.0 also can be used for accessing FTP and gopher sites, which use text-based formats.

TASK 1: TO LAUNCH INTERNET EXPLORER 4.0:

 Double-click the Internet Explorer 4.0 icon on the desktop.

If a message displays telling you that Internet Explorer 4.0 is currently not the default browser, you can choose Yes to make it the default. If you don't want Internet Explorer 4.0 to be the default browser, deselect "Always perform this check when starting Internet Explorer" so you don't have to see the message each time you start Internet Explorer 4.0.

> **Hint**   If the Quick Launch toolbar displays in the taskbar, click the Launch Internet Explorer Browser button to start Internet Explorer 4.0.

2   Respond to any prompts to log onto your service provider's network, if applicable.
The default start page displays.

> **Tip** You also can launch Internet Explorer 4.0 from within each module of Office 97. Just click the Web toolbar button to display an abbreviated Internet Explorer 4.0 toolbar. When you type an Internet address and press (ENTER), Internet Explorer 4.0 launches and goes to the specified site.

Identifying the Internet Explorer 4.0 Screen Elements

Figure I.1 shows the basic elements of the Internet Explorer 4.0 screen. Table I.3 describes the elements of the screen.

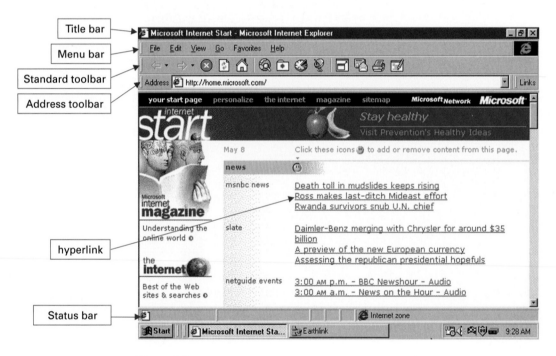

Figure I.1

Table I.3:   Screen Elements

Screen Element	Description
Title bar	Displays the name of the application and has the application minimize, maximize/restore, and close buttons.
Menu bar	Contains the options File, Edit, View, Go, Favorites, and Help.
Standard toolbar	Contains the buttons Back, Forward, Stop, Refresh, Home, Search, Favorites, History, Channels, Fullscreen, Mail, Print, and Edit. By default the Names of buttons appear below the button icons, but you can hide button names so the buttons are not as wide.
Address toolbar	Contains a text box in which you enter the address of the Internet site you want to visit.
Links toolbar	Contains buttons that jump to specific Web sites. If this toolbar is not fully displayed, you can double-click the vertical bar on the left side of the toolbar to expand the toolbar. If you drag the toolbar up or down, the toolbar moves to a new line.
Status bar	Displays information about what is happening at the moment.

Tip As you navigate to other sites on the Internet, the text box in the Address toolbar displays the address of the current site

Navigating the Internet

As soon as you launch Internet Explorer 4.0, you begin navigating the Internet automatically because Internet Explorer 4.0 takes you to its start page on the World Wide Web. To continue navigating on the Internet, you can use any of the following methods:

- Click a hyperlink
- Type the address of the Internet site
- Select a site from History
- Select a Favorite from the Favorites menu
- Click the Search button

Tip To change to a different start page, go to the desired page and choose View, Internet Options. Click the General tab, if necessary, and choose the option Use Current. Then click OK. For the sake of students who follow you, it is probably not advisable to change the start page in the computer lab.

Following Links

A Web page generally has text or graphic hyperlinks that jump to a different location. The location may be another location in the same Web page, another Web page located on the same server, or another Web page located on a server in another part of the world. Text hyperlinks are generally bright blue and underlined, but that will depend on how the page was designed. When you click a text hyperlink, the color changes to purple to show that you have followed the link.

Tip To find out whether text or a graphic is a hyperlink, point to the item with the mouse pointer. If the mouse pointer turns into a hand, then the item is a hyperlink and you can click on it.

TASK 2: TO USE A HYPERLINK:

1 Point to text or a graphic that you think is a hyperlink.

2 Click.

Tip To print what you see on the screen, click the Print button on the Standard toolbar.

Typing an Address

To connect with any site on the Internet, you can enter the site address in the text box on the Address toolbar.

Note Because Internet sites may close or move to a different location, the addresses used in the following task may be invalid when you try to use them. If you have difficulty visiting a particular address, ask your instructor for alternative addresses.

TASK 3: TO TYPE AN INTERNET ADDRESS:

1 Click in the Address text box on the Address toolbar.

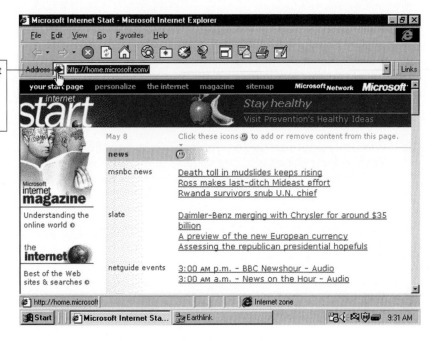

The insertion point is positioned in the text box and the address is highlighted.

2 Type **http://espnet.sportszone.com** and press (ENTER).
The ESPN SportsZone page displays.

3 Type **ftp://ftp.microsoft.com** in the Address text box and press (ENTER).
The Microsoft FTP site displays.

4 Type **gopher://gopher.tc.umn.edu** in the Address text box and press (ENTER).
The University of Minnesota Gopher site displays.

5 Click the Home button on the Standard toolbar.
The start page displays.

Tip Web pages with large graphic files (or other types of multimedia files) may take too long to display on the screen. You can turn off the downloading of multimedia by choosing View, Internet Options, and then clicking the Advanced page. Scroll down to the Multimedia section, deselect all options, and click OK. Check with your lab instructor before making changes to the computers in the lab.

Selecting a Site from History

Internet Explorer 4.0 maintains a history of the sites you visit each day so that you can return to them easily by using the *History* button.

TASK 4: TO RETURN TO A PAGE BY USING HISTORY:

1 Click the History 🌐 button on the Standard toolbar.
The Explorer bar opens. It is called the Explorer bar because it uses a hierarchical structure like Windows Explorer to display a history of the sites you visit, your favorites, channels, and searches.

2 Double-click Today's entry for ESPN's SportsZone.
The entry expands to show the pages visited at that site.

3 Click the hyperlink (espnet.sportszone.com).
The Web page displays in the pane to the right.

4 Click any hyperlink on the page in the right pane.
A new entry is added under the main entry for SportsZone.

5 Click the **X** beside History in the History pane.
The History pane closes.

Selecting a Favorite

Internet Explorer 4.0 calls shortcuts to Internet sites *Favorites* and lists them on the Favorites menu. You can create shortcuts for your favorite sites if you can't remember the addresses or you don't want to type them.

TASK 5: TO ADD A FAVORITE:

1 Ensure that you are on the SportsZone site and then click the Favorites 📁 menu on the menu bar.

2 Choose Add to Favorites.

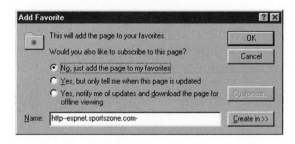

3 Click OK.
The dialog box closes, and the ESPNET SportsZone page is added to the Favorites menu.

4 Click .
The start page displays.

Using a Favorite

You can select a favorite from the Favorites menu or from the Explorer bar.

TASK 6: TO GO TO A FAVORITE:

1 Choose Favorites from the menu bar.
The Favorites menu displays.

2 Scroll, if necessary, and click the shortcut to the ESPN SportsZone page.
The Web page displays.

> **Note** Clicking the Favorites button displays Favorites in the Explorer bar.

Searching the Internet

The Internet is so vast that finding information can be a challenge. To meet that challenge, several organizations and companies have created *search engines*, programs that search the Internet for sites that have specified text. Internet Explorer 4.0 gives you access to several popular search engines.

> **Note** Your search query will result in a list of Web pages that relate to the text you specified in your query. When you look at these Web sites, you will notice that the text is not emphasized in any way to reflect your query. To find text on a Web page, use the Find command in the Edit menu.

TASK 7: TO SEARCH FOR INFORMATION USING A SEARCH ENGINE:

1 Click the Search 🔍 button.
The Explorer bar opens and displays one of the search engines.

> **Note** Unless you choose a default search engine, Internet Explorer 4.0 displays a different search engine each time you search.

2 In the Explorer bar, click Choose a Search Engine and click List of All Search Engines.

3 Click Infoseek under the Preferred Providers in the pane to the right.
The Infoseek search engine displays in the left pane. (If Infoseek is already displayed in the left pane, choose Yahoo in the right pane.)

4 Type **"beach resort"** in the text box (including the quotation marks) and click Seek.
The left pane displays the results of the search as hyperlinks.

> **Note** When sending and receiving information on the Internet, you may see security alerts to remind you that other users can obtain information about you while you are logged on unless you are using a secure connection.

5 Scroll down to see the results and click any item you want to read.
The page displays in the right pane.

Tip When you find a page you want to read, click ⊠ in the left pane so the page occupies the whole screen. When you are ready to go to another one of the hyperlinks in the search results, click ⊛ to redisplay the Explorer bar.

6 Scroll as necessary and click another hyperlink in the left pane.
A new page displays in the pane to the right.

7 Click the Back ⇐ · button.
The previous page displays in the right pane.

8 Click the Forward ⇒ · button.
The next page displays in the right pane.

9 Scroll to the bottom of the left pane and click "next 10."
The next ten hyperlinks display.

10 Click ⊠ in the Explorer bar.
The Explorer bar closes.

Downloading a File via FTP

Many organizations maintain anonymous FTP sites that contain files for public downloading. The sites are called anonymous because anyone can log on without a prearranged password.

FTP sites are text-based sites that look quite different from a Web page. They contain hierarchical lists of directories and files, much like the list of directories and files you see in Windows Explorer. Each directory or file-name in the list is a hyperlink. When you click a directory name, the directory displays its content. When you click a filename, the file opens (if Windows 95 recognizes the file type). Most text files on FTP sites use the txt format. Other files found on FTP sites are exe files (programs) and zip files (compressed files).

TASK 8: TO DOWNLOAD A FILE FROM AN FTP SITE:

1 Type **ftp://nis.nsf.net** in the Address text box and press (ENTER).
The FTP site displays.

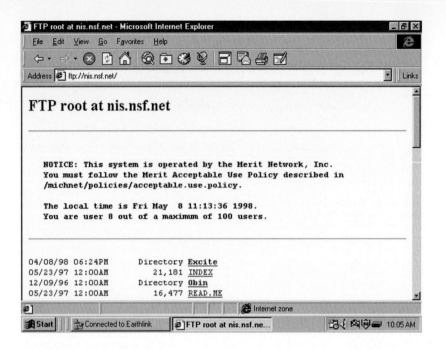

Note All FTP servers have a limit to the number of users that may log on at one time. This site is fairly busy, so you may have to try it again later.

2 Scroll down if necessary and click the directory named documents.

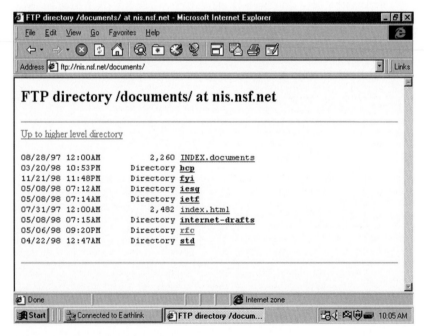

3 Click the directory named rfc.
A list of rfc (request for comment) files displays.

4 Scroll to *rfc1983.txt* and click it.

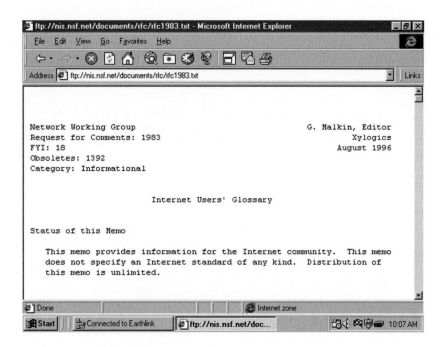

5 Choose File, Save As File.

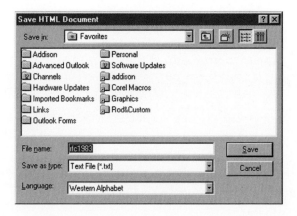

6 Select the desired folder where the file should be saved, type **Glossary** for File Name, and click Save.
The file is downloaded to the specified folder.

> **Note** Save HTML Document, the name for this dialog box, is a little misleading because most FTP sites do not have HTML files. Also, because the file is a text file, the txt format is automatically selected in the Save HTML Document dialog box.

Accessing Resources with a Gopher

A gopher site provides a character-based, hierarchical list that eventually leads to files you can download. Many gopher sites are linked to other gopher sites, so using a gopher is similar to using the Web because you can jump from one gopher site to another in your search for information. The difference is that with a gopher you move down through a hierarchy until you reach specific information; when using the Web, you may jump around in random fashion. Another difference between the Web and a gopher site is that the gopher site isn't graphical — it resembles an FTP site.

The gopher site at the University of Minnesota is a good place to start a gopher search because the site is linked to most gopher sites on the Internet. The University of Minnesota, home of the Golden Gophers, originated the gopher protocol.

> **Note** Many gopher sites have moved their information to Web servers and are concentrating their efforts on presenting data in the graphical format of the World Wide Web rather than the character-based format of gopher.

TASK 9: TO LOOK UP INFORMATION USING A GOPHER:

1 Type **gopher://gopher.tc.umn.edu** in the Address text box and press (ENTER).

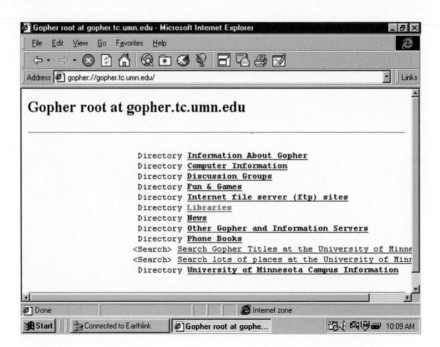

2 Click the Libraries listing.

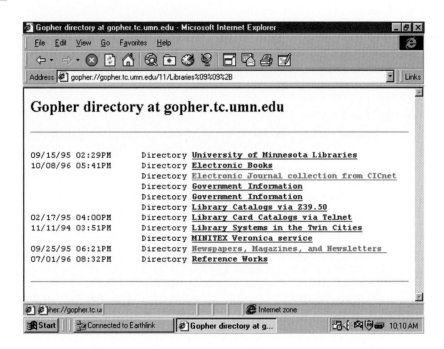

3 Click either of the Government Information listings.

4 Click Statistics and Census Data.

5 Click 1990 Census: US Summaries (via UMich).

6 Click 1990 U.S. selected population and housing data (STF1C).

7 Scroll through the page to find out what age group has the largest population.

8 Click 🏠.
The start page displays.

Using Channels

The new Internet feature called channels uses push technology to send Web-page content to your computer and store it on your system so you can view it anytime without actually being connected to the Internet. Of course, if you subscribe to too many channels you could fill up your hard disk very quickly. So don't go wild!

If you have the Active Desktop activated in Windows 95, you can display the Channel bar on the desktop. The Channel bar has a set of shortcuts to sites that have been preselected for you. You can add the sites you want to the Channel bar as well.

Using the Channel Bar on the Desktop

To use the Channel bar on the desktop, click the button for the site you want to open. Although Internet Explorer opens, you do not see the application window; instead the site occupies the full screen. When you are finished, click the Close button in the upper-right corner of the screen. (It may be difficult to see the Close button.)

> **Note** If the site you want to view has been downloaded to your local drive, you do not have to be connected to the Internet to view it.

Subscribing to a Channel

When you subscribe to a channel, any new content for the specific Web site can be sent to you automatically and stored on your local drive. When it is convenient, you can browse the Web content offline (when you are not connected to the Internet). If you don't want the content downloaded, you can simply instruct the system to notify you with an e-mail that the content has changed. The e-mail usually contains a link to the site so you can open it from the e-mail message.

TASK 10: TO SUBSCRIBE TO A CHANNEL:

1 Click the Channels 🌐 button.

2   Click Microsoft Active Channel Guide in the Explorer bar and then close the Explorer bar. (Your screen will not look exactly like this because the content of this page is constantly changing.)

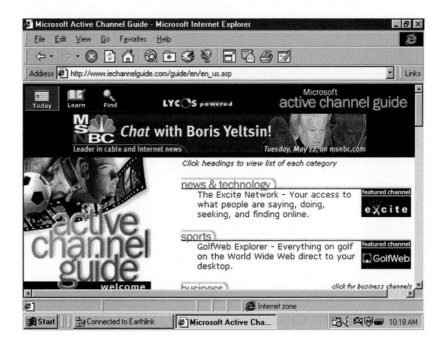

3   Click Search.
The Search screen displays.

4   Click a category and specify keywords, media type, country, and language, as desired. Then click Search.
Your screen displays the first set of icons for the channels in the selected category.

> **Note**   To see additional channel icons, click More.

5   Click the icon for the channel you want.
A preview of the channel displays.

6   Click Add Active Channel.
The Add Active Channel Content dialog box or the Modify Channel Usage dialog box opens if you select a channel that is already on the Channel bar.

> **Note**   You may have to scroll through the window to find the Add Active Channel button.

7   Choose "Yes, But Only Tell Me When Updates Occur" or choose "Yes, Notify Me of Updates and Download the Channel for Offline Viewing."
Choosing either option means that you will receive an e-mail message when the content of the page changes.

8 Click Customize.
The Subscription wizard opens.

9 Answer the questions in the wizard and choose Next to continue, if applicable.

> **Note** When given the opportunity in the Subscription Wizard to schedule the time when the computer will automatically connect to the site to download, select a time when you are not working on the computer or, if you're being billed for time online, when the rates are cheaper.

10 Choose Finish when done.
The previous dialog box reappears.

11 Choose OK.
The dialog box closes and the Explorer bar opens.

> **Note** If a message displays that says the channel subscription includes content for display by the Channel Screen Saver, choose Yes to replace your current screen saver or choose No.

Accessing Newsgroups

Newsgroups are collections of world-wide electronic discussion groups that enable network users to exchange ideas, opinions, and information. To participate in one of the many thousands of newsgroups available, you must have access to a news server and have a *newsreader* program.

Internet Explorer includes a newsreader program, so you're covered there. If you use an Internet Service Provider to connect with the Internet, then you probably have access to a news server as well because almost all ISPs have servers on their networks that are dedicated to newsgroups. If you connect to the Internet through your organization, you may or may not have access to a news server. Not all organizations find it valuable to provide a server on the network that is dedicated to newsgroups.

Usenet, the oldest organization of newsgroups, provides seven major categories:

comp	Computer-related topics
news	Newsgroup information
rec	Recreational topics
sci	Scientific research topics
soc	Social issues
talk	Controversial debates
misc	Everything else

Almost all news servers carry the seven major categories. Other categories that may or may not be carried by a news server include:

alt	Alternative subjects
bionet	Biological topics
bit	Miscellaneous topics
biz	Business-related topics and advertisements
gnu	Free Software Foundation topics
k12	Educational topics for kindergarten through 12th grade

Launching the Internet Explorer Newsreader

The newsreader program is part of the Outlook Express program that comes with Internet Explorer 4.0. You can start Outlook Express from the desktop with the Outlook Express icon or from within Internet Explorer 4.0.

TASK 11: LAUNCHING THE NEWS READER FROM INTERNET EXPLORER 4.0:

1 Click the Mail 🖂 button.
The Mail menu displays.

2 Click Read News.
Outlook Express starts and the News folder is selected in the left pane.

> **Note** The first time you use the News reader you will have to configure it. There is a Wizard to guide you, buy you may need to check with your instructor for specific instructions.

Reading a Message in a Newsgroup

Individual contributions to a newsgroup are called articles or **messages**. Submitting a message is called **posting**. Each posted message can become part of a discussion **thread**. Posting a reply to a message adds a message to the thread; posting a new message starts a new thread. Threads that have replies are marked with a plus sign (+).

TASK 12: TO READ A MESSAGE:

1 Click the News groups 🗐 button in the Outlook Express toolbar.

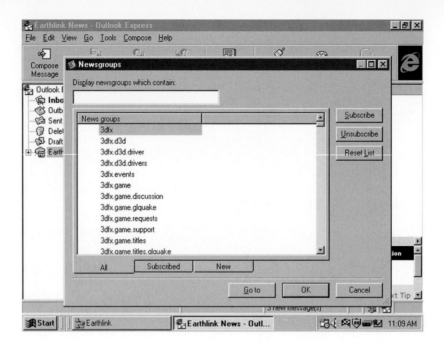

2 Scroll to rec.equestrian and click to select it. Then click Go to.
The dialog box closes, the group is added to the News folder in the left
pane, and the articles posted in the newsgroup are listed in the upper pane
on the right, as shown in this figure.

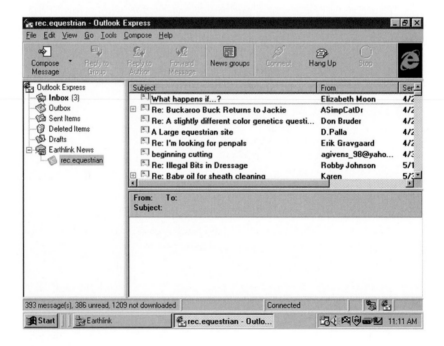

3 Click 🖻.
The Outlook Express window maximizes.

4 In the upper pane on the right, click an article you want to read.
The text appears in the lower pane.

> **Tip** If you double-click an article in the upper pane, the article opens in its own window.

5 Click .
The Newsgroup dialog box opens.

6 Scroll to rec.sport.golf and click Go to.
The newsgroup opens.

Subscribing to Newsgroups

Because so many newsgroups are available, you may want to subscribe to just the newsgroups that interest you so that you don't have to scroll through such a long list each time you want to participate in a group. Subscribing to a newsgroup is not like subscribing to a magazine — no money is involved! When you subscribe to a newsgroup, it is simply listed on a Subscription page in a dialog box so you can access it more easily.

TASK 13: SUBSCRIBING TO A NEWSGROUP:

1 Right click the rec.equestrian newsgroup in the left pane.
A shortcut menu opens.

2 Choose Subscribe to this Newsgroup.
The number of articles posted in the group appears beside the name of the group.

3 Using the same method, subscribe to the rec.sport.golf newsgroup.

4 Click .
The Newsgroup dialog box opens.

5 Scroll to and double-click rec.sport.tennis.
The newspaper icon appears next to the name. You are now subscribed to rec.sport.tennis.

> **Tip** Double-clicking also unsubscribes a newsgroup.

6 Click the Subscription tab.

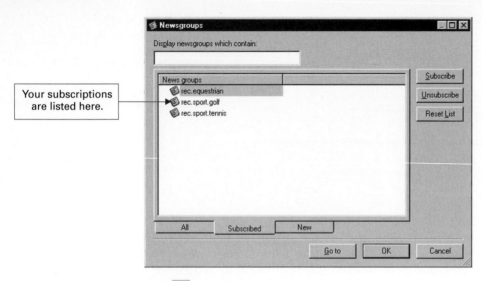

Your subscriptions are listed here.

7 Click **X**.

You will be prompted to save your changes. Go ahead and do so. Outlook Express closes, but Internet Explorer 4.0 remains open.

> **Warning** You shouldn't post messages to newsgroups unless you know the informal rules that govern the newsgroup and are familiar with proper Netiquette, news etiquette. Look for the rules in a FAQ (frequently asked questions) posted on the newsgroup. Also check the newsgroup news.announce.newusers for rules of net etiquette. Most importantly, "lurk" for a while. Lurking means to just read the messages for a few days or weeks to get comfortable with the messages before you actually participate.

Creating, Sending, and Reading E-mail

Electronic mail (e-mail) is the most widely used resource on the Internet.

Using e-mail, you can communicate with or send files to other people almost instantaneously without making expensive long-distance calls or using overnight delivery services.

To send and receive e-mail messages on the Internet, you must have an e-mail program; be connected to a *mail server*, a computer dedicated to the storage and handing of e-mail; and have an e-mail address. The e-mail program that comes with Internet Explorer 4.0 is included in Outlook Express. The mail server may be provided by your organization's network or by an Internet service provider. Your e-mail address is a combination of a user name, the "at" symbol (@), and the domain name of the server. For example, a student at the University of Illinois might have an e-mail address like this: saboggs@ux10.uiuc.edu.

Launching the E-mail Program

You can launch the e-mail program from the desktop with the Outlook Express icon or from within Internet Explorer 4.0.

TASK 14: TO LAUNCH THE E-MAIL PROGRAM FROM WITHIN INTERNET EXPLORER 4.0:

1 Click 🖾 and choose Read Mail.
Outlook Express starts, and the Inbox is selected in the left pane.

2 Click 🖻 if necessary.

Creating and Sending a New Message

To send an e-mail message, you must have a valid e-mail address for the recipient.

TASK 15: TO CREATE AND SEND A NEW MESSAGE:

1 Click the Compose Message button.

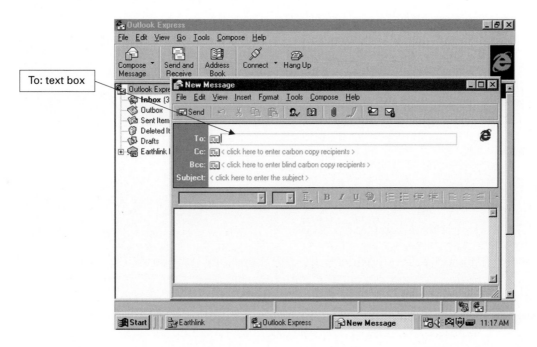

2 Type a valid e-mail address in the To: text box. (Type your own e-mail address, if desired.)

3 Click <click here to enter the subject> and type **Test**.

4 Click in the blank area under the Subject and type **This is a test.**

5 Click the Send button.
The message is sent immediately.

> **Note** If the Send option for sending messages immediately is de-selected, the message will be stored in the Outbox until you click the Send and Receive button.

6 Click ❌.
Outlook Express closes.

> **Tip** You can create and send a new e-mail message from within Internet Explorer 4.0 without opening Outlook Express by choosing New Message from the Mail menu.

Reading E-mail

The e-mail that you receive is stored in the Inbox.

TASK 16: TO READ AN E-MAIL MESSAGE:

1 Start Outlook Express, if necessary, and click any message in the upper pane.
The message displays in the lower pane.

> **Tip** If you double-click the message in the upper pane, the message opens in its own window.

2 Click ❌ when finished.
Outlook Express closes.

Exiting Internet Explorer 4.0

When you are finished using the Internet, exit Internet Explorer 4.0 and terminate your connection, if necessary.

TASK 17: TO EXIT INTERNET EXPLORER 4.0:

1 Click ❌.

2 Choose the option to disconnect if you are prompted to disconnect from your Internet Service Provider's network.

Summary and Exercises

Summary

- The Internet is a network of networks all communicating with the IP protocol.
- Services on the Internet include e-mail, World Wide Web, newsgroups, FTP, gopher, relay chat, and telnet.
- Internet Explorer 4.0 provides many ways to navigate the Internet.
- The World Wide Web presents data in a graphical format.
- FTP sites contain files for downloading.
- Gopher sites provide hierarchical menus to access resources.
- Newsgroups are discussion groups.
- E-mail is a fast, convenient, inexpensive way to communicate.

Key Terms and Operations

Key Terms

amortization	InterNIC
Key Terms	Links toolbar
Address toolbar	mail server
client	message
domain name	Netiquette
e-mail	newsgroups
FAQ	newsreader
Favorite	posting
FTP	search engine
gopher	server
History	telnet
HTTP	thread
Internet Protocol (IP)	URL
Internet Relay Chat (IRC)	World Wide Web
Internet Service Provider (ISP)	

Operations

download a file	print a Web page
exit Internet Explorer 4.0	read a newsgroup message
exit Outlook Express	read an e-mail message
follow a link	search the Internet
launch Internet Explorer 4.0	send an e-mail message
launch Outlook Express	subscribe to a newsgroup

Study Questions

Multiple Choice

1. URL is
   a. a protocol used on the World Wide Web.
   b. an acronym for Unspecified Resource Link.
   c. an acronym for Uniform Resource Locator.
   d. the organization that regulates the Internet.

2. The gopher protocol was originated at the
   a. University of Illinois.
   b. University of Minnesota.
   c. University of Wisconsin.
   d. National Science Foundation.

3. A Web browser is a
   a. user who browses the Web without actively participating.
   b. user who browses the Web an actively participates.
   c. program that accesses Web sites on the Internet.
   d. search engine on a gopher site.

4. The oldest organization of newsgroups is
   a. Internet.
   b. Usenet.
   c. BITNET.
   d. Clarinet.

5. The syntax for an e-mail address is
   a. domain_name@user_name.
   b. user_name@domain_name.
   c. site@logon_id.
   d. logon_id@school_name.

6. The Find command searches
   a. all Web sites for specified text.
   b. all FTP sites for specified text.
   c. only the current page for specified text.
   d. all gopher sites for specified text.

7. When you click a hyperlink,
   a. a pop-up box displays with a description of the hyperlink.
   b. the name of the hyperlinked file displays.
   c. another location on the Internet is accessed.
   d. you are automatically logged off the Internet.

8. The History stores
   a. a log of the dates and times you log on to the Internet.
   b. a list of Favorites.
   c. links to the Internet addresses you have accessed each day.
   d. a list of user names that log on to the Internet.

9. When the mouse pointer hovers over a hyperlink
   a. the link changes color.
   b. the link blinks.
   c. the pointer changes to a hand with a pointing finger.
   d. the pointer changes color.

10. Subscribing to a channel
    a. entails a fee.
    b. places an icon in the Channel box on the desktop.
    c. Both a and b.
    d. None of the above.

Short Answer

1. What was the name of the first network on the Internet, and who established it?

2. What protocol does the World Wide Web use?

3. What does FTP stand for?

4. What are newsgroups?

5. What is a thread?

6. What is a channel?

7. What is a hyperlink?

8. What is a FAQ?

9. What is an Internet Service Provider?

10. What Internet service/protocol is used to store files for downloading?

For Discussion

1. Discuss the advantages and disadvantages of using channels.

2. Do you think that the traditional culture on the Internet is justified in feeling some resentment toward the Commercial Internet Exchange? Why or why not?

3. In what ways can you benefit from the Internet personally?

4. Why do you think that e-mail is the most popular service on the Internet?

Review Exercises

1. Finding information with Gophers

The daily temperature is very important to the golf course manager, so you must check the temperature for your area on a daily basis. In this exercise, you will create a favorite for a resource you find on a gopher.

1. Launch Internet Explorer 4.0 and go to gopher://gopher.utdallas.edu.

2. Click Internet Services and Information.

3. Click Internet Information by Subject.

4. Click Weather.

5. Click Weather forecasts and maps (the U of I Weather Machine).

6. Add this site to the Favorites.

7. Click States and Provinces.

8. Click South Carolina, US.

9. Click Surface Summary (with names).

10. Click the Print button.

2. Using the World Wide Web

In this exercise, you will explore some of the links on the Links toolbar.

1. Launch Internet Explorer 4.0, if necessary, and display the Links toolbar by dragging it under the Address toolbar.

2. Click the Best of the Web button in the toolbar.

3. Print the page.

Assignments

1. Exploring newsgroups

Explore the newsgroups more thoroughly and visit newsgroups that might be interesting or helpful in the management of a resort. Make a list of the newsgroups that you find.

2. Exploring FTP sites

Explore several of the following FTP sites:

ftp://ftp.novell.com
ftp://ftp.microsoft.com
ftp://ftp.sco.com
ftp://ftp.digital.com
ftp://rtfm.mit.edu
ftp://nis.nsf.net
ftp://ds.internic.net

Use the Index files on each site to get acquainted with the site. Then look for the following types of files to download: helpful information about the Internet, free software programs, and graphic files. Make a list of the files that you would like to download.

Word Processing
Using Microsoft Word 97

Overview

Before you can become productive with Word 97, you need to get acquainted with the program and learn how to perform some of the most basic functions of word processing. After you are comfortable with starting and exiting the program and getting help, you will be ready to tackle the tasks in the projects that follow.

Objectives

After completing this project, you will be able to:

➤ **Identify the Word 97 features**

➤ **Launch Word 97**

➤ **Identify Word 97 screen elements**

➤ **Get help**

➤ **Close a document**

➤ **Exit Word 97**

Identifying the Word 97 Features

The primary purpose of a word processing program is to create documents such as memos, letters, envelopes, reports, manuals, and so on. Word 97 is a powerful program that has all the features you need to create the most complex documents (see Figure 0.1), yet it's easy to use and easy to learn. Word 97 includes many features such as creating headers and footers, tables of contents and indexes, and tables and forms; checking spelling and grammar; using a thesaurus; inserting graphics and other objects; and creating form letters that are merged with address lists. Additionally, you can cut, copy, and move text; find text for editing without reading through the document, format a document automatically by making a selection from a gallery of formats,

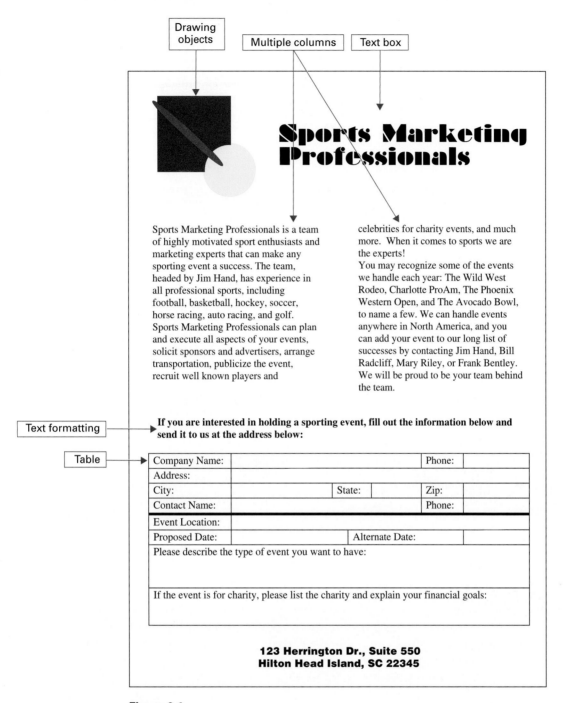

Drawing objects

Multiple columns

Text box

Sports Marketing Professionals

Sports Marketing Professionals is a team of highly motivated sport enthusiasts and marketing experts that can make any sporting event a success. The team, headed by Jim Hand, has experience in all professional sports, including football, basketball, hockey, soccer, horse racing, auto racing, and golf. Sports Marketing Professionals can plan and execute all aspects of your events, solicit sponsors and advertisers, arrange transportation, publicize the event, recruit well known players and

celebrities for charity events, and much more. When it comes to sports we are the experts!

You may recognize some of the events we handle each year: The Wild West Rodeo, Charlotte ProAm, The Phoenix Western Open, and The Avocado Bowl, to name a few. We can handle events anywhere in North America, and you can add your event to our long list of successes by contacting Jim Hand, Bill Radcliff, Mary Riley, or Frank Bentley. We will be proud to be your team behind the team.

Text formatting

If you are interested in holding a sporting event, fill out the information below and send it to us at the address below:

Table

Company Name:				Phone:	
Address:					
City:		State:		Zip:	
Contact Name:				Phone:	
Event Location:					
Proposed Date:			Alternate Date:		
Please describe the type of event you want to have:					
If the event is for charity, please list the charity and explain your financial goals:					

123 Herrington Dr., Suite 550
Hilton Head Island, SC 22345

Figure 0.1

change the look of a paragraph by applying a predefined style, preview a document before you print it, and make a common typing error or misspell a common word without worrying because Word 97 corrects the mistake automatically.

Launching Word 97

When you start your computer, you may have to log on to a network or perform some other steps before Windows 95 starts. After the Windows 95 desktop displays on the screen, you're ready to launch Word 97.

TASK 1: TO LAUNCH WORD 97:

1   Click the Start 🏁Start button and point to Programs.

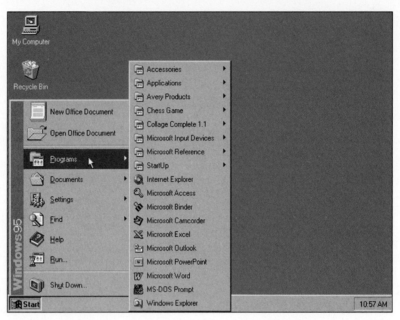

2   Point to the Microsoft Word program and click. The program opens in a window and creates a document called *Document1*.

Identifying Word 97 Screen Elements

The Word 97 screen has many of the common elements of a Windows 95 screen as well as some elements that are unique to the Word 97 program (see Figure 0.2). Because screen elements can be turned on and off, your screen may not look exactly like the screen in the figure.

Note The screen displays two Close buttons. The button in the title bar closes Word 97; the button in the menu bar closes the current document.

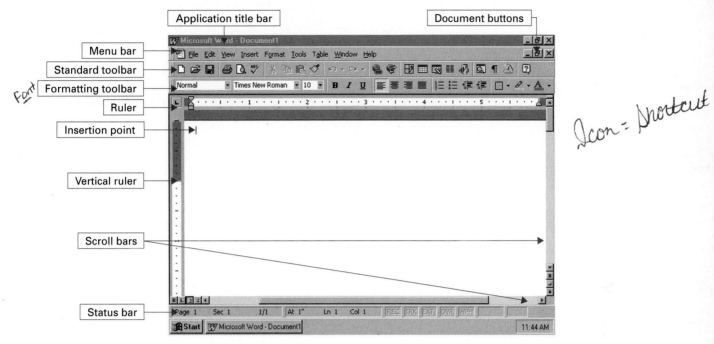

Font

Icon = Shortcut

Figure 0.2 The Word 97 Screen

Elements of the screen include the following:

Element	Description
Application title bar	Displays the name of the application and the Minimize, Maximize/Restore, and Close buttons. If the document window is maximized, as in Figure 0.2, the name of the document also displays in the application title bar.
Document title bar	Displays the document title and the Minimize, Maximize/Restore, and Close buttons. If the window is maximized, no document title bar displays and the document buttons display in the menu bar. This title bar is not shown in Figure O.2
Menu bar	Contains menu options. To use the menu, click an option to display a drop-down menu and then click an option on the drop-down menu to perform a command, view another menu, or view a dialog box.
Standard toolbar	Contains buttons for accomplishing commands. To use the toolbar, click a button to perform a command or view a dialog box.
Formatting toolbar	Contains buttons and controls for formatting. To use the toolbar, click a button to perform a command or view a dialog box.
Ruler	Displays the settings for the margins, tabs, and indents. The ruler also can be used to make these settings.
Insertion point	Marks the position with a blinking vertical line where a letter is inserted when you press a key.
Vertical and horizontal scroll bars	Scroll the screen vertically and horizontally.
Status bar	Displays information about the current document, including the page number and the position of the insertion point.

Working with Toolbars

Toolbars contain buttons that perform functions to accomplish a specific task or group of related tasks. Word 97 has several toolbars, but the Standard toolbar and the Formatting toolbar are the default toolbars, the ones that Word automatically displays. You can display or hide as many toolbars as you want.

You also can move toolbars to different locations on the screen. When a toolbar has been closed and then displayed again, Word places it where it was last located.

TASK 2: TO WORK WITH TOOLBARS:

1   Choose View, Toolbars.

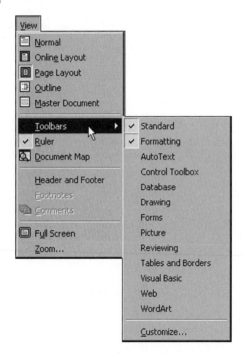

2   Click AutoText to display that toolbar.
The menu closes. Repeat for Control Toolbox, Database, and Drawing to display each toolbar (each time you choose a toolbar, the menu will close, requiring you to reopen it to select another toolbar).

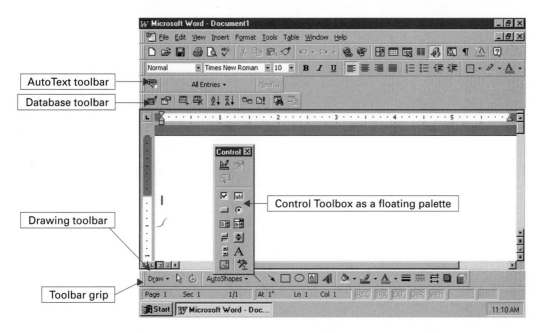

AutoText toolbar

Database toolbar

Drawing toolbar

Toolbar grip

Control Toolbox as a floating palette

Your screen may not look exactly like this if Word 97 has been used by someone who previously moved the toolbars.

Tip Some buttons on the Standard toolbar also display toolbars. The Web button displays the Web toolbar, for example, and the Drawing button displays the Drawing toolbar.

3 Point to the grip on any toolbar and drag the toolbar to the middle of the screen.

The grip

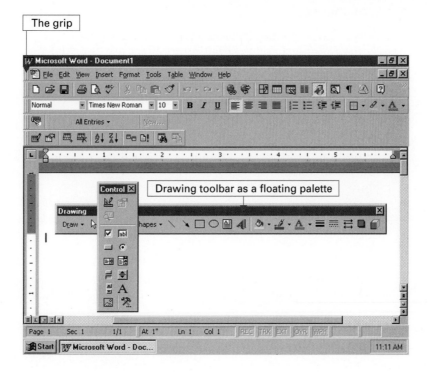

Drawing toolbar as a floating palette

4   Click the Close ✖ button of the palette you just moved.
The palette closes.

5   Point to the title bar of any floating palette and drag it to the top of the screen until it becomes a toolbar.
(If you don't have a floating palette, drag the toolbar until it becomes a palette and then drag it to the top of the screen until it becomes a toolbar.

6   Point to any toolbar and right-click.

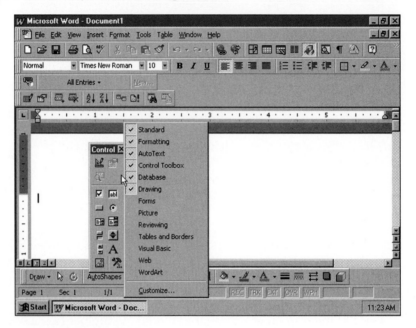

7   Click any toolbar that has a check mark beside it.
The toolbar closes.

8   Choose View, Toolbars and remove the check mark on each toolbar until only the Standard and Formatting toolbars are checked. (You may have to add check marks to the Standard and Formatting toolbars if you have closed them.)
Your screen should have the toolbars shown in Figure 0.2 displayed.

> **Note** If you want to hide a toolbar that you displayed by clicking a button on the Standard toolbar, just click the button again. The toolbar will disappear.

Hiding and Displaying the Ruler

The ruler provides an easy method of setting margins, tabs, and indents. If you don't need to use the ruler, you can hide it to provide more room on the screen. You use the same steps to hide or display the ruler.

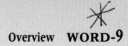

TASK 3: TO HIDE OR DISPLAY THE RULER:

read note

1 Choose View.

2 Choose Ruler.
The ruler displays if it wasn't displayed before.

3 Choose View, Ruler again, if necessary to redisplay the ruler.

Getting Help

Word 97 provides several ways to get help while you're learning and using the program. Previously, most software manufacturers went to great expense to produce printed user manuals that explained all the features of the program. Now the trend is to provide short Getting Started manuals and *online help* that explains all the features of the program. For online help, Word 97 offers several forms of help—the standard Windows 95 Help dialog box with three pages: Contents, Index, and Find; as well as What's This?, Office Assistant, and Help from the Microsoft Web site.

Note The term *online help* refers to the help that is provided by the software and is accessible on the computer. Online help doesn't refer to "going online," which implies connecting with the Internet or some other network.

TASK 4: TO USE THE WORD HELP DIALOG BOX:

1 Choose Help, Contents and Index, and click the Index tab.

2 Type **splitting windows**.

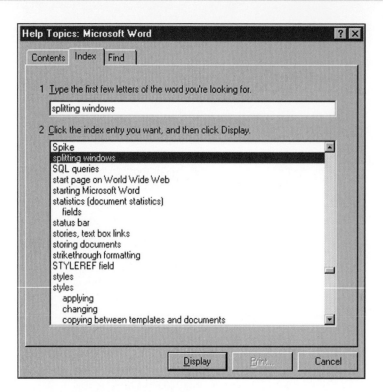

3 Double-click the topic "splitting windows" in the list.

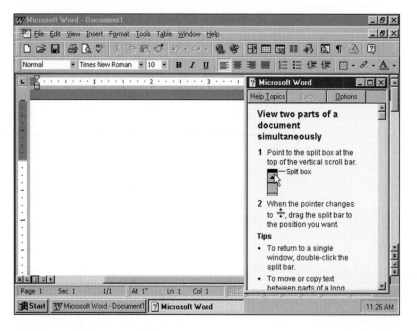

4 Read the Help information.

5 Click **X** when you finish reading the Help information. The dialog box closes.

Using the What's This? Help Feature

If you just want to know what something is, what something does, or what something means, you can use the *What's This?* Help feature. What's This? Help displays a short description in a pop-up box.

TASK 5: TO USE WHAT'S THIS? HELP:

1 Choose Tools, Language, Hyphenation.

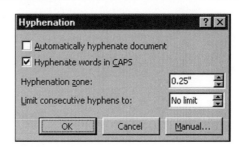

2 Click the What's This? [?] button.
A question mark is attached to the mouse pointer.

3 Click Hyphenation zone.

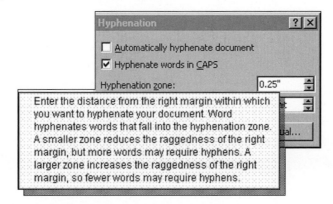

4 After reading the information, click the pop-up box. The pop-up box closes.

> **Tip** You can use What's This? help even if you aren't in a dialog box. Press Shift+F1 or choose Help, What's This? and then click the item you have a question about.

5 Click the Close button [X] to close the Hyphenation dialog box.

Using the Office Assistant

If you need some "hand-holding" help, use the new Help feature called *Office Assistant*. Whenever possible, the Office Assistant offers help on the task you are performing, and is often referred to as *context-sensitive help*. If the Office Assistant doesn't display the help you want, you can type a question to obtain the desired help.

TASK 6: TO USE THE OFFICE ASSISTANT:

1 Click the Office Assistant 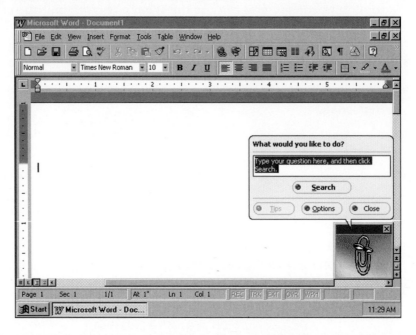 button.

2 Type **How do you count the number of words in a document?** and click Search.

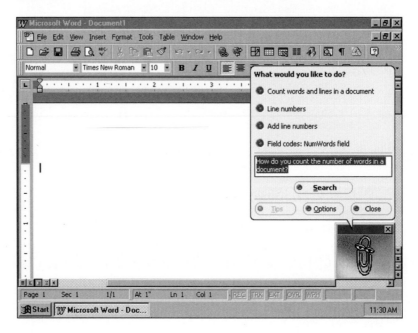

3   Click Count words and lines in a document.

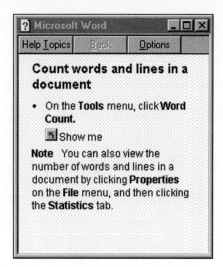

4   After reading the Help dialog box, click ☒.
The Help dialog box closes, but the Office Assistant window remains open.

5   Click the Office Assistant character in the Office Assistant window.
The Office Assistant asks what you want to do.

Note The default Office Assistant is a paper clip named Clippit. Other assistants include Shakespeare, a robot, and a cat—to name a few.

6   Click Close.
The "bubble" closes.

7   Click ☒ in the Office Assistant window.
The Office Assistant winks at you, and the window closes.

Getting Help from the World Wide Web

Microsoft maintains several sites on the Web that have useful information, user support, product news, and free programs and files that you can download. If your system is connected to the Internet, you can access this type of help easily. The Microsoft sites are open to all users.

Note When Microsoft is beta-testing a program, the company maintains "closed sites" open only to beta testers with a valid password.

TASK 7: TO READ ANSWERS TO FREQUENTLY ASKED QUESTIONS:

1   Choose Help, Microsoft on the Web.

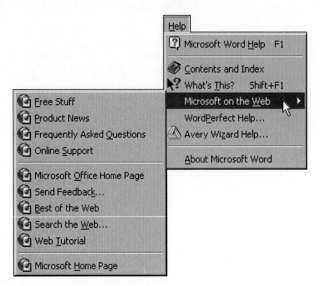

2   Choose Frequently Asked Questions. (If prompted, connect to your Internet Service Provider.)
The Internet browser program starts (usually Internet Explorer) and connects to the appropriate Web site.

3   When you finish browsing the Web, click **X** in the browser window.

Closing a Document and Exiting Word 97

Before you exit Word, you should always save any work that you want to keep and then close any open documents. When you exit Word 97, the program closes, and the Windows 95 desktop is visible again. If you have another program running in a maximized window, however, the program will be visible, not the desktop.

> **Tip** If you forget to save and close a changed file before you try to exit, Word 97 asks whether you want to save changes. You can choose Yes to save the changed file, No to exit without saving, or Cancel to cancel the exit request.

TASK 8: TO CLOSE THE DOCUMENT AND EXIT WORD 97:

1 Click ❌ in the document title bar.
Only the application window is open now.

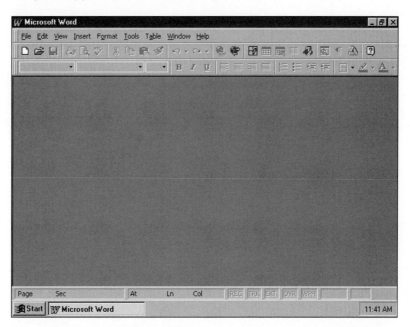

2 Click ❌ in the application title bar.
The Word 97 program closes.

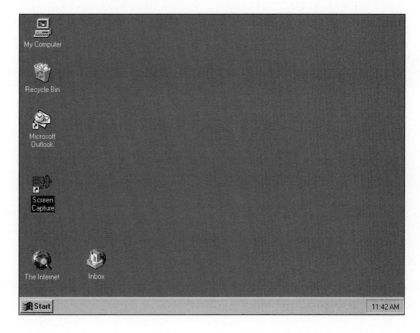

Summary and Exercises

Summary

- Word 97 is a full-featured word processing program that's easy to use.
- Many features of Word 97 streamline work by performing tasks automatically.
- You can hide or display many screen elements to suit your needs.
- If you don't understand a concept or you don't know how to do a task, you can get help from a variety of sources online or from the Web.
- Word 97 won't let you exit without reminding you to save a changed file if you haven't already done so.

Key Terms and Operations

Key Terms
application title bar
context-sensitive help
document title bar
floating palette
insertion point
menu bar
Office Assistant
online help
ruler
scroll bars
status bar
title bar

toolbar
toolbar grip
What's This?
word processing program

Operations
exit Word 97
get help from the Web
get online help
hide and display the ruler
hide and display toolbars
start Word 97
use Office Assistant

Study Questions

Multiple Choice

1. Which of the following methods starts Office Assistant?
   a. Choose Help, Office Assistant.
   b. Click the Office Assistant button.
   c. Press Shift+F1.
   d. Press F1.

2. To start Word 97,
   a. click Start and choose Run, Word 97.
   b. double-click the Outlook icon on the desktop.
   c. start Windows 95 and then press Alt+W.
   d. click Start and choose Programs, Microsoft Word.

3. Which two of the following aren't valid methods of moving a toolbar?
   a. Point to the toolbar and press the right mouse button while dragging the toolbar to a new location.
   b. Point to the toolbar grip and drag the toolbar to a new location.
   c. Point to the title bar of the toolbar and drag the toolbar to a new location.
   d. Choose View, Toolbar, Move.

4. To turn on the Web toolbar,
    a. point to the Standard toolbar, right-click, and click Web.
    b. point to any toolbar, right-click, and click Web.
    c. click the Web button on the Standard toolbar.
    d. All of the above.

5. The purpose of the ruler is
    a. to set the width of the page.
    b. to display the margins, tabs, and indents.
    c. to set the margins, tabs, and indents.
    d. Both B and C.

6. A shortcut menu
    a. appears when you right-click a toolbar.
    b. displays a list of shortcut keys.
    c. displays when you choose View, Shortcuts.
    d. displays shortcut icons.

7. To exit Word 97,
    a. choose File, Exit.
    b. click the Close button in the menu bar.
    c. click the Exit button in the Standard toolbar.
    d. Both A and B.

8. A question mark is attached to the mouse pointer when
    a. you press Shift+?.
    b. you press Shift+F1.
    c. you choose File, What's This?
    d. Both B and C.

9. To get help on the Web, you must
    a. be registered for support with Microsoft.
    b. have a connection to the Internet.
    c. know the password to logon to the Microsoft Web site.
    d. be a registered user of Office 97.

10. Which of the following is a false statement?
    a. The insertion point blinks.
    b. The insertion point marks the position where a letter will be inserted when you press a key.
    c. The insertion point is a vertical line.
    d. The insertion point can change shapes.

Short Answer

1. What are the two Word 97 default toolbars?

2. Can you exit Word 97 without saving your work?

3. What Help feature allows you to ask for help in your own words?

4. What's the grip on a toolbar?

5. What's the name of the document created automatically by Word 97 when you start the program?

6. What type of toolbar has a Close button?

7. What Help feature is equivalent to a printed user manual?

8. What's context-sensitive help?

9. How is it possible that Word 97 could be running on two different computers and the screens wouldn't look identical?

10. What happens if you click the Close button in the menu bar?

For Discussion

1. What features included in Word 97 do you think will be most useful for you?

2. What advantage is there to moving toolbars to different locations on the screen?

3. Discuss the pros and cons of using a printed user manual versus using online help.

4. Compare the value of the help information on the Web to the online help information that comes with Word 97.

Review Exercises

1. Customizing the Screen

Your work requires quite a bit of drawing, but you rarely make changes to margins, tabs, or indents. Customize your screen so that it accommodates your needs (see Figure 0.3).

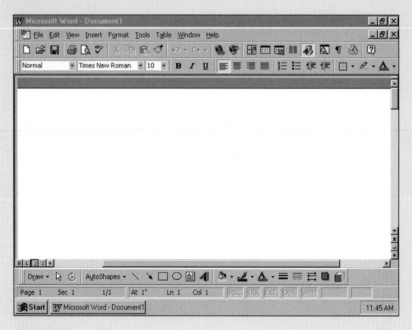

Figure 0.3

1. Start Word 97 if necessary.

2. Hide the Ruler if it's displayed.

3. Display the Drawing toolbar.

4. Drag the toolbar so it turns into a floating palette (if it isn't already floating) and move it to the location shown in Figure 0.3.

5. Exit Word 97 without saving the file.

2. Getting Help on the Web

Your company has a policy of upgrading software whenever a new release comes out. Find out whether Microsoft is developing any new software programs or upgrades at the current time.

1. Choose Help, Microsoft on the Web.

2. Choose Product News.

3. Follow appropriate hypertext links.

4. When you're finished, close Internet Explorer.

3. Using Word 97 features

1. Launch Word 97, if necessary.

2. Hide the Ruler if it's displayed; display the Ruler if it is not displayed.

3. Display the Web toolbar.

4. Drag the toolbar so it docks on the right side of the screen.

5. Use the Search the Web button on the Web toolbar to log onto the Internet and search for Free Stuff.

Note If you cannot connect to the Internet using the Search the Web button on the Web toolbar, choose Help, Microsoft on the Web, Free Stuff to connect and search the Web.

6. Follow appropriate hypertext links to locate something free that you find interesting and make a note of the URL address for the free item.

7. Print a copy of the page containing information about the free item.

8. When you're finished, close Internet Explorer.

9. Drag the Web toolbar back to the top of the screen and close the Web toolbar.

Assignments

1. Using Help to Explore and Use Buttons on the Drawing Toolbar

Display the Drawing toolbar, if necessary. Use What's This? help to display a description of the rectangle icon on the Drawing toolbar. Using the information What's This? provides, draw a rectangle as shown in Figure 0.4. Ask the Office Assistant how to add a fill color and then add a blue fill to the rectangle.

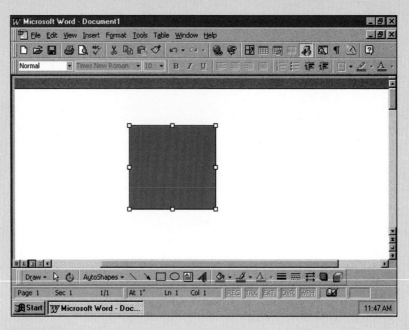

Figure 0.4

2. Exploring the Microsoft Home Page

The Microsoft home page has links to many interesting and helpful sites, and the home page changes frequently. Using Microsoft on the Web help, go to the Microsoft home page and see what's there. Print the page.

Creating a Document

Creating, saving, and printing are tasks that are basic to Word 97. Every user must have a good grasp of these skills in order to use Word 97 effectively.

Objectives

After completing this project, you will be able to:

- ➤ **Create a new document**
- ➤ **Enter text**
- ➤ **Undo changes**
- ➤ **Correct errors marked by SpellIt**
- ➤ **Save a document**
- ➤ **Preview a document**
- ➤ **Print a document**
- ➤ **Close a file**

The Challenge

In September, The Willows will host a golf tournament to benefit the Juvenile Diabetes Foundation. You must type a letter to a marketing firm asking Jim Hand to handle the tournament.

The Solution

Figure 1.1 shows the first draft of the document you will create and print on letterhead stationery. Because you will be enclosing the letter in a larger envelope with other enclosures, you don't need to create an envelope for this letter.

Figure 1.1

The Setup

So that your screen will match the illustrations and the tasks in this project will function as described, make sure that the Word 97 settings listed in Table 1.1 are selected on your computer.

Table 1.1   Word 97 Settings

Location	Make these settings:
View, Toolbars	Deselect all toolbars except the Standard and Formatting toolbars
View	Deselect the ruler
Standard toolbar	Deselect any buttons that are selected and set Zoom to 100%
Insert, AutoText, AutoText	Select the Show AutoComplete tip for AutoText and dates option
Tools, Options, Spelling & Grammar	Select the Check spelling as you type and the Check Grammar as you type options
My Computer: View, Options, View	Deselect Hide MS-DOS file extentions for file types that are registered

Creating a New Document

When you launch Word 97, a blank *new document* named Document 1 automatically opens for you and you can begin to type.

TASK 1: TO CREATE A NEW DOCUMENT:

1 Click the Start  button.

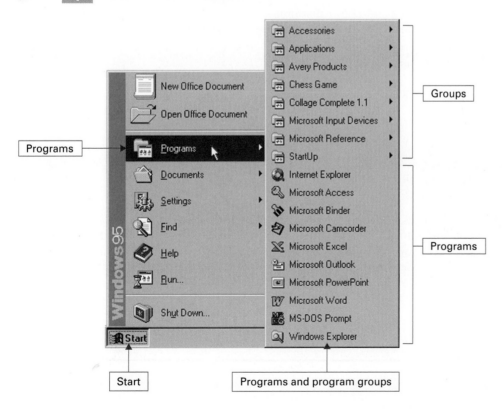

2 Point to Programs and choose the Microsoft Word program.
The program opens in a window and creates a document called Document1.

> **Troubleshooting** If Word is already started and you don't see a document on the screen, click the New button. Word creates a new document just for you.

Entering Text

Instead of typing the complete letter you see in Figure 1.1, you will type the letter in sections so that you can focus on some features and commands. As you type, you will be using the **Enter** key to end short lines and paragraphs and create blank lines. Don't press the Enter key at the end of each line in a paragraph, because the lines in the paragraph **wrap** around automatically.

> **Caution** When you want to move down through the text, use the down arrow, not the Enter key. Remember that you use the Enter key only when you want to start a new paragraph or create a blank line.

TASK 2: TO SPACE DOWN ENOUGH TO ALLOW FOR THE LETTERHEAD:

1 Press (CTRL)+(HOME) to ensure that the insertion point is in the upper-left corner of the document.
Notice that the status bar displays 1" for the vertical position of the insertion point; you need to allow space for the letterhead.

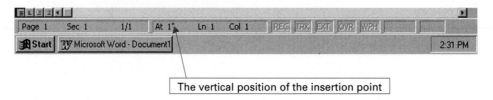

The vertical position of the insertion point

2 Press (ENTER) repeatedly until the vertical position 2.1" is displayed in the status bar. (Press (BACKSPACE) if you go too far.)

Inserting a Date

The date should appear on the first line of the letter. Instead of typing the date, you can have Word 97 insert it for you.

TASK 3: TO INSERT THE DATE:

1   Choose Insert from the menu bar.

2   Choose Date and Time.

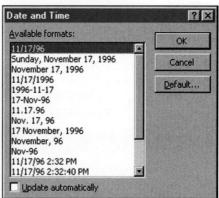

3   Select the third format.

Your computer will show the current date in this list

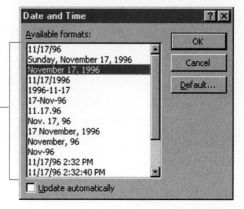

> **Tip** If you want to use the same date format in all your documents, click Default and choose Yes.

4 Click OK.
The current date (if the date in the computer is accurate) appears in the document.

Correcting Errors

As you type, you probably will make typos, but you may not see too many when you use this version of Word: the Word *AutoCorrect* feature automatically corrects many common typographical errors, such as *t-e-h* and *a-h-v-e*. When you see a word underlined with a wavy red line, you haven't gone crazy: Word is just pointing out a word that isn't in its dictionary. When you make a grammatical mistake, the Word Grammar feature underlines it with a wavy green line.

When you see a typo or a grammatical error, you can use the Backspace key to erase and then retype. Don't worry if you fail to catch and correct some mistakes while typing. You will have a chance in Project 2 to fix these little culprits when you are learning to make other revisions.

TASK 4: TO TYPE THE FIRST PART OF THE LETTER SHOWN IN FIGURE 1.1:

1 Press (ENTER) four times after the date.

2 Type **Sprots** (No, it's not a typo. Well, it is a typo, but it's deliberate so you can get some practice making corrections.)

3 Press (BACKSPACE) four times.
The last four letters you typed are erased.

4 Type **orts**.

5 Type **Marketing Professionals** and press (ENTER). Type each line of the remainder of the address, pressing (ENTER) after each line, as in:

Jim Hand
Sports Marketing Professionals
123 Harrington Dr., Suite 550
Hilton Head Island, SC 29928

6 Press (ENTER) again to create a blank line between the address and the greeting you are going to type.

7 Type **Dear Jim,** and press ⟨ENTER⟩ twice.

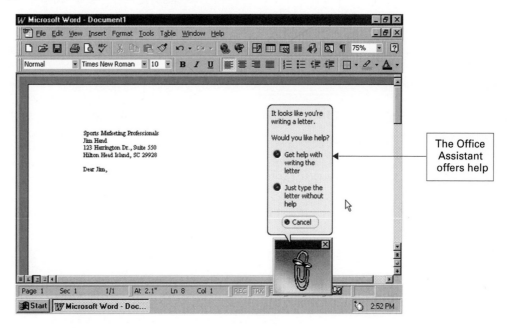

The Office Assistant offers help

8 Click Cancel on the Office Assistant message.

9 Type the first paragraph until you reach the word "the," as in:

We were so pleased with your work on our celebrity tournament last year that we want you to promote our ladies charity tournament scheduled for September 18–20 this year. (Profits will be donated to

10 Type **teh** and a space. AutoCorrect fixes your typo!

11 Type the following:

Juvenile Diabetes Fund.) We want to invite at least 15 of the top women PGA players and 10 national and local celebrities. This will give us a total of 25 foursomes with a player or a celebrity in each foursome.

12 Press ⟨ENTER⟩ twice.

13 Type the following:

You will need to line up the players and celebrities, obtain sponsors, and promote the tournament locally. Our goal is to realize $100,000 in profits.

14 Press ⟨ENTER⟩ twice.

Inserting Special Characters

The keyboard has a limited number of characters. Some of the characters you may want to include in text, such as © and ®, can't be typed from the keyboard, but you can insert them by using the Symbol dialog box.

TASK 5: TO INSERT A SYMBOL:

1 Type **I have enclosed several lists of names.** (Don't type the period.)

2 Choose Insert from the menu bar.
The Insert menu displays.

3 Choose Symbol and click the square that contains the em dash.

To select a symbol in a different font, click this drop-down list

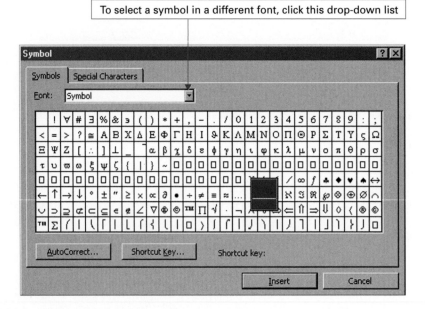

4 Click Insert and then click Close.
The em dash is inserted into the document.

5 Type the rest of the paragraph and press (ENTER) twice, as in:

sponsors, local celebrities, and local charitable contributors that will help you. Please call me to discuss the details.

Using AutoComplete

The Word *AutoComplete* feature automatically completes many frequently typed words and phrases for you, such as *Best regards*. A pop-up box displays the word or phrase, and you can either accept it or keep on typing.

TASK 6: TO USE AUTOCOMPLETE:

1 Type **Best r**.

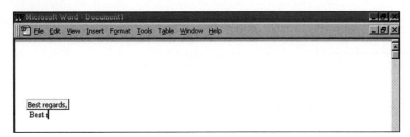

2 Press (ENTER).
Word automatically completes the phrase.

3 Press (ENTER) four times.

4 Type the rest of the text, as in:

Thomas Williams
Golf and Tennis Property Manager
The Willows

Undoing Changes

If you make a change to the text and decide that you shouldn't have, you can easily undo the change. Word 97 keeps a list of changes made in a document and allows you to undo all of them one by one.

> **Note** The Undo command is a lifesaver when some totally weird thing happens, and you don't know what you did to make it happen. Believe me; it will happen to you.

TASK 7: TO UNDO A CORRECTION:

1 Press (ENTER) twice and then type **Cc: John Gilmore**.

2 Press (HOME) and then press (DELETE) twice.
The insertion point moves to the beginning of the line and the first two characters are erased.

3 Point to the icon on the Undo ⤺▾ button (not the down arrow) and click it twice.
The two previously erased characters are inserted again. Somehow, I have a feeling that Undo will become your new best friend. Just remember—I introduced you.

> **Tip** If you undo something accidentally or you change your mind, you can click the Redo button and everything will be back the way it was before you used Undo so over-zealously.

Correcting Errors Marked by SpellIt

SpellIt is the automatic spell-checking feature that puts all those wavy red lines in your documents. As you type, Word 97 checks the spelling of each word against the words in its dictionary. When you type a word that isn't in its dictionary—ZAP—a wavy red line. Instead of erasing the word with the Backspace key, you can correct the word by selecting the correct spelling from a shortcut menu.

TASK 8: TO CORRECT A SPELLING ERROR MARKED BY WORD 97:

 Press (ENTER) twice, type **Encloseres**, and press the spacebar— another deliberate typo. (If you're like me, however, you make enough mistakes on your own! You really don't need to practice making them.)
The word is underlined with a wavy red line to indicate that it's misspelled.

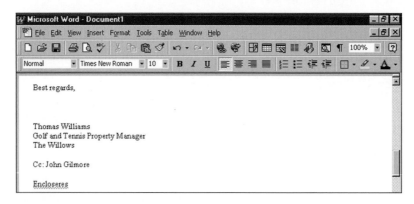

Point to the word and right-click.

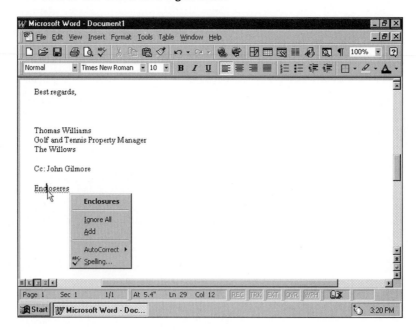

3   Click Enclosures.
Word corrects the spelling.

> **Tip** If a word is marked with a wavy red line but it isn't misspelled, you can add the word to the dictionary or ignore the word by right-clicking the word and choosing Add or Ignore. Don't add words to the dictionary when working in the lab, however, because the words that you add won't show up with wavy red lines for other students.

Saving a Document

If you want to keep a document for any period of time, you must save the document to disk. When saving the document, you specify a name for the document and a location where it will be stored.

> **Tip** Because Word 97 is written for Windows 95, the name can be a **long filename.** Long filenames (including the full path of the file) can have up to 255 characters. Although you can include as many spaces and periods in the filename as you want, you can't use ? or : or *. Older versions of Word (prior to Word 7.0) don't use long filenames, but a file with a long filename also has a conventional name that older versions of Word can read.

TASK 9: TO SAVE A NEW FILE:

1   Click the Save ⊟ button.

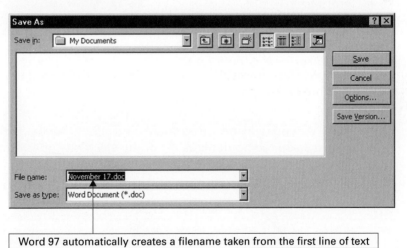

Word 97 automatically creates a filename taken from the first line of text

2 Type **Letter to Jim Hand** in the File Name text box.

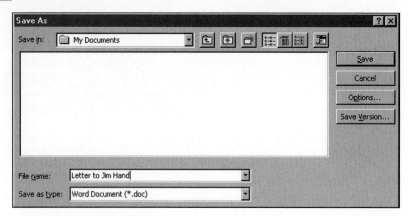

Word 97 automatically adds the default extension .doc to the filename when the document is saved.

3 Click the down arrow in the Save In text box and choose drive A (or the drive and folder designated by your professor or lab assistant).

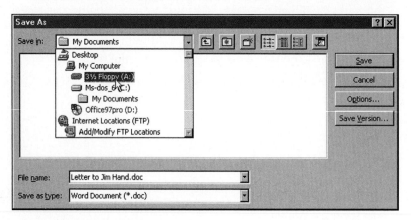

4 Click Save.
The dialog box closes, the file is saved on the disk, and the title bar displays the name of the file.

Tip As you work on a document, you should save it periodically just in case your computer crashes or the electricity goes off.

TASK 10: TO SAVE AN EXISTING FILE:

1 Press (ENTER) twice and type your initials to indicate that you are the typist of the letter.

2   Click 🖫.
The Save As dialog box doesn't display. The file is simply saved with the same name in the same location.

> **Note** To save an existing document in a different location or with a different name, choose File, Save As.

Previewing a Document

Before printing a document, you should preview it to see if it looks the way you want it to look. The Print Preview mode shows the full page of a document (see Figure 1.2). While you're working in the Print Preview mode, you can magnify the page, edit text, and print the document as well.

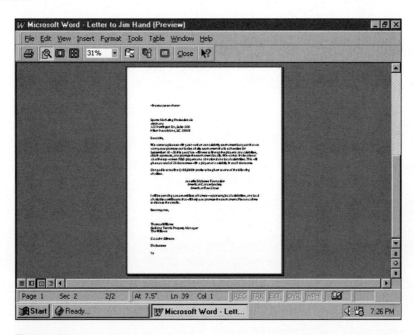

Figure 1.2

> **Tip** If you're previewing a multi-page document, you can show as many as six pages at a time.

TASK 11: TO VIEW A FILE IN PRINT PREVIEW MODE:

1   Click the Print Preview 🔍 button and notice the amount of blank space at the top of the page that is reserved for the letterhead.
The letter displays in the Print Preview mode, as shown in Figure 1.2.

2 Click the pointer, shaped like a magnifying glass, at the top of the letter where the address is typed.

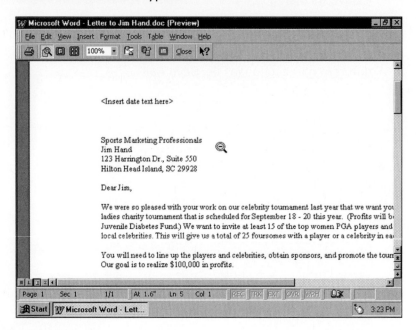

3 Click the Magnifier ⊛ button.
The pointer changes to its normal shape.

4 Click before the "a" in "Harrington" in the street address.
The insertion point is positioned before the "a."

5 Press (DELETE) and type **e**.
Word corrects the spelling.

6 Click Close in the Print Preview toolbar.
The Print Preview mode closes, and the document screen displays.

7 Click 🖫.
The revised document is saved under the same name.

Printing a Document

You can print a document from the Print Preview window or from the document window. Clicking the Print button prints one copy of the complete document. If you want to print only part of the document or more than one copy, you should use the Print command from the File menu.

TASK 12: TO PRINT THE LETTER TO JIM HAND:

1 Ensure that the computer you are using is attached to a printer and that the printer is online.

2   Choose File from the menu bar.

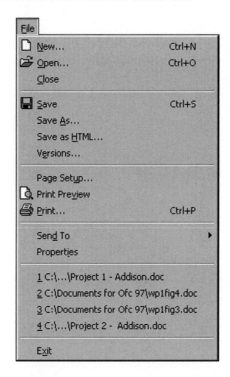

3   Choose Print.

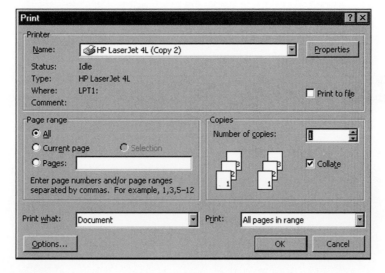

4   Click OK.
The document prints.

Closing a File

When you are finished with a file, you can close it to "put it away." If you have made changes to the file that you want to keep, you should save the file before closing it. Don't worry, though. If you forget to save a file, Word 97 asks if you want to save changes.

TASK 13: TO CLOSE A FILE:

1 Choose File from the menu bar.
The File menu displays.

2 Choose Close.

The Conclusion

You can exit Word 97 now by clicking the Close button, or you can work on the Review Exercises and Assignments.

Summary and Exercises

Summary

- When you launch Word 97, it automatically creates a new document named Document 1.
- Word 97 can insert the current date in several formats.
- When typing text, you press (ENTER) to end a short line or paragraph or to create a blank line.
- Characters that can't be created by pressing a key on the keyboard can be inserted from the Symbols dialog box.
- Simple typing errors can be corrected using the Backspace key.
- The Undo command can undo multiple commands and tasks that you have performed.
- Misspelled words are marked with a wavy red line by Word 97 and replacement words can be selected from a pop-up menu.
- Documents can be saved with long filenames.
- Before you print a document, you can preview it to see if it looks acceptable.
- You can print a document using the Print button or the Print command on the File menu.
- When you close a file, if you haven't saved changes to the file, Word 97 asks if you want to save the changes.

Key Terms and Operations

Key Terms	Operations
AutoComplete	create new document
AutoCorrect	indent
Enter	insert special characters
new document	undo
SpellIt	save a document
Tab	preview a document
Wrap	print a document
	close a document

Study Questions

Multiple Choice

1. Which of the following should *not* be done when typing text in a document?
   a. Press (BACKSPACE) to erase the character to the left.
   b. Press (ENTER) at the end of every line. p24
   c. Press (ENTER) to create a blank line.
   d. Click the Undo button to undo the last operation.

2. After Word 97 launches,
   a. the screen is blank until you create a new document.
   b. a dialog box displays with the options to create a new document or edit an existing document.
   c. Document 1 is created automatically.
   d. the New File dialog box displays.

3. The Undo command
   a. can undo the last operation.
   b. can undo deletions only.
   c. can undo the last five operations.
   d. can undo an unlimited number of operations.

4. A long filename
   a. is the name of a file that is more than ten pages long.
   b. can be as many characters as you want to use.
   c. can use a period only between the name and the extension.
   d. can't contain a question mark.

5. A word that has a wavy red line under it
   a. is misspelled.
   b. is marked for deletion.
   c. will print in bold.
   d. isn't in the Word 97 dictionary.

6. Which of the following names isn't a valid filename?
   a. *Letter to Mr. Hand . doc*
   b. *Letter to Mr. Hand.doc*
   c. *Letter:Mr. Hand.doc*
   d. *LttrHand.doc*

7. The Print Preview mode
   a. shows only one page at a time.
   b. can zoom to different magnifications.
   c. can display as many as ten pages.
   d. displays automatically before you print a document.

8. The Backspace key
   a. erases the character to the right.
   b. erases the character to the left.
   c. erases the character that the insertion point is on.
   d. moves the insertion point to the right but doesn't erase a character.

9. The status bar shows the
   a. left and right margins.
   b. vertical position of the insertion point.
   c. scroll bars.
   d. ruler.

10. If you click a word with a wavy red line,
    a. the line disappears.
    b. a menu displays.
    c. the Spell Checker starts.
    d. the insertion point is positioned in the word.

Short Answer

1. How do you save an existing file to a different location?

2. How many characters can a filename have, including the path?

3. How do you insert a date?

4. How do you insert a character that can't be entered from the keyboard?

5. How do you end a paragraph?

6. How do you magnify the document in the Print Preview mode?

7. What's the difference between using the Print command from the File menu and using the Print button?

8. What happens when you choose File, Close if you haven't saved the file?

9. Can you edit a document while viewing it in Print Preview mode?

10. Why don't you have to press Enter at the end of each line in a paragraph?

For Discussion

1. How does previewing a file before printing help the environment?

2. Why would you want to ignore a word that isn't in the dictionary rather than to add it to the dictionary?

3. Why is the Undo command so beneficial for novice users?

4. Under what circumstances would you click the New button to create a new document?

Review Exercises

1. Creating a new letter

After meeting with Jim Hand to discuss promoting the golf tournament, Thomas Williams wants you to type a follow-up letter to confirm some of the topics they discussed.

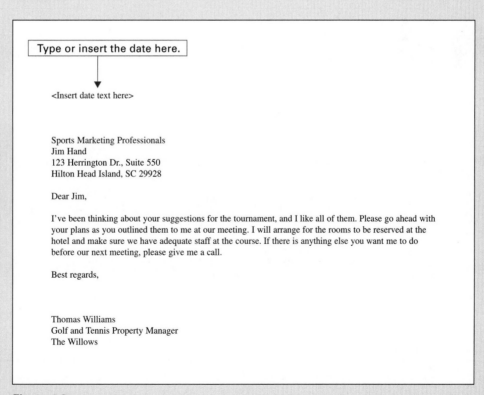

Figure 1.3

1. Create a new file and type the document shown in Figure 1.3. (Begin typing approximately 2 inches from the top of the page.)

2. Save the file as *Hand Follow-up.doc.*

3. Preview the file.

4. Add your initials to the end of the file while in Print Preview mode.

5. Save the file again and close it.

2. Getting information from the Internet

Mr. Williams wants you to search the Internet for some ideas for the upcoming golf tournament. If you find anything useful, print it and give it to him with a short memo.

1. Search the Internet for topics related to golf.

2. Print several appropriate pages or files that you find.

3. Create a new file and type the memo shown in Figure 1.4.

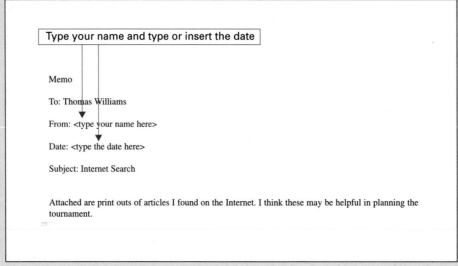

Figure 1.4

4. Save the file as *Internet Findings.doc* and close it.

3. Create, check, and print a document

1. Launch Word 97, if necessary.

2. Create the document displayed in Figure 1.5.
   - Start the letter 1.9″ from the top of the page.
   - Substitute the current date in the position indicated at the top of the letter.
   - Substitute your name and address in the inside address and salutation.
   - Use standard procedures to correct errors you type.

<Insert date text here>

<Your title> <Your first name> <Your last name>
<Your address>
<Your city, state, and Zip code>

Dear <Your title> <Your last name>:

When was the last time you yielded to temptation and set off on the vacation you'd always dreamed of. Imagine the beaches of the Bahamas, Tahiti, or Acapulco... or the splendor of the Mediterranean! Then consider exploring the Great Land -- Alaska!

It's time to join a tour that shows you the Alaska you want to see -- the mountains, the glaciers, and wildlife, and the Gold Rush Territory. Visit the wilds of the Yukon Territory, shiver among the glaciers, and view the peak of the majestic Mt. McKinley! Whether you choose to tour by domed railcar, luxury cruise ship, or comfortable motorcoach, you'll see all this Great Land has to offer... and if you book early, you'll take advantage of the special seasonal prices which can save you more than 50% off the tour's normal cost!

Make this your year to see Alaska by contacting your travel agent today! We guarantee you won't regret it!

Sincerely,

Mrs. Josephine Walters
Alaska Promotion Specialist

Figure 1.5

3. Spell check the document and correct all errors.

4. Save the document using the filename *Alaska Promotion xxx* (where xxx represents your initials).

5. Print a copy of the document.

Assignments

1. Creating a memo

Type a memo to the Grande Hotel manager's administrative assistant, Lois Parks, asking her to reserve a block of 100 rooms for the golf tournament on September 18, 19, and 20. Save and print the memo.

2. Creating a list of e-mail addresses

Mr. Williams needs a list of the names of famous people whom he can contact about playing in the charity golf tournament. Use Internet Explorer (or your Web browser) to search for between five and ten e-mail addresses for several famous people, including TV and movie personalities, comedians, musicians and singers, politicians, and so on. Create a document listing the e-mail addresses you find and print the document.

PROJECT

Editing a Document

Creating a document is just the beginning of your work in word processing. After you create a document, you usually revise it several times. In this project, you will explore some of the most commonly used revision techniques.

Objectives

After completing this project, you will be able to:

➤ **Open a document**

➤ **Move around in a document**

➤ **Select text to change the attributes**

➤ **Work with text**

➤ **Check spelling and grammar**

➤ **Create an envelope**

➤ **Change the view**

The Challenge

After typing a letter for Mr. Williams to the Sports Marketing Professionals, Mr. Williams wants the letter retyped with the changes shown in Figure 2.1. Instead of sending additional information with the letter as previously planned, Mr. Williams has decided to send the information separately, so you will have to create an envelope for the letter.

Thomas Williams
The Willows Resort
1000 Coast Highway
Willow Grove, SC 22345

Sports Marketing Professionals
Jim Hand
123 Herrington Dr., Suite 550
Hilton Head Island, SC 29928

<Insert date text here>

Sports Marketing Professionals
Jim Hand
123 Herrington Dr., Suite 550
Hilton Head Island, SC 29928

Dear Jim,

We were **so** pleased with your work on our celebrity tournament last year that we want you to promote our ladies charity tournament that is scheduled for September 18 - 20 this year. You will need to line up the players and celebrities, obtain sponsors, and promote the tournament locally. We want to invite at least 15 of the top women PGA players and 10 national and local celebrities. This will give us a total of 25 foursomes with a player or a celebrity in each foursome.

Our goal is to realize $100,000 in profits to be given to one of the following charities.

Juvenile Diabetes Foundation
American Cancer Society
American Red Cross

I will be sending you several lists of names—sponsors, local celebrities, and local charitable contributors that will help you promote the tournament. Please call me to discuss the details.

Best regards,

Thomas Williams
Golf and Tennis Property Manager
The Willows

Cc: John Gilmore

Enclosures

YJ

Figure 2.1

The Solution

You will revise the original letter using several of Word's common revision techniques, and you will use the automatic feature in Word to create an envelope.

The Setup

So that your screen will match the illustrations and the tasks in this project will function as described, make sure that the Word 97 settings listed in Table 2.1 are selected on your computer.

Table 2.1   Word 97 Settings

Location	Make these settings:
View, Toolbars	Deselect all toolbars except the Standard and Formatting toolbars
View	Deselect the ruler
Standard toolbar	Deselect any buttons that are selected and set Zoom to 100%
Tools, Options, View	Select the Horizontal and Vertical scroll bars
Tools, Options, Edit	Select the Typing replaces selection option; deselect the Drag-and-drop text editing option; and select the option When selecting, automatically select entire word
Tools, Options, Spelling & Grammar	Select the Check spelling as you type, Check Grammar as you type, and Check grammar with spelling options

Opening a Document

When you want to view or revise a document that you have saved, you must open the document first.

> **Tip** If the document is one that you have opened recently, you may see it listed at the bottom of the File menu. To open the file, simply choose it from the menu.

TASK 1: TO OPEN A DOCUMENT:

 Click the Open 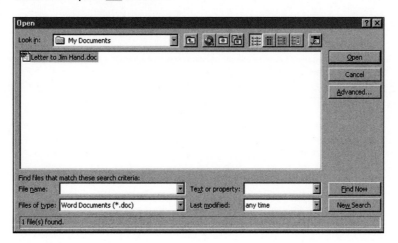 button.

Open dialog box showing:

Look in: My Documents

Letter to Jim Hand.doc

Open
Cancel
Advanced...

Find files that match these search criteria:
File name:
Text or property:
Find Now
Files of type: Word Documents (*.doc)
Last modified: any time
New Search
1 file(s) found.

2 Double-click *Letter to Jim Hand.doc*
The file opens.

> **Troubleshooting** If the filename doesn't appear in the Open dialog box, click the down arrow in the Look in text box and click the drive where the file is stored. Type the filename in the File Name text box and click Advanced. Click Search subfolders and then click Find Now. If the file is on the drive, Word will find it. You can bet on it. Click Open when the results appear.

> **Note** The view last used in a document is the view that displays when you open the document again.

Moving Around in a Document

If the complete document isn't visible on the screen, you can use the scroll bars to scroll the text or just move the insertion point up or down one line at a time by pressing the up or down arrow.

When you are making revisions in a document, you need to move the insertion point to a specific location. The easiest way to move the insertion point is to scroll to the line of text using the scroll bar and then click the mouse pointer (shaped like an I-beam) in the desired location.

Instead of using the mouse to position the insertion point, you can use the keystrokes listed in Table 2.2.

Table 2.2   Navigation Keystrokes

To Move	Press
Down one line	⬇
Up one line	⬆
Left one character	⬅
Right one character	➡
Left one word	CTRL + ⬅
Right one word	CTRL + ➡
End of line	END
Beginning of line	HOME
Down one screen	PGDN
Up one screen	PGUP
End of the document	CTRL + END
Beginning of the document	CTRL + HOME

TASK 2: TO SCROLL THROUGH THE DOCUMENT:

1 Press ⬇ to scroll through the document until you come to the bottom of the document.

2 Scroll back to the top of the document using the up arrow in the vertical scroll bar.
You can't see the insertion point because it's still at the bottom of the document. Scrolling with the scroll bar doesn't move the insertion point.

3 Press PGDN.
Now you can see the insertion point again.

Selecting Text to Change the Attributes

Several revision techniques, such as copying text or changing the text's size, require that you *select* the text first. Selected text is highlighted as shown in Figure 2.2. In most cases, the easiest way to select text is to drag the mouse pointer over the text, but Table 2.3 describes other ways of selecting text that are appropriate in many situations.

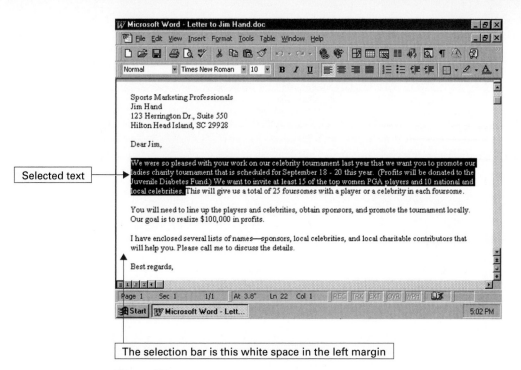

Selected text

The selection bar is this white space in the left margin

Figure 2.2

Table 2.3   Text Selection Methods

To Select	With the Mouse	With the Keyboard
A word	Double-click the word	Position the insertion point at the beginning of the word and press (SHIFT)+(CTRL)+(→)
A line	Click in the selection bar to the left of the line	Position the insertion point at the beginning of the line and press (SHIFT)+(END)
A sentence	Click anywhere in the sentence while pressing (CTRL)	None
A paragraph	Triple-click anywhere in the paragraph	Position the insertion point at the beginning of the paragraph and press (SHIFT)+(CTRL)+(↓)
An entire document	Click anywhere in the selection bar while pressing (CTRL) or Click Edit, Select All	Press (CTRL)+A or press (SHIFT)+(CTRL)+(END) at the top of the document
A block of text	Drag the mouse pointer through the text	Position the insertion point at the beginning of the block, press and hold down (SHIFT) as you press any combination of arrow keys to move to the end of the block
A vertical block of text	Drag the mouse pointer through the text while pressing (ALT)	None

TASK 3: TO CHANGE TEXT ATTRIBUTES:

1 Select the word "so" in the first paragraph of the letter.

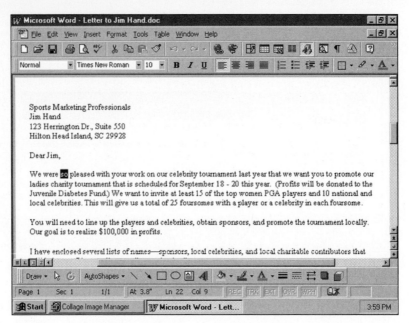

2 Click the Bold **B** button and then press ⊖ to deselect the text.

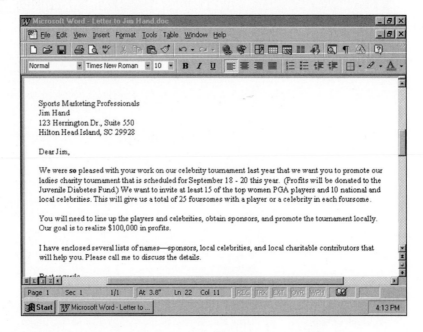

3 Select "so" again and then click the Underline **U** button.
The word is now **_bold_** and **_underlined,_** although it's a little difficult to tell because it's still selected.

4 Click **U** again.
The underline is removed.

5 Click the Italic **I** button and then press ⊕ to deselect the text.
The word is ***bold*** and ***italic***.

6 Select "so" and press ⌷CTRL⌷+**I**.
The word is just bold now.

7 Select the entire document.

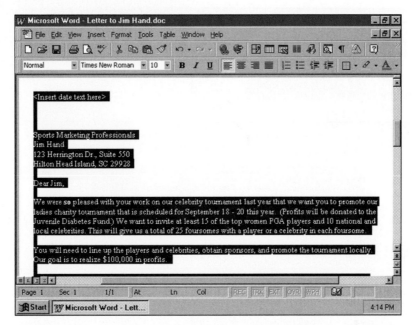

8 Click the down arrow in the Font Size drop-down list.

9 Choose 12.

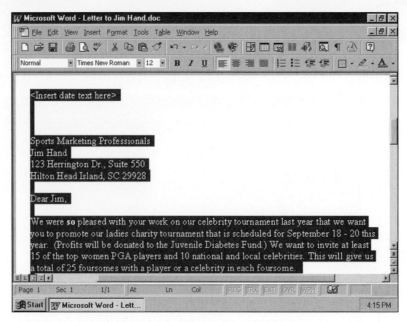

10 Click the down arrow in the Font drop-down list.

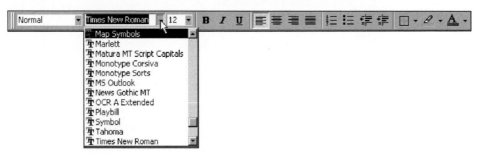

11 Scroll the list if necessary to display Arial.

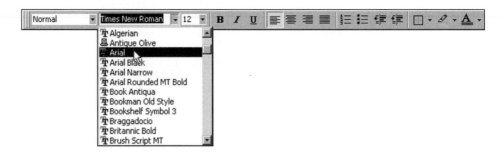

12   Click Arial.
All the text in the document changes to the Arial font.

> **Tip** To change the font, font size, and font attributes of selected text all at the same time, choose Format, Font to display the Font dialog box.

Working with Text

In addition to changing the appearance of text, often you have to delete, rearrange, realign, and copy text when you are making revisions. If you use a portion of text over and over again, you can make Word do your work for you by creating an AutoText entry for the text.

TASK 4: TO DELETE TEXT:

1   Select the text "(Profits will be donated to the Juvenile Diabetes Foundation.)"

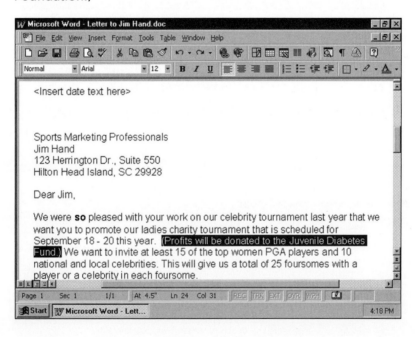

2   Press (DELETE).

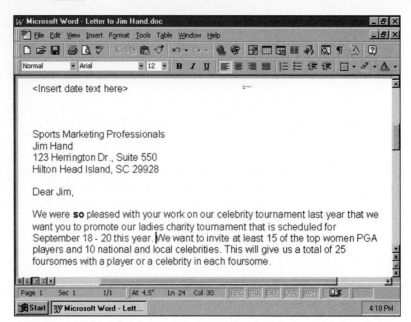

TASK 5: TO MOVE TEXT:

1   Select the text "You will need to line up the players and celebrities, obtain sponsors, and promote the tournament locally."

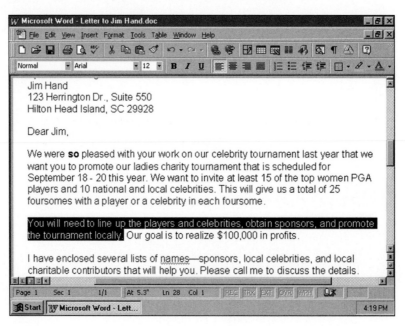

2 Click the Cut ✂ button.

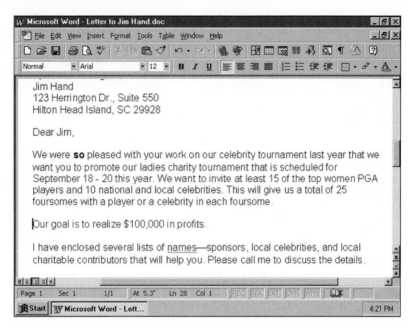

3 Click the insertion point after "September 18 - 20 this year."

The insertion point should be here

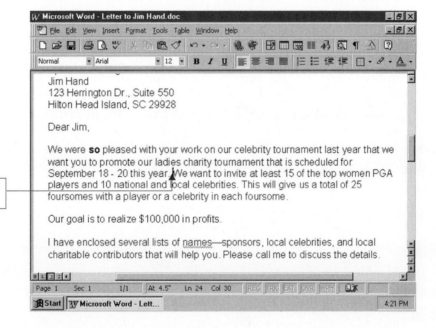

4   Click the Paste 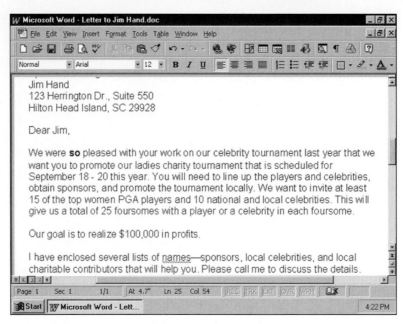 button. Press (SPACE) if necessary.

Tip Clicking the Cut button deletes text and stores it in a memory area called the Clipboard. When you delete text with the Delete key, the text isn't stored in the Clipboard, and you can't paste it in another location.

You can change the alignment of paragraphs in your document so that they are aligned at the left margin (*left-aligned*), at the right margin (*right-aligned*), *centered* between the margins, or *justified* (spread evenly between the margins). To align the text, you simply place the insertion point in the paragraph and click the Left, Right, Center, or Justify button on the Formatting toolbar. The paragraphs you type after setting the alignment keep the same alignment until you change it.

TASK 6: TO ALIGN TEXT:

1   Click the insertion point after "$100,000 in profits" just before the period and press (SPACE).

2   Type **to be given to one of the following charities**, and then press ⊕.

3   Press (ENTER) twice.

4 Type **Juvenile Diabetes Foundation** and then click the Center ≣ button to center that line. Press (ENTER) to continue entering centered text in a list.

5 Type **American Cancer Society** and press (ENTER).

6 Type **American Red Cross** and press (ENTER) again.
The completed list is centered in the document.

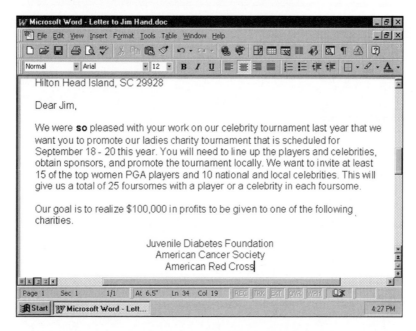

If you select text and then type something new, the selected text is replaced by the new text.

TASK 7: TO REPLACE TEXT:

1 Select the text "have enclosed."

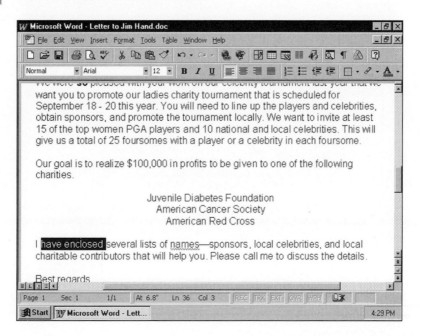

2   Type **will be sending you**.

If you want to have the same text repeated in the document, you can copy the text and paste it.

TASK 8: TO COPY TEXT:

1   In the first paragraph of the letter, select the text "promote the tournament."

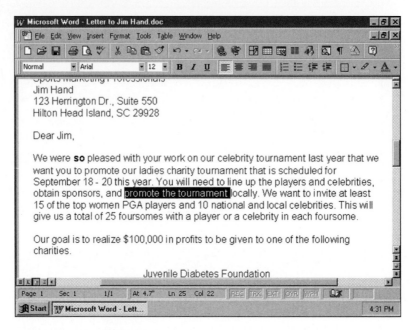

2   Click the Copy button.
The text is copied to the Clipboard.

3   Click the insertion point before the period in "that will help you."

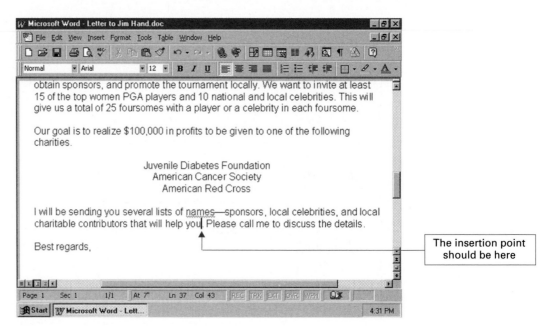

The insertion point should be here

4   Click 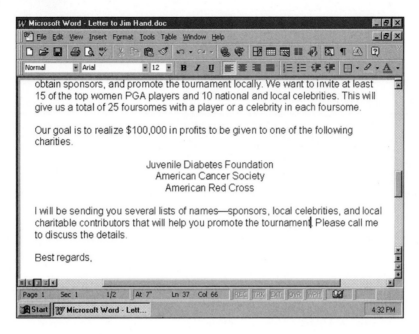.

Tip The content of the Clipboard can be pasted over and over again. The content can even be pasted in other documents.

An *AutoText entry* is a portion of text that you can recall with a single keystroke. In the next task, you will create an AutoText entry for a letter closing.

TASK 9: TO CREATE AN AUTOTEXT ENTRY:

1   Select the signature block at the end of the letter.

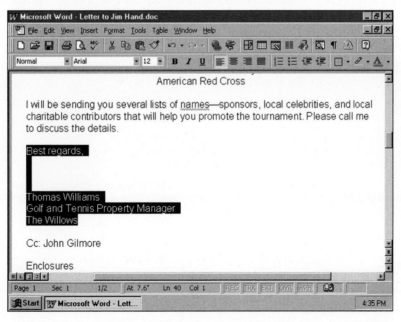

2   Choose Insert, Autotext, New.

Create AutoText   [?] [X]

Word will create an AutoText entry
from the current selection.

Please name your AutoText entry:

| Best regards, |

[OK]   [Cancel]

3   Type **twclose** and click OK.

4   Press (DELETE).
The signature block is deleted.

5   Type **twclose** and press (F3).
The signature block is inserted automatically.

> **Note** You can use this AutoText entry in any document. If you create enough AutoText entries, you may never have to type a complete sentence again.

Checking Spelling and Grammar

When you have made all the revisions in a document, you should give it one final check with the Spelling and Grammar checker. Because the automatic spelling and grammar features underline errors as you type, the final check will find only the errors you failed to correct as you went along.

TASK 10: TO CHECK SPELLING AND GRAMMAR:

1   Delete the "g" in the word "Marketing" in the address at the top of the letter.

2   Add another "s" in the middle of the word "Professionals."

3   Right-click on the word "Herrington" and choose Ignore All so it doesn't show up in the spell check.

4   Press (CTRL)+(HOME) to move to the beginning of the document.

5   Click the Spelling & Grammar ⟨ABC✓⟩ button.

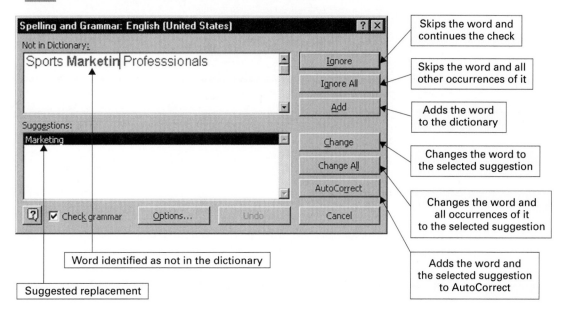

Skips the word and
continues the check

Skips the word and all
other occurrences of it

Adds the word
to the dictionary

Changes the word to
the selected suggestion

Changes the word and
all occurrences of it
to the selected suggestion

Word identified as not in the dictionary

Adds the word and
the selected suggestion
to AutoCorrect

Suggested replacement

6   Click Change.

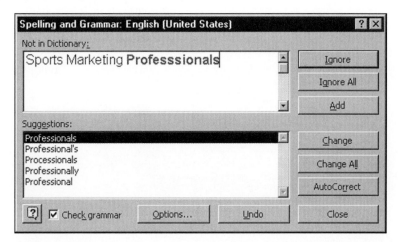

7   Click Change.

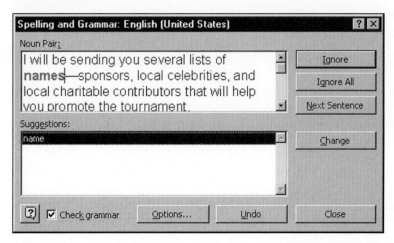

8 Click Ignore until you see the following message.

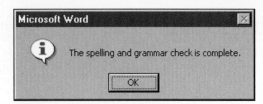

9 Click OK.
The dialog box closes.

Creating an Envelope

Word's Envelope tool makes it easy to create an envelope. In fact, you don't even have to type the address if you have an address at the top of the document.

TASK 11: TO CREATE AN ENVELOPE:

1 Choose Tools, Envelopes and Labels, and click the Envelopes tab if necessary.

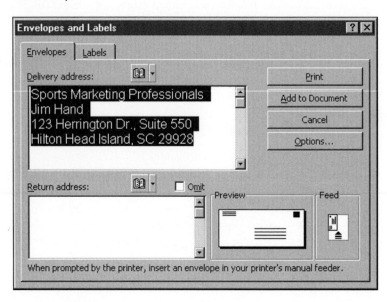

2 Click in the Return address area and type the address shown below.

Thomas Williams
The Willows Resort
1000 Coast Highway
Willow Grove, SC 22345

3   Click Add to Document and then click No when the message appears asking if you want to save the new address as the default address.

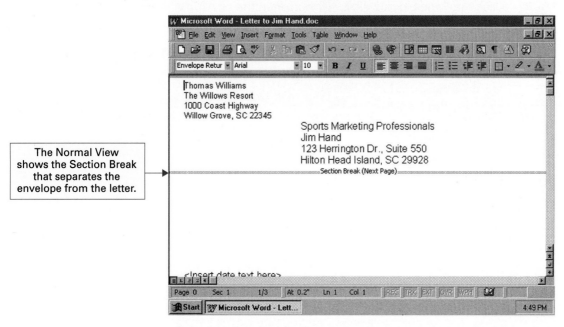

The Normal View shows the Section Break that separates the envelope from the letter.

Word adds the envelope at the beginning of the document, making the letter the second page.

> **Tip**   If you just want to print the envelope and not add it to the document, you can click Print instead of Add to Document.

Changing the View

Word provides several views for working with documents. Each view has features that are useful in different situations. The default view, Normal, doesn't show the white space for margins or the area on a page that hasn't been used; therefore, use the *Normal view* when you need to see the maximum amount of text. The *Page Layout view* shows margins and unused space as well as a visual *page break* between pages. Use the Page Layout view when you need an idea of what the page will look like when printed.

TASK 12: TO CHANGE THE VIEW TO PAGE LAYOUT VIEW:

1   Click the Page Layout View ⊟ button in the horizontal scroll bar, if necessary.

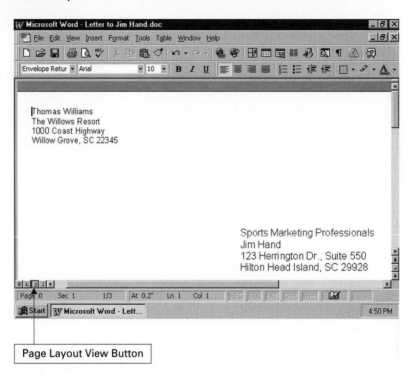

Page Layout View Button

2   Scroll down to see the page break.

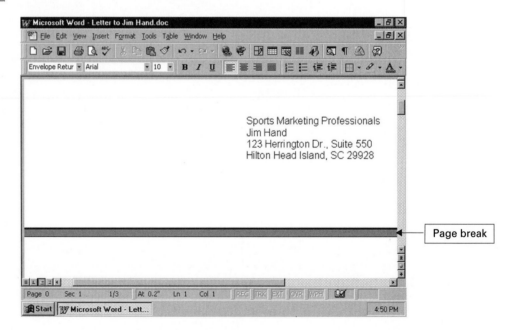

Page break

3 Scroll down to the bottom of the letter.
The letter won't fit on one page after you have revised it.

4 Scroll to the top of the letter and press (DELETE).
One line at the top of the letter is deleted.

5 Press (CTRL)+(END) to go to the bottom of the document.
The letter fits on one page now.

> **Note** Page breaks are determined in some degree by the printer. If the letter still does not fit on one page, you might want to change the font size to 11 or make some other adjustment, such as editing the text.

The Conclusion

Edit the inside address and closing lines so they conform to standard business letter format as directed by your instructor. When you are finished with the document, click the Save button to save it; then choose File, Close to close the file.

Summary and Exercises

Summary

- You open a file to view it or revise it.
- To make revisions in a file, you must move the insertion point to the point of the revision.
- You can move the insertion point by clicking the mouse or by using different keystrokes.
- Scrolling with the scroll bar doesn't move the insertion point.
- Several revision techniques require selecting text.
- You can select text by highlighting it with the mouse or by using different keystrokes.
- You can change text attributes by clicking buttons or drop-down lists in the Formatting toolbar.
- You also can change text attributes by using the Font dialog box.
- The alignment buttons in the Formatting toolbar are Left, Center, Right, and Justify.
- The Clipboard stores text that has been cut or copied.
- The Paste button inserts text from the Clipboard.
- When using the Spelling and Grammar Checker, you can ignore or change words or add words to the dictionary or to the AutoCorrect list.
- Word creates and formats an envelope for you.
- The Normal view is the default view.
- The Page Layout view shows margins and unused space on a page.

Key Terms and Operations

Key Terms	Operations
bold	align text
center	change the view
Clipboard	copy text
italic	create an envelope
justify	delete text
left-align	move text
Normal view	open a document
page break	paste text
Page Layout view	replace text
right-align	scroll
selection bar	select text
underline	spelling and grammar check

Study Questions

Multiple Choice
1. The selection bar is
   a. a toolbar.
   b. the blank area to the left of the text.
   c. the bar button in the status bar.
   d. the blank area to the right of the text.

2. Which of the following methods, if any, does *not* apply italic to text that's selected?
   a. Click the Italic button in the Formatting toolbar.
   b. Choose Format, Font, click Italic, and choose OK.
   c. Click the Italic button in the status bar.
   d. Press (CTRL)+I.

3. Which of the following should *not* be used to scroll down through a document?
   a. Press the down arrow repeatedly.
   b. Press Enter repeatedly.
   c. Press PageDown repeatedly.
   d. Click the down scroll arrow repeatedly.

4. The Clipboard
   a. is an area in memory.
   b. holds excess text that does not fit in a one-page document.
   c. is erased when you close a document.
   d. holds text that has been selected.

5. To store text in the Clipboard, you must first
   a. select the text.
   b. click the Copy or Cut button.
   c. click the Clipboard button.
   d. click the Paste button.

6. To move the insertion point to the end of a document,
   a. press (CTRL)+(PGDN).
   b. press (SHIFT) and click in the selection bar.
   c. double-click the box in the vertical scroll bar.
   d. press (CTRL)+(END).

7. To select a paragraph with the keyboard, position the insertion point at the beginning of the paragraph and press
   a. (SHIFT)+(CTRL)+(↓)
   b. (SHIFT)+(ALT)+(↓)
   c. (SHIFT)+(CTRL)+(PGDN)
   d. (SHIFT)+(↓)

8. Choosing Ignore All in the Spelling and Grammar dialog box
   a. ends the spell check.
   b. ignores all occurrences of the word.
   c. ignores all capitalization errors.
   d. ignores all suggestions.

9. The Copy button on the toolbar looks like
   a. a pair of scissors.
   b. two pieces of paper.
   c. a piece of paper with a magnifying glass.
   d. a clipboard with a piece of paper.

10. Which of the following methods, if any, does *not* select the entire document:
    a. Press Ctrl+A.
    b. Press and hold Ctrl and click in the selection bar.
    c. Position the insertion point at the top of the document and press Shift+Ctrl+Home.
    d. Choose Edit, Select All.

Short Answer
1. How do you remove bold, italic, or underline from text?
2. What do you choose in the Spelling and Grammar dialog box if you don't want to correct a word that has been identified as not being in the dictionary?
3. What two buttons do you use to move text?
4. What two buttons do you use to copy text?
5. How do you start the Spelling and Grammar checker?
6. How do you select a vertical block of text?
7. Describe two methods of selecting a word.
8. How can you open a document quickly if it has been opened recently?
9. Does scrolling with the vertical scroll bar move the insertion point?
10. How do you change the font of text?

For Discussion
1. Discuss the advantages of using the Normal view and the Page Layout view and when you would use both views.

2. In what circumstances would it be better to delete text with the Cut button than with the Delete key?

3. Describe the spelling and grammar checking tools available in Word.

4. How can you find a file and open it if you don't know where the file is located on the disk?

Review Exercises

1. Creating a list of possible sponsors
Mr. Williams has given you several Rolodex cards, some business cards, and some sticky notes with names, addresses, and phone numbers of potential sponsors in the area. He wants you to type a letter to Mr. Hand and include the alphabetical list (see Figure 2.3).

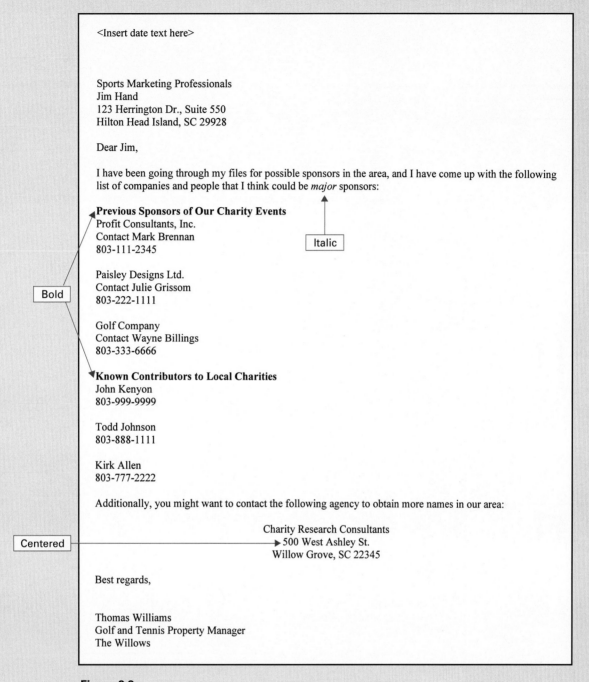

Figure 2.3

1. Create a new document and type the text shown in Figure 2.3, allowing approximately 1½ at the top for letterhead. Notice the font attributes and formatting that have been used in the document.

2. Create an envelope and add it to the document. (Don't type a return address because the envelope has a preprinted return address.)

3. View the document in Page Layout view.

4. Make the changes shown in Figure 2.4. Make the necessary adjustments to keep the text on one page.

5. Save the file as *Sponsors.doc* and close the file.

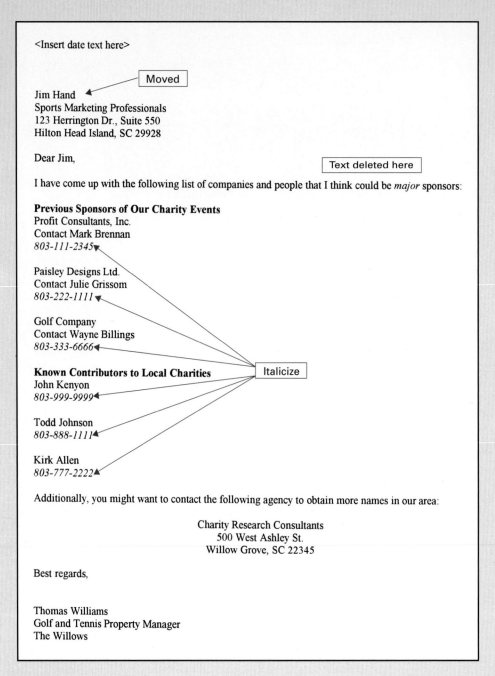

Figure 2.4

2. Creating a list of Web sites

Mr. Williams wants you to spend some time on the Web exploring sites that have information about golf clubs and then give him the addresses of the five most informative sites. You will use a memo template to create a memo listing the sites and summarizing them (see Figure 2.5).

The Willows Resort

Memo

To: Mr. Williams

From: <type your name here>

CC: [Click **here** and type name]

Date: 11/26/96

Re: Web Sites for Golf Clubs

Web Site Addresses and Summaries

Address:

Summary:

Address:

Summary:

Address:

Summary:

Address:

Summary:

Address:

Summary:

● Page 1

Figure 2.5

1. Choose File, New.

2. Click the Memos tab.

3. Select *Professional Memo.dot* and click OK.

4. Select the text "Company Name Here" and type **The Willows Resort**.

5. Click beside "To:" and type **Mr. Williams**.

6. Click beside "From:" and type your name.

7. Click beside "Re:" and type **Web Sites for Golf Clubs**.

8. Select all the text below the horizontal line and type the title **Web Site Addresses and Summaries**.

9. Type **Address:** and press Enter. Type **Summary:** and press Enter twice.

10. Copy the two lines you just typed in Step 3 and paste them four times.

11. Center the title and make it 12-point bold.

12. Fill in the addresses and summary with the information you obtain from the Web, making the Web addresses italic.

13. View the file in Page Layout view to see how much space is unused at the bottom of the page. If the text isn't centered under the horizontal line, move the text down by pressing Enter to insert blank lines after the horizontal line.

14. Save the file as *Golf Clubs.doc* and close the file.

3. **Revising, making formatting changes, and printing an envelope for your document**

1. Launch Word and open *Alaska Promotion xxx.doc* (where xxx represents your initials.

> **Note** If you do not have a document named *Alaska Promotion xxx.doc*, ask your instructor for a copy of the file you should use to complete this exercise.

2. Make the following changes to the document to that your letter appears as shown in Figure 2.6.
   - Change your title and last name to your first name in the salutation.
   - Add your name to the last paragraph as shown.
   - Delete the first sentence of paragraph two up to the first dash and type the word **Alaska** befor the dash.
   - Replace the word *Visit* in sentence two of the second paragraph with **Come with us to**.
   - Replace the dashes with em mark symbols in paragraphs one and two.
   - Search for each instance of the word *Alaska* in the letter body and bold and italicize the word.
   - Change the font for all text in the letter to Arial (or another sans serif font).
   - Right align the date.
   - Add the following text centered on the last typing line of the page and format the text using a 10-point italic font:
     Rediscover your heart in the Great Land—Alaska!

<Insert date text here>

<Your title> <Your first name> <Your last name>
<Your address>
<Your city, state, and Zip code>

Dear <Your first name>:

When was the last time you yielded to temptation and set off on the vacation you'd always dreamed of. Imagine the beaches of the Bahamas, Tahiti, or Acapulco…or the splendor of the Mediterranean! Then consider exploring the Great Land—*Alaska*!

Alaska—the mountains, the glaciers, and wildlife, and the Gold Rush Territory. Come with us to the wilds of the Yukon Territory, shiver among the glaciers, and view the peak of the majestic Mt. McKinley! Whether you choose to tour by domed railcar, luxury cruise ship, or comfortable motorcoach, you'll see all this Great Land has to offer…and if you book early, you'll take advantage of the special seasonal prices which can save you more than 50% off the tour's normal cost!

Make this your year to see *Alaska* by contacting your travel agent today, <Your first name>! We guarantee you won't regret it!

Sincerely,

Mrs. Josephine Walters
Alaska Promotion Specialist

Rediscover your heart in the Great Land—Alaska!

Figure 2.6

3. Save the revised document using the filename *Alaska Promotion Rev xxx*.

4. Spell check the document and correct all errors.

5. Create an envelope for the document.

6. Print a copy of the revised document and envelope and save the changes to the document.

Assignments

1. Creating an announcement
Create the announcement shown in Figure 2.7. Use bold as shown and use fonts that appeal to you if you don't have fonts similar to those shown in the figure. Be sure to center text as shown in the figure.

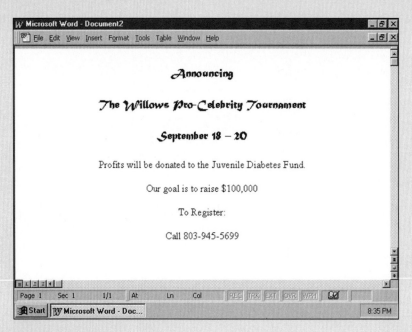

Figure 2.7

2. Modifying the announcement

Make the changes shown in Figure 2.8. Search the Web to find an appropriate address to use in the last line of the announcement.

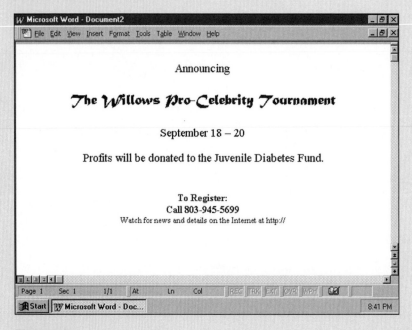

Figure 2.8

Using Advanced Formatting Features

In the first two projects, you worked with a simple document that used character formatting and alignment. In this project, you will use formatting techniques that produce a more sophisticated document that has multiple columns, a graphic, bulleted lists, indented paragraphs, styles, and more. You'll be out of breath when you finish this one!

Objectives

After completing this project, you will be able to:

- ➤ **Set up the page**
- ➤ **Create columns**
- ➤ **Insert and manipulate a graphic**
- ➤ **Format paragraphs**
- ➤ **Work with tabs**
- ➤ **Apply and modify styles**
- ➤ **Create bulleted and numbered lists**
- ➤ **Apply borders and shading**

The Challenge

The Willows needs a three-panel brochure for the summer camp program. The brochure gives the dates, ages, and costs; describes the facilities and excursions; lists items to bring; and provides directions for registering.

The Solution

You will format a document and set up the document to print across the long side of the paper in three columns. You will insert a graphic, modify and apply styles, create the bulleted and numbered lists, and format the brochure shown in Figure 3.1.

Camp Willows

Hit the bull's eye this summer at Camp Willows. You'll have plenty to say in that first school essay about what you did this summer - horseback riding, go-kart racing, hayrides, volleyball tournaments, fishing, jet-skiing, bicycling, golfing, camp fires, and more! The fun never stops at Camp Willows.

Space is limited, so make your reservations early. Each camp session is limited to 50 campers and 10 camp counselors - a maximum of five campers and one counselor per bungalow.

Camp Sessions

Date: June 9 - 13
Ages: 10 – 12
Cost: $500

Date: July 14 - 18
Ages: 13 – 15
Cost: $600

Date: August 4 - 8
Ages: 6 – 9
Cost: $400

Facilities

Campers stay in the Willow Beach Bungalows and all the facilities of The Willows are available for the campers' enjoyment.

Wild Hare Expo
Video games and electronic entertainment

Olympia Fitness Center
Free weights, exercise machines, saunas, whirlpools, indoor Olympic-size pool

Bye Bye Birdie and The Eagle's Nest
Two challenging miniature golf courses

Golf and Tennis
Three 18-hole PGA courses, two driving ranges, five putting greens, and ten tennis courses

Willow Pond Riding Stables
Guided horseback tours through open fields and wonderful wooded areas

Little Tree Playland
Playground equipment for younger children

Tree Top Water Park
Wave pool, water slides, swimming pools, diving pool

The Beach
White sand and the Board Walk, beach volleyball, jet skiing, water skiing

Excursions

Monday and Friday are camp excursion days. Campers are taken to outlying attractions that are located close to The Willows. Some excursions have an additional cost. Transportation is provided by hotel vans. Each camper may choose from the following excursions:

Cameron Caverns Tour
Cameron Caverns Tour is a 1 hour tour by an experienced guide through the complex maze of Cameron Caverns.

Haunted House Wax Museum
Nationally famous sculptor, Mark Hanson, fills the haunted house with life-like (and death-like) figures of your favorite ghosts and goblins.

Paul Bunyan's Action Park
Fun is guaranteed at Paul Bunyan's Action Park where you can race go-karts, play laser tag, ride bumper boats, ride the wild river, and test your batting skills in the cages.
Additional Cost $30

Carolina Science Center
Explore technology at work today. Many hands on exhibits demonstrate the fundamentals of aviation, space flight, genetics, ecology, computers, and more.

Spring Mill Park
Visit the historic gristmill, the apothecary, the train station, and other restored buildings in Spring Mill Park, one of the first settlements in the state.

Hannibal Lake
Hannibal Lake offers some of the best crappie fishing in the state. Anglers will also find largemouth bass, bluegill, and a variety of catfish.
Fishing license $11

What To Bring

Pack up your sense of adventure and these necessities:

- t-shirts and shorts
- tennis shoes
- a light jacket or sweatshirt
- socks and underwear
- bathing suit
- sunscreen and toiletries
- flashlight and batteries

How To Register

Follow these easy steps:

1. Fill out the enclosed registration.
2. Enclose a $100 non-refundable deposit.
3. Mail at least 60 days in advance.

Mail Your Registration Today!

Figure 3.1

The Setup

So that your screen will match the illustrations and the tasks in this project will function as described, make sure that the Word 97 settings listed in Table 3.1 are selected on your computer.

Table 3.1   Word 97 Settings.

Location	Make these settings:
View, Toolbars	Deselect all toolbars except the Standard and Formatting toolbars
View	Select the Ruler option and Page Layout view
Standard toolbar	Deselect any buttons that are selected and set Zoom to 100%
Tools, Options, View	Select the Vertical ruler option, the Horizontal scroll bar option, and the Vertical scroll bar option
Tools, Options, Edit	Select the Typing replaces selection option; deselect the Drag-and-drop text editing option; and select the option When selecting, automatically select entire word
Tools, Options, Spelling & Grammar	Select the Check spelling as you type and Check Grammar as you type options

Setting Up the Page

When you create a new document, Word chooses the setup options, including the margins, paper size, and orientation. The default margins are 1 for the top and bottom and 1.25″ for the left and right. The paper size is 8½″ by 11″, and the *orientation* is portrait, that is, the paper is oriented so it is taller than it is wide. Sometimes the defaults don't meet your needs, and you must change them.

> **Note** When the paper is oriented sideways, so that it is wider than it is tall, it is called landscape orientation.

TASK 1: TO CHANGE MARGINS AND ORIENTATION:

1 Click the Open button.

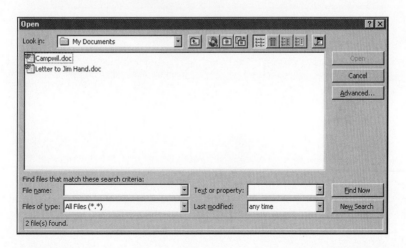

2 Change the Look in folder, if necessary, and then double-click *Campwil.doc.*

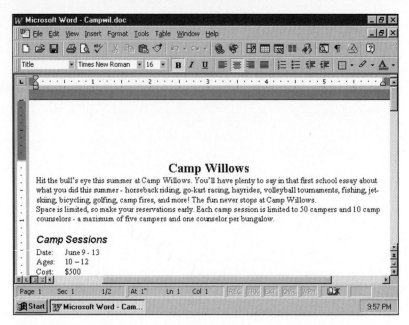

3 Choose File, Page Setup, and then click the Margins page tab, if necessary.

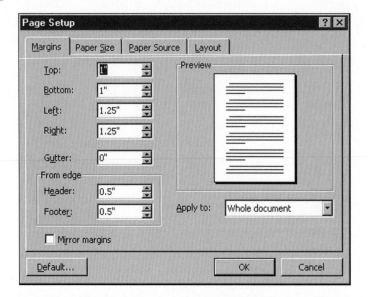

4 Change Top, Bottom, Left, and Right margins to .5".

5   Click the Paper Size page tab.

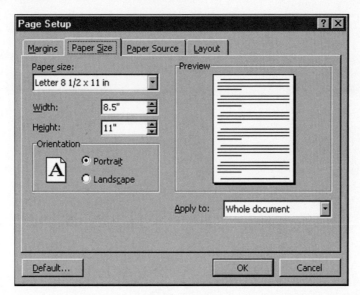

6   Select Landscape and click OK.
The dialog box closes.

Note Some older printers cannot print ½" from the edge of the page. If you get an error message, ignore it and continue.

Creating Columns

Word 97 can create multiple newspaper columns of equal or unequal widths. The text in newspaper columns flows from one column to the next when a column fills up.

TASK 2: TO CREATE THREE NEWSPAPER COLUMNS:

1   Choose Format.

2 Choose Columns and click the Presets Three icon.

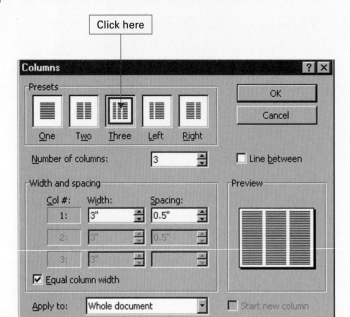

3 Click OK.
The dialog box closes.

4 Click the Print Preview button, view the new layout, and click the Close button.

> **Tip** To break a text column before it fills up, choose Insert, Break, Column Break, OK.

Inserting and Manipulating a Graphic

Graphics add interest to a document, and Word 97 provides a Clip Gallery of graphics, called *clip art*, for you to use.

TASK 3: TO INSERT A GRAPHIC:

1 Choose Insert, Picture.

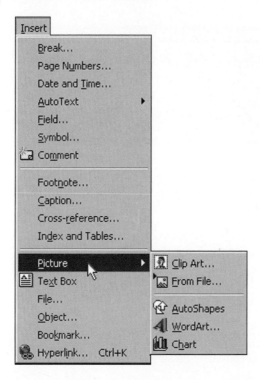

2 Choose Clip Art, choose OK if the "Additional Clips are Available on CD-ROM" message appears, and click the Clip Art page tab if necessary.

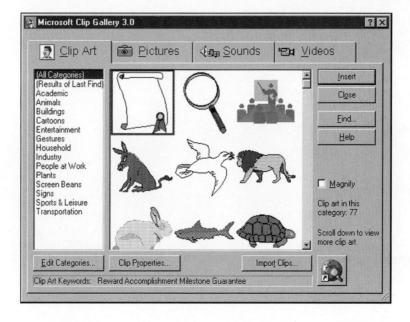

3 Click Sports & Leisure.

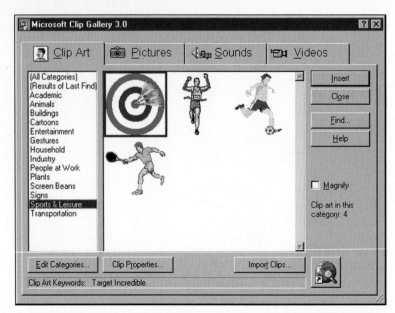

4 Click the graphic of the bull's eye if it isn't selected and click Insert.

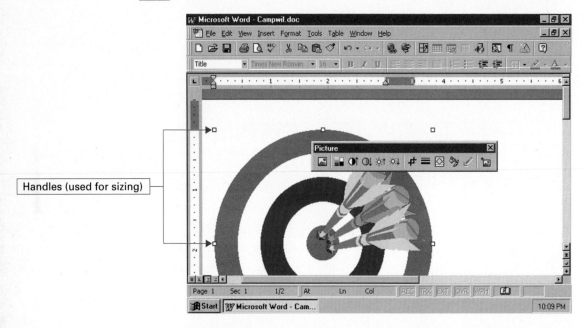

Handles (used for sizing)

The graphic inserted in the document is too large for the brochure. Also, you need to position it at the top of the first column. This looks to me like an excellent opportunity to practice manipulating graphics.

TASK 4: TO SIZE AND MOVE A GRAPHIC:

1 Click the down arrow in the vertical scroll bar until you can see the bottom of the graphic.

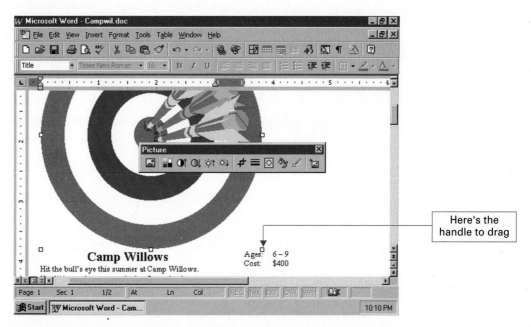

Here's the handle to drag

2 Drag the handle on the lower-right corner up and to the left until the graphic is about 1" wide. (While dragging the corner, the mouse pointer changes to a slanted 2-headed arrow.)

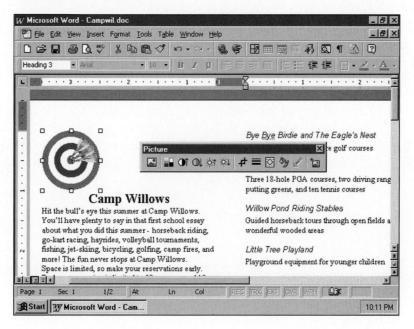

Tip Dragging a corner handle of a graphic keeps the graphic in proportion.

3 Click the up arrow in the vertical scroll bar to scroll to the top of the document, if necessary, and close the Picture palette.

4 Point to the middle of the graphic.
The mouse pointer changes to a four-headed arrow.

5 Drag the graphic to the center of the column.

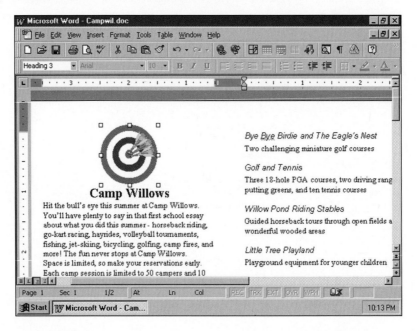

Formatting Paragraphs

In default paragraphs, all the lines line up with the left margin, are single-spaced, and have no spacing before or after them. By formatting a paragraph, you can indent the first line, indent all the lines of a paragraph on the left or right, change the line spacing, and add spacing before or after the paragraph.

TASK 5: TO INDENT THE FIRST LINE OF A PARAGRAPH AND ADD SPACING UNDER THE PARAGRAPH:

1 Click anywhere in the paragraph that begins "Hit the bull's eye...."

The clicked paragraph →

2 Choose Format.

3 Choose Paragraph and click the Indents and Spacing tab if necessary.

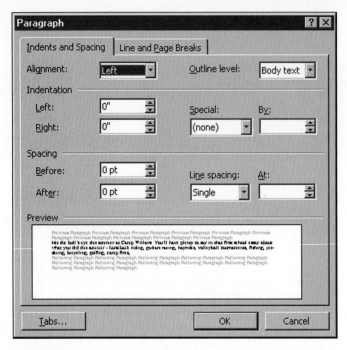

4 Click the down arrow in the Special text box.
A drop-down list displays.

5 Click First Line.
The Special text box displays your choice.

6 Click the down arrow in the By spinner box until the measurement is 0.3".
Click the up arrow in the After spinner box until the measurement is 6 pt.

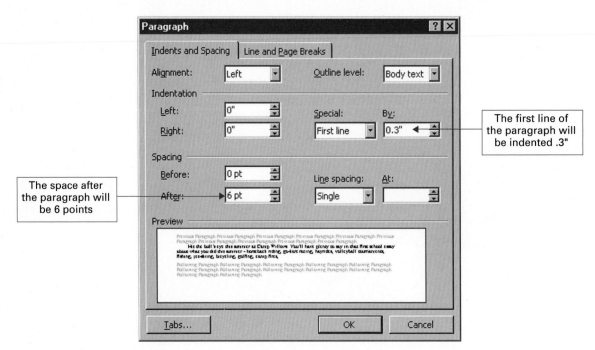

The space after the paragraph will be 6 points

The first line of the paragraph will be indented .3"

7   Click OK.
The dialog box closes.

8   Click anywhere in the paragraph that begins "Space is limited...."

9   Choose Format, Paragraph.
The Paragraph dialog box displays.

10   Click the down arrow in the Special text box and click First Line. Then click the down arrow in the By spinner box until the measurement is 0.3".

> **Note** There is no need to set space after this paragraph because the next paragraph already has space above it.

11   Click OK.
The two changed paragraphs should look like those in Figure 3.1.

Working with Tabs

When you want text within a paragraph to align differently, you can use *tabs*. They are shown as markers on the ruler. Table 3.2 describes the types of tabs available in Word 97.

Table 3.2   Types of Tabs

Type	Symbol	Description
Left	∟	Aligns text on the left.
Center	⊥	Centers text on the tab stop.
Right	⌐	Aligns text on the right.
Decimal	⊥·	Aligns text on the decimal.
Bar	I	Inserts a vertical bar at the tab stop.
Leader		Displays characters, such as periods, before the tab. Any type of tab can have a leader.

TASK 6: TO SET A TAB:

1 Select all the text under the "Camp Sessions" heading.

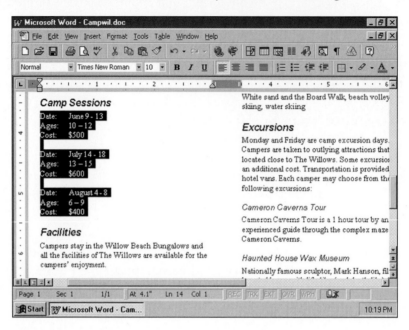

2 Click the dot in the ruler that is just to the left of the half-inch mark.

3 Scroll to the top of the third column by clicking the right arrow in the horizontal scroll bar and then clicking the up arrow in the vertical scroll bar.

4 Click after the period in "...in the cages." in the third column and then press (ENTER).

5 Click the tab selector ⌊ button until the right tab ⌟ button displays.

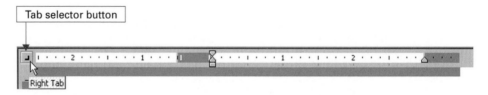

6 Click the second dot to the right of the 2½" mark on the ruler.

7 Type **Additional cost**, press (TAB), and type **$30**.

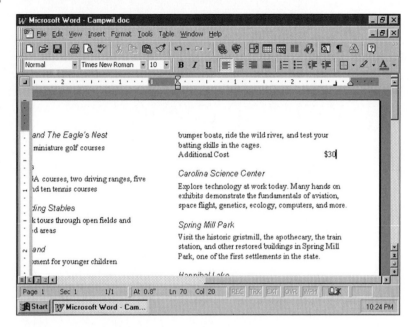

8 Choose Format, Tabs.

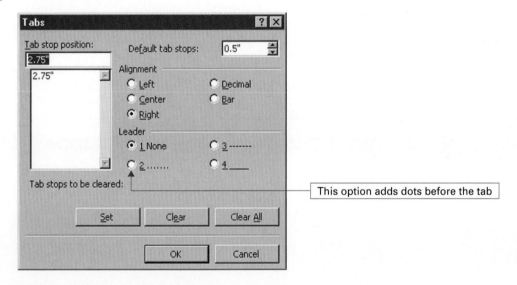

This option adds dots before the tab

9 Select 2 under Leader.

10   Click OK.

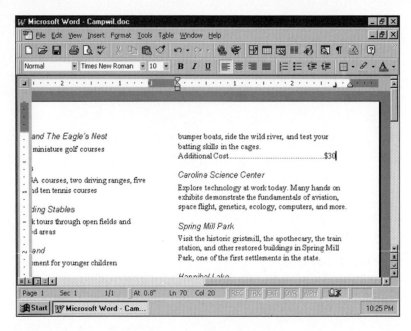

11   Click after the period in "...a variety of catfish." in the third column and press ENTER. A new, blank line is created.

12   Ensure that the tab selector button displays the right tab and click the second dot to the right of the 2½" mark on the ruler.

13   Type **Fishing license**, press TAB, and type **$11**.

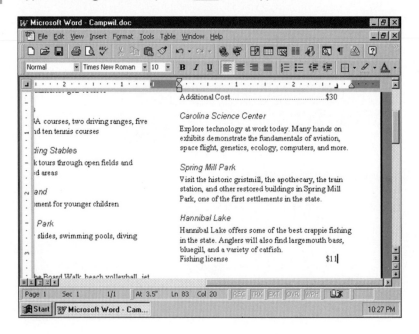

14   Choose Format, Tabs and select 2 under Leader again.

15   Click OK.

16   Press (ENTER).
The insertion point moves to the next line and inserts a new blank line.

Applying and Modifying Styles

A *style* is a collection of format settings that are grouped together and given a name. When you apply a style to a paragraph, the text of the paragraph takes on all the formatting stored in the style.

TASK 7: TO APPLY A STYLE:

1   Ensure the insertion point is on the line after "Fishing license..." and type **What To Bring**.

2   Press (ENTER), type **Pack up your sense of adventure and these necessities:** and press (ENTER).

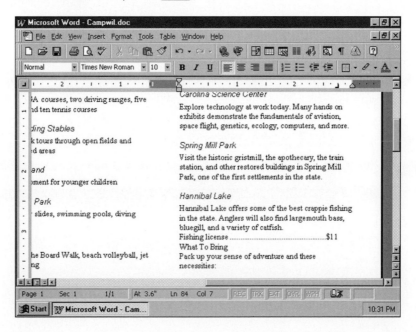

3 Type the list of items to bring, as in:

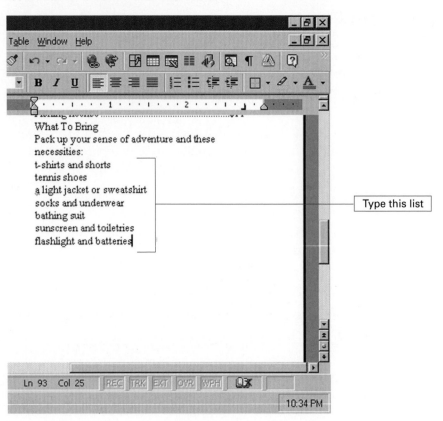

Type this list

4 Click anywhere in the text "What To Bring."

5 Click the down arrow in the Style list box in the Formatting toolbar.

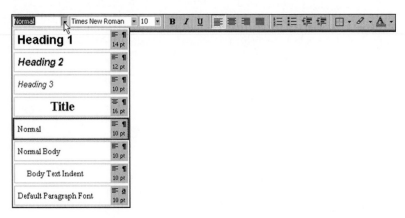

6   Click Heading 2.

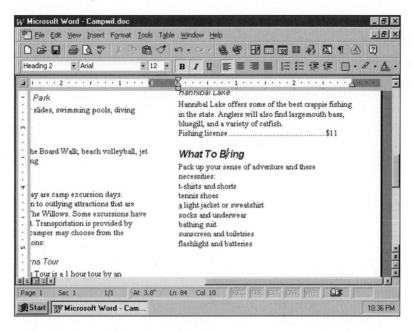

7   Click the insertion point anywhere in the paragraph that begins "Pack up your..."

8   Click the down arrow in the Style list box and click Normal Body.
You won't notice any change in the text when you complete this step; you'll just have to trust Word on this one.

In this document, the Normal Body style is used for paragraphs that follow Heading 2 styles. The format would look better if these paragraphs had a first line indent and some space after them like the paragraphs you formatted at the top of the first column. Instead of formatting each paragraph individually, you can modify the Normal Body style, and the paragraphs that already use the style will reflect the changes automatically—another example of how Word makes your life easier.

TASK 8: TO MODIFY A STYLE:

1 Choose Format, Style.

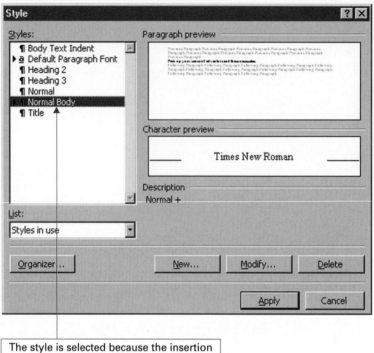

The style is selected because the insertion point is in a paragraph using that style

2 Click Modify.

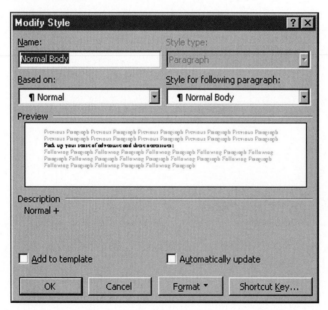

3 Click Format.

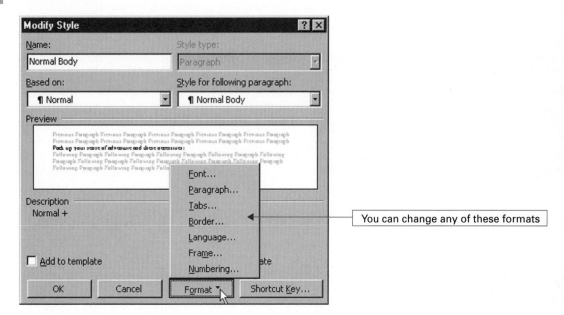

You can change any of these formats

4 Click Paragraph.
The Paragraph dialog box displays.

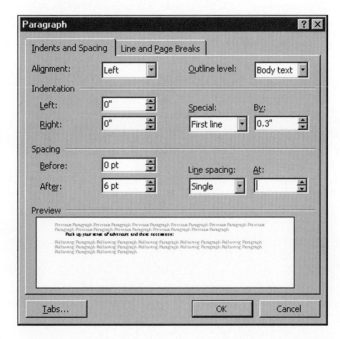

5 Under Specials, select First Line, specify 0.3" for the By option, and specify 6 pt for the After option.

6 Click OK.
The Modify Style dialog box redisplays.

7 Click OK.
The Style dialog box redisplays.

8 Click Close.

The modifications you made are applied to the paragraph that begins "Pack up your..." because you applied this style in the last task.

Creating Bulleted and Numbered Lists

To draw attention to a list, you can bullet the list or number it. A **bullet** is a symbol (usually a black circle) that precedes the text. Word 97 has two paragraph formats set up just for bulleting and numbering lists, and all you have to do is apply them.

> **Tip** Lists that have no particular order are usually bulleted rather than numbered.

TASK 9: TO CREATE A BULLETED LIST:

1 Select the text in the list under the "What To Bring" heading.

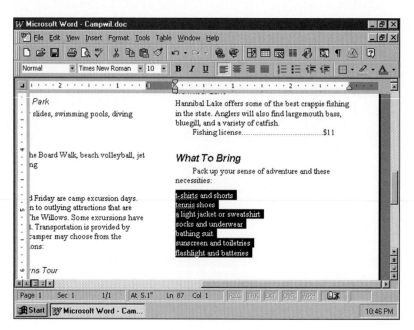

2   Click the Bullets ⊞ button in the Formatting toolbar.

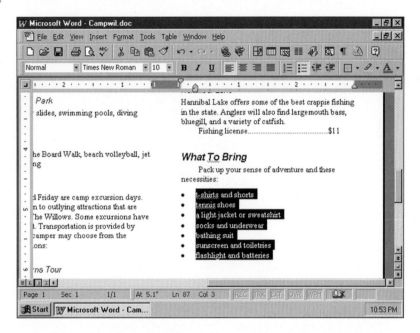

3   Click the Increase Indent 펜 button in the Formatting toolbar.

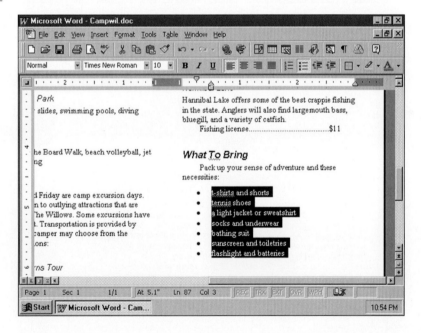

Tip If you don't like the bullet that Word automatically uses, choose Format, Bullets and Numbering to select a different bullet.

TASK 10: TO CREATE A NUMBERED LIST:

1 Click after "flashlight and batteries," press (ENTER), and type **How To Register**.

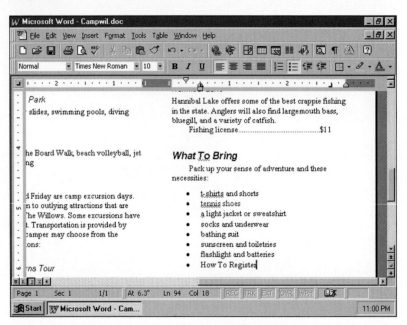

2 Select Heading 2 from the Styles drop-down list.

3 Press (ENTER), type **Follow these easy steps:**, and press (ENTER).

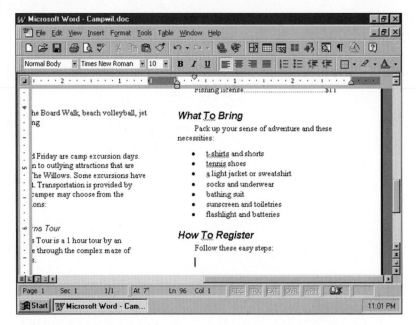

4 Choose Normal from the style drop-down list.

5 Click the Numbering ≣ button in the Formatting toolbar.
Word relieves you of the burden of numbering each item individually. Say thank you.

6   Type the following lines and press (ENTER) after each one:

Fill out the enclosed registration.
Enclose a $100 non-refundable deposit.
Mail at least 60 days in advance.

7   Click 📋 again.
The number is removed from the current line.

Applying Borders and Shading

Borders and shading draw attention to important text. *Borders* consist of a top, bottom, left, and right line, any of which can be displayed or hidden. *Shading* is available in various percentages of gray and in colors.

> **Caution** Be careful when you use shading. If the shading is too dark, people won't be able to read the text—especially if you're faxing the document.

TASK 11: TO APPLY A BORDER AND SHADING:

1   Press (ENTER), type **Mail Your Registration Today!** and press (ENTER).

2   Click the Show/Hide ¶ ¶ button in the Standard toolbar so that you can see the paragraph symbols.

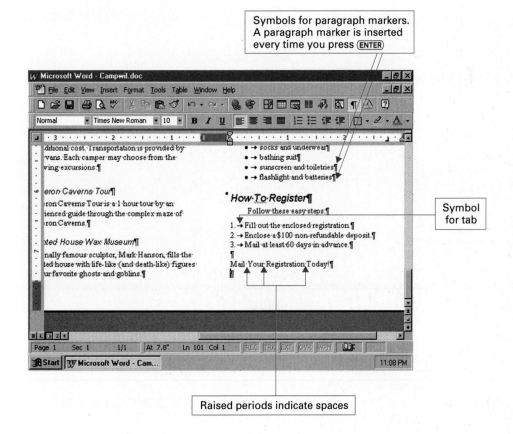

Symbols for paragraph markers. A paragraph marker is inserted every time you press (ENTER)

Symbol for tab

Raised periods indicate spaces

3 Select the paragraph symbol above the text, the text, and the paragraph symbol below the text.

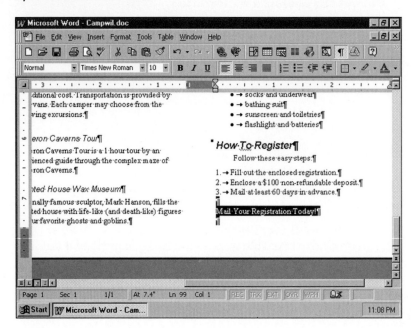

4 Choose Format, Borders and Shading, and click the Borders tab, if necessary.

Click this page tab to work with borders

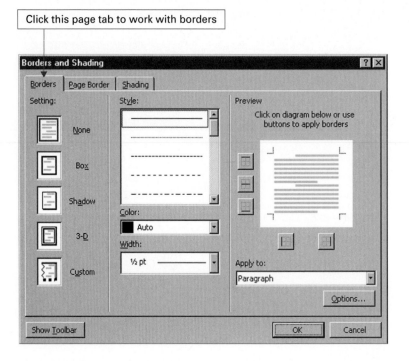

5   Click the icon beside the Box setting.

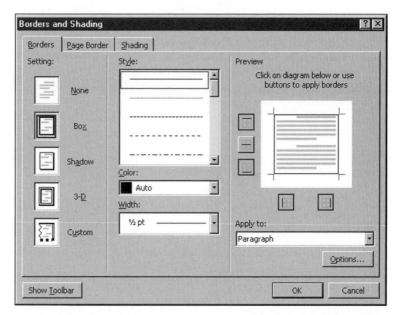

6   Click the Shading tab and click the fourth box in the first row.

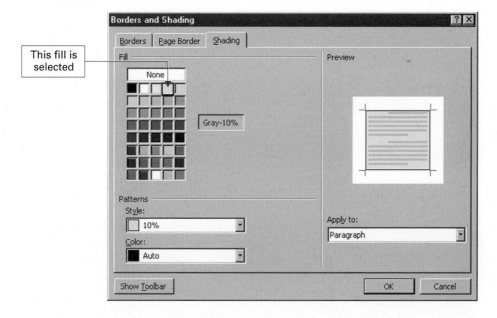

7 Click OK.

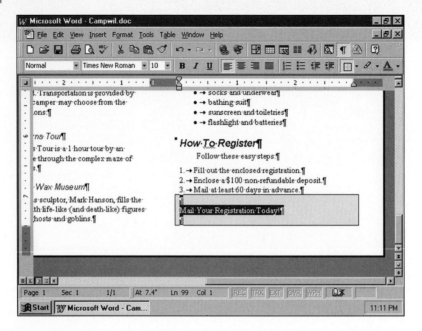

8 Click ¶.
Word hides the paragraph and space symbols.

9 Click the Center ☰ button.

> **Tip** To apply a border or shading to text within a paragraph, such as a single word, select the text before you choose Format, Borders and Shading.

The Conclusion

The document should have only one page. If your printer causes an additional page to be created, make adjustments by changing the space before and after the paragraphs. Check the file for spelling errors and then save the file as *Camp Willows.doc*. If you have access to a printer, preview the file and then print it and fold the paper in thirds to see how the brochure looks. If you don't have access to a printer, just preview the file. When you're finished, close the file.

Summary and Exercises

Summary

- Page setup options, including the margins, paper size, and orientation, are preset, but can be changed.
- The text in newspaper columns flows from column to column.
- The Clip Gallery has clip art for inserting in documents.
- Graphics can be sized and moved.
- Paragraph formats include alignment, line spacing, indention, and spacing before and after the paragraph.
- Tabs cause text to align in specific ways, depending on the type of tab.
- A leader can be added to any type of tab.
- A style is a collection of format settings.
- Word 97 has automatic formats for formatting bulleted lists and numbered lists.
- You can apply borders and shading to text.

Key Terms and Operations

Key Terms
border
bulleted list
center tab
clip art
decimal tab
graphic
indent
landscape
leader
left tab
line spacing
margin
newspaper column
numbered list
orientation
page setup
paper size
portrait
right tab
shading
style
tab

Operations
apply a border
apply a style
apply shading
create a bulleted list
create a numbered list
create columns
format a paragraph
insert a graphic
modify a style
move a graphic
set a tab
set margins
size a graphic

Study Questions

Multiple Choice

1. You can add borders and shading to
   a. a paragraph only.
   b. a page only.
   c. a paragraph and a page only.
   d. any text, paragraphs, and a page.

2. The default page orientation is
  a. 8½" by 11".
  b. portrait.
  c. landscape.
  d. upright.

3. By default paragraphs are aligned on the
  a. left.
  b. right.
  c. center.
  d. left and right.

4. A *leader* is
  a. a string of characters that displays before a tab.
  b. the first line of an indented paragraph.
  c. a type of bullet.
  d. a style.

5. To size a graphic,
  a. choose Format, AutoFormat.
  b. choose Insert, Picture, Clip Art, specify the size, and click Insert.
  c. right-click the graphic and choose Size.
  d. drag one of the handles.

6. To set a tab for a particular paragraph,
  a. position the insertion point at the beginning of the paragraph.
  b. position the insertion point at the end of the paragraph.
  c. position the insertion point anywhere in the paragraph.
  d. select the entire paragraph.

7. When you modify a style,
  a. the format changes aren't reflected in the paragraphs that already use the style.
  b. the format changes are reflected in the paragraphs that already use the style.
  c. you must give the style a new name.
  d. you must reapply the style to paragraphs that already use the style.

8. When you move a graphic, the mouse pointer has a
  a. two-headed arrow attached.
  b. three-headed arrow attached.
  c. four-headed arrow attached.
  d. five-headed arrow attached.

9. The default margins are
  a. 1" for the top, bottom, left, and right margins.
  b. 1.25" for the top and bottom margins and 1" for the left and right margins.
  c. 1" for the top and bottom margins and 1.25" for the left and right margins.
  d. 1.5" for the top margin and 1" for the bottom, left, and right margins.

10. When a style is applied to a paragraph,
    a. the name of the style appears in the selection bar.
    b. the paragraph takes on the formatting of the style.
    c. the paragraph can't be edited.
    d. the formatting of the paragraph can't be changed.

Short Answer

1. Can you apply a border to a single word in a paragraph? If so, how?

2. What kind of borders can be applied to a paragraph?

3. List the options available for paragraph line spacing.

4. What other format options are available, in addition to paragraph formats, when you modify a style?

5. How do you apply a style?

6. Where is the tab selector button located?

7. How do you set a left tab at 3"?

8. How do you insert a graphic?

9. What kind of tab would you use to align the following numbers: 10.987, 1.1, and 123.45?

10. What does the Show/Hide ¶ button do?

For Discussion

1. When would you use numbers instead of bullets in a list?

2. Discuss the advantages of using styles.

3. When would it be better to format a paragraph rather than create a style to apply to the paragraph?

4. List and describe the types of tabs provided by Word 97.

Review Exercises _____

1. Creating a list of rules
Now that you know how to format lists and work with styles, you can dress up the Rules document so that it looks like the one shown in Figure 3.2.

1. Open the file *Rules.doc*. Make sure the left and right margins are set to 1.5".

2. Insert the graphic from the Shapes category in the Clip Gallery.

3. Size and move the graphic so that it approximates the one in Figure 3.2.

4. Modify the Normal style and change the font to 12 and the spacing after the paragraph to 6 pt.

5. Go to the end of the document and create two equal columns. Select This point forward for the Apply to option.

6. Type the rules shown in the figure and apply numbering to the list.

7. Save the file as *Camp Willow Rules.doc* and close it.

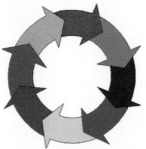

Team Rules

At Camp Willows, you are part of a team. Your mission is to be the best team player you can be and to help your team have the most fun it can have. To assist you in having a safe and fun-filled experience, we have some rules you must follow. These rules aren't like ordinary rules that are meant to restrain you. Just the opposite, these rules will knock down barriers and open doors.

1. Open doors slowly and watch out for buckets of water overhead.

2. Learn the names of at least two new people a day.

3. Don't lock your counselor in his or her room for more than two hours.

4. Eat whatever you want and as much as you want.

5. No jet skiing in the pool.

6. Write or call home at least once.

7. Don't pet the alligators on Tuesday unless they look like they're having a good day.

8. Don't put your team members' underwear in the freezer. Do it to members of opposing teams.

9. Stay with the group when we go on field trips to nearby attractions.

10. Don't play shuffleboard. Campers who break this rule will have to take Geritol and move to a retirement cottage.

11. All bonfires must be built on the beach and be approved by the fire marshall.

12. No skateboarding off the roof unless accompanied by an adult.

Figure 3.2

2. Creating a camp schedule

Now that you've created the brochure for Camp Willows, it's time to begin planning the Camp Willows schedule. Follow these easy steps to create the schedule shown in Figure 3.3.

1. Create a new document and type the title and the first paragraph as shown in Figure 3.3.

2. Set right tabs at 3.75″ and 5.5″. Set left tabs at 1″ and 4.5″. Type the schedule shown in the figure.

3. Explore the Internet for a historical site you can visit in South Carolina and describe it in the bordered box at the bottom of the document.

4. Save the file as *Schedule.doc* and close it.

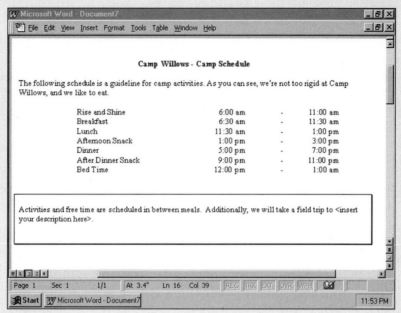

Figure 3.3

3. Formatting a document into columns and adding a graphic to the background

1. Open the document *Alaska Brochure.doc*.

2. Format the document in three evenly sized columns from the point *The Glaciers—An Age-Old Ice Show* forward to the end of the document.

3. Move to the end of the document and format from that point forward as one column.

4. Add the following text to the end of the document:

   Celebrate the Gold Rush Centennial by visiting Alaska and the Klondike. Retrace the footsteps taken by thousands who overcame unbearable hardships to seek their fortunes. Pan for gold... cruise the Yukon... tour the dredges... and experience the culture with a trip to Dawson City in the Yukon Territory. It's an experience of a lifetime--one you'll never forget!

   For more information about Alaska and tour packages available, contact your travel agent.

5. Change the margins for the one-column sections to 1″ left and right.

6. Remove the dashes from the features (such as The Glaciers) in the two-column section and move text which follows the dashes to a new line.

7. Format text in the two-column section of the document as follows:
   - Topic headings: Centered 15-point font
   - Glacier names: Bulleted 9-point font justified
   - Paragraph text: 11-point font for first two column text only
   - Columnar text: Justified for all three columns

8. Format the title text as centered 20-point font.

9. Replace the words *your travel agent* in the last paragraph with your name.

10. Insert an appropriate ClipArt image and size it appropriately. Change the order for the graphic so that it appears behind the text, as shown in Figure 3.4.

11. Save the document using the filename *Alaska Brochure Rev xxx.doc* and print a copy of the revised brochure.

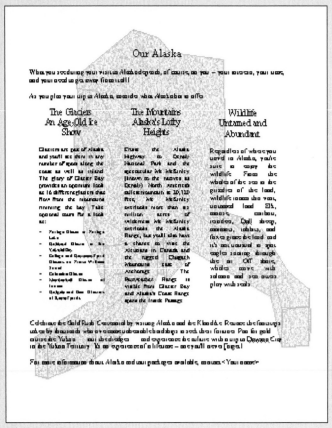

Figure 3.4

Assignments

1. Creating an award certificate

Create the award certificate shown in Figure 3.5. Choose Landscape for the orientation, use a page border, and insert the graphic from the Sports & Leisure category.

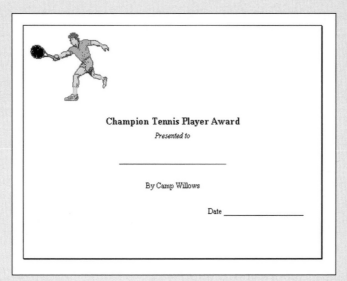

Figure 3.5

> **Note** If the Borders option is selected on the AutoFormat As You Type page of the AutoCorrect dialog box, typing underlines for the two lines in the certificate results in a thick line across the entire width of the page. To deselect the option, choose Tools, AutoCorrect, and click the AutoFormat As You Type tab.

2. Creating a list of summer camps

Search the Web for information on summer camps. Create a new document listing at least five camps and give the following information for each: name of camp, location, cost, dates, Web address. List the information in columns separated by tabs. You may find it helpful to use landscape orientation.

PROJECT

Creating a Table

A table is a versatile tool for presenting data in an easy-to-read format. Often tables are used instead of tabs to present columnar information.

Objectives

After completing this project, you will be able to:

➤ **Create a table**

➤ **Convert existing text to a table**

➤ **Move around in a table and enter data**

➤ **Insert and delete rows and columns in a table**

➤ **Format a table automatically**

➤ **Format a table manually**

➤ **Change the width of columns**

➤ **Position tables**

➤ **Draw a table**

The Challenge

Mr. Williams wants you to complete the document that he drafted pertaining to entry fees and tee times for the upcoming golf tournament.

The Solution

You will open the document and add the tee times information in a table, and you will also convert some of the existing text into a table.

Then you will format the tables to make them easier to read, and finally you will draw a table to create a form. The complete document is shown in Figure 4.1.

The Willows Pro-Celebrity Golf Tournament
to aid the
Juvenile Diabetes Foundation
September 18 - 20

Entry Fees

Type	Sept. 18	Sept. 19	Sept. 20	All Three Days
Celebrity Foursome	$200	$400	$500	$900
Pro Foursome	$300	$500	$600	$1000

The Willows will donate the green fees. Carts will be charged at the regular price for 18 holes.

Tee Times

Group	Hole	Time
1	1	7:00 am
2	1	1:00 pm
1	3	7:00 am
2	3	1:00 pm
1	6	7:00 am
2	6	1:00 pm
1	9	7:10 am
2	9	1:10 pm
1	12	7:10 am
2	12	1:10 pm
1	15	7:10 am
2	15	1:10 pm
1	18	7:10 am
2	18	1:10 pm

✂ ---

Please detach the following form and mail with your nonrefundable deposit of $100 to:

**The Willows Pro-Celebrity Tournament
The Willows Resort
1000 Coast Highway
Willow Grove, SC 22345**

Name							
Address							
City			State		Zip		

Indicate your first, second and third choices for the type of foursome you want by placing the numbers 1, 2, and 3 in the appropriate boxes. We will make every effort to give you your first choice.

Celebrity Sept. 18	Pro Sept. 18	Celebrity Sept. 19	Pro Sept. 19	Celebrity Sept. 20	Pro Sept. 20	Celebrity 3-days	Pro 3-days

Figure 4.1

The Setup

So that your screen will match the illustrations and the tasks in this project will function as described, make sure that the Word 97 settings listed in Table 4.1 are selected on your computer.

Table 4.1   Word 97 Settings

Location	Make these settings:
View, Toolbars	Deselect all toolbars except the Standard and Formatting toolbars
View	Deselect the Ruler option and select Page Layout view
Standard toolbar	Deselect any buttons that are selected and set Zoom to 100%

Creating a Table

A *table* contains *columns* and *rows* (like a spreadsheet). The intersection of a column and a row is called a *cell.* Word 97 provides three methods of creating a table. You can insert a blank table, convert existing text to a table, or draw a table freehand. In this section, you will use the first two methods. Later in this project, after you have become more comfortable with using tables, you will draw one.

TASK 1: TO INSERT A TABLE:

1 Open the file *Fees.doc.*

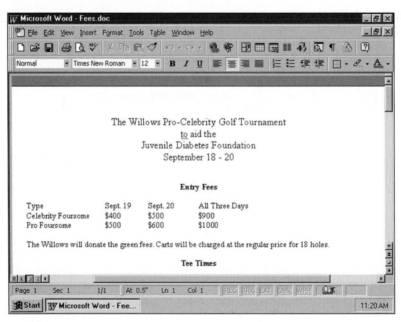

2   Click at the end of the line that says "Tee Times" and press . twice. The insertion point moves two lines below the text.

3   Choose Table.

4   Choose Insert Table.

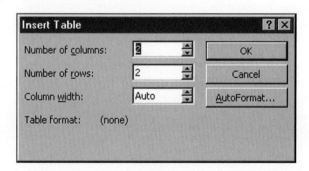

5 Type **4** for the number of columns; type **14** for the number of rows; and click OK.

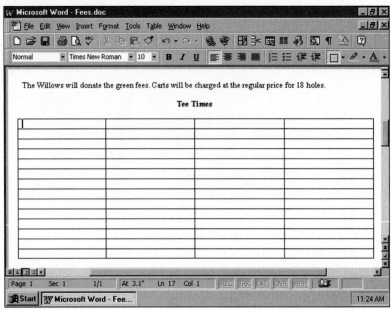

Moving Around in a Table and Entering Data

The easiest way to go to a particular cell in a table is to click in the cell, but when you are entering data in blank cells it's more efficient to move around with the keyboard techniques described in Table 4.2.

As you type data in a cell, the text wraps to the next line automatically if the cell isn't wide enough to contain the text on one line. To create a new line in a cell, press the Enter key. To indent text in a cell, press and hold down the Ctrl key while you press the Tab key.

Table 4.2   Keyboard Navigation Techniques for a Blank Table

To go to	Press
The next cell	(TAB) or (→)
The previous cell	(SHIFT)+(TAB) or (←)
The next row	(↓)
The previous row	(↑)

Note When a table contains data, using the keyboard techniques described in Table 4.2 produces different results. For example, pressing (TAB) and (SHIFT)+(TAB) moves to the next and previous cells, but it also selects the text; pressing ⊕ moves to the next cell only when the insertion point is positioned after the last character in the current cell; and pressing ⊕ moves to the next row only if the insertion point is positioned in the last line of the text in the current cell.

TASK 2: TO ENTER DATA IN A TABLE:

1 Click in the first cell of the blank table.
The insertion point blinks in the first cell.

2 Type **Group** and press (TAB).
The text appears in the cell, and the insertion point moves to the next cell.

3 Type **Hole** and press (TAB).
The text appears in the cell, and the insertion point moves to the next cell.

4 Type **Time** and press (TAB).
The text appears in the cell, and the insertion point moves to the next cell.

5 Type **Cart Number** and press (TAB).
The text appears in the cell, and the insertion point moves to the next cell, which in this case, is the first cell in the next row.

6 Type the remaining text as in:

Tee Times

Group	Hole	Time	Cart Number
1	1	7:00 am	1
2	1	1:00 pm	3
1	3	7:00 am	4
2	3	1:00 pm	5
1	6	7:00 am	7
2	6	1:00 pm	8
1	9	7:10 am	10
2	9	1:10 pm	12
1	12	7:10 am	13
2	12	1:10 pm	14
1	15	7:10 am	15
2	15	1:10 pm	16
1	18	7:10 am	20

Converting Existing Text to a Table

If you have already typed the text that you want to include in a table, you can convert the text to a table without having to insert a blank table and copy the text or retype it. Generally the text that you convert is formatted in columns using tabs.

> **Tip** Be sure that only one tab exists between each item in the list; each tab creates a column in the table.

TASK 3: TO CREATE A TABLE FROM TEXT:

1 Click the Show/Hide ¶ ⟦¶⟧ button so that you can see the tabs and paragraph returns.

2 Select the three lines of text under the "Entry Fees" heading.

3 Choose Table, Convert Text to Table.

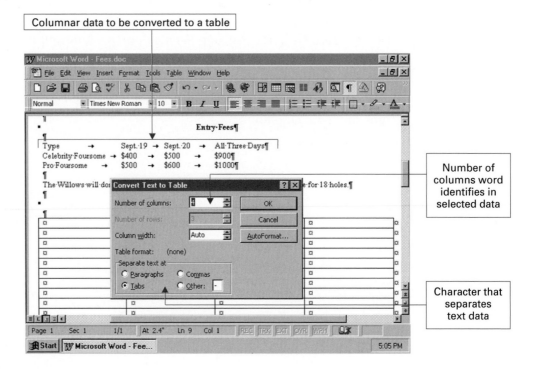

4 Click OK.

Inserting and Deleting Rows and Columns in a Table

After you have created a table, you may need to add more rows or columns to insert additional data. You also may have to delete unwanted rows or columns. When you delete a row or column, all the data in the cells is deleted. To insert or delete rows or columns, you must select the appropriate rows or columns as described in Table 4.3. An inserted row is inserted above the selected row(s). An inserted column is inserted to the left of the selected column(s).

Table 4.3   Selection Techniques

To select	Technique
The contents of a single cell	Triple-click.
A row	Point to the row in the selection bar and click. (The selection bar is the white space to the left of the table.) If you want to insert only one row, you also can simply click in any cell in the row to select the row.
Several contiguous rows	Drag the pointer in the selection bar for all the desired rows.
A column	Point to the top border of the column until the pointer turns to a black arrow and then click.
Several contiguous columns	Point to the top border of the first column until the pointer turns to a black arrow and then click and drag across the other columns.
A block of cells	Drag the pointer through the cells.
The entire table	Press (ALT)+(5). ((NUM LOCK) must be turned off.)

Tip Use the selection techniques in Table 4.3 when you want to select parts of a table for formatting.

TASK 4: TO INSERT AND DELETE ROWS AND COLUMNS:

1 Click in any cell in the row under the headings in the Tee Times table.
The insertion point blinks in the cell.

2 Choose Table, Insert Row.
A new row is inserted.

3 Click in the last cell in the last row of the table.
The insertion point blinks in the cell.

4 Press TAB.
A new row is added to the end of the table.

5 Type the following text in the new row at the bottom of the table:

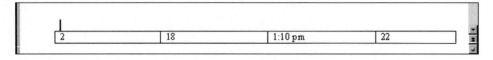

2	18	1:10 pm	22

> **Tip** If the insertion point is in the last cell in a table and you press the Tab key, Word adds a new row to the bottom of the table. To insert a new row below an existing row, click outside the table just to the right of the row's right border and then press the Enter key.

6 Select the second column in the Entry Fees table.

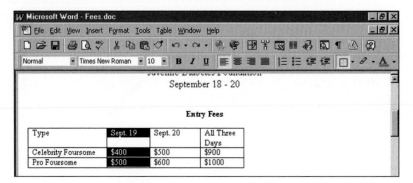

7 Choose Table, Insert Columns.
A new column is inserted to the left of the selected column, and the new Column is now the selected column.

8   Type the data in the column as in:

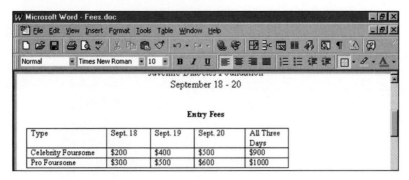

9   Click in the selection bar beside the second row in the Tee Times table.

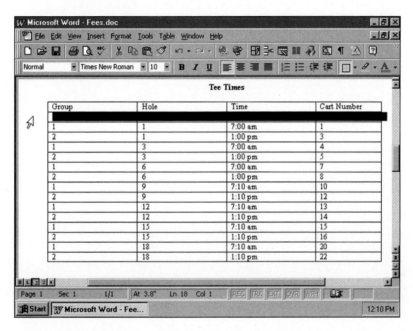

10   Choose Table, Delete Rows.
The row is deleted.

11 Select the fourth column in the Tee Times table.

```
W Microsoft Word - Fees.doc                                    _ 8 X
File Edit View Insert Format Tools Table Window Help           _ 8 X

Normal        Times New Roman   10    B  I  U
```

Tee Times

Group	Hole	Time	Cart Number
1	1	7:00 am	1
2	1	1:00 pm	3
1	3	7:00 am	4
2	3	1:00 pm	5
1	6	7:00 am	7
2	6	1:00 pm	8
1	9	7:10 am	10
2	9	1:10 pm	12
1	12	7:10 am	13
2	12	1:10 pm	14
1	15	7:10 am	15
2	15	1:10 pm	16
1	18	7:10 am	20
2	18	1:10 pm	22

```
Page 1   Sec 1   1/1   At 3.2"   Ln 17   Col 1   REC TRK EXT OVR WPH
Start   Microsoft Word - Fee...                              12:06 PM
```

12 Choose Table, Delete Columns.
The column is deleted.

Formatting a Table Automatically

Formatting a table is easy with Word 97's **AutoFormat** feature. AutoFormat provides many different formats for a table and allows you to preview the format before you select it.

TASK 5: TO FORMAT A TABLE WITH AUTOFORMAT:

1 Click in any cell in the Tee Times table.
The insertion point blinks in the cell.

2   Choose Table, Table AutoFormat.

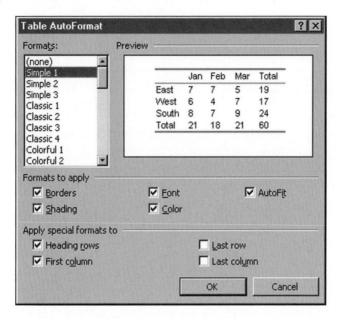

3   Scroll the Formats list, choose 3D effects 2, and deselect the First Column option.

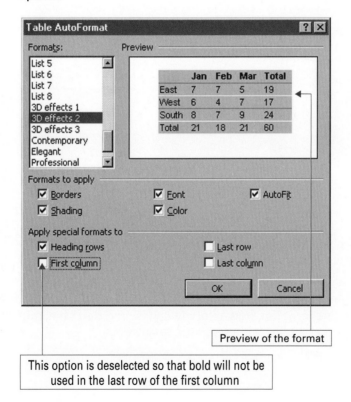

Preview of the format

This option is deselected so that bold will not be used in the last row of the first column

4   Click OK.

Formatting a Table Manually

In addition to using AutoFormat, you can manually apply other formatting techniques, such as bold and center, to text in a table. The steps to apply any type of formatting to text in a table are the same as those for formatting paragraph text. Usually, you select the text in the table and then apply the formatting.

Note Remember to select all the text in a cell, triple-click. To select a block of cells, drag the pointer through the cells.

TASK 6: TO CENTER TEXT IN A COLUMN:

1 Select the first and second columns in the Tee Times table.

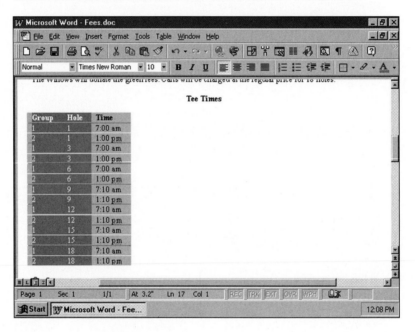

2 Click the Center ▇ button.
Text and numbers in each cell are centered.

Tip You can also apply styles to the text in a table. Refer to Project 3 if you have forgotten how to apply styles, and don't feel guilty. You can't remember all this without a little review.

Changing the Width of Columns

If the text in a column wraps to another line, you can widen the column to keep the text on the same line. If the width of a column is too wide for the data it contains, you can narrow the column.

TASK 7: TO WIDEN A COLUMN:

1 Point to the cell border between "Hole" and "Time" in the first row of the Tee Times table until you see the double-headed arrow.

It is not necessary to select the column to change the width; however, if the column is selected, all the cells in the column should be selected

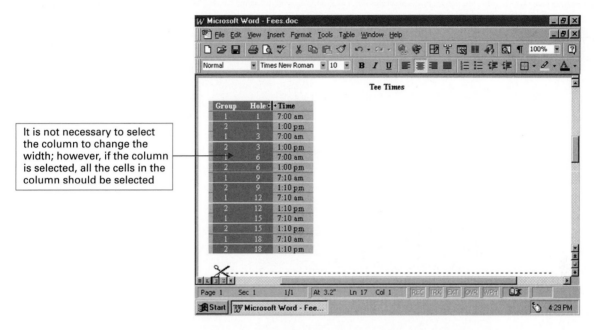

2 Drag to the right just a little bit to increase the width of the "Hole" column so it's about as wide as the first column.

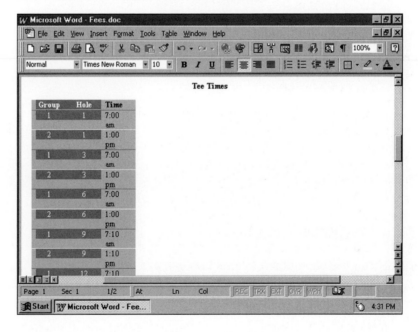

3 Point to the upper-right edge of the table until you see the double-headed ◄‖► arrow.

4 Drag to the right until the text in the last column doesn't wrap.

Positioning Tables

You can align tables on the left or right margins, center, or indent them a specific amount.

TASK 8: TO CENTER A TABLE:

1 Click in the first cell of the first row in the Tee Times table. The insertion point blinks in the cell.

2 Choose Table, Cell Height and Width.

3 Select the Row tab if not already displayed.

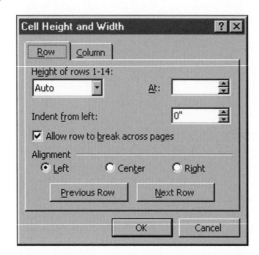

4 Choose Center for Alignment and click OK.

Drawing Tables

Sometimes you will want to create a table that has a very complex structure. Although you can create one by splitting and merging cells, why waste your time? Word 97 gives you a far easier method: You can draw the table so it looks perfect. Word even supplies an eraser you can use to remove unwanted lines and merge cells. When you draw a table, the Tables and Borders toolbar displays automatically.

TASK 9: TO DRAW A TABLE:

1 Scroll the page down so that you can see only the text "Willow Grove, SC 22345" at the top of the screen.

2 Choose Table, Draw Table.

If the Office Assistant displays, cancel it; you'll get all the help you need right now from this book.

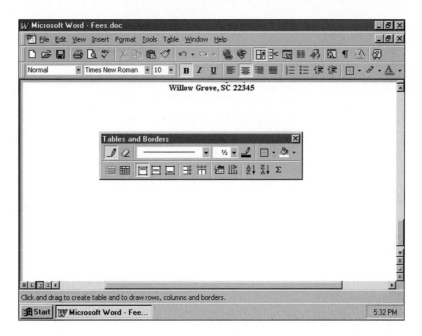

3 If the Tables and Borders toolbar appears as a palette, drag it to the bottom of the screen so that it becomes a bar.

4 Draw a rectangle below the text, starting at the left margin and extending to the right margin, that takes up most of the remainder of the screen.

5 Type **Name**, click the Draw Table ✎ button, and then draw a horizontal line under the text and a vertical line after the text.

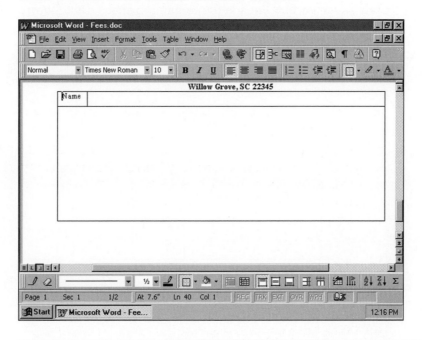

Tip If you draw a vertical line that's too close to the text and the text wraps, you can deselect the Draw Table button and then drag the column border to widen the column.

6 Click 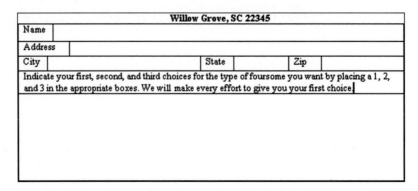.

The pointer changes to the insertion point.

7 Click under "Name" and type **Address**.

8 Click ✐ and draw a horizontal line under "Address" and a vertical line after "Address."

9 Continue using the same steps to type the following text and draw the following cells:

Willow Grove, SC 22345					
Name					
Address					
City			State		Zip
Indicate your first, second, and third choices for the type of foursome you want by placing a 1, 2, and 3 in the appropriate boxes. We will make every effort to give you your first choice.					

> **Note** If you make a mistake, you can erase a line by clicking the Eraser button and dragging the mouse pointer over the line.

10 Draw seven vertical lines in the remaining space. Don't worry if the lines aren't equally spaced; Word will even them up for you later.

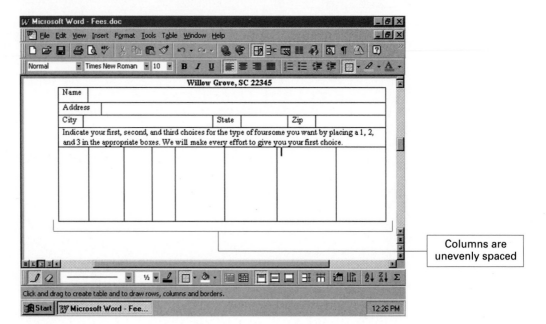

Columns are unevenly spaced

11 Select the last row by clicking in the selection bar.

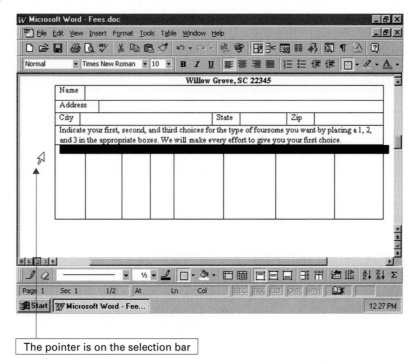

The pointer is on the selection bar

> **Note** You can't select text, cells, columns, or rows when the Draw Table button is selected.

12 Click the Distribute Columns Evenly 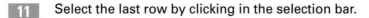 button on the Drawing bar.

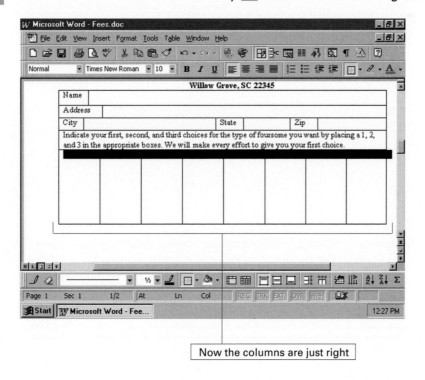

Now the columns are just right

13 Type the following text shown in the last row.

Name							
Address							
City				State		Zip	
Indicate your first, second, and third choices for the type of foursome you want by placing a 1, 2, and 3 in the appropriate boxes. We will make every effort to give you your first choice.							
Celebrity Sept. 18	Pro Sept. 18	Celebrity Sept. 19	Pro Sept. 19	Celebrity Sept. 20	Pro Sept. 20	Celebrity 3-days	Pro 3-days

14 Select the first four rows of the table.

15 Click the Distribute Rows Evenly ⊞ button and then click the Center Vertically ⊟ button.
The text is centered vertically in the rows.

16 Click the down arrow for Line Style and choose the line style shown here:

Choose this style

17   Click 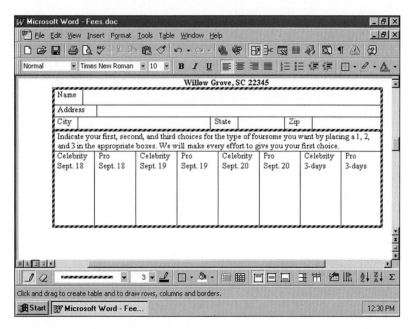 and trace over the top border line.
The line changes to the new style.

18   Trace over the other lines so that the form looks like the following:

The Conclusion

Make adjustments to the table size if necessary. Widen the last column in the first table and then center the table. Save the file as *Fees-Times-Form.doc,* and then preview the file. If you have access to a printer, print the file and then close it.

Summary and Exercises

Summary

- You can insert a blank table, convert text to a table, or draw a table.
- To go to a cell in a table, you click in the cell.
- Text automatically wraps in a cell.
- You can insert and delete rows and columns.
- AutoFormat provides many formats for formatting a table automatically.
- You also can format a table manually.
- You can change the width of a column by dragging it.
- Tables can be aligned on the left or right margin, centered, or indented.
- The Tables and Borders toolbar contains the tools for drawing a table.

Key Terms and Operations

Key Terms	Operations
AutoFormat	align (position) a table
cell	AutoFormat a table
column	change the width of a column
row	convert text to a table
selection bar	create a table
table	delete a column
Tables and Borders toolbar	delete a row
	draw a table
	insert a column
	insert a row

Study Questions

Multiple Choice

1. To create a table, you
   a. must first type the text of the table.
   b. must create space for the table by inserting blank lines.
   c. choose Table, Insert Table.
   d. choose Table, Create Table.

2. To select a column,
   a. triple-click the first cell in the column.
   b. point to the top border of the column and click when the pointer is a black arrow.
   c. point to the top border of the column and click.
   d. point to the top border of the column and press (SHIFT) while you click.

3. To draw a horizontal or vertical line in a table, use
   a. the Draw Table button.
   b. the Draw Line button.
   c. the Line button.
   d. the Straight Line button.

4. You can't select a row
   a. if a column is selected.
   b. if a group of cells is selected.
   c. if the Draw Table button is selected.
   d. unless the table is selected.

5. To go to the previous cell, press
   a. (ALT)+(TAB)
   b. (SHIFT)+(TAB)
   c. (CTRL)+(TAB)
   d. (TAB)

6. If a table is blank, what keystroke moves down in a column from cell to cell?
   a. (↓)
   b. (ENTER)
   c. (TAB)
   d. (SHIFT)+(↓)

7. Which of the following statements are true, if any?
   a. An inserted row is inserted below the selected row(s).
   b. An inserted column is inserted to the left of the selected column(s).
   c. When you delete a row, all the data is added to the next row.
   d. When you delete a column, all the data is deleted as well.

8. Before using AutoFormat, you
   a. can click in any cell in the table.
   b. must select all the cells in the table.
   c. must manually align cells.
   d. must select the first row of the table.

9. To insert a row below the selected row,
   a. choose Table, Insert Rows.
   b. click in the last cell in the row and press (ENTER).
   c. click in the last cell in the row and press (TAB).
   d. click to the right of the right border of the last cell and press (ENTER).

10. The Eraser button erases
   a. text in the document.
   b. text in a table only.
   c. lines in a table.
   d. any object in a table.

Short Answer

1. Describe two ways to add a row after the last row in the table.

2. What method of creating a table would you most likely use to create an employment application form?

3. How can you keep text from wrapping in a column?

4. How do you select multiple rows?

5. How do you indent text in a cell?

6. How do you center a table?

7. How do you change the style of a line in a table?

8. How do you widen a column?

9. How do you select multiple columns?

10. What's the name of the dialog box that has the options for positioning a table?

For Discussion

1. In what ways is the AutoFormat feature flexible?

2. Discuss the advantages of drawing a table.

3. Discuss the formatting that you can manually apply to the text in a table.

4. Describe the following AutoFormats: Simple 1, Classic 1, Columns 5, and List 1.

Review Exercises

1. Creating a script for a commercial

Mr. Williams has requested that you type up the script for a TV commercial about the golf tournament. Follow these steps to create the script.

1. Create a new document, using Figure 4.2 as your guide.

2. Type and format the text shown above the table, and press (ENTER) three times at the end of the text.

3. Create a table with 2 columns and 10 rows. Make the width of the first column narrower.

4. Type the following text:

Camera	Aerial view of golf course. Pan 9th hole. Zoom in on tee.
Action	Golfer 1 (back to the camera) seems to hit a terrific tee shot.
Golfer 2	Boy, you're having a good round. What's the secret?
Action	Other three golfers move closer to Golfer 1 to listen. (Golfer 1 still has back to camera)
Golfer 1	(Back is still to the camera) I think it's the environment. The course is great, the weather is beautiful, the resort is relaxing—everything a golfer could want.
Camera	Circles to reveal identity of Golfer 1.
Golfer 2	Yeah, and being a pro didn't hurt either, did it?
Action	Laughter from all golfers.
Camera	Fade out sound and zoom in on clubhouse.
Voice of announcer	Get together with friends at any one of the fine courses at The Willows Resort. You never know who might be in your foursome. Reservations accepted three days in advance. Call 803–945–5699 for available tee times.

5. Save the file as *Commercial* and close it.

Script for 30 Second TV Spot

Characters: Golfer 1 (a well known professional), Golfers 2, 3, and 4 (unknowns), Announcer
Setting: 9th hole overlooking Green Jacket Clubhouse

Camera	Arial view of golf course. Pan 9th hole. Zoom in on tee.
Action	Golfer 1 (back to the camera) seems to hit a terrific tee shot.
Golfer 2	Boy, you're having a good round. What's the secret?
Action	Other three golfers move closer to Golfer 1 to listen. (Golfer 1 still has back to camera)
Golfer 1	(Back is still to the camera) I think it's the environment. The course is great, the weather is beautiful, the resort is relaxing – everything a golfer could want.
Camera	Circles to reveal identity of Golfer 1.
Golfer 2	Yeah, and being a pro didn't hurt either, did it?
Action	Laughter from all golfers.
Camera	Fade out sound and zoom in on clubhouse.
Voice of announcer	Get together with friends at any one of the fine courses at The Willows Resort. You never know who might be in your foursome. Reservations accepted three days in advance. Call 803-945-5699 for available tee times.

Figure 4.2

2. Comparing the competition

To ensure that golf course standards at the Willows keeps up with the competition, the golf pro would like for you to check out fees at other resort courses. Follow these steps to create the *Competition* document:

1. Search the Web using the search string **"PGA golf course"** (include the quotation marks in the search).

2. Gather the information that appears in the table shown in Figure 4.3 for five golf courses.

3. Create a new document and change the page orientation to landscape.

4. Create a table with 8 columns and 6 rows.

5. Type the headings shown in the first row in Figure 4.3.

6. Delete the sample text in the second row and enter the information that you have found for the five golf courses.

7. Choose the Grid 5 AutoFormat.

8. Save the file as *Competition.doc* and close it.

Other Courses

Name	City	State	# of Courses	Lessons	Green Fees	Cart Fees	Annual Tournament
Sandy Beach Pines	Savannah	GA	3	Yes	$22	$18	None

Figure 4.3

3. Creating and formatting tables

1. Launch Word and create a new document.

2. Add the title *1998 Alaska Tours* in centered, 20-point bold font 1.5" from the top of the page.

3. Create the table shown in Figure 4.4.

Tour Start Date	Tour Completion Date	Cost
May 12	May 22	$2,995
May 24	May 30	$2,795
June 2	June 12	$3,095
June 14	June 24	$3,495
July 5	July 15	$3,195
July 17	July 27	$3,095
August 4	August 10	$2,795
August 13	August 19	$2,595
August 21	August 31	$2,895
September 8	September 18	$2,095

Figure 4.4

4. Save the document using the filename *Alaska Tour Dates xxx*.

5. Format the table using an appropriate AutoFormat and adjust the column widths to fit the data contained in the table columns.

6. Center the table between the left and right margins.

7. Add the following text centered below the table:

For more information about our 1998 Alaska Tours, tear off and send the form below to:

Alaska Tours International
1545 Eash Highway
Waymouth, NH 19876

8. Add the divider line a double space below the mailing information and draw the table pictured in Figure 4.5 below the divider line. Use symbols to represent the check boxes.

Please send the latest brochure on your Alaska Tours to:			
Name and address			
Check the tour features for which you would like more information			
☐ Ocean Cruises		☐ Glacier Bay	
☐ Gold Rush Sites		☐ Mountain Ranges	
☐ Denali		☐ Yukon Territory	
☐ Inside Passage		☐ Native Alaskans	

Figure 4.5

9. Save the changes to the table and print a copy of the document.

Assignments

1. Creating a form

Create the form shown in Figure 4.6. The table should be approximately 6½″ by 9″. The rows that appear to be the same height have been evenly distributed and the text is aligned vertically.

Employment Application Form						
For what position with our company are you applying?						
Last Name		First Name		Middle Initial		
Street Address				Phone		
City		State		ZIP		
Education						
Institution Name				Dates	Diploma/Degree	
Current Employer				Phone		
Employment History						
Company Name		Date/Position				
Military Experience						
Have you ever been convicted of a felony?						
Will you submit to periodic drug testing?						
What skills do you have that qualify you for this position?						
References						
Name		Phone Number				

Figure 4.6

2. Creating a golf FAQ

The golf pro wants to have a FAQ sheet to give to novices who are taking golf lessons. Create a document with a two-column table. List the questions in the first column and the answers in the second column.

Search the Web for **"golf FAQ"** to answer the following questions. (Be sure to include the quotation marks in the search string.)

- What is *par*?
- What is a *foursome*?
- What is a *wood*?
- What is an *iron*?
- What does the number on the club mean?
- What is a *handicap*?
- What is a *hook*?
- What is a *slice*?

Apply an AutoFormat of your choice.

Formatting a Long Document

When working with long documents—documents that have several pages—you will have to use some features and techniques that aren't frequently used with one-page documents.

Objectives

After completing this project, you will be able to:

➤ **Navigate in a long document**

➤ **Insert and delete page breaks**

➤ **Insert section breaks**

➤ **Create headers and footers**

➤ **Create footnotes**

The Challenge

The golf pro has a file that's an excerpt from the PGA rule book written by the United States Golf Association (USGA). He wants you to add a title page as the first page and then number the second and subsequent pages starting with the number 1. He also wants a copyright notice on each page, and he wants to add some examples to the file as footnotes. No problem; you and Word 97 can handle anything.

The Solution

You will revise the file and add a page break to create the title page. Then you will create headers and footers for the file and insert the footnotes as shown in Figure 5.1.

The Rules of Play

The rules published within this document are a subset of the rules that belong to the United States Golf Association (USGA). This document is not intended to replace the complete set of rules as published by the USGA. The intent of this document is to promote the interests of golf and the rules of golf.

Rule 14. Striking the Ball

Definition

A "stroke" is the forward movement of the club made with the intention of fairly striking at and moving the ball, but if a player checks his downswing voluntarily before the clubhead reaches the ball, he is deemed not to have made a stroke.

14-1. Ball to Be Fairly Struck At

The ball shall be fairly struck at with the head of the club and must not be pushed, scraped or spooned.[1]

14-2. Assistance

In making a stroke, a player shall not accept physical assistance or protection from the elements.[2]

14-4. Striking the Ball More than Once

If a player's club strikes the ball more than once in the course of a stroke, the player shall count the stroke and add a penalty stroke, making two strokes in all.

Rule 18. Ball at Rest Moved

Definitions

A ball is deemed to have "moved" if it leaves its position and comes to rest in any other place.

An "outside agency" is any agency not part of the match or, in stroke play, not part of the competitor's side, and includes a referee, a marker, an observer or a fore-caddie. Neither wind nor water is an outside agency.

"Equipment" is anything used, worn or carried by or for the player except any ball he has played at the hole being played and any small object, such as a coin or a tee, when used to mark the position of a ball or the extent of an area in which a ball is to be dropped. Equipment includes a golf cart, whether or not motorized. If such a cart is shared by two or more players, the cart and everything in it are deemed to be the equipment of the player whose ball is involved except that, when the cart is being moved by one of the players sharing it, the cart and everything in it are deemed to be that player's equipment.

Note: A ball played at the hole being played is equipment when it has been lifted and not put back into play.

---

[1] You cannot push a short putt all the way into the hole, for example.
[2] For example, a caddie cannot hold an umbrella over the golfer.

1

A player has "addressed the ball" when he has taken his stance and has also grounded his club, except that in a hazard a player has addressed the ball when he has taken his stance.

Taking the "stance" consists in a player placing his feet in position for and preparatory to making a stroke.

18-1. By Outside Agency

If a ball at rest is moved by an outside agency, the player shall incur no penalty and the ball shall be replaced before the player plays another stroke.

18-2. By Player, Partner, Caddie or Equipment

a. General

When a player's ball is in play, if:

1. the player, his partner or either of their caddies lifts or moves it, touches it purposely (except with a club in the act of addressing it) or causes it to move except as permitted by a rule, or
2. equipment of the player or his partner causes the ball to move, the player shall incur a penalty stroke. The ball shall be replaced unless the movement of the ball occurs after the player has begun his swing and he does not discontinue his swing.

Under the Rules no penalty is incurred if a player accidentally causes his ball to move in the following circumstances:

- In measuring to determine which ball farther from hole -- Rule 10-4
- In searching for covered ball in hazard or for ball in casual water, ground under repair, etc. -- Rule 12-1
- In process of repairing hole plug or ball mark -- Rule 16-1c
- In process of removing loose impediment on putting green -- Rule 18-2c
- In process of lifting ball under a Rule -- Rule 20-1
- In process of placing or replacing ball under a Rule -- Rule 20-3a
- In complying with Rule 22 relating to lifting ball interfering with or assisting play
- In removal of movable obstruction-- Rule 24-1

b. Ball Moving After Address

If a player's ball in play moves after he has addressed it (other than as a result of a stroke), the player shall be deemed to have moved the ball and shall incur a penalty stroke. The player shall replace the ball unless the movement of the ball occurs after he has begun his swing and he does not discontinue his swing.

2

---

c. Ball Moving After Loose Impediment Touched

Through the green, if the ball moves after any loose impediment lying within a club-length of it has been touched by the player, his partner or either of their caddies and before the player has addressed it, the player shall be deemed to have moved the ball and shall incur a penalty stroke. The player shall replace the ball unless the movement of the ball occurs after he has begun his swing and he does not discontinue his swing.

On the putting green, if the ball or ball-marker moves while removing a loose impediment, the ball or ball-marker shall be replaced. There is no penalty provided the movement of the ball or the ball-marker is directly attributable to the removal or the loose impediment. Otherwise, the player shall incur a penalty stroke under Rule 18-2a or 20-1.

18-3. By Opponent, Caddie or Equipment in Match Play

a. During Search

If, during search for a player's ball, it is moved by an opponent, his caddie or his equipment, no penalty is incurred and the player shall replace the ball.

b. Other Than During Search

If, other than during search for a ball, the ball is touched or moved by an opponent, his caddie or his equipment, except as otherwise provided in the Rules, the opponent shall incur a penalty stroke. The player shall replace the ball.

18-4. By Fellow-Competitor, Caddie or Equipment in Stroke Play

If a competitor's ball is moved by a fellow-competitor, his caddie or his equipment, no penalty is incurred. The competitor shall replace his ball.

18-5. By Another Ball

If a ball in play and at rest is moved by another ball in motion after a stroke, the moved ball shall be replaced.

Penalty for Breach of Rule:

Match play -- Loss of hole; Stroke play -- Two strokes.

*If a player who is required to replace a ball fails to do so, he shall incur the general penalty for breach of Rule 18 but no additional penalty under Rule 18 shall be applied.

Note 1: If a ball to be replaced under this Rule is not immediately recoverable, another ball may be substituted.

Note 2: If it is impossible to determine the spot on which a ball is to be placed, see Rule 20-3c.

3

Figure 5.1

© USGA

Rule 24. Obstructions

Definition

An "obstruction" is anything artificial, including the artificial surfaces and sides of roads and paths and manufactured ice, except:

1. Objects defining out of bounds, such as walls, fences, stacks and railings.
2. Any part of an immovable artificial object which is out of bounds.
3. Any construction declared by the Committee to be an integral part of the course.

24-1. Movable Obstruction

A player may obtain relief from a movable obstruction as follows:

1. If the ball does not lie in or on the obstruction, the obstruction may be removed. If the ball moves, it shall be replaced, and there is no penalty provided that the movement of the ball is directly attributable to the removal of the obstruction. Otherwise, Rule 18-2a applies.
2. If the ball lies in or on the obstruction, the ball may be lifted, without penalty, and the obstruction removed. The ball shall, through the green or in a hazard, be dropped, or on the putting green be placed, as near as possible to the spot directly under the place where the ball lay in or on the obstruction, but not nearer the hole.

The ball may be cleaned when lifted under Rule 24-1.

When a ball is in motion, an obstruction which might influence the movement of the ball, other than an attended flagstick or equipment of the players, shall not be removed.

24-2. Immovable Obstruction

a. Interference

Interference by an immovable obstruction occurs when a ball lies in or on the obstruction, or so close to the obstruction that the obstruction interferes with the player's stance or the area of his intended swing. If the player's ball lies on the putting green, interference also occurs if an immovable obstruction on the putting green intervenes on his line of putt. Otherwise, intervention on the line of play is not, of itself, interference under this Rule.

b. Relief

Except when the ball lies in or touches a water hazard or a lateral water hazard, a player may obtain relief from interference by an immovable obstruction, without penalty, as follows:

4

© USGA

1. Through the Green: If the ball lies through the green, the point on the course nearest to where the ball lies shall be determined (without crossing over, through or under the obstruction) which (a) is not nearer the hole, (b) avoids interference (as defined) and (c) is not in a hazard or on a putting green. The player shall lift the ball and drop it within one club-length of the point thus determined on ground which fulfills (a), (b) and (c) above.

    Note: The prohibition against crossing over, through or under the obstruction does not apply to the artificial surfaces and sides of roads and paths or when the ball lies in or on the obstruction.

2. In a Bunker: If the ball lies in or touches a bunker, the player shall lift and drop the ball in accordance with Clause (i) above, except that the ball must be dropped in the bunker.

3. On the Putting Green: If the ball lies on the putting green, the player shall lift the ball and place it in the nearest position to where it lay which affords relief from interference, but not nearer the hole nor in a hazard.

The ball may be cleaned when lifted under Rule 24-2b.

Exception: A player may not obtain relief under Rule 24-2b if (a) it is clearly unreasonable for him to play a stroke because of interference by anything other than an immovable obstruction or (b) interference by an immovable obstruction would occur only through use of an unnecessarily abnormal stance, swing or direction of play.

Note: If a ball lies in or touches a water hazard (including a lateral water hazard), the player is not entitled to relief without penalty from interference by an immovable obstruction. The player shall play the ball as it lies or proceed under Rule 26-1.

c. Ball Lost

Except in a water hazard or a lateral water hazard, if there is reasonable evidence that a ball is lost in an immovable obstruction, the player may, without penalty, substitute another ball and follow the procedure prescribed in Rule 24-2b. For the purpose of applying this Rule, the ball shall be deemed to lie at the spot where it entered the obstruction. If the ball is lost in an underground drain pipe or culvert the entrance to which is in a hazard, a ball must be dropped in that hazard or the player may proceed under Rule 26-1, if applicable.

5

Figure 5.1   *(continued)*

The Setup

So that your screen will match the illustrations and the tasks in this project will function as described, make sure that the Word 97 settings listed in Table 5.1 are selected on your computer.

Table 5.1   Word 97 Settings.

Location	Make these settings:
View, Toolbars	Deselect all toolbars except the Standard and Formatting toolbars
View	Deselect the Ruler option and select the Normal view
Standard toolbar	Deselect any buttons that are selected and set Zoom to 100%

Navigating Within a Long Document

Word 97 provides several ways to navigate within a document—Go To, Find, and Word's cool new Document Map feature. You can use buttons or scroll bars to go to each page, heading, graphic, or table. If you want to revise specific text in a long document, the easiest way to go to the text is to use the Find command. You also can use the Document Map to move to text under a specific heading.

TASK 1: TO GO TO A PAGE:

1   Open *Glfrules.doc*.
The first page of a multiple-page document displays.

2   Drag the box in the vertical scroll bar until you see Page 5 and then click the cursor in "b. Relief" in the document. (You may have to scroll up to find the text.)

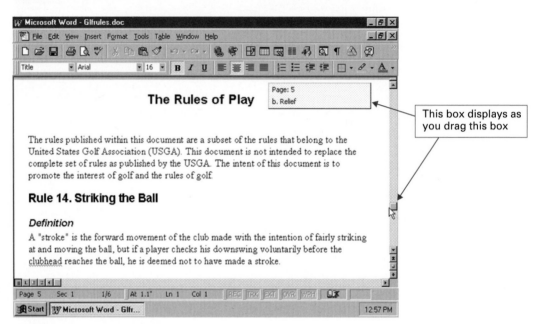

3   Choose View, Page Layout.
The view changes to Page Layout.

> **Tip** In Normal view, a page break that Word inserts automatically is a dotted line; in Page Layout view, the page break is a thick gray line with a thin black line at the top.

4   Click the Previous Page 🔼 button twice.
Page 3 displays (as shown in the status bar).

5   Click the Next Page 🔽 button.
Page 4 displays.

The new browsing feature allows you to navigate a document by jumping from one element to another. For example, you can jump from heading to heading or from table to table.

TASK 2: TO BROWSE BY HEADINGS:

1   Press (CTRL)+(HOME).
The insertion point moves to the top of the first page.

2   Choose Edit, Go To.

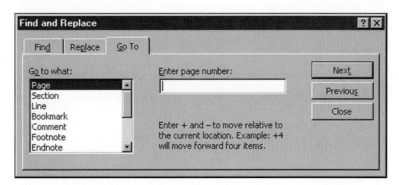

3   Choose Heading for Go to what, type **+1**, and click Close.
The dialog box closes, and the Previous Page and Next Page buttons turn blue, indicating that their functions have now changed to Previous Heading and Next Heading.

> **Tip** Pointing to the blue navigational buttons displays the current name of the button in a pop-up box.

4   Click the Next Heading ⬆ button.
The insertion point moves to the first paragraph with a heading style. (Notice the name of the style in the Style box in the Formatting toolbar.)

5   Click ⬆ repeatedly to browse through the entire document.
The insertion point moves to each paragraph with a heading style until it reaches the last paragraph with a heading style at the end of the document.

Finding a specific word or string of words is an efficient way to navigate in documents of more than one page, especially if you want to go to a specific portion of text to edit the text.

TASK 3: TO FIND TEXT IN A DOCUMENT:

1   Choose Edit, Find.

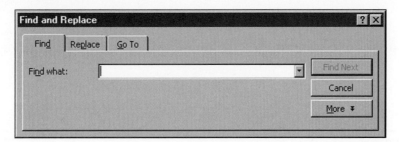

2 Type **club** and click Find Next.

The next occurrence of the word is highlighted and the dialog box remains open. If you get a message saying that Word has reached the end of the document, click Yes to continue searching from the beginning.

3 Click Find Next.

The word "clubhead" is highlighted.

4 Click More.

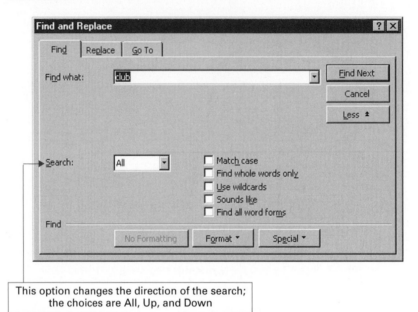

This option changes the direction of the search; the choices are All, Up, and Down

5 Choose the Find whole words only option and click Find Next.

The next occurrence is highlighted, but it's hidden by the dialog box.

6 Click ✕.

The dialog box closes, the Previous Heading button changes to the Previous Find/Go To button, and the Next Heading button changes to the Next Find/Go To button.

7 Click ⬇.

The next occurrence is highlighted.

> **Tip** To quickly change the navigation buttons back to Previous Page and Next Page, click the Select Browse Object button ⊙ and click the Browse by Page button.

The ***Document Map*** is a new tool in Word 97 that lists all the document headings, similar to an outline, in a pane on the left. The headings are linked to the document so that you can click a heading and go directly to the text in the document.

TASK 4: TO NAVIGATE WITH THE DOCUMENT MAP:

1 Click the Document Map button.

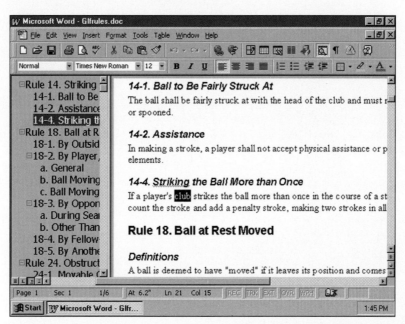

Note You can make the left pane wider, but it is not necessary because when you point to a heading that is partially hidden, the complete text displays.

2 Click "Rule 14. Striking the Ball" in the left pane.

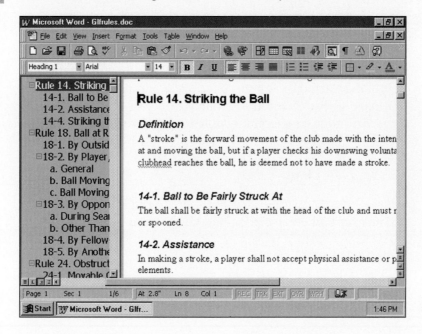

3 Click "Rule 24. Obstructions" in the left pane.

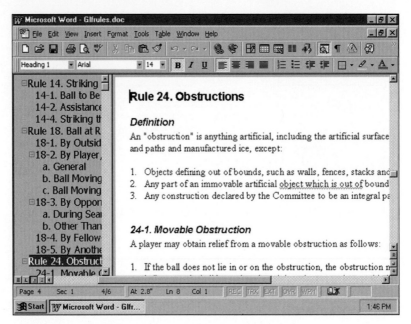

4 Click .
The view changes to Page Layout, the view originally selected.

> **Tip** To collapse a heading in the Document Map pane so that the sub-headings are hidden, click the minus sign that appears to the left of the heading. To expand a heading to show the subheadings, click the plus sign that appears to the left of the heading.

Inserting and Deleting Page Breaks

When a page fills up with text, Word 97 automatically inserts a page break, referred to as a *soft page break,* and creates a new page. If you want a page to break before it's filled, you can insert a page break yourself. A user-defined page break is called a *hard page break.*

TASK 5: TO INSERT A PAGE BREAK FOR THE TITLE PAGE AND FOR EACH RULE

1 Press (CTRL)+(HOME) and click before "Rule 14. Striking the Ball."
The insertion point is positioned before the "R" in the text.

2   Press (CTRL)+(ENTER).

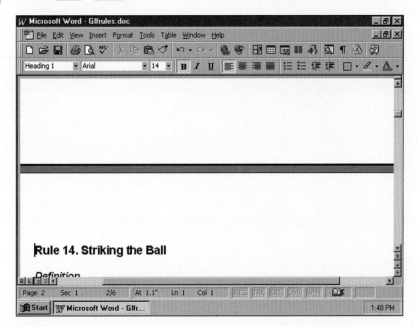

3   Choose View, Normal.
The view changes from Page Layout to Normal.

> **Tip** In Normal view, a hard page break has the words "Page Break" centered on the dotted line; a soft page break is simply a dotted line.

4   Choose Edit, Find.
The Find and Replace dialog box displays.

5   Type **Rule 18,** click Less, and then click Find Next.
"Rule 18" is highlighted.

6   Click Cancel.
The Find and Replace dialog box closes.

7   Press (←).
The insertion point moves to the beginning of the highlighted text, and the text is no longer highlighted.

8   Press (CTRL)+(ENTER).
You just forced Word 97 to insert another page break. What power! What control!

9   Choose Edit, Find.
The Find and Replace dialog box displays.

10   Type **Rule 24,** click Find Next, and then click Find Next again to go to the next occurrence.
The text is highlighted.

11   Click Cancel.
The dialog box closes.

12 Press ⬅.
The insertion point moves to the beginning of the highlighted text, and the text is no longer highlighted.

13 Press CTRL+ENTER.
A page break is inserted.

TASK 6: TO DELETE A PAGE BREAK:

1 Press CTRL+HOME.
The insertion point moves to the top of the document.

> **Tip** If you want to delete a page break that you have inserted, it's advisable—though not mandatory—to switch to the Normal view. In the Normal view, you can actually see a symbol that you can delete.

2 Click the Select Browse Object ⊙ button.

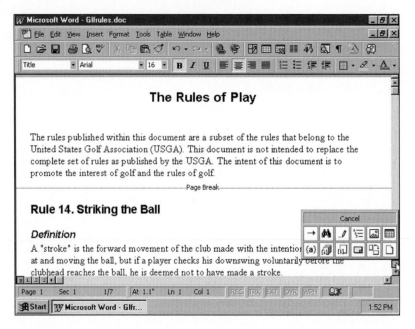

3 Click the Browse by Page ▢ button.
The Browse palette closes, and the navigational buttons change from blue to black and the insertion point advances to the next page.

4 Click ⬇ once.
The insertion point is blinking at the top of page 3.

5 Scroll up until you can see the page break.

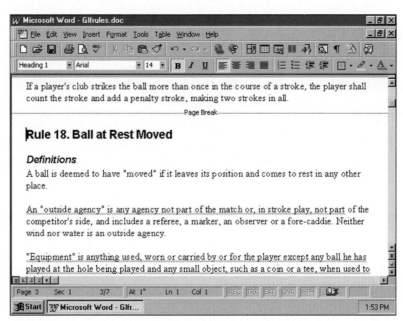

6 Click anywhere on the page break's dotted line.
The insertion point is positioned at the left margin on the dotted line.

7 Press (DELETE).
Zap! The page break is gone. Out of there. History.

8 Click ⬇ three times to move to page 5, and scroll up so that you can see the page break.

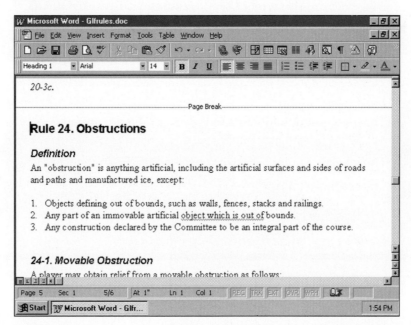

9   Click anywhere on the page break's dotted line.
The insertion point is positioned at the left margin on the dotted line.

10   Press (DELETE).
The page break is deleted.

> **Note** You can't delete a soft page break.

> **Tip** To delete a hard page break in the Page Layout view, click after the last character on the previous page and press Del or click before the first character on the page and press Backspace.

Inserting Section Breaks

A *section break* defines a new *section* in a document. You need to create a new section in a document if you want to use different formats, such as paper size and orientation, or if you want to create different headers and footers for each section.

> **Note** A *header* is text that prints at the top of every page in a section. A *footer* is text that prints at the bottom of every page in a section.

In the Rules of Play document, you will insert a section break between the title page and the first page so that you can create different headers and footers for these sections later. Not all section breaks have page breaks. But, because the type of section break you will insert carries a page break with it, you will have to delete the page break you inserted earlier, to avoid having a blank page.

TASK 7: TO INSERT A SECTION BREAK:

1   Press (CTRL)+(HOME).
The insertion point moves to the top of the document.

2   Click before "Rule 14. Striking the Ball."
The insertion point is blinking before the "R" in the text.

3   Choose Insert, Break.

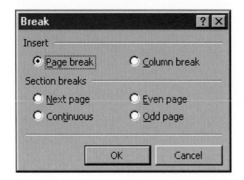

4 Select Next page and click OK.

The section break carries a page break with it, so the previous page break isn't needed.

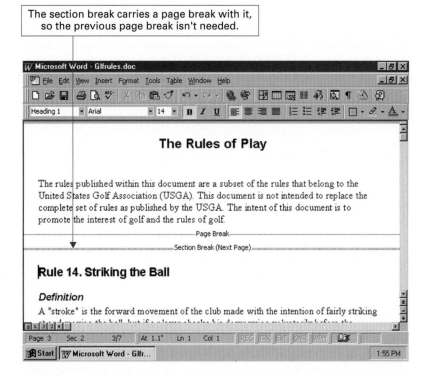

5 Click the page break above the section break and press (DELETE). The page break is deleted.

> **Tip** To delete a section break, change to Normal view, click the section break, and press (DELETE).

Creating Headers and Footers

When you create a header or a footer, a toolbar displays, and a header or footer space opens. Because text in a header or footer is normally printed in the center or flush with the left or right margins, the space has a center tab in the center and a right tab on the right margin.

TASK 8: TO CREATE A HEADER AND A FOOTER:

1 Click anywhere on page 2. "Page 2 Sec 2" displays in the status bar.

2   Choose View, Header and Footer.

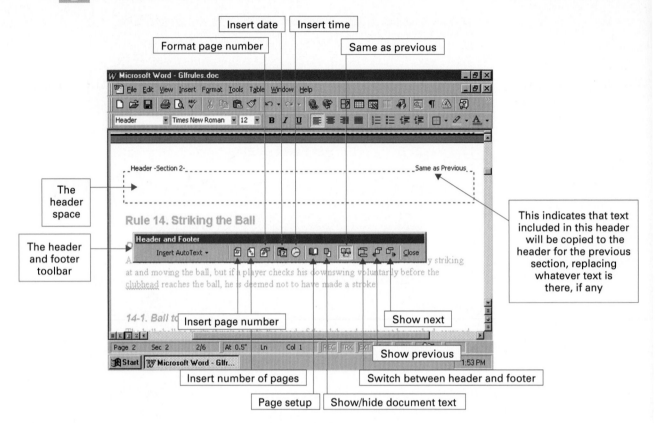

3   Click the Same as Previous button to deselect it so that this header doesn't influence the header in the previous section.
The words "Same as Previous" in the upper-right corner of the header are deleted.

4   Press ⌐TAB⌐ twice.
The insertion point moves to the right margin in the header space.

5   Type **(c) USGA**.

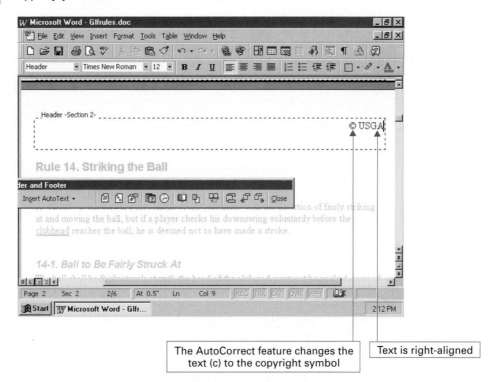

The AutoCorrect feature changes the text (c) to the copyright symbol

Text is right-aligned

6   Click the Show Previous 🔲 button.

This is the header for Section 1. You can enter different data in this header.

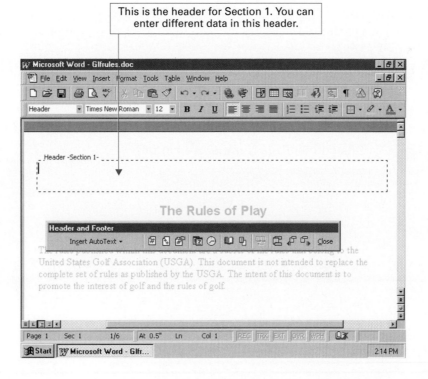

7 Click the Show Next ⬚ button.
The header for Section 2 displays.

8 Click the Switch Between Header and Footer ⬚ button.

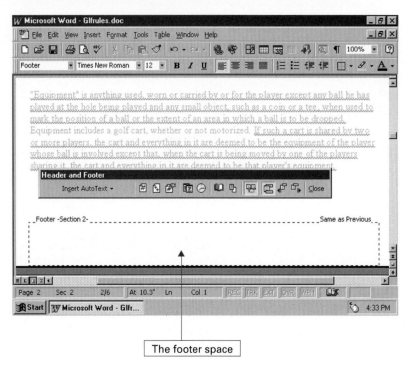

The footer space

9 Click ⬚.
The words "Same as Previous" in the upper-right corner of the footer are deleted.

10 Press TAB.
The insertion point moves to the middle of the footer space.

11 Click the Insert Page Number ⬚ button.
The number "2" is inserted because Section 2 starts on page 2.

12 Click the Format Page Number ⬚ button.

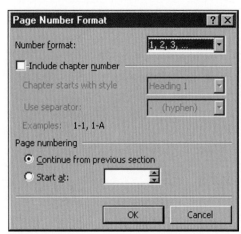

13 Select Start at.

14 Click OK.

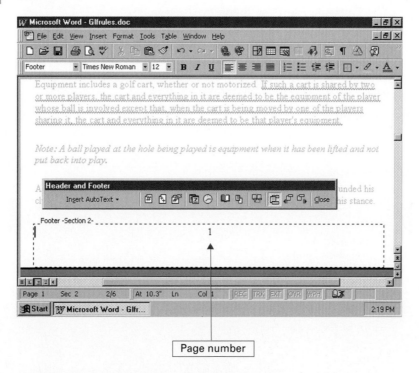

Page number

15 Click Close on the Header and Footer toolbar.
The footer space closes.

> **Tip** Headers and footers aren't visible in the Normal view.

16 Choose View, Page Layout, press (CTRL)+(HOME), and then scroll through the document to see the headers and footers.
No header or footer appears on the first page, but headers and footers appear on subsequent pages, and the page numbers are incremented.

17 Choose View, Normal.
The view changes to Normal and the headers and footers are no longer visible.

Creating Footnotes

A *footnote* is a comment or reference that appears at the bottom of the page. The reference in the text to which the footnote applies is generally numbered, and the footnote displays the same number. When you create a footnote, Word automatically numbers the footnote in the text and provides sufficient space at the bottom of the page for the footnote. You can create multiple footnotes on the same page. If you group the footnotes together at the end of the document, they're called *endnotes*.

You can insert footnotes in any order, and Word will number or renumber them consecutively throughout the document. Word is one accommodating word processing program.

TASK 9: TO INSERT A FOOTNOTE:

1 Choose Edit, Find.
The Find and Replace dialog box displays.

2 Type **protection from the elements.** and click Find Next.
The text is highlighted.

3 Click Cancel.
The Find and Replace dialog box closes.

4 Press ⊙ twice.
The insertion point moves to the end of the sentence and the highlight is removed.

5 Choose Insert, Footnote.

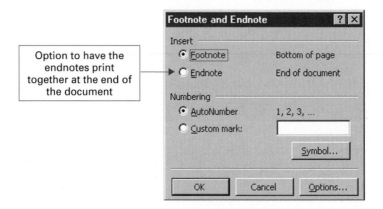

Option to have the endnotes print together at the end of the document

6 Click OK.

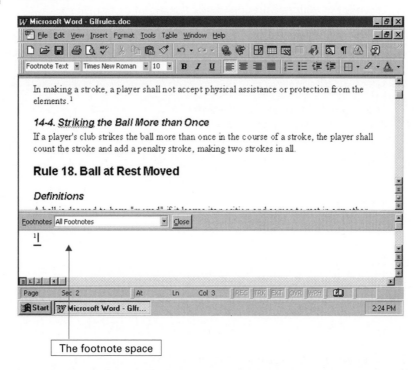

The footnote space

7 Type **For example, a caddie cannot hold an umbrella over the golfer.**

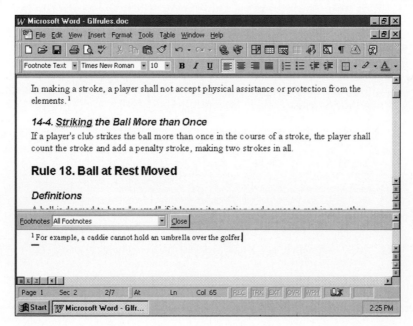

8 Click the up arrow in the document's vertical scroll bar until the previous heading is visible and click after "scraped or spooned."

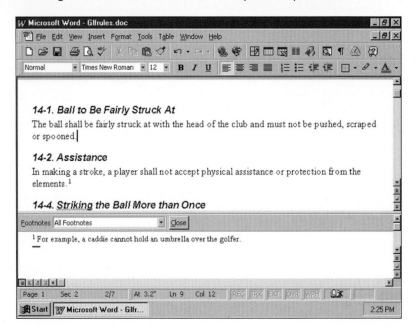

9 Choose Insert, Footnote, and click OK.
The reference number 1 is inserted and the previous reference changes to 2.

10 Type **You cannot push a short putt all the way into the hole, for example**.

11 Click Close.
The footnote space closes.

12 Change to Page Layout view if necessary and scroll to the end of the page to see the footnote.

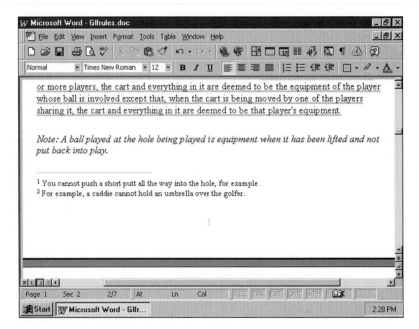

Tip If you can't see a footnote, you're not blind. Just switch to Page Layout view. Footnotes aren't visible in Normal view.

The Conclusion

Save the file as *Rules of Golf.doc*. If you have access to a printer, practice printing portions of the document such as the current page or pages 2 and 3. When finished, close the file.

Summary and Exercises

Summary

- Word 97 provides several ways to navigate in a long document: Go To, Find, and Document Map.
- A page break creates a new page.
- A section break creates a new section.
- A header prints at the top of every page in a section.
- A footer prints at the bottom of every page in a section.
- Word 97 automatically numbers footnotes.

Key Terms and Operations

Key Terms	Operations
Document Map	delete a page break
endnote	delete a section break
footer	find text
footnote	go to text
hard page break	insert a page break
header	insert a section break
page break	select Browse Object button
section break	
soft page break	

Study Questions

Multiple Choice

1. A footnote
   a. is automatically renumbered if you insert another footnote.
   b. is automatically renumbered if you insert another footnote before it.
   c. displays a subscripted number.
   d. doesn't display in Page Layout view.

2. A page break
   a. is inserted automatically by Word when a page fills up.
   b. is never inserted in the middle of a paragraph.
   c. can only be inserted by the user.
   d. allows you to use different orientation for different pages in the same document.

3. A footnote prints
   a. at the end of the document.
   b. at the bottom of the page on which the reference appears.
   c. only in the Page Layout view.
   d. only in the Normal view.

4. The Document Map
  a. is an outline.
  b. lists all the document headings in the right pane.
  c. displays headings that are linked to the document.
  d. displays all the headers, footers, footnotes, and other objects that aren't actually part of the body of the text.

5. A header prints
  a. at the top of every page.
  b. at the bottom of every page.
  c. at the top of every page in a section.
  d. at the top of every page in every section.

6. A section break
  a. always inserts a page break.
  b. allows you to use a different page orientation for different pages in the same document.
  c. is another name for a page break.
  d. must be applied to even or odd pages.

7. "Same as Previous" indicates that
  a. the section break will be like the one before it.
  b. the footnote will be like the one before it.
  c. the page break will be like the one before it.
  d. the header will be like the one before it.

8. A dotted line that spans the width of the screen indicates
  a. a soft page break.
  b. a section break.
  c. the footnote space.
  d. the header space.

9. The Select Browse Object button
  a. is located on the Standard toolbar.
  b. is located in the horizontal scroll bar.
  c. displays a palette.
  d. displays the Object toolbar.

10. If you want the first page of a document to have a portrait orientation and the next page to have a landscape orientation, you must
  a. insert a page break.
  b. create two different documents.
  c. insert a section break.
  d. insert a footer.

Short Answer

1. What happens if you click the Select Browse Object button?

2. List all the elements that you can go to using the Go To command.

3. What additional options are displayed in the Find dialog box if you click the More button?

4. What happens to the footnote numbers if you insert a footnote between two existing footnotes?

5. How can you change the navigational keys back to Previous Page and Next Page?

6. What elements can be automatically inserted in a header or footer?

7. How can you use two different page numbering formats in the same document?

8. How do you collapse the headings in the Document Map?

9. How do you display the Document Map?

10. What's the difference between footnotes and endnotes?

For Discussion

1. If you want to find several occurrences of a word, what's the best way to find the occurrences and read them in context?

2. Discuss the advantages of using a section break.

3. Why is it better to use a header or footer than to simply type the text that you want at the top or bottom of every page?

4. Discuss the benefits of using a word processing program to create a document that has many footnotes versus typing the document on a typewriter.

Review Exercises _____

1. Creating a document with two sections

For the golf tournament, you need to type the memo and table pictured in Figure 5.2. Follow these steps to complete the task.

1. Create a new document using the *Professional Memo.dot* template.

2. Type the text for page 1 as shown in Figure 5.2.

3. Insert a Next Page section break at the end of the page.

4. Click page 2 and change the orientation to landscape.

5. Type the title and the footnote.

6. Format the titles as shown in Figure 5.2.

7. Create a table that's 13 columns by 7 rows.

8. Enter the data in the table as shown in Figure 5.2.

9. Save the file as *Golf Ball Sales.doc* and close it.

The Willows Resort

Memo

To: Thomas Williams

From: <type your name here>

Date: 11/29/96

Re: Golf Ball Sales for Last Year

I have looked up the sales records for last year for all sales of golf balls. The attached table includes sales in the pro shop **and all other** shops in The Willows Resort. If you want just the sales for the pro shop, let me know. I can easily obtain that information as well.

Golf Ball Sales for Last Year[1]

	Jan	Feb	Mar	Apr	May	Jun	Jul	Aug	Sep	Oct	Nov	Dec
MaxFli	500	900	700	760	800*	900	840	880	800	760*	900	900*
Titleist	520	610	720*	750	790	800*	910*	900	790	760	610*	800*
Dunlop	500	570	580	600*	510	400	500	600	510*	600	570	400*
Wilson	520	660	760	780	790	850	760	720*	790	820	660	850*
X-Out	540*	590*	600	580	590	600	780	800	590	580	590	600
Total	2580	3330	3360	3470	3480	3550	3790	3900	3480	3520	3330	3550

---
[1] Asterisk denotes that a sales promotion was run for that brand in that month.

● Page 2

Figure 5.2

2. Revising a multi-page document

The Games.doc needs to be revised and references added for some of the information contained in the document. Follow these steps to edit the document.

1. Open the file named *Games.doc*.

2. Add this footnote to the title:

   See The Complete Book of Golf Games by Scott Johnston

3. View the Document Map so you can get an idea of what's contained in the file.

4. Click the Tournament Formats heading in the left pane.

5. Delete the page break after the "Tournament Formats" heading.

6. Insert a page break before the heading "Tournament Formats" heading.

7. Insert a Next Page section break between the first and second page.

8. On page 2, create a footer that contains a centered page number (starting with the number 2). Be sure there's no page number on page 1.

9. Insert a page break before the "Pink Ball" heading.

10. Search for "blind bogey" on the Web and add the definition to the end of the document under the "Blind Bogey" heading.

11. Save the file as *Games of Golf* and close it.

Games of Golf[1]

Games for Twosomes, Threesomes, and Foursomes

Pick Up Sticks
Comment: Requires some strategy and is also quite entertaining; highly recommended for beginners because it forces you to create shots
Handicap: Full handicap

Play is match play. Each time a player loses a hole, he may take one club in his opponent's bag out of play. (Best club to take away: the sand wedge, unless the player also carries a lob wedge.) Most players agree before the game to give the putter immunity because it's too much of a handicap not to have one.

Variation: Use a club handicap instead of a "stroke" handicap. For example, before the game begins, the higher-handicapped player can remove one club from his opponent's bag for every two strokes in their handicap differential. The game then progresses in the same manner as described above.

No Alibis
Also known as Criers & Whiners

Instead of using handicaps, players may replay shots during the round. The number of shots replayed is usually equal to three-fourths of a player's handicap. When replaying, the golfer must use the second shot, regardless of where it goes, and he can't replay the same shot twice.

Wolf
Also known as Wolfman
Comment: Wolf is a three-player game
Handicap: Full handicap

On each hole, the golfer with the drive that lands between the other two drives is the *wolf*. His opponents are the *hunters*. On par-three holes, the wolf is the second-closest to the pin after the first shot.

[1] See *The Complete Book of Golf Games* by Scott Johnston.

The wolf must match twice his net score on the hole against the combined net scores of the hunters. If there's a tie, players decide whether the points carry to the next hole. Any points carried over go to the next winning team.

Scotch Foursome
Also known as Alternative Shot
Comment: A popular game in Great Britain, where it's simply called a *Foursome*; a fast game because partners tend to walk ahead to the next shot
Handicap: Use one-half of combined handicaps

To play, a two-man team alternates shots from tee to green until the ball is in the hole. One player should drive all the odd holes and the other all the even. You must put some thought into who drives which holes.

Bridge
Comment: Excellent golf game for foursomes

At the tee, one pair makes a bid on how many strokes (net or gross) it will take their team to complete the hole. For instance, if they bid 9, they are saying they can play the hole in 9 strokes or fewer combined.

The other team then has three options:

1. Bid lower than 9.
2. Take the bid.
3. Take the bid and double it.

The first team may then double it back, if they wish.

Variation: Add a penalty point for each stroke that the winning bidder incurs over bogey.

Selected Score
Comment: A fun, leisurely format to use over a weekend
Handicap: two-thirds or three-fourths handicap

Each golfer plays 36 holes. The final score is the combination of the two rounds, selecting the best net score from each of the 18 holes. Lowest score wins.

2

Figure 5.3

Tournament Formats

Medal Play
Also known as Stroke Play
Comment: No gimmes
Handicap: Use handicaps from 80-100% - preferably on the lower side to prevent sandbagging.

Golfers play 18 holes and the winner is the player with the best gross scores and net scores.

Scramble
Comment: A shotgun start is generally used; seven or eight under is usually the score to beat
Handicap: Used to create teams but not used during play

Each foursome is a team competing against all other foursomes. Each player in the group drives off the tee, then all four golfers play their second shots from the best-driven ball. All then play their third shots from the best second ball, and so on. Each player in a foursome must have at least four of his or her drives used by the group during the game.

Flag Tournament
In a Flag Tournament, each player receives a certain number of strokes - usually the course par plus two-thirds of the player's full handicap. So, a 15-handicapper on a par-72 course gets 82 strokes.

There are then two options for play. The golfer can play all 82 shots and stops, planting a flag with her name on it on the spot where her 82nd shot landed, or she can stop when she has played 18 holes. The winner is the one who has planted the flag the farthest on the course or who has the most shots remaining after 18 holes. If the farthest two players both finish on the same green, the winner is the golfer closer to the hole.

Additional rule: You can't plant a flag past a hole that you haven't completed. For example, if you're five feet short of a green with one stroke left, you can't hit the ball onto the next fairway.

3

Pink Ball
Comment: A game for foursomes

Each foursome has a pink ball that rotates among players on each hole. Player 1 uses it on the first hole, player 2 on the second, and so on. Take the best net score on each hole and add it to the score of the player who used the pink ball.

Variation: Keep the overall net score for the pink ball separately, and give a prize to the team with the best pink ball score. If a team loses the pink ball, it's disqualified.

Trouble
Also known as Disaster
Comment: An excellent game for the intermediate player; encourages smart golf

Trouble is a point game in which the goal is to collect the least number of *trouble points* possible during a round.

Points are assigned as follows:

- out of bounds - 1
- water hazard - 1
- bunker - 1
- three-putt - 1
- leaving ball in bunker - 2
- hitting from one bunker to another - 2
- four-putt - 3
- whiffed ball - 4

A player can erase all the points accumulated on a given hole by making par. At the end of the round, simply net all the points against each other to see who wins.

Blind Bogey
<type your description here>

4

Figure 5.3   *(continued)*

3. Creating headers, footers, and footnotes

1. Open *Alaska Highway.doc*.

2. Use the Document Map to identify all level 2 headings.

3. Insert Next Page section breaks before each level 2 heading except Quote.

4. Create a header for each section that contains the level 2 heading right aligned.

5. Add a right-aligned document page number to the footer and position your name on the next line of the footer, left-aligned.

6. Create a different first-page footer and remove the page number and your name from the first page footer.

7. Cut the last line of the document (the Copyright line) to the Windows Clipboard and insert a footnote after the document title. Paste the Windows Clipboard contents as the footnote text.

8. Save the document using the filename *Alaska Highway Rev xxx* and print a copy of the document.

Assignments

1. Creating a document with two sections on the same page

Create a new document and type the text that you see above the two columns in Figure 5.4. Insert a Continuous section break after the text. Create two columns and copy the remaining text from the *Games.doc* file.

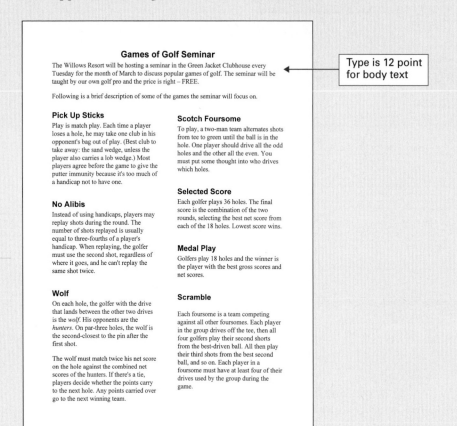

Figure 5.4

2. Downloading and formatting a file

Go to the Microsoft FTP site (ftp://ftp.microsoft.com) and download a file with an extension of .doc or .txt. Open the file in Word. View the headers and footers, if it has any. Add headers and footers of your own if the file doesn't have them. Add this footnote at the end of the document:

Downloaded from the Microsoft FTP site

Creating a Mail Merge

Mail merging is a process that inserts text from one file which contains a list of information into a second file such as a form letter. The process involves three steps: creating the file that contains the list of information, creating the form, and merging the two files.

Objectives

After completing this project, you will be able to:

➤ **Create the Data Source document**

➤ **Create the Main document**

➤ **Merge the documents**

➤ **Create another Main document to use with a Data Source document**

➤ **Create and use another Data Source document with a Main document**

The Challenge

The Olympia Fitness Center at The Willows Resort wants to offer a limited number of memberships to the general public in the surrounding area. Before advertising the memberships, the manager, Laura Carr, wants to send out personalized letters to a list of previous guests to give them an opportunity to join the club.

The Solution

You will create a *Data Source document* that contains the names and addresses of the guests to whom the letters will be sent. Then you will create the letter as a *Main document* and merge the letter with the list of names. Figure 6.1 shows a sample of a merged letter.

May 10, 1997

Mr. John A. Cartwright
ABC Printing
101 Main Street
Willow Grove, SC 22345

Dear Mr. Cartwright:

A limited number of memberships to the Olympia Fitness Center at The Willows Resort are available for local patrons at a very reasonable price. Because you have been a guest at the fitness club in the past, we would like to give you an opportunity to join the club before we advertise the memberships publicly. A one-year membership is $1,500, and it includes full access to all the fitness club facilities as well as discounts on the use of our golf and tennis facilities.

If you would like to take advantage of this special offer, please fill out and return the enclosed membership form with a down payment of $500. You will be billed in two installments for the balance.

Sincerely,

Laura Carr
Manager, Olympia Fitness Center

Figure 6.1

The Setup

So that your screen will match the illustrations and the tasks in this project will function as described, make sure that the Word 97 settings listed in Table 6.1 are selected on your computer.

Table 6.1   Word 97 Settings

Location	Make these settings:
View, Toolbars	Deselect all toolbars except the Standard and Formatting toolbars
View	Deselect the Ruler option and select the Normal view
Standard toolbar	Deselect any buttons that are selected and set Zoom to 100%

Creating the Data Source Document

The Data Source document contains the variable information, such as the list of names and addresses. Each category of information in the Data Source document must be labeled by a field name. The variable information that comprises all the data for one person, group, etc. is called a record. For example, the field named Address might contain the variable information "101 Main Street," "512 Southwinds Avenue," and so on in different records.

TASK 1: TO CREATE THE DATA SOURCE DOCUMENT:

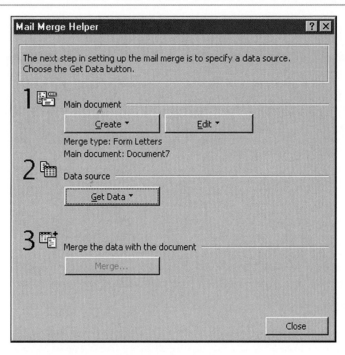

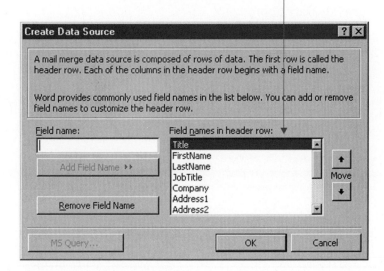

1 In a blank document, choose Tools, Mail Merge.

2 Select Create, Form Letters, Active Window.

3 Select Get Data.
A drop-down list displays.

4 Select Create Data Source.

5 Select JobTitle in the Field names in header row list box.
The field is highlighted.

6 Click Remove Field Name.
The field is removed, appears in the Field name text box, and the next field is highlighted.

7 Following the same process, remove the Country, HomePhone, and WorkPhone fields.

8 Type **MiddleI**.
The name "WorkPhone" is replaced with the name "MiddleI" in the Field name text box.

9 Click Add Field Name.
The field name is added to the end of the Field names in header row list, and it's highlighted.

Note A field name can't have a space in it.

10 Click the ⊡ button (above the word "Move") seven times.
The field name moves up in the list until it's positioned after FirstName.

11 Click OK.
The Save As dialog box displays.

12 Type **Fitness List** for the filename, specify the Save in location that you're using for your work, and then click Save.

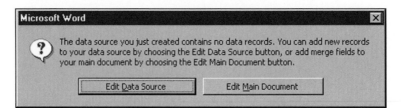

13 Choose Edit Data Source.

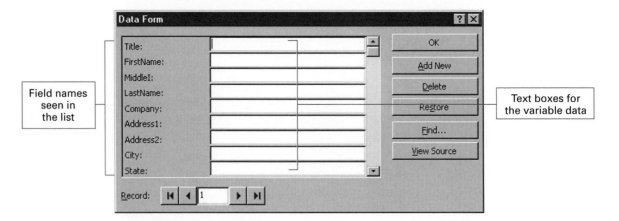

Field names seen in the list

Text boxes for the variable data

14 Type **Mr.** and press (ENTER).
The text displays in the Title text box, and the insertion point moves to the next text box.

15 Type **John** and press (ENTER), type **A.** and press (ENTER), and then type **Cartwright** and press (ENTER).
The text displays in the appropriate name text boxes, and the insertion point moves to the Company text box.

16 Type **ABC Printing** and press (ENTER).
The text displays in the Company text box, and the insertion point moves to the next text box.

17 Type **101 Main Street** and press (ENTER) twice.
The text displays in the Address1 text box, and the insertion point moves to the City text box.

> **Note** When Word 97 prints a letter that has a record with a blank field, Word skips the field without leaving a blank space or a blank line.

18 Type **Willow Grove** and press (ENTER), type **SC** and press (ENTER), and then type **22345** and press (ENTER).
Record 1 is finished, and a new blank form displays for the next record.

19 Continue typing the following records:

Title	Ms.
FirstName	Cynthia
Middlel	
LastName	Baker
Company	
Address1	18 Winding Willows Road
Address2	
City	Willow Grove
State	SC
PostalCode	22345

Title	Mrs.
FirstName	Jackie
Middlel	B.
LastName	Taylor
Company	
Address1	Macon Estates
Address2	546 Seagrove Lane
City	Willow Grove
State	SC
PostalCode	22345

Title	Mr.
FirstName	Earl
Middlel	W.
LastName	Thomas
Company	Highland Oil
Address1	2700 Highway 91
Address2	
City	Willow Grove
State	SC
PostalCode	22345

20 Click OK.

The word processing document displays. In it, you will type the Main document for the mail merge in the next task. The Mail Merge toolbar displays automatically.

Mail Merge toolbar →

> **Note** At this point, the data you have typed in the Data Source document hasn't been saved. Only the field names have been saved.

Creating the Main Document

The Main document contains the text (usually a letter) to be merged with the names in the Data Source document. You insert the field names in the text of the Main document where you want the variable information to appear.

TASK 2: TO CREATE THE MAIN DOCUMENT:

1 Type or insert the current date and press (ENTER) four times.

The date appears at the top of the letter, and the insertion point is moved to the position where the inside address should appear.

2 Click Insert Merge Field.

A drop-down list of the fields in the Data Source document displays.

3 Click Title

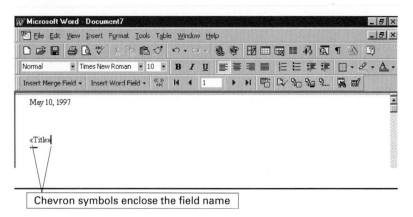

Chevron symbols enclose the field name

4 To complete the full name, press (SPACE), click Insert Merge Field, and click FirstName. Press (SPACE), click Insert Merge Field, and click Middlel. Press (SPACE), click Insert Merge Field, and click LastName. Then press (ENTER).

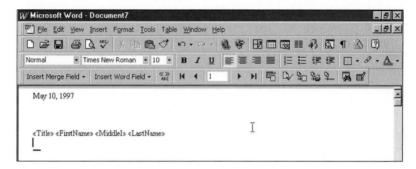

5 Click Insert Merge Field and click Company. Then press (ENTER).

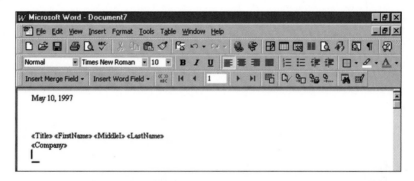

6 Click Insert Merge Field and click Address1. Then press (ENTER).

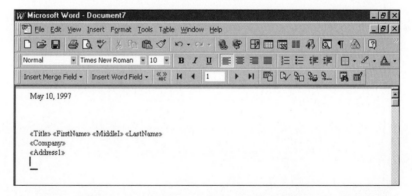

7 Click Insert Merge Field and click Address2. Then press (ENTER).

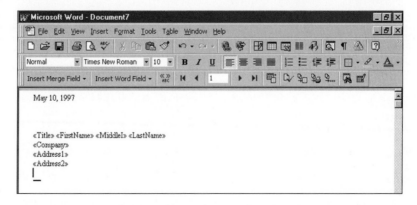

8 Click Insert Merge Field and click City. Type a comma, press (SPACE), click Insert Merge Field, and click State. Press (SPACE) twice, click Insert Merge Field, and click PostalCode.

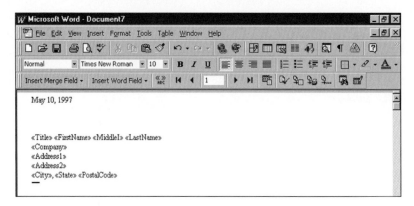

9 Press (ENTER) twice.
The insertion point moves into the position where the salutation should appear.

10 To create the salutation, type **Dear** and press (SPACE). Click Insert Merge Field and click Title. Press (SPACE), click Insert Merge Field, and click LastName. Type a colon and press (ENTER) twice.

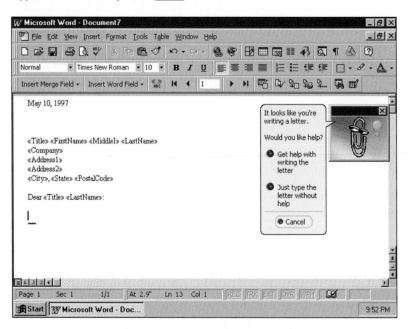

11 Click Cancel in the Office Assistant, and then type the text of the letter.

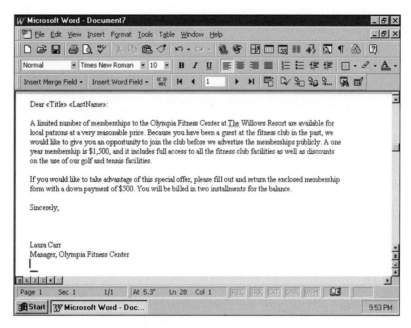

12 Save the file as *Membership Form Letter.doc* in the Save in location that you're using for your work. Leave the file open for the next exercise.

Merging the Documents

When you merge the Main document with the Data Source document, Word 97 matches the field names in the Main document with the field names in the Data Source document and inserts the appropriate data. Before you merge the Main document with the variable information in the Data Source document, you can see the variable information in the Main document by clicking the View Merged Data button.

TASK 3: TO MERGE THE DATA SOURCE DOCUMENT WITH THE MAIN DOCUMENT:

1 Click the Merge to New Document button.
A new document is created with a page for every record in the Data Source document.

> **Tip** If you don't want to create a new document, click the Merge to Printer button, and the merged documents will be printed instead.

2 Make desired revisions to the file.

3 Save the file if you want.

4 Print the file if you want.

5 Close the file when finished.

6 Close the Main document.

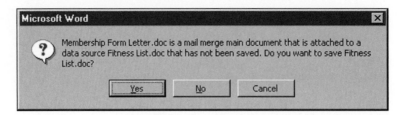

7 Click Yes.
The Data Source document is saved, and a message displays asking if you want to save changes made to the Main document.

8 Click Yes.
The Main document closes.

Creating Another Main Document
to Use with a Data Source Document

You can create multiple Main documents to use with the same Data Source document. For example, you can create a series of several letters that you send to the same mailing list.

TASK 4: TO CREATE ANOTHER MAIN DOCUMENT
TO USE WITH THE SAME DATA SOURCE DOCUMENT:

1 Click the New ☐ button.
A new file is created.

2 Choose Tools, Mail Merge, Create, Form Letters, Active Window.

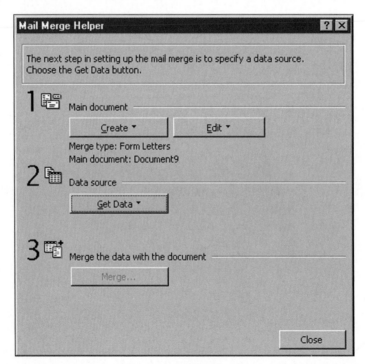

3   Select Get Data, Open Data Source.
The Open Data Source dialog box displays.

4   Double-click the file named *Fitness List.doc.*

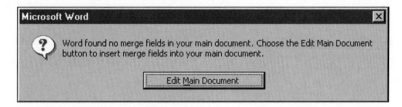

5   Click Edit Main Document.
A blank Main document displays.

6   Type the following document:

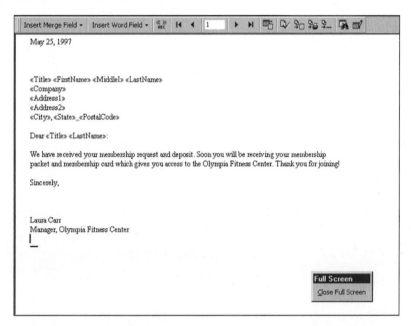

7   Save the file as *Thank You.doc.*

8   Click .
A new merged document displays.

9   Close the file without saving.

10 Close *Thank You.doc.*

11 Choose Yes to save the changes.

Creating and Using Another Data Source Document with a Main Document

Just as you can create multiple Main documents to merge with the same Data Source document, you also can create multiple Data Source documents to merge with the same Main document. The Data Source document may have fields that aren't used in the Main document, but all the fields used in the Main document must be contained in the Data Source document.

TASK 5: TO CREATE ANOTHER DATA SOURCE DOCUMENT FOR A MAIN DOCUMENT:

1   Open the file *Membership Form Letter.doc*.

2   Click the Mail Merge Helper 📇 button.

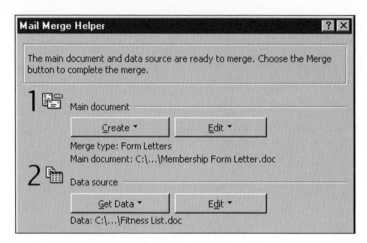

3   Select Get Data, Create Data Source.

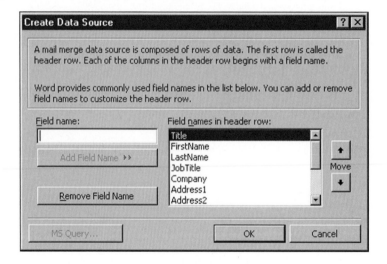

4   Remove the fields Job Title, Country, HomePhone, and WorkPhone. Add the field Middlel and move it up under FirstName. Click OK.
The Save As dialog box displays.

5   Type **Fitness List 2** for the filename, specify the Save in location that you're using for your particular work, and click Save.
The Mail Merge Helper dialog box redisplays.

6   Click Edit (under Data source) and click Fitness List 2.
The Data Form displays.

7   Type the information for at least two records, and click OK when finished.
The Main document redisplays.

8   Save and close the Main document. A message displays asking if you want to save changes to the Data Source file.

9   Click Yes.

TASK 6: TO SELECT A DIFFERENT DATA SOURCE DOCUMENT:

1 Open the file *Membership Form Letter.doc*.

2 Click 🔲.

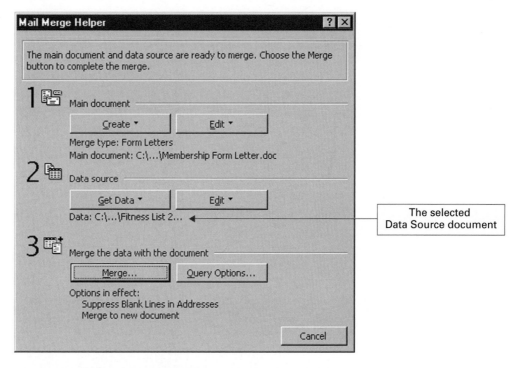

3 Click Get Data and click Open Data Source.
The Open Data Source dialog box displays.

4 Double-click the file *Fitness List.doc*.
The selected Data Source document name changes from *Fitness List 2.doc* to *Fitness List.doc*.

5 Click Close.
The Main document redisplays.

6 Click 🔲.
A new merged document displays.

The Conclusion

Make any desired revisions and then save the document. Print the document, if desired, and then close the file.

Close the Main document.

Summary and Exercises

Summary

- The Data Source document contains the field names of the variables as well as the variable information for each record.
- The Main document contains the text to be merged with the names in the Data Source document.
- During the merge process, Word 97 matches the field names in the Main document with the field names in the Data source document and inserts the appropriate data.
- You can create multiple Main documents to use with the same Data Source document.
- You can create multiple Data Source documents to merge with the same Main document.

Key Terms and Operations

Key Terms	Operations
Data Source document	add records to the Data Source document
field	create a Main document
Main document	create a Date Source document
mail merging	merge
record	

Study Questions

Multiple Choice

1. The two documents used in a mail merge are
   a. the List document and the Form document.
   b. the Data Source document and the Form document.
   c. the List document and the Main document.
   d. the Data Source document and the Main document.

2. The file that contains the list of variable information is called the
   a. List document.
   b. Data Source document.
   c. Main document.
   d. Form document.

3. The file that contains the text (usually a letter) and the field names is called the
   a. List document.
   b. Data Source document.
   c. Main document.
   d. Form document.

4. To display the Mail Merge Helper dialog box,
   a. click the Mail Merger Helper button.
   b. choose Tools, Mail Merge.
   c. Both A and B.
   d. None of the above.

5. When you perform a merge,
   a. a new document is always created.
   b. the merged documents are always printed.
   c. you can choose to create a new document or send the document directly to the printer.
   d. the merged document replaces the form document.

6. Fields
   a. contain variable information.
   b. appear in the Data Form.
   c. can be inserted in the document that contains the form letter.
   d. All of the above.

7. When creating the list of fields,
   a. you must use the default list of fields.
   b. you can add your own fields to the default list and remove fields from the default list.
   c. you can remove fields from the default list, but you can't add fields.
   d. you must use only the fields in the default list, but you can move the fields to different locations.

8. To insert a field in a form letter,
   a. select the field from the Insert Merge Field drop-down list.
   b. choose Insert, Field.
   c. click the toolbar button that represents the field you want.
   d. None of the above.

9. Which two of the following statements are true?
   a. You can create several Data Source files to be used with a Main document.
   b. You can create only one List document to be used with a Form document.
   c. You can create several Main documents to be used with the same Data Source document.
   d. You can use the same Form document with several Main documents.

10. The merged document
   a. has one page for each record.
   b. displays all records on the same page.
   c. must be paginated to divide the records into pages.
   d. is saved automatically.

Short Answer

1. What happens when you click the Merge to New Document button?

2. What's the Data Form?

3. What's a field?

4. What's a record?

5. What happens when you click the Insert Merge Field button?

6. What's the Mail Merge Helper?

7. How can you see the variable information in the document that contains the form letter?

8. What symbols enclose an inserted field name?

9. If a record has a blank field, will the field print?

10. Can a field name be two words?

For Discussion

1. What process would you perform to create the same result as a mail merge if you didn't have the mail merge feature to use?

2. In what ways is the mail merge process flexible?

3. Open the file *Fitness List.doc* and discuss its structure.

4. Under what circumstances would you merge to a new document, and under what circumstances would you merge to the printer?

Review Exercises

1. Creating a data source

When equipment at the fitness center is replaced with new equipment, the used equipment is often sold to Fitness Club members who have expressed an interest. Create a Data Source which contains names of members who have asked to be notified when equipment is replaced.

1. Create a new file.

2. Create a Data Source document with the following fields: Title, FirstName, LastName, Address1, Address2, City, State, PostalCode, Salutation.

3. Save the Data Source as *Sale List.doc*.

4. Add these records to the Data Source document:

Title	Mr.	Ms.
FirstName	Alan	Barbara
LastName	Sheppard	Mavis
Address1	55 Frederick Lane	98 Jones Hollow Road
Address2		
City	Willow Grove	Willow Grove
State	SC	SC
PostalCode	22345	22345
Salutation	Dear Buzz,	Dear Ms. Mavis:

Title	Mrs.	Mr.
FirstName	Judy	William
LastName	Puckett	Turner
Address1	4351 Bay View Drive	Greenbriar Towers
Address2		101 Broad Way, Suite 100
City	Willow Grove	Willow Grove
State	SC	SC
PostalCode	22345	22345
Salutation	Dear Judy,	Dear Bill,

March 12, 1997

«Title» «FirstName» «LastName»
«Address1»
«Address2»
«City», «State» «PostalCode»

«Salutation»

From time to time the fitness center replaces equipment with newer or more advanced equipment. As a courtesy to our membership, we offer the equipment that we are replacing for sale. This month we are replacing all the Trimline 2200 treadmills.
Here are the specs on the treadmill:

Motor HP	
Continuous/Peak Speed	
Incline	
Belt Size	
Speed Control	
Deck	
Display	

The sale price is $500. If you are interested in purchasing one of the three machines we are replacing, please contact me.

Sincerely,

Laura Carr
Manager, Olympia Fitness Center

Figure 6.3

5. Save the blank document as *Sale Form Letter.doc* and close the file.

6. Save the Data Source document.

2. Creating a main document and merging

Create the letter shown in Figure 6.3 to notify members about the equipment scheduled for replacement. Follow these steps to complete the document and merge the letter with names in the Data Source file.

1. Open *Sale Form Letter.doc*.

2. Type the letter shown in Figure 6.3, and insert the fields indicated.

3. Go to the Advanced Fitness home page (http://www.advancedfitness.com), and click the Fitness Equipment link. Click the Treadmills link, and find the information to fill in the second column in the table.

4. Merge the Main document with *Sale List.doc* and create a new document with the merged letters.

5. Save the new document as *Sale.doc* and close the file.

6. Close *Sale Form Letter.doc*.

3. **Creating a mail merge data source and adding records to the data source file**

1. Launch Word 97 and create a new plain document, if necessary.

2. Create a mail merge data source which contains the following fields:

   - Title
   - FirstName
   - Last Name
   - School

   - Address1
   - City
   - State
   - PostalCode

3. Save the Data Source using the filename *1998 Cruise Aps Data xxx.*

4. Add the following data records to the Data Source file:

   \<Your Name\>
   \<Your School\>
   \<Your Address\>
   \<Your City, State, PostalCode\>

   Mr. Samuel Adams
   Southern Illinois University
   123 Nealy Hall
   Carbondale, IL 62901

   Ms. Susan Williams
   Louisiana State University
   159 College Avenue, Apt. 4

   Baton Rouge, LA 70803 Ms. Edith Combs
   The Pennsylvania State University
   204 Beaver Hall
   University Park, PA 16802

5. Create the main document shown in Figure 6.4.

<Insert date text here>

«Title» «FirstName» «LastName»
«School»
«Address1»
«City», «State» «PostalCode»

Dear «Title» «LastName»:

Thank you for your interest in working with our cruise line during its summer tours of
Alaska. We begin scheduling and interviewing new personnel in January.

Please complete and return the enclosed application and release form at your earliest
convenience. To be considered for open positions, we must have the application and
release forms on file.

Again, thank you for your interest in American Cruises. We look forward to reviewing
the talents you offer.

Sincerely,

Mrs. Elizabeth Adams
Summer Personnel Coordinator

Figure 6.4

6. Save the main document using the filename *1998 Cruise Aps Letter xxx*.

7. Merge the letters with the Data Source and print a copy of all four letters.
   Close the merged letters without saving them.

Assignments

1. Creating a form letter to send to family and friends

Merging data to documents can also improve your efficiency in corresponding
with friends and family. Use your personal files to develop each of the following:

1. Create a Data Source document with the names and addresses of friends and
   family.

2. Create a Main document that contains general news about yourself and
   what you're doing.

3. Merge the Data Source document and the Main document to create a
   merged document.

2. Creating a form letter requesting catalogs

In your search for new items to sell in the shops at The Willows, you must keep up with the new items available from different vendors. Complete the following tasks to obtain information and catalogs from several vendors:

1. Go to the Web site http://www.yahoo.com, and click the Shopping link. Find the names and addresses of several companies. Create a Data Source file for the companies.

2. Create a form letter asking for information and/or catalogs from the companies, and merge the files to a new document.

3. Save the new file as *Catalogs*.

More Word 97

This section contains additional topics that are necessary for you to know if you plan to take the Microsoft Proficient exam for Word. The topics are listed in the same order as the Skill Sets outlined in the *Microsoft Word 97 Exam Preparation Guide*, which you can download from Microsoft's Web site (www.microsoft.com/office/train_cert). All other topics necessary for successful completion of the exam are covered in Projects 1 through 6 of this book.

Processing Text

Inserting Text

The insert mode is the default typing mode in Word. This means that when you type, text is inserted at the insertion point. Any text located to the right of the insertion point moves to the right as you type.

Overtyping Text

To type over existing text, you can activate the overtype mode by pressing the Insert key. When overtype is activated, the status bar displays "OVR" in bold. To return to insert mode, press the Insert key again. (OVR changes to gray.)

> **Note** In the first release of Office 97, the Insert key does not work. To turn the overtype feature on and off, double-click "OVR" in the status bar.

Formatting Characters

Using All Underline Options

The Underline button **U** in the Formatting toolbar applies only the single underline, but Word has several other underlining formats that you can apply. To apply a different type of underline, select the text and choose Format, Font. Select the underline format from the Underline list, as shown in the figure on the next page, and choose OK.

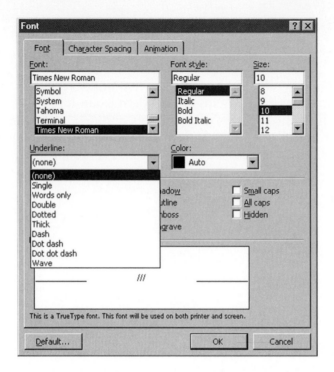

Applying Character Effects

In addition to making characters bold, italic, or underlined, you can apply other character formats such as small caps, shadow, embossed, and engraved. You also can raise the text above the baseline to create a superscript, as in $a^2+b^2=c^2$, or lower the text below the baseline to create a subscript, as in H_2O.

To apply a character effect, select the text and choose Format, Font. Select the desired options from the Effects section of the dialog box and choose OK.

Placing and Aligning Text

Using Hyphenation

By default, words do not hyphenate automatically at the end of a line. If you want more text to fit on a line, you should activate the hyphenation feature. To turn on hyphenation in a document, choose Tools, Language, Hyphenation. The Hyphenation dialog box appears, as shown in the figure at the top of the next page.

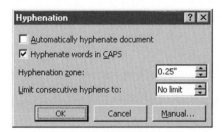

Choose Automatically Hyphenate Document. Select the other options as desired and choose OK. When automatic hyphenation is activated, Word hyphenates words with "soft" hyphens, which are automatically removed if the word no longer falls at the end of the line due to edits.

When a hyphenated word, such as father-in-law, falls at the end of the line, Word breaks it across the line at the hyphens. If you don't want the word to be broken, insert nonbreaking hyphens instead of regular hyphens by typing (CTRL) + (SHIFT) + the regular hyphen.

Aligning Text Vertically

The vertical alignment feature centers text vertically on the page. To align text vertically on a page, move the insertion point to the page and choose File, Page Setup. Your screen should look like the one shown in the following figure. Click the Layout tab, select Center for Vertical Alignment, select Whole Document or From this Point Forward for Apply To, and click OK. Word automatically inserts a section break before the page if you select From this Point Forward.

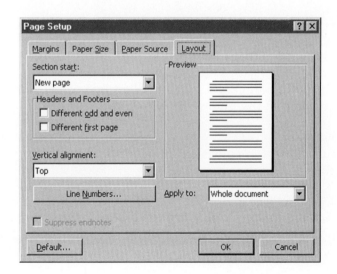

Using Paragraph Formatting

Using Indentation Options

In addition to indenting the first line of a paragraph, as described in Project 3, you can indent a paragraph on the left and/or right and create a hanging indent. To indent on the left and right, first select the paragraph(s) and choose Format, Paragraph. Click the Indents and Spacing tab shown in the following figure, if necessary, and enter a value for Left and/or a value for Right. Click OK.

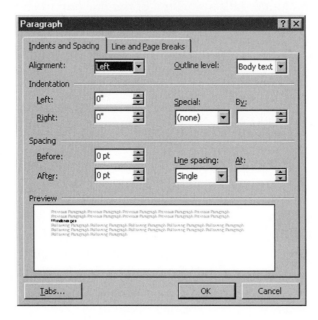

A hanging indent is used automatically in Word's built-in styles for bulleted and numbered lists. The hanging indent indents the second and subsequent lines in a paragraph, while the first line of the paragraph "hangs" out on the left as in the following:

Four score and seven years ago, our fathers brought forth on this continent a new nation conceived in liberty and dedicated to the proposition that all men are created equal.

To create a hanging indent, select the paragraph and choose Format, Paragraph. Click the Indents and Spacing tab, if necessary, and select Hanging for Special. Specify a measurement for By and click OK.

Using Headers and Footers

Creating Alternating Headers and Footers

Alternating headers or footers can vary in content on odd and even pages. To create alternating headers or footers, choose File, Page Setup. Click the Layout tab, choose Different Odd and Even, and choose OK. To enter the text in the alternating headers or footers, display the header or footer with the View, Header and Footer command. Then use the toolbar to navigate to the first header or footer. Type the desired text and then navigate to the next header or footer and type the text.

Using Styles and Templates

Creating Styles

A style is a set of formatting options that are saved with a style name. When a style is applied to text, the text is formatted with the formatting options included in the style.

To create a style, choose Format, Styles, and click New. Your screen should look like the one shown in the following figure. Type the name you want to give the style. Then specify the type of style (usually Paragraph), the style on which you want to base the new style (if any), and the style that should be applied to the paragraph that follows. Then click Format, choose any of the formatting categories that you want, select the formats, and click OK. Repeat this last step for each of the desired formatting categories. Then click OK and click Close.

> **Note** If you base a new style on an existing style, changing the base style also changes the new style. This can work for you or against you. If you don't want the style to be changed unless you change it intentionally, then base your style on "no style."

Using Templates

A template may contain specific styles, toolbars, macros, and AutoText that are available and applicable only to the type of document that the template creates. Word provides several ready-made templates in several categories. To apply a template to a new document, choose File, New, click the tab that contains the template you want, and double-click the template, as shown in this figure. Respond to any prompts presented by the template.

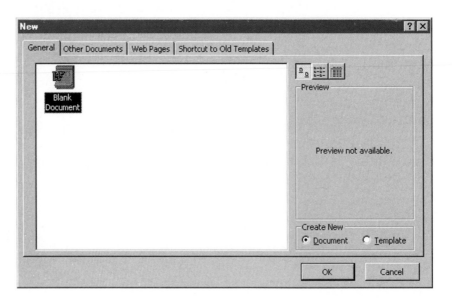

Editing Text

Finding and Replacing Text

If you have to make the same change to a word or phrase that appears in a document several times, you can use the Find and Replace command. With this command, you can make all the changes at once or review each word or phrase and decide if you want to make the change on an individual basis.

To use the Find and Replace command, choose Edit, Replace. Your screen should look like the one shown in the following figure. Type the word or phrase you want to find in the Find What text box; type the replacement text in the Replace With text box. To set additional options, click More if necessary and select the options you want, such as Match Case, or Find Whole Words Only. Click Replace All to replace all occurrences without reviewing each one. If you want to review each change, click Find to go to the first occurrence, and then either click Replace to replace it or click Find to skip it and go to the next occurrence. When Word notifies you that all occurrences have been found or all replacements have been made, click OK and close the Find and Replace dialog box.

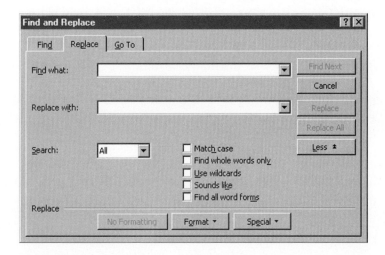

Setting AutoCorrect Exceptions

Word corrects some of your typing errors automatically using the Auto-Correct feature. If you want to specify some exceptions to the AutoCorrect feature, choose Tools, AutoCorrect and click Exceptions. Type the exception in Don't Capitalize After and click Add. Add as many exceptions as you want and then click the INitial CAps tab. Type the exception for Don't Correct and click Add. Add as many of these exceptions as you want and then click OK.

Generating an Outline

Creating an Outline

Word's Outline feature enables you to create more than an outline—you can actually include the text of the document in the outline. To create an outline, create a new file and switch to the Outline view by clicking the Outline button ⊞. The first line in the document is assigned the Heading 1 style. Type the first heading and press Enter. Word automatically assigns the style Heading 1 to the new line. You can type another one-level heading or type a subheading by clicking the Demote button ⇨ in the toolbar so that Word assigns the Heading 2 style to the current line.

Each time you type a heading and press Enter, Word assigns the same heading level to the new line. You can then demote the line to the next lower level (as described previously) or promote the line to the next higher level by clicking the Promote button ⇦. You can include a maximum of nine levels in the outline; each level corresponds to the styles Heading 1 through Heading 9.

To type the text of the document that appears under each heading, click the insertion point at the end of the desired heading and press Enter. Then click the Demote to Body Text button ⇨. Word assigns the Normal style to the text. Type as much text as desired. Another way to enter the text of the actual document is to switch to Normal view or Page Layout view and then enter text as you normally would. When using either of these two views, Word automatically assigns the Normal style to the text that you type, as long as you begin typing under each heading by first positioning the insertion point at the end of the heading and then pressing Enter.

To apply numbering to the outline, select all the text in the outline, choose Format, Bullets and Numbering, and click the Outline Numbered tab, as shown in this figure. Select the numbering style you want to use and click OK.

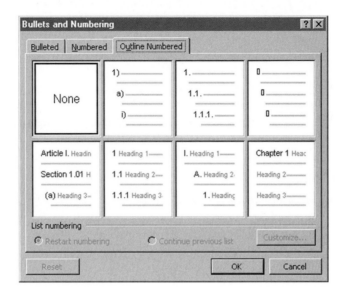

Modifying an Outline

When modifying an outline in Outline view, you may want to collapse or expand the headings. To collapse an individual heading, click anywhere in the heading and click the Collapse button ▬ as many times as desired. (Each click collapses an additional level.) To expand an individual heading, click anywhere in the heading and click the Expand button ✚ as many times as desired. To collapse all levels at once, click the button in the toolbar that corresponds to the number of levels you want to see. For example, to collapse to only main headings, click the button with the 1 on it. To collapse to the main headings and only the first-level subheadings under the main headings, click the button with the 2 on it. To see all levels, click the All button.

To move headings in an outline, select the heading (and its subheadings, if desired) and click the Move Up button ⬆ or Move Down button ⬇.

Creating Documents for Use on Internet/Intranet

Saving as HTML

Because Word is an HTML editor, it has HTML editing tools that you can use in a graphical interface without having to enter HTML code. To create an HTML file, first create the file in Word and then save it as HTML by choosing File, Save as HTML. Specify the path and the name of the file and click Save. Word may ask you if you would like to check the Internet to see whether there are any new HTML tools available for download before you continue. Then Word writes the HTML code for the file that you have created, but it displays the results of the code in the graphical interface, not the code itself. You can then make modifications to the file using the HTML tools provided by Word. Word translates all the modifications that you make to the file in the graphical interface to HTML code.

To see the actual HTML code, choose View, HTML Source. If the document has not been saved since the last changes, Word prompts you to save the file. To return to the graphical interface, choose View, Exit HTML Source.

Creating a Hyperlink

A hyperlink is an instruction that's activated by a mouse click. The hyperlink instruction tells the computer to open a page on the Web or to open another document on your system. You can create a hyperlink in a Word document or in an HTML document.

To create a hyperlink, select the text or a graphic that you want the user to click to activate the link. Click the Insert Hyperlink button 🔗. Your screen should appear similar to the one shown in this figure. Specify the path and file name or the URL. If desired, specify a location in the file (such as a bookmark or a named range in a worksheet). Select Use Relative Path for the Hyperlink if the current file and the hyperlinked file could be moved to different folders. Click OK.

Note Text that has a hyperlink assigned to it appears blue and underlined. When you point to a hyperlink — whether it is text or a graphic — the mouse pointer changes to a pointing finger.

Browsing through Files

Even if you do not have an intranet, you can browse through files as if you did (even on a stand-alone system) by using the Web toolbar in Word. (Click the Web Toolbar button ▒ to display the toolbar.) To open another file, type the path and filename of the file in the address text box of the Web toolbar and press Enter. (The file can be a Word or HTML file.) After you have opened files, you can move back and forth between them by clicking the Back button or Forward buttons on the Web Toolbar. In addition, you can navigate by clicking the arrow in the address box and selecting a file from the drop-down list.

> **Note** If the file you open has a hyperlink, you can click the hyperlink to open the linked file.

Using Writing Tools

Using the Thesaurus

The Thesaurus feature looks up synonyms and antonyms of a selected word. You can replace the selected word with any of the words that the Thesaurus finds. To replace a word with a synonym, select the word and choose Tools, Language, Thesaurus. Your screen should appear similar to the one shown in this figure. Select the correct part of speech in the list on the left to display the synonyms on the right. Select the synonym in the list on the right and click Replace.

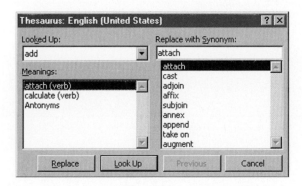

Creating Tables

Adding Borders and Shading

To add emphasis and organization to a table, use borders and shading. When you create a table, Word automatically applies a line to all sides of all cells in the table. To change the border for the entire table or for specific cells, click in the table or select the cells. Then choose Format, Borders and Shading, and click the Borders tab, if necessary. You can change the border's style, color, and width. To change a specific border for the table or selected cells, select the desired options for style, color, and width, as shown in the following figure; then click the border in the preview to which you want to apply the modification.

To apply shading to the table, select the table or the specific cells, choose Format, Borders and Shading, and click the Shading tab, if necessary. Select the Fill color. If desired, select a Style (which determines the number of dots in the fill) and select a Color (for the dots). Click OK.

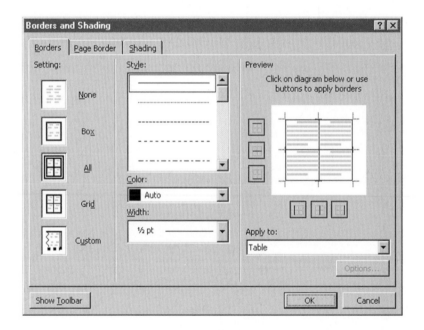

Merging and Splitting Cells

Often it is necessary to merge or split cells in a table. To merge cells, select the cells and choose Table, Merge Cells. To split a cell, select the cell(s) and choose Table, Split Cells. Specify the number of columns and/or rows and click OK. When splitting multiple cells, you can select the option to merge before splitting, if appropriate.

Note When splitting cells that already contain text, all the text is moved to the first cell if you choose the option to merge cells before splitting.

Changing Row Height

The height of a row is determined automatically by Word based on the largest font used in the row. To change the height of a row, click in any cell in the row and choose Table, Cell Height and Width. Click the Row tab, if necessary, so that your screen appears similar to the one shown in this figure. For the option Height of Row n (where n equals the row number), select At least or Exactly from the drop-down list. Specify the desired height and click OK.

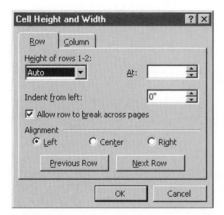

Rotating Text

To rotate the text in a cell, select the cell(s) and choose Format, Text Direction. Select the desired Orientation from the dialog box that appears in this figure, and click OK.

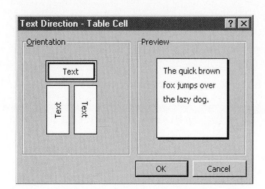

Managing Files

Creating a Folder

If you want to save a file in a new folder, you can create the folder when you save the file. To create a folder, choose File, Save, or choose File, Save As. Open the drive or folder where you want to create the new folder. Click the Create New Folder button, type the name of the new folder, and click OK. Double-click to open the folder and continue with the save operation as usual.

Using Draw

Creating and Modifying Lines and Objects

Word provides several drawing tools in the Drawing toolbar, which can be displayed by clicking the Drawing Toolbar button in the Standard toolbar. Drawing tools include the Line tool, Arrow tool, Rectangle tool, and Oval tool. To draw a shape with any of these tools, click the tool in the toolbar and drag the shape in the desired location. Additional drawing tools are available on the AutoShapes menu, including additional line styles, basic shapes, block arrows, flowchart symbols, stars, banners, and callouts. To draw with one of these tools, click the arrow in the AutoShapes button, point to a category, and click the desired tool. Then drag to draw the shape.

Creating and Modifying 3D Shapes

With the 3-D tool, you can add a three-dimensional look to shapes that you have drawn. First draw the shape; then click the 3-D button and select the desired shape.

You can modify a 3-D shape with the 3-D Settings toolbar, which contains buttons for changing tilt, depth, direction, lighting, surface, and color of the 3-D object. To display the 3-D Settings toolbar, click the 3-D button in the Drawing toolbar and choose 3-D Settings. Then select the drawing object and use the buttons in the toolbar to modify the object. For example, to change the direction of the light on the object (and thus the shading of the object), click the Lighting button and select a lighting direction and intensity.

Printing Documents and Envelopes

Creating and Printing Labels

Word supports several popular label brands and sizes. You can create and print a single label or a whole page of labels that have the same address.

To create and print labels, open an existing document or create a new one, and choose Tools, Envelopes and Labels. Click the Labels tab, if necessary, so that your screen appears similar to the one shown in the following figure. If the document that is open has an address at the top, this address appears in the Address box in the dialog box. If no address appears, type the correct address in the box. Click Options. Specify the printer information, select the label product (brand), select the label number, and click OK.

To print a single label, select Single Label and identify the Row and Column on the sheet of labels where you want the label to print. Load the labels in the printer, and click Print. To print a full page of labels with the same address, select Full Page of the Same Label, load the labels in the printer, and click Print. Instead of printing a full page of labels immediately, you can choose New Document to create a document that you can save and print any time.

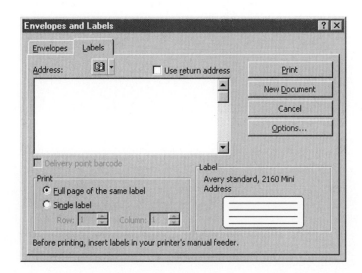

Notes

Notes

Notes

Notes

Notes

Notes

Notes

Notes

Notes

Notes

Notes

Spreadsheets
Using Microsoft Excel 97

Overview

Excel is a tool you can use for organizing, calculating, and displaying numerical data. You might use Excel to record your checking account transactions, plan a budget, prepare a bid, control inventory, track sales, or create an expense report. Before you can become proficient with Excel 97, however, you need to get acquainted with the program and learn how to perform some of the most basic functions. Then you will be ready to start working on the projects in this part of the book.

Objectives

After completing this project, you will be able to:

➤ **Identify Excel 97 Features**

➤ **Launch Excel 97**

➤ **Identify Excel 97 Screen Elements**

➤ **Get help**

➤ **Close a workbook**

➤ **Exit Excel 97**

Identifying Excel 97 Features

Excel 97 is the electronic equivalent of one of those green (or buff color) columnar pads that bookkeepers and accountants use. Excel calls the area in which you work a *worksheet* — other programs call this a spreadsheet. An Excel worksheet has 256 *columns* and 65,536 *rows*, for a whopping total of 16,777,216 cells. Is that big or what?

Note A *cell* is the intersection of a column and a row.

An Excel worksheet is actually a page in a *workbook* file. By default, a new workbook file has three worksheets, but you can add additional worksheets if you need them — as many as your computer memory allows.

You can do more than store numbers with Excel 97; you can use it to perform calculations, recalculate formulas when numbers are changed, analyze data, and create charts and maps from the data that you enter. Many of the same text features available in a word processing program are also available in Excel. For example, you can check the spelling of words, use text styles, add headers and footers, and insert graphics and other objects. Figure 0.1 shows a worksheet with numbers, calculations, text formatted with styles, a graphic, and a chart.

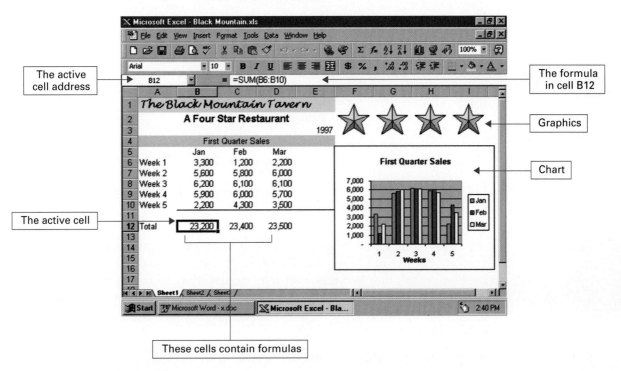

Figure O.1

Launching Excel 97

When you start your computer, you may have to log on to a network or perform some other steps before Windows 95 starts. After the Windows 95 desktop displays on the screen, you're ready to launch Excel 97.

TASK 1: TO LAUNCH EXCEL 97:

1. Click the Start button and point to Programs.

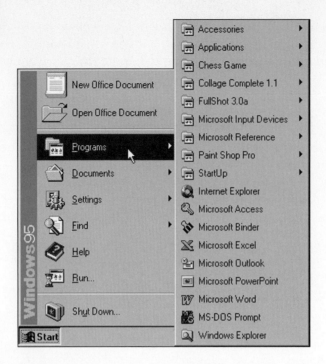

2 Point to Microsoft Excel and click.
The program opens in a window and creates a workbook called *Book1*.

Identifying Excel 97 Screen Elements

When you create a new workbook, the screen should look similar to the one shown in Figure 0.2. The Excel 97 screen has many of the common elements of a Windows 95 screen as well as some elements that are unique to the Excel 97 program.

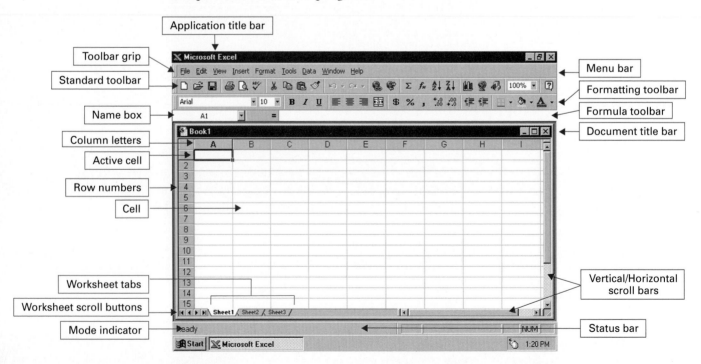

Figure O.2

Note The screen displays two Close buttons. The button in the Application title bar closes Excel 97; the button in the document title bar closes the current workbook. If the document window is maximized, the Close button appears in the menu bar.

Table 0.1 lists the elements of the Excel 97 screen.

Table O.1   Elements of the Excel 97 Screen

Element	Description
Application title bar	Displays the name of the application and the Minimize, Maximize/Restore, and Close buttons. If the document window is maximized, the name of the workbook also displays in the application title bar.
Document title bar	Displays the name of the workbook file and the Minimize, Maximize/Restore, and Close buttons. If the window is maximized, there is no document title bar and the document buttons display in the menu bar.
Menu bar	Contains menu options. To use the menu, click an option to display a drop-down menu, and then click a command on the drop-down menu to perform the command, view another menu, or view a dialog box.
Standard toolbar	Contains buttons for accomplishing commands. To use the toolbar, click the button for the command you want to perform.
Formatting toolbar	Contains buttons and controls for formatting. To use the toolbar, click the button for the command you want to perform or click a drop-down list arrow to make a selection.
Name box	Displays the address of the active cell.
Formula bar	Displays the cell address and the contents of the active cell. Also used to enter and edit formulas.
Active cell	Marks the cell where data will be entered with a black border.
Scroll bars	Vertical and horizontal Scroll bars scroll the screen vertically and horizontally.
Worksheet tabs	Display the names of worksheets in the current workbook. Clicking a tab displays the worksheet.
Worksheet scroll buttons	Scroll the worksheet tabs (if you have too many worksheets to display all the tabs).
Status bar	Displays information about the current workbook. The Mode indicator displays on the far left side of the status bar. The right side of the status bar displays "NUM" if the Num Lock Key is on and "CAPS" if the Cap Lock key is on.
Row numbers	Indicate the numbers associated with the rows.
Column letters	Indicate the letters associated with the columns.
Cell	The intersection of a column and a row, referred to with an address that combines the column letter(s) with the row number, such as A1, AA223, and so on.
Mode	Displays on the left side of the status bar and shows a word that describes the current working condition of the workbook. For example, the word *"Ready"* means that the worksheet is ready to receive data or execute a command. Other modes include *Edit*, *Enter*, *Point*, *Error*, and *Wait*.

Note Although you can turn off the display of certain screen elements (toolbars, the Formula bar, and the Status bar), generally all the screen elements are displayed in Excel 97 because they are used so often.

Web toolbar →

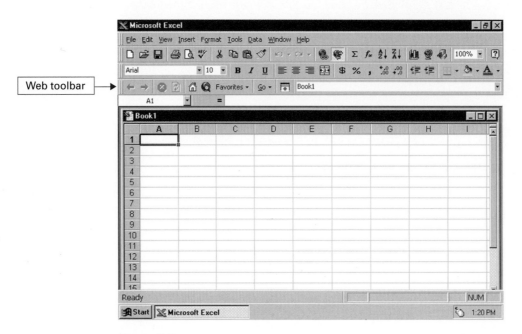

Figure O.3

Working with Toolbars

Toolbars contain buttons that perform functions. Usually the tools grouped together on a toolbar perform tasks that are all related. For example, the buttons on the Chart toolbar all perform tasks related to creating and modifying charts.

The Standard toolbar and the Formatting toolbar are the default toolbars, the ones that Excel 97 automatically displays. You can display or hide as many toolbars as desired. You also can move toolbars to different locations on the screen. When a toolbar is displayed, Excel places it where it was last located.

If you use the Internet frequently, you may want to display the **Web toolbar** by clicking the Web Toolbar button 🌐 in the Standard toolbar. With the Web toolbar displayed, your screen should look like Figure O.3. To hide the Web toolbar, click the Web Toolbar button again.

TASK 2: TO WORK WITH TOOLBARS:

1 Choose View, Toolbars.

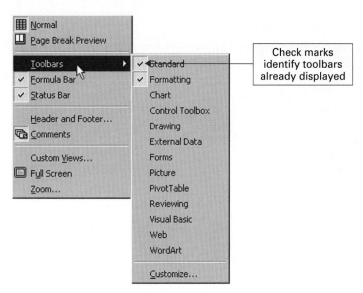

Check marks identify toolbars already displayed

2 Choose Chart.

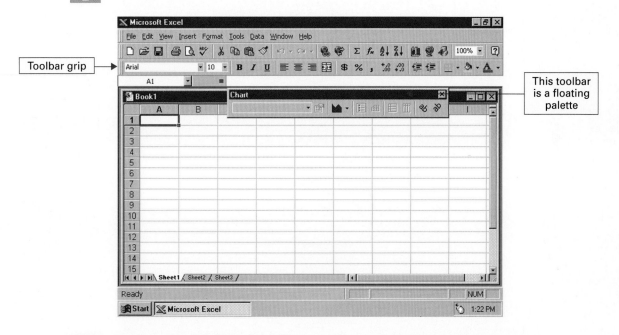

Toolbar grip

This toolbar is a floating palette

3 Point to the title bar of the Chart toolbar and drag the toolbar to a new location. If the toolbar doesn't appear as a palette, drag the toolbar by grabbing the grip. The toolbar moves.

4 Choose View, Toolbars, Chart.
The toolbar no longer displays.

Getting Help

Excel 97 provides several ways to get help. You can use the standard Windows 95 help dialog box that contains the Contents, Index, and Find pages and the What's This Help feature. Additionally, you can use the Office Assistant and Microsoft on the Web, both help features unique to Office 97.

Using the Office Assistant

The Office Assistant offers help on the task you are performing, often referred to as *context-sensitive help*. If the Office Assistant doesn't display the help you want, you can type a question to obtain the desired help.

> **Note** Sometimes the Office Assistant offers unsolicited help. When this happens, you can choose to read the help or just close the Office Assistant. Unfortunately, there is no way for a user to deactivate the Office Assistant.

TASK 3: TO USE THE OFFICE ASSISTANT:

1 Click the Office Assistant 🔲 button if you don't see the Office Assistant.

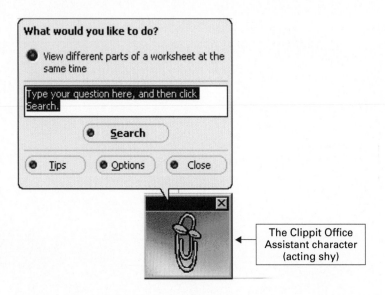

The Clippit Office Assistant character (acting shy)

2   Type **How do you enter a formula?**

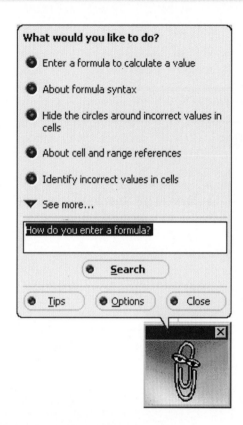

3   Click Search and then click About formula syntax.

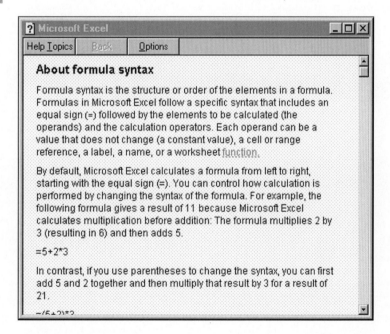

4   Read the Help dialog box and then click ☒ on the Help title bar.
The Help dialog box closes, but the Office Assistant window remains open.

5   Click the Office Assistant character in the Office Assistant window.
The Office Assistant asks what you want to do.

> **Note** The default Office Assistant is a paper clip named Clippit. Other assistants include Shakespeare, a robot, and a cat — to name a few.

6 Click Close.
The "bubble" closes.

7 Click **X** on the Office Assistant title bar.
The Office Assistant window closes.

Getting Help from the World Wide Web

Microsoft maintains several sites on the Web that have useful information, user support, product news, and free programs and files that you can download. If your system is connected to the Internet, you can access this type of help easily. The Microsoft sites are open to all users.

> **Note** When Microsoft is beta testing a program, the company maintains "closed sites" open only to beta testers with a valid password.

TASK 4: TO READ ANSWERS TO FREQUENTLY ASKED QUESTIONS:

1 Choose Help, Microsoft on the Web.

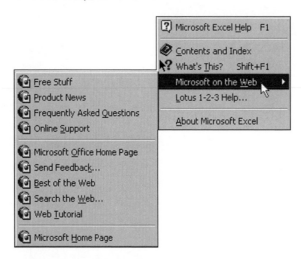

2 Choose Frequently Asked Questions.
The Internet browser program Internet Explorer starts and connects to the appropriate Web site. (You may be prompted to connect to the Internet.)

3 When you finish browsing the Web, click **X** in the browser window. (I know you're tempted to start browsing around, but you can do that later.)

Closing a Workbook and Exiting Excel 97

Before you exit Excel, you should always save any work that you want to keep and then it's a good idea to close any open workbooks. When you exit Excel 97, the program closes, and the Windows 95 desktop is visible unless you have another program running in a maximized window, however, the program will be visible, not the desktop.

> **Tip** If you forget to save a changed file before you try to exit, Excel 97 asks whether you want to save changes. You can choose Yes to save the changed file, No to exit without saving, or Cancel to cancel the exit request. If you exit without closing a file that does not need to be saved, Excel closes the file for you.

TASK 5: TO CLOSE THE WORKBOOK AND EXIT EXCEL 97:

1 Click the Close **X** button in the menu bar (if the document window is maximized) or in the document title bar (if the window is not maximized).

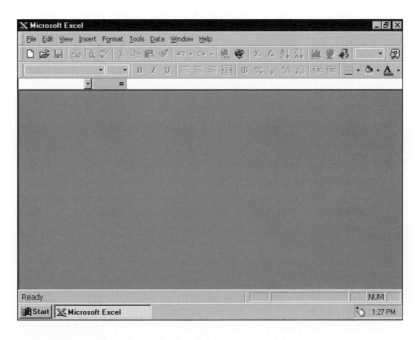

2 Click **X** in the application title bar.
The Excel 97 program closes.

Summary and Exercises

Summary

- Excel 97 is a full-featured spreadsheet program that's easy to use.
- An Excel workbook includes three worksheets by default.
- Worksheets enable you to store numbers, perform calculations and recalculations, analyze data, and create charts and maps.
- Many features found in Word processing are also available in Excel 97.
- Excel 97 provides a variety of Help features.
- Excel 97 warns you if you try to exit the program without saving your work.

Key Terms and Operations

Key Terms
active cell
cell
column
column indicators
Edit mode
Enter mode
Error mode
Formatting toolbar
formula bar
menu bar
mode indicator
Office Assistant
Point mode
Ready mode
row
row indicators
scroll bars
Standard toolbar
status bar
title bar
toolbar
Wait mode
Web toolbar
What's This?
workbook
worksheet
worksheet scroll buttons
worksheet tab

Operations
exit Excel 97
get help from the Web
start Excel 97
use Office Assistant

Study Questions

Multiple Choice

1. Another name for a columnar worksheet is a
   a. workbook.
   b. spreadsheet.
   c. cell.
   d. booksheet.

2. The intersection of a column and a row is
   a. a worksheet tab.
   b. a cell.
   c. an active cell.
   d. an indicator.

3. The number of worksheets in a workbook is limited
   a. by default.
   b. to three.
   c. by memory.
   d. to 256.

4. The size of an Excel worksheet is
   a. 128 columns by 9,999 rows.
   b. 65,536 columns by 256 rows.
   c. over 256 million cells.
   d. 256 columns by 65,536 rows.

5. The name of a worksheet displays
   a. in the column letters.
   b. on the worksheet tab.
   c. in the row number.
   d. in the status bar.

6. Which of the following applications would most likely be created in Excel?
   a. a letter
   b. a budget
   c. a memo
   d. a meeting report

7. The standard Windows 95 help features used in Excel include all of the following except
   a. What's This?
   b. Contents.
   c. Index.
   d. Office Assistant.

8. Before exiting Excel 97, you should
   a. save all files and then close all files.
   b. close all files, saving only those that you want to keep.
   c. close all files without saving because Excel saves them automatically.
   d. close the Office Assistant.

9. Which of the following statements are false?
   a. The Office Assistant gives context-sensitive help and unsolicited help.
   b. The Office Assistant is an animated character.
   c. The Office Assistant can be deactivated.
   d. The Office Assistant displays help in a bubble.

10. Which of the following are false statements?
    a. The formula bar displays the cell address and the cell contents of the active cell.
    b. The formula bar is a floating palette.
    c. The formula bar is used for typing formulas.
    d. The formula bar can be hidden.

Short Answer

1. How do you start Excel?

2. What is a cell address? Give examples.

3. How are columns and rows identified?

4. How do you display the Web toolbar?

5. Why are screen elements not usually hidden in Excel?

6. Name some of the things that Excel can do.

7. Name some of the word processing features that are found in Excel.

8. Name and describe the different help features in Excel.

9. Name some of the mode indicators in Excel.

10. How many cells are in a worksheet?

For Discussion

1. Name some tasks that you could perform in Excel for your own personal use.

2. Discuss the advantages of using a program like Excel over keeping columnar records manually.

3. Name examples of situations that would benefit from having multiple worksheets in the same file.

4. Discuss the value of a chart in a worksheet.

Review Exercises

1. Starting Excel and exploring the workbook

In this exercise, you will start Excel 97 and move around in the workbook.

1. Start Excel 97.

2. Turn on the Web toolbar if it isn't displayed.

3. What text is displayed in the status bar?

4. What text is displayed in the Name box?

5. Click the tab that says Sheet2.

6. Is there any change in the status bar and in the Name box?

7. Turn the Web toolbar on if necessary and then turn it off.

2. Getting help on the Web

In this exercise, you will explore the help feature on the World Wide Web.

1. Choose Help, Microsoft on the Web.

2. Choose Product News.

3. Print the initial Web page that displays.

4. Disconnect from the Internet and exit Internet Explorer.

3. Displaying and docking toolbars and getting help from the Office Assistant

1. Launch Excel 97, if necessary.

2. Display the Control Toolbox toolbar.

3. Float the Excel 97 menu bar.

4. Display the Office Assistant and move the Office Assistant to a different location on-screen.

5. Ask the Office Assistant how to change the name of a worksheet.

6. Select a topic from among those the Office Assistant identifies about renaming a worksheet and print a copy of the topic.

7. Dock the menu bar at its original position.

8. Close the Control Toolbox toolbar and the Office Assistant.

9. Exit Excel without saving the worksheet.

Assignments

1. Getting online help

Start Excel 97 and use the Office Assistant to find and open a help topic about the Text Import Wizard. Choose Options and print the topic. When finished, close the Help dialog box.

2. Using the Web toolbar

Start Excel 97 and display the Web toolbar in the new workbook if it isn't already displayed. Go to this address: http://www.dominis.com/Zines/ and explore the site. Give a brief description of what you find. When finished, close Internet Explorer, disconnect from the Internet, and exit Excel 97.

Creating a Workbook

In order to use Excel 97 effectively, you must know how to create, save, and print workbooks. In this project, you will enter text and numbers and calculate the numbers with formulas and functions to create a simple worksheet. (This might sound like a lot, but I promise you won't have to use all 16,777,216 cells!)

Objectives

After completing this project, you will be able to:

➤ **Create a new workbook**

➤ **Move around in a worksheet and a workbook**

➤ **Name worksheets**

➤ **Enter data**

➤ **Enter simple formulas and functions**

➤ **Save a workbook**

➤ **Preview and print a worksheet**

➤ **Close a worksheet**

The Challenge

Mr. Gilmore, manager of The Grande Hotel, wants a down-and-dirty worksheet to compare the January receipts to the February receipts for both restaurants in the hotel (the Atrium Café and the Willow Top Restaurant). Since the worksheet is just for him, you won't have to worry about formatting right now.

The Solution

You will create a workbook with a page for the Atrium Café and a page for the Willow Top Restaurant as shown in Figure 1.1. (For now, don't worry about aligning headings such as Jan and Feb. You'll learn this in a later project.)

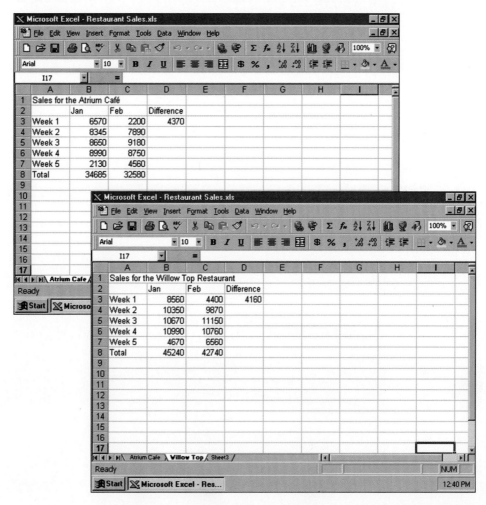

Figure 1.1

The Setup

So that your screen will match the illustrations in this chapter and to ensure that all the tasks in this project will function as described, you should set up Excel as described in Table 1.1. Because these are the default settings for the toolbars and view, you may not need to make any changes to your setup.

Table 1.1   Excel Settings

Location	Make these settings:
View, Toolbars	Deselect all toolbars except the Standard and Formatting.
View	Use the Normal view and display the Formula Bar and the Status Bar.

Creating a New Workbook

When you launch Excel 97, a new blank workbook named Book1 automatically opens for you, and you can begin to enter data.

TASK 1: TO CREATE A NEW WORKBOOK:

1 Click the Start button and point to Programs.

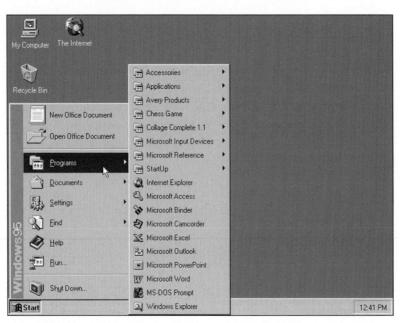

2 Choose Microsoft Excel.
The program launches and creates a workbook called Book1.

> **Note** If Excel is already started and you don't see a workbook on the screen, click the New button on the standard toolbar, and Excel will create one for you.

Moving Around in a Worksheet and a Workbook

To enter data in a worksheet like the one shown on the next page in Figure 1.2, you must move to the desired cell. The *active cell* is outlined with a black border. You make a cell the active cell by clicking in the cell or by moving to the cell with keystrokes. Table 1.2 lists the navigational keystrokes used to move to the desired cell.

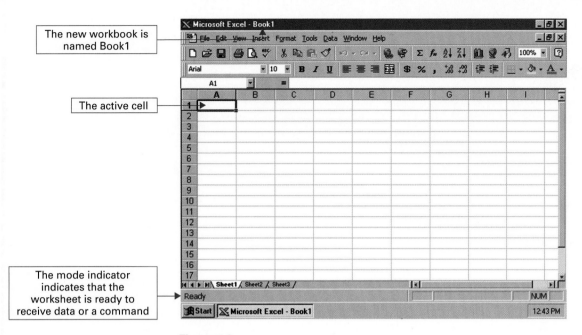

The new workbook is named Book1

The active cell

The mode indicator indicates that the worksheet is ready to receive data or a command

Figure 1.2

Note If you want to click in a cell you can't see on the screen, use the vertical or horizontal scroll bar to scroll the worksheet until you see the cell.

Table 1.2   Navigational Keystrokes

Target Location	Keystroke
Cell to the right of the active cell	→ or TAB
Cell to the left of the active cell	← or SHIFT+TAB
Cell below the active cell	↓ or ENTER
Cell above the active cell	↑ or SHIFT+ENTER
Upper-left corner of the worksheet	CTRL+HOME
Lower-right corner of the active area of the worksheet	CTRL+END
Down one screen	PGDN
Up one screen	PGUP
Right one screen	ALT+PGDN
Left one screen	ALT+PGUP

To display a different worksheet, click the worksheet tab. If you can't see the tab for the worksheet that you want to display, click the appropriate scroll button (the arrows just to the left of the worksheet tabs) to display the tab.

TASK 2: TO MOVE AROUND IN A WORKSHEET AND A WORKBOOK:

1 Press (PGDN).

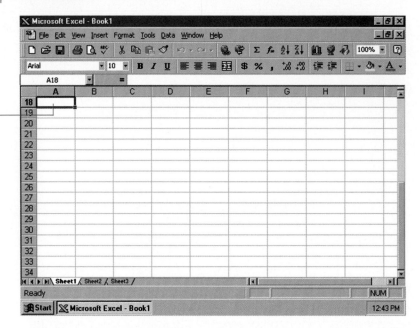

Cell A18 becomes the active cell

Note The monitor's size and resolution determine the number of columns and rows displayed on a screen. When you press (PGDN), (PGUP), (ALT)+(PGDN), or (ALT)+(PGUP), the active cell may be different from those shown in the illustrations.

2 Press ⊝ five times.

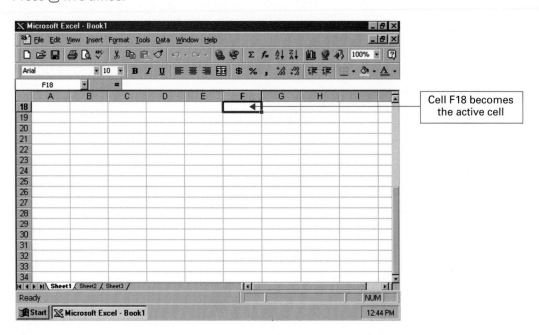

Cell F18 becomes the active cell

3 Type **88** and press (ENTER).
The number displays in cell F18, and cell F19 becomes the active cell.

> **Note** Instead of pressing the (ENTER) key to enter data in a cell, you can press any one of the arrow keys ((↑), (↓), (←), or (→)) or any key that moves the cell pointer, such as the (PGUP) key or the (PGDN) key. When you enter data across a row, it's more efficient to use the (→) key than to use the (ENTER) key.

4 Press (CTRL)+(HOME).
Cell A1 becomes the active cell.

5 Drag the box in the vertical scroll bar until you see Row 4 in the ScrollTip box.

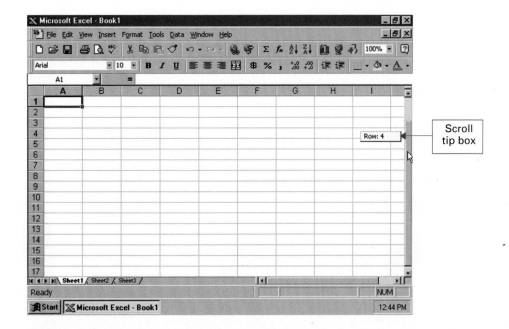

6 Click in cell D5.
Cell D5 becomes the active cell.

7   Press CTRL + END.

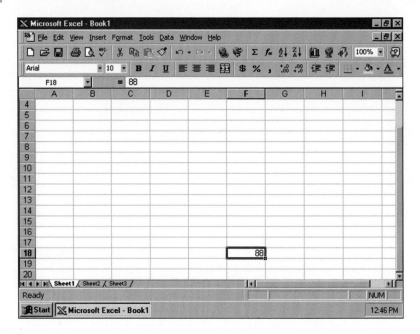

Note The lower right corner of the active worksheet is always the cell at the intersection of the last row and the last column used, and it doesn't necessarily contain data.

8   Press DEL.
The number is deleted.

9   Click the Sheet2 tab.
Sheet2 displays.

Naming Worksheets

The three worksheets created by default in a new workbook are named Sheet1, Sheet2, and Sheet3. Not very imaginative or meaningful names, are they? You can give the worksheets better names to help you identify the content of the worksheet.

TASK 3: TO NAME A WORKSHEET:

1   Point to the Sheet1 tab and right-click.

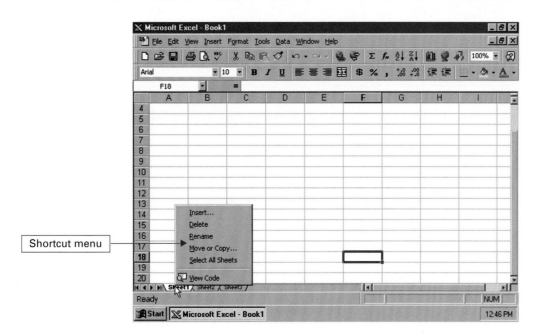

Shortcut menu

2 Choose Rename.
The current name on the tab is highlighted.

3 Type **Atrium Cafe** and press (ENTER).

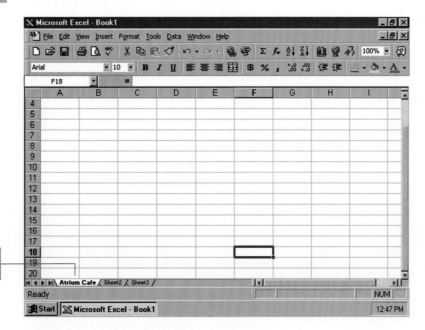

The new worksheet name appears on the tab

4 Point to the Sheet2 tab and right-click.
The shortcut menu displays.

5 Choose Rename.
The current name on the tab is highlighted.

6 Type **Willow Top** and press (ENTER).
The name displays on the tab.

Entering Data

Excel 97 recognizes several different types of data—text, dates, numbers, and formulas. Text can include any characters on the keyboard as well as special characters such as the symbols for the British pound or the Japanese Yen. Dates can be entered with numbers separated with a slash or a dash. Numbers can include only these characters:

1 2 3 4 5 6 7 8 9 0 + – ( ) , / $ % . E

Tip To enter a fraction instead of a date, precede the fraction with a zero. For example, to enter the fraction one-half, type 0 1/2 instead of 1/2 which Excel interprets as a date.

Entering Text

When you enter text in a cell, if the cell isn't wide enough to hold the text, the text will spill over into the next cell (if it's empty).

Tip Any time you enter data that doesn't fit in a cell, you can widen the column and the data will display, or you can wrap the text in the cell.

TASK 4: TO ENTER DATA IN THE WORKSHEET:

1 Click the Atrium Cafe tab.
The Atrium Cafe worksheet displays.

2 Click in cell A1.
Cell A1 becomes the active cell.

3 Type **Sales for the Atrium Cafe**.
Notice that the mode changes to **Enter** because you are entering data.

4 Press (ENTER). Notice that Excel adds an accent to the "e" in "cafe" after you press the (ENTER) key to accept your data entry.

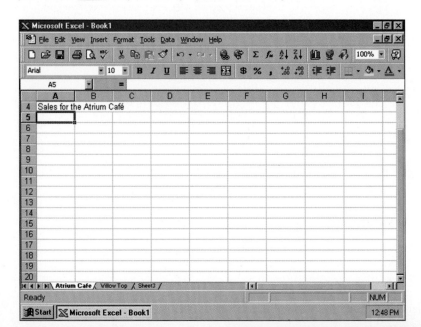

Tip If you make a mistake while typing, simply press the Backspace key and retype the text before you press Enter. If you change your mind about entering the data in the current cell, press (ESC) before Excel enters the data.

5   Click the Willow Top tab.
The Willow Top worksheet displays.

6   Click in cell A1 if necessary.
Cell A1 becomes the active cell.

7   Type **Sales for the Willow Top Restaurant** and press (ENTER).

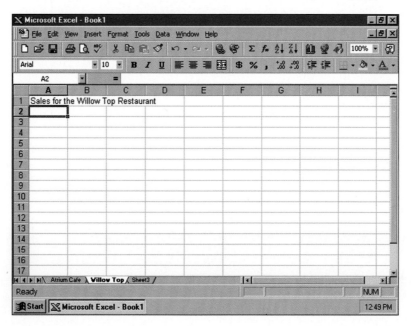

Entering Data on Multiple Worksheets

Sometimes the worksheets that you create have the same data entered several times. If the repetitive data that you are entering is text, the *Auto-Complete* feature of Excel 97 may complete the entry for you if the repetitive text appears in the same column. If the automatic completion isn't appropriate, just continue typing the text that you want.

If you are creating multiple worksheets in a workbook, you may want to use the same data for the column and row headings. To save time, you can enter the data that is the same on all worksheets at the same time.

TASK 5: TO ENTER THE SAME DATA ON MULTIPLE WORKSHEETS AT THE SAME TIME:

1   Press (CTRL) and click the Atrium Cafe tab.
Both the Atrium Cafe worksheet and the Willow Top worksheet are selected.

2   Click in cell B2 and type **Jan.**

Note The Group indicator displays in the title bar when multiple worksheets are selected.

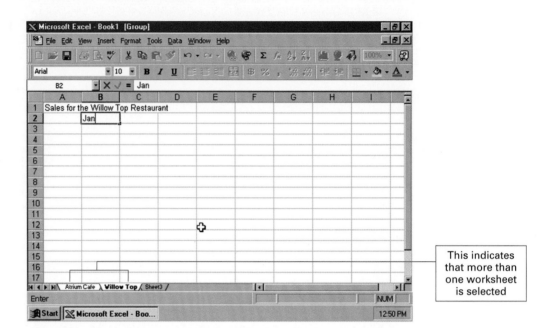

This indicates that more than one worksheet is selected

3 Press ⊕ and type **Feb**.

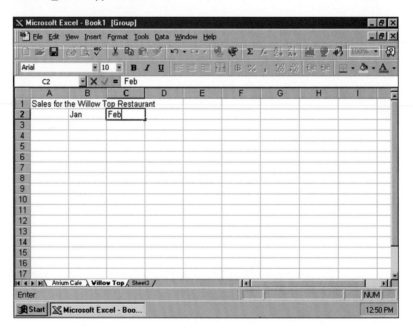

4　Press → and type **Difference**.

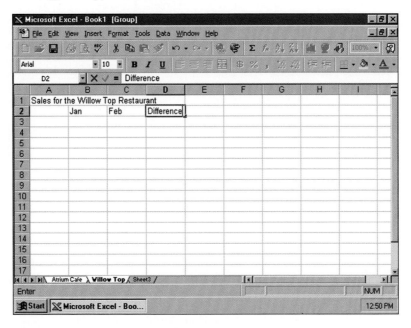

5　Click in cell A3 and type **Week 1**.

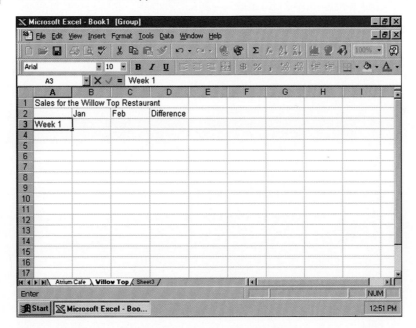

6　Press (ENTER) and type **Week**.
The AutoComplete feature completes the entry as Week 1.

7 Continue typing so that the entry is "Week 2" and then press (ENTER).

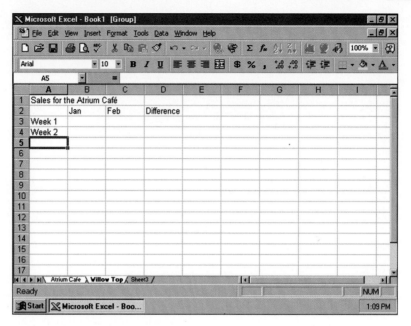

8 Click in cell A4.
Cell A4 becomes the active cell.

9 Point to the handle in the lower right corner of the cell.

Note The pointer appears as a plus when you point to the handle.

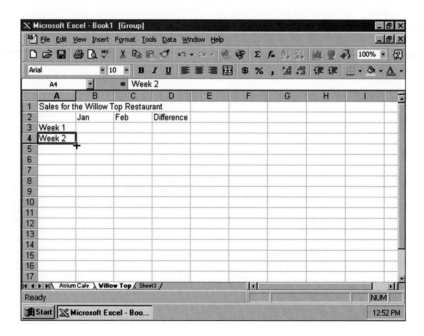

10   Drag the handle to cell A7.

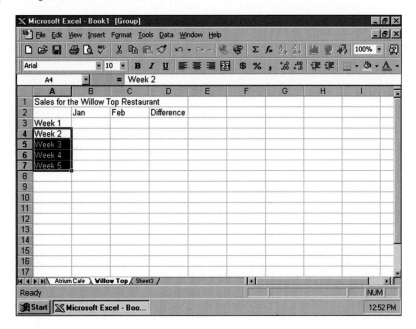

> **Tip** You can use the dragging technique to enter almost any type of series (except the World Series, of course).

11   Click in cell A8, type **Total** and press ⟨ENTER⟩.

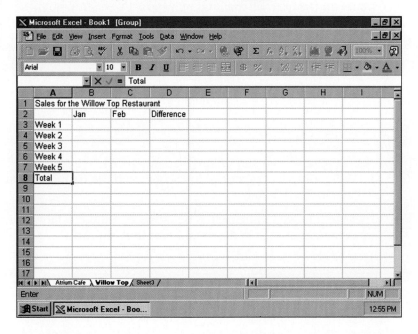

12   Click the Atrium Cafe tab to verify that the information appears on both worksheets.

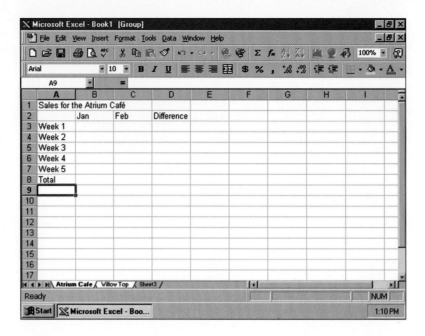

Entering Numbers

If you enter a number that doesn't fit in a cell, Excel 97 either converts the number to *scientific notation* or displays pound signs (#) in the cell. If you enter a date that doesn't fit in a cell, Excel 97 displays pound signs.

> **Note** Scientific notation is a number format used for very large numbers and very small decimal numbers. For example, the scientific notation for 1,000,000,000 is 1E+09 which means 1 times 10 to the ninth power. Perhaps our government should consider using scientific notation to express the national debt; maybe it wouldn't look so bad.

TASK 6: TO ENTER NUMBERS IN THE WORKSHEETS:

1. Press (CTRL) and click the Willow Top tab.
    The Willow Top worksheet is deselected and the Group indicator no longer displays in the title bar.

2. Enter the following numbers in columns B and C on the Atrium Cafe worksheet, as shown in the illustration that follows.

COLUMN B	COLUMN C
6570	2200
8345	7890
8650	9180
8990	8750
2130	4560

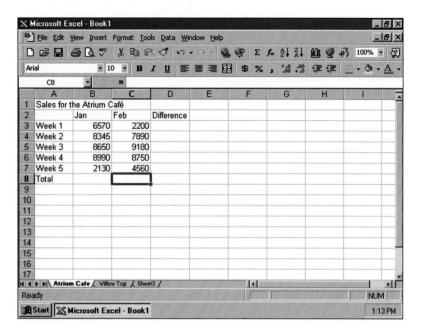

3   Click the Willow Top tab.
The Willow Top worksheet displays.

4   Enter the following numbers in columns B and C on the Willow Top worksheet:

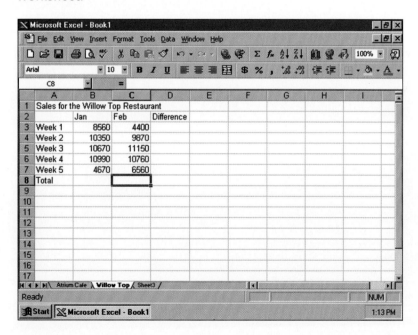

Entering Simple Formulas and Functions

Formulas and *functions* are mathematical statements that perform calculations. Formulas are made up and entered by the user to perform the specific calculation needed. Functions are formulas that are included in Excel 97. They perform calculations that are commonly used such as calculating a sum or an average. Functions require specific information, called *arguments,* to perform the calculations. Formulas and functions must start with the equal sign (=), and they can contain cell addresses, numbers, and *arithmetic operators.* Table 1.3 describes the arithmetic operators and gives examples. Table 1.4 lists some of the commonly used functions.

> **Tip** Some formulas and functions refer to a block of cells, called a *range.* The address of a range includes the first and last cells in the range separated by a colon. For example, the address of the range from cell A1 through cell B10 is A1:B10.

Table 1.3   Arithmetic Operators

Operator	Meaning	Example	Result (if A1 = 20 and A2 = 2)
+	Addition	=A1+A2	22
−	Subtraction	=A1−A2	18
*	Multiplication	=A1*10	200
/	Division	=A1/A2	10
%	Percent	=A1%	.2
^	Exponentiation	=A1^A2	400

Table 1.4   Commonly Used Functions

Function	Meaning	Example	Result (if A1 = 1, A2 = 2 and A3 = 3)
=SUM(*argument*)	Calculates the sum of the cells in the argument	=SUM(A1:A3)	6
=AVERAGE(*argument*)	Calculates the average of the cells in the argument	=AVERAGE(A1:A3)	2
=MAX(*argument*)	Finds the largest value in the cells in the argument	=MAX(A1:A3)	3
=MIN(*argument*)	Finds the smallest value of the cells in the argument	=MIN(A1:A3)	1
=COUNT(*argument*)	Counts the number of cells in the argument that have a numeric value	=COUNT(A1:A3)	3

TASK 7: TO ENTER FORMULAS AND FUNCTIONS:

1 Press ⟨CTRL⟩ and click the Atrium Cafe tab.
Both worksheets are selected, and the data you enter will display on both worksheets. Notice that the Group indicator displays in the title bar.

2 Click in cell D3 and click the equal sign in the formula bar. (If the Office

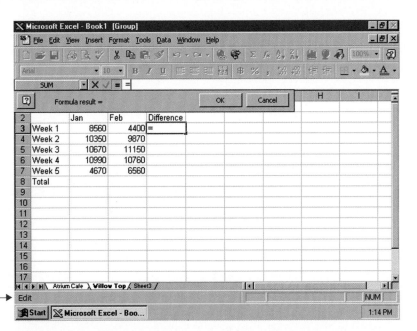

The mode changes to Edit because the data is being entered in the formula bar

Assistant opens, choose No, don't provide help now.)

3 Click in cell B3.
The mode changes to **Point** because you are pointing to cells to build the formula.

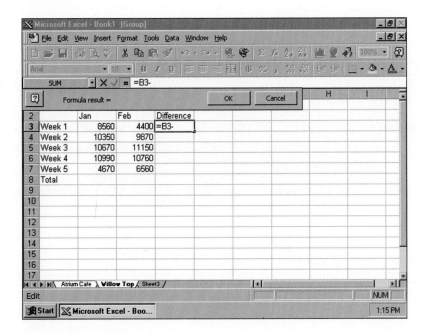

4 Type a minus sign (−).

5 Click in cell C3 and then click the Enter 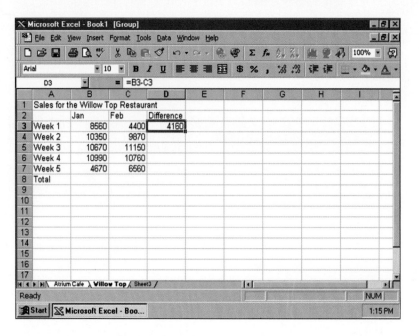 button in the formula bar.

6 Click in cell B8 and type **=sum(**

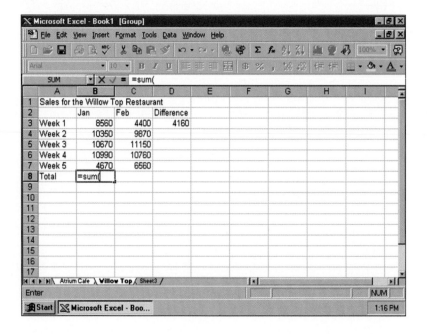

7   Drag the cursor from cell B3 through cell B7.

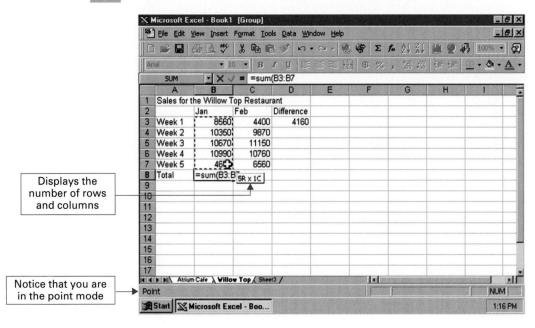

Displays the number of rows and columns

Notice that you are in the point mode

8   Press (ENTER).

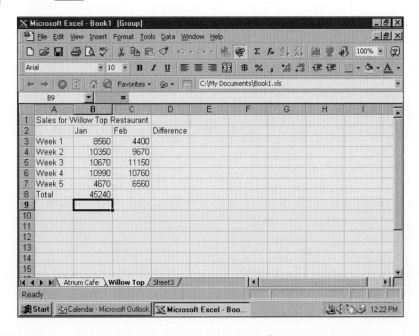

9   Click in cell C8 and click the AutoSum Σ button on the Standard toolbar.

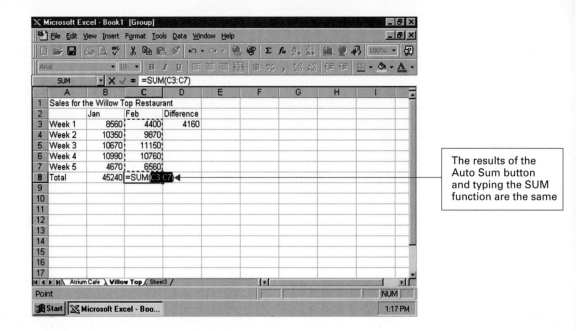

The results of the Auto Sum button and typing the SUM function are the same

10 Press ENTER.
The numbers in column C are totaled.

Note If you change a number in a cell, Excel 97 automatically recalculates all formulas or functions that might be affected.

Key Concept When a formula has more than one operation, Excel 97 follows an *order of precedence* to determine the sequence in which each operation should be performed. The order is as follows: exponentiation first, then multiplication or division (from left to right), and finally addition or subtraction (from left to right). If the formula has parentheses, the operation(s) in the parentheses are performed first. You can use the phrase "Please excuse my dear Aunt Sally" to remember "p" for parentheses, "e" for exponent, "m" for multiplication, "d" for division, "a" for addition, and "s" for subtraction.

Saving a Workbook

If you want to keep the data that you have entered in a workbook, you must save the file. When saving the file, you specify a name for the document and a location where it will be stored.

Tip Because Excel 97 is written for Windows 95, the name of a workbook can be a *long filename.* Long filenames (including the full path of the file) can use up to 255 characters. Although you can use as many spaces and periods in the filename as you want, you can't use ? or : or *. Older versions of Excel prior to Excel 7.0 do NOT use long filenames and will convert a long filename to eight characters (plus the extension).

TASK 8: TO SAVE A WORKBOOK:

1 Click the Atrium Cafe tab if it isn't the displayed worksheet.
The Atrium Cafe worksheet displays.

2 Press (CTRL) and click the Willow Top tab.
The Willow Top worksheet is deselected.

> **Tip** When you are ready to save and close a workbook and you have more than one worksheet selected, you might want to deselect all but one worksheet by pressing (CTRL) and clicking the tabs you want to deselect. If you don't deselect worksheets, the next time you open the workbook, the worksheets will still be selected and any changes you make will be made on all worksheets.

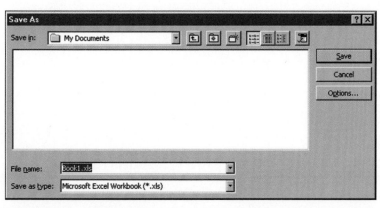

3 Click the Save 🖫 button.

4 Type **Restaurant Sales** in the File Name text box.
Excel 97 adds the default extension xls to the filename when the file is saved.

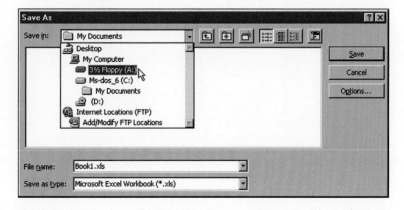

5 Click the down arrow in the Save In text box and choose drive A: (or the drive and folder designated by your professor or lab assistant).

6 Click Save.
The dialog box closes, the file is saved on the disk, and the title bar displays the name of the file.

Tip After saving a file for the first time, you should save the document periodically as you continue to work on it in case your system goes down for some reason. After a file has a name, you can save the file again simply by clicking the Save button.

Note To save a file in a different location or with a different name, choose File, Save As.

Previewing and Printing a Worksheet

Before you print a file, you should preview it to see if it looks like what you expect. (You don't want any surprises.) The ***Print Preview*** shows the full page of the current worksheet and allows you to zoom in on the worksheet so you can actually read the data, if necessary.

You can print a worksheet in the Print Preview mode or in Normal view. Clicking the Print button prints one copy of the complete workbook. If you want to print only part of the workbook or more than one copy, you should use the Print command from the File menu because it allows you to make selections from the Print dialog box.

TASK 9: TO PREVIEW AND PRINT A WORKSHEET:

1 Click the Print Preview button on the Standard toolbar.

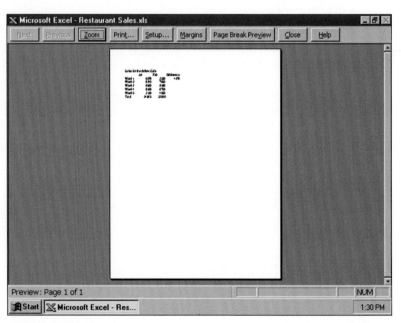

2 Click the pointer, now shaped like a magnifying glass, at the top of the worksheet.

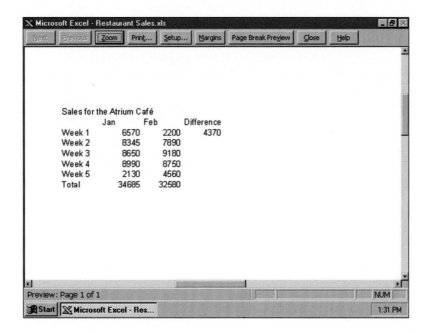

3 Click again.
The full page displays again.

4 Click Close in the Print Preview toolbar.
The Print Preview mode closes and the worksheet screen displays.

5 Ensure that the computer you are using is attached to a printer and that the printer is online.

6 Choose File from the menu bar.

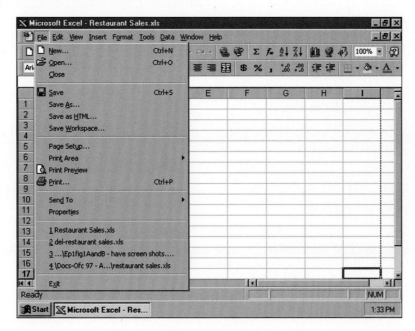

7   Choose Print.

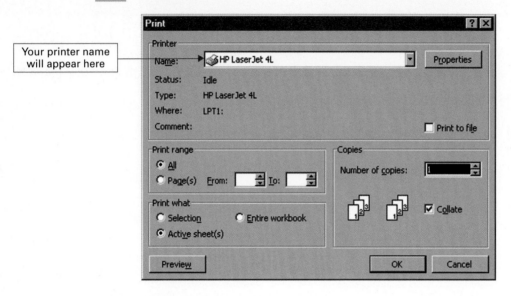

Your printer name will appear here

8   Click OK.
The workbook prints.

Closing a Workbook

When you are finished with a workbook, you can close it. If you have made changes that you want to keep, you should save the workbook before closing it. If you forget to save a workbook before closing, Excel 97 asks if you want to save changes.

TASK 11: TO CLOSE A FILE:

1   Click 🖫.
The worksheet is saved.

2   Click ☒ on the Menu bar.
The file closes.

The Conclusion

You can exit Excel 97 now by clicking ☒ on the application title bar, or you can work on the Review Exercises and Assignments.

Summary and Exercises

Summary

- When you launch Excel 97 a workbook named Book1 is created automatically.
- To enter data in a worksheet, the cell pointer must be positioned in the desired cell.
- By default, a new workbook has three worksheets.
- Excel 97 recognizes several different types of data: text, dates, numbers, and formulas.
- Formulas and functions are mathematical statements that perform calculations.
- Files can be saved with long filenames.
- Before you print a worksheet, you can preview it to see if it looks acceptable.
- When you close a file, if you haven't saved changes to the file, Excel 97 asks if you want to save the changes.

Key Terms and Operations

Key Terms
active cell
arithmetic operators
AutoComplete
Edit mode
Enter mode
formula
function
order of precedence
Point mode
Print Preview mode
range
scientific notation

Operations
close a workbook
create a workbook
enter data
enter formulas and functions
move in a workbook
name a workbook
name a worksheet
preview a worksheet
print a worksheet
save a workbook

Study Questions

Multiple Choice

1. Using the order of precedence, solve the formula 5–2*(8+2). What is the answer?
   a. 26
   b. −15
   c. −9
   d. 30

2. To move to the cell below the active cell, press
   a. (ENTER).
   b. (PGDN).
   c. (TAB).
   d. (CTRL)+(↓).

3. Which of the following is a range address?
   a. D1;D10
   b. D1,D10
   c. D1 D10
   d. D1:D10

4. Which of the following can not be included in numeric data?
   a. 1
   b. 2
   c. E
   d. =

5. Which of the following is an example of scientific notation?
   a. 1.5E+11
   b. 1^10
   c. 7.8!
   d. $A$2

6. If A1 is 10, A2 is 15, and A3 is 20, what is the result of =SUM(A1:A2)?
   a. 10
   b. 15
   c. 25
   d. 45

7. If A1 is 10, A2 is 15, and A3 is 20, what is the result of =AVERAGE(A1:A3)?
   a. 10
   b. 15
   c. 25
   d. 45

8. If A1 is 10, A2 is 15, A3 is 20, and A4 says "Total," what is the result of =COUNT(A1:A4)?
   a. 3
   b. 15
   c. 45
   d. 4

9. The Preview mode shows
   a. all pages of a workbook.
   b. the current page of the workbook.
   c. the formulas.
   d. the formulas and functions.

10. When you press (CTRL)+(END), what cell becomes the active cell?
   a. IV65536
   b. The last cell in the current column.
   c. The cell in the lower right corner.
   d. The cell in the lower right corner of the active area of the worksheet.

Short Answer

1. What happens when you change a number in a cell that is included in a formula?

2. What should you do before you close a workbook?

3. How do you rename a worksheet?

4. What is the order of precedence?

5. What displays in a cell if you enter 1/10?

6. How can you make 1/10 display as a fraction in a cell?

7. Write the formula to add the numbers from cell A1 through cell A5.

8. Write the function to add the numbers from cell A1 through cell A5.

9. How do you enter the same data on more than one worksheet?

10. What function finds the smallest value?

For Discussion

1. Describe a situation in which you would use several worksheets in the same workbook.

2. The cell displays #######. What caused the problem and how can you solve it?

3. Discuss the reasons you might rename worksheets in a workbook.

4. What is a range and how is it addressed?

Review Exercises

1. Creating an expense account

Your good friend Karl Klaus, the head chef at the 4-star restaurant in *The Grande Hotel*, has asked you to create an expense report for him because he can't type. In this exercise, you will create a worksheet that lists the expenses Karl had on a recent trip for the hotel.

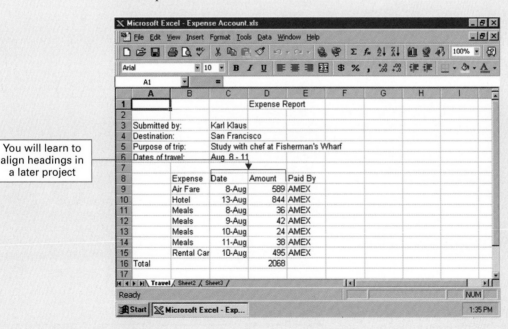

Figure 1.3

1. Create a new workbook.

2. Rename Sheet1 to Travel.

3. Enter the data shown in Figure 1.3 except for Row 16.

> **Note** The format for dates might be different on your computer.

4. Use the AutoSum button to calculate the total expenses.

5. Save the workbook as *Expense Account.xls*.

2. Calculating savings

In this exercise, you will use a worksheet to calculate the amount of money you will have in twenty years, based on different variables such as the amount you can save each year and the rate of interest you earn.

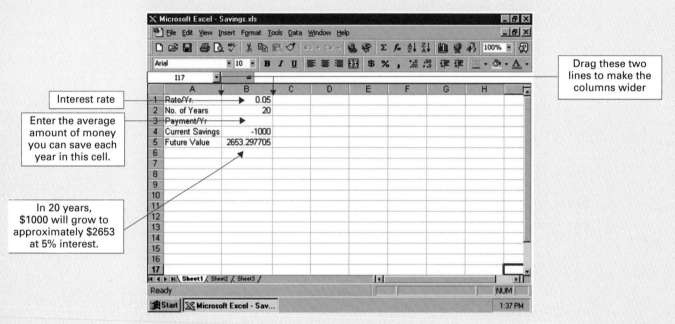

Figure 1.4

1. Go to this address on the Web:
http://www.finaid.org/finaid/calculators/finaid_calc.html.

2. Select the Savings Plan Designer.

3. If you currently have $1000 in savings and you can get 5 percent interest, how much will you have to save each month to have $200,000 in 20 years?

4. Create a new worksheet and enter the data for A1, A2, A3, A4, A5, B1, B2, and B4 as shown in Figure 1.4. Be sure to enter the data in the same cells shown in the figure.

> **Note** The values for current savings is a negative number due to the use of debits and credits in standard accounting procedures.

5. In cell B5, type this function: =FV(B1,B2,B3,B4,1).

6. In cell B3, enter the number that is 12 times the answer you got in step 3. Precede the number with a minus sign. The answer in cell B5 should be approximately 200,000.

7. Change the Payment/Yr amount to −2000 and change the Rate/Yr to .15.

8. Save the worksheet as *Savings.xls*.

3. Creating a sales analysis worksheet

1. Launch Excel 97, if necessary, or create a new blank workbook.

2. Create the worksheet displayed in Figure 1.5.

> **Tip** The product description of rows 5–7 contains the word cardboard.

	A	B	C	D	E	F
1	Multi-Size Container Corporation					
2	Sales Analysis					
3						
4	Product #	Product	Actual	Expected	Actual-Expected	
5	3-453	3" Cardboa	145300	156900		
6	3-455	5" Cardboa	132900	186700		
7	3-457	7" Cardboa	865330	163300		
8	5-852	2" Glass	655900	567000		
9	5-854	4" Glass	754980	641500		
10						

Figure 1.5

3. Name the worksheet *<Current year> Sales*, substituting the current year as indicated.

4. Save the workbook using the filename *Container Corporation Sales xxx* (where *xxx* represents your initials).

5. Add a formula to Column E that calculates the difference between the actual sales and the amount expected.

6. Add a formula to Row 10 that calculates the total actual sales, the total expected sales, and the total difference.

7. Save the changes to the workbook and print a copy of the worksheet.

8. Close the workbook and exit Excel.

Assignments

1. Creating a timesheet

Create a workbook with a worksheet for each of your classes. List the dates and the number of hours that you spend for each class (including class time, lab time, and homework) in a week. Total the number of hours. Save the worksheets and workbook, using an appropriate filename.

2. Creating a worksheet that compares menu prices

Go to http://www.metrodine.com and follow links to find restaurant menus that list entrees and prices. Search for "menu." Create a worksheet that lists the entrees and prices for at least two restaurants. Use the MIN and MAX functions to show the lowest and highest priced entree for each restaurant. Save the worksheets and workbook, using an appropriate filename.

Editing a Workbook

Moving a title to a different location, deleting last week's totals, copying this month's totals to the summary worksheet, adding comments to a cell, checking the spelling — an Excel user's work is never done! In this project, you will edit a workbook and modify the data using some basic editing tasks.

Objectives

After completing this project, you will be able to:

- ➤ **Open a workbook**
- ➤ **Find data**
- ➤ **Edit data**
- ➤ **Work with data**
- ➤ **Add comments**
- ➤ **Check spelling**

The Challenge

Mr. Gilmore was impressed at how quickly you created his "down-and-dirty" worksheet, but he wants a few changes made to it. Specifically, he wants you to add some comments and create a new worksheet that includes the January sales figures from both restaurants.

The Solution

To make the changes Mr. Gilmore wants, you will open the Restaurant Sales workbook, revise some of the data, move and copy some of the cells, add comments, and check the spelling. The finished workbook will look like Figure 2.1.

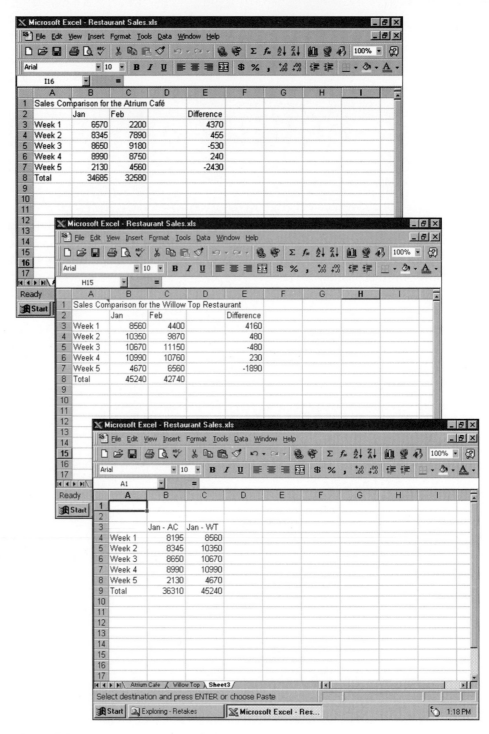

Figure 2.1

The Setup

So that your screen will match the illustrations in this chapter and to ensure that all the tasks in this project will function as described, you should set up Excel as described in Table 2.1. Because these are the default settings for the toolbars and view, you may not need to make any changes to your setup.

Table 2.1   Excel Settings

Location	Make these settings:
View, Toolbars	Deselect all toolbars except Standard and Formatting
View	Use Normal and display the Formula Bar and the Status Bar.

Opening a Workbook

When you want to view or revise a workbook that you have saved, you must open the workbook first. The worksheet and cell that were active when you last saved and closed the workbook are active when you open the workbook.

> **Tip** If the workbook is one that you have opened recently, you may see it listed at the bottom of the File menu. To open the file, simply select it from the menu.

TASK 1: TO OPEN A WORKBOOK:

1   Click the Open 📂 button.

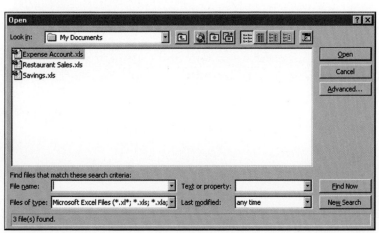

Click on the arrow in the Look in text box to display the drop down list.

2   Select the correct path and folder.
The folder name appears in the Look in text box.

3 Double-click *Restaurant Sales.xls.*

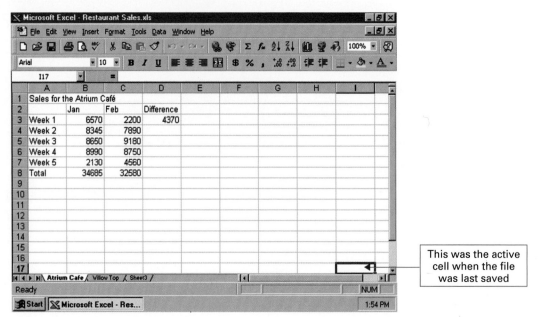

This was the active cell when the file was last saved

When you open a workbook, it opens to the location where you were when you last saved and closed it.

4 Click the Atrium Cafe tab if necessary.
The Atrium Cafe worksheet displays.

Finding Data

The Find command helps you find specific text or values in a worksheet. The command is very useful if the worksheet is large, but it also can be useful in small worksheets to find text and values that aren't shown on the screen. For example, you can use the Find command to find a word, number, or cell address that is in a formula.

TASK 2: TO FIND DATA:

1   Press CTRL+HOME.

2   Choose Edit.

3   Choose Find.

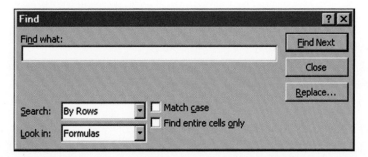

4   Type **Sum** in the Find what text box and ensure that Formulas is selected in the Look in text box.

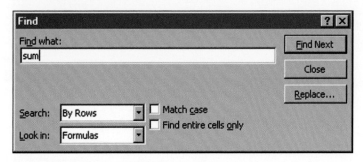

5   Click Find Next.
Cell B8 becomes the active cell.

6 Click Find Next.
Cell C8 becomes the active cell.

7 Click Find Next.
Cell B8 becomes the active cell again even though the next worksheet has a SUM function.

> **Tip** The Find command searches only the current worksheet.

8 Click Close.
The Find dialog box closes.

Editing Data

If you want to change the data that is entered in a cell, just click in the cell and type the new data. If the data is lengthy, it is more efficient to edit the existing data unless the new data is completely different. If the cell that you edit is used in a formula or function, Excel 97 recalculates automatically to update the worksheet.

TASK 3: TO EDIT DATA IN A CELL:

1 Click in cell A1 in the Atrium Cafe worksheet.
Cell A1 becomes the active cell.

2 Click in the formula bar before the "f" in "for."

> The insertion point should be here

X Microsoft Excel - Restaurant Sales.xls

File Edit View Insert Format Tools Data Window Help

Arial   10   **B** _I_ <u>U</u>   = Sales for the Atrium Café

	A	B	C	D	E	F	G	H	I
1	Sales for tl								
2		Jan	Feb	Difference					
3	Week 1	6570	2200	4370					
4	Week 2	8345	7890						
5	Week 3	8650	9180						
6	Week 4	8990	8750						
7	Week 5	2130	4560						
8	Total	34685	32580						
9									
10									

3 Type **Comparison** and then press (SPACE BAR).

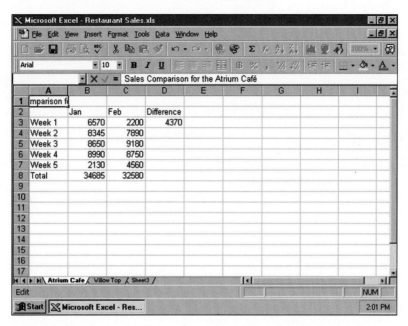

4 Press (ENTER).

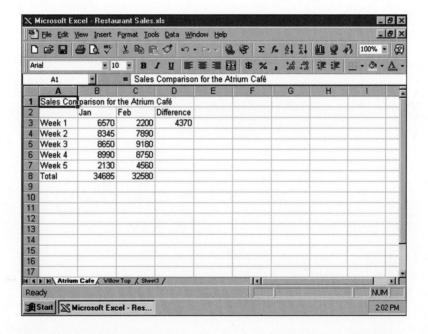

5 Click the Willow Top tab.
The Willow Top worksheet displays.

6 Click in cell A1.
Cell A1 becomes the active cell.

7 Click in the formula bar before the "f" in "for."

The insertion point should be here

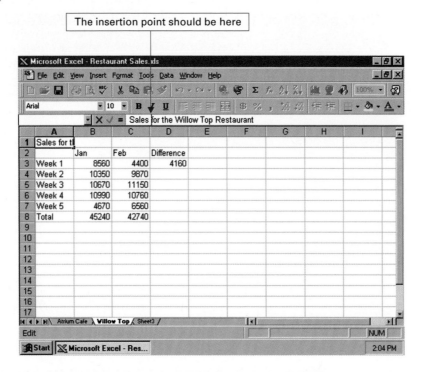

8 Type **Comparison**, press (SPACE BAR), and press (ENTER).

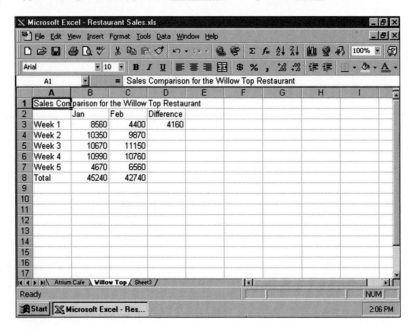

9 Click in cell B3.
Cell B3 becomes the active cell.

10   Type **8195** and press (ENTER).

Working with Data

After you have entered data in a worksheet, you may find that you need to make some changes. You may have to copy, delete, or move the data. All of these types of revisions require selecting cells.

Selecting Cells

When you select cells, they are highlighted. In most cases, the easiest way to select cells is to drag the mouse pointer over the cells, but Table 2.2 describes other ways of selecting cells that are appropriate in many situations.

Table 2.2   Selection Methods

Selection	Method
Entire column	Click the column letter at the top of the column.
Entire row	Click the row number at the left of the row.
Entire worksheet	Click the blank button above the row numbers and to the left of the column letters.
Adjacent columns	Drag the pointer through the column letters.
Adjacent rows	Drag the pointer through the row numbers.
Non-adjacent ranges	Select the first range (the range can be an entire column or row) and then press (CTRL) while you select additional ranges.

TASK 4: TO SELECT RANGES:

1 Click the column letter above column A.

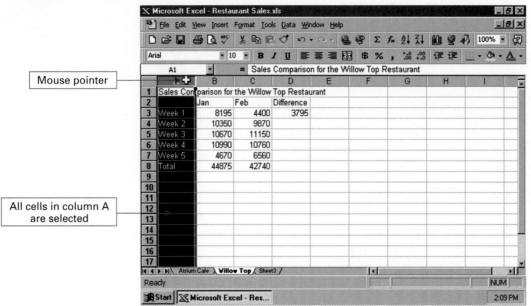

2 Drag the pointer through row numbers 3 and 4.

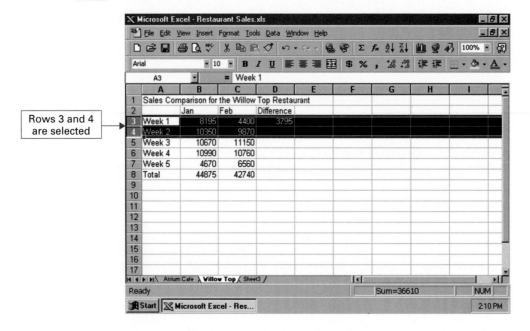

3 Select column C and then press (CTRL) while you select column F, row 8, and the range from cell H6 through cell I9.

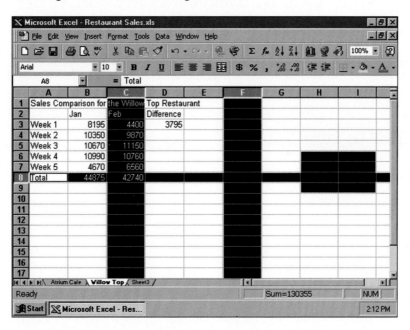

4 Select cell B3 through cell B7.

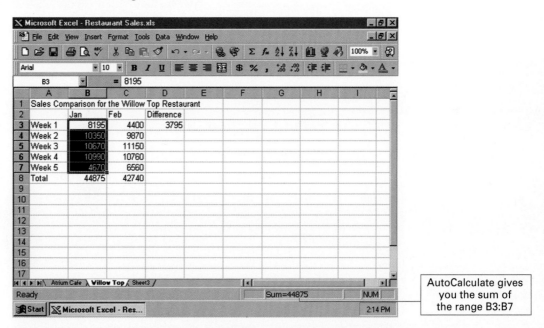

AutoCalculate gives you the sum of the range B3:B7

Tip When you select a range with values, the *AutoCalculate* feature displays a calculation in the status bar. To change the type of calculation, right-click the calculation and choose a different one.

Copying Data

When you copy data, Excel 97 stores the data in a memory area called the **Clipboard.** Data in the Clipboard can be pasted in any cell, or range of cells in any worksheet or any workbook. If you copy or cut additional data, the new data replaces the existing data in the Clipboard. The Clipboard is erased when you exit Excel 97. Pasting data from the Clipboard does not remove data from the Clipboard; therefore, you can paste it repeatedly.

TASK 5: TO COPY DATA:

1 Press (CTRL) and click the Atrium Cafe tab.
The Atrium Cafe worksheet and the Willow Top worksheet are both selected, and the Willow Top worksheet still displays.

2 Click in cell D3.
Cell D3 becomes the active cell.

3 Click the Copy button.

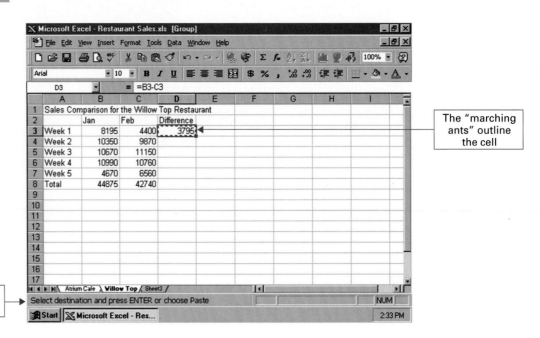

The "marching ants" outline the cell

The status bar tells you what to do next

4 Select the range from cell D4 through cell D7.

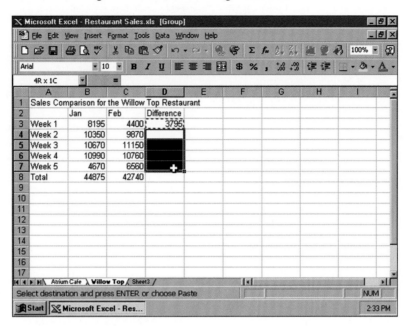

5 Click the Paste button.

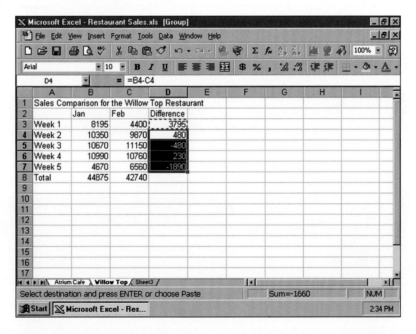

6 Click the Atrium Cafe tab.
The Copy command has been executed on this worksheet, too.

7 Press (CTRL) and click the Willow Top tab.
The Willow Top worksheet is deselected.

8 Select the range from cell B2 through cell B8.

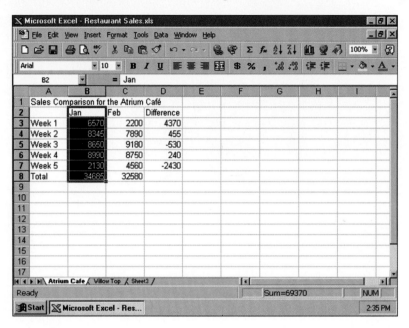

9 Click .
The cells are copied to the Clipboard.

10 Click the Sheet3 tab.
The Sheet3 worksheet displays.

11 Click in cell A3.
Cell A3 becomes the active cell.

12 Click .

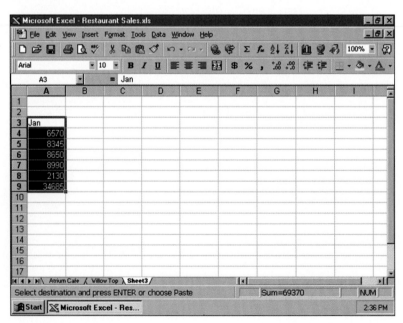

Caution Pasting data into cells automatically replaces data already contained in the cells — without notice. Use the Undo feature to restore data, if necessary.

13 Copy and paste the same range from the Willow Top worksheet to cell B3 in Sheet3.

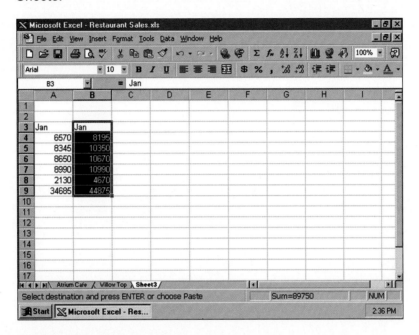

14 Rename Sheet3 to "January."
The name January appears on the tab.

Deleting Data

To erase the data in a cell or a range of cells, simply select the cells and press the Delete key. If you change your mind, click the Undo button.

Warning Some users try to erase cells by passing the space bar. Although the cell looks blank, it really isn't; it contains the character for a space. You should never use this method to erase a cell; you could get arrested by the SSP (Special Spreadsheet Police).

Note The Edit, Clear command accomplishes the same as pressing the (DEL) key.

TASK 6: TO DELETE DATA:

1   Select cell A8 through cell B8 on the January worksheet.

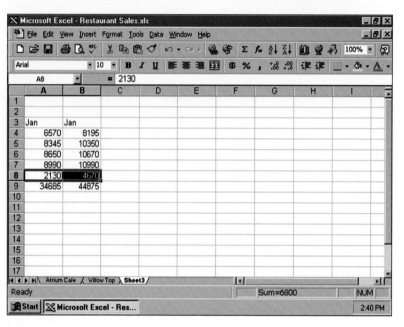

2   Press (DEL).

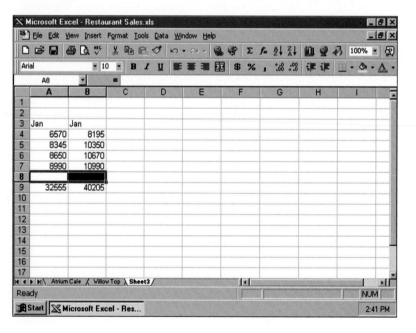

3   Click the Undo button.
The data appears again.

> **Tip** When you delete text with the ⌐DEL⌐ key, the text isn't stored in the Clipboard and therefore it can't be pasted in another location. You can press ⌐SHIFT⌐+⌐DEL⌐ if you want deleted text placed in the Clipboard.

Moving Data

You can move data to a different location in the same worksheet or to a location in a different worksheet.

TASK 7: TO MOVE DATA:

1   Click on the Atrium Cafe tab.
The Atrium Cafe worksheet displays.

2   Select cell D2 through cell D7.

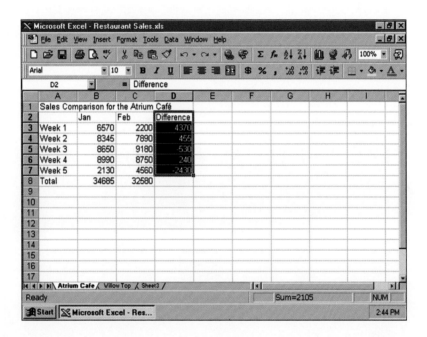

3 Click the Cut ✂ button.

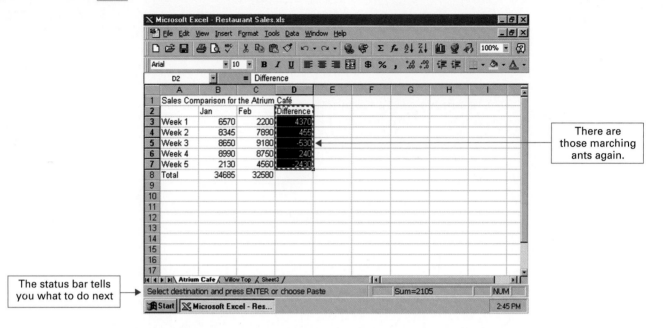

There are those marching ants again.

The status bar tells you what to do next

4 Click in cell E2.
Cell E2 becomes the active cell.

5 Click 📋.

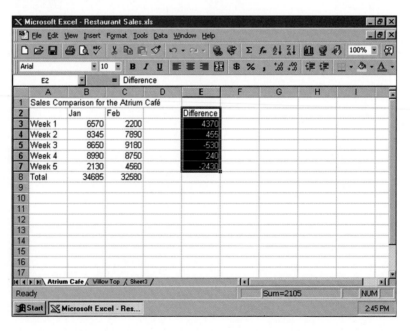

Warning Pasting anything that has been cut (or copied) to a new location that contains data overwrites the data.

6 Display the Willow Top worksheet and move the range D2 through D7 to cell E2.

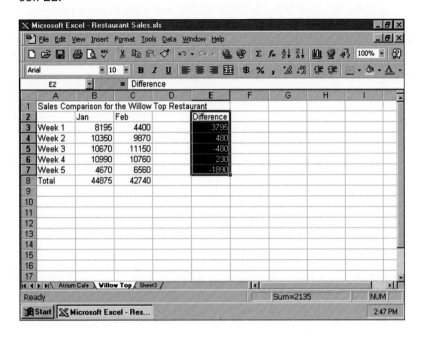

Adding Comments

You can attach **comments** to cells in a worksheet to provide additional information. The comment will contain the user name that is specified on the General page of the Options dialog box accessed from the Tools menu. The text in a comment displays on the screen and it can be made to print as well.

TASK 8: TO ADD COMMENTS:

1 Click in cell A1 on the Willow Top worksheet.
Cell A1 becomes the active cell.

2 Choose Insert from the Menu bar.

3 Choose Comment.

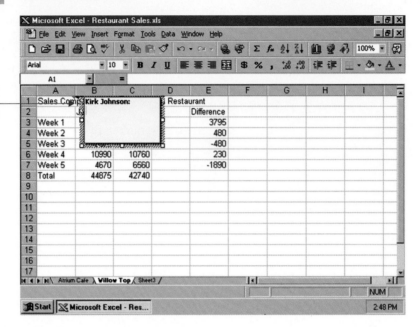

The user name precedes the comment

4 Type **Open for dinner only.**

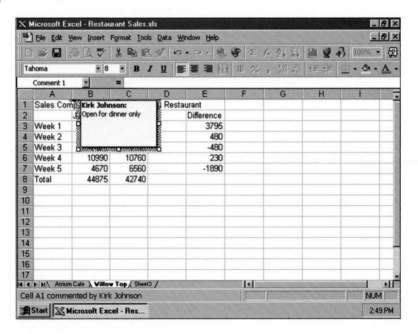

5 Click anywhere outside the comment box.

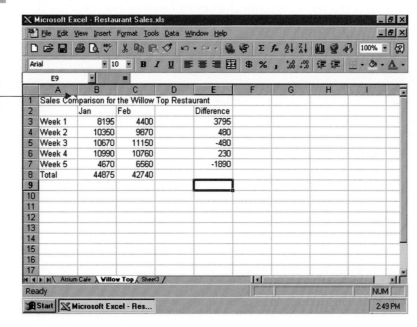

The red mark denotes a comment

6 Click the Atrium Cafe tab.
The Atrium Cafe worksheet displays.

7 Click in cell A1.
Cell A1 becomes the active cell.

8 Choose Insert, Comment, and type **Open for breakfest, lunch, and dinner.**
Do not correct the spelling of "breakfast."

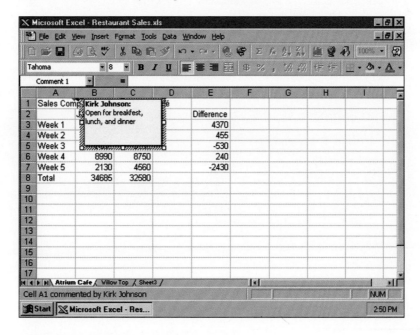

9 Click anywhere outside the comment box.
A red mark appears in cell A1.

If you want to see the comments on a worksheet, you can point to the cell that has a red mark and the comment box will pop up, or you can turn on the Comment view and all the comments will be visible.

TASK 9: TO TURN ON THE COMMENT VIEW AND TURN IT OFF AGAIN:

1 Choose View.

2 Choose Comments.

The Reviewing toolbar displays when you turn on the Comments view

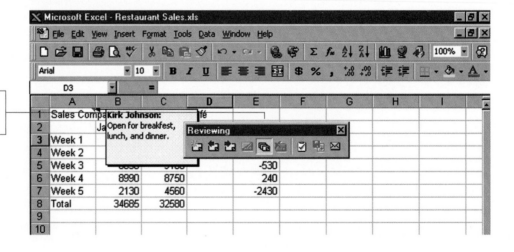

3 Click the Willow Top tab.

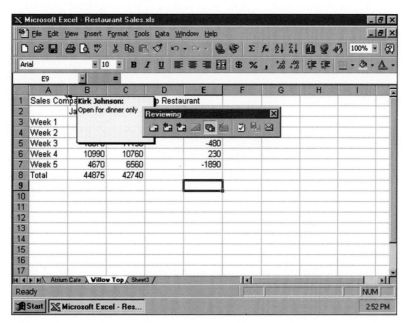

4 Click ☒ on the Reviewing toolbar.
The toolbar closes.

5 Choose View, Comments.
The comments are hidden.

> **Tip** Use the Find command to find text or values in comments by selecting Comments from the Look in drop-down list.

Checking Spelling

When you have made all the revisions in a worksheet, it is a good idea to check the spelling, especially since Excel 97 doesn't underline spelling errors as you make them (as Word 97 does).

> **Note** Even though Excel 97 doesn't check your spelling as you go, it does make automatic corrections for many typing errors.

TASK 10: TO CHECK THE SPELLING:

1 Click the Atrium Cafe tab.
The Atrium Cafe worksheet displays.

2 Click in cell A1 so that Excel 97 will begin its check of the spelling with cell A1.

3 Click the Spelling 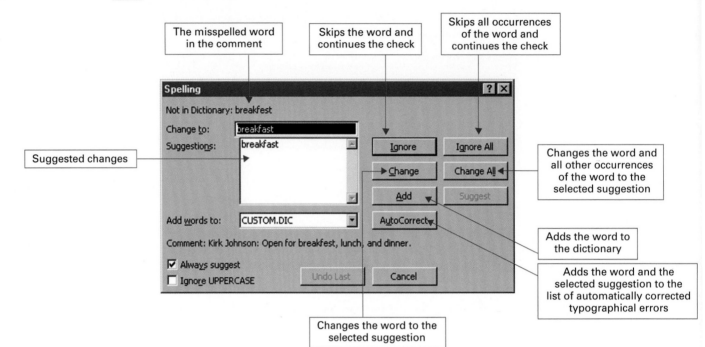 button.

The misspelled word in the comment

Skips the word and continues the check

Skips all occurrences of the word and continues the check

Suggested changes

Changes the word and all other occurrences of the word to the selected suggestion

Adds the word to the dictionary

Adds the word and the selected suggestion to the list of automatically corrected typographical errors

Changes the word to the selected suggestion

4 Choose Change.
If there is another word not found in the dictionary, Excel 97 lists it, but if there are no more words, a message displays telling you that the spell check is complete.

5 Click OK.
The worksheet redisplays.

> **Note** If you have used multiple worksheets, you must spell check each sheet individually. Sorry!

Conclusion

If you have time, you may want to spell check the other worksheets. Then save the file and close it.

Summary and Exercises

Summary

- The Find command finds specific text or values in a worksheet.
- You can edit the data in a cell or simply reenter the data.
- Excel 97 automatically recalculates formulas if the numbers in the cells change.
- When you copy data it is stored in the Clipboard.
- Comments provide additional information in a workbook.
- You can check the spelling of worksheets in a workbook.

Key Terms and Operations

Key Terms
AutoCalculate
Clipboard
comment

Operations
add comments
copy data
delete data
edit data
find data
move data
open a workbook
paste data
select cells
spell check a worksheet

Study Questions

Multiple Choice

1. A workbook's name may appear at the bottom of the File menu,
   a. if it is in the current path.
   b. if the workbook has multiple worksheets.
   c. unless it is on a floppy disk.
   d. if it has been opened recently.

2. To edit a cell, first
   a. select the cell.
   b. click in the formula bar.
   c. activate the edit mode.
   d. press F4.

3. The easiest way to select the entire worksheet is to
   a. triple-click in any cell.
   b. click the button above the row numbers and to the left of the column letters.
   c. drag the pointer through all the cells in the worksheet.
   d. select all the rows in the worksheet.

4. The Find command can find
   a. only text.
   b. only numbers.
   c. only cell addresses.
   d. text in comments.

5. The Spell Checker will
   a. not check all worksheets at once.
   b. not check comments.
   c. only start in the first cell of a worksheet.
   d. not add words to the dictionary.

6. When you press (DEL), the
   a. contents of the selected cells are erased.
   b. selected cells are removed from the worksheet.
   c. contents of the selected cells are stored in the Clipboard.
   d. same result is achieved as when you choose Edit, Delete.

7. The Find command
   a. searches only the current worksheet.
   b. searches all worksheets in the workbook.
   c. searches only formulas.
   d. is useful only in large worksheets.

8. Which of the following do not require pressing the (CTRL) key?
   a. non-adjacent columns
   b. non-adjacent rows
   c. adjacent columns
   d. selecting non-adjacent ranges.

9. To move data, use the
   a. Cut and Paste buttons.
   b. Copy and Paste buttons.
   c. Move and Paste buttons.
   d. Cut and Insert buttons.

10. A comment
   a. is attached to the worksheet.
   b. is attached to a cell.
   c. is only visible when you point to the cell.
   d. displays when you click a cell.

Short Answer

1. When you open a workbook, what is the location of the active cell?

2. How do you use the AutoCalculate feature?

3. What happens if you copy data to a range that already contains data?

4. What toolbar displays when you turn on the Comments view?

5. How would you select both Column C and the range A1 through A10?

6. How do you move data?

7. What happens to the data in the Clipboard when you copy new data?

8. What happens to the data in the Clipboard when you exit Excel 97?

9. How do you select several consecutive rows?

10. How do you insert a comment?

For Discussion

1. What do you do if you need to find all the formulas that reference cell B3?

2. Discuss the two methods of changing data in a cell and when you use each method.

3. Describe several scenarios in which comments are useful.

4. Describe several scenarios in which the AutoCalculate feature could be used.

Review Exercises

1. Revising the restaurant sales worksheet

In this exercise, you will revise the Restaurant Sales worksheet, revising data and adding a comment.

1. Open the workbook named *Restaurant Sales.xls*, unless it is already open.

2. Make the revisions (highlighted in yellow) shown in Figure 2.2.

3. Add a comment to cell A7 in the Atrium Cafe worksheet that says "This

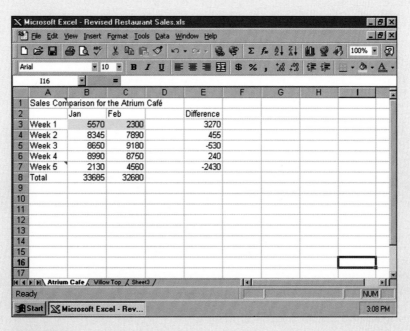

Figure 2.2

week had 4 days in January and 3 days in February."

4. Make sure the numbers on the January worksheet match the numbers on the Atrium Cafe and Willow Top worksheets.

5. Save the file as *Revised Restaurant Sales.xls* and close it.

2. Revising a timesheet

In this exercise, you will revise a timesheet workbook.

1. Ask your instructor how to obtain the file *Tmsheet.xls*. (If you have Internet access, you can download this file from the Addison Wesley Longman website at http://hepg.awl.com/select and follow the appropriate links).

2. Open the file and find the word "sum" in a formula in the Smith worksheet. Copy the formula to the next six cells on the right.

3. Delete the text in row 4.

4. Move the data in cell B1 to cell D1.

5. Copy A1:H9 to the same location in the Jones worksheet.

6. Save the file as *Times.xls* and close it.

3. Moving and copying data in a worksheet

1. Launch Excel and open *Container Corporation Sales xxx.xls* (where *xxx* represents your initials).

> **Note** If you do not have a workbook named *Container Corporation Sales xxx.xls*, ask your instructor for a copy of the file you should use to complete this exercise.

2. Make the following changes to the workbook:
- Delete *Multi-Size* from the name of the container company in Cell A1.
- Move the data in Columns C, D, and E and place the data in Columns D, E, and F.
- Copy the data in Columns A, B and F to the second and third worksheets in the workbook.
- Copy the data in Rows 4 and 10 to the second and third worksheets.
- Rename Sheet2 *<Last Year> Sales*, substituting last year's date as indicated.
- Rename Sheet3 *Sales Increase*.

3. Add a comment note that contains your name and the current date to Cell A1.

4. Spell check the workbook and make appropriate corrections.

5. Save the workbook using the filename *2 Container Corporation Sales xxx*.

6. Print a copy of each worksheet in the workbook and then close the workbook and exit Excel.

Assignments

1. Creating and revising a budget

Create a worksheet that lists expenses for your personal budget. List expense items in column A starting in row 4. List the projected amounts for the next three months in columns B through D. Total each month at the bottom of the column. Save the worksheet as *My Budget.xls*. Revise the amounts so they are more conservative. Move the totals to row 3. Add comments for expenses that need further explanation. Save the revised worksheet as *Lower Budget.xls*.

2. Tracking the American Stock Exchange (Optional Exercise)

Go to the web site http://www.amex.com and explore the site. Create a worksheet to track individual stocks or the market summary. Save the worksheet as *Amex.xls*. Check the site on several different days and add the information to the worksheet.

Enhancing the Appearance of a Workbook

Now that you can create and edit a worksheet, it's time for you to add a little pizzazz to the worksheet with various formatting techniques. In this project you will use borders and colors to give the worksheet a classy look.

Objectives

After completing this project, you will be able to:

➤ **Format text**
➤ **Change cell alignment**
➤ **Format numbers**
➤ **Format dates**
➤ **Format numbers as text**
➤ **Add borders and fill**
➤ **View and change a page break**
➤ **Use AutoFormat**

The Challenge

Mr. Williams, the manager of the golf and tennis property at The Willows, has created a worksheet named *Income.xls* that estimates the income for the upcoming Pro-Celebrity Tournament. He has entered all the data and formulas, but he wants you to format the worksheet so it looks better and is easier to read.

The Solution

You will open the workbook, format the numbers and dates, add a border to the important information and emphasize the totals with shading. Additionally, you will format and align the data in some of the cells and use AutoFormat to format a group of cells automatically. The formatted worksheet will look like Figure 3.1 when you are finished. (The Full Screen view is used in Figure 3.1.)

Before you can begin you must download *Income.xls* from the Addison Wesley Longman web site. The file can be found at http://hepg.awl.com/select. (Follow the appropriate links.). If you are unable to download, obtain the file from your instructor.

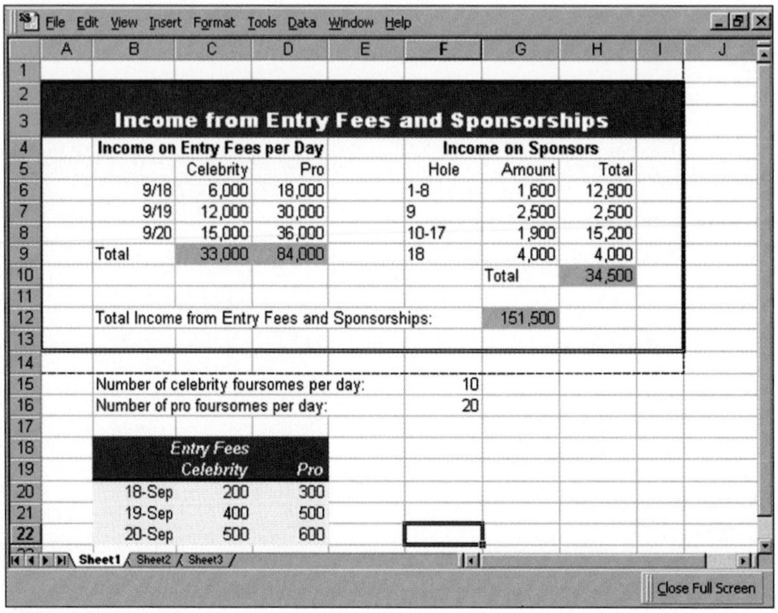

Figure 3.1

The Setup

So that your screen will match the illustrations in this chapter and to ensure that all the tasks in this project will function as described, you should set up Excel as described in Table 3.1. Because these are the default settings for the toolbars and view, you may not need to make any changes to your setup.

Table 3.1   Excel Settings

Location	Make these settings:
View, Toolbars	Deselect all toolbars except Standard and Formatting.
View	Use the Normal view and display the Formula Bar and Status Bar.

Formatting Text

You can format text in a number of ways. You can make it bold, italic, or underlined, or change the font, the font size, and the font color. The Formatting toolbar includes buttons for many of the text formatting options. Before you begin formatting the worksheet, you will save it as *Income2.xls* so you can use the original again later.

TASK 1: TO FORMAT TEXT:

1 Open *Income.xls* and choose File, Select the drive or folder, type *Income2.xls* in the filename text box and click Save.

2 Select cells D3, B4, and F4.

> Click the first cell to select it and then press Ctrl when you click the other cells

	A	B	C	D	E	F	G	H	I	J
1										
2										
3				Income from Entry Fees and Sponsorships						
4		Income on Entry Fees per Day				Income on Sponsors				
5			Celebrity	Pro		Hole	Amount	Total		
6		18-Sep	6000	18000		#1 - #8	1600	12800		
7		19-Sep	12000	30000		#9	2500	2500		
8		20-Sep	15000	36000		#10 - #17	1900	15200		
9		Total	33000	84000		#18	4000	4000		
10							Total	34500		
11										
12		Total Income from Entry Fees and Sponsorships:					151500			
13										
14										
15		Number of celebrity foursomes per day:					10			
16		Number of pro foursomes per day:					20			
17										

Microsoft Excel - Income 2.xls — F4 = Income on Sponsors — Sheet1 / Sheet2 / Sheet3 — Ready — NUM — Start   Microsoft Excel - Inc...   4:44 PM

3 Click the Bold **B** button.
The text in all three cells changes to bold.

4 Select cell D3. Click the drop-down arrow for Font Size and choose 12.
The text in the cell changes from 10 point to 12 point.

5   Click the drop-down arrow bar Font and choose Arial Black.

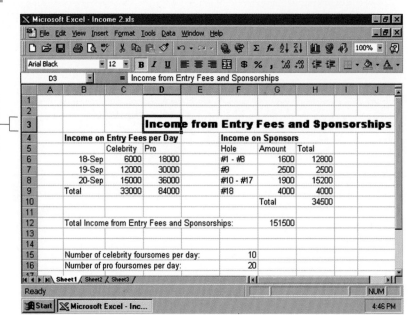

The height of the row increases automatically to accommodate the size of the font

Changing Cell Alignment

Data in a cell can be aligned on the left, in the center, or on the right. Each type of data that you enter uses a default alignment—text is left aligned and numbers and dates are right aligned.

You can change the alignment of data in a selected cell by clicking on one of the alignment buttons in the Formatting toolbar. Sometimes you may want to align data across several cells; for example, you might want to center a title in the first row so that the title spans the columns used in the worksheet. In this case, you can merge the cells into one wide cell, and then center the data in the wide cell.

TASK 2: TO CHANGE THE CELL ALIGNMENT:

1   Select A3:I3.
The cells are highlighted.

2   Choose Format.

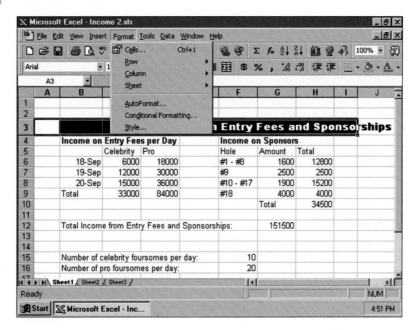

3   Choose Cells.

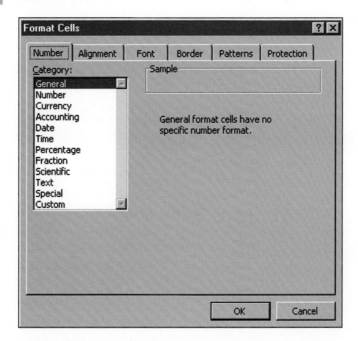

4   Click the Alignment tab.

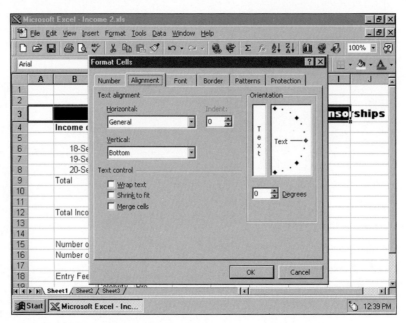

5   Choose Merge cells and click OK.
The cells become one cell.

6   Click the Center ≣ button on the Formatting toolbar.

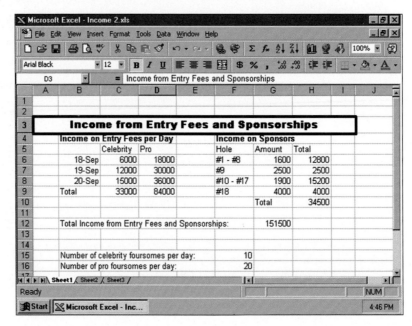

Tip To merge and center at the same time, select the cells and click the Merge and Center button ⊞.

7   Merge and align the remaining cells:
Merge the cells B4:D4 into one cell and center the text in the cell. Merge the cells F4:H4 into one cell and center the text in the cell. Center the text in cell F5. Select cells C5, D5, G5, and H5 and click the Align Right ≡ button.

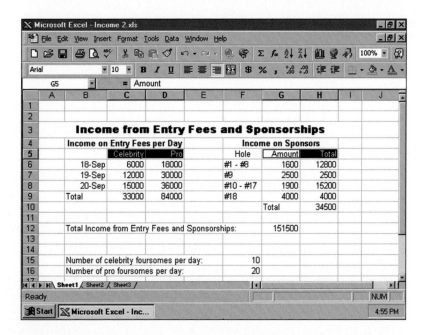

Formatting Numbers

The numbers you enter in a workbook can be "dressed up" with several different formats. As with text, you can make numbers bold, italic, change the font size, and font color. But there are other formatting options available for numbers. Table 3.2 describes the formats that are available in Excel and Figure 3.2 shows some examples.

Table 3.2   Number Formats

Format	Description
General	Numbers appear as entered except for fractions in the form of 1/2 which must be entered as **0 1/2**. Commas and decimal points can be entered with the numbers. If commas are not entered, they will not display automatically as in other formats. You can enter a minus or parentheses for negative numbers.
Number	Numbers have a fixed number of decimal places, comma separators can be displayed automatically, and negative numbers can be displayed with a minus, in red, with parentheses, or in red with parentheses.
Currency	Numbers have thousands separators and can have a fixed number of decimal places, a currency symbol, and negative numbers can be displayed with a minus, in red, with parentheses, or in red with parentheses.
Accounting	Numbers have thousands separators, a fixed number of decimal places, and can display a currency symbol. Currency symbols and decimal points line up in a column.
Date	Dates can display with numbers, such as 3/4/97 or 03/04/97, or with numbers and text, such as March 4, 1997 or March-97. Some date formats also display the time.
Time	Times can display as AM or PM or use the 24-hour clock, as in 13:15 for 1:15 PM. Some Time formats also display dates.
Percentage	Numbers are multiplied by 100 and display a percent sign.
Fraction	Numbers display as one, two, or three digit fractions.
Scientific	Numbers display as a number times a power of 10 (represented by E).
Text	Numbers display exactly as entered but are treated as text; therefore, the number would not be used in a calculation.
Special	These formats are used for zip codes, phone numbers, and social security numbers.
Custom	Numbers display in a format created by the user.

	A	B	C	D	E	
1	This column is formatted with the **General** Format which is the default.	This column is formatted with the **Number** format with two decimal places.	This column is formatted with the **Currency** format, two decimal places, a dollar sign, and negative numbers in red.	This column is formatted with the **Accounting** format and two decimal places.	This column is formatted with the **Scientific** format with two decimal places.	
3	1.37512349	1.38	$1.38	$ 1.38	1.38E+00	
4	1000000000	1000000000.00	$1,000,000,000.00	$ 1,000,000,000.00	1.00E+09	
5	-98	-98.00	$98.00	$ (98.00)	-9.80E+01	
6	12345.6	12345.60	$12,345.60	$ 12,345.60	1.23E+04	
7	10	10.00	$10.00	$ 10.00	1.00E+01	
8						

Figure 3.2

TASK 3: TO FORMAT NUMBERS:

1 Select cells C6:D9, G6:H9, H10, and G12.
The cells are highlighted.

2 Choose Format, Cells, click the Number tab, and select Currency from the Category list.

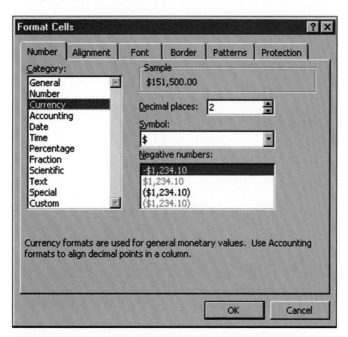

3 Select 0 for Decimal places and None for Symbol.

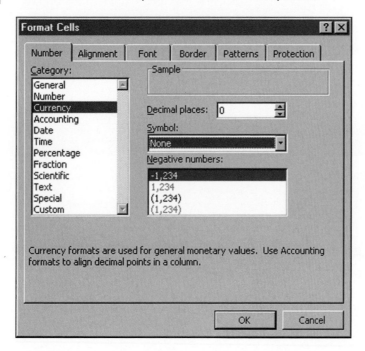

4 Click OK.
The format is applied.

Formatting Dates

The date format is included in the number formats because Excel stores dates as numbers. You can format dates in several ways. For example, if you enter the date 3/4/98, you can format it to look like any of the following:

3/4	Mar-98
3/4/98	March-98
03/04/98	March 4, 1998
4-Mar	M
4-Mar-98	M-98
04-Mar-98	

Some numbers that you enter are really text. For example, in Figure 3.1, shown on page 77 and again below, the range of 1–8 refers to holes 1 through 8 on the golf course. If you do not format "1–8" as text, Excel will interpret the entry as a date. You will learn how to format dates in Tasks 4 and 5.

File Edit View Insert Format Tools Data Window Help										
	A	B	C	D	E	F	G	H	I	J
1										
2										
3		**Income from Entry Fees and Sponsorships**								
4		**Income on Entry Fees per Day**				**Income on Sponsors**				
5			Celebrity	Pro		Hole	Amount	Total		
6		9/18	6,000	18,000		1-8	1,600	12,800		
7		9/19	12,000	30,000		9	2,500	2,500		
8		9/20	15,000	36,000		10-17	1,900	15,200		
9		Total	33,000	84,000		18	4,000	4,000		
10							Total	34,500		
11										
12		Total Income from Entry Fees and Sponsorships:					151,500			
13										
14										
15		Number of celebrity foursomes per day:				10				
16		Number of pro foursomes per day:				20				
17										
18			**Entry Fees**							
19			Celebrity	Pro						
20		18-Sep	200	300						
21		19-Sep	400	500						
22		20-Sep	500	600						

Sheet1 / Sheet2 / Sheet3

Close Full Screen

Figure 3.1

TASK 4: TO FORMAT DATES:

1 Select B6:B8.
The cells are highlighted.

2 Choose Format, Cells, and click on the Number tab (if necessary).
The default Date format is selected.

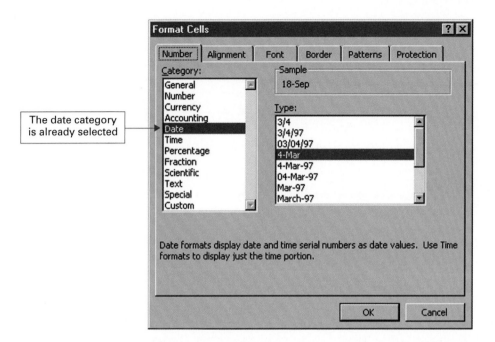

The date category is already selected

3 Select the first option from the Type list (3/4) and click OK.

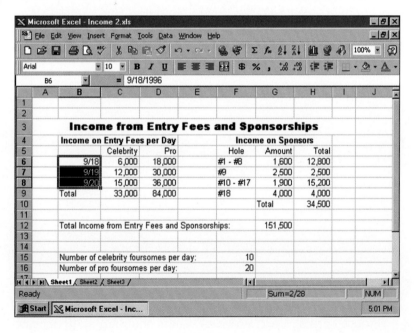

Formatting Numbers as Text

When you enter numbers with dashes or slashes in a worksheet, as we did in golf course holes 1–8 and 10–17 shown below, Excel interprets the entry as a date. To avoid this, you must format the numbers as text.

TASK 5: TO FORMAT NUMBERS AS TEXT:

1 Reenter the data in cells F6:F9 exactly as shown:
F6: **1 - 8**
F7: **9**
F8: **10 - 17**
F9: **18**

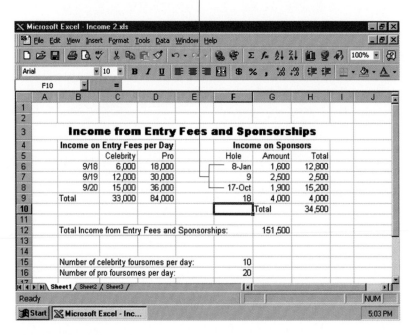

Excel has interpreted the text in these two cells as dates

2 Select cells F6:F9.
The cells are highlighted.

3 Choose Format, Cells, and click on the Number tab (if necessary). Select Text for the Category and click OK.

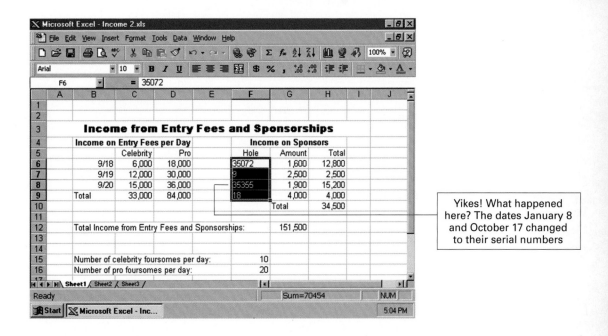

Yikes! What happened here? The dates January 8 and October 17 changed to their serial numbers

Note A serial number is a sequential number given to every day of every year since the turn of the century. So the number 35072 means that January 8, 1997 is the 35,072nd day of the 20th century.

4   Type **1 - 8** in cell F6. Type **10 - 17** in cell F8.

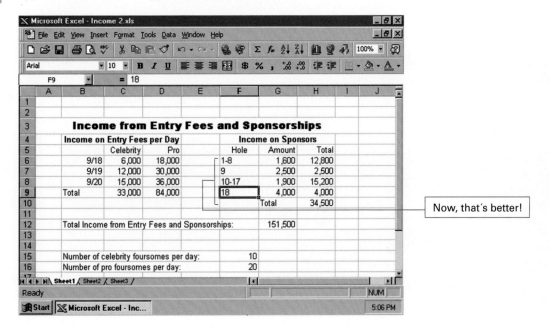

Now, that's better!

Adding Borders and Fill

A **border** is a line that displays on any side of a cell or group of cells. You can use borders in a variety of ways: to draw rectangles around cells, to create dividers between columns, to create a total line under a column of numbers, and so on.

Fill, also called **shading** or **patterns**, is a color or a shade of gray that you apply to the background of a cell. Use fill carefully if you do not have a color printer. Sometimes it doesn't look as good when it prints in black and white as it does on screen.

TASK 6: TO ADD A BORDER AND FILL:

1 Select cells A2:I13.
The cells are highlighted.

2 Choose Format, Cells, and click the Border tab.

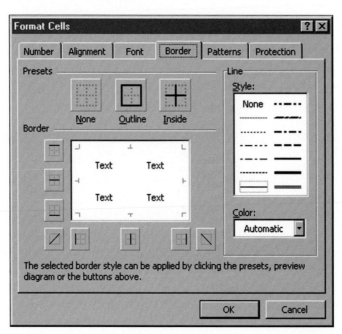

3 Select the double line in the Style box, click the Outline button, and click OK.

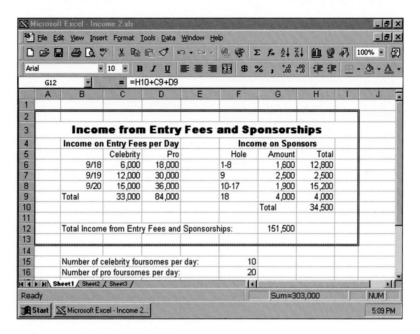

4   Select cells C9:D9, H10, and G12.
The cells are highlighted.

5   Choose Format, Cells, and click the Patterns tab.

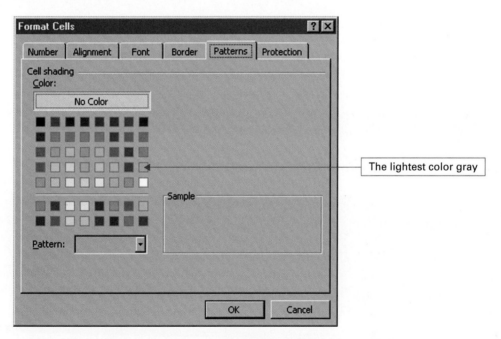

The lightest color gray

6   Select the lightest color gray and click OK.

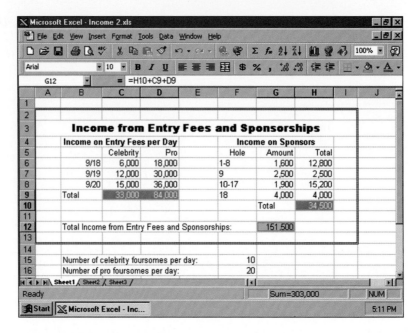

7 Select cells A2:I3 and format them with the first color on the second row of the color chart on the Patterns page.

The cells are shaded with the selected color, but you cannot tell because the cells are still selected.

> **Tip** You also can apply color by clicking the down arrow on the Fill Color 🏷️ · button on the Formatting toolbar and selecting a color from a smaller palette.

8 Select cell A3.

The cell is highlighted.

9 To change the text color, click the down arrow in the Font Color 🔺 · button and click the white rectangle in the color palette.

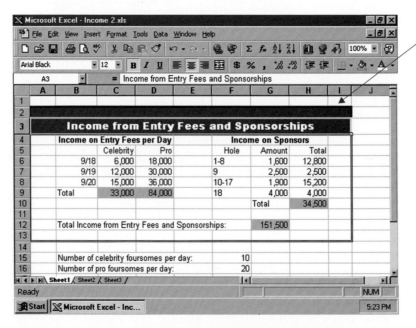

The border is in the same place, but it is hard to see because of the selected cells

Viewing and Changing a Page Break

Unlike word processing documents, worksheets are not represented on the screen by pages. The complete worksheet, all 16,777,216 cells of it, is one big page on the screen. So that you can see where the pages will break when the worksheet prints, Excel provides a *Page Break view*. You can adjust the location of the *page breaks* in this view.

TASK 7: TO VIEW THE PAGE BREAK IN THE INCOME WORKSHEET AND CHANGE IT:

1 Click the Print Preview button.

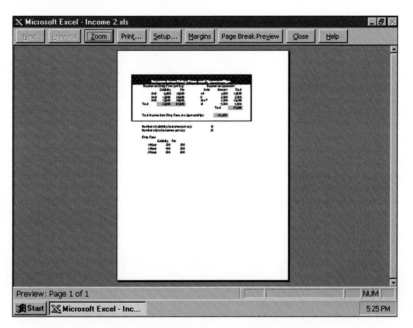

2 Click the Page Break Preview button. (Click OK if a message displays.)

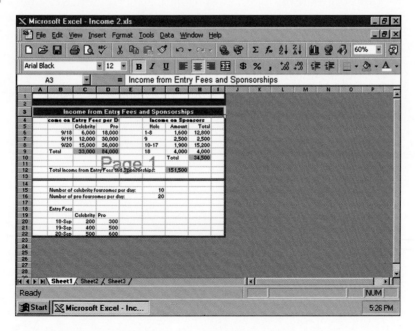

3   Drag the blue line at the bottom to just below row 14.

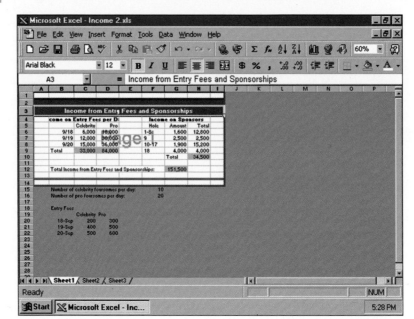

4   Click ▣.
Now, only the bordered text displays in the print preview for page 1.

5   Click the Normal View button.
The worksheet displays in Normal view. Notice that the page break location is indicated with a dotted line.

Using AutoFormat

Excel provides several formats that you can apply to a complete work-sheet or to a single range. The **AutoFormat** feature enables you to apply many formatting features automatically, creating very professional look-ing worksheets without much effort on your part. (Excel works hard so you don't have to.)

> **Note** AutoFormats are designed for worksheets or ranges that have row headings in the first column and column headings in the first row.

TASK 8: TO APPLY AN AUTOFORMAT:

1   Select B18:D22.
The cells are highlighted.

2   Choose Format, AutoFormat.

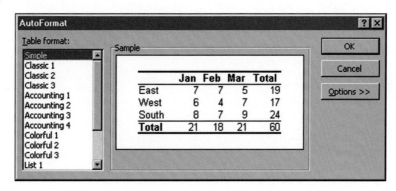

3   Select Colorful 2. Click Options, deselect Width/Height, and click OK. Click in a cell outside the selected range to see the true colors.

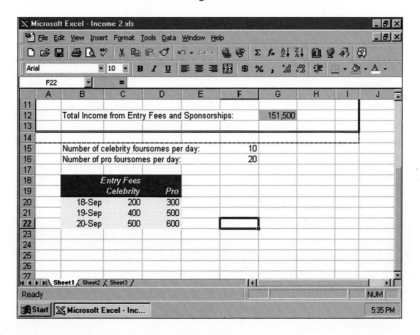

The Conclusion

If you have access to a printer, print page 1 of the worksheet. Save the workbook and close it.

Summary and Exercises

Summary

- You can format text with bold, italic, underline, different fonts and font sizes, and so on.
- Data in a cell can be left, right, or center aligned.
- Excel provides many formats for displaying numbers.
- You can apply a border to any side of a cell.
- You can apply a background color to a cell.
- You can apply a color to text.
- The Page Break view shows where page breaks are located.
- You can rearrange page breaks in the Page Break view.
- An AutoFormat can be applied to a worksheet or a range.

Key Terms and Operations

Key Terms	Operations
border	add a border
fill	add fill
page break	align cells
Page Break view	AutoFormat
pattern	change a page break
shading	format dates
	format numbers
	format text
	view a page break

Study Questions

Multiple Choice

1. If you type text in cell A1 and you want to center the text across cells A1 through A5,
   a. merge the cells and click the Center button.
   b. select A1:A5 and click the Center button.
   c. select A1:A5 and choose Format, Cells, Alignment, Center, and click OK.
   d. merge the cells, and choose Format, Align, Center.

2. You can apply an AutoFormat
   a. to a cell.
   b. only to a complete worksheet.
   c. to a single range.
   d. to noncontiguous ranges.

3. To make text bold,
   a. click in the cell, type the text, click the Bold button, and press Enter.
   b. select the cell and click the Bold button.
   c. select the cell and choose Format, Bold.
   d. All of the above.

4. Borders can be applied to
   a. any side of a range.
   b. all sides of a range.
   c. the top and bottom sides of a range.
   d. All of the above.

5. To add shading to a cell, select the cell and
   a. click the drop-down arrow on the Shading button and choose the color.
   b. choose Format, Cells, Shading, select the color, and click OK.
   c. choose Format, Cells, Patterns, select the color, and click OK.
   d. choose Format, Shading, select the color, and click OK.

6. A page break is marked with
   a. a dotted line in the worksheet.
   b. a blue line in the Print Preview.
   c. a dotted line in the Page Break Preview.
   d. a blue line in the worksheet.

7. Which of the following format(s) (if any) would be used to achieve this format: $ 1,200.00?
   a. general format with a dollar sign symbol and two decimal places
   b. accounting format with a dollar sign symbol and two decimal places
   c. currency format with a dollar sign symbol and two decimal places
   d. number format with a dollar sign symbol and two decimal places

8. When you increase the point size of text,
   a. you must first increase the height of the row.
   b. the text may wrap in the cell if the cell is not wide enough to accommodate the new size.
   c. the row height increases automatically to accommodate the size of the text.
   d. the cell width increases automatically to accommodate the size of the text.

9. The option to rotate text in a cell is found
   a. on the Orientation page of the Format Cells dialog box.
   b. on the Format menu.
   c. on the Rotate button in the Formatting Toolbar.
   d. on the Alignment page of the Format Cells dialog box.

10. Excel stores a date as
   a. a number.
   b. a date.
   c. text.
   d. a mixture of text and numbers.

Short Answer

1. How are numbers aligned in a cell?

2. How can you enter 1–2–97 and make it appear as January 2, 1997?

3. How do you change the font of the text entered in a cell?

4. How do you change the color of the text entered in a cell?

5. Under what circumstances do you have to format a cell as text?

6. How do you merge cells?

7. How are dates aligned in a cell?

8. The entry 1.2E103 is an example of what number format?

9. What is a serial number?

10. What is the default alignment for text in a cell?

For Discussion

1. Describe the AutoFormat feature and discuss the advantages of using it.

2. How can you designate where the pages will break when the worksheet prints?

3. Compare the Page Break Preview with the Print Preview view.

4. Give examples of ways you could use borders.

Review Exercises

1. Enhancing the restaurant sales worksheet

In this exercise, you will enhance the worksheet with border, shading, and number formats.

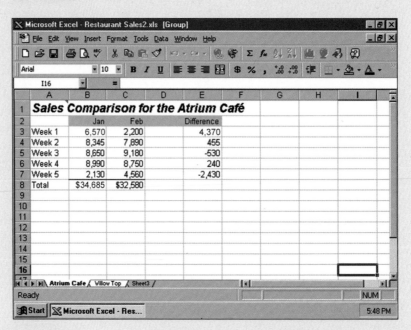

Figure 3.3

1. Open *Restaurant Sales.xls,* the file you saved at the end of Project 2.

2. Right align cells B2 and C2 on both worksheets.

3. Format all numbers on both worksheets (except for cells B8 and C8) with the Currency format, using no decimal places and no dollar sign. Format B8 and C8 on both worksheets with Currency, no decimal places, and a dollar sign.

4. Format cell A1 on both worksheets with bold, italic, 14 point.

5. Add a border to the bottom of cells B7 and C7 on both worksheets.

6. Add light gray fill to cells B2:E2 on both worksheets.

7. Save the file as *Restaurant Sales2.xls* and close it.

2. Creating a concert list

In this exercise, you will create a workbook for a list of concerts and enhance the worksheet with formatting.

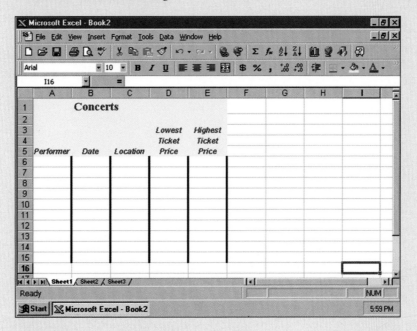

Figure 3.4

1. Go to http://www.ticketmaster.com and follow the link to the Box Office.

2. Search for at least 10 concerts by groups or performers that you like. Obtain information about when and where the concert will be and how much the tickets cost.

3. Create a worksheet based on Figure 3.4, with these column headings: Performer, Date, Location, Lowest Ticket Price, Highest Ticket Price.

4. Format the title with 14 point Times New Roman.

5. Format the column headings in bold, italic, 9 point and center them.

6. Use a thick border between each column.

7. Fill the range A1:E5 with light blue and change the color of the text in the range to dark blue.

8. Save the file as *Concerts.xls* and close it.

3. Enhancing the Container Corporation sales worksheet

1. Launch Excel and open *2 Container Corporation Sales xxx.xls* (where *xxx* represents your initials).

> **Note** If you do not have a workbook named *2 Container Corporation Sales xxx.xls*, ask your instructor for a copy of the file you should use to complete this exercise.

2. Make the following changes to all three worksheets in the workbook:
   - Center the data contained in Cells A1 and A2 across Columns A through F.
   - Change the color of text in Cells A1 and A2.
   - Format the text in Cell A1 to 26-point bold.
   - Format the text in Cell A2 to 16-point italics.
   - Format cells containing dollar values as Currency with 0 decimal points.
   - Center the column headings in Row 4 and add a fill color to cells containing data in Row 4.
   - Center the Produce #s in Column A and add a different fill color to cells containing product numbers.
   - Center the data contained in Column B across Columns B and C.

3. Save the workbook using the filename *3 Container Corporation Sales xxx* and print a copy of each worksheet.

Assignments

1. Reformatting the *Income.xls* File

Open the Income.xls file. Move the data in cells B15:F22 to cell A1 Sheet2. Format the data on Sheet1 using your own ideas for borders, shading, fonts, and so on. When finished, save the file as *Income 3.xls*.

2. Using AutoFormat

If you have Internet access, download *Revenues.xls* from http://hepg.awl.com/select. If you are unable to download this file, ask your instructor how to obtain it. Experiment with different AutoFormats. Choose one of the formats you like and save the file as *Revenues2.xls*. Open *Revenues.xls* again and save it with another format that you like as *Revenues3.xls*. Open *Revenues.xls* and save it with another format that you like as *Revenues4.xls*.

Editing the Structure of a Worksheet and a Workbook

Think of yourself as an Excel architect. You design workbooks using the Excel "materials" — cells, columns, rows, and worksheets. When you want to edit the structure of a worksheet or a workbook, you have to request that materials be added to or removed from the file. Sometimes the design you want calls for different-sized materials or special materials — such as headers and footers. This project introduces you to the tools you'll need to modify the structure of a worksheet.

Objectives

After completing this project, you will be able to:

➤ **Insert, delete, and arrange worksheets**

➤ **Change the size of columns and rows**

➤ **Insert columns, rows, and cells**

➤ **Delete columns, rows, and cells**

➤ **Create headers and footers**

The Challenge

You have a workbook that contains March and April restaurant sales information that you have been preparing for the hotel manager, Mr. Gilmore.

You need to delete some information, add some information, make some adjustments in the columns and rows, and add a header and footer.

The Solution

You will begin your edits by deleting one of the worksheets, inserting a new worksheet, and rearranging worksheets. Then you will adjust the width of columns and the height of rows as needed. Next, you will insert and delete columns, rows, and cells, and, finally, you will add the headers and footers. Figure 4.1 shows the first worksheet in the workbook.

To obtain the files you need for this project, download them from the Addison Wesley Longman web site (http://hepg.awl.com/select or obtain them from your instructor.

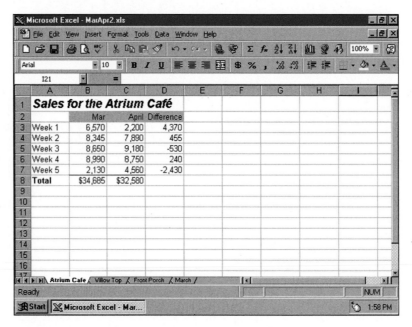

Figure 4.1

The Setup

So that your screen will match the illustrations and the tasks in this project will function as described, make sure that the Excel settings listed in Table 4.1 are selected on your computer. Because these are the default settings for the toolbars and view, you may not need to make any changes to your setup.

Table 4.1:   Excel Settings

Location	Make these settings:
View, Toolbars	Deselect all toolbars except Standard and Formatting.
View	Use the Normal view and display the Formula Bar and Status Bar.

Inserting, Deleting, and Arranging Worksheets

As you remember (if you don't remember, just keep it to yourself and no one will be the wiser), a workbook starts out with three worksheets. You can add more worksheets or delete up to two of the three. You also can re-arrange the order of worksheets.

TASK 1: TO INSERT AND DELETE PAGES:

1   Open *MarApr.xls.*

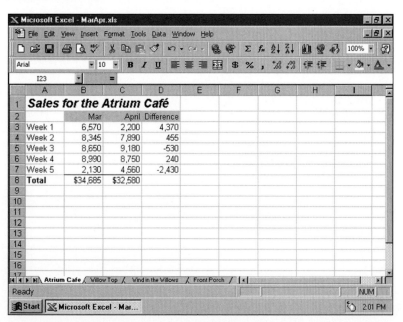

2   Click each worksheet tab to see each page of the workbook.

3   Right-click the tab for Wind in the Willows.

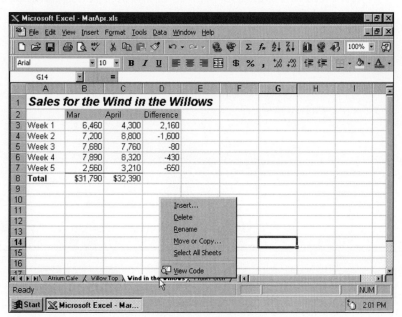

4 Choose Delete from the shortcut menu.

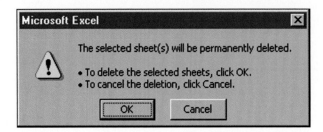

5 Click OK.
The worksheet is permanently deleted from the workbook, and no amount of clicking the Undo button will bring it back.

6 Right-click the Atrium Café tab and choose Insert from the shortcut menu.

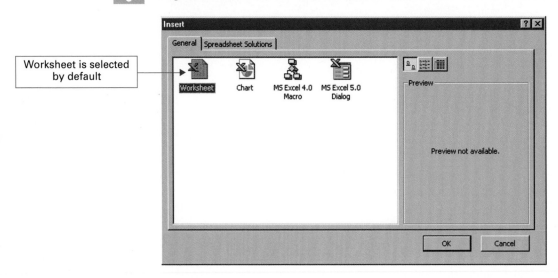

7 Click OK.
A new blank worksheet is inserted before the selected worksheet.

8 Rename the new worksheet **March**.

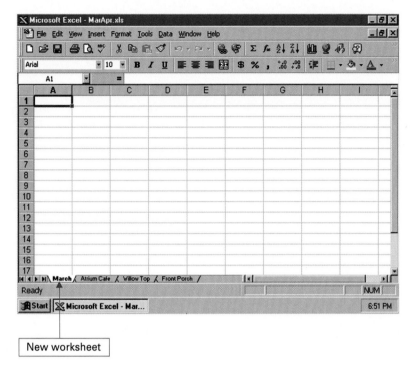

New worksheet

9 Drag the March tab to between the Atrium Café tab and the Willow Top tab, but don't release the mouse button yet.

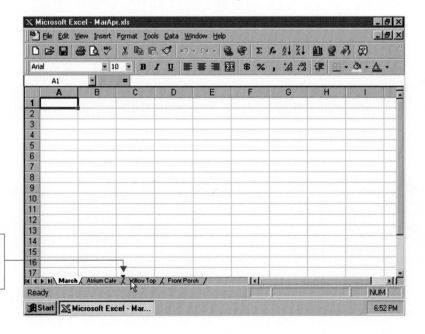

The black triangle marks the location where the new worksheet will be positioned

10 Continue dragging to the end of the tabs and then release the mouse button.

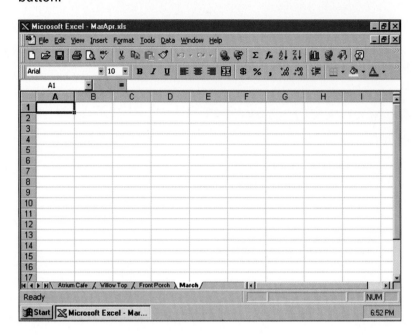

Changing the Size of Columns and Rows

When you create a new workbook, all the columns are the same width, and all the rows are the same height. When you add data to a worksheet, you often must change the row heights and column widths to accommodate the data. As you have already seen in a previous project, the height of a row increases or decreases automatically when you change the point size of the data; however, you may want to change the height of a row just to improve the spacing.

TASK 2: TO CHANGE THE WIDTH OF COLUMNS BY DRAGGING:

1 Type the following in the designated cells of the March worksheet:
A1: **March Sales**
A2: **Atrium Café**

> **Note** Excel will add the accent to the "e" in "café" automatically.

A3: **Willow Top Restaurant**
A4: **Front Porch Restaurant**

2   Point to the line that divides column letters A and B in the Column heading row.

The pointer changes to a double-headed arrow

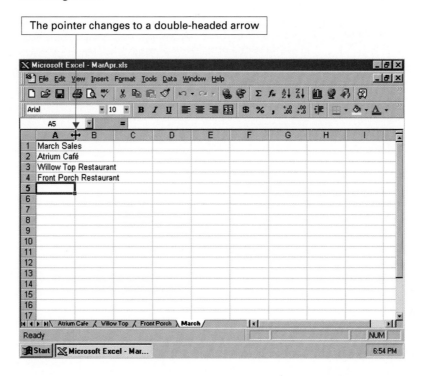

3   Drag the line to the right until the column is wide enough to hold the text.

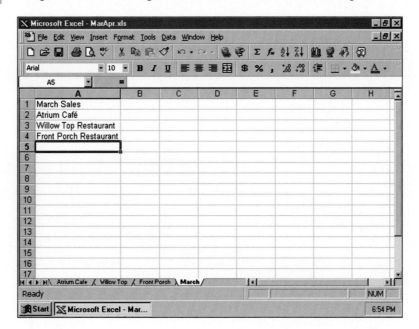

4 Drag the column until it is too wide as shown:

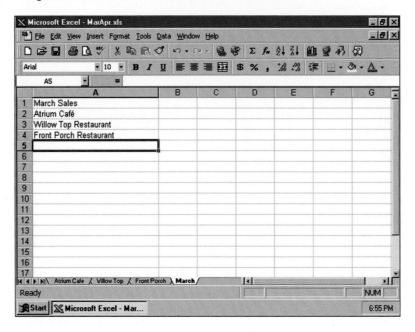

5 Type the following in the designated cells:
B2: **34685**
B3: **45240**
B4: **30835**

6 Drag the line between column letters B and C until column B is too wide as shown:

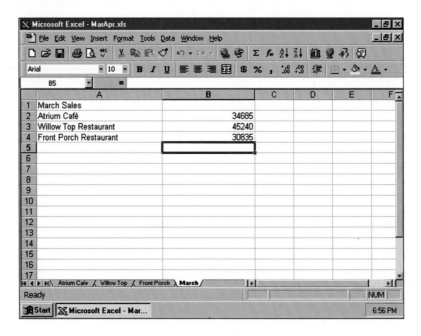

Using AutoFit

Another way to change the width of a column is to use AutoFit. **AutoFit** automatically adjusts columns to be just wide enough to accommodate the widest entry and can adjust the widths of several columns at once.

TASK 3: TO CHANGE THE WIDTH OF COLUMNS BY USING AUTOFIT:

1 Select columns A and B by dragging the mouse pointer through A and B at the top of the columns.
The columns are highlighted.

2 Choose Format, Column.

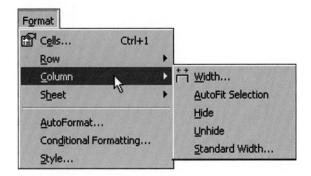

3 Choose AutoFit Selection.

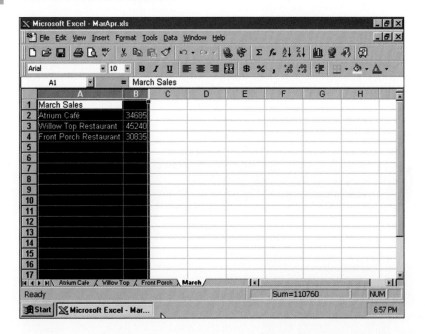

> **Tip** You can select multiple columns and double-click the line between the column letters to AutoFit the selections.

Adjusting Row Height

If you want to control the spacing in a worksheet, you can make rows taller or shorter by dragging them to the desired height.

TASK 4: TO CHANGE THE HEIGHT OF ROWS:

1 Point to the line that divides row numbers 1 and 2 in the row indicators column.

The pointer changes to a double-headed arrow

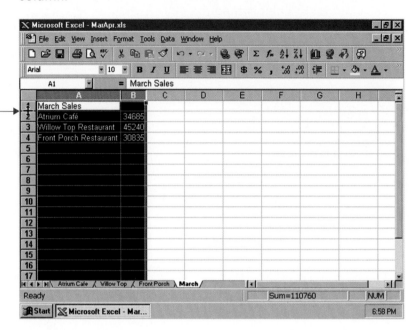

It doesn't matter if columns are selected when you change the row height because you don't have to select anything to change the height.

2 Drag down to make the row taller.

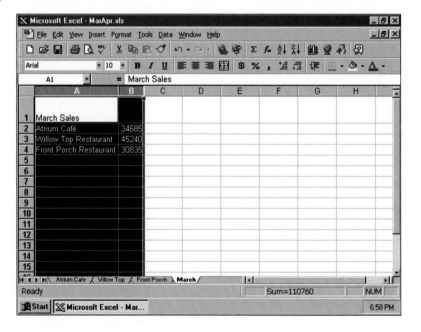

Tip You also can size rows with AutoFit. As you probably can guess, the command is under Format, Row or you can select the rows and double-click the line between the row numbers.

Inserting Columns, Rows, and Cells

When you insert a column, all the other columns move to the right to give the new column room. When you insert rows, all the other rows move down, and when you insert cells, the other cells move to the right or move down. Excel is so polite!

TASK 5: TO INSERT A COLUMN, A ROW, AND A CELL:

1   Click anywhere in column A.
The cell is selected.

2   Choose Insert.

3   Choose Columns.

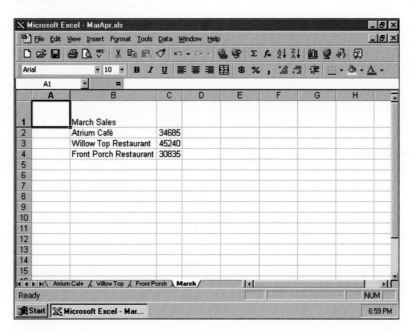

Tip To insert multiple columns, select the number of columns you want to insert in the location where you want to insert them, and then choose Insert, Columns.

4   Click anywhere in row 2.
The cell is selected.

5   Choose Insert, Rows. (The new rows take on the dimensions of the row above.)

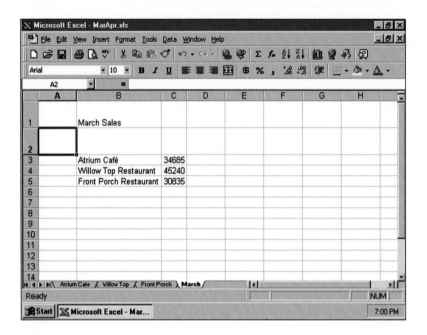

Tip To insert multiple rows, select the number of rows you want to insert in the location where you want to insert them, and then choose Insert, Rows.

6 Type the following in the designated cells:
D1: **March Banquets**
D3: **D.A.R.**
D4: **L.W.V.**
D5: **B.S.A**
E3: **2560**
E4: **1500**
E5: **900**

7 Select cells D4 and E4.

8 Choose Insert, Cells.

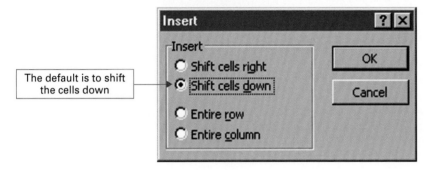

The default is to shift the cells down

9 Click OK.

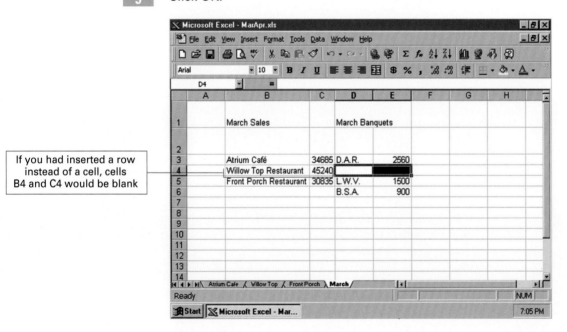

If you had inserted a row instead of a cell, cells B4 and C4 would be blank

10   Type **G.S.A.** in cell D4, press ⊕, type **950**, and press (ENTER).

```
X Microsoft Excel - MarApr.xls                                    _ 5 X
 File  Edit  View  Insert  Format  Tools  Data  Window  Help       _ 5 X

 D 🖆 🖬  🖨 🗅 ✎   ✕ 🗎 🖺 ⬩   ⭮ ▾ ⭯ ▾   🗐 ⭐ Σ ƒ ᷂ ↓ ᷂↑  🔲 🌐 ⥅ 🗒

 Arial         ▾ 10 ▾   B  I  U   ▤ ▤ ▤ ▦   $ %  ,  ⁍⁌ ⁍⁌  ⥯  ▦ ▾ 🎨 ▾ A ▾
      E5        ▾        =  1500
      A         B              C      D         E      F      G      H

 1             March Sales           March Banquets

 2
 3             Atrium Café      34685 D.A.R.      2560
 4             Willow Top Restaurant 45240 G.S.A.  950
 5             Front Porch Restaurant 30835 L.W.V. 1500
 6                                  B.S.A.       900
 7
 8
 9
 10
 11
 12
 13
 14
 |◄ ◄ ► ►|\ Atrium Cafe / Willow Top / Front Porch \ March /   |◄|            ►|
 Ready                                                      NUM

 🟦 Start   X Microsoft Excel - Mar...                              7:06 PM
```

Deleting Columns, Rows, and Cells

When you delete columns, rows, or cells, you actually cut the space they occupy out of the worksheet. You don't just delete the data they contain.

> **Caution** When you delete a column or row, the entire column or the entire row is deleted. Before deleting, be sure that the column or row doesn't contain data in a location that is off screen.

TASK 6: TO DELETE A COLUMN, A ROW, AND A CELL:

1   Select row 2 by clicking the row 2 button — at the left of the row. The row is highlighted.

2   Choose Edit, Delete.

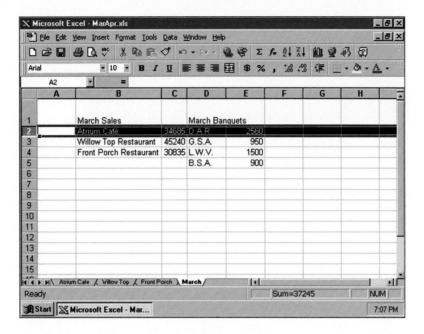

3   Select column A by clicking the column button A above the column. The column is highlighted.

4   Choose Edit, Delete.

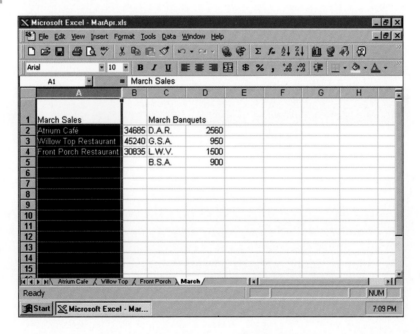

5 Select cells C2 and D2 and choose Edit, Delete.

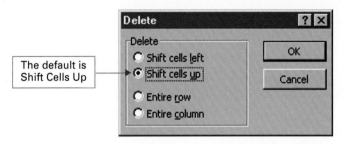

6 Click OK.

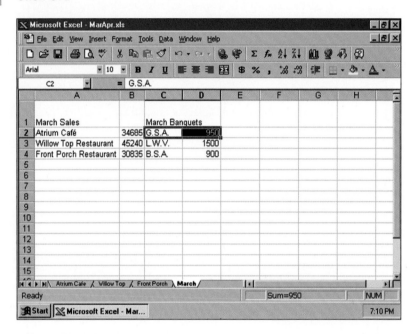

Creating Headers and Footers

A *header* prints at the top of every page of a worksheet, and a *footer* prints (you guessed it) at the bottom of every page. If the workbook has multiple worksheets, you can create headers and footers for each worksheet. A header or footer created for one worksheet doesn't print on any other worksheets in the same workbook.

TASK 7: TO CREATE A SIMPLE HEADER AND A FOOTER:

1 Choose View.

2 Choose Header and Footer.

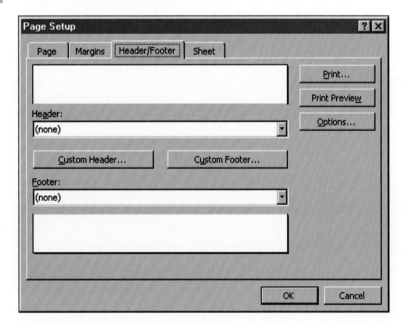

3 Click the down arrow for the Header list and choose Page 1.

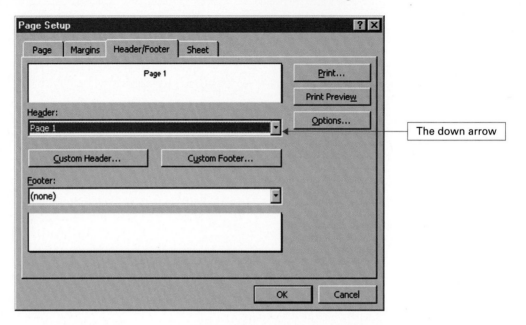

4 Click the down arrow for the Footer list and choose MarApr.xls.

5 Click Print Preview.

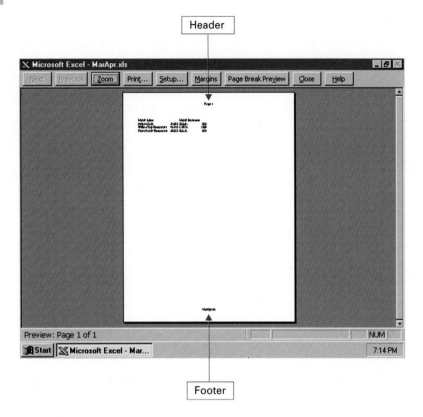

6 Click Close.
The preview closes, and the worksheet displays in Normal view.

Creating a Custom Header and Footer

If you don't want to use the text supplied for a simple header or footer, you can create a custom header or footer and type the text that you want. Custom headers and footers are divided into three typing areas. The area on the left is left-justified, the area in the middle is centered, and the area on the right is right-justified.

TASK 8: TO CREATE A CUSTOM HEADER AND FOOTER:

1 Click the Atrium Café tab.
The Atrium Café worksheet displays.

2 Choose View, Headers and Footers. The Page Setup dialog box displays.

3 Click Custom Header.

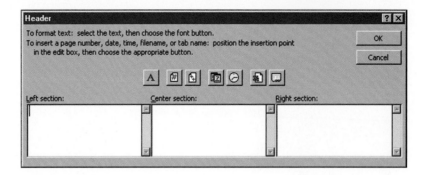

4 Type **Sales Report** in the left section, press (TAB) twice, and click the Date button. (When you click the Date button instead of typing the date, Excel adjusts the date to the current date each time the workbook is used.)

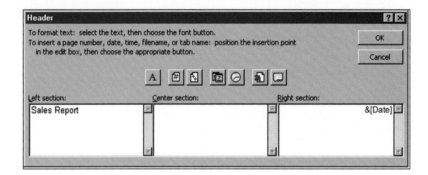

5 Click OK.
The Header dialog box closes and the Page Setup dialog box reappears.

6 Click Custom Footer.

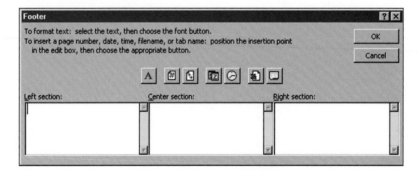

7 Press (TAB) and type **Prepared by Accounting** in the center section.

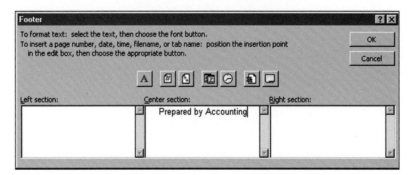

8   Click OK.
The Footer dialog box closes.

9   Click Print Preview.

Custom header

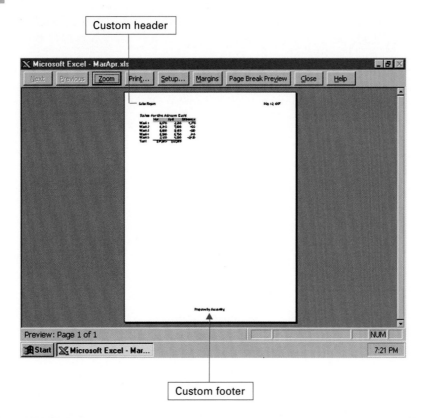

Custom footer

10   Click Close.
The Print Preview closes, and the worksheet displays in Normal view.

The Conclusion

Save the worksheet as *MarApr2.xls* and close the file.

Summary and Exercises

Summary

- You can insert and delete worksheets, as well as rearrange them.
- You can change the width of columns and the height of rows.
- You can insert columns, rows, and cells.
- You can delete columns, rows, and cells.
- You can create a header that prints at the top of the page and a footer that prints at the bottom of a page. Headers and footers do not appear on screen in Normal view.

Key Terms and Operations

Key Terms	Operations
AutoFit	change the height of a row
footer	change the width of a column
header	create a footer
	create a header
	delete a cell
	delete a column
	delete a row
	delete a worksheet
	insert a cell
	insert a column
	insert a row
	insert a worksheet
	move a worksheet

Study Questions

Multiple Choice

1. A header prints at the
   a. top of every page in a workbook.
   b. bottom of every page in a workbook.
   c. top of every page in a worksheet.
   d. bottom of every page in a worksheet.

2. When you delete a column,
   a. the data in the column is deleted but the cells remain in the worksheet.
   b. the data in the column is deleted and so are the cells.
   c. the column is really just hidden.
   d. the column is moved to the end of the worksheet.

3. When you insert a cell, the other cells move
   a. down.
   b. to the left.
   c. to the right.
   d. down or to the right, as specified by the user.

4. A footer prints at the
   a. top of every page in a workbook.
   b. bottom of every page in a workbook.
   c. top of every page in a worksheet.
   d. bottom of every page in a worksheet.

5. AutoFit can adjust the width of
   a. only one column at a time.
   b. only a row.
   c. columns or rows.
   d. the page.

6. A custom header
   a. is divided into three typing areas.
   b. is created by choosing Format, Header and Footer.
   c. isn't visible in Print Preview mode.
   d. only uses default data, such as the page number or the name of the file.

7. If you delete a cell,
   a. the data is deleted.
   b. the cell is deleted and the data displays in the next cell.
   c. the data and the cell are deleted.
   d. None of the above.

8. When you delete a cell, the other cells move
   a. up.
   b. down.
   c. to the left.
   d. up or to the left, as specified by the user.

9. When you drag to change the column width, the pointer displays as
   a. a four-headed arrow.
   b. an arrow.
   c. a two-headed arrow.
   d. a hand.

10. To insert a column, first
    a. select the column where you want the new column to go.
    b. click in the column where you want the new column to go.
    c. A or B
    d. None of the above.

Short Answer

1. How do you insert multiple rows?

2. How do you insert multiple columns?

3. What is a custom header?

4. How do you delete a worksheet?

5. How do you delete a row?

6. How do you delete a cell?

7. How do you create a header with the filename in the center?

8. If the row height adjusts automatically, why would you need to change the height of a row?

9. How do you move a worksheet?

10. How do you see a header or footer without actually printing the worksheet?

For Discussion

1. When would it be an advantage to use AutoFit instead of dragging columns to change the width?

2. Discuss the advantages of using a custom header or footer.

3. Describe a circumstance in which it would be preferable to insert a cell instead of a row.

4. What precautions should you take before deleting a column or a row?

Review Exercises

1. Editing the *MarApr2* workbook

In this exercise you will enhance the worksheet and create a footer.

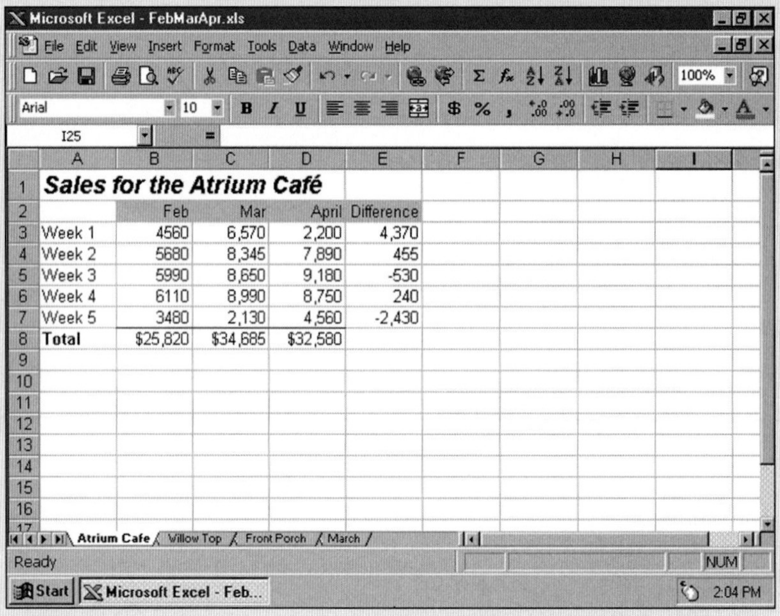

Figure 4.2

1. Open *MarApr2.xls* and click the Atrium Café tab, if necessary.

2. Insert a column before column B and type this information:

    B2: **Feb**

    B3: **4560**

    B4: **5680**

    B5: **5990**

    B6: **6110**

    B7: **3480**

    B8: **=SUM(B3:B7)**

3. Apply a gray fill to cell B2, apply a border to the bottom of cell B7, and format cell B8 with a Currency format (no decimal places) and remove the bold.

4. Create a footer for the Willow Top worksheet that says "Located in The Grande Hotel" and center the footer.

5. Save the file as *FebMarApr.xls* and close it.

2. Creating a sales workbook for the sandwich shops and snack bars
In this exercise, you will create a workbook that can be used to track the sales of all the sandwich shops and snack bars at The Willows Resort.

1. Download the file *Willows.doc* from the Addison Wesley Longman web site (http://hepg.awl.com/select), or ask your instructor for this file. Open the file and find the list of sandwich shops and snack bars.

2. Create a workbook with a worksheet for each of the nine shops and name each worksheet with the name of the shop.

3. Type a title on each worksheet that says "Sales for *xxx*," where *xxx* is the name of the sandwich shop or snack bar. In column A, starting in cell A3, list the weeks in the month (Week 1, Week 2, and so on) and the word "Total" (as in Figure 4.2). In cells B2, C2, and D2, list the first three months of the year (Jan, Feb, and Mar).

4. Create a footer with a centered page number for each worksheet.

5. Save the file as *ShopSales.xls*.

3. Editing and enhancing the Container Corporation sales worksheet

1. Launch Excel and open the workbook *3 Container Corporation Sales xxx.xls*.

> **Note** If you do not have a workbook named *3 Container Corporation Sales xxx.xls*, ask your instructor for a copy of the file you should use to complete this exercise.

2. Make the following changes to the Sales Increase worksheet:
   • Move the *Sales Increase* worksheet so that it appears as the first worksheet in the workbook.
   • Search for the word Actual and replace it with the current year.
   • Search for the word Expected and replace it with the last year.

3. Copy the *<Last Year> Sales* worksheet to create a new worksheet at the end of the workbook.

4. Rename the worksheet *Projected <Next Year> Sales*.

5. Delete the *Sales Increase* worksheet.

6. Make the following changes to all worksheets in the workbook:
   • Change the data in Cell B4 to *Product Description*.
   • Change the width of Column C to accommodate the new column heading.
   • Change the height of Row 5 and Row 10 so that there is more room between Row 4 and Row 5 and between Row 9 and 10.

- Add a bottom border to Cells D9, E9, and F9 and center the word *Total* in bold in Cell A10.

- Change the fill color for cells in Row 10 to the same color added to Cells A5–A9.

7. Save the workbook using the filename *4 Container Corporation Sales xxx*.

8. Add a header that contains your name right aligned to the workbook and print a copy of each worksheet in the workbook.

Assignments

1. Creating a banquet workbook

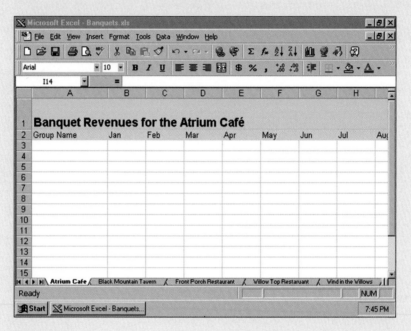

Figure 4.3

Create a workbook with five worksheets and name each worksheet as follows: Atrium Café, Willow Top Restaurant, Wind in the Willows, Front Porch Restaurant, and Black Mountain Tavern. Arrange the worksheets in alphabetical order. Add the text and formatting shown in Figure 4.3 to all the worksheets. (Remember, you can enter the same data on multiple worksheets at the same time.) Save the file as *Banquets.xls* and close it.

2. Creating a shopping list (Optional Exercise)

Take an international shopping trip via the Planet Shopping Network (http://www.planetshopping.com). Create a workbook that lists the items you would like to buy, their prices (including any shipping, handling, taxes, and duties), and their Web addresses. Use the SUM formula to total the prices and other costs. Create a worksheet for each shopping category (apparel, books, music, jewelry, automobiles, and so on). Save the workbook as *ShopTilYouDrop.xls*.

Creating a More Complex Workbook

Well, you're getting pretty good at this, so you're probably ready for something more challenging. This project provides both challenge and fun.

Objectives

After completing this project, you will be able to:

➤ **Copy data from another workbook**

➤ **Sort data**

➤ **Enter formulas with relative references**

➤ **Use headings in formulas**

➤ **Enter formulas with absolute references**

➤ **Create and modify a chart**

The Challenge

Ruth Lindsey, the manager of most of the gift shops at The Willows Resort, would like for you to work on an inventory of the ten top selling items and create some charts for the first quarter sales.

The Solution

You will copy data from an existing workbook into the inventory workbook, enter new data, and create formulas to calculate the number of items that you need to order and the wholesale prices of the items. Additionally, you will create a chart for the first quarter sales and a chart for the January sales. Figure 5.1 shows the results.

You can download the files needed for this project form the Addison Wesley Longman web site (http://www.aw.com./is/select) or you can obtain them from your instructor.

The Setup

So that your screen will match the illustrations in this chapter and to ensure that all the tasks in this project will function as described, you should set up Excel as described in Table 5.1. Because these are the default settings for the toolbars and view, you may not need to make any changes to your setup.

Table 5.1: Excel Settings

Location	Make these settings:
View, Toolbars	Deselect all toolbars except Standard and Formatting.
View	Use the Normal view and display the Formula Bar and Status Bar.

Copying Data from Another Workbook

You have copied data from one range to another on the same worksheet, and you have copied data from one worksheet to another in the same workbook. Now you will copy data from one workbook to another. The procedure is very similar to what you have already learned.

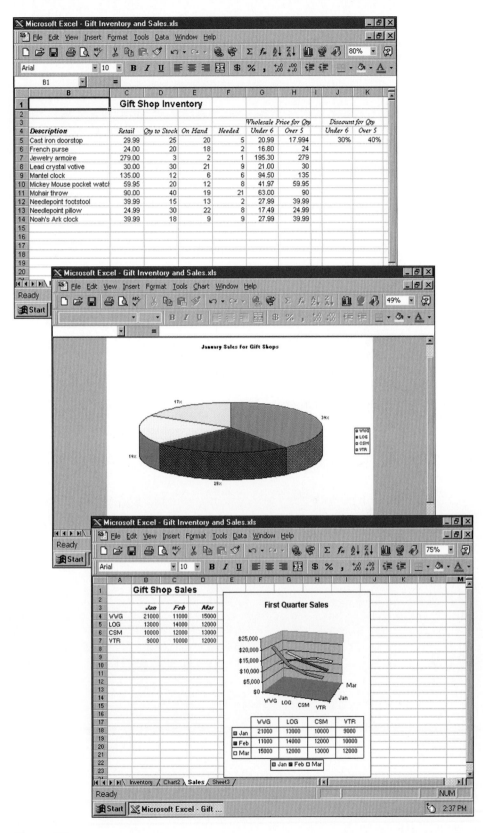

Figure 5.1

TASK 1: TO COPY DATA FROM ANOTHER WORKBOOK:

1 Open *Giftinv.xls*.

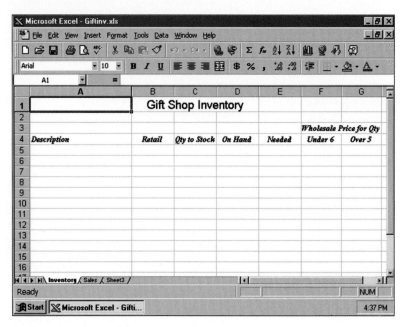

2 Open *TopTen.xls* and select the range A4:B13.

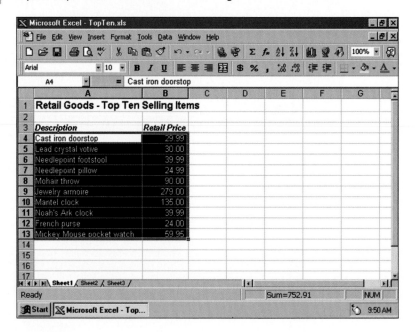

3 Click 📋.
The data is copied to the Clipboard.

4 Choose Window from the menu bar and then choose Giftinv.xls.
The *Giftinv.xls* workbook displays.

5   Click in cell A5 and click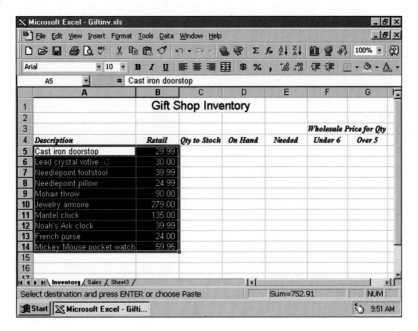

6   Choose Window, TopTen.xls.
The *TopTen.xls* workbook displays.

7   Click ❌ in the menu bar.
The *TopTen.xls* workbook closes, and the Giftinv.xls workbook displays.

Sorting Data

You can sort columns of data in an Excel worksheet in ascending order or descending order. The Standard toolbar has a button for each function.

TASK 2: TO SORT DATA:

1   Make sure that the range A5:B14 is still selected.
When you sort data, you must be careful to select all the columns that should be included in the sort. When selecting the rows to include, don't include the row with the column headings.

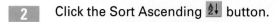

2   Click the Sort Ascending 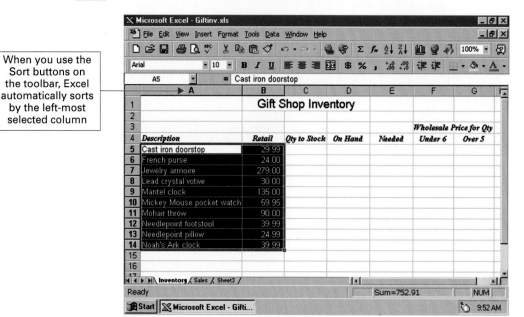 button.

When you use the
Sort buttons on
the toolbar, Excel
automatically sorts
by the left-most
selected column

Tip If you want to sort a range by any column other than the first column, you must use the Sort command on the Data menu. This command displays a dialog box that allows you to specify the column you want to sort on and the order of the sort. You also can specify two other columns to sort on after the first column is sorted. Check it out. Choose Data, Sort to see the dialog box.

Entering Formulas with Relative References

All the formulas you have used so far have included cell addresses that are relative references. A *relative reference* is an address that Excel automatically changes when the formula is copied to another location to make it true for its new location. For example, if the formula =A1+A2 is in cell A3 and you copy it to cell B3, Excel changes the formula in column B to refer to the corresponding cells in column B, and the formula becomes =B1+B2. Generally, this is precisely what you want, and you are happy that Excel can make such intelligent decisions on its own.

Perhaps you are wondering how this works. Here's the scoop: Excel doesn't interpret a relative cell address in a formula as the actual cell address but rather as a location relative to the location of the formula. For example, Excel interprets the formula =A1+A2 in cell A3 as "Add the cell that is two rows above the formula in the same column to the cell that is one row above the formula in the same column." Therefore, when you copy the formula to any other column, the formula will add the cells that are two rows and one row above the location of the formula.

TASK 3: TO ENTER AND COPY A FORMULA WITH RELATIVE ADDRESSES:

1 Enter the following data in the *Qty to Stock* column and the *On Hand* column so that you can write a formula to calculate the value for the *Needed* column.

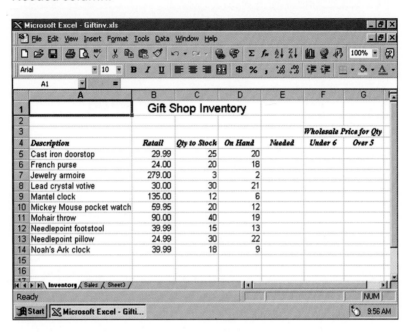

2 Click in cell E5, type **=C5–D5**, and press (ENTER).

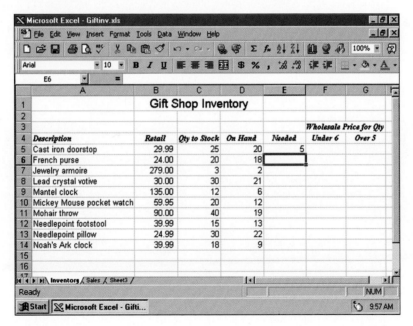

3 Copy cell E5 to the range E6:E8.

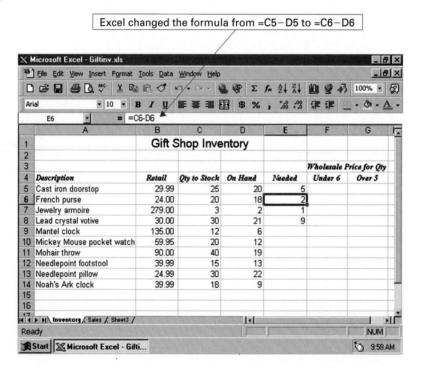

Click + drag lower right corner

4 Click in cell E6 and notice the formula in the formula bar.

Excel changed the formula from =C5−D5 to =C6−D6

Using Headings in Formulas

Using headings in formulas instead of cell addresses is a new feature in Excel 97. The *headings* feature is helpful in two ways: when you create a formula, you can think in logical terms (such as "quantity times cost") and you can easily recognize the purpose of the formula. When you see the formula "Quantity*Cost," you know immediately what it does, but the formula A1*B1 gives you very little information.

TASK 4: TO ENTER A FORMULA THAT USES HEADINGS:

1 Click in cell E9, type **=qty to stock−on hand**, and press ⟨ENTER⟩.
The cell displays the correct calculation.

> **Tip** You do not have to capitalize the headings in formulas, but spelling and spaces must be exact.

2 Copy cell E9 to the range E10:E14.
The range also displays the correct calculations relative to the rows.

3 Click in cell E10 and look at the formula in the formula bar.
The formula in cell E10 is the same as in E9.

Entering Formulas with Absolute References

As you have already seen, when formulas with relative references are copied, the cell addresses change appropriately; however, sometimes formulas refer to a cell or range that should never be changed when the formula is copied. To prevent the cell or range address from changing, you must make the address an *absolute reference*. An absolute reference is denoted with the dollar sign symbol, as in $A$1.

TASK 5: TO ENTER AND COPY A FORMULA WITH AN ABSOLUTE REFERENCE:

1 Scroll the worksheet so that columns B through J are visible.

2 Click in cell F5, type **=B5−(B5*I5)**, and press ⟨ENTER⟩.
This formula calculates the wholesale price of the item using the discount that applies if you are ordering a quantity of less than six. The wholesale price is the retail price minus the discount (which is determined by multiplying the retail price by 30%).

3 Copy cell F5 to F6.
The answer is obviously not correct.

4 Click in cell F6 and look at the formula in the formula bar.

Excel changed the formula to =B6−(B6*I6).
The reference to B6 is correct, but the reference to I6 isn't.

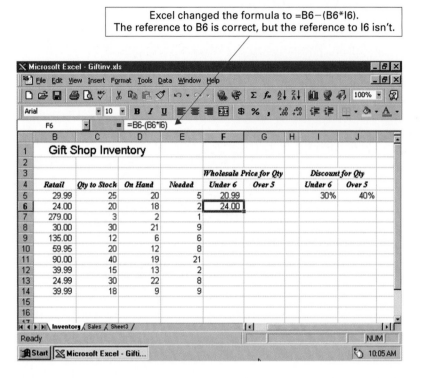

5 Edit the contents of cell F5 and insert dollar signs before and after "I" so the formula looks like **=B5−(B5*$I$5)** and press ENTER.
The result in cell F5 is the same as before, but watch what happens when you copy it.

6 Copy cell F5 to the range F6:F13.

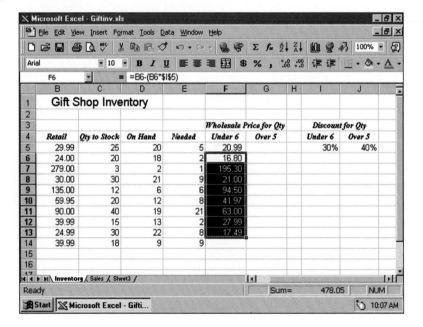

Pointing to Enter Absolute References

In the previous task, you typed the complete formula in the cell, but, as you have seen in other projects, you can enter a formula with the pointing method. When you use this method, you can designate an absolute reference with the F4 key.

TASK 6: TO ENTER A FORMULA WITH AN ABSOLUTE REFERENCE USING THE POINTING METHOD:

1   Click in cell F14, type an equal sign (=), move to cell B14 using ←, and then type a minus sign followed by an open parenthesis.

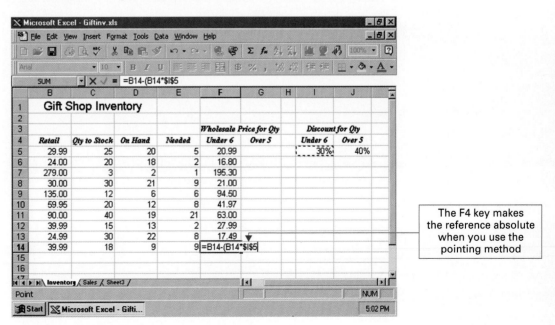

2   Move to cell B14 again, type an asterisk (*),move to cell I5, and then press F4.

The F4 key makes the reference absolute when you use the pointing method

3 Type a closing parenthesis and press (ENTER).
The correct calculation (27.99) displays in the cell.

Using Headings with Absolute References

The heading feature in Excel 97 also works with absolute references. When designating an absolute reference for a heading, only one dollar sign is used, and it precedes the heading.

TASK 7: TO ENTER AND COPY A FORMULA WITH AN ABSOLUTE REFERENCE USING HEADINGS:

1 Copy cell J5 to the range J6:J14.

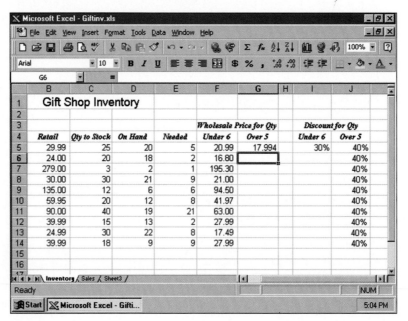

2 Click in cell G5, type **=retail−(retail*$over 5)**, and press (ENTER).

3 Copy cell G5 to the range G6:G14.
The cells display the correct computations.

Creating and Modifying a Chart

Charts present data in a worksheet in a way that numbers never can — visually. Seeing trends and data relationships is so much easier when you look at a chart than when you read numbers. To put a new spin on a tired, old saying, you might say, "A chart is worth 16,777,216 cells." The *Chart Wizard* helps you create charts in Excel.

TASK 8: TO CREATE A COLUMN CHART:

1 Click the Sales tab.

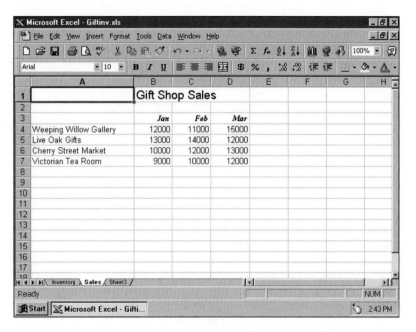

2 Select the range A3:D7 and click the Chart Wizard 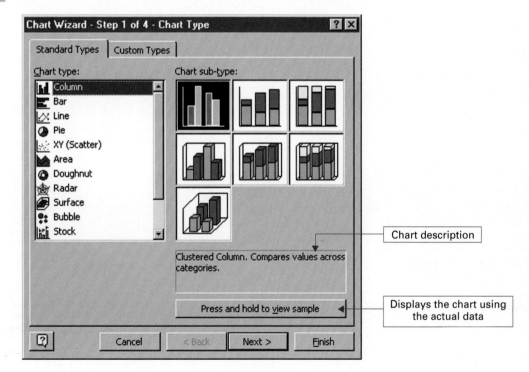 button.

3 Click Next to accept the chart type.

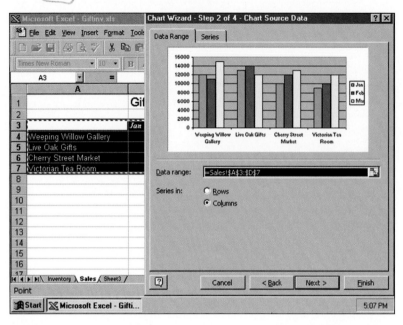

4 Click Next to accept the data range.

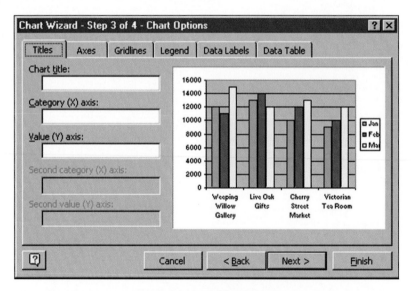

5 Type **First Quarter Sales** for the Chart title and click Next.

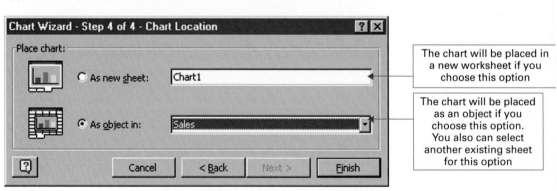

The chart will be placed in a new worksheet if you choose this option

The chart will be placed as an object if you choose this option. You also can select another existing sheet for this option

6   Click Finish.
The chart displays in the current worksheet with **selection handles**. You may want to close the Chart toolbar to see the complete chart.

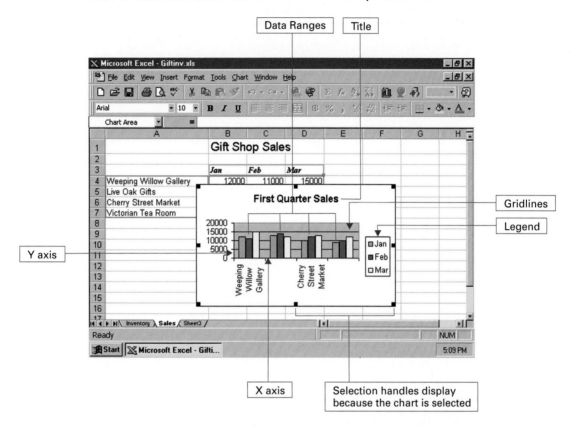

Note The Chart Wizard arbitrarily displays every other data label (in this example, Weeping Willow Gallery and Cherry Street Market), because there is too much text to show all the labels.

Moving and Sizing a Chart

When you place a chart on the same page as the worksheet, the Chart Wizard may place the chart in a location that obscures the data in the worksheet, and it may make the chart too small. Because the chart is an object, you can move it and size it however you want.

TASK 9: TO MOVE AND SIZE THE CHART:

1   Point to a blank area of the chart and drag the chart to the right of the data that created the chart.
The chart moves to the new location.

2 Point to a handle at the bottom of the chart and drag the handle down to make the chart about three rows taller.

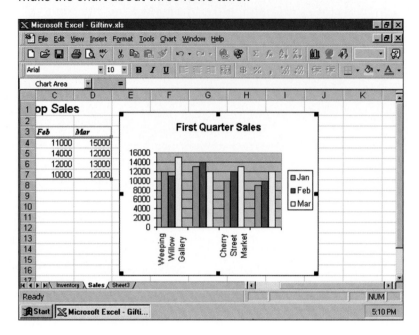

Changing Chart Data

The chart is linked to the data in the worksheet; when you change the data in the worksheet, the chart reflects the change. By the same token, when you change a value in a *data range* in the chart, the data in the worksheet reflects the change.

TASK 10: TO CHANGE CHART DATA:

1 In the worksheet, change the names of the gift shops to abbreviations as follows:
Weeping Willow Gallery: **WWG**;
Live Oak Gifts: **LOG**;
Cherry Street Market: **CSM**;
Victorian Tea Room: **VTR**.
After changing the names, make column A narrower.

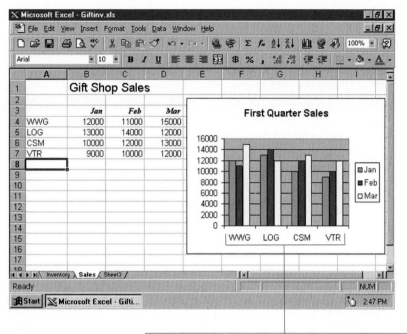

The names on the X axis reflect the change in the worksheet

2   Change the value in cell B4 to 18000 and notice the change in the chart as you press (ENTER).
The height of the first column increases when you change the value.

3   Click the first column in the chart to select the data range for January.

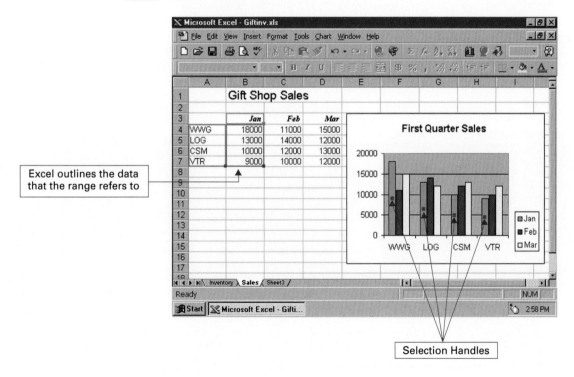

Excel outlines the data that the range refers to

Selection Handles

4   Click the first column again.

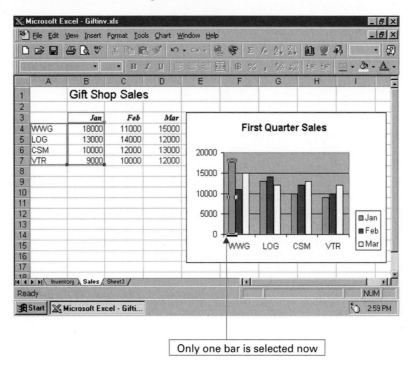

Only one bar is selected now

5   Drag the top of the column up until the value is 21000.

The data in cell B4 changes

The values in this axis and the size of the chart changes

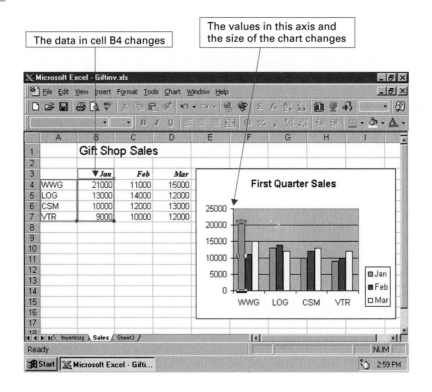

Formatting Chart Elements

> When you create a chart with the Chart Wizard, the Chart Wizard decides how the chart elements will look. For example, the Chart Wizard uses the General number format for the scale on the Y axis. After the chart is created, you can format each element of a chart and use the settings that you want.

TASK 11: TO FORMAT CHART ELEMENTS:

1   Right-click the legend, choose Format Legend from the Shortcut menu, and click the Placement tab.

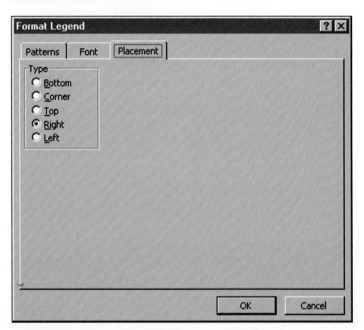

2   Select Bottom and click OK.

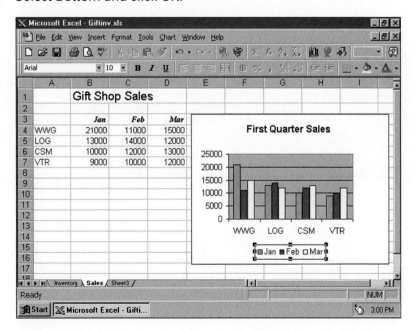

3 Right-click the numbers on the Value axis (Y axis), choose Format Axis from the Shortcut menu, and click the Number tab.

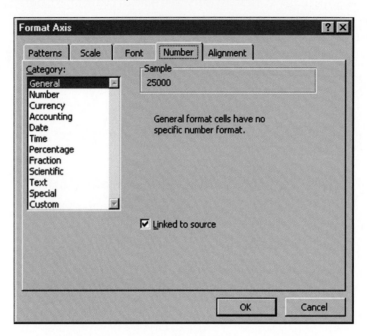

4 Select Currency, 0 decimal places, and click OK.

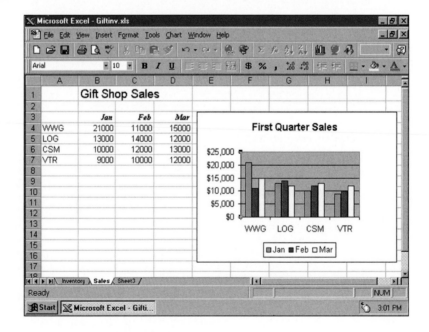

5 Right-click the text on the Category axis (X axis), choose Format Axis, and click the Font tab.

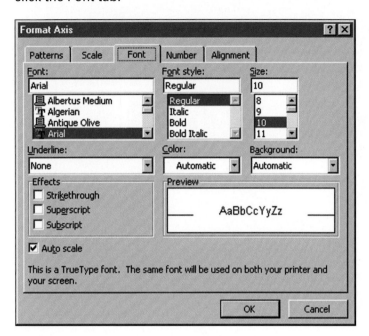

6 Select 8 for the Size and click OK.
The font size of the text is decreased.

Changing the Chart Type

Excel 97 provides many *chart types* and *chart sub-types*. Not all chart types are appropriate for the data in a workbook. Some charts are designed especially for certain types of data. For example, the Stock chart requires three series of data which must be arranged in a specific order: high, low, and close (a stock's high and low values for the day and the closing price of the stock).

TASK 12: TO CHANGE THE CHART TYPE:

1 Right-click a blank area of the chart and choose Chart type from the Shortcut menu.

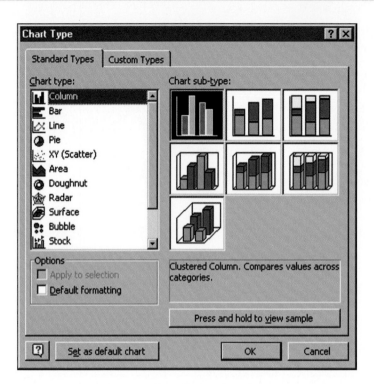

2 Select Line for Chart Type, select the 3-D line sub-type, and click OK.

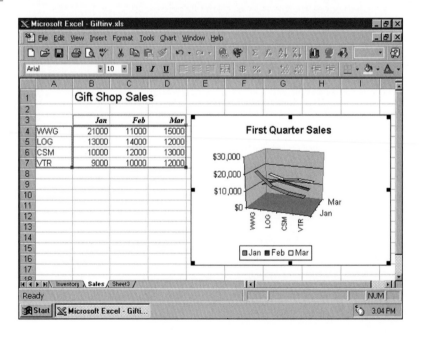

Changing the Chart Options

Settings for the chart *titles*, *X axis*, *Y axis*, *gridlines*, *legend*, *data labels*, and *data table* are all contained in the Chart Options dialog box. After you have created a chart, you can select the options that you want.

TASK 13: TO CHANGE THE CHART OPTIONS:

1 Right-click a blank area of the chart, choose Chart Options from the Shortcut menu, and click the Data Table tab.

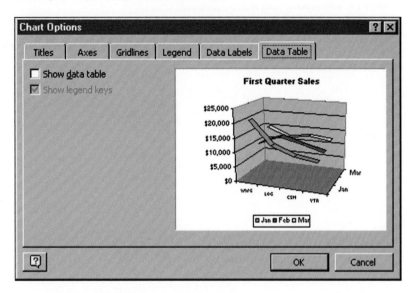

2 Select Show data table and click OK.

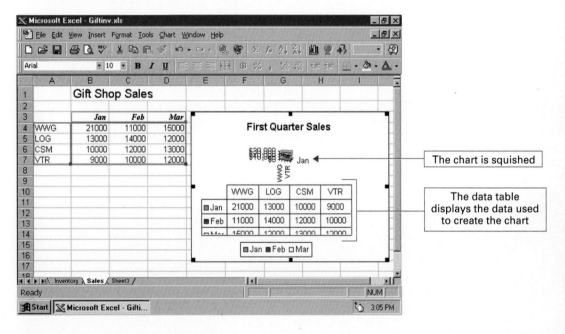

3 Make the chart about 9 rows taller.
The graph returns to its former size.

Creating a Pie Chart

A pie chart is a popular type of chart that shows the relationship of parts to the whole. When selecting data for a pie chart, you will select only one data range.

TASK 14: TO CREATE A PIE CHART:

1 Select the range A4:B7, click 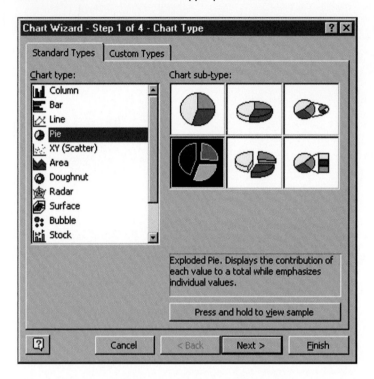, and select Pie as the Chart type and Exploded pie as the sub-type. (A description of the selected chart sub-type shows below the chart sub-type pictures.)

2 Click but don't release the button named Press and hold to view sample. A preview of the chart using your data displays in a Sample box.

3 Release the mouse button and click Next.

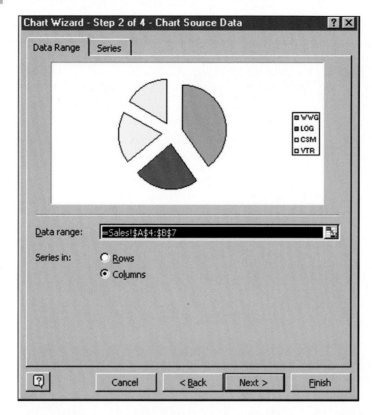

4 Click Next.

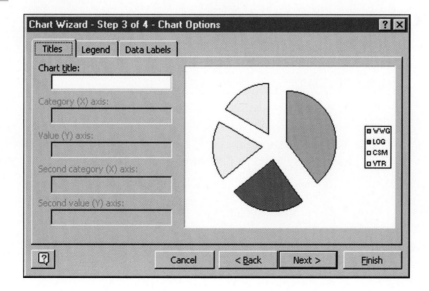

5 Type **January Sales for Gift Shops** for Chart title and click Next.

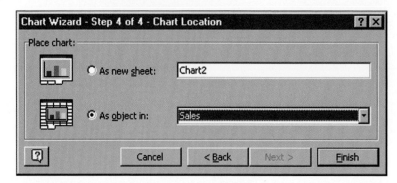

6 Select As new sheet and click Finish.

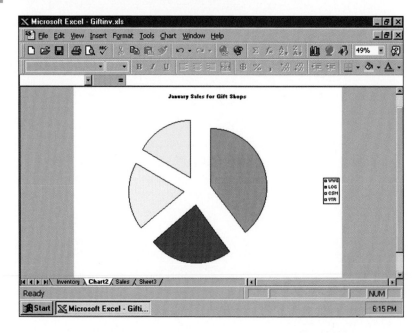

Tip You can change the name of the worksheet that the chart appears on just as you would any other worksheet name.

7   Change the chart sub-type to Pie with a 3-D visual effect.

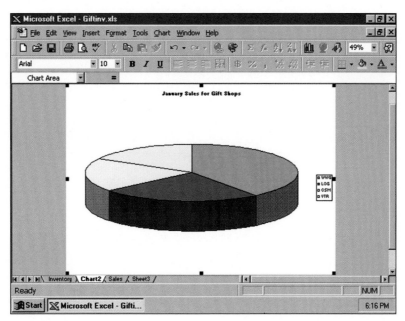

8   Right-click the pie, choose Format Data Series, and click the Data Labels tab.

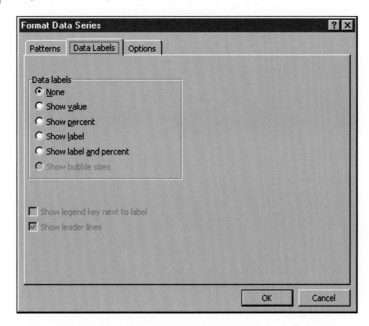

9 Select Show percent and click OK.

The Conclusion

Save the file as *Gift Inventory and Sales.xls*. Preview each page of the work-book and print each page if you have access to a printer. Close the file.

Summary and Exercises

Summary

- You can copy data from one workbook to another.
- You can sort data in ascending or descending order.
- Formulas use relative references, headings, and absolute references to refer to particular cells on the worksheet.
- Excel can change the address of relative references when a formula is copied, but it cannot change the address of an absolute reference.
- Charts represent the data in a worksheet visually.
- Charts can be displayed on any worksheet in a workbook.
- Once a chart has been created you can change the type, format the elements, or choose different chart options.

Key Terms and Operations

Key Terms	Operations
absolute reference	change the chart type
chart	copy data from another workbook
chart sub-type	create a chart
chart type	enter formulas with relative or absolute addresses
Chart Wizard	format a chart
data labels	move a chart
data range	size a chart
data table	sort data
gridlines	
heading	
legend	
relative reference	
selection handles	
title	
X axis	
Y axis	

Study Questions

Multiple Choice

1. Which of the following categories isn't included in the Chart Options dialog box?
   a. Data Labels
   b. Data Table
   c. Axes
   d. Pattern

2. When you sort by using the Sort Ascending button on the Standard toolbar,
   a. columns are sorted individually.
   b. you can sort on only one row.
   c. the first column must be the key column.
   d. you can sort by as many as three columns.

3. Which of the following statements about the Chart Wizard is false?
   a. The Chart Wizard creates charts by guiding you through a step-by-step process.
   b. The Chart Wizard can create only a limited number of charts that are available in Excel 97.
   c. The Chart Wizard is launched by a button on the Standard toolbar.
   d. The Chart Wizard doesn't give you an opportunity to format the chart before it is created.

4. Which of the following formulas is written in incorrect form?
   a. =A1/A10
   b. =A1/$A$1
   c. =quantity*retail
   d. =quantity*$retail$

5. A relative reference
   a. is the actual address of a cell.
   b. is the range that contains the data labels for a chart.
   c. can be changed by Excel when the formula that contains it is copied to another location.
   d. is denoted by a dollar sign.

6. When a chart is selected,
   a. it has selection handles.
   b. the outline of the chart is blue.
   c. it opens in a separate window.
   d. None of the above.

7. An exploded pie chart is a chart
   a. type.
   b. sub-type.
   c. option.
   d. element.

8. To designate a cell address as an absolute reference when entering a formula using the pointing method, press
   a. (F2).
   b. (F3).
   c. (F4).
   d. (F5).

9. If you want to show the relationship of individual values to a total, which chart type would you use?
   a. column
   b. stock
   c. line
   d. pie

10. To prevent a cell address from changing when the formula that contains it is copied to a new location,
   a. use a relative address for the cell.
   b. use an absolute address for the cell.
   c. use the value of the cell instead of the address.
   d. copy the formula with the Edit, Copy command.

Short Answer

1. When you create a chart, where are the two locations that you can place the chart?

2. What is a data table?

3. Where can a legend be placed on a chart?

4. What command do you use if you want to sort on more than one column?

5. How do you move a chart?

6. How do you size a chart?

7. What is the difference between a relative and an absolute reference?

8. Can you use an absolute reference in a formula that uses headings instead of cell addresses?

9. What happens if you change the data in a worksheet after you have created a chart that uses the data?

10. What happens in the worksheet when you select the data ranges in a chart?

For Discussion

1. Discuss the advantages of using headings in formulas.

2. Discuss the advantages of presenting information in charts as opposed to numbers.

3. Name and describe the elements of a chart.

4. Explain how Excel interprets the following formula if it were located in cell H10: =I5+I6*$A$1.

Review Exercises

1. Revising the gift inventory and sales workbook
In this exercise, you will make changes to an existing chart.

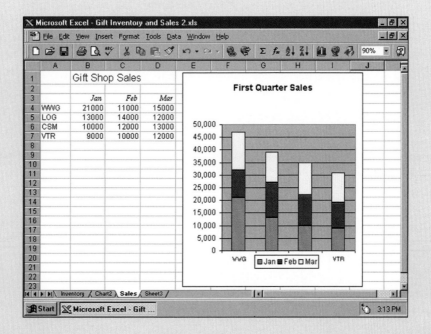

1. Open *Gift Inventory and Sales.xls*.

2. Click the Sales tab if necessary.

3. Change the chart type to a stacked column.

4. Remove the data table.

5. Remove the dollar sign from the numbers on the Y axis.

6. Save the file as Gift Inventory and Sales 2.xls and close the file.

2. Creating a new items workbook

In this exercise, you will create a workbook that lists five possible new items and computes the discount on the items.

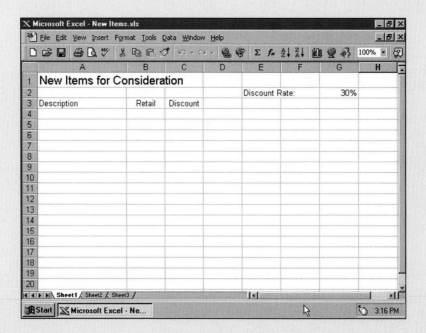

1. Create the workbook shown above.

2. Find five items on the Web that you can suggest as new items for the gift shops to carry. Enter the descriptions of the items and their retail prices in the worksheet in the appropriate columns.

3. In cell C4, enter the formula that multiplies the discount rate in cell G2 times the retail price in cell B4. Copy the formula to the range C5:C8.

4. Save the file as *New Items.xls* and close the file.

3. Sorting data and creating a sales chart in a worksheet

1. Launch Excel and open the workbook *Container Corporation Regional Sales.xls*.

2. Sort the data so that it appears in order by total sales per region with the region with the highest sales at the top.

3. Print a copy of the worksheet after sorting.

4. Create a column chart which displays a comparison of sales by quarter according to region and format the chart as follows:

- Add a chart title *Regional Sales by Quarter*.

- Place the chart in the workbook as a new sheet.

5. Save the workbook using the filename *Container Corporation Regional Sales xxx*.

6. Print a copy of the chart.

Assignments

1. Creating a chart of expenditures

Create a workbook that lists your expenditures for the past month. Create a pie chart for the data. Are you spending too much on pizza?

2. Completing a vacation package workbook

Download the workbook *Vacation.xls* from the Addison Wesley Longman web site (http://hepg.awl.com/select) or ask your instructor for this workbook file. Sort the data in ascending order in the range A4:C8. Enter a formula in cell D4 that multiplies the Price/Person times the appropriate discount rate (cell H4). Copy the formula to the other cells in the column. Enter appropriate formulas for the Travel Agency discounts and the Resort Club discounts. Use headings in the formulas for the Resort Club discounts.

Using Financial Functions

One of the advantages of electronic spreadsheets is that the user has the capability of performing "What if" analyses. The computer can easily store and retrieve data and perform calculations, so Microsoft Excel can be used to develop sophisticated models to assist in decision making.

One decision that individuals and managers often undertake involves assessing the terms under which they will borrow money. Loan payments are amortized; *amortization* is the process of distributing monthly payments over the life of a loan. The factors determining a loan's repayment include the amount of the loan, the percent interest charged by the bank or lending organization, and the length of time over which the loan will be repaid. Each of these factors has a technical name:

- The amount borrowed is the *principal*.
- The percent interest is the *rate*.
- The time period over which payments are made is the *term*.

Depending on the values associated with each factor, varying portions of each loan payment apply to the principal and the interest payment. In general, borrowers aim to pay off the principal in as short an amount of time as financially possible.

An *amortization schedule* lists the outstanding balance, monthly payment, amount of each payment that applies to the principal, and the amount of each payment that applies to the outstanding principal for the life of a loan. In this project, you will learn to use financial functions to create an amortization schedule.

Objectives

After completing this project, you will be able to:

➤ **Define the structure of the amortization schedule**

➤ **Enter the numeric data for the loan**

➤ **Calculate the monthly payment using the PMT function**

➤ **Calculate the remaining balance using the PV function**

➤ **Calculate the principal and interest paid in each loan payment using the PPMT and IPMT functions**

➤ **Construct formulas to calculate the cumulative principal, cumulative interest, total payments, and ending balance**

➤ **Use the Fill Handle to complete the amortization schedule**

➤ **Freeze worksheet panes to assist in viewing the amortization schedule**

➤ **Create and apply a macro**

The Challenge

The Atrium Café will expand next year, so Mr. Gilmore has asked you to construct an amortization schedule so he can compare different loan scenarios. After you complete the workbook, Mr. Gilmore will determine the optimum loan scenario before contacting specific lending institutions for funding.

The Solution

Excel has a number of financial functions that will make creating this workbook a simple task! By entering four numeric constants and using the PMT, PPMT, IPMT, and PV financial functions, you can create the workbook Mr. Gilmore needs. Your completed amortization schedule will look like the one shown in Figure 6.1.

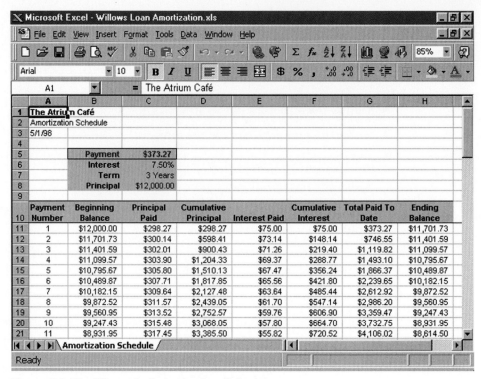

Figure 6.1: Mr. Gilmore's Amortization Schedule

The Setup

Make sure that the Excel settings listed in Table 6.1 are selected on your computer. This will ensure that your screen matches the illustrations and that the tasks in this project function as described.

Table 6.1   Excel Settings

Location	Make these settings
Office Assistant	Close the Office Assistant
View, Toolbars	Display the Standard and Formatting toolbars
View, Formula bar	Display the Formula bar
View, Status bar	Display the Status bar
Maximize	Maximize the Application and Workbook windows
Tools, Options	In the General tab, set the default worksheet font to Arial, 10 point
File, Page Setup	Click the Page tab and set the orientation to landscape
Worksheet Tab for Sheet1	Double-click and rename this tab as Amortization Schedule, and delete the remaining worksheets

Defining the Structure of the Amortization Schedule

The amortization schedule's structure is defined by entering constants to specify where the payment, interest, term, and loan repayment data appear in the worksheet. Excel uses two categories of constants: *text constants* define the structure of the worksheet and *numeric constants* comprise the data upon which the *loan scenario* is based.

When you enter the constants, you format them to enhance the appearance of the worksheet.

TASK 1: DEFINE THE STRUCTURE OF THE AMORTIZATION SCHEDULE:

1 Type **The Atrium Cafe** in cell A1, and change the format to bold.

2 Type **Amortization Schedule** in cell A2.

3 Type **=NOW()** as a formula in cell A3 and click the Enter button ✔ on the Formula Bar.

> **Comment** The =NOW() function is a Date & Time function that displays the date and time according to the computer's system clock. This date is dynamic; as the system clock changes, the date is updated.

4 Select Cells from the Format menu. Select the Number tab in the Format Cells dialog box, select Date as the category, and select the date type shown in the figure below.

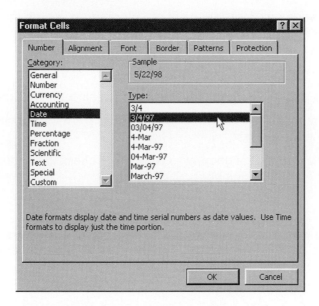

5 Set the alignment of the cell to left.

6 Click OK.

7 Type **Payment** in cell B5, **Interest** in cell B6, **Term** in cell B7, and **Principal** in cell B8. Set the alignment of these cells to right aligned.

8 Type **Payment Number** in cell A10, **Beginning Balance** in cell B10, **Principal Paid** in cell C10, **Cumulative Principal** in cell D10, **Interest Paid** in cell E10, **Cumulative Interest** in cell F10, **Total Paid To Date** in cell G10, and **Ending Balance** in cell H10.

TASK 2: APPLY ADDITIONAL FORMATS TO THE TEXT CONSTANTS:

1 Select the range A10:H10, and set the font style to bold. Using the Fill Color button ⬛ ▾ on the Formatting toolbar, set the fill color of the selection to 25% Gray.

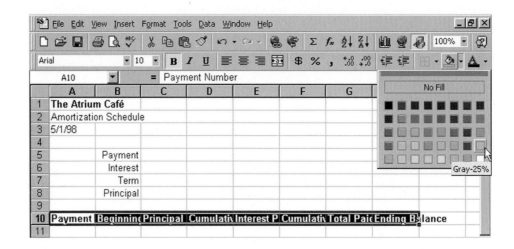

2 Select the range B5:C8. Set the fill color of the selection to 25% gray.

3 Select the range B5:C5. Using the Font Color button **A** ▾ on the Formatting toolbar, set the font color of this selection to dark red.

4 Select the Borders button ⬜ ▾ on the Formatting toolbar. Insert a thin border around the selection.

5 Select the range B5:B8. Set the font style of the selection to Bold.

6 Highlight the range A10 to H10, and select Cells from the Format menu. Select the Alignment tab.

7 Set the Horizontal text alignment to center, and check the option to wrap text, as shown on the next page. Click OK.

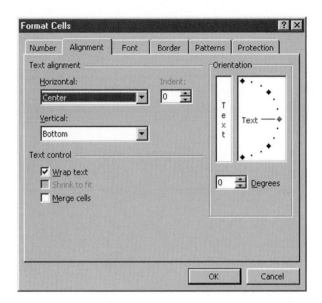

8 Select the Borders tool on the Standard toolbar. Select the option to add a thin border to the top and bottom of the selection.

9 Use the column headings to select columns B through H. Set the width of the selected columns to 12.00. Save your workbook to your floppy disk as *Willows Loan Amortization.xls*.

10 Change the Zoom control 85% on the Standard toolbar to 85%. Your workbook should look like the one shown below.

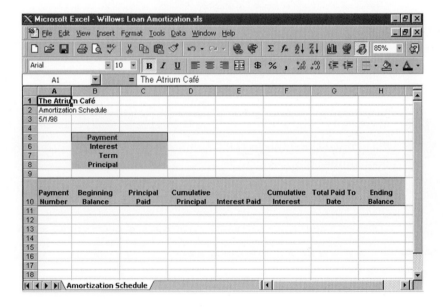

Entering Numeric Constants

A loan payment is calculated using three factors: the loan principal, the interest rate, and the term. These values are entered in the range C6:C8 of your worksheet. All loan repayment data is calculated using these values.

TASK 3: ENTERING NUMERIC CONSTANTS:

1 Place the cell pointer in cell C6, type **.075**, and press (ENTER).

2 Click cell C6 again to make it the active cell, select Cells from the Format menu, and click the Number tab.

3 Select Percentage as the category, and specify two decimal places. Click OK.

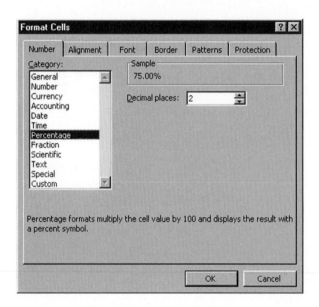

4 Make cell C7 the active cell, type the value **3**, and press (ENTER).

5 Place the cell pointer in cell C7, select Cells from the Format menu, and click the Number tab.

6 Select Custom as the category, and place the insertion point in the Type: text box.

7 Enter **## "Years"** as the custom format and click OK, as shown on the next page. This places the text string "Years" after the numeric value in the cell.

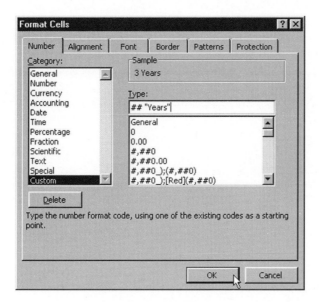

Tip   When specifying a custom format, the dialog box displays a sample of the current cell with the custom format applied.

8   Place the cell pointer in cell C8, type **12000** and press (ENTER).

9   Make cell C8 the active cell and select Cells from the Format menu. Click the Number tab, and select Currency as the category. Make sure two decimal places are specified. Click OK.

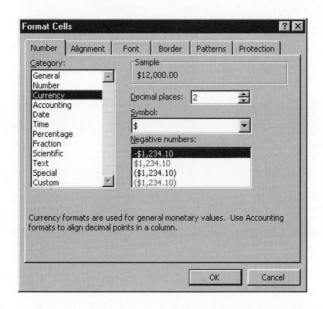

10   After entering and formatting the three numeric constants, the worksheet should look like the one on the next page.

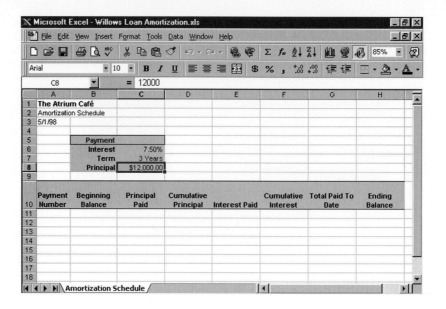

Calculating the Loan Payment

After you specify the rate, term, and principal, you can calculate the loan payment. The PMT (payment) function is a financial function used to calculate the periodic payment of a loan, assuming a constant interest rate and constant payments over the life of the loan. Functions perform calculations by using specific values, called **arguments**, in a particular order, called the syntax. The PMT function uses five arguments, three of which are required. A function's **syntax** specifies the order in which the arguments must appear. Each argument is separated from the others with a comma. The general syntax for the PMT function is:

=PMT(interest rate, number of payments, present value)

> **Note** Search for PMT in the Help system for more information about the arguments accompanying this function.

TASK 4: CALCULATE THE LOAN PAYMENT USING THE PMT FUNCTION:

1. Place the cell pointer in cell C5 to make it the active cell. Select Function from the Insert menu.

2. In the Paste Function dialog box, select Financial as the function category and select PMT as the function name, as shown on the next page. Note that the Paste Function dialog box also displays the arguments used by the function.

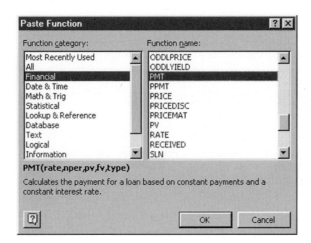

3   Click OK. The function's arguments can be entered in the box that appears.

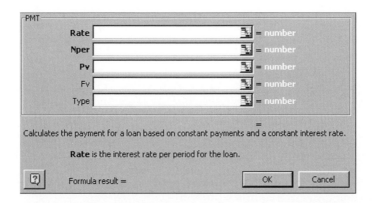

4   Click the button 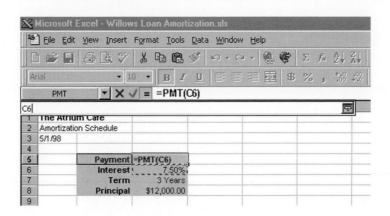 immediately to the right of the text box for specifying the rate.

5   Point to cell C6 and click the left mouse button, as shown in the figure below. Notice that the reference C6 appears both in the Formula bar and the text box below the Formula bar.

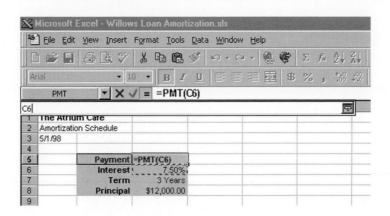

6 The interest rate specified in the worksheet is an annual interest rate. Therefore, it must be divided by 12 (the number of interest periods in one year) for the function to calculate the correct payment.

7 Place the insertion point in the text box that appears under the Formula bar, and type **/12**.

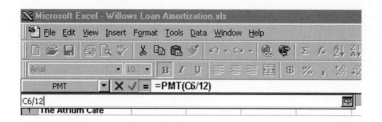

8 Press (ENTER).

The pointing method is one way of entering the arguments the PMT function needs. Because you know the term appears in cell C7 and the payment appears in cell C8, you can enter these values directly.

9 Enter the remaining required arguments, as shown below.

> **Troubleshooting** Note that the term "numeric constant" specifies years. The PMT function requires monthly payments, so you must multiply the value by 12. The PV is the present value of the loan, which is the same as the loan principal. In *annuity functions* (functions that involve payments that are constant), the cash you pay out is represented as a negative value. Therefore, you must precede the reference to cell C8 with a minus sign.

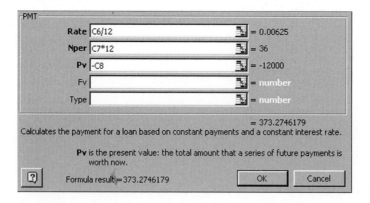

10 Click OK to enter the formula containing the PMT function in cell C5, and save your workbook. The results of the formula should appear as shown on the next page.

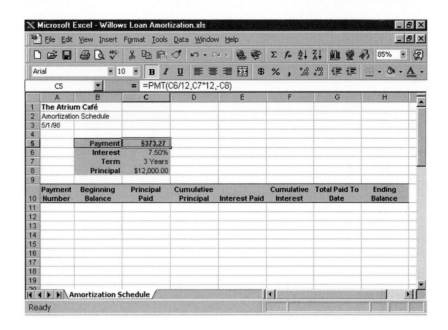

Calculating the Beginning Balance Using the PV Function

Although the beginning balance of the loan that appears in cell B11 is the same as the principal displayed in cell C8, the PV function can be used to enter a "check" into the worksheet. By using the PV function in cell B12 rather than merely including a reference to cell C5, you verify the accuracy of the worksheet.

As with the PMT function, the PV (present value of an annuity) function requires three arguments: rate, term, and payment. The general syntax for the PV function is:

=PV(interest rate, number of payments, periodic payment)

TASK 5: CALCULATE THE BEGINNING BALANCE USING THE PV FUNCTION:

1   Place the cell pointer in cell B11.

2   Type **=PV(C6/12,C7*12,–C5)** and press (ENTER).

Tip As with the PMT function, the annual interest rate must be divided by the number of annual periods (12) per year. In addition, the term (in years) must be multiplied by the number of payments made each year (12), and the payment must be preceded by a minus sign.

The value displayed in cell B11 should appear as shown below.

3 Save your workbook.

Calculating the Principal Paid in Each Payment

The amount of each loan payment that applies to the loan principal (rather than the accrued interest) varies throughout the term of the loan. As with most annuity functions, the actual variance depends upon the loan's rate, term, and principal. The PPMT (periodic principal payment) returns the payment on the principal for a given period. The PPMT function requires four arguments: the rate, the specific period, the number of payments, and the present value of the annuity for the period.

In this function, the **present value** refers to the total amount that a series of future payments is worth now—this is the loan principal. The general syntax is:

=PPMT(interest rate, payment period, number of payments, present value)

This function, which is copied to other cells in the amortization schedule, includes both absolute cell references and one mixed cell reference. A **mixed reference** means that the column reference remains constant, but the row reference varies. The function also will need to reference the specific payment (by payment number) within the period. This data is supplied to the function from column A of the amortization schedule.

> **Tip**   The term *mixed reference* is a carryover from Lotus 1-2-3 and is not used in Microsoft Excel. Therefore, this term will not be found in the Help System. It is a useful term, however, because it conveys the idea that part of the reference is relative and part is absolute. In Excel, mixed references are also referred to as absolute references.

TASK 6: CALCULATE THE PERIODIC PRINCIPAL PAYMENT USING THE PPMT FUNCTION:

1   Click cell A11 to make it the active cell.

2   Type **1** as a numeric constant representing the first periodic payment.

3   Place the insertion point in cell C11, making it the active cell.
Type **=-PPMT($C$6/12,$A11,$C$7*12,$C$8)** and press (ENTER).

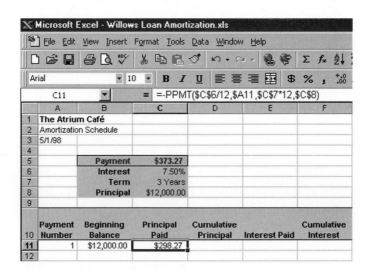

Now let's analyze this formula. The entire payment is preceded by a minus sign, because annuity payments must be specified as a negative value. The references to the rate (cell C6), term (cell C7), and present value (cell C8) are absolute, because the formula must always reference the same cells, regardless of where the formula is copied in the worksheet. Cell C11 contains a mixed reference: The row reference must change to reflect the periodic payment as the formula is copied down the amortization schedule, but column A must be referenced when the formula is copied to cell E11 to construct the IPMT function.

> **Tip** It is not mandatory that cells C6, C7, and C8 contain absolute references. Technically, these could contain mixed references to specify which part of the reference should remain constant (C$6, for example); only the row designation must remain constant as the formulas are copied. The worksheet also uses the IPMT function, which shares the same arguments as the PPMT function, so absolute references are used to assist in creating these formulas. In general, it is a good practice to use absolute references unless the column reference must change if the formula is copied to another column in the worksheet.

Calculating the Interest Paid in Each Payment

The method for calculating the portion of a loan payment that applies to the interest payment is almost identical to the method for calculating a periodic principal payment. The only difference is that the IPMT (periodic interest payment) function is used. The general syntax for the IPMT function is:

=IPMT(interest rate, payment period, number of payments, present value)

TASK 7: CALCULATE THE PERIODIC INTEREST PAYMENT:

1 Select cell C11.

2 Copy the contents of the cell.

3 Place the insertion point in cell E11.

4 Select Paste using either the Edit menu or the Standard toolbar.

5 Edit the formula in the Formula bar by changing the function from PPMT to IPMT.

Your worksheet should now look like the one shown below.

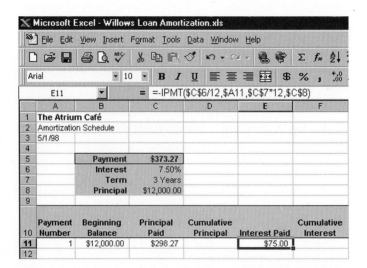

Constructing Formulas to Calculate the Cumulative Principal, Cumulative Interest, Total Payments, and Ending Balance

When building an amortization schedule, it is helpful to display not only the current principal and interest payments, but the cumulative payments as well. For the first payment, the periodic principal and interest payment equal the cumulative payments. In subsequent rows, however, the cumulative payment figures increase. The total payments to date can be calculated by adding the cumulative principal and the cumulative interest payments.

TASK 8: CONSTRUCT FORMULAS TO DETERMINE THE CUMULATIVE INTEREST, CUMULATIVE PRINCIPAL, TOTAL PAYMENTS, AND ENDING BALANCE:

1   Select cell D11 as the active cell.

2   Type =C11.

3   Place the insertion point in cell F11, and type =E11.

4   Place the insertion point in cell G11, and type =D11+F11.

> **Reminder** The value displayed in cell G11 should be identical to the value in cell C5. This provides another "check" to verify the accuracy of your worksheet.

5   Place the insertion point in cell H11.

6   Type =B11–C11. The ending balance is the principal that must be paid to fulfill the repayment obligation. This is equal to the beginning balance minus the principal payment. Your worksheet should now look like the one shown on the next page.

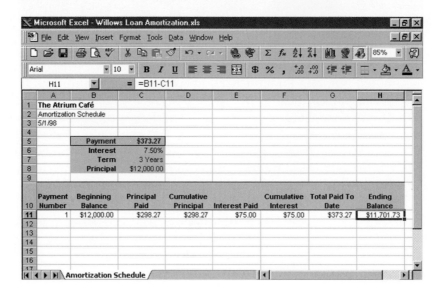

7   Save your worksheet.

Using the Fill Handle to Complete the Amortization Schedule

After you enter formulas in row 12 of the amortization schedule, you can use the Fill Handle to copy the formula to other portions of the worksheet. The default amortization schedule covers a loan with a term of three years, a principal of $12,000, and an annual interest rate of 7.50%.

TASK 9: USE THE FILL HANDLE TO COMPLETE THE AMORTIZATION SCHEDULE:

1   Place the insertion point in cell A12 to make it the active cell.

2   Type **=A11+1**.

3   Type **=H11** in cell B12. The beginning balance for this payment equals the ending balance after the last payment was made.

4   Highlight the range C11:H11. Using the Fill Handle, copy the range down to row 12, as shown on the next page.

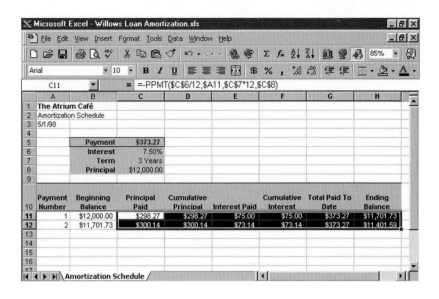

5   Highlight cell D12, and change the formula to **=D11+C12**.

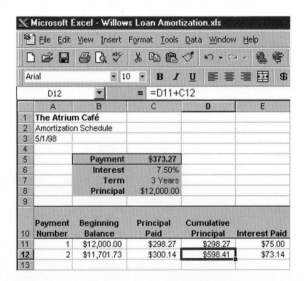

6   Highlight cell F12, and change the formula to **=F11+E12**.

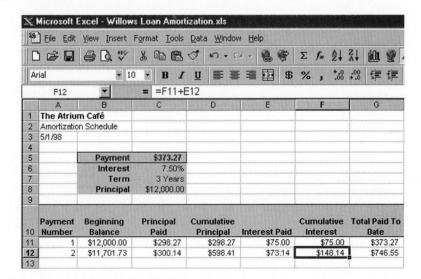

7 Highlight the range A12:H12. Using the Fill Handle, copy this row of formulas through row 46, as shown below.

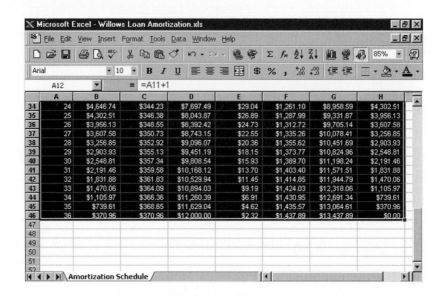

Tip Notice that the Ending Balance equals zero at payment 36. This verifies that the amortization schedule is calculating the loan repayment figures correctly.

8 Highlight Column A and set the alignment of the selection to center.

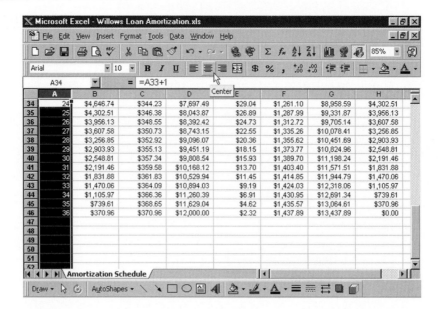

9   Highlight the range A1:A3. Set the alignment to left.

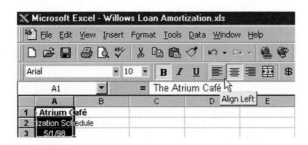

10   Save your changes. Your workbook should now look like the one shown in the figure below.

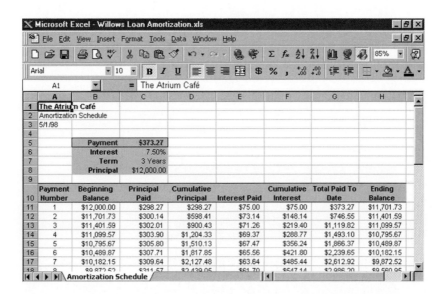

Freezing Worksheet Panes to Assist in Viewing Large Worksheets

Your amortization schedule is now fully functional. Take a moment to note the power of Microsoft Excel. By using financial functions and copying these formulas down the worksheet, the entire loan repayment table is based upon four numeric constants—even though your worksheet presently contains almost 300 formulas.

Viewing large worksheets can be problematic because the heading rows scroll out of view as you move down the worksheet. To alleviate this problem, certain rows can be "frozen" so they always appear on the screen. In the next task, you will freeze the worksheet headings so the entire amortization schedule can be viewed with the headings visible on the screen.

TASK 10: FREEZE WORKSHEET PANES TO ASSIST VIEWING:

1 Place the insertion point in cell A11.

2 Select Freeze Panes from the Window menu.

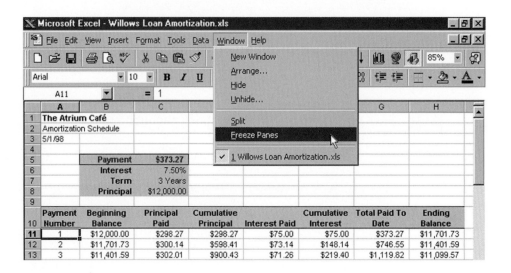

3 Select Go To from the Edit menu.

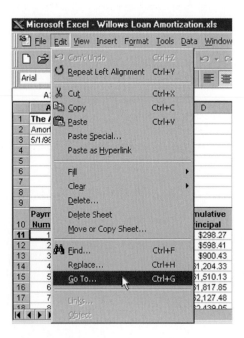

4 Type **A46** in the Reference text box of the Go To dialog box.

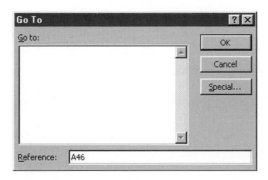

5 Click OK. Cell A46 becomes the active cell, and rows 1 through 10 and additional rows up to row 46 become visible.

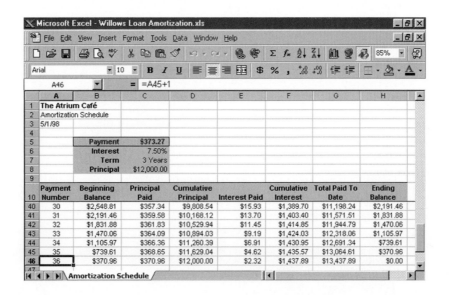

As you scroll through the worksheet, rows 1 through 10 always remain visible.

Tip To unfreeze the panes, select Unfreeze Panes from the Window menu.

Changing the Loan Scenario

Using this workbook, Mr. Gilmore can easily compare alternative loan scenarios. To see how easy it is to view another loan scenario, simply change the principal and term values, and then add additional rows to the worksheet.

TASK 11: TO CHANGE THE LOAN SCENARIO:

1 Enter **4** in cell C7 and press (ENTER).

2 Type **10000** in cell C8 and press (ENTER). Notice that the monthly payment changes to $241.79.

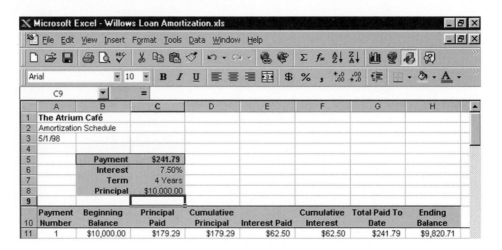

3 Scroll to the bottom of the worksheet, and highlight the range A46:H46.

4 Using the Fill Handle, drag the selection through row 58 and release the left mouse button. Your amortization schedule should now resemble the one shown in the figure below.

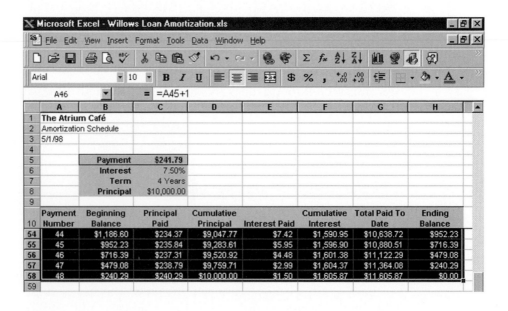

5 Using the vertical scroll bar, move to the top of the worksheet, and make cell A1 the active cell.

6 Save your workbook.

Creating Excel Macros

When using Excel you often may need to complete a series of tasks more than once. By recording a macro, you can easily apply these procedures again by simply playing the macro. A **macro** is a series of commands and functions stored in a Visual Basic module that can be run whenever you need to perform the task again. (**Visual Basic** is the programming language used throughout the Office environment for recording macros. If you know Visual Basic, you can easily edit a macro you have created.)

It would be nice if your amortization worksheet could easily be returned to a predictable state after the loan's term is changed, because the worksheet will either display errors or not display the entire repayment schedule. You can create a macro to set the default values and create the appropriate number of loan repayment formulas.

TASK 12: TO RECORD A MACRO:

1 Select Macros from the Tools menu, and choose Record New Macro.

2 Type **SetDefaults** as the name of the macro, and make sure the macro is stored in the current workbook, as shown in the figure below. Click OK.

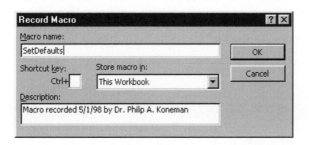

> **Tip** Every procedure you now apply will become a part of the macro. You will also notice that the Stop Recording toolbar is now visible on the screen.

3 Click cell A13 to make it the active cell.

4 While simultaneously holding down the (SHIFT) and (CTRL) keys, press the (END) key. The range A13:H56 is now selected.

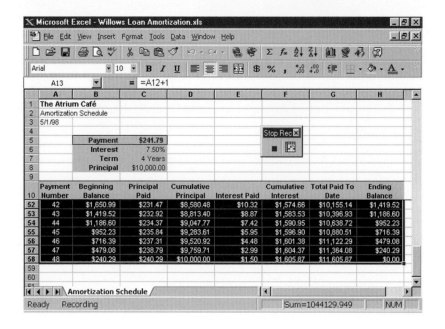

5   Press the (DELETE) key to delete the selected portion of the amortization schedule.

6   Type **3** in cell C7 as the term, and type **12000** in cell C8 as the principal.

7   Select the range A12:H12 and use the Fill Handle to copy the formulas through row 46.

8   Scroll to the top of the worksheet and make cell A1 the active cell.

9   Click the Stop Recording button.

10   You have now successfully recorded a macro. Save your workbook.

Running a Macro

After you have recorded a macro, it can be run. When you **run** a macro, each step included in the macro is applied to the workbook. Before running the macro, you will change the loan scenario to see the results of applying the macro.

TASK 13: TO RUN A MACRO:

1   Type **10** in cell C7 and **50000** in cell C8.

2   Scroll to the bottom of the worksheet and select the range A46:H46.

3   Using the Fill Handle, copy the selection through row 130, as shown on the next page.

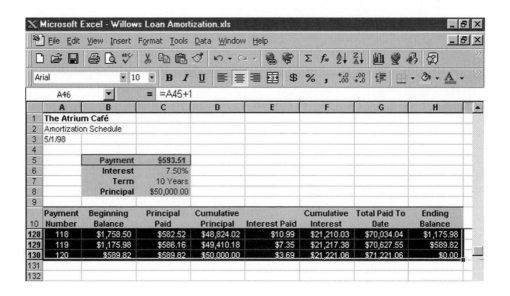

4 Select Macro from the Tools menu, and then choose Macros.

5 Select the SetDefaults macro and click the Run command button.

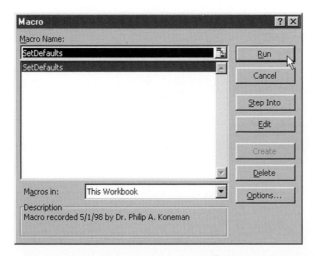

The macro will change the term and principal of the loan, and modify the amortization schedule accordingly. You can easily change the loan scenario to a predictable state at any time by simply running the SetDefaults macro.

The Conclusion

The worksheet you have created in this project serves as a powerful tool for analyzing different loan scenarios. The numeric constants in the upper portion of the Amortization Schedule worksheet can easily be changed to compare alternate loan scenarios.

Summary and Exercises

Summary

- Text constants are used to define a workbook's structure.
- Excel contains many financial functions.
- In an amortization schedule workbook, numeric constants for the principal, rate, and term are used to calculate the loan payment.
- The PMT function is used to calculate a loan payment.
- The PV function is used to calculate the present value of an annuity.
- The PPMT function is used to calculate the portion of a loan payment that applies toward the loan principal.
- The IPMT is used to calculate the portion of a loan payment that applies toward the accrued interest.
- A complex workbook such as an amortization schedule will often contain hundreds of formulas.
- Once created, formulas are easily copied using the Fill Handle.
- Worksheet panes can be frozen to assist in viewing large worksheets.
- A macro is used to record redundant tasks that can be applied again and again.

Key Terms and Operations

Key Terms

amortization	present value
amortization schedule	principal
annuity functions	rate
argument	run
loan scenario	syntax
macro	term
mixed reference	text constants
numeric constants	Visual Basic

Operations

construct a formula using the IPMT (interest payment) function
construct a formula using the PMT (payment) function
construct a formula using the PPMT (periodic payment) function
construct a formula using the PV (present value of an annuity) function
create an amortization schedule
create formulas to calculate the cumulative interest and cumulative principal
determine the ending balance
freeze worksheet panes
record a macro
run a macro
use AutoFill to copy formulas

Study Questions

Multiple Choice

1. A worksheet is being constructed to determine the monthly payment required to return $250,000 in the year 2025. Which financial function should be used to perform this calculation?
   a. PMT
   b. IPMT
   c. PV
   d. FV
   e. PPMT

2. A worksheet includes a formula for calculating the payment on a loan. To see the amount of the monthly payment that applies to the interest payment, you will use which function?
   a. PMT
   b. PV
   c. NOW()
   d. PPMT
   e. IPMT

3. Which statement concerning the use of the PV annuity function is false?
   a. An annuity payment should be entered as a negative value.
   b. The present value of the investment is required.
   c. The total number of payment periods in the annuity is required.
   d. Parentheses are not used when constructing this function.
   e. The interest rate cannot change over the life of the annuity.

4. Which of the following most likely refers to the principal of a loan in a financial function?
   a. H6/12
   b. I7*12
   c. –J7
   d. g3/12
   e. –a1*24

5. Which of the following formulas includes an absolute reference to an annuity payment?
   a. =PMT(a1/12,c7*12,d7)
   b. =PPMT(a1/12,c7*12,e7)
   c. =PMT(h6/12,I$7*12,–j7)
   d. =IPMT(a1/12,c7*12,–e7)
   e. =PMT(a1/12,$b7*12,–$r$5)

6. Which of the following is true about macros?
   a. After a macro is created, it cannot be edited.
   b. Macros aren't very useful in worksheets containing financial functions.
   c. Macros are used to record a series of redundant tasks.
   d. Macros cannot perform copy and paste operations.
   e. Macros are rarely used in Excel workbooks.

7. The Principal Payment (PPMT) function is similar to which function?
    a. PMT
    b. PV
    c. IPMT
    d. PPMT
    e. NOW()

8. Which function calculates the portion of a loan payment applied toward the principal?
    a. PMT
    b. PV
    c. IPMT
    d. PPMT
    e. FV

9. You can freeze worksheet panes using which menu?
    a. Format
    b. Edit
    c. Data
    d. View
    e. Window

10. The =NOW() function is in which category of functions?
    a. Financial
    b. Statistical
    c. Date/Time
    d. Logical
    e. String

Short Answer

1. Examine the function =PMT(H6/12,I7*12,−J7). Which element refers to the present value of the loan? How is it identified?

2. Explain how the term of a loan impacts the total amount paid.

3. What does the PMT function calculate?

4. What is a mixed cell reference?

5. Why should the formulas in an amortization schedule contain absolute references?

6. What is the maximum number of arguments that can be included with the PMT function?

7. What value does the PPMT function return?

8. If you are having difficulty viewing the headings in a large worksheet, what should you do?

9. What happens when you record a macro?

10. How should annuity payments be entered in a formula?

For Discussion

1. What is the FV function? How does the data it returns differ from the PV function?

2. What is a macro? How is a macro recorded and applied?

3. How can worksheets, such as the amortization schedule you created in this project, be protected from changes?

4. What arguments are required by the PMT function? Is the order in which these appear in a formula significant?

Review Exercises

1. Protecting cells in a workbook

In many settings, portions of a worksheet should be protected to prohibit users from inadvertently making destructive changes to the workbook. By unlocking the cells to which users need access and protecting the worksheet, this objective can easily be achieved. Open the *Willows Loan Amortization* workbook and do the following:

1. Select the following nonadjacent ranges: C6:C8 and A13:H370.

2. Select Cells from the Format menu.

3. Click the Protection tab.

4. Deselect the Locked check box in the Format Cells dialog box.

5. Click the OK button.

6. Select Protection from the Tools menu.

7. Select Protect Sheet from the cascading menu.

8. Do not enter a protection password in the Protect Sheet dialog box.

9. Click OK.

10. Save the updated workbook as *Protected Loan Analysis.xls*.

2. Creating a worksheet to predict the future value of an investment

The FV function is similar to the PV function, except that it returns the future value of an investment, assuming a constant interest rate. Create the workbook shown below as follows:

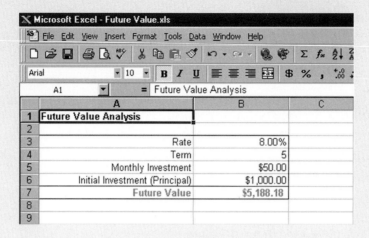

1. Launch Excel if isn't already running.

2. Create a new workbook.

3. Save the workbook as *Future value.xls*.

4. Enter the text and numeric constants shown in the figure on the previous page into the worksheet.

5. Type **=FV(B3/12,B4*12,–B5,–B6,1)** as the formula in cell B7. Look up FV in the Excel Help System for information about the arguments.

Assignments

1. Creating macros to enable and disable protection for a worksheet
Open the *Protected loan analysis.xls* workbook. Create two macros: one that sets the protection for the worksheet, and one that removes the worksheet protection. Save the workbook as *Protected Loan Y-N.xls*.

2. Repaying a loan early
Visit Microsoft's New Spreadsheet Solutions site, which contains spreadsheet solutions created by Village Software. (http://www.microsoft.com/excel/ freestuff/templates/villagesoftware/). Download the Loan Manager file self-extracting file(*Loan.exe*), and install the *Loan.xlt* template to your floppy diskette. Open the *Loan.xlt* file, and enter the loan data from this project. Make three additional payments of $100.00 each. Save the workbook as *Prepaid.xls*.

More Excel 97

This section contains additional topics that are necessary for you to know if you plan to take the Microsoft Proficient exam for Excel. The topics are listed in the same order as the Skill Sets outlined in the *Microsoft Excel 97 Exam Preparation Guide*, which you can download from Microsoft's Web site(www.microsoft.com/office/train_cert). All other topics necessary for successful completion of the exam are covered in projects one through six of this book.

Modifying Workbooks

Rotating and Indenting Text

Sometimes, for the sake of format, it is better to rotate the text in a cell. For example, if a column heading is much wider than the data in the column, you can rotate the heading to make the column narrower. To rotate the text in cell(s), select the cell(s), choose Format, Cells, and click the Alignment tab. Using the mouse, drag the Text line in the Orientation box to the desired angle or specify the angle in the Degrees spin box. Then click OK.

To indent text in a cell, select the cell(s), choose Format, Cells, and click the Alignment tab. Specify the number of characters the text should be indented in the Indent spin box and click OK.

Revise Formulas

You can edit a formula with the same technique described in Project 2, Task 3. Basically, you edit a formula with these steps: select the cell that contains the formula, click in the Formula bar, make the desired changes, and press (ENTER).

Print Workbooks

Printing the Screen and Ranges

Although you can use the PrintScreen key to print what you see on the screen (including the column and row headings), you generally will want to print a range, especially if the worksheet is too large to print on one page. To print a range, first select the range and then choose File, Print. For Print What, choose Selection and click OK.

Creating and Applying Ranges

Creating and Naming Ranges

In Project 1, you learned how to use ranges in formulas. In doing so, however, you either pointed to the range or typed the address of the range. The third way to refer to a range in a formula is to use the name of the range.

To name a range, select the cells and choose Insert, Name, Define. Type the desired name for the range and click OK. To use a range name in a formula, simply type the name where you would normally specify the range address. For example, if the range A1 through A10 is named "January," you would use the formula =sum(january) instead of =sum(a1:a10).

> **Note** Range names are not case-sensitive.

Using Draw

Creating and Modifying Lines and Objects

Excel provides several drawing tools in the Drawing toolbar, which can be displayed by clicking the Drawing button ▨ in the Standard toolbar. Drawing tools include the Line tool, Arrow tool, Rectangle tool, and Oval tool. To draw a shape with any of these tools, click the tool in the toolbar and drag the shape in the desired location. Additional drawing tools are available on the AutoShapes menu. The AutoShape tools include additional line styles, basic shapes, block arrows, flowchart symbols, stars, banners, and call outs. To draw with one of these tools, click the arrow in the AutoShapes button, point to a category, and click the desired tool. Then drag to draw the shape.

Creating and Modifying 3D Shapes

With the 3-D tool, you can add a three-dimensional look to shapes that you have drawn. First draw the shape; then click the 3-D button ▨ and select the desired shape.

You can modify a 3-D shape with the 3-D Settings toolbar, which contains buttons for changing tilt, depth, direction, lighting, surface, and color of the 3-D object. To display the 3-D Settings toolbar, click the 3-D button in the Drawing toolbar and choose 3-D Settings. Then select the drawing object and use the buttons in the toolbar to modify the object. For example, to change the direction of the light on the object (and thus the shading of the object), click the Lighting button ▼ and select a lighting direction and intensity.

Using Charts

Previewing and Printing Charts

If a chart is an object on a worksheet page, the chart will print when you print the page. If the chart is a completely separate page, you can print just that page. Before printing a chart, however, you can preview it to make sure the format and information is correct.

To preview and print a chart that is an object on a worksheet, choose File, Print. Select the page that contains the chart in the print range. Then click Preview. After viewing, click Close or click Print. To preview and print a chart located on a Chart page, select the page and choose File, Print. Select Active Sheet(s) for Print What and then click Preview. After viewing, click Close or click Print.

Saving Spreadsheets as HTML

Saving Spreadsheets as HTML Documents

Excel can save a worksheet as an HTML file that can be used either as an independent Web page or as a table that can be inserted into an existing Web page. To create an HTML file, select the range you want to convert to HTML and choose File, Save As HTML. The Internet Assistant Wizard opens. Click Add to add an additional range; then specify the range and click OK. Click the Next button. Select either the option to create an independent Web page or the option to create a file that can be inserted as a table. Click the Next button. The next steps in the wizard depend on whether you are creating an independent Web page or a table.

If you are creating an independent Web page, specify the title text, the header text, and the description text, if desired; select horizontal lines, if desired; and specify the update and e-mail information, if desired. Click Next. Type the path and name for the file and click Finish.

> **Note** By default, the wizard uses the extension "htm" instead of "html," but you can change the extension, if desired.

If you are creating a file to be inserted as a table, specify how you want the file to open, and specify the path and name of the existing file that will contain the Excel table. (The existing file must already contain the code described at the top of the dialog box.) Click Next. Specify the name of the path and the name of the new HTML file that will be created by the wizard. (The new file will combine the existing Web page and the Excel table.) Click Finish.

To view the independent Web page you created or to see the table that was inserted in the existing Web page, you must open the HTML file in an HTML viewer. You can open the files in either Word or Internet Explorer.

Formatting Worksheets

The following topic, Applying Outlines, has not been clearly defined in the Microsoft guidelines. It may refer to one of two features—a border or collapsible data. If the topic refers to applying a border, the topic is covered in Project 3. If the topic refers to collapsible data, the following topic explains the procedure.

Applying Outlines

You can apply outline groupings to data in worksheets that contain summary rows arranged consistently above or below related detail data or summary columns arranged consistently to the left or right of related detail data. By applying outline groupings, you can collapse or expand the detail data.

To outline a worksheet automatically, choose Data, Group and Outline, Auto Outline. To apply an outline level to a range of cells manually, select the range and choose Data, Group and Outline, Group. Choose Rows or Columns (whichever is appropriate) and click OK. The outline symbols appear beside the data.

To collapse an outline level, click the minus sign. The detail (denoted by the period symbols) is hidden, and the minus sign changes to a plus sign. To expand a level, click the plus sign. To expand or collapse all the levels, click an appropriate number button. The previous figure, shows only two number buttons above the outline symbols: 1 and 2. When you click the 2 button, all the data displays. When you click the 1 button, the data collapses.

To turn off the outlining, choose Data, Group and Outline, Clear Outline.

Integrating Word and Excel

One of the advantages of using software programs that are part of a suite is that the programs are designed to work together as a team. You've already discovered a few of the shared components in Microsoft Office — the spelling dictionary, Find, and so on. Now it's time to see how you can use data from an Excel worksheet in a Word document or enhance an Excel worksheet with WordArt.

Objectives

After completing this project, you will be able to:

- ➤ **Create an Excel worksheet**
- ➤ **Create an Excel chart**
- ➤ **Create a Word document**
- ➤ **Add WordArt to a Word document**
- ➤ **Copy Excel data to a Word document**
- ➤ **Link an Excel chart to a Word document**

The Challenge

The golf tournament is now complete, and you need to create a worksheet to display the profits from the tournament. You also need to prepare a report for The Willows Board of Directors that includes the profit figures.

The Solution

To create the documents shown in Figure 1.1, you will enter the final figures for the golf tournament revenues in a new Excel worksheet. Then you will create a chart to visually display profits. After you complete the Excel worksheet and chart, you will create a report in Word that includes the data and chart from Excel.

Integrating data from the worksheet with text in the report is as easy as dragging the data from the worksheet and dropping it on the report. You can also copy the Excel chart to the report and create a link so that the chart in the Word document automatically updates when you change data in the Excel worksheet.

The Setup

To accomplish the tasks outlined in this project, you need to work with both Word and Excel. So that they are available when you need them, launch both applications. Table 1.1 shows the settings you should choose.

Table 1.1   Word and Excel Settings

Element	Setting
Office Assistant	Close Office Assistant in both programs
View, Toolbars	Display the Standard and Formatting toolbars in both programs
View, Ruler	Display the vertical and horizontal rulers in Word
Maximize	Maximize the document windows in both programs
Minimize	The Word program until you are ready for it

When you complete the basic documents in both applications, you can arrange the Excel and Word windows on the screen so that you can drag information from one application to the other and see immediate results.

Creating the Excel Worksheet

The first step to accomplishing your goal is to create the Excel worksheet and use the data to create a chart. If necessary, refer to the Excel Function Guide for detailed instructions on tasks required to complete the worksheet.

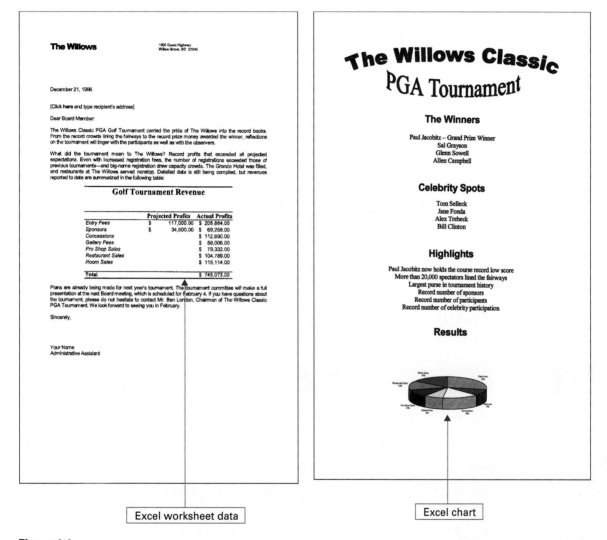

Excel worksheet data

Excel chart

Figure 1.1

TASK 1: TO CREATE THE PROFITS WORKSHEET AND CHART:

1   Select the cells identified on the following illustration and type new data into cells of the worksheet.

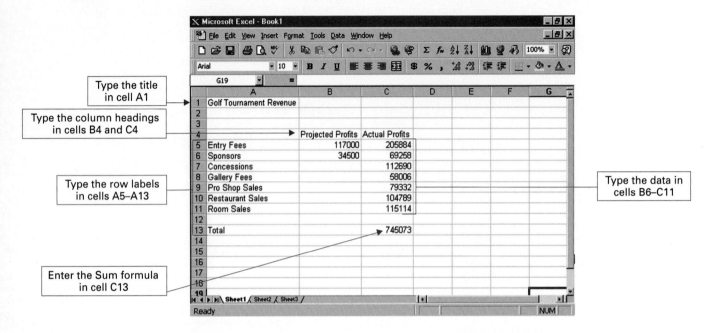

Type the title in cell A1

Type the column headings in cells B4 and C4

Type the row labels in cells A5–A13

Type the data in cells B6–C11

Enter the Sum formula in cell C13

2   Save the worksheet using the filename *Tournament Profits.*

3   Select cells A1 through C13, then choose Format, AutoFormat, and double-click the Simple Table format.

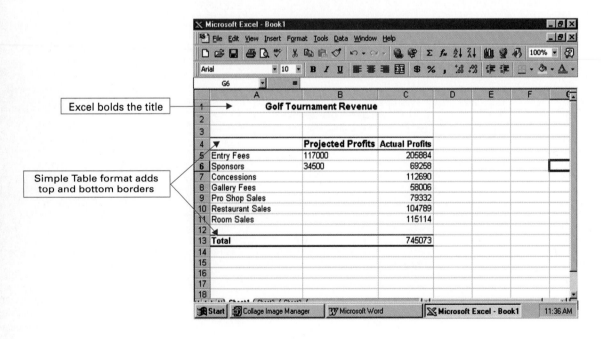

Excel bolds the title

Simple Table format adds top and bottom borders

4   Format cells and text as shown in the following illustration:

Change the title font to 16 point Times Roman and center it across Columns A through C

Change the column headings font to Times Roman 12 point and bold the headings

Italicize the row labels

Bold the word Total

Format the values for currency

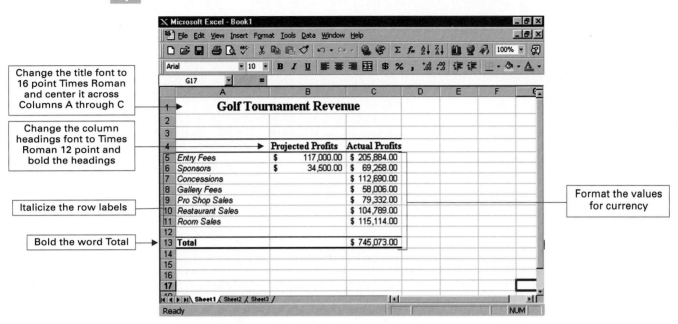

5   Save the changes to the worksheet.

Creating an Excel Chart

Now that you have the data stored in the worksheet, you can select the Actual Profits data and create a pie chart. If necessary, refer to the Excel Function Guide for information about accomplishing specific tasks.

TASK 2: TO CREATE AN EXCEL CHART:

1   Select the data in cells A5 through A11, press (CTRL) and then select cells C5 through C11, and then click the Chart Wizard button on the Standard toolbar.

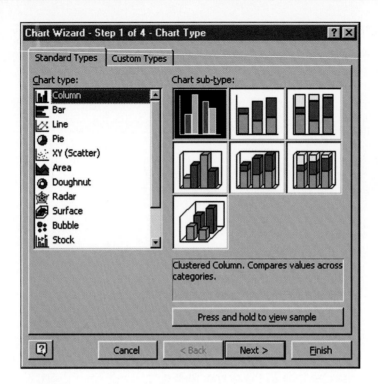

2   Select Pie from the Chart type list, click the 3-D pie on the Chart sub-type palette, and then click Next.

3   Click Next to accept the default values on Steps 2 and 3.

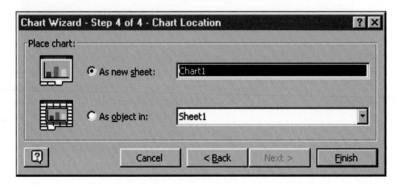

4   Select As new sheet on the Step 4 Wizard page, type **Actual Profits** as the sheet name, and then click Finish.

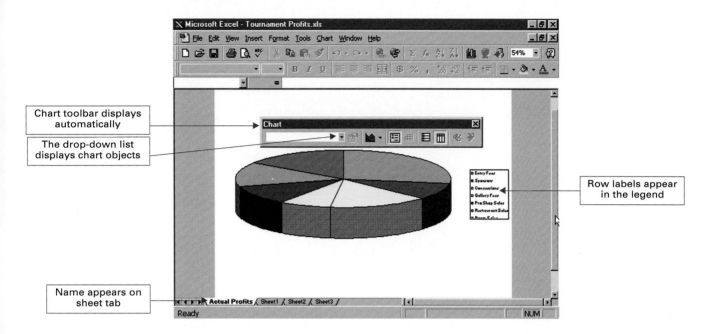

Chart toolbar displays automatically

The drop-down list displays chart objects

Row labels appear in the legend

Name appears on sheet tab

5   Click the Legend 🗐 button on the Chart toolbar to turn the legend off, click the drop-down list arrow on the Chart toolbar, select Series 1, and then click the Format Data Series 🖼 button on the Chart toolbar.

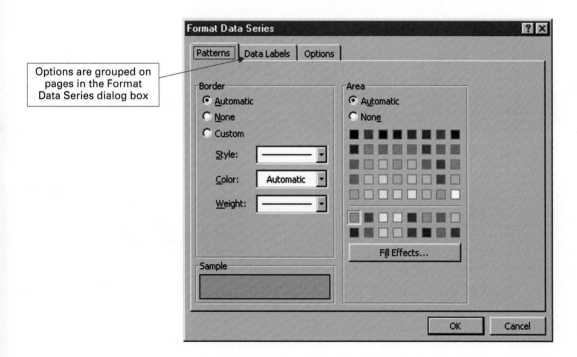

Options are grouped on pages in the Format Data Series dialog box

6 Click the Data Labels tab, select Show label and percent, and then press ⟨ENTER⟩.

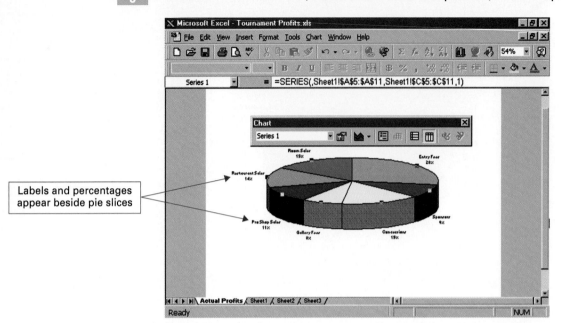

Labels and percentages appear beside pie slices

7 Click the Sheet 1 tab, click cell A1, save changes to the workbook and minimize Excel so that it displays as a button on the Taskbar.

Creating a Word Document

Now that you have completed the Excel worksheet and chart, you need to create the Word document. Refer to the Word and Excel Function Guides for information about how to complete specific tasks.

TASK 3: TO CREATE THE WORD DOCUMENT:

1 Maximize Word and choose File, New to create a new document, if necessary.

> **Tip** If you don't already have Word open, launch the program.

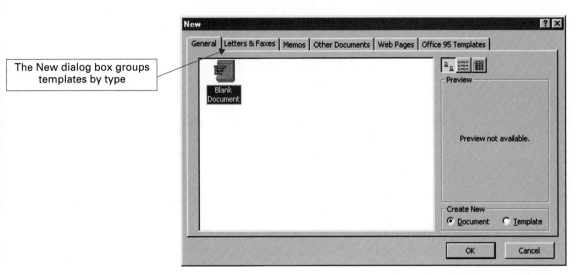

The New dialog box groups templates by type

2 Click the Letters & Faxes tab and double-click the Professional Letter template.

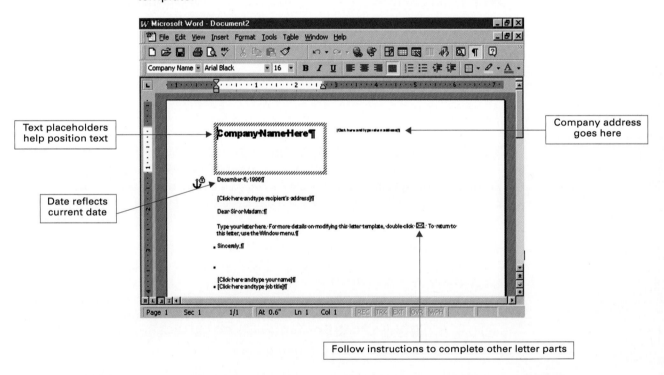

Text placeholders help position text

Date reflects current date

Company address goes here

Follow instructions to complete other letter parts

3 Press (SHIFT)+(END) to select "Company Name Here" and type **The Willows**.

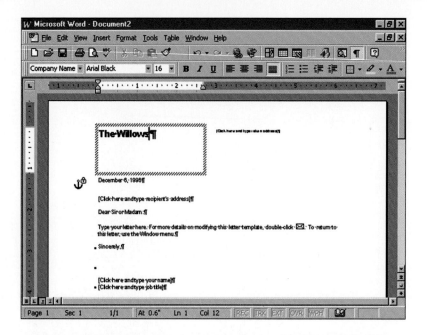

After Step #4
Select the area
(click here + type
recipients address)
+ delete

4 Choose a view of 100%, then click [Click here and type return address], type **1000 Coast Highway**, press (ENTER), and type **Willow Grove, SC 22345**.

5 Select "Dear Sir or Madam:" and type **Dear Board Member:** to replace existing text.

6 Select the "Type your letter here . . ." text and type:

The Willows Classic PGA Golf Tournament carried the pride of The Willows into the record books. From the record crowds lining the fairways to the record prize money awarded the winner, reflections on the tournament will linger with the participants as well as with the observers.

What did the tournament mean to The Willows? Record profits that exceeded all projected expectations. Even with increased registration fees, the number of registrations exceeded those of previous tournaments - and big-name registration drew capacity crowds. The Grande Hotel was filled, and restaurants at The Willows served nonstop. Detailed data is still being compiled, but revenues reported to date are summarized in the following table:

7 Press (ENTER) seven times after the second paragraph to leave room for the Excel worksheet and then type the following paragraph:

Plans are already being made for next year's tournament. The tournament committee will make a full presentation at the next Board meeting, which is scheduled for February 4. If you have questions about the tournament, please do not hesitate to contact Mr. Ben London, Chairman of The Willows Classic PGA Tournament. We look forward to seeing you in February.

8 Type your name as the sender, type **Administrative Assistant** as your job title, and then press (CTRL)+(ENTER) to create a new page.

9 Double-click the header text at the top of page 2 and select the text in the header.

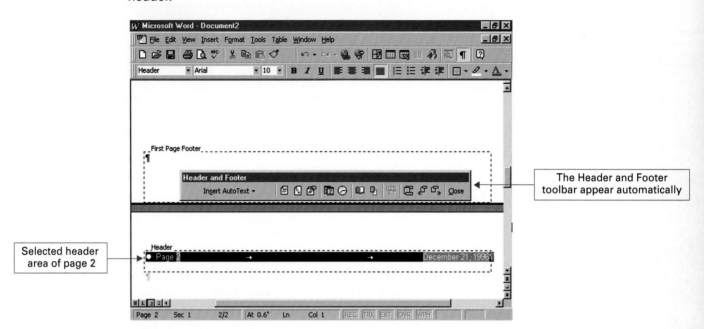

Selected header area of page 2

The Header and Footer toolbar appear automatically

10 Press (DEL) to delete header text, click the Close button on the Header and Footer toolbar, and change the text style to *Normal*.

11 Press (ENTER) eight times and then type:

The Winners
Paul Jacobitz - Grand Prize Winner
Sal Grayson
Glenn Sowell
Allen Campbell
Celebrity Spots
Tom Selleck
Jane Fonda
Alex Trebeck
Bill Clinton
Highlights
Paul Jacobitz now holds the course record low score
More than 20,000 spectators lined the fairways
Largest purse in tournament history
Record number of sponsors
Record number of participants
Record number of celebrity participation
Results

12 Format the text as shown in the following illustration:

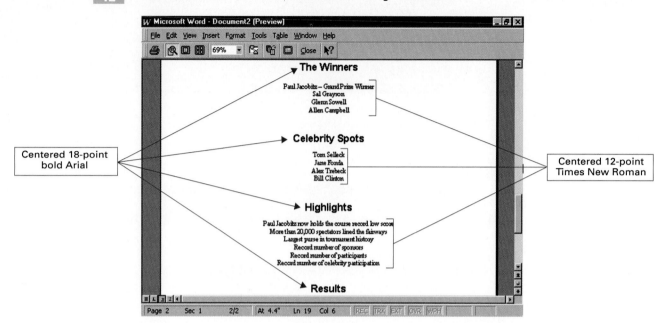

13 Save the document using the filename *Tournament Results to the Board*.

Adding WordArt to a Word Document

WordArt, a feature shared by Word, Excel, and other applications enables you to dress up your Excel worksheets and charts and your Word documents. You can use WordArt to create the graphic text shown in Figure 1.1 at the top of page two on the Word document.

TASK 4: TO ADD WORDART TO A WORD DOCUMENT:

1 Click the Show/Hide ¶ button on the Standard toolbar to turn paragraph symbols on, position the insertion point at the top of Page 2 of the Word document (not in the header area), and click the Drawing 🔁 button on the Standard toolbar.

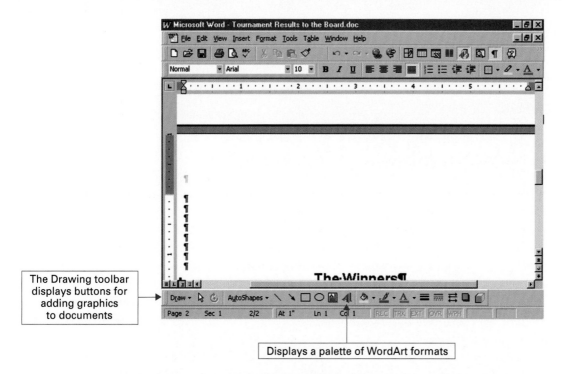

The Drawing toolbar displays buttons for adding graphics to documents

Displays a palette of WordArt formats

2 Click the Insert WordArt button.

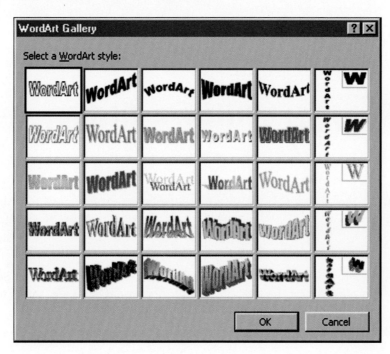

3 Click the third format on the top row and click OK.

4 Type **The Willows Classic** and click OK.

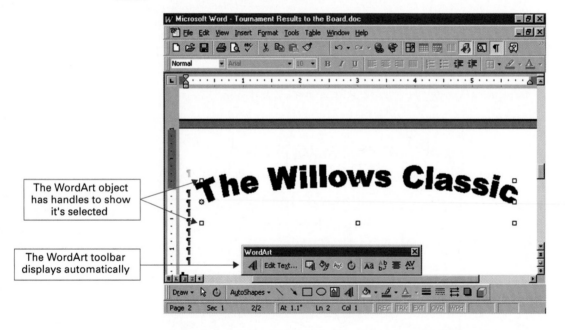

The WordArt object has handles to show it's selected

The WordArt toolbar displays automatically

5 Position the insertion point beside the fourth paragraph symbol just below the WordArt on the left side of your document, click ◀, select the fifth format on the top row, and click OK.

6 Type **PGA Tournament** and click OK.

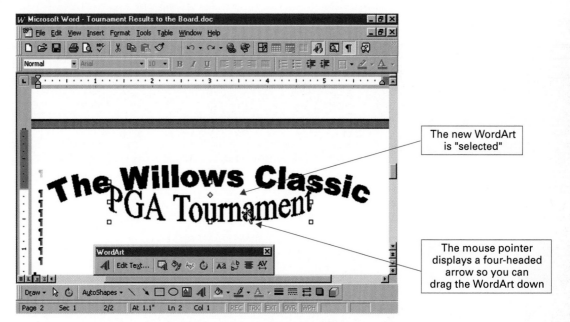

The new WordArt is "selected"

The mouse pointer displays a four-headed arrow so you can drag the WordArt down

7 Point to the new WordArt object, click and drag the WordArt down so that the top left handle appears at about the 0" mark on the vertical ruler, and then press (ESC).

8 Preview your document. Click 🖫 to save the changes.

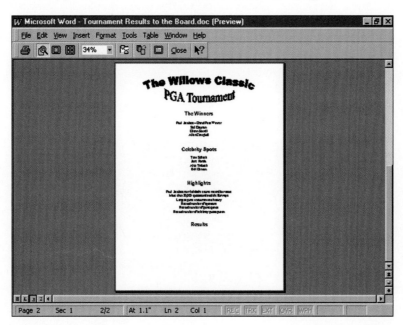

Copying Excel Data to a Word document

After completing and saving the Excel worksheet and the Word documents, you're ready to *integrate,* or combine, the data from the worksheet with the Word document. You can copy the Excel worksheet into the

The task Bar is the bottom clar on your desktop. (it includes the Start button + Novel)

Word document and actually embed the data in the document. The file you copy is called the **source document** and the file receiving the data is called the **target document**. **Embedded data** (called an **object**) stays with the target document and doesn't change when data in the source document changes.

TASK 5: TO COPY EXCEL DATA TO A WORD DOCUMENT:

1   Close all applications you have opened except Word and Excel, maximize both applications, and ensure that the Tournament Profits worksheet is open and active in Excel and that Tournament Results to the Board document is open and active in Word.

2   Point to an area of the Taskbar away from program buttons and right-click.

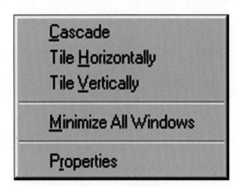

> **Troubleshooting** If your mouse pointer is positioned on a pro-gram button on the Taskbar, you get a different pop-up menu. Press (ESC), reposition the mouse pointer, and try again.

3   Choose Tile Vertically.

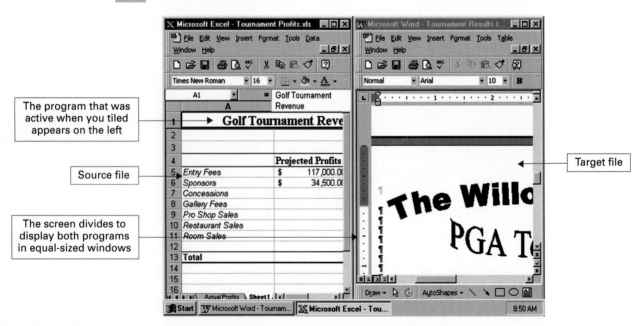

The program that was active when you tiled appears on the left

Source file

The screen divides to display both programs in equal-sized windows

Target file

4   Click the Word title bar to make it active and scroll so that page 1 of the document displays.

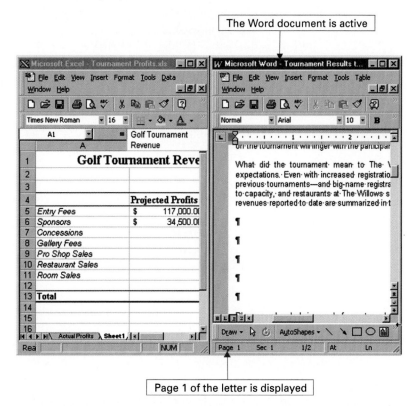

The Word document is active

Page 1 of the letter is displayed

5   Click cell A1 in Excel and drag to select cells A1 through C13.

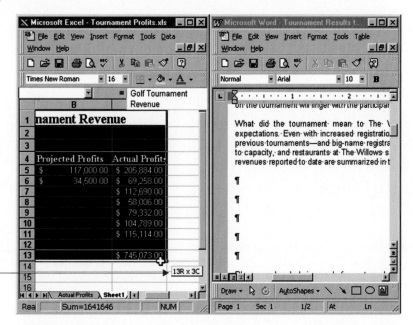

Excel tells you the size of the selected range

6   Position the mouse pointer close to the edge of the selected range so that you see a hollow arrow pointer, press (CTRL) and drag the selection to Word, placing the cursor at the end of the first blank line:

read caution before doing # 6

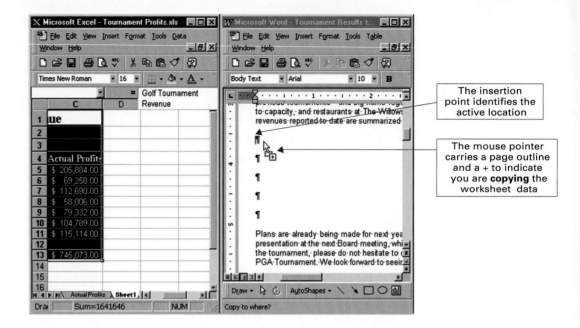

The insertion point identifies the active location

The mouse pointer carries a page outline and a + to indicate you are **copying** the worksheet data

Caution If you don't see a + beside the mouse pointer, you are *moving, not copying,* the data from Excel to Word. Move the mouse pointer back to the worksheet and drop the data. Click Undo, if necessary, and then start over.

7 Release the mouse button to drop the data into Word.

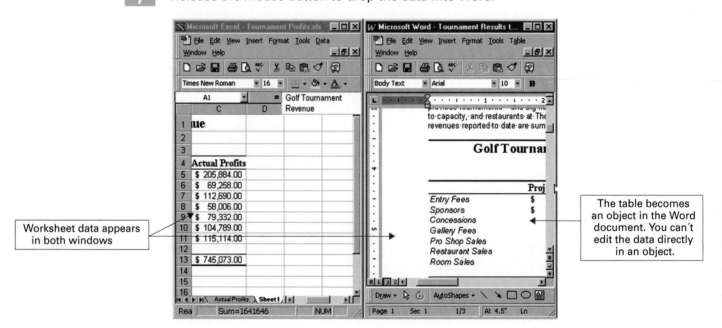

Worksheet data appears in both windows

The table becomes an object in the Word document. You can't edit the data directly in an object.

8 Maximize Word, click the Excel object to select it, click the Center ☰ button on the Formatting toolbar, delete extra paragraph symbols between the object and the last paragraph; then preview the letter and print the first page.

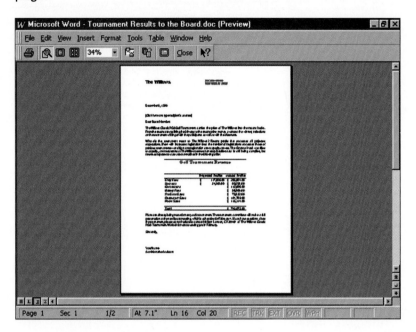

Linking an Excel Chart to a Word Document

The data you copied from the worksheet to the letter is now an embedded object in the letter, and the data in the Word document remains the same regardless of what happens to the worksheet. When you want data in a document to change as data in the original worksheet changes, you have to create a *link* between the worksheet and the document. When you create a link, the document where you place the data checks the original file each time you open the document to see whether changes were made since the data was last updated. You can create a link between the Excel chart and the Word document when you copy the chart to the document.

TASK 6: TO LINK AN EXCEL CHART TO A WORD DOCUMENT:

1 Tile the program windows again, display the Actual Profits chart sheet in Excel, close the Chart toolbar, and scroll the Word document until you see "Results" at the bottom of page 2.

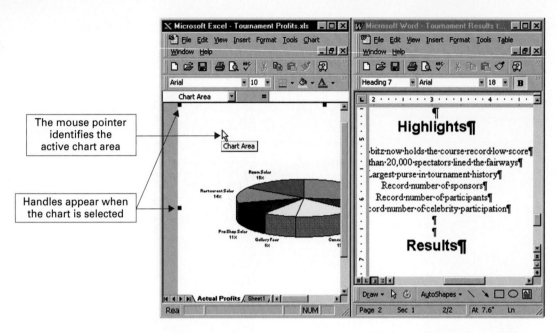

The mouse pointer identifies the active chart area

Handles appear when the chart is selected

2 Click to select the Chart Area of the Excel chart and click 🗎.
A marquee that looks like marching ants displays around the chart area.

3 Click the Word title bar, position the insertion point after the word "Result,"
and press (ENTER).
The insertion point moves to the left margin of the document and displays a
new paragraph symbol.

4 Choose Edit, Paste Special.

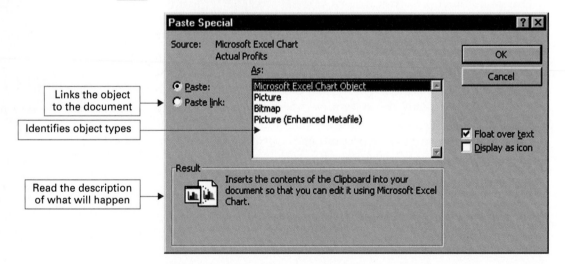

Links the object to the document

Identifies object types

Read the description of what will happen

5 Click the Paste link option, ensure that Microsoft Excel Chart Object is
selected in the As list, and click OK.
Wow! Did your screen seem to go nuts? You need to make some
adjustments to the size of the chart to bring it back onto the previous page.

6 Maximize Word, click 🔍, scroll to preview the chart, and then close the
Preview window.

7 Click the chart to ensure that it is selected, and change the Zoom to Page
width.

8   Make the chart smaller, and position it at the bottom of page 2.

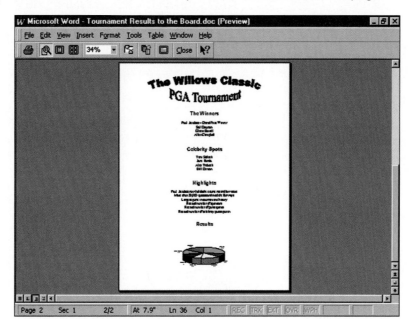

9   Save changes to the document and print a copy of the second page.

The Conclusion

To see the effects of linking the chart to the document, display the Excel worksheet and change a value in the Actual Profits column. View the changes on the chart and then display the Word document. Choose Edit, Links, Update Now to view the changes to the chart in the Word document. Close the Excel worksheet and the Word document without saving the change you made to the data. If you have completed your work, exit Excel and Word and shut down your computer as instructed.

By the way, when you create a WordArt object or an Excel chart, you are actually embedding new objects in the documents. WordArt is created using the Microsoft WordArt program and the chart is created using the Microsoft Chart.

Double-clicking embedded objects opens the source file in the source program so that you can edit data.

Summary and Exercises

Summary

- One advantage of using programs that are part of an office suite is that the shared features make integrating information quick and easy.
- You can share data between applications using a variety of different techniques: dragging and dropping, copying and pasting, and linking.
- Linking data between applications ensures that data updated in one application is reflected in the other application.
- Embedding creates a copy of the data and places it in the target document without creating a link. Embedded data isn't updated automatically when data changes in the other application.

Key Terms and Operations

Key Terms	Operations
embed	Create WordArt objects
integrate	Drag data from Excel and drop it into a Word document
link	Link data from Excel to a Word document
source document	
target document	
tile windows	
WordArt	

Study Questions

Multiple Choice

1. To artistically design text in a document, use
   a. graphics.
   b. the mouse and draw the text.
   c. WordArt.
   d. regular text and change the size.

2. Using data from an Excel worksheet in a Word document is called
   a. integrating data.
   b. AutoFormatting.
   c. tiling.
   d. WordArt.

3. Objects created in one application that are copied to a document in another application are said to be
   a. embedded.
   b. linked.
   c. copied.
   d. placed.

4. The application that created the original file is called the
   a. document.
   b. source.
   c. original.
   d. target.

5. The application into which you copy data from another application is called the
   a. document.
   b. source.
   c. original.
   d. target.

6. To ensure that changes to the source document are automatically reflected in the receiving file, create a(n)
   a. embedded file.
   b. link.
   c. copy.
   d. new object.

7. When you want to link source data to a target file, use the
   a. Clipboard.
   b. Edit, Paste command.
   c. Edit, Paste Special command.
   d. drag and drop technique.

8. The easiest way to arrange the windows so that you can easily drag data from one application to another is to
   a. size the windows separately.
   b. switch back and forth between windows.
   c. close one application and open the other.
   d. open both applications and use the Tile command on the Taskbar shortcut menu.

9. An example of a component shared by all applications contained in an office suite of products is
   a. Office.
   b. Excel.
   c. Word.
   d. WordArt.

10. When you want to use one application to create data that will eventually go into another application,
   a. you should always create the target document first.
   b. you should always create the source document first.
   c. complete and save both documents before linking or embedding the data.
   d. create the data in the target application and then drag it to the source application to save it.

Short Answer

1. What feature in both Word and Excel enables you to create special text effects by graphically arranging and designing text?

2. How do you display the Taskbar shortcut menu?

Current Date

The Willows Board of Directors
P. O. Box 5456
Willow Grove, SC 22345

Ladies and Gentlemen:

The monthly sales figures for our restaurant are reflected in the following table:

Sales for the Atrium Café

	Mar	April	Difference
Week 1	6,570	2,200	4,370
Week 2	8,345	7,890	455
Week 3	8,650	9,180	-530
Week 4	8,990	8,750	240
Week 5	2,130	4,560	-2,430
Total	$34,685	$32,580	

If you have questions about these figures or would like to receive additional in
please do not hesitate to contact me at the number shown above.

Sincerely,

Your Name

Current Date

The Willows Board of Directors
P. O. Box 5456
Willow Grove, SC 22345

Ladies and Gentlemen:

The monthly sales figures for our restaurant are reflected in the following table:

Sales for the The Front Porch Restaurant

	Mar	April	Difference
Week 1	5,460	4,400	1,060
Week 2	7,250	8,870	-1,620
Week 3	7,670	7,750	-80
Week 4	7,990	8,100	-110
Week 5	2,465	3,100	-635

If you have questions about these figures or would like to receive additional information,
please do not hesitate to contact me at the number shown above.

Sincerely,

Your Name

Current Date

The Willows Board of Directors
P. O. Box 5456
Willow Grove, SC 22345

Ladies and Gentlemen:

The monthly sales figures for our restaurant are reflected in the following table:

Sales for the Willow Top Restaurant

	Mar	April	Difference
Week 1	8,560	4,400	4,160
Week 2	10,350	9,870	480
Week 3	10,670	11,150	-480
Week 4	10,990	10,760	230
Week 5	4,670	6,560	-1,890
Total	$45,240	$42,740	

If you have questions about these figures or would like to receive additional i
please do not hesitate to contact me at the number shown above.

Sincerely,

Your Name

Current Date

The Willows Board of Directors
P. O. Box 5456
Willow Grove, SC 22345

Ladies and Gentlemen:

The monthly sales figures for our restaurant are reflected in the following table:

Sales for the Wind in the Willows

	Mar	April	Difference
Week 1	6,460	4,300	2,160
Week 2	7,200	8,800	-1,600
Week 3	7,680	7,760	-80
Week 4	7,890	8,320	-430
Week 5	2,560	3,210	-650
Total	$31,790	$32,390	

If you have questions about these figures or would like to receive additional information,
please do not hesitate to contact me at the number shown above.

Sincerely,

Your Name

Figure 1.2

Follow these steps to complete your task:

1. Launch Word so that you can create the letter pictured here, save the letter using the filename *Restaurant Sales to the Board,* and leave the letter open.

December 6, 1996

The Willows Board of Directors
P. O. Box 5456
Willow Grove, SC 22345

Ladies and Gentlemen:

The monthly sales figures for our restaurant are reflected in the following table:

If you have questions about these figures or would like to receive additional information, please do not hesitate to contact me at the number shown above.

Sincerely,

Your Name

---

2. Launch Excel and open your MarApr.xls worksheet.

3. Tile the two applications on-screen.

4. Select the data in the Atrium Cafe worksheet, and copy it to the Clipboard. Then paste the data as a link into the Word document.

5. Format, center, and align the table with paragraphs in the letter and then save the letter using the filename *Atrium Cafe Sales to the Board.*

6. Follow the same procedure to create letters for the Willow Top restaurant, the Wind in the Willow, and the Front Porch restaurant, saving each letter separately with the restaurant name as part of the filename.

7. Print copies of the letters and exit Word and Excel when you have completed your work.

Assignment

Dragging and dropping Word table data to an Excel worksheet and adding WordArt

Figure 1.3 displays data for entry fees for the upcoming golf tournament formatted as a new worksheet which contains WordArt.

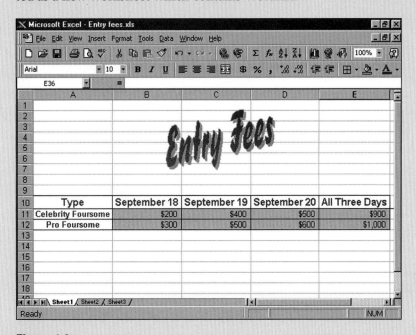

Figure 1.3

The entry fees for the golf tournament were added to a table in your Word Fees-Times-Form.doc document. Use tools presented in this Project to drag the first data table in the document into Sheet 1 of a new Excel workbook. Add a WordArt object, formatting it as shown in Figure 1.3. Save the worksheet using the filename *Tournament Entry Fees* and print a copy of the worksheet. Close the worksheet and exit Excel when you have completed your work.

Notes

Notes

Notes

Notes

Notes

Databases
Using Microsoft Access 97

Overview

Microsoft Access is the database management tool that ships with Microsoft Office 97 Professional. Because Access is based upon the relational database model, you can create powerful applications that can be implemented in a variety of ways. This overview introduces you to basic database concepts and the Microsoft Access user interface.

Objectives

After completing this project, you will be able to:

➤ **Define database terminology**

➤ **List the steps required to design a database**

➤ **Launch Microsoft Access and create a new database**

➤ **Identify Microsoft Access screen elements**

➤ **Work with Access menus and the Database toolbar**

➤ **Get Microsoft Access help**

➤ **Close a database and exit Access**

Defining Database Terminology

A *database* is a collection of information related to a particular subject or purpose. For example, most people keep a list of the names, addresses, and phone numbers of the people they contact frequently. The categories of information that you keep on each individual are most likely consistent. In database terms, each individual item of information in the list such as first name or last name is called a *field*. The collection of field information for one person in the list is a *record*. Therefore, a database contains fields and records. Figure O.1 refers to five fields and one record in a sample phone list.

When using Microsoft Access to store information, field and record information is contained in a grid called a *table*. Figure O.2 displays employee name, address, and phone number data in a Microsoft Access table.

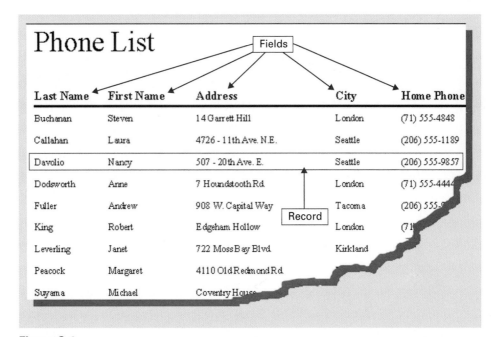

Figure O.1

Figure O.2

A computer application that you use to create and maintain databases is a *database management system (DBMS)*. With Access, you can store information in separate tables and then use the data from one or more tables through relationships, which combine field data from one or more tables. A database management system that enables you to establish relationships among tables is a *relational database management system (RDBMS)*. Relational database management systems are the most powerful kinds of database applications available for microcomputers.

Access Database Objects

In addition to tables, Microsoft Access databases contain other components, each of which is called an object. A **database object** is a component of the database that gives it functionality. Each database object belongs to a category of objects, known as a *class*. For example, a table used for storing phone list information is a table object. Microsoft Access has six classes of database objects. These six classes are tables, queries, forms, reports, macros, and modules. The purpose of each object is listed in Table O.1.

Table O.1   Six Classes of Database Objects

Object Class	Purpose
Table	An organized collection of rows and columns used to store field data. Tables are the primary database object in that they hold the data.
Query	An object that allows the user to view, change, or organize data. Queries are often used as the data source for a screen form or a printed report.
Form	A graphical object that displays data from a table or a query on the screen. Forms make it easy for database users to add, edit, and delete table data.
Report	The database object used to present data in a printed format. Reports can be based upon either tables or queries.
Macro	A set of one or more actions used to automate common tasks, such as opening a form or printing a report.
Module	A collection of Visual Basic for Applications programming components that are stored together as a unit. Programmers create modules to customize an Access database.

Tip Macros and modules are complex database objects. In this book you will learn to design and use tables, queries, forms, and reports.

In Microsoft Access, the database objects you create are stored in a single database file with an *mdb* extension, which stands for "**M**icrosoft **d**atabase."

Before you design a database, you must understand how Access database objects relate to one another. Because tables are used to store field and record information, you must create at least one table before you create any other object. For instance, queries are always based upon one or more tables because they enable you to organize and view data in different ways. Queries can also display data from other queries.

Working with records in a row-and-column format is often tedious, because you often have to scroll horizontally or vertically to display information on the screen. For this reason, forms are used to make table or query data more accessible. In a well-designed database, users work with record and field data via forms, not at the table level. While forms are appropriate for viewing data on the screen, reports are used to format table or query data for printed output. Macros and modules are resources you can use to add more functionality to a database application. Working with these objects requires a solid working knowledge of Microsoft Access and Visual Basic, though, so this book does not cover them.

Designing a Database

Creating a database that is easy to use requires careful consideration, and the time you spend planning one will greatly benefit you in the long run. In general, you must complete five steps when designing a database.

1. **Defining the purpose**
   Define the overall purpose of the database, including a list of user specifications for input and output. Specifications include tasks such as entering data from a common source (such as employment applications) or printing a report of payroll data for the current pay period.

2. **Planning the database objects**
   The objects contained in your database must be carefully planned. You must determine the appropriate number of tables, the ways in which the records will be reorganized using queries and the kinds of forms and reports your database will contain. Make sure you talk with the people who will actually use the database, as they will often give you the most appropriate information about which fields will be needed for input and output.

3. **Creating and relating tables**
   As you know, tables are the primary database objects in Access. As you will see in Project 1, you must specify the kind of data each field will contain before you design a table. If your database contains more than one table, you will need to establish relationships among the tables.

4. **Creating queries to reorganize data**
   You rarely need to see all the field data in a database for all records at the same time. For this reason, queries are used to reorganize or manipulate data to fulfill a specific request. For instance, you may need a listing of all customers from California, or you may want to perform a calculation of a member's outstanding balance.

5. **Creating forms and reports**
   Users can access forms and reports to work with records both onscreen and in printed format, so they are essential to a database. Forms and reports obtain their data from tables and queries.

> **Tip** Designing a full-fledged database is a complex and time-consuming process that requires careful planning and documentation. For the databases you design in this book, use either paper and pencil or a word processor such as Microsoft Word to document your intended design.

In the projects that follow you will create a simple database in which the data is stored in one table. After launching Microsoft Access, you will see that the user interface has been designed to facilitate the creation and maintenance of relational databases.

Launching Microsoft Access and Creating a New Database

As with each of the Office applications, you can launch Microsoft Access in a variety of ways from the Windows desktop. In Task 1, you use the Start button to launch Access and create a new database.

TASK 1: TO LAUNCH MICROSOFT ACCESS AND CREATE A NEW DATABASE:

1. Click the Start ⊞Start button.

2. Select Programs from the Cascading Start menu, and select Access.

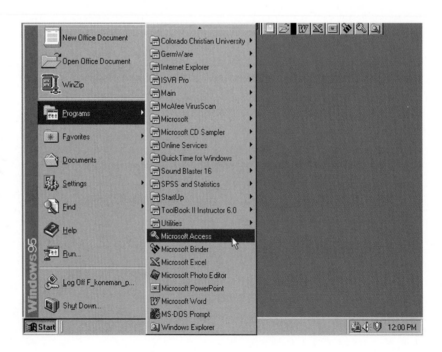

The dialog box shown below appears. You have three options: to open an existing database using the list of recently used databases, to create a new database using the Database Wizard, or to create a blank database.

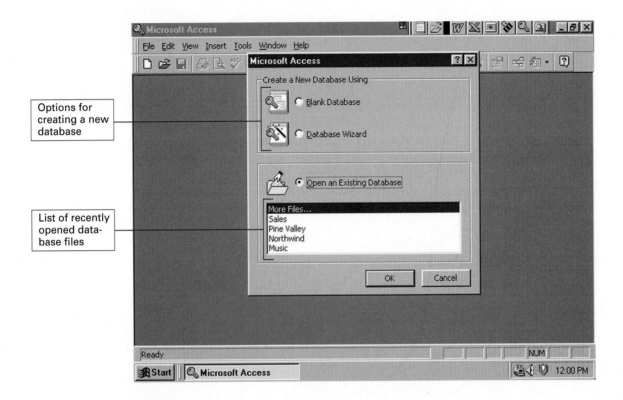

Options for creating a new database

List of recently opened data-base files

3   Select the Blank Database option and click OK.

The File New Database dialog box appears. Notice that the dialog box specifies a default location and default filename.

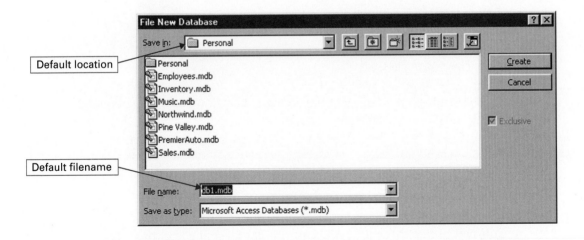

Default location

Default filename

4   Select your floppy disk as the storage location, and type **Willows Membership** as the database name.

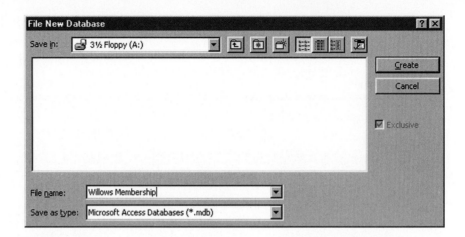

> **Tip** When you name your database file, Access automatically adds a *.mdb* extension to the filename.

5 Click the Create button. Access creates a new database and displays the Database window shown below.

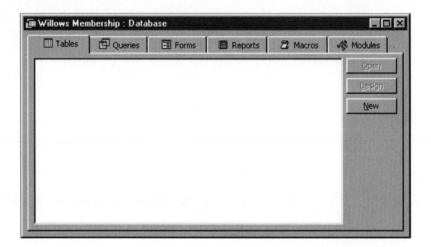

> **Tip** Unlike other applications in the Office suite, only one database file can be open at a time.

Identifying Microsoft Access Screen Elements

You will notice three things about the database file you have just created:

- The Database window appears in a restored state within the Application window (although you can maximize or minimize the Database Window in Access, it will always appear as shown when you create a new database).

- The name of the database appears in the title bar of the Database window.

- The Database window contains tabs that display the database objects you will create; the leftmost Tables tab is active.

You will notice that the Microsoft Access application window shown below has unique elements not seen in other Office applications.

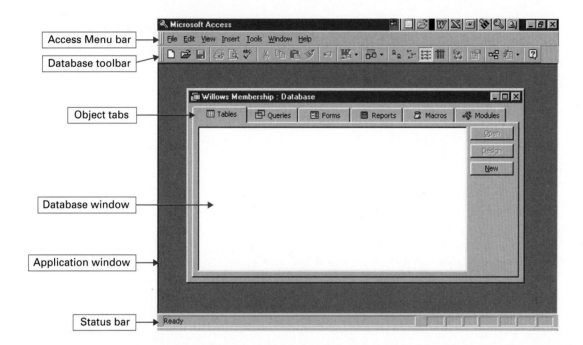

The most striking feature of the Access interface is the Database window. As you create database objects, they are displayed in the appropriate Object tab. You will also notice that the Application Window contains only one toolbar. You use this in the same way as other Toolbars in the Windows environment. Table O.2 identifies the purpose of each screen element you see.

> **Tip**   Notice that the object tabs in the Database window appear in the same order as the kinds of database objects listed in steps for designing a database (see Table O.1). Because tables are the primary repositories for the data in a database, the Tables tab is listed first.

Table O.2 Access Screen Elements

Screen Element	Purpose
Access Menu Bar	Provides access to the commands used to perform tasks.
Application Title Bar	Identifies the current application and contains Control menu items for minimizing the Application Window, maximizing and restoring the Application Window, and exiting the application.
Database Toolbar	Provides shortcuts to the most common database commands and tasks.
Database Window	Displays Object tabs for the six kinds of database objects you can create.
Object Tabs	Display the specific objects you create. You can use the Object tabs to design or open each object.
Status Bar	Displays program status as well as instructions and information for performing specific tasks.

Working with Access Menus

The Microsoft Access menus and the Database toolbar provide access to the tasks you perform when creating and maintaining databases. Many of these procedures display dialog boxes in which you can specify exactly how to accomplish a task or procedure.

TASK 2: TO USE THE ACCESS MENU:

1 Select the File menu by clicking it. The menu opens.

2 Select Database Properties.

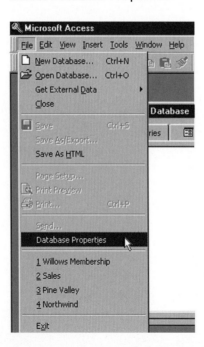

The Database Properties dialog box appears.

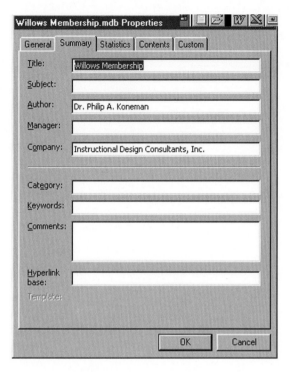

3 Place the insertion point inside the Subject: line, and type **The Willows Membership Roster**.

4 Click OK.

TASK 3: TO USE THE DATABASE TOOLBAR:

1 Click the New Database icon, as shown below.

The New dialog box appears.

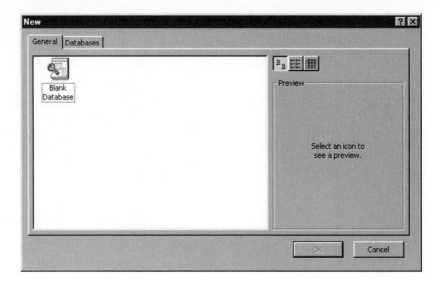

2 Click the Databases tab. The dialog box now displays the available database templates.

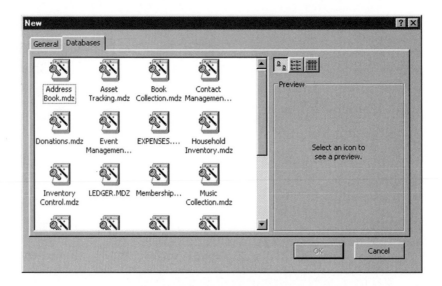

Troubleshooting If the database templates do not appear as shown in the figure above, check to make sure the Large Icons option is active by clicking the Large Icons button.

3 Click the *Address Book.mdz* icon. A graphic depicting the structure of the database should display in the Preview window shown on the next page.

Tip The *mdz* file extension identifies this file as an Access Wizard template.

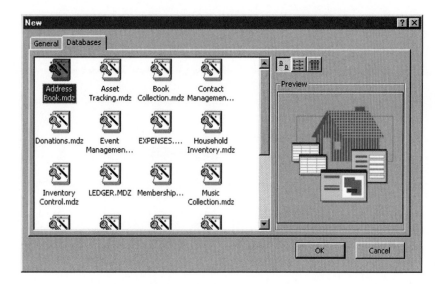

4　Click Cancel to return to the Database window.

Getting Help

Microsoft Access provides numerous options for getting help online as you work. To get help, select Help from the Access menu. Access includes four ways of obtaining help:

- Office Assistant
- Contents and Index
- What's This?
- Microsoft on the Web

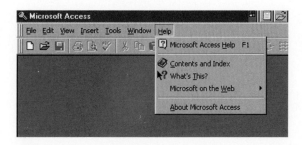

The Office Assistant

The Office Assistant can answer your questions, offer tips, and provide Help for a variety of features specific to Access. To open the Office Assistant, select Microsoft Access Help from the menu. When using the Office Assistant, you can either select an option from the list or type a word or phrase to display new options.

TASK 4: TO USE THE OFFICE ASSISTANT:

1 Select Microsoft Access Help from the Help menu.

2 The Office Assistant opens, as shown below.

3 Type **Tables** as a search term in the text box.

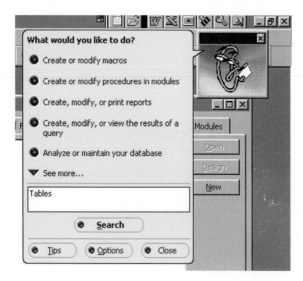

4 Click the Search button. The topics in the list change.

5 Click the first option, *Create a table*. The Help system displays the topic shown on the next page.

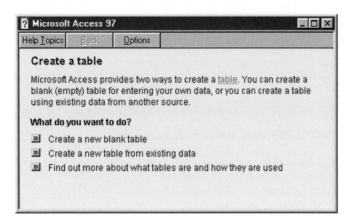

6   Use the Close button in the upper right-hand corner of the Help Topics window to close it.

Obtaining Help Using Contents and Index

Contents and Index is the familiar Help system that has been available in all Microsoft applications. Select Contents and Index from the Help menu. When using this option, Access displays the standard Windows Help system interface.

TASK 5: TO USE CONTENTS AND INDEX:

1   Select Contents and Index from the Help menu. The Help Topics dialog box appears.

2   Click the Index tab and type **queries** in the list.

3 Select the *creating* index entry and then click the Display button, as shown below.

4 In the Topics Found dialog box shown in the figure on the next page, select the *Create a query* topic and then click the Display button.

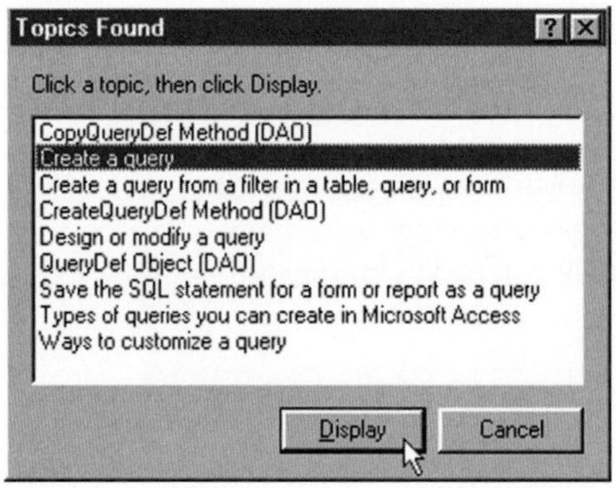

The Create a query topic appears.

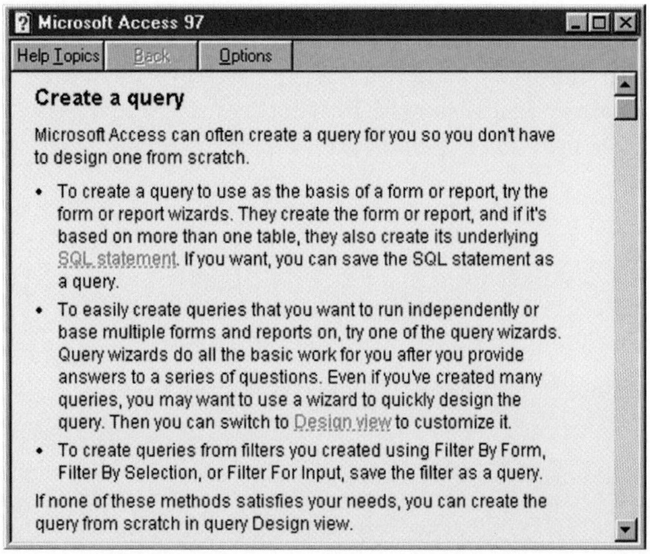

5 Click the Close button in the Help Topics window to close it.

Getting Help Using What's This?

You can easily view tips on menu commands, toolbar buttons, and other screen items using What's This?. When you select What's This? from the Help menu, the Office What's This icon is displayed. You can obtain help on any screen element by simply clicking this icon.

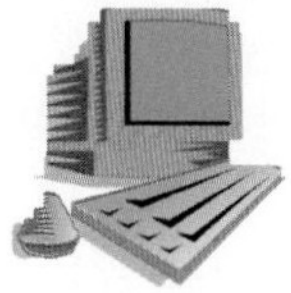

TASK 6: TO USE WHAT'S THIS?:

1 Select ***What's This?*** from the Help menu. The mouse pointer icon changes ? to indicate that What's This? is active.

2 Place the mouse pointer directly over the title bar of the Database window, and click the left mouse button.

Information about the Database Window appears onscreen, as shown on the next page.

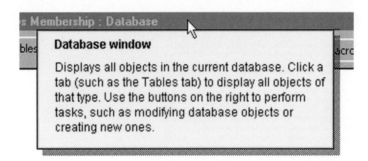

Database window

Displays all objects in the current database. Click a tab (such as the Tables tab) to display all objects of that type. Use the buttons on the right to perform tasks, such as modifying database objects or creating new ones.

3 Click the left mouse button to close the information window.

Obtaining Help Using Microsoft on the Web

Extensive help is available online through Microsoft on the Web. This help option enables you to link to the Microsoft Web site for the latest information about using Access. To use this feature, you must have access to the Internet and a Web browser such as Internet Explorer or Netscape Navigator.

TASK 7: GETTING HELP FROM THE MICROSOFT WEB SITE:

1 Select Microsoft on the Web from the Help menu.

2 Choose Online Support from the cascading menu.

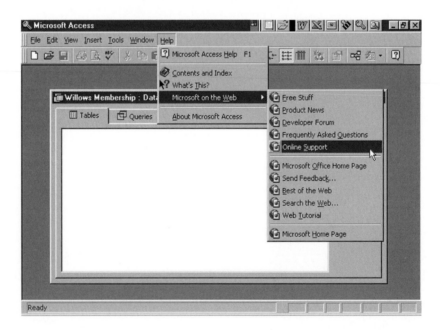

3 A Web page similar to the one displayed in the figure on the next page appears. You can use this resource to search for any topic in Access.

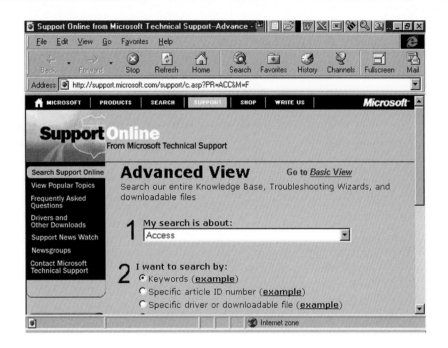

4 When you are finished using Microsoft's Web help system, close your Web browser by clicking the Close button.

Closing Your Database File and Exiting Microsoft Access

You are finished with your database for the present, so you can close it and exit Microsoft Access. You have not yet created any database objects, so you have nothing to update in the file.

> **Tip** Any time you close a database that you have modified, it is updated automatically.

TASK 8: TO CLOSE YOUR DATABASE FILE AND EXIT MICROSOFT ACCESS:

1 Click the Close button of the Database window to close the open database file.

2 Select Exit from the File menu, or click the Close button in the Application window to exit Microsoft Access.

Summary and Exercises

Summary

- Microsoft Access is a relational database management system (RDBMS).
- A database is a collection of information related to a common purpose.
- When launching Access, you must specify whether you want to open an existing database or create a new one.
- Access includes two methods for creating a new database: opening a blank database or using the database wizard.
- An Access database file contains multiple objects, including tables, queries, forms, reports, macros, and modules.
- Tables are the primary kind of database object in Access.
- Only one database can be open at a time.
- The Database window provides a graphical interface for designing and opening database objects.
- You can obtain online help in Access in four ways: the Office Assistant, Contents and Index, What's This?, and Microsoft on the Web. All types can be accessed through the Help menu.

Key Terms and Operations

Key Terms
class
database
database management system (DBMS)
database object
field
form
macro
module
query
record
relational database management system (RDBMS)
report
table

Operations
close a database file and exit Microsoft Access
display and change database properties
launch Access and create a new database
obtain online help using the Contents and Index option
use the Access File and Help menus
use the Office Assistant in Access to search for online help
use the What's This? help feature
view the available New Database templates
use Microsoft on the Web to search the World Wide Web

Study Questions

Multiple Choice

1. Which Access object is considered primary?
   a. table
   b. query
   c. form
   d. report

2. Which screen element is used to easily design or open the objects within a database?
   a. Close button
   b. Status bar
   c. Database toolbar
   d. Database window

3. Which online help option requires Internet access?
   a. What's This?
   b. Microsoft on the Web
   c. Contents
   d. Index

4. How many database files can be open simultaneously?
   a. one
   b. two
   c. three
   d. four

5. Which of the following terms describes all the data for one entity in a table?
   a. record
   b. file
   c. field
   d. query

6. Which database object is used to create printed output?
   a. table
   b. query
   c. form
   d. report

7. During which phase of the database design are the output specifications identified?
   a. defining the purpose
   b. planning the objects
   c. creating and relating tables
   d. creating queries

8. In a well-designed database, the end user almost never interacts directly with
   a. tables
   b. queries
   c. forms
   d. both a and b

9. A database contains the first name, last name, and phone number for a group of students. The first name is what kind of data?
   a. field
   b. record
   c. query
   d. table

10. A table object is an instance of what?
    a. a form
    b. a query
    c. a report
    d. a class

Short Answer

1. How do fields and records differ?

2. Which Access object is considered the primary object?

3. What is a relational database management system?

4. How is a query differ from a table?

5. Which Access object is used to make data in a database more visually appealing on the screen?

6. When you name a database file, on which screen element does the filename appear?

7. What is the Database window?

8. How are the Access menus and the Database toolbar related?

9. Why is it important to determine output specifications before creating a database?

10. How does the Office Assistant differ from the Contents and Index online help option?

For Discussion

1. What is the primary database object in a Microsoft Access database, and how does it differ from other Access objects?

2. What are the six classes of database objects? How is each category of object used?

3. What is required to use Microsoft on the Web to obtain help about Access?

4. What steps are required to design a database?

Review Exercises _____

1. Creating a new database using the New Database Wizard
One of the databases you will create for the Willows is an employee database. This database will be used to keep track of the names, addresses, phone numbers, and salary or wage information for each employee.

Using the design steps outlined in this Overview, plan a table to list employee data. Create a Microsoft Word document entitled *Employee Table Specifications.doc* that includes answers to the following questions:

1. What is the purpose of this database?

2. What are two potential input specifications?

3. What are two potential output specifications?

4. What fields would be appropriate for this table?

Save your document before exiting Microsoft Word.

2. Getting Help about Wizards

Microsoft Office 97 Professional incorporates Wizards to simplify common tasks. In an assignment for Project 1, you will use the New Database Wizard to create an employee database.

Use the online help system to obtain information about creating a database using Wizards. Follow these steps:

1. Select Microsoft Access Help from the Help menu.

2. Type **What is the database wizard** in the question box, and then click the Search button.

3. Select the Create a Database topic. In the Microsoft Access 97 help dialog box, select *Create a database using a Database Wizard* from the help topic and review the necessary steps to use this Wizard.

3. Creating a new database and exploring object windows

1. Launch Access 97 and create a new blank database named **High Point Foods xxx** (where **xxx** represents your initials).

2. Display each page of the blank database object window.

3. Display a list of toolbars available and display one of the toolbars available.

4. Close the toolbar.

5. Maximize the database window; then restore the window.

6. Close the database and exit Access.

Assignments

1. Using the Microsoft Web site to obtain help on Access

Connect to the Microsoft Access Web site, and search for information about publishing Microsoft Access data on the Web. If time permits, create a Word document explaining the process of publishing table data to a static Web page.

2. Designing a membership database

One of your tasks at the Willows is to design a database for tracking information about the current members. Using the same strategy from the Overview and Assignment 1, develop a set of specifications for a membership database. Save your specifications in a Microsoft Word document.

PROJECT

Building an Access Table

Now that you have created a database file, your first step in building the database itself is to create individual database objects. In this project you will build a table to hold membership information.

Objectives

After completing this project, you will be able to:

➤ **Open an Access database**

➤ **Create an Access table using Design view**

➤ **Define a table structure**

➤ **Add records to an Access table in Datasheet view**

➤ **Create an AutoForm**

➤ **Navigate among records and add records to a table using the navigation controls on a form**

The Challenge

As a member of the IT (Information Technology) department at the Willows, Mr. Gilmore has asked you to design a database containing information about current members of the club. The Willows has three membership categories, each with corresponding dues. A member can receive a discount on his or her membership based upon current age and length of membership. Mr. Gilmore wants the database to print a list of each member's current status and membership dues.

The Solution

Before creating a table, you must determine the appropriate data types for each field of information. Using Table Design view you can quickly create the table design by naming each field and selecting the appropriate data type and field size. After you add a few records to the table in Datasheet view, you can create a simple AutoForm to work with records in the database one at a time. Your completed table and a form displaying table data appears in Figure 1.1.

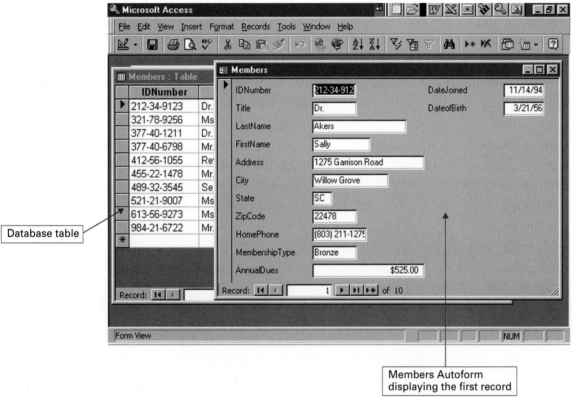

Figure 1.1

The Setup

After you launch Access and open your database, you should set up Access as shown in Table 1.1 so that your screen matches the illustrations in

Table 1.1   Access Settings

Location	Make These Settings:
View, Toolbars	Display the Database toolbar
Tools, Options	Display the Status bar

this project. The following table lists the default settings in Access, but they may have been changed on your computer.

> **Troubleshooting** If you do not see the Database toolbar on the screen when you launch Access and open your database, choose Toolbars from the View menu. Select the Database toolbar to display it. If any additional toolbars are visible, close them. If you do not see the Status Bar at the bottom of the Application Window, choose Options from the Tools menu, click the View tab and change the Status Bar check box option.

Opening an Access Database

When you launch Access, the Microsoft Access dialog box shown in Figure 1.2 appears onscreen. This dialog box enables you to either create a new database or open an existing one. Remember that a list of recently opened databases appears at the bottom of the dialog box.

Figure 1.2

TASK 1: TO OPEN A DATABASE:

 Launch Access.

> **Troubleshooting** If Access is running and the Microsoft Access dialog box is not visible, select Open Database from the File menu.

2 Select the Open an Existing Database option and click OK.

3 When the Open dialog box appears, select your floppy disk drive in the Look in: drop-down list.

4 Click *Willows Membership.mdb* in the file list, as shown opposite, if it is not already selected.

5 Click Open.
Access opens the database file, displays the name of the database in the Title bar of the Database window, and makes the Tables tab active, as shown below.

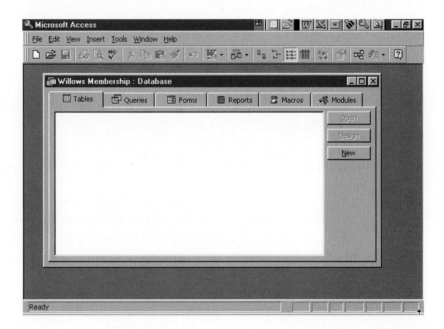

Creating a Table

As you will recall from the Overview, you must first plan a database before designing it. This database will list members and will provide a printed list of each member's current membership status, dues, and discounts. You will need at least one table and one report. To simplify the process of modifying membership data, you will also create a screen form. The discount data will be calculated using a query.

An Access table object is the primary repository for data, so you must create a table to hold the record data. When creating a table, you must specify the kind of data each field will contain. The name of each field, the kind of data it contains, and the number of characters each field can store are known as the *table structure*. You must follow Access naming conventions when determining a table's structure.

Naming Fields and Determining Data Types

Access does not place many restrictions on naming the fields in a table. A field name can be up to 64 characters in length and can include any combination of letters, numbers, spaces, and special characters except a period (.), an exclamation point (!), an accent grave (`), and brackets ([ ]).

> **Tip** If your database will include Visual Basic code or more complex expressions, consider omitting spaces from the field name.

To store your table data in the most efficient manner, Access supports different data types. A *data type* is a characteristic of how data is stored in a database. Various data types correspond to the kind of data your fields will contain. For example, a text data type is required to store name and address information. If you need to perform calculations involving monetary units, you will need to use the currency data type. Table 1.2 summarizes the 10 data types you can use for table data.

Determining an Appropriate Table Structure

Now that you know what Mr. Gilmore wants, you can design a table that stores information about the club's members. In most databases that contain name and address information, you create separate fields for first and last name, and for address, city, state, and zip code. This ensures that you can sort the data in different ways, such as by last name, by state of residence, or by zip code.

Your table will contain text, currency, and data/time data types. In the tasks that follow, you will create a new table with the table structure shown in Figure 1.3.

Table 1.2   Access Data Types

Data Type	Description
Text	Any combination of alphabetic and numeric characters, such as names, addresses, and phone numbers. The text data type holds a maximum of 255 characters, which is the default data type.
Memo	Used for long text entries that exceed 255 characters. Holds up to 64 kilobytes of data in a random format.
Number	Numeric values, such as inventory quantity or the number of items ordered. Numeric data can be used in calculations.
Date/Time	Date and time values for the years 100 through 9999.
Currency	Currency values and numeric data used in mathematical calculations that involve data with one to four decimal places.
AutoNumber	Access feature that assigns a unique and sequential number to records as they are created and added to a table. AutoNumber data cannot be changed, edited, or deleted.
Yes/No	This data type displays a checkbox and allows for Yes/No (Boolean) data. If the checkbox is empty, the value is No or False (0). If the checkbox is checked, the value is Yes or True (1).
OLE Object	Fields that contain embedded or linked objects, such as Microsoft Excel spreadsheet, a Microsoft Word document, graphics, or sounds.
Hyperlink	Text, or combinations of text and numbers, used as a hyperlink address. This data type is used to link to Web pages or other documents.
Lookup Wizard	A wizard that walks you through the process of defining a field that allows you to choose a value from another table or from a list of values.

Field Name	Data Type	Field Length / Format
IDNumber	Text	11
Title	Text	10
LastName	Text	25
FirstName	Text	15
Address	Text	50
City	Text	20
State	Text	2
ZipCode	Text	10
HomePhone	Text	14
MembershipType	Text	10
AnnualDues	Currency	
DateJoined	Date/Time	Short Date
DateofBirth	Date/Time	Short Date

Figure 1.3

TASK 2: TO CREATE FIELDS IN A TABLE WITH A TEXT DATA TYPE:

1 With the Tables tab active, click the New button in the Database window.

2 In the New Table dialog box, select Design view and click OK.

The Table Design window will appear.

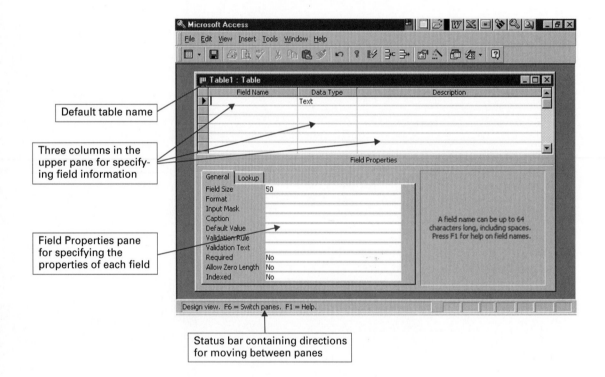

The **Table Design window** is a visual workspace in which you can enter information about each field in your table. **Table Design view** always displays this window.

3 The insertion point appears in the left column of the first row of the upper pane. Type **IDNumber** in the left column of the first row, as shown on the following page.

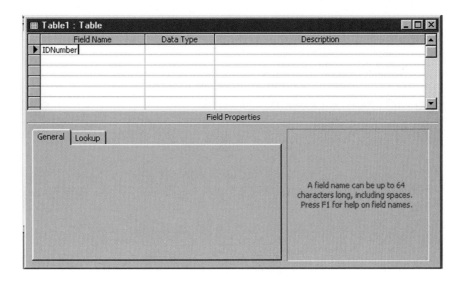

4 Press (F6) once to activate the Properties pane (the lower half of the window) for the current field. You will notice that the data type is set to text by default, and that the default field size entry is selected.

5 Type **11** as the field size for the IDNumber field.

6 Press (F6) to move back to the upper pane.

7 Click the Primary Key 🔑 button on the toolbar, as shown.

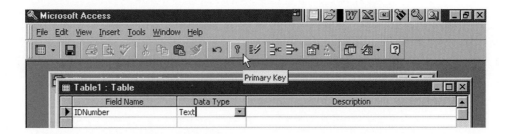

> **Tip** The power of a relational database system such as Access comes from its ability to quickly find and bring together information stored in separate tables. In order to do this, each table should include a field or set of fields that uniquely identify each record in the table. This information is called the primary key of the table. Once you designate a primary key for a table, to ensure uniqueness, Microsoft Access will prevent any duplicate or Null values from being entered in the primary key fields.

An icon representing this field as the primary key appears in the upper pane, as shown on the next page.

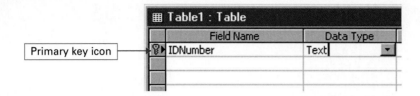

Primary key icon

8 Using the specifications listed in Figure 1.3, add field names and change the default field size for all fields through MembershipType. When you are finished, your Table Definition window will look similar to the figure shown below.

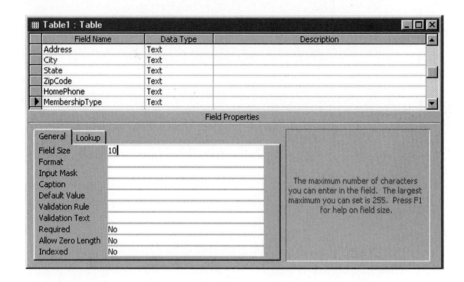

> **Troubleshooting** If you make a mistake while defining one or more fields, use the scroll bar in the upper pane and place the insertion point into the appropriate cell in the upper pane or the row in the lower pane that must be corrected. After a table is saved, you can always return to the Table Design window to modify its structure.

9 Click the Save 🖫 icon on the toolbar.
The Save As dialog box shown below appears. Notice that the default table name Table1 is highlighted.

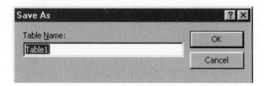

10 Type **Members** as the table name, and click OK. The name of the table changes in the Table Title bar.

Name of table
displayed in
Title bar

Field Name	Data Type
Address	Text
City	Text
State	Text
ZipCode	Text
HomePhone	Text
▶ MembershipType	Text

Members : Table

TASK 3: DEFINING FIELDS WITH CURRENCY AND DATE/TIME DATA TYPES:

1   Type **AnnualDues** as the field name in the next available row in the upper pane. Press the ⟨TAB⟩ key once to activate the Data Type column.

2   Click the drop-down list button next in the Data Type column, and select Currency as the data type.

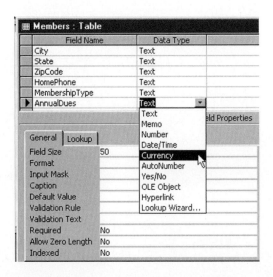

You will notice that the available properties for this field change in the lower pane.

3   Press the ⟨TAB⟩ key twice until the insertion point appears in the "Field Name" column of the next row. Then type **DateJoined** as the next field name, and set its data type to Date/Time. The data field appears, as shown on the next page.

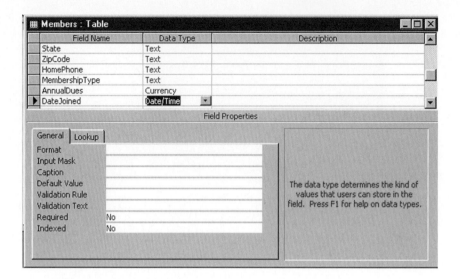

4 Type **DateofBirth** as the name of the last field. Set the data type to Date/Time.

5 Save the changes to your table design.

6 Select Datasheet view ▦ from the View menu.

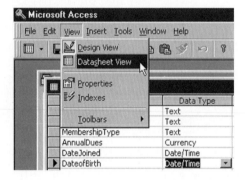

The table is now displayed in Datasheet view, as shown on the next page. *Datasheet view* is a display format in which field data appears in columns and record data appears in rows. Notice that the name of each field appears above the columns near the top of the window. A horizontal scroll bar appears along the bottom of the window. You can use this scrollbar to reveal the remaining fields in the table.

Tip You can also use the Up and Down directional arrow keys to move among records.

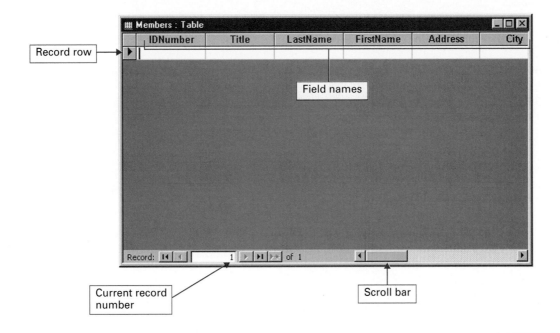

7   Use the Close button in the upper right-hand corner of the Table window to close the table and return to the Database window.

Adding Records to a Table Using Datasheet View

Now that you have successfully created a table, you can easily add records about specific members using Datasheet view. Notice that the Database window shown below displays an icon representing the table you just created. In addition, the Open and Design buttons are now enabled.

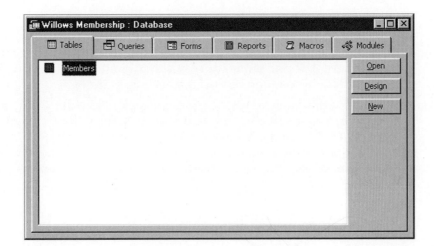

Remember that every Access object has at least two views: one for creating or editing the object's design, and one for viewing record data by the object. You will use Datasheet view to add records to the table.

TASK 4: TO ADD RECORDS TO A TABLE USING DATASHEET VIEW:

1 Highlight the *Members* table in the Tables tab of the Database window, and click the Open button.

> **Tip** You can also open a table in Datasheet view by double-clicking the table's icon in the Database window.

2 Type **455-22-1478** as the membership ID number for the first member's record.

3 Press the TAB key once to move to the next field.

4 Type **Mr.** as the title for this member.

5 Type **Jenkins** as the last name and **Adley** as the first name.

> **Troubleshooting** If you inadvertently move to the next field, you can use the SHIFT+TAB combination to move to the previous field in the datasheet. You can also click the mouse in any field to edit its contents.

6 Type **250 Windjammer Drive**, **Almont**, **SC**, **22217**, and **(803) 551-2770** respectively, as the address and phone information for this member. (Remember that you don't type in the commas.)

7 Type **Charter** as the membership type, **775** as his annual dues, **1/25/87** as the date this member joined the Willows, and **10/16/31** as this member's date of birth.

> **Troubleshooting** When adding currency data, you do not need to enter a dollar sign before the value. If the value is an integer, Access adds two zeros to the right of the decimal place.
>
> When entering dates, place a forward slash character (/) or a hyphen (-) between the month, day, and year values. If you use the hyphen character, Access will convert it to a forward slash character when you move out of the field.

8 Press the TAB key. The insertion point moves to the first field of the second record.

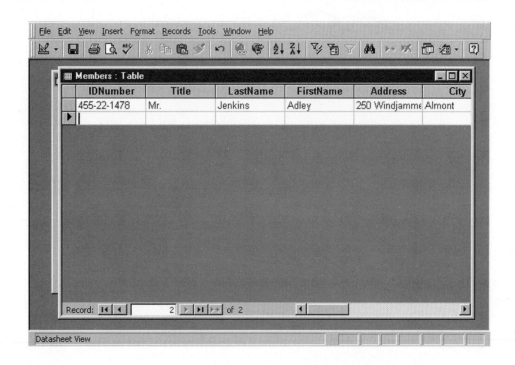

9   Using the data shown in the figure below, add four additional records to the database by following the same process as in Steps 1–8.

Record	ID Number	Title	Last Name	First Name	Address	City	State
2	212-34-9123	Dr.	Akers	Sally	1275 Garrison Road	Willow Grove	SC
3	521-21-9007	Ms.	Bock	Anita	14563 Greenridge	James Way	SC
4	412-56-1055	Reverend	Barclay	William	9007 Leesburg Pike	Smithfield	SC
5	321-78-9256	Ms.	Williams	Sandy	14419 Brooke Street	James Way	SC

Record	Zip Code	Home Phone	Membership Type	Annual Dues	Date Joined	Date of Birth
2	22478	(803) 211-1275	Bronze	$525.00	11/14/94	3/21/56
3	24382	(803) 555-1212	Gold	$650.00	2/1/64	5/3/35
4	24491	(803) 744-7611	Silver	$575.00	1/9/97	7/14/65
5	24381	(803) 555-8272	Charter	$775.00	6/29/82	4/15/30

After you add four more records, the Datasheet will appear as shown below.

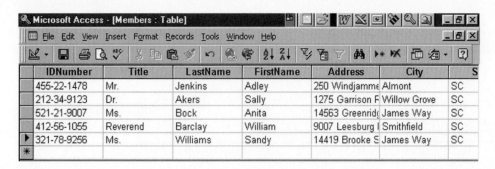

10   Close the table.

Creating an AutoForm

As you can see, working with records in Datasheet view is tedious. Not only do you have to scroll back and forth to see all fields, but navigation between fields is limited. Therefore, most databases include screen forms for editing table data. In this context, a form is a visual representation of record and field data that usually displays only one record on the screen at a time. Just as with tables, forms include multiple views.

It is not difficult to create a form in Access. In fact the *AutoForm* option for new forms can create a form for you after you specify the form layout you want and which table to use as the source for your form.

TASK 5: TO CREATE AN AUTOFORM:

1 Click the Forms tab in the Database window.

2 Click the New button.

3 In the New Forms dialog box, select the AutoForm: Columnar option, as shown below.

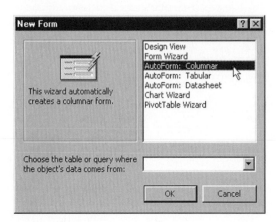

4 In the lower portion of the form, click the drop-down list button to specify a table or query.

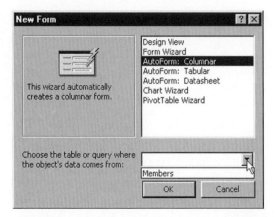

5 Because the Members table is the only object in your database that you can use as the source for an AutoForm, select Members in the list of available tables and queries. Members should now appear in the listbox, as shown below.

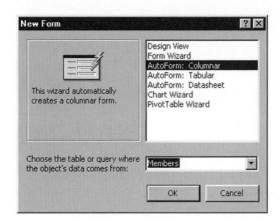

6 Click OK. AutoForm generates a form that looks similar to the one shown below.

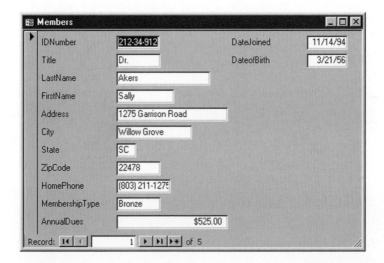

Troubleshooting Depending upon how Access is configured on your computer, your form may contain a background image or display different colors. In addition, some of the fields may not display completely.

7 Click the Save button 🖫 on the toolbar to save your form. The Save As dialog box appears.

8 Accept the default name by clicking OK.

Navigating Among Records and Adding Records to a Table Using the Navigation Controls on a Form

The form you created in the last task includes navigation buttons for moving among records in the underlying Members table. To **navigate** among records is to move from one record to another in a table. By default, the form displays the first record in the table when it is created or opened. You can use these controls to move to the first, previous, next, and last records in the table. You can also use the New Record button to add records to the table. The figure below explains the navigation buttons that appear on the Members form.

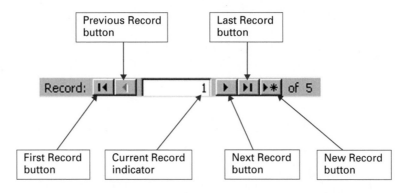

TASK 6: TO NAVIGATE AMONG RECORDS IN A TABLE USING A FORM:

1 Click the Last Record button on the Members form. Record 5 appears in the form.

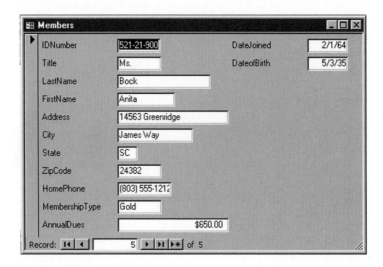

2 Click the Previous Record button. The form displays record number 4.

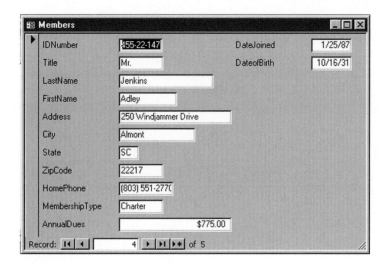

3   Select the number 4 inside the text box displaying the current record, and type **2**. When you press (ENTER), the form displays the second record in the table.

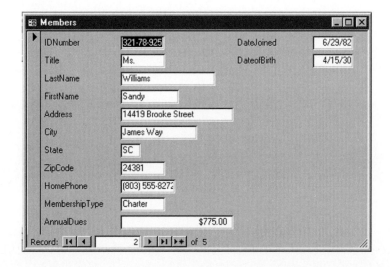

Troubleshooting As you navigate through the table the record numbers will not correspond to the order in which you entered the records. This is because the records are ordered according to the primary key.

TASK 7: TO ADD RECORDS TO THE TABLE USING THE NEW RECORD BUTTON ON THE FORM:

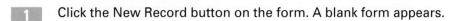

1   Click the New Record button on the form. A blank form appears.

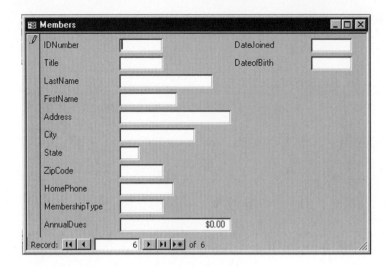

Notice that the insertion point appears inside the IDNumber field, and that the current record is record 6.

2 Type **377-40-6798** as the ID Number for the sixth member in the table.

3 Press the (TAB) key to move to the next field on the form.

4 Using the data shown below, complete the sixth record and add four additional records to the Members table.

Record	ID Number	Title	Last Name	First Name	Address	City	State
6	377-40-6798	Mr.	Gill	Samuel	9575 Kingsley Road	Altamont	SC
7	984-21-6722	Mr.	Thomas	Michael	15065 Knicker Drive	Fordham	SC
8	489-32-3545	Senator	Lilley	William	13411 Reardon Lane	Adamsville	SC
9	377-40-1211	Dr.	Bolts	Raymond	5622 Forest Glen	Freeman	NC
10	613-56-9273	Ms.	Adams	Jennifer	14419 Brook Street	Willow Grove	SC

Record	Zip Code	Home Phone	Membership Type	Annual Dues	Date Joined	Date of Birth
6	24122	(803) 343-2100	Bronze	$525.00	9/6/92	6/5/55
7	22786	(803) 555-2190	Gold	$650.00	1/21/96	12/11/71
8	24112	(803) 788-2131	Charter	$775.00	4/10/69	3/25/45
9	29120	(802) 522-9011	Silver	$575.00	9/27/66	7/18/32
10	22512	(803) 525-2341	Bronze	$525.00	4/21/78	5/19/56

Tip After you complete a record entry in Access, the record is automatically saved to the database file when you move to a new or a different record.

5 When you are finished, your table should look like the datasheet shown on the next page.

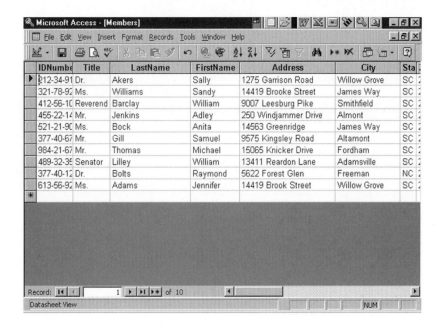

6   Close the *Members* form.

7   Close the *Willows Membership.mdb* database.

The Conclusion

In this project, you learned how to create a table using Design view, and you then learned how to enter records directly into the table. You created an AutoForm based upon the table to assist with data entry. Finally, you learned how to navigate among records and add new records to the table using the controls on a form.

Summary and Exercises

Summary

- Tables are the primary repositories for data in an Access database.
- Table structure includes field names, data types, field lengths, and field formats.
- Access supports 10 data types.
- Tables are created using Design view, and the record data is edited or displayed in Datasheet view.
- Forms are often used to display and edit database records.
- An AutoForm is an automatically generated form based upon a table (or tables).
- Forms contain controls for navigating among records and adding new records to a table.

Key Terms and Operations

Key Terms

AutoForm	navigate
controls	numeric
currency	OLE
data type	table
date/time	Table Design view
Datasheet view	Table Design window
Design view	table structure
hyperlink	text
memo	yes/no

Operations

open a database
create a table using Design view
add text data fields to a table
add currency and date/time fields to a table
add records to a table using Datasheet view
create an AutoForm
use form controls to navigate among records
use form controls to add new records to a table

Study Questions

Multiple Choice

1. Which data type is used to store long text entries?
   a. text
   b. memo
   c. numeric
   d. OLE

2. The upper pane in the Table Design Screen is used to enter:
   a. field names
   b. field data types
   c. field properties
   d. both a and b

3. Which of the following statements is false?
   a. When you open an Access database, the Database window normally is displayed.
   b. To create tables, you must first open an existing database file or create a new one.
   c. All Access database objects are contained in one file.
   d. When you open a database file, a new table is automatically created.

4. What field type uses a checkbox to store field data?
   a. text
   b. number
   c. date/time
   d. yes/no

5. Which of the following data types enables you to specify a field size?
   a. text
   b. number
   c. date/time
   d. currency

6. You are designing a table containing name and address information. How many characters should you reserve for the Last Name field, which is a text data type?
   a. 255
   b. 100
   c. 15
   d. 5

7. You have been commissioned to create a database for a hardware store. The table listing inventory items must display the current quantity in stock. Which data type will you use for this field?
   a. text
   b. currency
   c. numeric
   d. memo

8. Your database contains a form created using the Columnar AutoForm option. Which statement is false concerning this form?
   a. The form displays only one record in the form.
   b. You can use the New Record button in the navigation controls to add a record to the underlying table.
   c. The form displays the records from the underlying table as a datasheet.
   d. The form contains a text box displaying the current record number.

9. Which of the following controls does not appear on a Columnar AutoForm?
   a. First Record
   b. Delete Record
   c. Last Record
   d. Previous Record

10. When navigating among records in a table using a form, which control displays any record you specify by record number?
   a. the Add New Record button
   b. the Current Record text box
   c. the First Record button
   d. the Previous Record button

Short Answer

1. How does a table differ from a database?

2. How does a table differ from a form?

3. What is the default data type listed in the Table Design window?

4. Where do you change the properties of a field in a table?

5. Which option do you select to create an AutoForm?

6. How do you create a table in Access?

7. What is displayed onscreen when you open an Access database file?

8. Where in the Database window are forms displayed?

9. When displaying records in a form, if there are 10 records and you are positioned at record 2 and want to move to record 5, how do you display this record?

10. How do you add a new record to a table using a form?

For Discussion

1. How do text and memo data types differ? When is each appropriate?

2. Why does a form require a table?

3. What additional fields might you want to include in the Members table, and why?

4. Could the Willows Membership database include any additional tables? What data might an additional table contain?

Review Exercises

1. Creating a database per design specifications
In Review Exercise 1 from the Overview, you listed the specifications for an Employee database. Create the database and use the Table Wizard to create a table.

1. Launch Access if it is not currently running. Create a blank database named Willows Employees, and save it to your floppy diskette.

2. Make sure the Tables tab is selected in the Database window. Click the New button.

3. Select Table Wizard in the New Table dialog box and click OK, as shown on the next page.

4. In the Table Wizard dialog box, select Employees from the Sample Tables: list, and check the option button for Business. You now must specify which fields to add to the table. Select SocialSecurityNumber from the Sample Fields: list, and click the single arrow button to add this field to the Fields in my New Table: list.

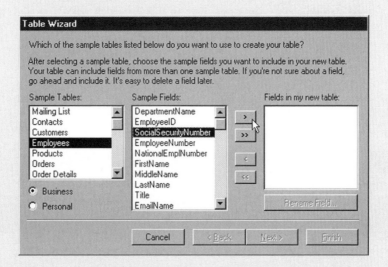

5. Add the following additional fields to your table, in the order specified: Title, LastName, FirstName, Address, City, StateOrProvince, PostalCode, and Salary. The Table Wizard dialog box should now appear.

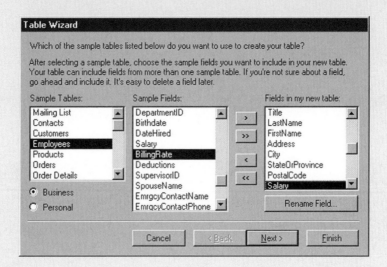

6. Click the Next button. In this step of the Table Wizard, specify Employees as the name for the table, and select the option to set your own primary key. Click Next.

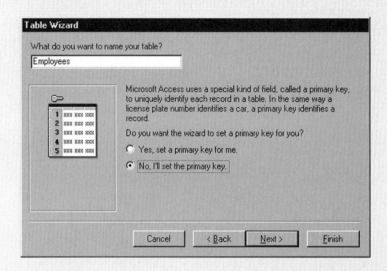

7. By default, the Table Wizard should specify SocialSecurityNumber as the primary key field since it was the first field entered. Select the last option button for the kind of data the field will contain, and click Next.

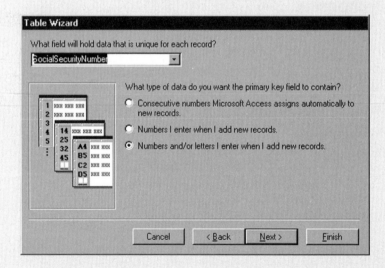

8. In the last step of the Table Wizard, select the option to enter data via a form the Wizard will create. Click the Finish button.

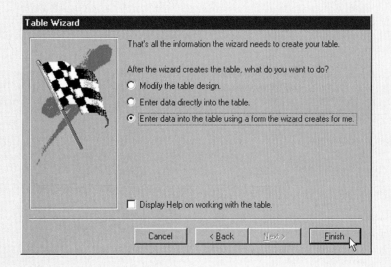

The Wizard automatically creates a table and the data entry form shown here.

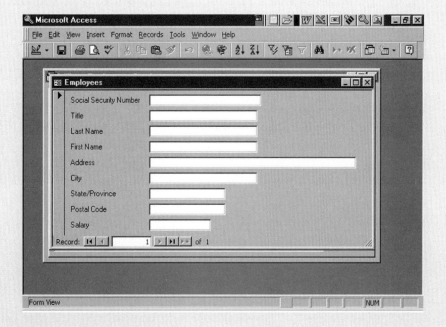

9. Close the form, and accept **Employees** as the name when you are prompted to save changes to the form.

10. Close the Willows Employees database.

2. Adding Records to a table using a form

Open the *Willows Employees.mdb* database file you created in the previous exercise. Complete the following steps to add records for five employees.

1. Click the Forms tab in the Database window.

2. Click the Open button to open the *Employees* form.

3. Using the procedures you learned in this project, add records for five employees into the table using this form.

Tip Notice that as you add records, you do not need to add hyphens in each employee's Social Security Number. You will learn how to create an input mask like this in Project 3.

4. Close the form.

5. Close the database.

3. Creating a new table, adding records, and creating an AutoForm for the table

1. Launch Access 97, if necessary, and open the database *High Point Foods xxx.mdb* (where *xxx* represents your initials).

Note If you do not have a database named *High Point Foods xxx.mdb*, ask your instructor for a copy of the file you should use to complete this exercise.

2. Create a new table containing fields and field descriptions displayed as follows:

Field Name	Data Type	Description
CategoryID	AutoNumber	Number automatically assigned to a new category
CategoryName	Text	Name of food category
Description	Memo	

3. Save the table using the table name *Food Categories* with no primary key defined.

ID	Category Name	Description
1	Beverages	Soft drinks, coffees, teas, beers, and ales
2	Condiments	Sweet and savory sauces, relishes, spreads, and seasonings
3	Confections	Desserts, candies, and sweetbreads
4	Dairy Products	Cheeses
5	Grains/Cereals	Breads, crackers, pasta, and cereal
6	Meat/Poultry	Prepared meats
7	Produce	Dried fruit and bean curd
8	Seafood	Seaweed and fish

5. Spell check the table and make the necessary corrections.

6. Create an AutoForm for the table and save the form using the form name *Food Categories*.

7. Print a copy of the *Food Categories* table and the *Food Categories* form.

8. Close the database and exit Access.

Assignments

1. Creating a database using the hyperlink data type

The hyperLink data type is new in Access 97. In this assignment, you will create a new database that incorporates this data type. Create a new database with the name *Web Sites.mdb*. Create a table named **Sites** with the following structure:

Field Name	Data Type	Size
Company	Text	50
Primary Product	Text	50
Company URL	Hyperlink	N/A

When you save the table, allow Access to create a primary key. Access will add an AutoNumber field for the primary key data. As you add records to the table, tab through this field, since Access will supply a value automatically. Close the database when you are finished.

2. Creating an AutoForm and adding records to a table

In this assignment, you will modify the database you created in Assignment 1 for this project. Open the database, and create a Columnar AutoForm based upon the Sites table. Name the form **Sites**. Add the following three records to the table using the Sites form:

Company	Primary Product	Company URL
Microsoft	Software	http://www.microsoft.com
Adobe	Graphics software	http://www.adobe.com
Fidelity	Financial services	http://www.fidelity.com

After you have added these records, use the navigation controls on the form to move to the first record. If you can access the World Wide Web from your lab or computer, click the company URL field for Microsoft. When you are finished, close your Web browser and the database.

2 PROJECT

Manipulating and Maintaining Tables

After you have created database tables and added records to them, you frequently need to edit the record data or view it in different ways. In this project, you will learn how to manipulate and maintain table data.

Objectives

After completing this project, you will be able to:

➤ **Use the Find feature to locate a specific record**

➤ **Update records in a table**

➤ **Use the Replace feature**

➤ **Sort table data**

➤ **Filter records by selection**

➤ **Filter records by form**

➤ **Compact the database**

The Challenge

As the database developer at the Willows, you are responsible for implementing and maintaining the database of the club's members. As with any database, Mr. Gilmore will expect you to be able to customize the database as the need for information in new formats arises. For instance, just this week two members reported a change of address. The board of directors also just voted to raise the membership fees. Finally, Mr. Gilmore has requested that the data in the *Members* table display Charter members alphabetized by last name.

The Solution

Although well-designed databases shield users from having to interact with records at the table level, Access includes a number of features that make manipulating records a straightforward task. For example, you can use the Search feature to find records for members with an address change, and you can use the search and replace feature to change fee structures. Finally, you can filter the table either by selection or by form to display the records by type of membership. Figure 2.1 shows how the *Members* table datasheet appears when the table has been filtered and sorted by charter membership and then last name.

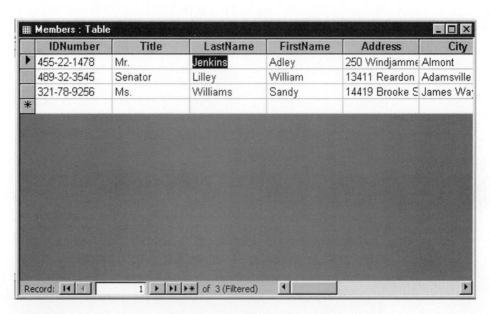

Figure 2.1

The Setup

After you launch Access and open your database, you should make sure the Database toolbar and the Status toolbar are displayed. These are the default settings in Access, but they may have been changed on your computer. (If you have forgotten how to do this, refer to Table 1.1 in Project 1.)

> **Troubleshooting** If you do not see the Database toolbar on the screen when you launch Access and open your database, choose Toolbars from the View menu. Select the Database toolbar to display it. If any additional toolbars are visible, close them. If you do not see the Status bar at the bottom of the Application window, choose Options from the Tools menu, click the View Page tab, and change the Status bar check box option.

Using the procedures you learned in Task 1 of Project 1, open the *Willows Membership.mdb* file from your disk.

Searching a Table for a Specific Record

As with many databases, record data changes over time. This is particularly true for database tables containing address information. Although it is not difficult to find a specific record in a table that contains a small number of records, this method becomes impractical when a table contains hundreds or thousands of records.

Fortunately, Access contains search capabilities. You can use the **Find** dialog box to search for a specific record and **edit**, or change, its data. Editing field data is one way of updating records, but **updating** also includes adding and deleting records. You will need to update the *Members* table by changing the address for Reverend Barclay and Ms. Adams.

TASK 1: TO SEARCH A TABLE FOR A SPECIFIC RECORD:

1 From the Database window, click the Forms tab to make it active.

2 Double-click the *Members* form to display the first record in the underlying table.

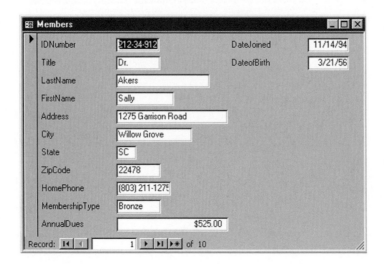

3   Click inside the LastName field on the form, to make it active.

4   Click the Find button 🔍 on the Form View toolbar as shown below.

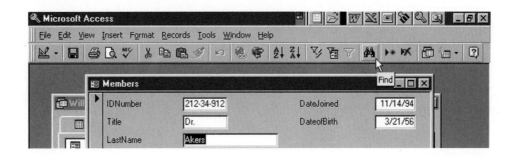

Tip You can also use the (CTRL) +F keyboard shortcut to open the Find dialog box.

5   Type **Barclay** as your search term in the Find What: textbox.

Tip The other two check box options allow you to find records with a specific upper and lower case combination, or to find data based upon its display format (date or currency, for example).

6   Accept the default settings in the Find dialog box. When your screen matches the figure on the next page, click the Find First button.

Below

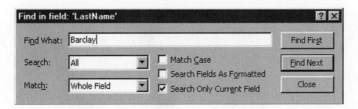

Tip Notice that you can find multiple records for your search term, if more than one record matches the search term. You can review any additional matches by clicking on the Find Next button.

7   Record 5 should now be displayed in the *Members* form. Click the Close button.

Updating Records in a Table

After you find a record using the Find option, you can edit it in the same way you edit any record displayed in a form. By moving the insertion point to the appropriate text box for a specific field, you can replace the text with a new entry.

> **Tip** Whenever you replace the data in a field using either a table's datasheet or the Form View for a form, the changes you make to the data are stored to disk as soon as you either move to another record or close the datasheet or the form.

TASK 2: TO UPDATE RECORDS IN A TABLE:

1 Select the current address, and type **4001 Cactus Circle** as the new address for this member.

2 Click the Find button 🔍 again and type **Adams** as the search term.

3 Deselect the option to search the current field only, as below. By doing so, you can search for the address even if another field has the focus.

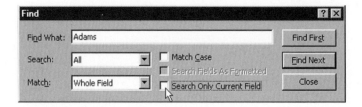

4 Click the Find First button.

5 When the form displays record 9, change the address, city, state, zip code, and phone data.

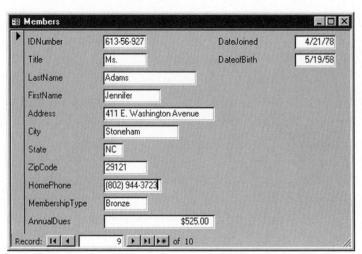

doesn't say to change Birth?

6 Close the form when you are finished.

Using the Replace Feature

As you can see, the Find feature provides a simple method for changing specific records. But what if you need to change data that occurs more frequently in the table? Consider the work it would take to change the area code for 1,500 customers if the local phone company added a new area code. Obviously, you need a method for changing all fields that contain a specific value.

Fortunately, Access utilizes the same Find and Replace feature found in the other Office applications. Consider Mr. Gilmore's request, that you change the annual membership fees. The new annual membership fees for Charter, Gold, Silver, and Bronze memberships cost $800, $675, $600, and $550, respectively. By using the *replace* feature, you can globally replace one value with another.

> **Tip** Both the Find and Replace features can be used with tables and forms.

TASK 3: TO REPLACE THE CURRENT MEMBERSHIP FEES WITH NEW VALUES:

1 Click the Tables tab in the Database window.

2 Double-click the *Members* table to open it in Datasheet view.

3 Select Replace from the Edit menu.

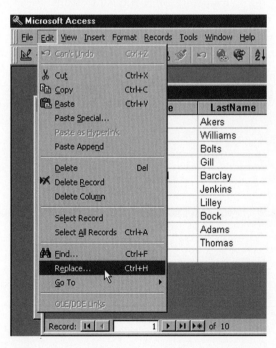

4 Type **$775.00** as the value for which to search in the Find What: text box.

> **Troubleshooting** The Replace feature searches for a text string as it is formatted, so make sure you enter a dollar sign, a decimal point, and two zeros to the right of the decimal place when searching for a currency value.

5 Click the Find Next button. The membership value in record 2 should now be highlighted.

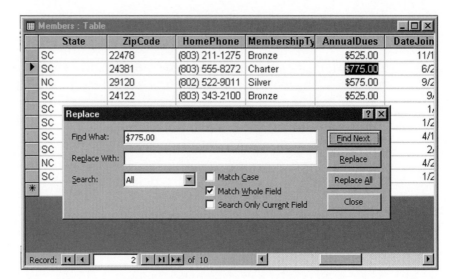

6 Type **800** in the Replace With text box. Do not add a dollar sign or decimal places, because the field is formatted to currency and Access will supply these for display. Then click on the Replace All button.

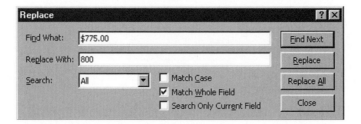

7 The warning shown below will appear. Click Yes.

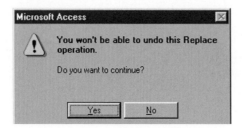

8 Verify that your datasheet looks like the one shown in the following figure. Access has replaced all instances of the value 775 in the AnnualDues field with 800.

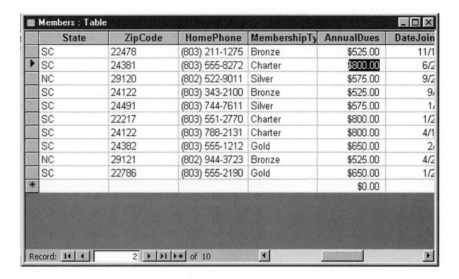

9 Use the Replace feature to change all instances of $650.00 to 675, $575.00 to 600, and $525.00 to 550.

> **Troubleshooting** Make sure you do not type a dollar sign or a decimal point in the Replace With text box of the Replace dialog box to search for the specified values, which are integers in this case. Although the new value will be displayed in currency format, Access will add these characters, because you specified a currency format when you created the table design.

10 Close the Replace dialog box. Your datasheet should now display the values shown below. Close the datasheet to return to the Database window.

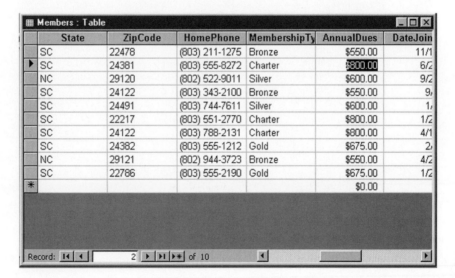

Sorting Records

Another common database maintenance task involves sorting records. When you apply a *sort*, you reorder the records in a table or form according to the entries in a specific field. The field you select for a sort specifies the *sort criteria*. Although Access objects such as forms and reports can be designed to display data in a sorted format, at times you may want to quickly verify the data on the screen. Records can be sorted in either ascending or descending order. When you sort in *ascending order*, names and terms are sorted from A to Z, and dates and times are sorted from earliest to latest. When you sort by *descending order*, the opposite is true.

> **Tip** When sorting text, capital letters are sorted before lowercase letters.

When you sort records, Access saves the sort order when the form or datasheet is saved, and then reapplies it automatically when you reopen the object or base a new form or report on that object.

TASK 4: TO SORT RECORDS IN A TABLE:

1 Open the *Members* table in Datasheet view.

2 Click the LastName field heading to select the entire column, as shown below.

> **Tip** You can also sort on a specific field by simply placing the insertion point anywhere in the field.

	IDNumber	Title	LastName	FirstName	Address	City
▶	212-34-9123	Dr.	Akers	Sally	1775 Garrison F	Willow Gro
	321-78-9256	Ms.	Williams	Sandy	14419 Brooke S	James Wa
	377-40-1211	Dr.	Bolts	Raymond	5622 Forest Gle	Freeman
	377-40-6798	Mr.	Gill	Samuel	9575 Kingsley F	Altamont
	412-56-1055	Reverend	Barclay	William	4001 Cactus Cii	Smithfield
	455-22-1478	Mr.	Jenkins	Adley	250 Windjamme	Almont
	489-32-3545	Senator	Lilley	William	13411 Reardon	Adamsville
	521-21-9007	Ms.	Bock	Anita	14563 Greenridç	James Wa
	613-56-9273	Ms.	Adams	Jennifer	411 E. Washinç	Stoneham
	984-21-6722	Mr.	Thomas	Michael	15065 Knicker [	Fordham

Members : Table

Record: 1 of 10

[Handwritten note: Does not stay in ABC order]

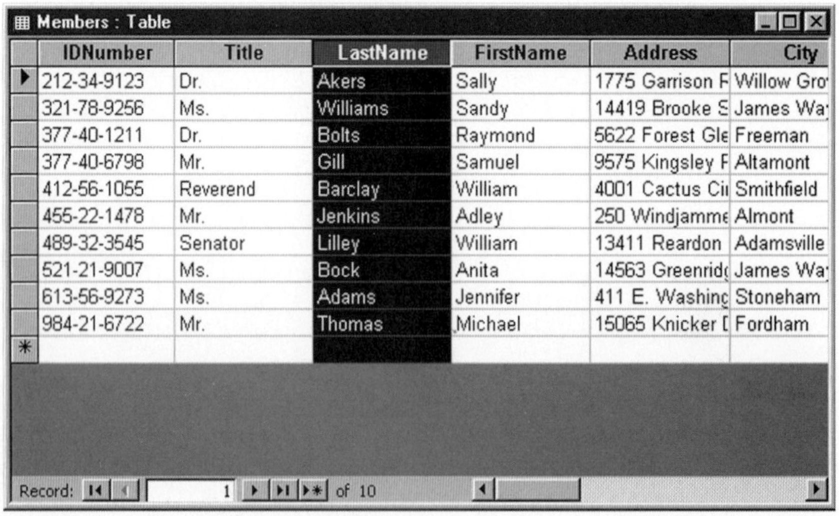

3 Click the Sort Ascending button on the Table Datasheet toolbar.

4 The records are now sorted in ascending order by last name, as shown on the next page. Close the table.

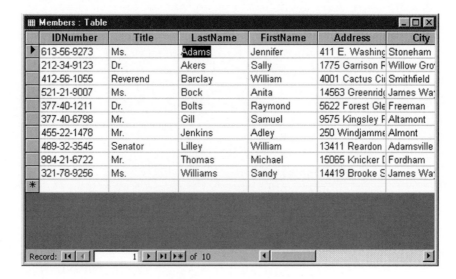

5 The Microsoft Access dialog box shown in the next figure appears. You do want the table design to be modified, so click Yes.

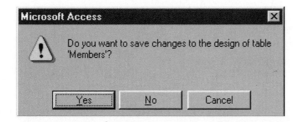

Any time you open the table, the data will now appear in alphabetical order by last name. This is because you modified the table structure by specifying a sort property for the table. A *property* is some characteristic of a database object. In the event that you want to change this property, you need to know where to change it.

TASK 5: TO VIEW THE TABLE PROPERTIES:

1 Click the Tables tab in the Database window.

2 Click the Design button.

3 In the Table Design window, place the insertion point inside the title bar, and click the right mouse button. The context menu shown below appears.

primary
Keys

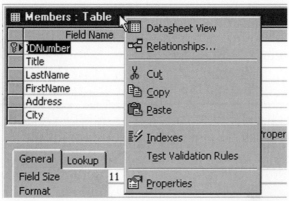

4 Select the Properties option.

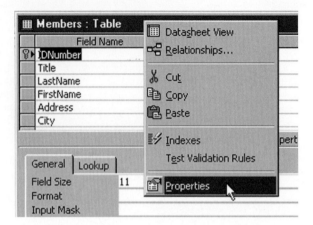

The Table Properties dialog box shown below appears. Notice the setting for the Order By row. To remove or change the sort specifications, delete this entry or select another field name.

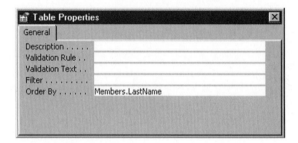

5 Close the Table Properties dialog box without making any changes.

6 Close the form.

> **Tip** To sort on more than one field, you must use either the Advanced Filter option, construct a query, or create a report, as you will do in Project 6.

Filtering Records

Sometimes you need to retrieve a subset of records from an underlying table, such as when Mr. Gilmore requests a list of charter members. With a *filter*, you can temporarily view or edit a subset of records while you're viewing a form or datasheet. Access supports two methods for quickly filtering records. With **Filter By Selection**, you select all or part of a value, and then click the Filter by Selection button on the toolbar to find all records with the selected value. If you would rather specify a value you're searching for by typing it or picking it from a list in the field, you can use the **Filter By Form** option. This option also enables you to specify multiple criteria for a filter.

When you are finished viewing the filtered data, you remove the filter to restore the datasheet or form to its previous order.

TASK 6: TO USE FILTER BY SELECTION TO DISPLAY ALL CHARTER MEMBERS:

1 Click the Tables tab in the Database window.

2 Click the Open button to open the *Members* table in Datasheet view.

3 Use the horizontal scrollbar to display the MembershipType field.

4 Select the word Charter in the seventh record.

	ZipCode	HomePhone	MembershipTy	AnnualDues	DateJoined	DateofBi
	29121	(802) 944-3723	Bronze	$550.00	4/21/78	5/1
	22478	(803) 211-1275	Bronze	$550.00	11/14/94	3/2
	24491	(803) 744-7611	Silver	$600.00	1/9/97	7/1
	24382	(803) 555-1212	Gold	$675.00	2/1/64	5/
	29120	(802) 522-9011	Silver	$600.00	9/27/66	7/1
	24122	(803) 343-2100	Bronze	$550.00	9/6/92	6/
▶	22217	(803) 551-2770	Charter	$800.00	1/25/87	10/1
	24122	(803) 788-2131	Charter	$800.00	4/10/69	3/2
	22786	(803) 555-2190	Gold	$675.00	1/21/96	12/1
	24381	(803) 555-8272	Charter	$800.00	6/29/82	4/1
*				$0.00		

Record: 7 of 10

5 Click the Filter By Selection button on the Table Datasheet toolbar. The filter is applied, as shown below. Notice that *FLTR* appears in the Status bar and the word *Filtered* appears in parentheses following the New Record button.

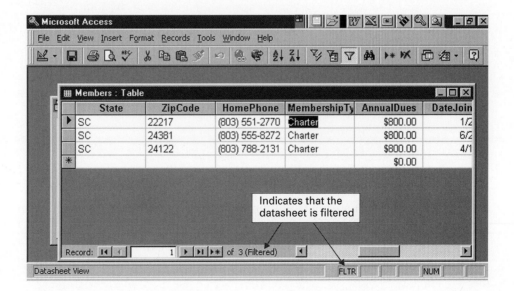

Indicates that the datasheet is filtered

6   Click the Remove Filter button ▽ on the toolbar to remove the filter.

TASK 7: TO USE FILTER BY FORM TO DISPLAY ALL CHARTER MEMBERS IN SORTED ORDER:

1   Click the Filter By Form button 🖿 on the Table Datasheet toolbar.

2   Use the Tab key or the mouse to select the MembershipType field.

3   Click the button that appears in the field.

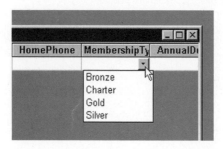

4   Select Charter in the list.

The word Charter now appears in quotes in the field.

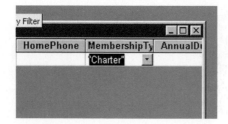

5   Click the Apply Filter button ▽ on the Table Datasheet toolbar. Once again, the datasheet displays records for charter members only.

6   Use the horizontal scrollbar to display the LastName field.
The three filtered records are now displayed in ascending order.

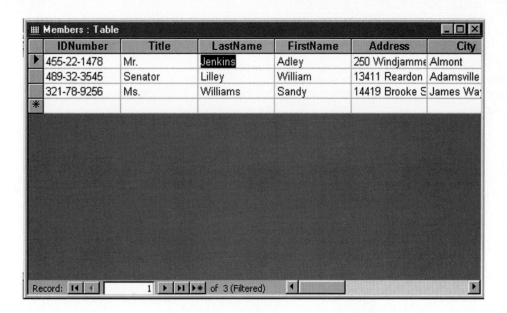

7 Close the datasheet. When the Microsoft Access dialog box shown in the next figure appears, click the No button.

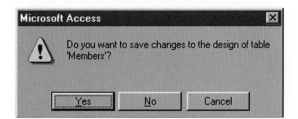

Tip Had you clicked the Yes button, the filter and sort information would have been stored with the table design. Whenever you apply sort or filter criteria and then update a table, these properties can always be edited or deleted at a later time.

Using the Database Utilities to Compact a Database

Whenever you modify your database objects, the database file contains empty space and grows in size. If you open your database from a disk, it is a good idea to periodically compact it, which will remove the empty space and reduce the file size. By keeping the file size as small as possible, you can locate and manipulate records more quickly.

TASK 8: TO COMPACT THE DATABASE:

1   Select Database Utilities from the Tools menu.

2   Select Compact Database from the cascading menu.

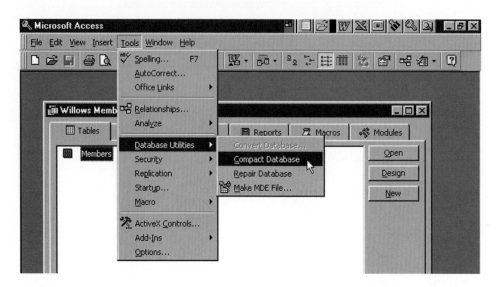

Records can't be read; no permission on A'Willows

As the database is compacting, the mouse pointer displays an hourglass icon; during this time various messages appear in the Status bar.

3   When control returns to the Database window, the database has been compacted. Close the database file.

The Conclusion

As you can see, Access offers you several methods for manipulating database tables and maintaining the entire database. Although you can accomplish much when working with tables, most databases are designed so that the typical user never has to interact with a table object directly. In the projects that follow, you will learn how to create additional database objects that also support some of the tasks you learned here for manipulating records.

Summary and Exercises

Summary

- You can use the Find dialog box to locate one or more records displayed in a table or form. You will often use this feature to update a record.
- You can use the Replace dialog box to replace information in one or more records displayed in a table or form. You will often use this feature in order to update a record.
- If you select the Replace All button in the Replace dialog box, all occurrences of a text string (any combination of letters, numbers, and symbols) or numeric value are replaced with another string or value.
- You can easily sort records by a specific criterion. Records can be sorted in ascending or descending order according to the letters, dates, or numbers occurring in a field.
- By applying a filter, you can view a specific subset of a table's records. The two easiest methods for applying a filter are Filter By Selection and Filter By Form.
- As you work with Access database objects, the database file grows in size. You can compact the database file using one of the Access database utilities.

Key Terms and Operations

Key Terms
ascending order	property
descending order	replace
edit	sort
filter	sort criteria
find	update

Operations
locate and update a table or form using the Find feature
locate and update a table or form using the Replace feature
organize a table or form using the Sort Ascending feature
organize a table or form using the Sort Descending feature
organize a table or form using the Filter By Selection feature
organize a table or form using the Filter By Form
optimize your database file by compacting it using a database utility

Study Questions

Multiple Choice
1. To quickly locate a record in a table or form, use the
   a. Find dialog box.
   b. Replace All button.
   c. Table Datasheet view.
   d. Apply Filter button.

2. Updating records in a table includes all of the following except
   a. changing an employee's address.
   b. creating a new table.
   c. inserting records.
   d. deleting records.

3. The easiest way of making a global change in a database is by using the
   a. Replace All feature.
   b. Sort Ascending button.
   c. Remove Filter button.
   d. Compact Database option in the Database utilities.

4. Which of the following is not true concerning the sort feature in Access?
   a. Records can be sorted in ascending or descending order according to the values in a specific field.
   b. Information about the sort can be saved with the table design properties.
   c. Dates are sorted from most recent to least recent when using the sort-descending feature.
   d. The case of text entries does not matter when sorting records.

5. The filter option that enables you to select records that match multiple criteria is the
   a. Apply filter.
   b. Filter By Form.
   c. Remove Filter.
   d. Filter By Selection.

6. The filter feature that enables you to select records containing the same text or value as one highlighted in a specific field is the
   a. Apply filter.
   b. Filter By Form.
   c. Remove Filter.
   d. Filter By Selection.

7. If a database file grows in size, what should you do to remedy this situation?
   a. Create a new table.
   b. Split the database into two files.
   c. Create a new database and copy all the records into it.
   d. Compact the database.

8. To identify the field you want to use for sorting records, you should
   a. click the Sort Ascending button.
   b. select the entire table.
   c. position the insertion point somewhere in the desired field.
   d. click the Sort Descending button.

9. Which feature enables you to select criteria for viewing records by using a drop-down list?
   a. Sort Ascending
   b. Filter By Selection
   c. Sort Descending
   d. Filter By Form

10. Which feature enables you to use a selected entry in a field to specify which records in the table to display?
    a. Sort Ascending
    b. Filter By Selection
    c. Sort Descending
    d. Filter By Form

Short Answer

1. What is the difference between finding and replacing data?

2. How does sorting records differ from applying a filter?

3. How does the case of a text entry affect the sort order?

4. How many criteria can you specify when using the Filter By Selection option?

5. Does the Replace All feature conduct a global search and replace?

6. What is an easy method for locating records to update?

7. Which option should you use to view a record in a table that meets a specific criterion?

8. How can you reduce the size of a database file without deleting any data?

9. Can you include multiple criteria when using the Filter By Form option?

10. How do date values appear if a database is sorted in descending order?

For Discussion

1. When should you consider using Filter By Form rather than Filter By Selection?

2. How does the data type of a field affect how the records are ordered when you sort a table?

3. What happens to a database file as you modify its objects and what can you do to remedy any potential problems?

4. Explain how editing, filtering, and sorting records differ.

Review Exercises

1. Deleting Records from a Table

Deleting records from a table is a common database maintenance task. In this exercise you will learn how to delete records from a table in Datasheet view. Complete the following tasks:

1. Open the *Willows Employees.mdb* file from your disk.

2. Click the Tables tab, and open the *Employees* table in Datasheet view.

3. Place the insertion point in the record selector for the third record, as shown below.

Employees : Table	
Social Securit	**Title**
321-22-1345	Mr.
322-11-8912	Dr.
412-55-6798	Ms.
477-22-9102	Mr.
522-11-8273	Ms.

> **Tip** The Record Selector allows you to easily select an entire record. Depending upon the current task, the Record Selector will display an icon indicating the current record 🖉 , a record currently being edited ▶ , or a new record ✳ .

4. Click the Record Selector. The entire record is now selected, as shown below.

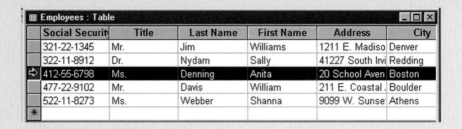

5. Click the Delete Record button 🗙 on the Table Datasheet toolbar.

6. The Microsoft Access dialog box appears. Click Yes to delete the record.

7. Select Database utilities from the Tools menu, and then select Compact Database from the cascading menu. This action closes the table.

2. Filtering a Table by Multiple Criteria

As you may guess, at times you may need to filter a table by multiple criteria. In this exercise, you use the Filter By Form method to filter a table by two criteria.

1. Open the *Employees* table in the *Willows Employees.mdb* database in Datasheet view.

2. Click the Filter By Form button 🖼 on the Table Datasheet toolbar.

3. Select Mr. in the Title field.

4. Select CO in the State/Province field.

5. Click the Apply Filter button ▽ on the Table Datasheet toolbar. The database now displays records that meet the criteria you specified.

6. Click Yes in the Microsoft Access dialog box to save the filter information with the table. Now whenever you open the table this filter will be available. To apply the filter, simply click the Apply Filter button.

7. Close the *Willows Employees.mdb* database.

3. Sorting and filtering records in a table

1. Launch Access 97 and open *High Point Foods xxx.mdb* (where *xxx* represents your initials).

> **Note** If you do not have a workbook named *High Point Foods xxx.mdb*, ask your instructor for a copy of the file you should use to complete this exercise.

2. Make the following change using the *Food Categories* form:
   - Find the record for *Seafood* and add *Shellfish* to the Description field.

3. Print a copy of the *Food Categories* table.

4. Sort the *Food Categories* table in reverse alphabetical order based on the Category Name field and print a copy of the table.

5. Close the table without saving the changes.

6. Filter the records in the table to locate all records containing the word *bread* in the Description field and print a copy of the filtered table.

7. Remove the filter and close the table without saving the changes.

8. Close the database and exit Access.

Assignments

1. Adding Records to a Table and Specifying Sort Criteria

In this assignment, you will modify the Web Sites database by adding records and then sorting the datasheet according to software category. After you open the *Web Sites.mdb* database file from your disk, add the following records using either the datasheet view or the form:

Company	Primary Product	Company URL
Macromedia	Multimedia software	http://www.macromedia.com
Asymetrix	Multimedia software	http://www.asymetrix.com
E-Trade	Financial services	http://www.etrade.com

Sort the Sites table in ascending order by company name. Note that the Auto-Number record for each record does not change when the records are sorted. Save the table design when you close the table.

2. Filtering the Sites Table in the Web Sites Database

As you learned in this project, both sort and filter specifications can be saved as a part of a table's design. In this assignment you will add filter specifications to the Sites table in the Web Sites database.

Open the Sites table in datasheet view. Select Filter By Form, and specify Multimedia Software as the filter criterion. Apply the filter. Update the table design when you close the table. Reopen the table and click the Apply Filter option again. Close the database and exit Access when you are finished.

3

Modifying Table Design

Most database developers periodically refine their databases to improve performance, increase accuracy, or to meet the changing needs of an organization. Because tables serve as the primary storage location in Access, many database enhancements involve modifying a table's design.

Objectives

After completing this project, you will be able to:

➤ **Add fields to a table**

➤ **Delete a field**

➤ **Change field properties**

➤ **Change a table's primary key**

➤ **Create data input masks**

➤ **Add data validation rules to a table**

The Challenge

Mr. Gilmore is pleased with the progress you have made in developing a membership database for the Willows. He has made a few suggestions for improving the database after reviewing the initial design specifications. First, he wants you to add two additional fields to the database: one to assign each member a unique membership number, and one to specify the number of family members included in the membership. Second, he wants you to assign a new field as the primary key, because many organizations are moving away from using a patron's Social Security number for identification. Finally, he wants you to find a way to simplify the data entry process.

The Solution

You can easily modify the *Members* table to fulfill all of Mr. Gilmore's recommendations. You can create an AutoNumber field that will automatically assign each member a unique number, and you can create a numeric field to store the number of family members included in the membership. By setting the AutoNumber field as the primary key, you will no longer need to use Social Security number as a unique identifier. Finally, by adding validation rules and input masks to the table design, you can simplify data entry and protect against certain data entry errors. Figure 3.1 displays a new *Members* form created using the updated table.

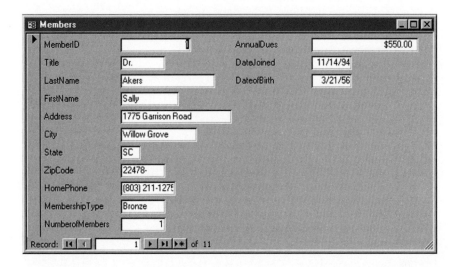

Figure 3.1

The Setup

After you launch Access and open your database, you should make sure the Database toolbar and the Status toolbar are displayed. These are the default settings in Access, but they may have been changed on your computer. (If you have forgotten how to do this, refer to Table 1.1 in Project 1.)

> **Troubleshooting** If you do not see the Database toolbar on the screen when you launch Access and open your database, choose Toolbars from the View menu. Select the Database toolbar to display it. If any additional toolbars are visible, close them. If you do not see the Status bar at the bottom of the Application window, choose Options from the Tools menu, click the View Page tab and change the Status bar check box option.

Using the procedures you learned in Task 1 of Project 1, open the *Willows Membership.mdb* file from your disk.

Modifying a Table's Design

Any enhancements you make to your database tables are table **design modifications**. Remember that tables are where Access stores record data; all other objects—queries, forms, and reports—are based upon the table data. Therefore, any changes you make to a table's design affect the objects that derive their data from a table.

In this project you will change the *Members* table in two ways. Adding fields, deleting fields, and changing the primary key field will change the underlying **table structure**, or how the table is physically arranged. When you add input masks and data validation, you are changing specific **field properties**, which affect how the field data is entered and displayed.

Modifying the *Members* Table Structure

Mr. Gilmore has asked you to make three modifications to the *Members* table structure. You will add an AutoNumber field, add a numeric field, and change the primary key and delete the IDNumber field.

When you delete the IDNumber field, you lose any data that the field contains, which is the Social Security number of each member. If you will ever need this data in the future, it is a good idea to first create a copy of the *Members* table before you modify its structure.

TASK 1: TO CREATE A BACKUP OF THE *MEMBERS* TABLE:

1 Verify that the Tables tab is active and that the *Members* table is selected in the Database window.

2 Select Save As/Export from the File menu.

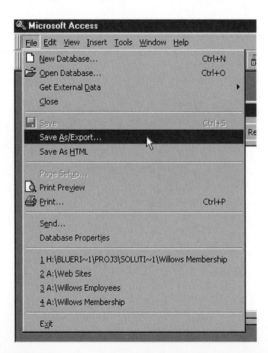

3 In the Save As dialog box, select the option button to save the *Members* table in the current database. Accept the default name shown in the figure below, and click OK.

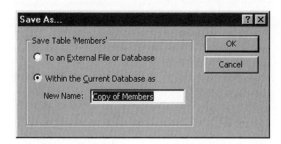

Two table objects now appear in the Database window.

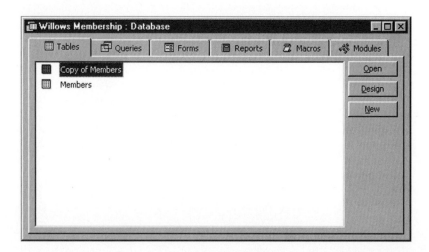

You are now ready to add fields to the *Members* table. For the rest of this project, you will modify the *Members* table, not the copy you just created.

TASK 2: TO ADD FIELDS TO THE *MEMBERS* TABLE:

1 Highlight the *Members* table in the Database window, and click the Design button to open the table in Design view.

2 Place the insertion point over the Row selector for the Title field, as shown below and click.

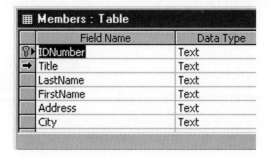

The entire field should now be selected.

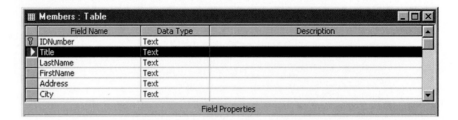

3 Click the Insert Rows button ⋑ on the Table Design toolbar.
A row is inserted in the upper pane of the Table Design window above the Title field.

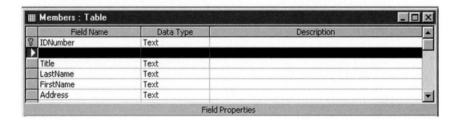

4 Type **MemberID** as the name of this field, and select AutoNumber as the data type.

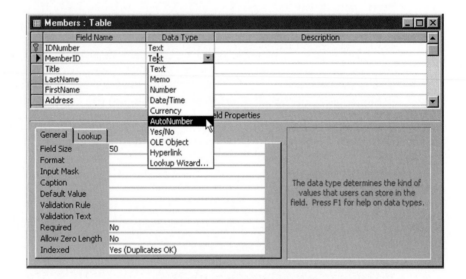

5 Use the vertical scroll bar in the upper pane of the Table Design window to display the MembershipType and Annual Dues fields.

6 Highlight the Annual Dues field and add a new row between it and the MembershipType field. The Table Design window should now look similar to the window shown in the following figure.

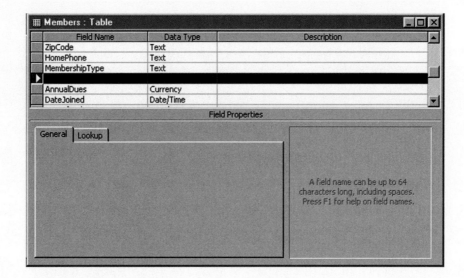

7   Type **NumberofMembers** as the name of this field, and select Number as
    the data type.

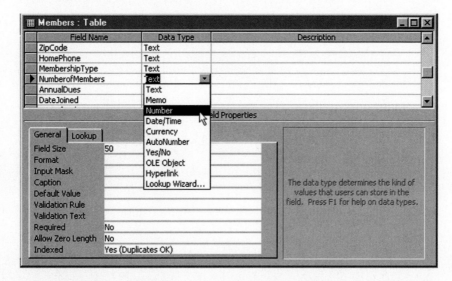

8   Click the Save button 🖫 on the Table Design toolbar.
    This saves the table design to your database file.

9   Click the View button 🛅 on the Table Design toolbar.
    This switches the view from Design view to Datasheet view. Your datasheet
    now appears as shown in the figure below.

IDNumber	MemberID	Title	LastName	FirstName	Addres
212-34-9123	1	Dr.	Akers	Sally	1775 Garris
321-78-9256	2	Ms.	Williams	Sandy	14419 Broc
377-40-1211	3	Dr.	Bolts	Raymond	5622 Fores
377-40-6798	4	Mr.	Gill	Samuel	9575 Kings
412-56-1055	5	Reverend	Barclay	William	4001 Cactu
455-22-1478	6	Mr.	Jenkins	Adley	250 Windja
489-32-3545	7	Senator	Lilley	William	13411 Rear
521-21-9007	8	Ms.	Bock	Anita	14563 Gree
613-56-9273	9	Ms.	Adams	Jennifer	411 E. Wa:
984-21-6722	10	Mr.	Thomas	Michael	15065 Knic
*	(AutoNumber)				

member ID Not same (handwritten annotation)

You will notice that Access added a numeric value for each record in the table. An ***AutoNumber field*** adds a number value for each record in the database, starting with 1 and increasing by 1.

10   Close the table.

Changing the Primary Key for the *Members* Table

In many businesses and organizations, it has become common to use a patron's Social Security number as a unique identifier. This number is a logical candidate for a primary key in a database, because no two individuals can ever have the same number. Lately, however, this practice is changing because it is fairly easy to obtain confidential information, such as credit history, about a person by using this number.

Mr. Gilmore has requested a unique identification number other than the Social Security number for each member, because some members have alerted him to the problems this can create. After you designate a new field as the primary key, you will delete the IDNumber field.

> **Caution** Remember that a primary key field cannot contain a null value (blank entry) or any duplicate values!

TASK 3: TO CHANGE THE PRIMARY KEY:

1   Open the *Members* table in Design view. The IDNumber field is now selected.

2   Click the Primary Key button ░ on the Table Design toolbar. This removes the primary key icon from the field.

3   Select the MemberID field by clicking the Row selector.

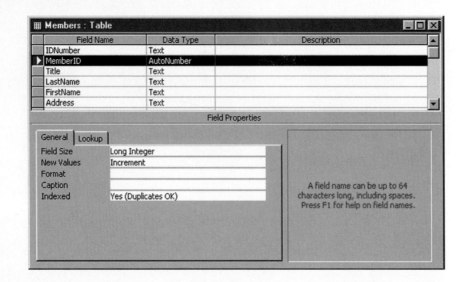

Tip In Project 2 you used the Row Selector to select a record in Datasheet view. You can also use the Row Selector to select fields in Table Design view.

4 Click the Primary Key button ⚷ . The primary key is now set to the Member ID field.

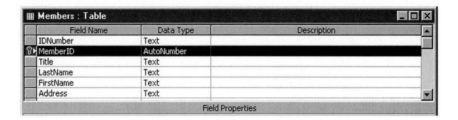

5 Click the Save button 🖫 to update the table.

TASK 4: TO DELETE THE IDNUMBER FIELD:

1 Select the IDNumber field by clicking its Row Selector.

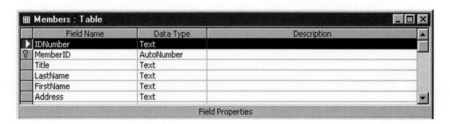

2 Click the Delete Rows button ☰ on the Table Design toolbar.

3 The dialog box shown below appears. Verify that you want to delete the field by clicking the Yes button.

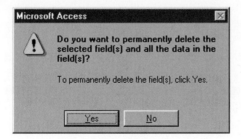

The dialog box displayed in the figure at the top of the next page appears. Because this field was previously the primary key, Access indexed the table by this field. An *index* is a method for speeding up record access in a table. Access uses indexes in a table as you use an index in a book: to find data, it looks up the location of the data in the index. The primary key field of a table is automatically indexed.

4   Click Yes.

5   The field is now deleted. Click the Save button 🖫 to update the table design.

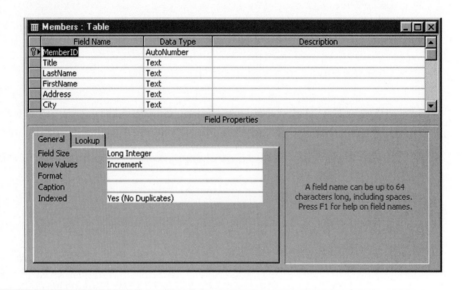

Changing Field Properties for the *Members* Table

Now you have made all the necessary changes to the structure of the *Members* table. You can think of table structure as the physical description of the table — the number of fields, data types, field sizes, indexes, and primary key designation. Sometimes you modify a table's structure by changing the field properties.

Other field properties in Access do not change the physical structure of the table, but they affect how the records are displayed in a datasheet or form, or limit the actual values that can be entered in the field. Mr. Gilmore has asked you to make data entry as simple as possible, and to minimize the chance for data entry errors. Entering data into some fields is simpler if the field contains an input mask. An ***input mask*** is a template that uses literal display characters (spaces, dots, dashes, or parentheses) to control how data is entered in a field. The ZipCode and HomePhone fields should use an input mask. Access will supply additional characters to make it easier to enter data into these fields.

Data validation is the process of checking field data as it is entered into a table or form. A ***validation rule*** is a field property that limits what the user can enter into a field. If what the user types violates the validation rule, the *validation text* property displays a message that explains the data entry error. The NumberofMembers, AnnualDues, DateJoined, and DateofBirth fields should all utilize a validation rule.

TASK 5: TO SPECIFY AN INPUT MASK FOR THE ZIPCODE AND HOMEPHONE FIELDS:

1   Select the ZipCode field in the upper pane of the Table Design window, and click the Input Mask property row. The Table Design window should appear similar to the window shown below.

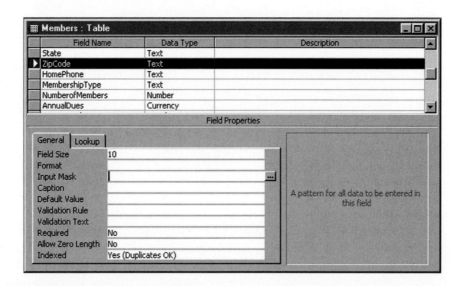

2   Click the ellipsis button ... that appears next to the Input Mask row. Access starts the Input Mask Wizard and displays the Input Mask Wizard dialog box.

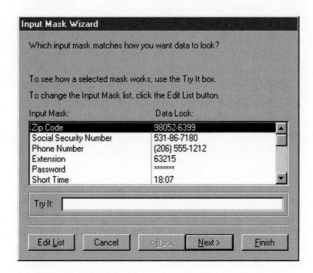

Troubleshooting If the Wizards are not installed on your computer or network, enter **00000\-9999;0;_** as the value for this property. For more information about these input mask characters, search for Input masks in the Help System, select the topic, and then select Examples of input masks from the topics found list.

3 The ZipCode field should be selected. Click Next.

4 Accept the default setting for the name, the mask, and the placeholder by clicking on the Next button.

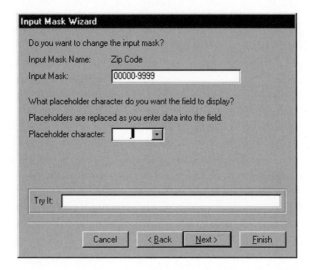

5 Select the option to store the symbols with the mask. Click Next.

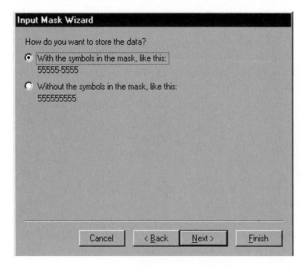

6 The last dialog box in the Input Mask Wizard appears. Click Finish.

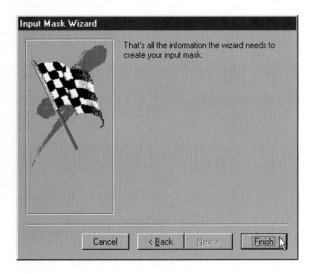

The text string shown below has been entered as the ZipCode Input Mask property.

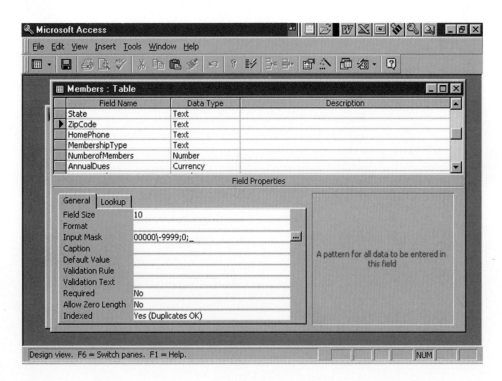

7   Select the HomePhone field in the upper pane of the Table Design window.

8   Type !(999) 000-0000;0;_ as the input mask property for this field. The input mask should appear as shown in the following figure.

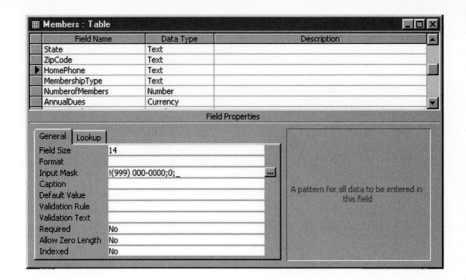

Troubleshooting Make sure you type the input mask exactly as specified, including the trailing underscore.

9 Click the Save button 🖫 to update the table design.

10 Close the table.

TASK 6: TO CHANGE THE VALIDATION PROPERTIES FOR THE *MEMBERS* TABLE:

1 Open the *Members* table in Datasheet view.

2 Scroll until the NumberofMembers field is visible. For records 1 through 10, type **1,1,4,2,3,1,2,2,1,1**, respectively, as the value for each record. When you are finished, the table should look similar to the datasheet shown below.

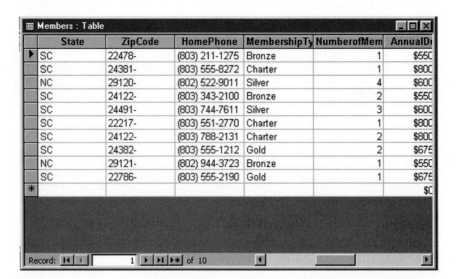

3 Click the View button 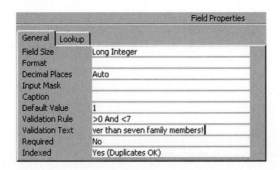 to switch to Design view.

4 Select the NumberofMembers fields in the upper pane of the Table Design window to activate this field's properties.

5 In the Properties pane, click the Default Value row. Type **1** as the default value. The default value must meet the conditions of the validation you create in the next step.

6 Click the Validation Rule row. Type **>0 and <7** as the validation rule.

> **Tip** This validation rule specifies that a value entered in this field for any existing or new record must be greater than zero and less than seven.

7 Click the Validation Text row. Type **Must be fewer than seven family members!** in the Validation Text row. The Field Properties pane for the NumberofMembers field should now appear as shown below.

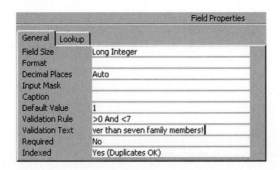

Field Size	Long Integer
Format	
Decimal Places	Auto
Input Mask	
Caption	
Default Value	1
Validation Rule	>0 And <7
Validation Text	ver than seven family members!
Required	No
Indexed	Yes (Duplicates OK)

8 To specify additional validation rules, type the entries shown in Table 3.1 into the specified fields.

> **Tip** For more information about these validation rule characters, search for ValidationRule property in the Help System, select the topic, and then select ValidationRule, ValidationText Properties (Microsoft Access) in the Topics Found list.

9 When you are finished, click the Save button 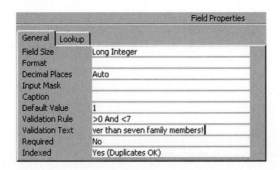. The dialog box shown on the next page appears. Click Yes.

10 Close the table.

Table 3.1 Additional Validation Rules and Text

Field Name	Validation Rule	Validation Text
Annual Dues	550 or 600 or 675 or 800	Invalid Fee!
DateJoined	<=CDate(Now())	Invalid Date!
DateofBirth	>=#1/1/1910#	Invalid Date!

Testing the Validation Rules

You are now ready to test the validation rules you have set by adding a new record to the table.

TASK 7: TO ADD A NEW RECORD TO THE TABLE:

1 Open the *Members* table in Datasheet view.

2 Click the New Record button. A blank record will be selected.

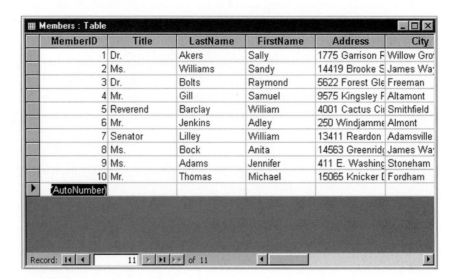

MemberID	Title	LastName	FirstName	Address	City
1	Dr.	Akers	Sally	1775 Garrison F	Willow Gro
2	Ms.	Williams	Sandy	14419 Brooke S	James Wa
3	Dr.	Bolts	Raymond	5622 Forest Gle	Freeman
4	Mr.	Gill	Samuel	9575 Kingsley F	Altamont
5	Reverend	Barclay	William	4001 Cactus Cir	Smithfield
6	Mr.	Jenkins	Adley	250 Windjamme	Almont
7	Senator	Lilley	William	13411 Reardon	Adamsville
8	Ms.	Bock	Anita	14563 Greenridg	James Wa
9	Ms.	Adams	Jennifer	411 E. Washing	Stoneham
10	Mr.	Thomas	Michael	15065 Knicker [	Fordham
(AutoNumber)					

3   Press the (TAB) key to move the focus to the Title field. Type **Ms.** as this new member's title.

4   Using the (TAB) key to move to the appropriate fields, type **Hopkins** as the last name, **Jennifer** as the first name, **31101 S.E. Quail** as the address, **James Way** as the city, **SC** as the state, and **24382** as the zip code. Notice that the input mask for the zip code displays the digits and the placeholder as you type.

5   Press the (TAB) key. Type **8005552131** as the phone number. The input mask supplies the parentheses and the hyphen character.

6   Press (TAB). Type **Silver** as the membership type.

7   Press the (TAB) key twice. Type **900** as the membership fee. The figure below shows the validation text that appears on the screen. Click OK.

8   Change the entry to **600**, and press (TAB).

9   Type today's date (in MM/DD/YY format) into the DateJoined field.

10 Press (TAB). Type **6/5/68** as the date of birth for Ms. Hopkins. Close the table.

Creating an Autoform for the Updated Table

In Project 1 you created an Autoform based upon the *Members* table. If you open the *Members* form, the form will try to display an IDNumber for each member, because this field was included in the form's design. Because you have modified the table design, you must either modify the form design, or delete the form and create a new one. In this case, it will be easiest to create a new form.

TASK 8: TO CREATE AN AUTOFORM:

1   Click the Forms tab in the Database Window.

2   Select the *Members* form and press the (DEL) key to remove the form from the database. When the Microsoft Access dialog box shown on the next page appears, click Yes to verify that you want to remove the form from the database.

3 Click the New button to create a new form.

4 In the New Form dialog box, select Form Wizard as the form, and select the *Members* table as the source of the form's data. Your selection should match the one shown in the figure below. If it does, click OK.

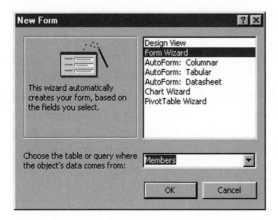

5 Add all fields in the Available Fields: list to the Select Fields: list by clicking the double-arrow button. Click Next.

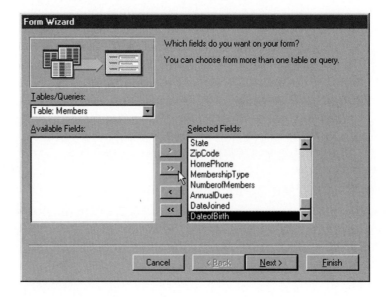

6   Select Columnar as the form type. Click Next.

7   Select Standard as the style. Click Next.

8   Accept *Members* as the name for the form, and click Finish. Your form should look similar to the one displayed below.

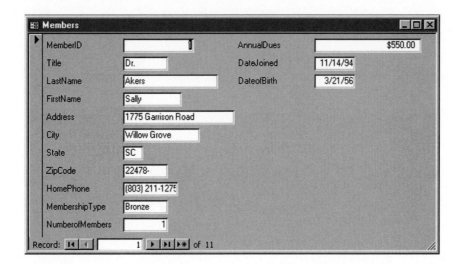

9   Close the form. Before you exit Access, select Database Utilities from the Tools menu, and select the Compact Database option. This stores the database file in the smallest size possible.

The Conclusion

Modifying a database often entails modifying the underlying tables. This might include modifying the physical structure of a table, changing the field properties, or both. Be mindful that altering a table's structure affects any database objects that use the table's data.

Summary and Exercises

Summary

- If you are planning to change the structure of a table, you may want to create a backup copy of the table first.
- Modifying a database entails both changing the physical structure of tables and altering the field properties that specify how data is entered and displayed in tables.
- Maintaining a database often requires adding fields to a table or removing fields from a table.
- You can change a table's primary key, as long as the new field does not contain any null or duplicate values.
- Input masks are used to simplify data entry and increase data accuracy.
- Validation Rules help to increase data accuracy by limiting a field entry to a specified value or range.
- A field's Validation Text property specifies the message that will appear if a validation rule is violated.

Key Terms and Operations

Key Terms

AutoNumber field	index
data validation	input mask
design modifications	table structure
field properties	validation rule
	validation text

Operations

add fields to a table
change a table's primary key
create a backup copy of a table
create an AutoForm based upon the updated table
create input masks
delete a field from a table
delete an existing form
specify validation rules
test validation rules by adding a record to the table

Study Questions

Multiple Choice

1. To insert a field into a table, you must use the
   a. Datasheet view.
   b. Design view.
   c. Form view.
   d. Database window.

2. A warning appears when you
   a. insert a field.
   b. change fields.
   c. edit field data.
   d. delete a field.

3. A primary key cannot contain
  a. a numeric value.
  b. an AutoNumber value.
  c. a null value.
  d. a patron's Social Security number.

4. To add validation rules to a field, you use
  a. the upper pane of the Table Design window.
  b. the table's datasheet.
  c. the properties pane of the Table Design window.
  d. the Database window.

5. An input mask is used to
  a. limit the data that is entered into a field.
  b. supply a template for entering data into a field.
  c. limit the data entry to a specific range.
  d. both a and b.

6. Records in a table can contain how many instances of a primary key value?
  a. one
  b. two
  c. four
  d. eight

7. When you create a validation rule, it's also a good idea to include
  a. a primary key.
  b. validation text.
  c. an input mask.
  d. an AutoNumber field.

8. Which data type ensures that a primary key always contains a unique value?
  a. currency
  b. text
  c. number
  d. AutoNumber

9. When you add a field to a database, it automatically contains a value if it is which data type?
  a. currency
  b. text
  c. number
  d. AutoNumber

10. Mr. Gilmore is concerned with finding a good primary key for the *Members* table that protects each member's confidentiality. Which field is a logical candidate, but should not be used?
  a. home phone number
  b. work phone number
  c. Social Security number
  d. zip code

Short Answer

1. Which button do you use to switch between table views?

2. Does a validation rule require validation text?

3. How many records in a table can contain the same primary key value?

4. What happens if you delete a field from a table that contains data?

5. Should you consider validating numeric field data?

6. If you want to improve the accuracy of data entered into a table, which field property or properties should you modify?

7. Which data type ensures that a primary key is always unique?

8. Many organizations have used what common identifier as a primary key in their databases?

9. Which property setting supplies a template that assists in data entry?

10. Which field property specifies a range of acceptable values for the field?

For Discussion

1. What is the difference between an input mask and a validation rule?

2. When you add a field to a table, what happens to the existing records?

3. In many Access database tables, an AutoNumber field is used as the primary key. Is this a good choice, and if so, why?

4. If you add a validation rule to a field, should you add validation text as well? Explain your answer.

Review Exercises

1. Creating an additional table and relating tables

You cannot appreciate the power of a relational database such as Access until you see why being able to relate table data is so significant. In this exercise, you will copy the Willows Membership database file, create an additional table, and relate the two tables. In Project 4, you will create a query that lists data from both tables. Complete the following:

1. Using the Windows Explorer or My Computer, copy the *Willows Membership.mdb* file. Rename the copy as **Membership Payments.mdb**.

2. Select the copy of *Members* table, and press the ⬡DEL key. Then click Yes on the confirmation alert box to delete the copy.

3. Create a new table using Design view. Use the field specifications in Table 3.2, set PaymentNumber as the primary key, and save the table as **Payments**.

   When you are finished defining the table structure and naming the table, the Table Design window should appear as below.

Table 3.2   Payments Table Field Specifications

Field Name	Data Type
PaymentNumber	AutoNumber
MemberID	Number
PaymentDate	Date/Time
Amount	Currency

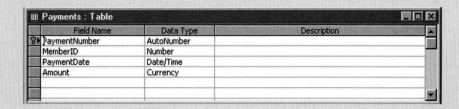

4. Close the table.

5. Click the Relationships button 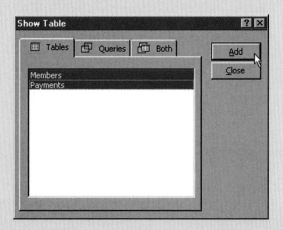 on the Database toolbar. The Show Table dialog box appears, and the *Members* table will be selected. Hold down the (SHIFT)key and click the *Payments* table to select it as well. Click the Add button.

6. Click the Close button. The two tables appear in the Relationships window. Click the MemberID field in the *Members* table, hold down the left mouse button, and drag it toward the Member ID field in the Payments table. Notice the icon representing the field, shown below.

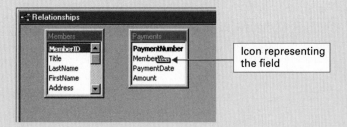

7. Release the left mouse button. Click the Create button in the Relationships dialog box.

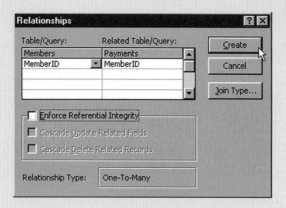

The line that extends between the fields in the two tables represents the relationship.

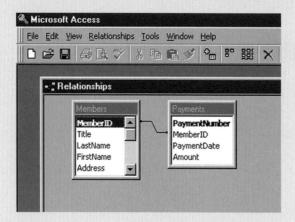

8. Close the Relationships window, and save your changes.

9. Close the table.

Comment You may have noticed a check box for maintaining referential integrity. You will learn more about this in Project 4, but in this example you may want to think about problems that could potentially arise if a data entry person entered a MemberID entry incorrectly. By enforcing referential integrity, this would never happen.

2. Adding Records to the Payments Table

The *Payments* table you created in Assignment 1 of this project does not contain any records. In this assignment, you will add records to the table that lists each member's payments toward his or her total dues. Add 10records to the table as follows:

1. Open the *Membership Payments.mdb* database if it is not currently open.

2. Open the *Payments* table in Datasheet view.

3. Add the records listed in Table 3.3 into the table. Remember that the PaymentNumber value is automatically entered, because this is an AutoNumber data type.

Table 3.3

Payment Number	MemberID	PaymentDate	Amount
1	1	1/5/98	275
2	1	6/1/98	275
3	2	1/5/98	200
4	2	4/20/98	200
5	2	6/1/98	400
6	3	1/5/98	600
7	4	1/5/98	500
8	4	3/16/98	50
9	5	1/5/98	300
10	5	6/1/98	300

4. Close the table.

5. Close the database.

3. Changing a table design and creating an AutoReport

1. Launch Access and open *High Point Foods xxx.mdb*.

> **Note** If you do not have a database named *High Point Foods xxx.mdb,* ask your instructor for a copy of the file you should use to complete this exercise.

2. Make the following changes to the *Food Categories* table design:

   - Make CategoryID the primary key field.

   - Add a field named **Quantity Consumed** as a text field and position it at the end of the table. Include the following description for the field: **Average number of pounds of food used per month.**

3. Save the changes to the table and add the following information to the *Quantity Consumed* field:
   6391 Gallons
   50 Pounds
   500 Servings
   903 Pounds
   2548 Pounds
   8192 Pounds
   1500 Pounds
   2164 Pounds
   12495 Pounds

4. Create an AutoReport named *Food Categories* for the table and print a copy of the AutoReport.

5. Save changes to the database and exit Access.

Assignments

1. Adding Validation Rules to the Willows Employees database

The Willows Employees database contains at least one field that requires a value within a specific range. Open the database, and then open the *Employees* table in Design view. Add a validation rule to the Salary field that specifies a salary greater than or equal to 25,000 and less than 100,000. Add validation text specifying that the value entered falls outside the salary range. Save your changes to the table, and close the table.

2. Changing Field properties in the Willows Employees database

When the Database Wizard created the Employees database, it set some of the field sizes to a value that is larger than necessary. Open the Willows Employees database if it is not currently open, and then open the *Employees* table in Design view. Change the field properties for the fields specified in Table 3.4.

For the StateOrProvince field, type **>LL** as the input mask. The mask requires an entry of two letters—A through Z—and if the user enters lowercase letters, they will be displayed in uppercase. Save your changes to the table, close it, and close the database.

Table 3.4   Field Size Property Values

Field Name	Field Size Property
SocialSecurityNumber	9
Title	10
LastName	20
FirstName	15
Address	50
City	15
StateOrProvince	2
PostalCode	9

Creating Queries

Most databases contain much more information than is useful at any given time. End users need some way of viewing information from the database that meets specific conditions, such as all members who live in a specific zip code. Although filters are useful, designing and running queries offers a much more flexible and powerful way for seeing the data you need.

Objectives

After completing this project, you will be able to:

➤ **Create a new query using Design View**

➤ **Add fields to a query**

➤ **Add calculated fields to a query**

➤ **Modify the format of a calculated field**

➤ **Run a query**

➤ **Specify query criteria and conditions**

➤ **Sort data in a query**

➤ **Create a form to display the results of a query**

The Challenge

Mr. Gilmore is very pleased with the work you have done on the membership database. Now he wants to see a list of the exact fees each member will pay this year. Membership fees include a base fee that varies depending upon the type of membership, plus a surcharge for each family member. Members over 65 years of age receive a 15 percent discount of the base membership fee. Finally, Mr. Gilmore wants a separate listing of the membership fee paid by charter members who also received a qualifying discount. As usual, this information will be sorted by last name.

The Solution

Fortunately, Access has powerful database query capabilities that enable you to deliver the exact information that Mr. Gilmore has requested. You can create a query that will calculate each member's total membership fee, based upon the specifications Mr. Gilmore gave you. In addition, you can specify criteria that will return records that meet specific conditions. Figure 4.1 shows a form displaying the total membership fees for one member.

Figure 4.1

The Setup

After you launch Access and open your database, you should make sure the Database toolbar and the Status toolbar are displayed. These are the default settings in Access, but they may have been changed on your computer. (If you have forgotten how to do this, refer to Table 1.1 in Project 1.)

> **Troubleshooting** If you do not see the Database toolbar on the screen when you launch Access and open your database, choose Toolbars from the View menu. Select the Database toolbar to display it. If any additional toolbars are visible, close them. If you do not see the Status Bar at the bottom of the Application window, choose Options from the Tools menu, click the View Page tab and change the Status Bar check box option.

Using the procedures you learned in Task 1 of Project 1, open the *Willows Membership.mdb* file from your diskette. Delete the *Copy of Members* table from the database.

Creating Queries

An Access *query* is a database object that you create to view, change, and analyze data in different ways. You can also use queries as the source of records for forms and reports. Sometimes you will want to see information from the database that requires a *calculated field*—a field that displays data resulting from a calculation that you specify rather than stored data.

Think of a query as a set of specifications that returns a subset of data from one or more tables. Data returned by a query isn't stored in the query; it is stored in the tables underlying the query, and the query stores the specifications. Therefore, the query always displays the most recent data in the database. Queries can also be used to add or edit table data.

Creating a Select Query

The most common kind of query is a *select query*—a query that retrieves data from one or more tables and displays the results in a datasheet where you can update the records.

TASK 1: TO CREATE A SELECT QUERY USING DESIGN VIEW:

1 Click the Queries tab in the Database window.

2 Click the New button.

3 In the New Query dialog box, select Design View.

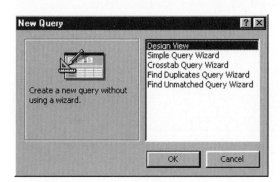

4 When the Show Table dialog box appears, click the *Members* table to select it. Then click Add. Notice that the *Members* table appears in the query window behind the Show Table dialog box.

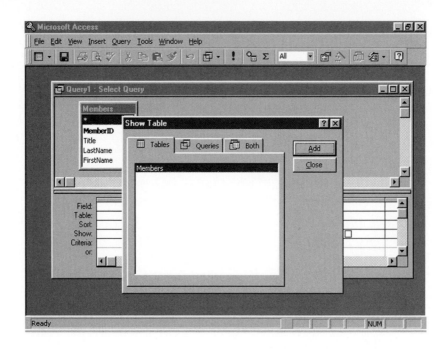

5 Click the Close button. The Query Design window should now be displayed.

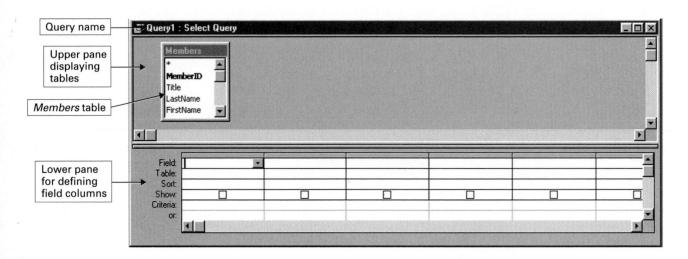

The Query Design window consists of two panes. The upper pane includes the tables containing the fields that you will use in the query. The lower pane consists of columns where you can define the fields of data the query displays. This is the *query design grid*. This view is called the *Query Design View*. Notice that the default name of the query is displayed in the query's title bar.

Tip You can add additional tables to the upper pane at any time by clicking the Show Table button on the toolbar.

6   Click the Save button 🖫 on the Query Design toolbar.

7   Type **Membership Fees** in the Save As dialog box.

8   Click OK.

Adding Fields to a Select Query

As with a table, an Access query has multiple views. You use Query Design View to create the query specifications before you *run* a query, which is the process of loading your specifications and displaying the results in a query datasheet. A *query datasheet* appears almost identical to a table datasheet; you can use it to modify field data and add records to the underlying table or tables.

Before a query datasheet will display any records, you must specify which fields the query will return. These are then added to the query design grid. You can add fields in a variety of ways.

TASK 2: TO ADD FIELDS TO THE QUERY DESIGN GRID USING TWO DIFFERENT METHODS:

1   Click the MemberID field in the field list of the Members table in the upper pane of the Query Design window.

2   While holding down the left mouse button, drag the field name from the upper pane to the first available row and column in the lower pane.

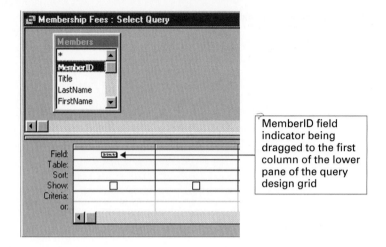

MemberID field indicator being dragged to the first column of the lower pane of the query design grid

3 Release the left mouse button.
The MemberID field is now displayed in the leftmost column of the query design grid. The name of the table from which the field is referenced is listed immediately under the field name.

This click-and-drag method is one way you can add fields to your query design grid. Another method follows:

4 Move the mouse pointer inside the first row of the next available column in the lower pane and click the left mouse button.
A drop-down list button appears.

5 Click the drop-down list button and select the Title field.

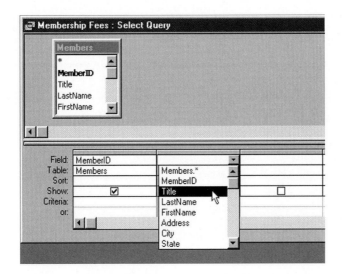

The Title field is added to the lower pane and the *Member* table is listed directly under it.

6   Using either the drag method or the drop-down list method, add the LastName, FirstName, MembershipType, and AnnualDues fields to the query design grid. When you are finished, six fields are displayed.

> **Tip** Notice that the Show: checkbox for each field is checked. If you need to use a field for the query but do not want it to show in the query datasheet, deselect the field's Show: button.

7   Click the Save button 🖫 on the Query Design toolbar to update the changes to your query.

Viewing the Results of a Query

So far you have not seen how the query datasheet will look when you run the query. One of the advantages of using a graphical query design tool such as the Query Design window is that you can run your query at any time while you are designing it to see what data it will display.

TASK 3: TO VIEW THE RESULTS OF A QUERY:

1   Click the Run button 🟦 on the Query Design toolbar.
The query switches to Datasheet View. The following figure shows what your datasheet will look like after you run the query.

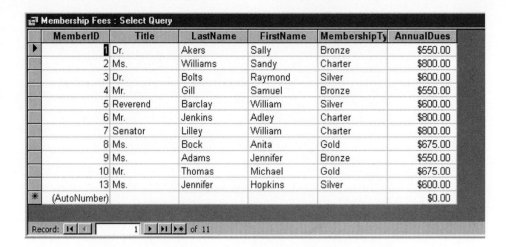

Tip You can also use the View menu or the View button on the toolbar to switch between views.

Notice that the title bar identifies the datasheet as belonging to a select query.

2 Click the View button 🔲▾ on the Query Datasheet toolbar.

3 Close the query.
The query object name appears in the Database window.

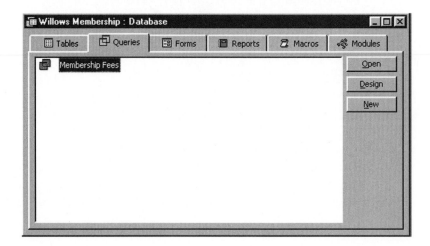

4 Click the Design button. The query again opens in Query Design View.

Adding Calculated Fields to a Query

To determine each member's total membership fee, you must first determine which members receive a discount or pay a surcharge for additional family members.

You can create calculated fields in the query design grid. You should recall that a calculated field is a field that returns data according to a certain expression. An *expression* is a combination of object identifiers such as table and field names, arithmetic or logical operators such as an addition sign or a less than (<) symbol, and numeric values that produce a result. Access includes an *Expression Builder* that is a graphical workspace you can use to create an expression.

TASK 4: TO ADD AN EXPRESSION TO CALCULATE THE MEMBER SURCHARGE:

1   Use the scroll bar in the query design grid to display additional columns in the pane.

2   Place the insertion point over the next available column and click the left mouse button.

3   Click the Build button ⚒ on the Query Design toolbar. The Expression Builder appears.

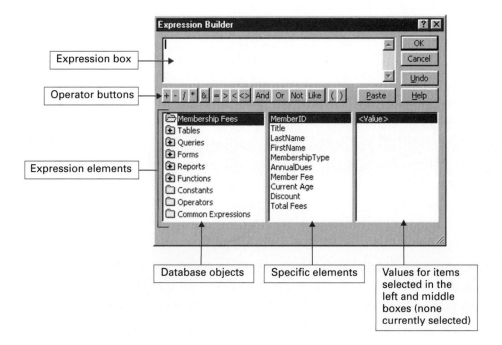

4   Double-click the Plus sign ⊞ Tables on the folder immediately to the left of the Tables list in the leftmost pane of the Expression Builder.

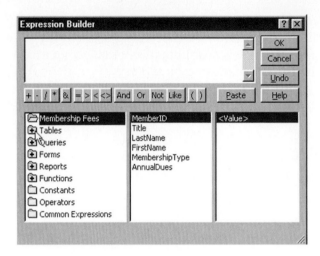

5   Click the *Members* table name. The list of fields in the table now appears in the middle pane of the Expression Builder.

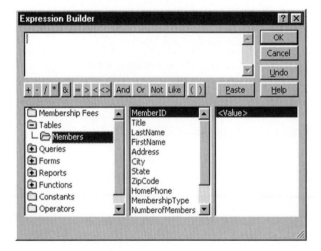

6   Place the insertion point inside the Expression box in the upper portion of the Expression Builder.

7   Click the Equals Sign button = appearing on the toolbar inside the Expression Builder. You will note that an equals sign appears in the workspace.

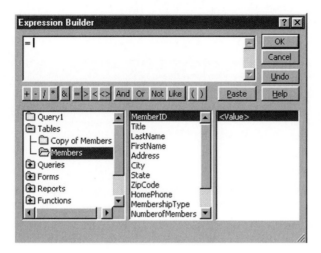

Tip For many expressions, the equals sign is optional. For more information about the Expression builder and the syntax required for specific expressions, click the Help button in the Expression Builder and select the Read more about expressions option.

8 Highlight the NumberOfMembers field name in the middle pane of the Expression Builder, and click the Paste button Paste .

9 Type ***25** at the end of the equation that is forming in the workspace. The expression displayed in the Expression Builder specifies that the value in the NumberOfMembers field will be multiplied by the value 25.

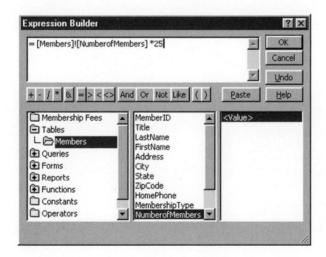

Tip In this expression, [Members]! [NumberofMembers] represents a field in the *Members* table. The ampersand character is the arithmetic operator for multiplication, and 25 is the literal value by which all field data is multiplied for each record.

10 Click OK. The expression appears in the query design grid.

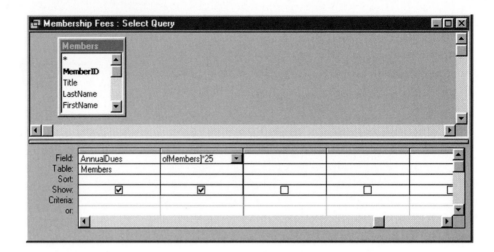

Troubleshooting The expression will appear truncated because it is too wide to appear in the current column width.

TASK 5: TO VIEW THE RESULTS OF THE EXPRESSION AND MODIFY ITS FORMAT:

1 Click the Run button **!** on the Query Design toolbar.

2 Using the scrollbar in the datasheet, position the columns so that you can see the calculated field data. Your results should match the results shown in the figure below.

Title	LastName	FirstName	MembershipTy	AnnualDues	Expr1
Dr.	Akers	Sally	Bronze	$550.00	25
Ms.	Williams	Sandy	Charter	$800.00	25
Dr.	Bolts	Raymond	Silver	$600.00	100
Mr.	Gill	Samuel	Bronze	$550.00	50
Reverend	Barclay	William	Silver	$600.00	75
Mr.	Jenkins	Adley	Charter	$800.00	25
Senator	Lilley	William	Charter	$800.00	50
Ms.	Bock	Anita	Gold	$675.00	50
Ms.	Adams	Jennifer	Bronze	$550.00	25
Mr.	Thomas	Michael	Gold	$675.00	25
Ms.	Jennifer	Hopkins	Silver	$600.00	25
*				$0.00	

Record: 1 of 11

You will notice that the calculated field has the default name of *Expr1*, and that the data does not appear in currency format.

3   Click the View button 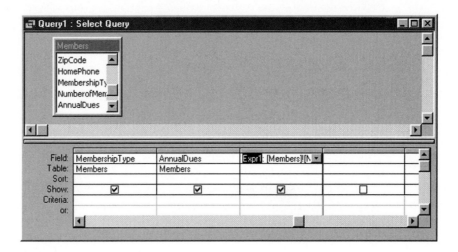 on the Query Datasheet toolbar.

4   Highlight the text *Expr1* in the first row of the column containing the calculated field expression.

Troubleshooting Make sure you do not highlight the colon character! This character is needed to separate the name of the calculated field from its expression.

5   Type **Member Fee** in place of *Expr1*.

6   Click the Properties button 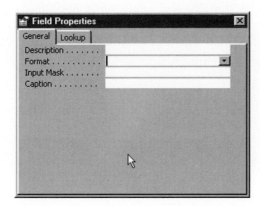 on the Query Datasheet toolbar.

7   Click the Format row in the Field Properties dialog box.

8   Click the drop-down list ▼ button. Drag the scroll bar until the Currency option is visible. Select Currency from the list.

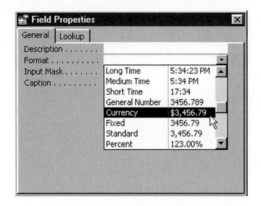

9 Close the Field Properties dialog box and run the query ▮ to view your changes. Adjust the view using the scroll bar if necessary.
Compare your results with the figure below. Note that the column title now reads "Member Fee" and that the data in that column is formatted for currency.

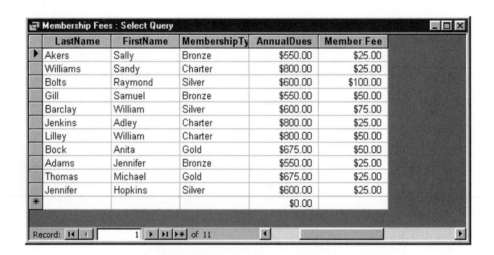

10 When you are finished, switch to Design view ▮▮.

Building Additional Calculated Fields

You can create expressions in the Expression Builder in a variety of ways. One method is to type the expression directly in the upper pane of the Expression Builder dialog box.

Tip You can also type expressions directly in the lower pane of the Query Design window when you know the proper syntax. Search for Expression in the Help system, and select the Creating topic. Then select the Create an expression topic.

TASK 6: TO BUILD AN EXPRESSION TO CALCULATE EACH MEMBER'S AGE:

1 Select the first row of the next available column in the query design grid.

2 Click the Build button on the Query Design toolbar.

3 Type **Current Age: DateDiff("d",[DateofBirth],Now())/365** as the expression in the upper portion of the Expression Builder.

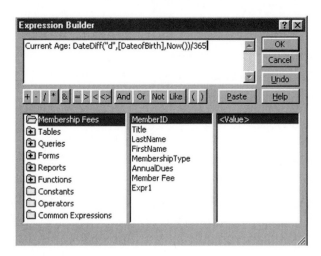

Hint This field calculates each member's current age, based upon his or her date of birth. For more information on the syntax for this expression, select Contents and Index from the Help menu, and search for DateDiff.

4 Click the OK button and run the query. Your results should be similar to those shown below. Note that the number of decimal places you see may differ.

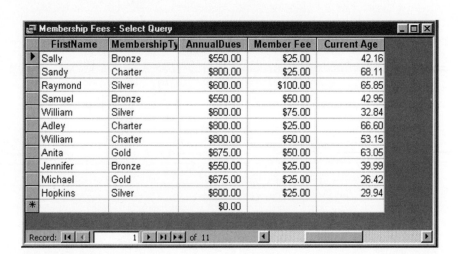

FirstName	MembershipTy	AnnualDues	Member Fee	Current Age
Sally	Bronze	$550.00	$25.00	42.16
Sandy	Charter	$800.00	$25.00	68.11
Raymond	Silver	$600.00	$100.00	65.85
Samuel	Bronze	$550.00	$50.00	42.95
William	Silver	$600.00	$75.00	32.84
Adley	Charter	$800.00	$25.00	66.60
William	Charter	$800.00	$50.00	53.15
Anita	Gold	$675.00	$50.00	63.05
Jennifer	Bronze	$550.00	$25.00	39.99
Michael	Gold	$675.00	$25.00	26.42
Hopkins	Silver	$600.00	$25.00	29.94
*		$0.00		

Record: 1 of 11

5   Click the View button to return to Design View. Click the Properties button on the Query Design toolbar.

6   Select Fixed as the format.

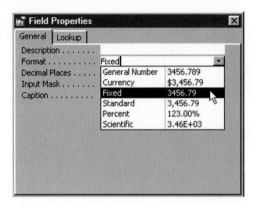

7   Set the decimal places to zero.

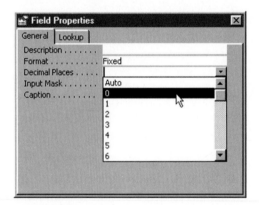

8   Close the Field Properties dialog box, and update the query design by saving the file.

9   Run the query. Use the scroll bar to display the results of the calculation.

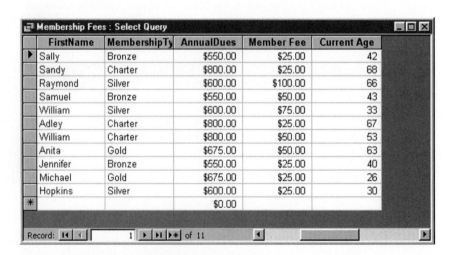

Troubleshooting The expression you created uses the computer's system clock to calculate each member's current age. If your computer's clock is set differently, the values will change.

10 Switch to Design view.

TASK 7: TO BUILD AN EXPRESSION TO CALCULATE THE AGE DISCOUNT:

1 Select the first row of the next available column in the query design grid.

2 Click the Build button 🔨 on the Query Design toolbar.

3 Type **Discount: IIf([Current Age]>=65,0.15*[AnnualDues],0)** as the expression in the Expression box of the Expression Builder.

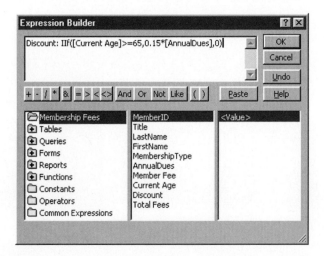

Tip This expression calculates a 15 percent discount for members who are 65 years of age or older, and no discount for members under 65 years of age.

4 Click OK to close the Expression Builder and run the query.

5 Switch to Design view and place the insertion point inside the Discount field. Click the Properties 🖹 button. Select the Format row in the Field Properties dialog box.

6 Change the format to Currency.

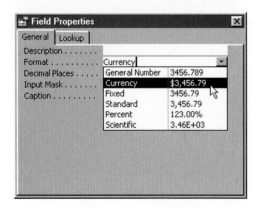

7 Close the Field Properties dialog box.

8 Run the query. The results should appear as shown below.

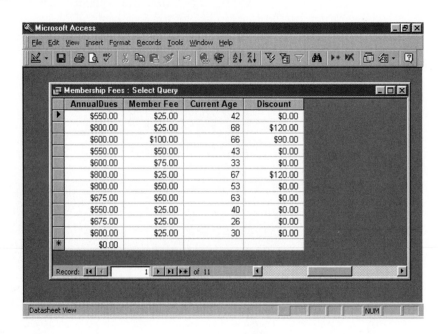

9 Update your query by saving the file 🖫.

TASK 8: TO BUILD AN EXPRESSION TO CALCULATE THE TOTAL FEE FOR EACH MEMBER:

1 Select the first row of the next available column in the query design grid.

2 Click the Build button 🔧 on the Query Design toolbar.

3 Type **Total Fees: [AnnualDues]+[Member Fee]-[Discount]** as the expression in the workspace of the Expression Builder.

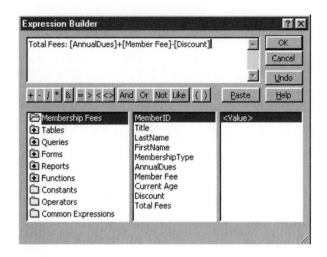

4   Click the OK button to close the Expression Builder.

5   Using the same procedure as in the previous task, change the format of this field to Currency.

6   Save your changes 🖫.

7   Run the query ❗. Use the scroll bar in the datasheet window to display each of the calculated fields you created.

Enter Parameter value

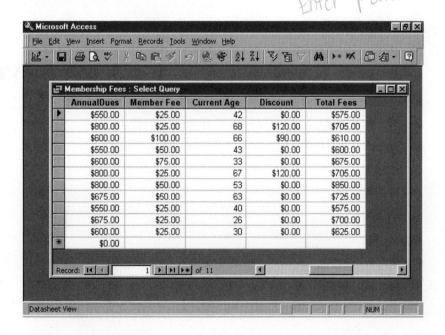

8   Close the query.

Defining the Sort Order and Criteria for a Query

You will frequently need to see records in a query that meet certain conditions and appear in a specific order. Remember that Mr. Gilmore requested a listing of the total fees for all charter members who also received a qualifying discount. He also wants this list alphabetized by last name. Query data can be sorted in either ascending or descending order.

TASK 9: TO ADD SORT ORDER AND FIELD CRITERIA TO THE QUERY DESIGN:

1 Open the Membership Fees query in Design View.

2 Place the insertion point in the Sort: row of the LastName field in the query design grid.

3 Click the drop-down list button ▾.

4 Select Ascending as the sort order.

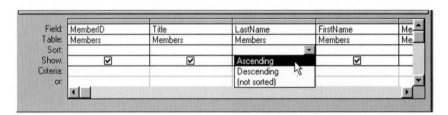

5 Use the scroll bar in the query design grid to display the MembershipType field.

6 Type **Charter** in the Criteria row.

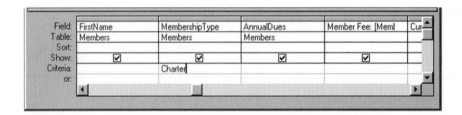

7 Use the scroll bar to display the Current Age calculated field.

8 Type **>=65** as the field criteria.

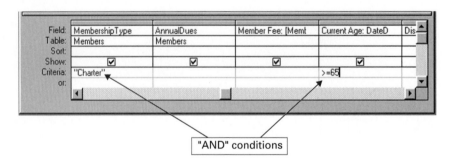

"AND" conditions

This is known as an *AND condition*, since both conditions (records with Charter members who are not older than 65) must be met for any records to be returned. The criteria specifying an AND condition always occupy only one row in the Query Design window.

Tip You can also create OR conditions in Access, where records are returned that meet either one or the other condition. When constructing OR conditions, you will use more than one criteria row in the Query Design window. For more information, search for the topic *Ways to specify multiple criteria in a query* in the Access Help System.

9   Update the query design by pressing the save button 🖫 on the toolbar and run the query ❗. Two records meet the multiple conditions you specify.

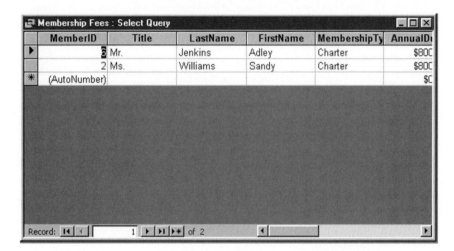

	MemberID	Title	LastName	FirstName	MembershipTy	AnnualD⬧
▶	5	Mr.	Jenkins	Adley	Charter	$80C
	2	Ms.	Williams	Sandy	Charter	$80C
*	(AutoNumber)					$C

Record: ⏮ ◀ [1] ▶ ▶⏭ ▶✱ of 2

10 Use the scrollbar in the datasheet to verify that the conditions have been correctly met. When you are finished, close the query.

Creating an Autoform Based upon a Query

You can think of an Access query as being similar to a table because you can base other database objects upon it. Remember how easy it was to create a form based upon a table? It's just as easy to create an AutoForm from a query.

TASK 10: TO CREATE AN AUTOFORM BASED UPON THE *MEMBERSHIP FEES* QUERY:

1   Click the Forms tab in the Database window and then press New.

2   In the New Form dialog box, select AutoForm: Columnar as the form type, and select Membership Fees as the object upon which the query will be based.

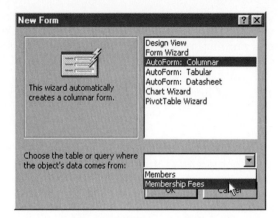

3 Click OK. After a moment, the form will appear.

4 Close the form. Click Yes to save the changes, and accept the default name of Membership Fees

> **Tip** By default, an AutoForm always uses the name of object upon which it was created as its own name.

5 Select Database Utilities from the Tools menu. Choose Compact Database from the cascading menu.

6 Close the Willows Membership database.

The Conclusion

As you can see, queries are much more powerful than filters for extracting information from a database. This is because in addition to supporting multiple criteria, queries can also include calculated fields that utilize the data stored in one or more tables to create additional fields. Calculated fields are not stored in the database, but are calculated whenever a query is displayed based on the commands that have been embedded in the query. Therefore, query results are always current even if users have changed information in the tables.

Summary and Exercises

Summary

- Queries are database objects that you use to view, change, and analyze data in different ways.
- Queries are often used as the source of records for forms and reports.
- A select query retrieves data from one or more tables and displays the results in a datasheet.
- You use the Query Design window to create queries in Access.
- The Query Design window consists of two panes — the upper pane contains a list of tables and fields; the lower pane contains the query design grid.
- Fields that appear in the query design grid return information in a query datasheet when the query is run.
- Queries can contain calculated fields that return data according to an expression.
- You can easily create expressions using the Expression Builder.
- You can add sort order and criteria specifications to return specific records in a specified order.
- A query object can be the source for an Access AutoForm.

Key Terms and Operations

Key Terms

AND condition	query datasheet
calculated field	query design grid
expression	Query Design View
Expression Builder	run
query	select query

Operations

add calculated fields to a query using the Expression Builder
add fields to a query using the query design grid
add tables to a query
create a new query
create an Autoform based upon a query
define the sort order and criteria for a query
run a query
specify sort order and criteria

Study Questions

Multiple Choice

1. The query design grid appears in the
   a. Database window.
   b. Query datasheet.
   c. upper pane of the Query Design window.
   d. lower pane of the Query Design window.

2. To sort the data returned by a query, you specify sort order in the
   a. Database window.
   b. query design grid.
   c. Query datasheet.
   d. upper pane of the Query Design window.

3. When you run a query based upon one table, the results are displayed in
   a. the Database window.
   b. a Query datasheet.
   c. a Table datasheet.
   d. the query design grid.

4. In Access, an AutoForm can be based upon
   a. tables only.
   b. queries only.
   c. tables and queries.
   d. neither tables nor queries.

5. Where do you add fields when designing a query?
   a. the Database window.
   b. the upper pane of the Query Design window.
   c. the query design grid.
   d. the query datasheet.

6. What do you use to create a calculated field in a query?
   a. an AND condition.
   b. an expression.
   c. a filter.
   d. an OR condition.

7. Which of the following statements is true?
   a. Select queries cannot be used to enter or edit field data in tables.
   b. Queries return records in a datasheet.
   c. Select queries do not reflect the most recent changes to an underlying table.
   d. Queries cannot be used as the source object for an Access form.

8. The expression =[Quantity]*[Cost] will most likely return the
   a. purchases made by an employee.
   b. total membership fee charged to a club member.
   c. total number of members belonging to a club.
   d. value of an inventory item.

9. Where is the data in a calculated field stored?
   a. The data comprising calculated fields are stored in the Database window.
   b. The data comprising calculated fields are stored in a query datasheet.
   c. The data comprising calculated fields are stored in a table.
   d. The data comprising calculated fields are not stored anywhere in a database.

10. Which of the following statements is false?
   a. Query results are returned in a datasheet.
   b. A query must be based upon one or more tables or another query.
   c. A query is similar to a filter in that it can be used to return specific records from a database.
   d. A query cannot be saved.

Short Answer

1. What is the query design grid?

2. What does the upper pane of the Query Design window display?

3. What do the columns in the query design grid represent?

4. How do you run a query?

5. What two options are available for sorting records returned by a query?

6. When you run a query, where is the data displayed?

7. How many criteria rows are required in the query design grid for an AND condition?

8. How do you specify conditions in a query?

9. What database objects can be used to create an AutoForm?

10. What kind of query returns data from one or more tables?

For Discussion

1. How does a query datasheet differ from a table datasheet?

2. What is a calculated field and where does it store data?

3. How do you specify the sort order for a query?

4. How does an AND condition differ from an OR condition?

Review Exercises

1. Enforcing referential integrity in table relationships

As you learned in this project, queries can be used to edit and modify data in the table or tables upon which a query is based. This can lead to potential problems in a database when data in two or more tables is related. By enforcing referential integrity, you can specify that tables related by a specific field MUST contain field data for the related field. In this exercise you will learn why referential integrity is important, and how to enforce referential integrity in table relationships. Complete the following steps:

1. Open the *Membership Payments.mdb* database from your floppy diskette.

2. Click the Relationships button 品 on the Database toolbar.

3. Place the insertion point immediately over the line extending between the two tables.

4. Right-click to edit the relationship. Select Edit Relationship from the right-click menu.

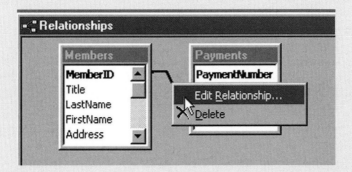

5. Click the Enforce Referential Integrity checkbox in the Relationships dialog box, which enforces referential integrity. Click OK.

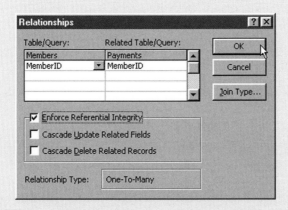

You will notice that the appearance of the line between the tables has changed. The graphical representation depicts a one-to-many relationship. In a one-to-many relationship, the related table (the "many" table) can contain one or more records that relate to the table on the "one" side of the relationship. In other words, there can be more than one payment record for each member.

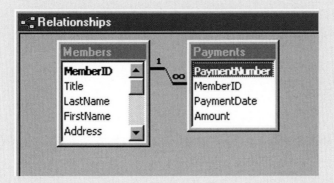

Enforcing referential integrity means that all records in the Payments table must have a MemberID entry that matches a primary key value in the *Members* table. Thus, you will never be able to enter a payment that is not related to a specific member.

6. Close the Relationships dialog box.

7. Close the database.

2. Creating a query based upon two tables

In this exercise you will see how a query can return data from more than one table. Complete the following:

1. Open the *Membership Payments.mdb* database.

2. Click the Queries tab in the Database window.

3. Click the New button and select Design View then press OK.

4. Select both tables, click the Add button, and click Close.

> **Tip** You can select more than one table by dragging the pointer over all the tables you want to select, or pressing the (SHIFT) key as you click on the additional tables. Or you can click each table individually and then click the Add button after you have selected each one.

5. Add the MemberID field from the Payments table to the query design grid.

6. Add the LastName field to the query design grid from the Members table.

7. Add the PaymentDate and Amount fields to the query design grid from the Payments table.

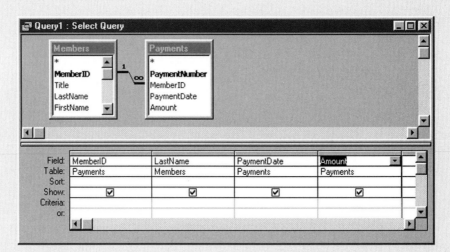

8. Click the Save button 💾. Type **Payments (Query)** as the name for the query.

> **Tip** A query cannot have the same name as an existing table object.

9. Run the query by pressing the Run button 📍. Your screen should resemble the one shown in the next figure.

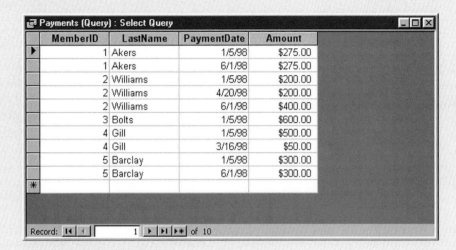

10. Close the query and the database.

3. Creating and running a query

1. Launch Access and open the *High Point Food Orders.mdb* database.

> **Tip** If you do not have a database named *High Point Food Orders.mdb*, ask your instructor for a copy of the file you should use to complete this exercise.

2. Create a query that includes the *Food Categories* table and the *Food Products* table, that provides a list of each product by product category. Save the query using the query name **Food Products by Category**.

3. Run the query and print a copy of the query run.

4. Run the query again, sorting the product names alphabetically and print a copy of the query run.

5. Run the query again to obtain a list of beverages only; print a copy of the list.

6. Save the changes to the query design and close the database.

7. Exit Access.

Assignments

1. Creating a query containing an OR condition

Open the *Willow Employees.mdb* database file. Create a new query in design view based upon the Employees table. Add the SocialSecurityNumber, LastName, StateOrProvince, and Salary fields to the query design grid. Type **CO** in the first criteria row for the StateOrProvince field, and **CA** in the next criteria row (labeled "or") for this field. Save the query as **Current Salary for CO and CA**. Run the query. Only record for employees from either Colorado or California will be returned. After you view the results, close the query and the database.

2. Creating an AutoForm based upon a query

Open the *Web Sites.mdb* database file from your diskette. Create a new query named *Financial Services* that contain all fields but returns only those records in which the primary product is financial services. After you save this query, create an AutoForm based upon it. Save the AutoForm, close the database, and exit Access.

Creating and Modifying Forms

After you have designed tables and queries in a database, it is usually a good idea to create forms for users. Tables hold data, queries return data, and forms make it easy to work with records in a database. Most of the information in a form comes from an underlying record source—a table or query. Other information in the form is stored in the form's design.

Objectives

After completing this project, you will be able to:

➤ **Delete a form from a database and rearrange fields on a form**

➤ **Select and remove fields from a form**

➤ **Create a new form in Design View**

➤ **Add controls to a form in Design View**

➤ **Save a form**

➤ **Modify a form's controls**

➤ **Add unbound controls to a form**

➤ **Add a picture to a form**

The Challenge

Mr. Gilmore has reviewed the forms in your database. He wants you to create a new form listing information about members at the Willows that will be as easy as possible for the data entry team to use. He wants a simpler layout that has fewer descriptive labels. Finally, he wants the Willows logo to appear on the Members form.

The Solution

You can easily modify existing forms and create new ones using Form Design View. Rather than modifying the Members form, it is easier to delete the existing one and create a new one in Design View that will meet Mr. Gilmore's specifications. You can use Design View to add fields to a form, modify the appearance of the form and add the Willows logo. Figure 5.1 shows the form you will create in this project.

Figure 5.1

The Setup

After you launch Access and open your database, you should make sure the Database toolbar and the Status toolbar are displayed. These are the default settings in Access, but they may have been changed on your computer. (If you have forgotten how to do this, refer to Table 1.1 in Project 1.)

> **Troubleshooting** If you do not see the Database toolbar on the screen when you launch Access and open your database, choose Toolbars from the View menu. Select the Database toolbar to display it. If any additional toolbars are visible, close them. If you do not see the Status Bar at the bottom of the Application Window, choose Options from the Tools menu, click the View Page tab and change the Status Bar checkbox option.

Using the procedures you learned in Task 1 of Project 1, open the *Willows Membership.mdb* file from your floppy diskette.

Creating Forms

In Project 1 you used the Autoform Wizard to create the Members form that is currently in the database. Remember that a form is always based upon a *record source*—a table or query that contains the records the form displays. You create the link between a form and its record source by using graphical objects called controls. A *control* is an object such as a text box that displays information in a form.

Although you have the option of modifying the current Members form in Design View, it is easier to delete the existing one and create a form in Form Design View.

TASK 1: TO DELETE AN EXISTING DATABASE FORM:

1 Click the Forms tab in the database window.

2 Select the *Members* form in the database window, if it is not currently highlighted.

3 Select Delete from the Edit menu or press the (DELETE) button on your keyboard.

> **Tip** You can also delete a database object using the Cut button ✄.

4 Click Yes when you are asked for confirmation.

> **Troubleshooting** Make sure you have selected the Members form, as you cannot reverse this action with Undo!

The form is no longer visible in the database window.

Creating a New Form in Design View

You are now ready to create a form. As you will see, Access provides numerous tools for creating a form in Design View. As with tables and queries, you create a form by adding controls to the form's *Detail section*, which is the area of the Form Design window that appears when you create a new form in *Design View*.

TASK 2: TO CREATE A NEW FORM USING DESIGN VIEW:

1 Click the New button in the Form tab of the database window.

2 Select Design View to create a form without using a Wizard, and base the form upon the *Members* table.

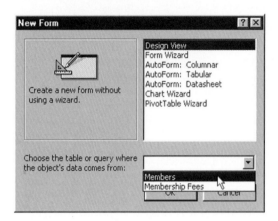

3 A blank form will appear in Form Design View.

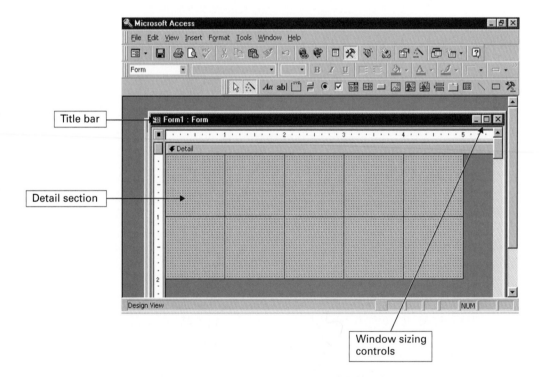

Note that a default name for the form appears in the form's title bar. The form design window contains the standard buttons in the upper right-hand corner for minimizing, maximizing, and closing the form. You will add form controls in the Detail section.

4 Click the Maximize button in the form's Title bar.

TASK 3: TO ADD CONTROLS TO THE FORM:

1 Click the Field List button 🔳 on the Form Design toolbar.

2 Resize the Field List box so that all field names are visible.

3 Click the MemberID field name to select it. While holding the left mouse button, begin to drag the field name toward the form's Detail section. Notice that as you drag, the mouse pointer changes to a graphic representation of the field.

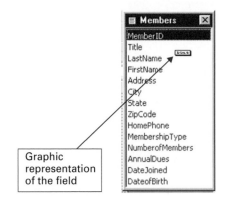

Graphic representation of the field

4 Drag the MemberID field into the upper left portion of the Detail section.

5 Release the mouse button. Two controls appear on the form.

Notice that both controls contain MemberID. The control on the right is a **bound control**, which means that it is bound, or linked to a specific database object (in this case, a field). The leftmost control is a **label control,** which displays descriptive text. The bound control is a **text box control**, which is used to display or enter field data from the underlying table or query.

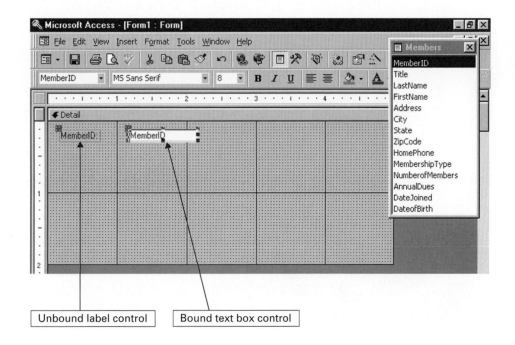

Unbound label control   Bound text box control

6 Using the same procedure as in the previous step, drag the remaining controls to the detail section of the form, approximately in the positions shown below.

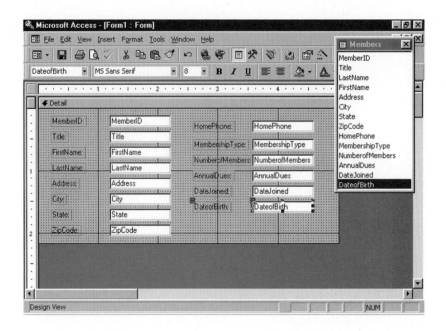

Troubleshooting Be careful not to place controls too close to the side of the form or the controls may overlap. Also, as you move the controls on the form you will notice that the label and the text box for each field move as a unit. If you inadvertently click the square selection handle in the upper-left portion of each control, it will move independently of the associated control.

TASK 4: TO SAVE THE FORM AND SWITCH TO FORM VIEW:

1 Save the form 🖫. Type **Members** in the Save As dialog box, and click OK.

2 Click the View button on the Form Design toolbar 🖽▾. The form displays the first record in the *Members* table in Form view.

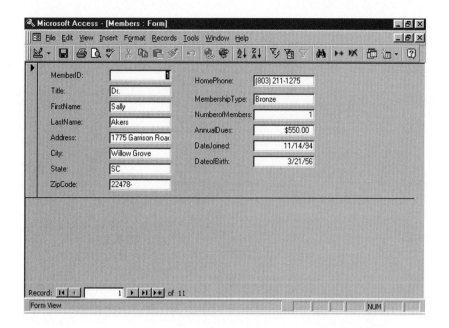

Tip The form is maximized, because you maximized the Form Design window.

3   Click the View button on the Form View toolbar to return to Design View.

Modifying a Form's Controls

Form Design View gives you complete control over the location and format of each control on a form. After you add controls to a form in Design View, the next step in designing a form is modifying the controls.

Some of the labels appearing on the Members form are not really necessary, and the size and location of each textbox should be changed as well. In the tasks that follow you will delete some of the labels on the form and change the text property of others. You will also reposition the text box controls to make the form easier to read. Finally, you will add a ControlTip to the text boxes that no longer have labels. A *ControlTip* is a descriptive message that appears when you move the mouse pointer over a control.

TASK 5: TO DELETE LABEL CONTROLS FROM THE MEMBERS FORM:

1   Move the mouse pointer over the MemberID label.

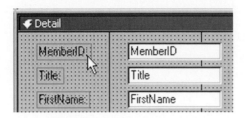

2   Click the left mouse button. The control is now selected. You can tell that it is selected because the sizing handles appear.

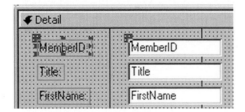

3   Click the Cut button ✄ on the Form Design toolbar.

4   Click the Title label. While holding the (SHIFT) key, click the FirstName, LastName, Address, City, State, ZipCode, and HomePhone labels.

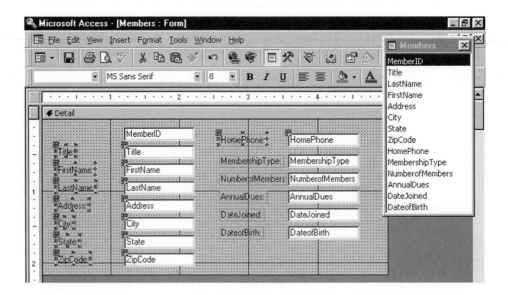

5   Select Cut ✄.

6   Click the Close button on the field list to close it. The results of these actions are shown on the next page.

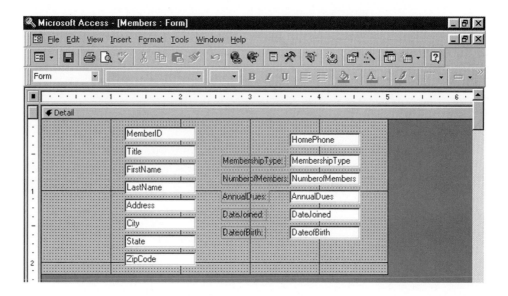

7   Save your changes .

TASK 6: TO REPOSITION TEXT BOX CONTROLS ON THE FORM:

1   Select the MemberID text box and move the insertion point to an edge until the pointer changes to a hand. You may now reposition the text box.

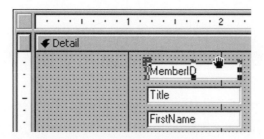

2   Move the MemberID text box to the left and below its present position.

3   Move the Title text box immediately below the MemberID control.

4 With the text box still selected, move the insertion point over the selection handle on the right border of the text box until the resizing double arrow appears.

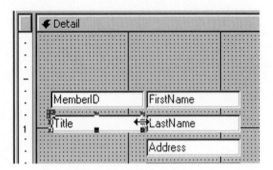

5 Use the left mouse button to resize the control.

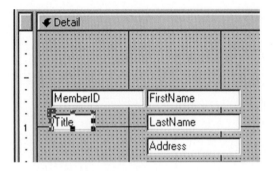

6 Using the figure below as a guide, reposition and resize the remaining controls as shown.

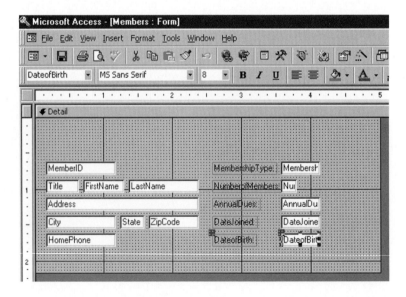

7   Click the Restore button in the Form's Title bar.

8   Resize the form as shown.

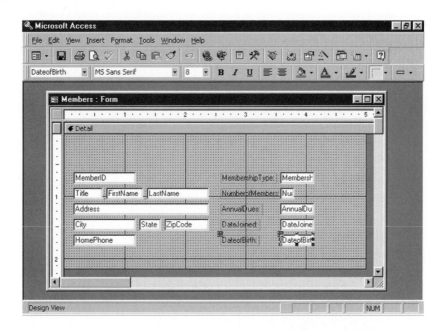

9   Click the View button to view your changes 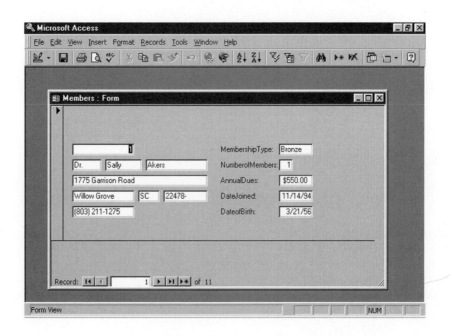.

10   Save your form and switch to Form Design View.

Using ControlTips to Improve Data Accuracy

When the form displays a record, you can see from the field data which control is bound to which field. If you were to add a new record, you may not know exactly what to enter into some of the text boxes. A ControlTip tells users exactly what information to enter into a text box control when a form is used to add records to a database.

TASK 7: TO ADD CONTROLTIPS TO THE MEMBERS FORM:

1 Select the Title text box and click the Properties button 🖼 on the Form Design toolbar.

2 Select the Other tab, and place the insertion point inside the ControlTip Text row.

3 Type **Enter the Member's Title Here** in the row.

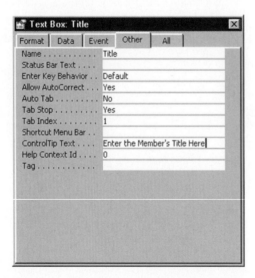

4 Close the Properties dialog box and switch to Form View ⊞▾.

5 Move the insertion point over the Title text box to see the ControlTip. Your screen should display the control tip shown in the next figure.

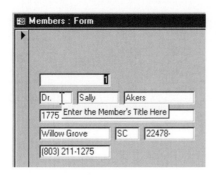

6 Switch to Design View ⊠▾.

7 Using the same procedure as in Steps 1–5, add a ControlTip to the FirstName, LastName, Address, City, State, ZipCode, and HomePhone text box controls. Type the appropriate field name in the text for the ControlTip.

8 Save your changes to the form 🖫.

Adding and Modifying Unbound Controls

Remember that a text box control is a bound control because it is bound, or linked to a specific record source. Labels, however, are **unbound controls**, because they do not return data from a table or a query. Unbound controls are often used to add descriptive information to a form.

Working with Unbound Label Controls

When you added fields to the form using the field list, Access created a label to accompany each bound text box control. The text for each label corresponds to the name of the field the text box displays. You will now modify the text in the existing labels, and add a label control as a title for the form.

TASK 8: TO MODIFY EXISTING LABELS AND ADD A LABEL CONTROL:

1 Select the MembershipType label. Selection handles will appear on each of the label's borders.

2 Place the insertion point immediately after the letter *p* in the caption, and click the left mouse button.

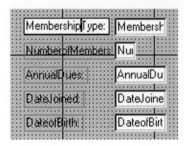

3 Press the (DEL) key five times to remove the remaining characters.

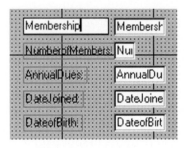

4 Using the same procedure, change NumberOfMembers: to Total Members, AnnualDues: to Base Fee, DateJoined to Member Since, and DateofBirth to Date of Birth. Note that the label width changes with your alterations.

5 Click the Toolbox button ⚒ if it is not currently visible.

Troubleshooting The Toolbox may appear either as a docked toolbar, which is fixed at the top, bottom, or side of the Form Design window, or in an undocked state, and "float" anywhere within the Form Design window.

6 Click the Label button *Aa* in the Toolbox.

7 Click inside the upper-left portion of detail section of the form, and drag the control down and to the right, approximately to the position shown in the figure below.

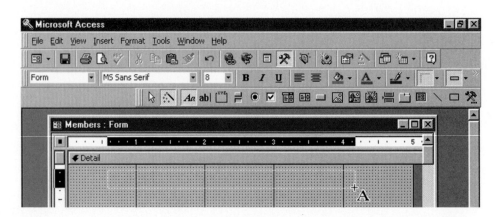

8 Release the mouse button. Type **The Willows Membership Roster** as the caption for the label and press (ENTER).

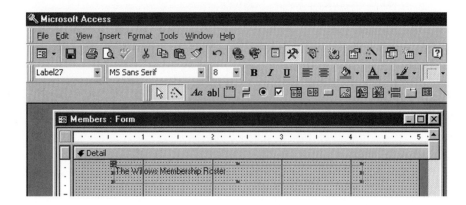

9 With the label control still selected, open the Properties dialog box 🖆. In the Format tab, change the Font Size property to 14 and the Text Align property to Center. You may have to scroll down in order to see these two properties.

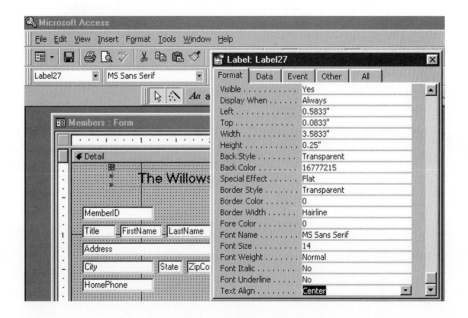

Tip Many of the properties can be set using a drop-down list. Click inside the property row to display the drop-down list button.

10 Save your changes 🖫. Now view the form 🖼. Your screen should look similar to the next figure.

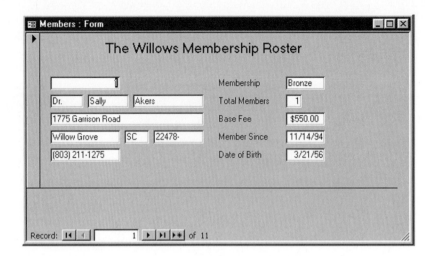

Adding an Image to the Form Using an Unbound Control

You can enhance the appearance of a form by adding an image to it. If the image will not need to be updated, you can insert or embed it into the form using an unbound image control, and the picture is stored with the database. An *image control* displays the embedded image file.

TASK 9: EMBEDDING AN IMAGE INTO THE FORM USING AN UNBOUND CONTROL:

1 Switch to Design View 🔍 ▾.

2 Close the Properties dialog box.

3 Select the image control 🖼 from the Toolbox.

4 Drag an image control immediately to the right of the form's label.

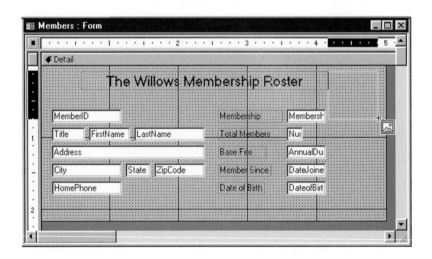

5 In the Insert Picture dialog box, select the *Willow.bmp* file from your diskette. Click OK.

Troubleshooting If you do not have a copy of the *Willow.bmp* file on your diskette, ask your instructor where it can be found.

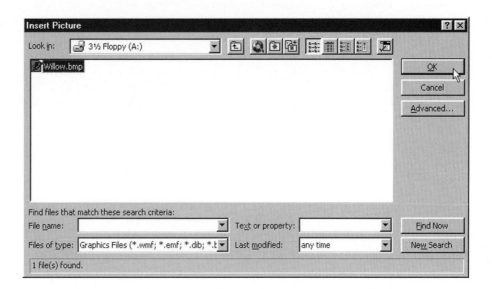

6   Position the image control as necessary using the method illustrated below.

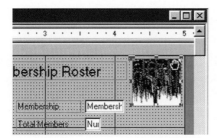

7   Update the form 💾 and switch to Form View 📋▾. Your form should look similar to the one shown on the next page.

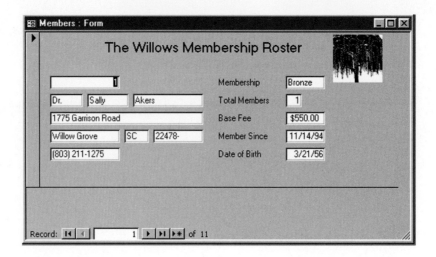

8   Close the form.

9   Select Database Utilities from the Tools menu and compact the database.

10   Close the database and exit Access.

The Conclusion

Mr. Gilmore should be pleased with how you have redesigned the Members form. Not only is the layout more visually appealing than the Auto-Form you created in Project 1, but it is more user-friendly as well, because the ControlTips will assist users in entering the appropriate information in the form when it is used for data entry.

Summary and Exercises

Summary

- You have a great deal of flexibility in how you create a form using Design View.
- Forms often contain both bound and unbound controls.
- Bound controls are linked to an underlying record source such as a table or a query.
- Unbound controls are typically used to add descriptive information to a form.
- When a form will be used to enter data into a record source, ControlTips are useful for providing instructions for users.
- You can embed an image in a form using an unbound image control.

Key Terms and Operations

Key Terms

bound control
control
ControlTip
detail section
Form Design View

image control
label control
record source
text box control
unbound control

Operations

add fields to a form
add unbound controls to a form
create a new form using Design View
delete a form
embed an image in a form using an unbound control
modify bound controls
view a form

Study Questions

Multiple Choice

1. Which form element displays a message when a mouse drifts over a text box control?
   a. label control
   b. image control
   c. bound control
   d. ControlTip

2. To add controls to a form, you use
   a. Form View.
   b. the Toolbox.
   c. Design View.
   d. both B and C.

3. In Access, a form typically
   a. is bound to a field.
   b. is based upon a record source.
   c. uses another form as its record source.
   d. contains only unbound controls.

4. You can easily add fields to a form using
   a. the Toolbox.
   b. Form View.
   c. the field list.
   d. the View button.

5. Label controls are used to display
   a. descriptive text.
   b. data that is bound.
   c. field data.
   d. images or graphics.

6. A form displays records in
   a. Form Design View.
   b. Form Datasheet View.
   c. the database window.
   d. Form View.

7. To embed an image on a form, you generally use a
   a. label control.
   b. text box control.
   c. image control.
   d. bound control.

8. Which of the following statements is false?
   a. Label controls can be deleted from a form.
   b. A label can be resized on a form.
   c. A label can be moved on a form using the mouse.
   d. A label is a bound control.

9. You created a form using Form Design View and specified a table as the form's data source. How many record sources does the form have?
   a. one
   b. two
   c. four
   d. eight

10. A form can be based upon all except which of the following?
    a. a table
    b. a query
    c. a table and a query
    d. a form.

Short Answer

1. What do you use to add fields to a form in Design View?

2. What kind of control do you use to add descriptive text to a form?

3. What database objects can be used to create a form?

4. A text box is which kind of control?

5. What screen element assists in adding fields to a form?

6. Where do you find the tools you need to add controls to a form?

7. Do you use a bound or an unbound control to display field data?

8. A label is which kind of control?

9. The data in a form is displayed on the screen using which view?

10. What kind of control is used to display a bitmap graphic on a form?

For Discussion

1. How does Form Design View differ from Query Design View and Table Design View?

2. How do you remove controls from a form?

3. How do bound controls differ from unbound controls?

4. What is a ControlTip? Why is it sometimes helpful to include ControlTips on a form?

Review Exercises

1. Creating a form with data from two tables

At times you will want to create a form that contains controls bound to more than one table. For instance, the query you created in the Membership Payments database creates a record source based upon fields from two tables. In this exercise you will create a form with controls bound to that record source. You will then print the form. Complete the following:

1. Open the *Membership Payments.mdb* database file from your diskette.

2. Click the Forms tab, then click the New button.

3. Create a form in Design View using the Payments (Query) query as the record source as shown below. Click OK.

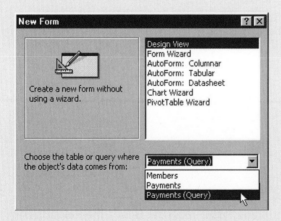

4. Add a label control at the top of the form. Type **Membership Payments** as the caption for the label. Change the Font Size property to 14 and the Text Align property to Center. Close the Properties dialog box.

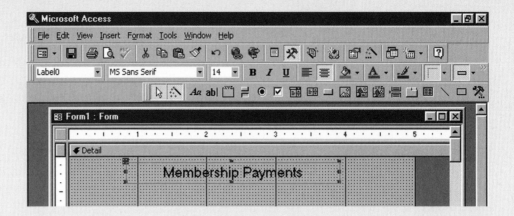

5. Display the Field List 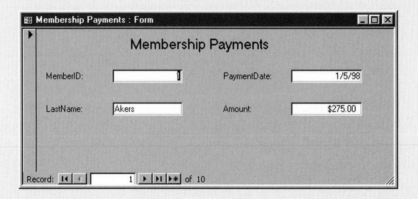. Add the MemberID, LastName, PaymentDate, and Amount fields to the form. Modify the position of each control and resize the form as necessary.

6. Save the form design 💾. Type **Membership Payments** as the name for the form.

7. Switch to Form View 🔲▾ to view the form. It should look similar to the form shown in the figure below.

8. Click the Print button 🖨 on the Form View toolbar to print the form.

9. Close the form.

10. Close the database.

2. Creating a main form with a subform using the Form Wizard

At times you will want to display multiple records in one table that relate to one record in another table. Recall from Review Exercises 1 in Project 4 that in a one-to-many relationship the related table (the "many" table) can contain one or more records that relate to the table on the "one" side of the relationship. You can display records from one table in a one-to-many relationship by creating one form that displays a single record and by creating a subform that contains one or more related records in another table. In this exercise you will create a form that lists each member in the Member Payments database. This form will include a subform that displays each member's payments.

1. Open the *Membership Payments.mdb* database file from your diskette.

2. Click the Forms tab, and create a new form using the Form Wizard. Base the form upon the *Members* table.

3. Click OK. In the Form Wizard dialog box, add the MemberID, Title, FirstName, and LastName fields to the Selected Fields list. Note that we are selecting the FirstName field before the LastName field.

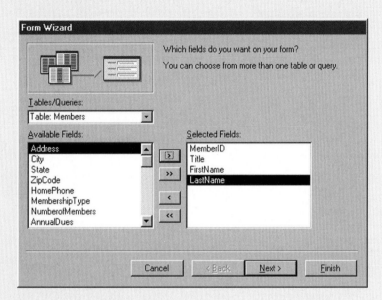

4. In the Tables/Queries list, select the Payments table.

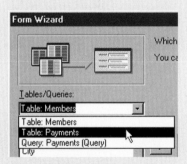

5. Add the PaymentNumber, PaymentDate, and Amount fields to the Selected Fields list.

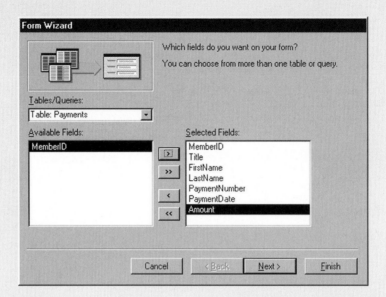

6. Click the Next button. Accept the defaults shown below and click the Next button.

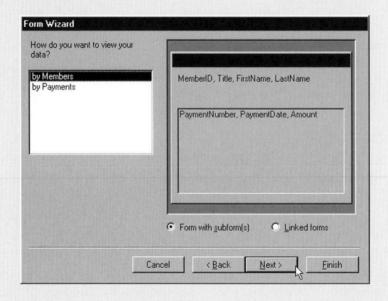

7. Select Datasheet as the layout for the subform. Click Next.

8. Select Standard as the style. Click Next.

9. Type **Payments by Member** as the name of the form, and accept the default name for the subform. Click Finish.

10. The form is displayed as shown on the next page. Close the form and the database when you are finished.

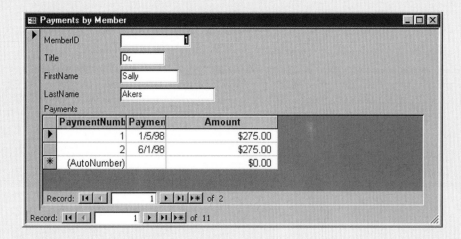

3. Creating and changing an AutoForm

1. Launch Access and open the database *High Point Food Orders.mdb*.

> **Notes** If you do not have a database named *High Point Food Orders.mdb*, ask your instructor for a copy of the file you should use to complete this exercise.

2. Create a new AutoForm named *Food Orders* based on the *Food Orders* table.

3. Use the Food Orders AutoForm to create the following form. Be sure to
   - Move fields to the positions shown.
   - Delete fields not shown on the figure.
   - Add a title to the form.
   - Adjust the length of fields so that they appear approximately as shown in the figure.
   - Change the field names so that they appear as shown on the figure.

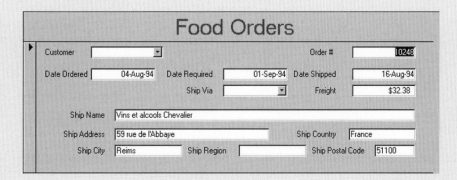

4. Print a copy of one record using the form design.

5. Close the database and exit Access.

Assignments

1. Creating a form using the Form Wizard

Open the *Willows Employees.mdb* file from your diskette. Using the Form Wizard, create a new form based upon the Current Salary for CO and CA query. Add all available fields to the form, use the tabular layout, and select a colorful style. Accept the default name when you finish the form. View the form and close the database when you are finished.

2. Modifying an AutoForm

Open the *Web Sites.mdb* database file from your diskette. Modify the controls to enhance the appearance of the Financial Services form. Add an image control to the form, and embed the *FSLogo.bmp* file on your disk in the control. Save your changes to the form and display it. Use the form to add one more record to the database for a financial service you located on the World Wide Web. Close the database when you are finished.

6

Creating and Modifying Reports

A report provides an effective way to present your data in a printed format. Because you have control over the size and appearance of everything included in a report, you can display the information exactly how you want to see it printed.

Objectives

After completing this project, you will be able to:

➤ **Create a report using the Report Wizard**

➤ **View a report in the Print Preview window**

➤ **Modify a report**

➤ **Print a report**

➤ **Create a report using Report Design View**

➤ **Sort data in a report**

➤ **Add a calculated control to a report**

The Challenge

Mr. Gilmore is very pleased with the work you have done on the membership database, and now he wants to begin distributing printed information from it. He has requested two reports: The first is a member address list that will be distributed to each of the club's committees. The second is a report listing the total fees each member owes the club, with the sum of all fees listed at the end of the report.

The Solution

You can easily create the first report using the Report Wizard. After you have designed the report, you can modify its appearance using Report Design View. You can create the second report using Report Design View in a manner similar to how you created forms. After adding the appropriate controls to the report's design, you can determine the total membership dues using a calculated expression in a text box control. Figure 6.1 shows the report listing each member's total membership fees that you will create in this project.

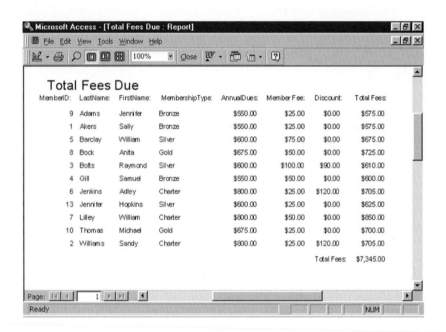

Figure 6.1

The Setup

After you launch Access and open your database, you should make sure the Database toolbar and the Status toolbar are displayed. These are the default settings in Access, but they may have been changed on your computer. (If you have forgotten how to do this, refer to Table 1.1 in Project 1.)

Troubleshooting If you do not see the Database toolbar on the screen when you launch Access and open your database, choose Toolbars from the View menu. Select the Database toolbar to display it. If any additional toolbars are visible, close them. If you do not see the Status Bar at the bottom of the Application window, choose Options from the Tools menu, click the View Page tab and change the Status Bar check box option.

Using the procedures you learned in Task 1 of Project 1, open the *Willows Membership.mdb* file from your disk.

Creating Reports

The process of creating reports is similar to that of creating forms. The ***Report Design window*** contains a graphical workspace displaying the report's bound and unbound controls. This window contains five sections where you can add controls. You add the controls to a specific section depending upon whether the information should appear at the beginning or end of the report; this requires a control in either the ***Report Header*** or ***Report Footer*** section, respectively. If your information should appear on every page of the report, add a control to the ***Page Header*** or ***Page Footer*** section. For information that is bound to a specific field in the record source, use a bound control such as a text box, and add this to the Report ***Detail section*** in the Report Design window. These sections are identified in Figure 6.2.

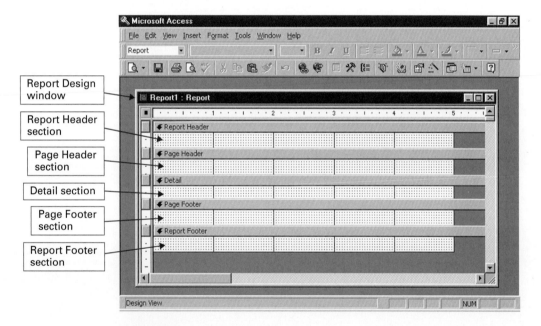

Figure 6.2

Creating a Report Using the Report Wizard

The easiest way to create a report is to use the Report Wizard, view the report, and then switch to the Report Design window to make any necessary modifications.

TASK 1: TO CREATE A REPORT USING THE REPORT WIZARD:

1 Click the Reports tab in the database window.

2 Click the New button.

3 Select the Report Wizard, and base the report upon the *Members* table.

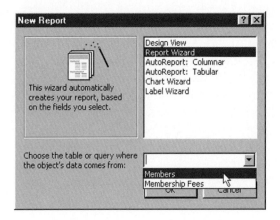

4 Move the MemberID, Title, LastName, FirstName, Address, City, State, ZipCode, and HomePhone fields from the Available Fields list to the Selected Fields list.

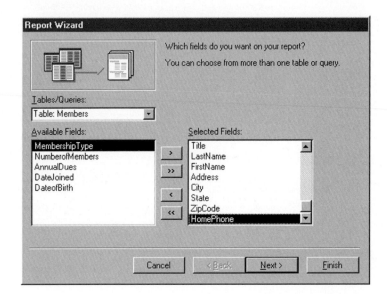

5 Click the Next button. The Report Wizard now asks if you want any grouping levels. Accept the default settings as shown below.

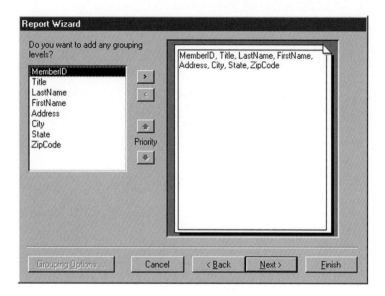

6 Click Next. Select LastName in the first sort drop-down list and select FirstName in the second list.

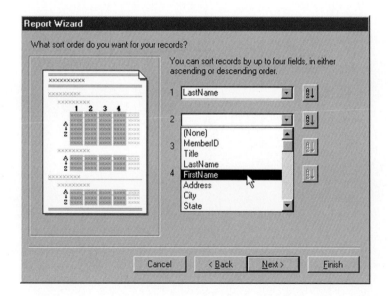

7 Click Next. Select a Tabular layout in Landscape orientation. Also select the check box to adjust all fields to fit on the page.

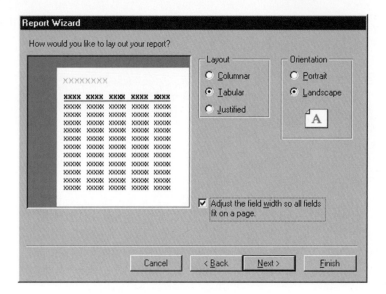

8 Click Next. Select Formal as the style.

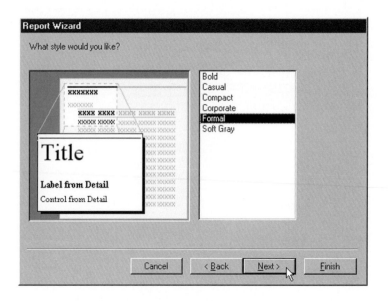

9 Click Finish to accept the default name for the report.

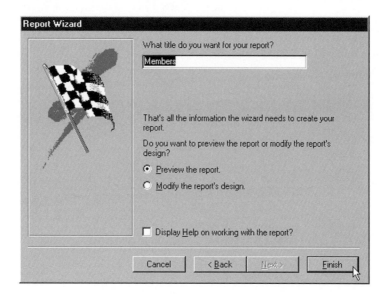

10   Access will display the report in Print Preview.

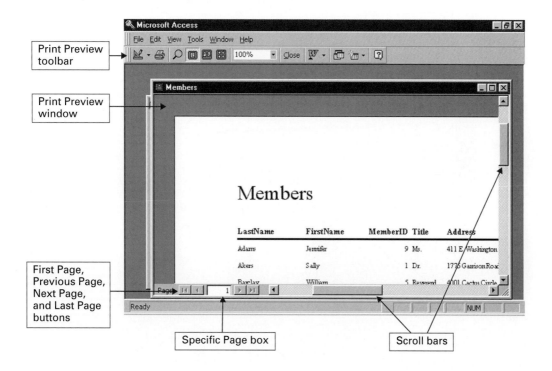

Viewing a Report in the Print Preview Window

When you create a new report using the Report Wizard, or when you preview an existing report, Access displays the report information in the Print Preview/Layout window. The information is displayed here exactly as it will appear when printed.

The preview typically displays at 100 percent of its size. You can use the scroll bars in the Print Preview window or the Zoom box on the Print Preview toolbar to change how the preview displays.

TASK 2: TO CHANGE THE PREVIEW DISPLAY:

1 Drag the horizontal scroll bar to reposition the preview. At 100 percent, it is difficult to see the entire layout of the report.

2 Click the Zoom box 100% ▾ on the Print Preview toolbar and change the view to 75 percent.

3 Reposition the preview using scrollbars. The entire report layout is now visible, as shown below.

> **Tip** You can also maximize the Report Preview window to view more of the report on the screen.

4 Close the report.

Modifying the Report Design for Printing

Rarely does a Wizard create a report that does not need modification. You can easily modify a report's layout by adjusting the size and position of its bound and unbound controls in the Report Design window. After you have modified the Members report, it will be ready for printing.

TASK 3: TO MODIFY THE DESIGN OF THE MEMBERS REPORT FOR PRINTING:

1   Click the Report tab in the database window if it is not currently active, click the Members report, and then click the Design button. Maximize the Report Design window.

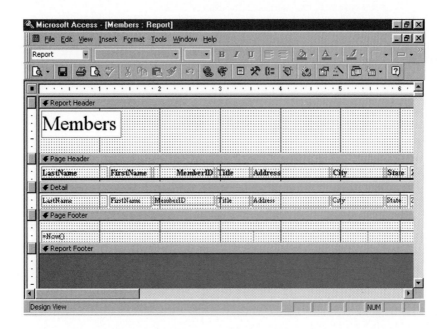

Notice that the current report used four report sections.

2   Double-click the caption of the label in the Report Header section to select the caption. This will bring up the label's property box. Type **The Willows Address List** as the new caption for the control, as shown in the next figure. Resize the label if necessary.

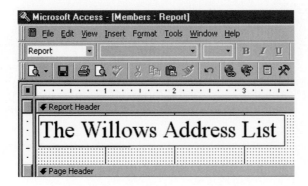

3   Select the MemberID text box control in the Detail section. Move the insertion point to the border of the control so it changes to the hand icon.

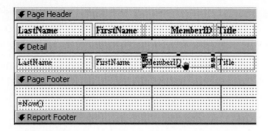

4 Hold the left mouse button and drag the control immediately under the LastName text box control.

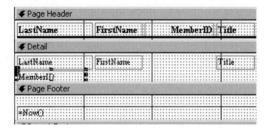

Troubleshooting Depending upon where you move controls in the report, the sections may resize automatically. You can also manually resize any of the report sections.

5 Reposition and resize the MemberID, Title, LastName, and FirstName text box controls so that they correspond with the controls shown below.

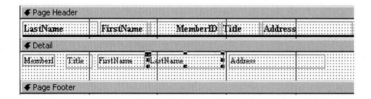

6 Select the FirstName label in the Page Header section, hold the (SHIFT) key, and select the Title label. Both labels should now be highlighted.

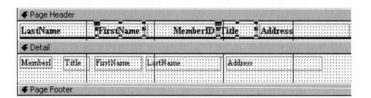

7   Select Cut ✂. Reposition, rename, and change the captions for the
MemberID, LastName, and Address label controls so that they correspond
with the controls shown in the next figure.

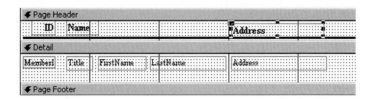

8   Move the insertion point to the lower edge of the Detail section, and hold
the left mouse button to resize it. Your screen should now look similar to the
one shown below. Save your changes 💾.

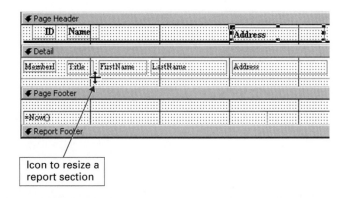

Icon to resize a
report section

9   Click the View button 🔍 on the Report Design toolbar to preview the
report.

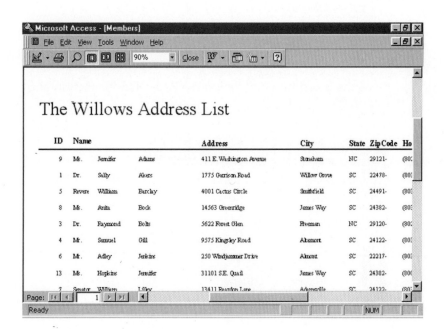

> **Tip** Reports have three views: Design, Print Preview, and Layout Preview. You use Design View to create or change a report. Print Preview displays the report's data as it will appear on the printed page. Layout Preview displays the report's layout, which includes just a sample of the data in the report.

10 Click the Print button 🖨 on the Print Preview toolbar to print the report. Close the report when it is finished printing.

Creating a Report Using Report Design View

Although the Report Wizard quickly generates reports, you have the greatest control over what a report contains when you create a new report using Design View. By placing bound and unbound controls in the various sections of the report, you specify exactly how you want the report to look.

TASK 4: TO CREATE A NEW REPORT USING DESIGN VIEW:

1 Click the New button in the database window.

2 Select Design View, and base the report on the Membership Fees query.

3 Click OK. Click the Field List button 🖾 on the Report Design toolbar to display the field list if it's not already visible.

4 Drag the MemberID, LastName, FirstName, MembershipType, AnnualDues, Member Fee, Discount, and Total Fees fields into the Detail section.

> **Tip** Don't be concerned with where these fields are currently placed, because you will modify the report design.

5 Select the MemberID label, and click the Cut button ✂.

6 Place the insertion point inside the Page Header section and click the Paste button 📋.

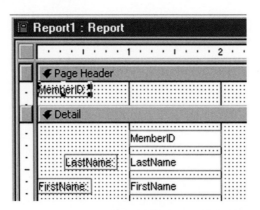

7   Cut the remaining labels from the Detail section, paste them into the Page Header section, and reposition each one. Resize the report as necessary, so it appears similar to the one shown below.

> **Troubleshooting** You will have to reposition each control when you paste it into the Page Header section, because by default Access pastes the control in the upper-left corner of the section.

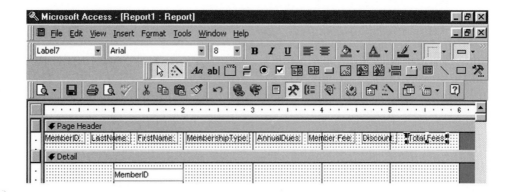

8   Position the text box controls as shown below. Make sure you resize the lower edge of the Detail section so that there isn't too much empty space at the end. If you leave a lot of space at the end of the detail section, you will find that your report has the same amount of space between each record.

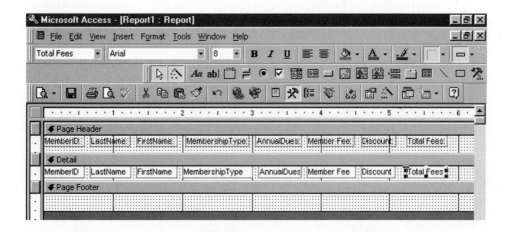

9   Save the report 🖫. Type **Total Fees Due** as the name of the report, and click OK.

10 Click the View button 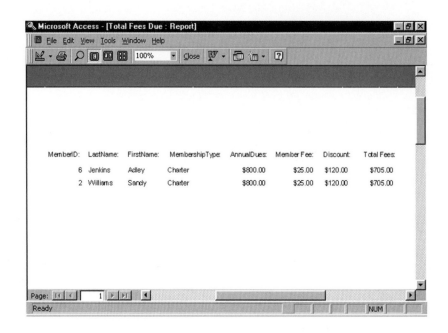 to preview the report. Depending upon how you sized the controls on your report, you may receive an error message stating that all of the information may not fit on the page.

Tip You will notice that the report returns only two records. This is because in Project 4 you set multiple criteria for the Membership Fees query.

Adding a Calculated Control to the Report

Mr. Gilmore wants the report to display the total membership fees that are due by all members. You can add this figure at the end of the report in a *calculated control*, which is a control containing an expression.

TASK 5: TO CREATE A CALCULATED CONTROL TO SUM THE TOTAL MEMBERSHIP FEES:

1 Click the view button on the Print Preview toolbar to return to Design view.

2 Select Report Header/Footer from the View menu.

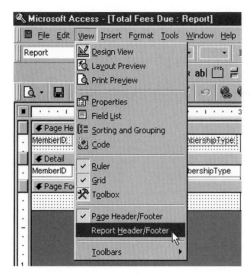

3 Select the Text Box control tool [abl] from the toolbox.

4 Add a text box control to the right side of the Report Footer section, immediately below the Total Fees text box in the Detail section.

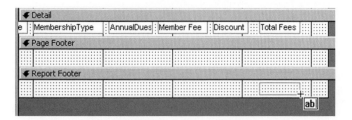

Tip Notice that the text box is currently not bound to a specific object.

5 Delete the label that is associated with the text box control.

6 Select the text box control, and click the Properties button 🖳 on the Report Design toolbar.

7 Click the Data tab in the Text Box Properties dialog box to display the data properties. Click the ellipsis button ..., as shown on the next page.

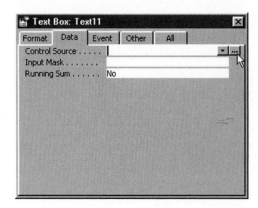

8 Type **=sum([Total Fees])** in the Expression box, then click OK.

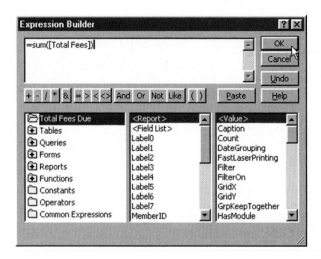

Tip For more information about the Expression builder and the syntax required for specific expressions click the Help button in the Expression Builder and select the Read more about expressions option.

9 Click the Format tab in the Properties dialog box, and set the Format property to Currency.

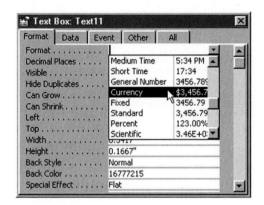

10 Save 🖫 and preview 🔍 ▾ your report. Your report should look similar to the one shown below.

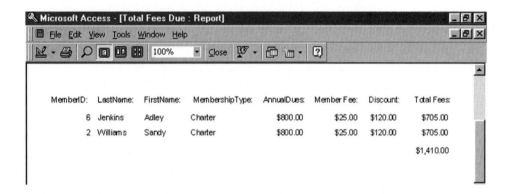

Modifying the Report

The report still needs slight modification: It will look better if you add a label in the Report Header section and add a descriptive label explaining exactly what information the calculated control displays. Finally, the query underlying the report needs to be modified so that the report lists records for all members.

TASK 6: TO MODIFY THE REPORT:

1 Click the View button 🖳 ▾ to return to the Report Design window.

2 Add a label control to the Report Header section. Type **Total Fees Due** as the caption in the label.

3 Change the Font Size property to 16.

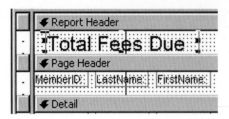

4   Add a label to the Report Footer section to the left of the calculated control.

5   Type **Total Fees:** as the caption.

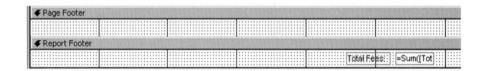

6   Save your changes to the report design, and close the report.

7   Open the Membership Fees query in Design View, and remove the entries in the criteria row from the MembershipType and Current Age fields. Close the query and save these changes.

8   Click the Reports tab in the database window, and preview the Total Fees Due report.

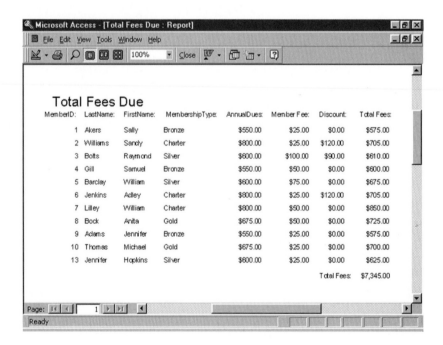

You will notice that the report is ordered according to MemberID. You can easily specify a different sort order for the report.

TASK 7: TO SPECIFY A DIFFERENT SORT ORDER FOR THE REPORT:

1. Click the View button 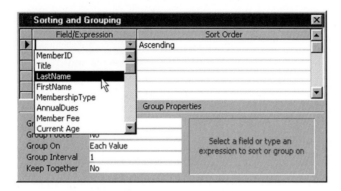 to return to the Report Design window.

2. Click the Sorting and Grouping button on the Report Design toolbar.

3. Select LastName in the Field/Expression drop-down list.

4. Make sure the settings in the Sorting and Grouping dialog box match those shown below.

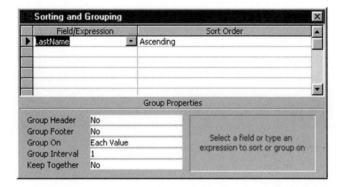

5. Close the Sorting and Grouping dialog box.

6. Save your changes to the report design and preview the report.

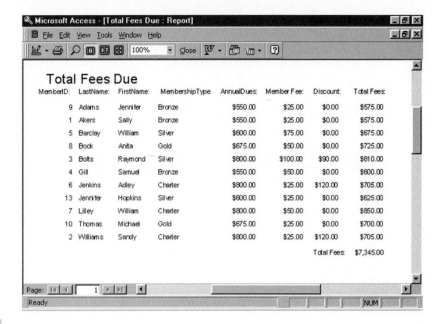

Print Before

7 Close the report.

8 Close the database.

The Conclusion

Mr. Gilmore should be pleased with the reports you have designed. As you have seen, creating reports is similar to creating forms; you can quickly generate a report with the Report Wizard, which you used to create a printed address list, or you can create a report in Design View by adding controls to the various report sections. You can also add calculated controls to a report, such as the expression listing the total fees owed to the club.

Summary and Exercises

Summary

- Database reports are used to print information from a database.
- You can create a report by using one of the Report Wizards or by using Report Design View.
- A report contains bound and unbound controls that specify where information will appear on the report.
- After you create a report, you can view it in the Print Preview window.
- You can modify a report by changing the properties of each control in the report.
- Calculated controls perform calculations based upon an expression.
- A report can be sorted on up to four fields when you create a report using the Report Wizard.
- You can change the sort order of information in a report by using the Sorting and Grouping option.

Key Terms and Operations

Key Terms
calculated control
Detail section
Page Footer
Page Header

Report Design window
Report Footer
Report Header

Operations
change the datasource
change the Preview display
create a calculated control
create a new report using Report Design View
create a report using the Report Wizard
modify a report in Design view
modifying a report
specify sort order

Study Questions

Multiple Choice
1. Which view displays all the data in a report exactly as it will be printed?
   a. Design View
   b. Preview View
   c. Layout View
   d. Form View

2. When you create a report using the Report Wizard, how many fields can you specify for the sort order?
   a. one
   b. two
   c. three
   d. four

3. To arrange controls on a report you must use
   a. Design View
   b. Layout View
   c. Form View
   d. Preview View

4. In which section of a report do bound controls generally appear?
   a. Page Header
   b. Detail
   c. Page Footer
   d. Report Header

5. You can add fields to a report easily using the
   a. toolbox
   b. Properties dialog box
   c. database window
   d. field list

6. Unbound controls usually appear in all sections of a report except which section?
   a. Page Header
   b. Report Header
   c. Page Footer
   d. Detail

7. Data entered in the Page Header section of a report appears at the
   a. beginning of the report only.
   b. end of the report.
   c. top of every page
   d. bottom of every page.

8. Field data from a query appears in which section of a report?
   a. Page Header
   b. Detail
   c. Page Footer
   d. Report Header

9. A query displays an employee's last name, first name, address, Social Security number, and annual salary. To easily locate a given employee in a report based upon the query, the report should be sorted on which field?
   a. Last Name
   b. Social Security Number
   c. First Name
   d. Annual Salary

10. You want to add a descriptive title to a report that appears only on the first page of the report. To which section should you add the control?
    a. Page Header
    b. Detail
    c. Page Footer
    d. Report Header

Short Answer

1. What is the main purpose of a report?

2. What is a calculated control?

3. Where do bound controls generally appear in a report?

4. When should you use a query versus a table as the basis for a report?

5. How do you specify sort order in a report?

6. What is the fastest method for creating a report?

7. What control do you use to create a calculated control in a report?

8. How do you move labels from the Detail section of a report to the Page Header section?

9. How do you save a report?

10. What kind of unbound controls does a report usually contain?

For Discussion

1. What two database objects can you use to create a report? When might you use one rather than the other?

2. What are some ways you might use calculated controls in a report?

3. When do you use bound versus unbound controls on a report?

4. Describe the three views associated with reports.

Review Exercises

1. Modifying a query and creating a report

Because an Access report is always based upon a record source, it always displays the most recent changes to the table or query upon which it is based. In this exercise, you will copy the Current Salary for CO and CA query, modify it, and create a report that lists the salary paid to each employee. The figure below displays the report.

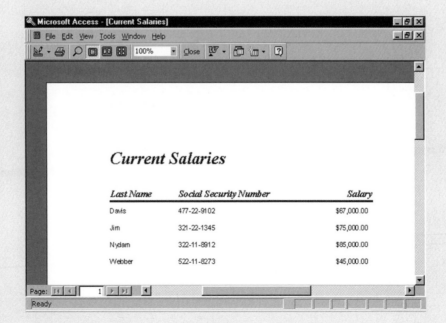

> **Troubleshooting** Your data will be different than what is shown here.

1. Open the *Willows Employees.mdb* database from your disk.

2. Click the Queries tab in the database window.

3. Copy and Paste the Current Salary for CO and CA query. Type **Current Salaries** as the name for the copy of the query.

4. Open the query in Design View, and remove the criteria for the StateOrProvince field. Close the query, and save the changes to its design.

5. Click the Reports tab in the database window.

6. Using the Report Wizard, create a new report that is based upon the Current Salaries query.

7. Add the LastName, SocialSecurityNumber, and Salary fields to the Selected Fields: list. Press the Next button.

8. Do not add any grouping levels. Press the Next button.

9. Set the sort order by the LastName field. Press the Next button.

10. Choose a Tabular report in Portrait Orientation. Press the Next button.

11. Choose Corporate as the style for the report. Press the Next button.

12. Accept the default name for the report. Press the Finish button.

13. Close the report after you preview it.

14. Compact the database and close the file.

2. Grouping and Sorting Data in a Report

Mr. Gilmore wants a report listing the payments each member has made toward his or her annual dues. This report must be sorted by each member's last name, with each payment listed according to the date it was paid. The following figure shows a preview of the report.

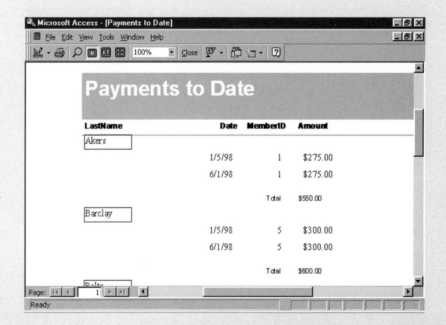

Complete the report as follows:

1. Open the *Membership Payments.mdb* database file from your disk.

2. Create a new report using the Report Wizard option. Base the report upon the Payments (Query) query. Click the Close button.

3. Add all the available fields to the Selected Fields: list. Click the Next button.

4. Group the report by Members, as shown below. Click the Next button.

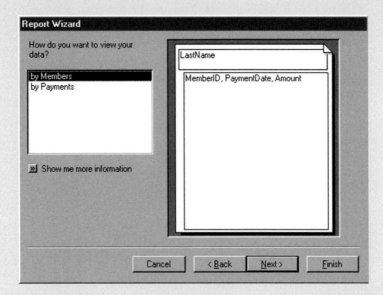

5. Do not add any grouping levels. Click the Next button.

6. Select PaymentDate as the sort order for the report.

7. Click the Summary Options button. Check the Sum box, and then select the option to show both the detail and the summary. Click OK. Then Click the Next button.

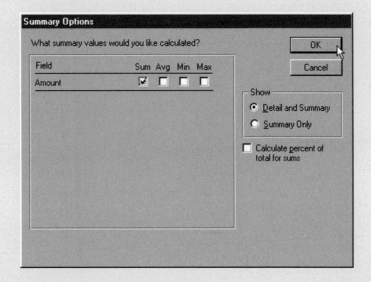

8. Choose the Stepped layout in Portrait Orientation. Click the Next button.

9. Select Soft Grey as the style. Click the Next button.

10. Type **Payments to Date** as the title for the report and click Finish.

11. Switch to Design View and modify the report design as necessary.

12. Close the report and save your changes.

13. Select Database Utilities from the Tools menu and compact the database.

14. Close the database.

3. Creating, saving, and printing a report

1. Launch Access and open the database *High Point Food Orders.mdb*.

> **Note** If you do not have a database named *High Point Food Orders.mdb*, ask your instructor for a copy of the file you should use to complete this exercise.

2. Create the report layout as pictured based on the *Food Products by Category* query.

Food Products
by Category

Category Name	Product Name
Beverages	Chai
Beverages	Chang
Beverages	Chartreuse verte
Beverages	Côte de Blaye
Beverages	Guaraná Fantástica
Beverages	Ipoh Coffee
Beverages	Lakkalikööri
Beverages	Laughing Lumberjack Lager

3. Save the report using the report name *Food Products by Category*.

4. Print a copy of the report.

The Integrity of Dates in Microsoft Access

And what about the integrity of dates in your Access database? Is Access safe from the Y2K (Year2000) problem? Yes it is, as long as your computer's BIOS chip will accept dates after 1999.

The Date/Time data type in Access uses an integer value to represent dates ranging from 1 January 100 to 31 December 9999, so your data is safe, even if the date is formatted in the short data format.

Improving the Presentation of a Database by Using a Switchboard

Finally, you may want to think about ways to keep users from opening tables or queries in which they might inadvertently change data or the object's design. By adding a *Switchboard* — a form with buttons that you can click to open forms and reports — you effectively limit the presentation of the database to those objects users need to use to enter, edit, and print information.

Analyzing Data with Queries

As you learned in Project 4, queries enable you to extract data from one or more tables based upon any criteria you specify. Queries also enable you to perform calculations using existing data and to summarize your data in different ways.

Summarizing Data with Queries

A *summary query* summarizes information in the underlying record source, such as counting the number of inventory items of a particular category currently in stock. A *crosstab query* is a specific summary query that displays summarized values (sums, counts, and averages) from one field in a table and then groups them by two sets of facts supplied from the data — one listed down the left side of the datasheet and another listed across the top of the datasheet. An example of a crosstab query is a datasheet listing the ages of the members at the Willows in rows, with separate columns displaying the membership categories. At the intersection of each row and column the average fees for members of an age and membership category appears. The format of a crosstab query is similar to a PivotTable, which is a method for designing cross tabulations in Microsoft Excel.

Modifying Queries

As you know, a query can be modified in the Query Design Window any time after you have created it. This means you can add or delete fields by either dragging them to the appropriate column or deleting the column completely from the Query Design grid.

Joining Tables in Queries

A query based upon multiple tables does not require a permanent relationship among the tables to display fields in a query datasheet. You can join two or more tables in the Query Design window by dragging a field from the field list in one table or query to the equivalent field in the field list for the other table or query. With this type of join, Access selects records from both tables only when the values in the joined fields are equal. You can remove a join in a query by deleting the line representing the relationship between tables.

Using Forms that Contain Subforms

If you completed Exercise 1 of Project 5, you know that a subform is a form within a form, and is useful when you want to show data from tables or queries with a one-to-many relationship. A subform is linked to a main form so that the subform displays only records that are related to the current record in the main form.

Entering Data into a Subform

When you use a form with a subform to enter new records, Microsoft Access saves the current record in the main form when you enter (display a record in) the subform. This ensures that the records in the "many" table have a related record in the "one" table. This method also automatically saves each record as you add it to the subform. Therefore, you can use a main form/subform combination to permit the user to enter data into multiple tables and still ensure that the data integrity constraints are met. See Exercise 3 of Project 5 for an example of how to create a form containing a subform.

Customizing Reports

As you may guess, reports are just as easy to modify as tables, queries, or forms. You can customize the pages in a report by selecting Page Setup from the File menu in Report Design view. You can also customize a report to display a chart. If Microsoft Graph 97 was installed with Access, you can use the Chart Wizard to create a chart from table or query data.

It is easiest to create a chart using the Chart Wizard. The Chart Wizard analyzes the existing data and determines whether it should display data from all fields in one global chart, or whether it is more appropriate to show a record-bound chart. If you use a record-bound chart, it represents only the data in the current record.

Sharing Information with Other Applications

One of the advantages of Microsoft Office Professional is that it enables you to easily share data among applications. You can add pictures to records, link your database to existing data, or import Excel or ASCII-delimited files into Access.

Using Object Linking and Embedding to Add Pictures to a Record

To add pictures to a record, you must use the OLE (Object Linking and Embedding) data type. The field will be bound to a specific bitmap image file that can be displayed on a form or in a report. You can also use the OLE data type to link an Excel or Word object to a bound or an unbound control. When information is linked, the source file is external to the database, and any changes to the source file are seen when the database displays this information. When you use embedding to share information with Access, the data becomes an Access object that does not change if the original information is subsequently changed.

Importing Data into Access

To import data from another source into Access, one or more import filters must be installed. Access can import text, existing workbooks, and data from a variety of database formats.

Access and the World Wide Web

One of the most exciting advances in the Office 97 suite is the degree of Web integration throughout. The End of Chapter Assignments in this book show you how to export the hyperlink data type, which you can use to link your Access form or report to the Web or other documents on your computer or network.

You can also develop static or dynamic HTML documents from your database, depending upon your application needs. Consider using static HTML format when your data does not change frequently and when your World Wide Web application does not require a form. If your data changes frequently and your Web application needs to store and retrieve live data from your Microsoft Access database using a form, you will need to use dynamic HTML. Dynamic HRML pages are more complex than static HTML pages. Search the Microsoft web site for more information about Dynamic HTML in Access.

Notes

Notes

Notes

Notes

Notes

Notes

Notes

Notes

2

Integrating Word, Excel, and Access

In Integrated Project 1, you learned how to share Word and Excel data using linking and embedding techniques. Many of the techniques you used to copy and paste data between Word and Excel can also be used when you want to share data between Access and Word or Excel. In addition, you'll appreciate the features built into Access that make sharing data automatic.

Objectives

After completing this project, you will be able to:

➤ **Copy Excel data to an Access database**

➤ **Update the Access table design**

➤ **Merge data from an Access database table with a Word document**

The Challenge

Ruth Lindsey, Manager of the retail shops at The Willows, would like to thank distributors of the top ten selling items by sending each distributor a thank-you letter.

The Solution

To fulfill Ms. Lindsey's simple request, you'll need to jump through quite a few hoops. First you will take the data for the top ten items stored in the Topten worksheet you created in Excel Project 5 and use it to create a database. Then you will add fields to the database so you can merge the data to a Word document.

Figure 2.1 displays one of the thank-you notes you'll create.

Current Date

Iron Works Unlimited
1550 North State Street
Ogden, Utah 84404

Ladies and Gentlemen:

It is with pleasure that we announce the success of one of your products in our retail shops at The Willows resort. Your Cast iron doorstop (Product Number CID 11126) was recently listed as one of the top ten selling products at the resort.

The success of your products is a reflection of the dependability of your staff in meeting the demands of your customers. Such service does not go unnoticed.

Best wishes for continued success in all your endeavors.

Sincerely,

Ms. Ruth Lindsey, Manager
Retail Sales

Figure 2.1

The Setup

To accomplish the tasks outlined in this project, you need to work with Word, Excel, and Access. So that they are available when you need them, launch all three applications and create a new blank database named *Retail Sales* in Access. As you work with each application, maximize the application and document windows. Minimize applications you aren't using. Table 2.1 shows the settings you need to use.

Table 2.1   Settings in Word, Excel, or Access

Element	Setting
Office Assistant	Close Office Assistant in all programs.
View, Toolbars	Display the Standard and Formatting toolbars in Word and Excel and the default toolbar in Access.

Copying Excel Data to an Access Database

You can drag data from Excel into the Access database using the same basic techniques you used to drag Excel data into Word. When you drag the Excel worksheet into Access, Access creates a new table using the worksheet data. Access *imports* the data, converting it to a format you can use to perform standard database activities.

TASK1: TO IMPORT EXCEL DATA TO A NEW ACCESS DATABASE:

1   Maximize Excel and open your *Topten.xls* worksheet.

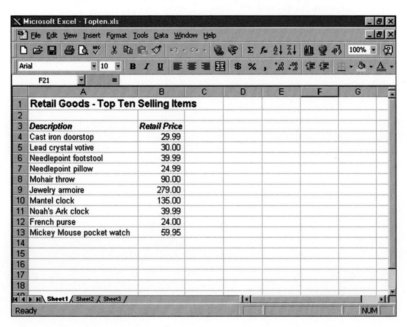

2   Maximize Access.

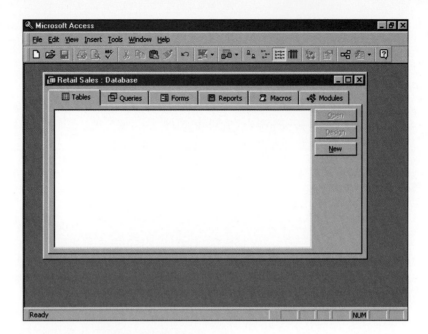

3 Position the mouse pointer on the Taskbar and right-click.

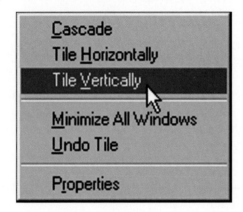

4 Choose Tile Vertically.

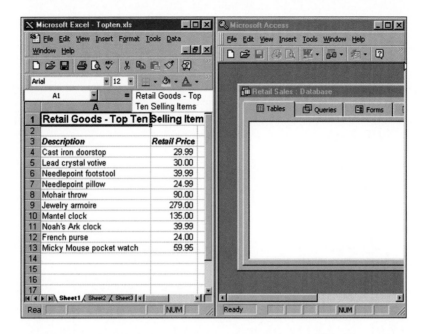

5 Select the Excel data in rows 3 through 13 and columns A and B.

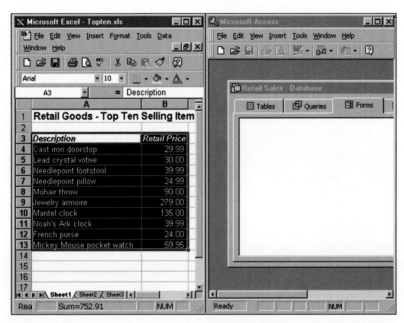

6 Position the mouse pointer on the right border of the selected Excel data, press (CTRL), and drag the data to the Access database window.

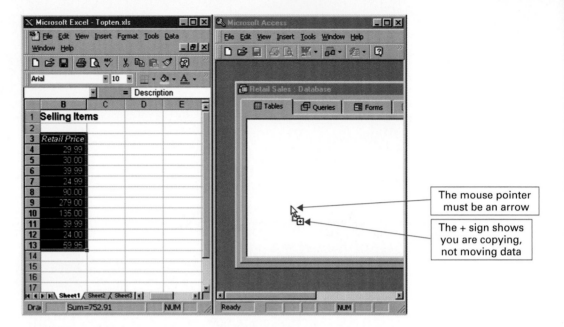

The mouse pointer must be an arrow

The + sign shows you are copying, not moving data

7   Release the mouse button and then the (CTRL) key.

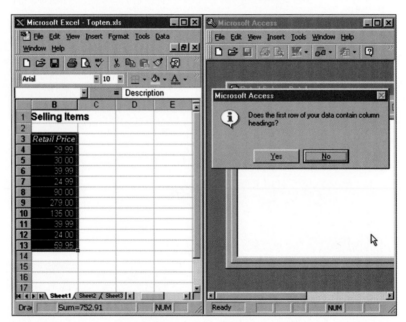

8   Select Yes to indicate that the top row does contain column headings.
Access informs you that the import was successful.

9   Click OK to acknowledge the import message.
Sheet1 appears as the table name in the database window.

10   Click Sheet1, type **TopTen Selling Products** as the table name, and
press (ENTER).
The table name in the database window changes.

11   Close Excel and maximize Access.

Updating the Access Table Design

Dragging worksheet data into Access creates a new table that identifies fields by column headings contained in the Excel worksheet. You can add fields to the table design and update table data without affecting the data or structure of the worksheet.

TASK 2: TO UPDATE THE ACCESS TABLE DESIGN:

1   Click the Design button on the Retail Sales database window.

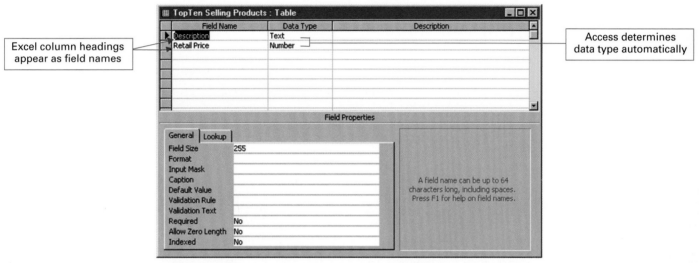

Excel column headings appear as field names

Access determines data type automatically

2   Position the mouse pointer on the first blank row of the table design and add the field names and data types shown in the following illustration:

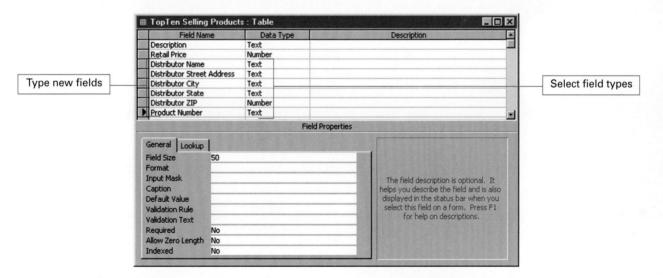

Type new fields

Select field types

3   Click 💾 to save design changes and then click 📖 ▼ to display table data.

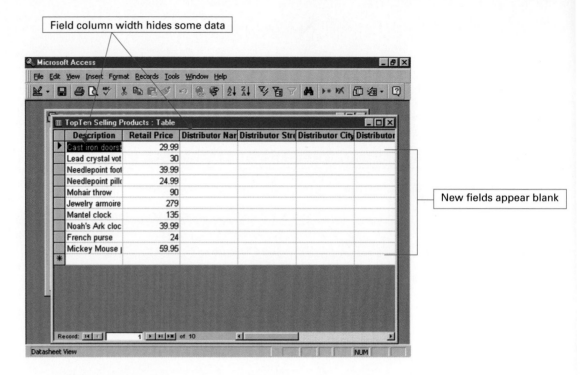

Field column width hides some data

New fields appear blank

4 Type the following data for the ten products:

Description	Distributor	Product Number
Cast iron doorstop	Iron Works Unlimited 1550 North State Street Ogden, Utah 84404	CID 11126
Lead crystal votive	Anna's China & Crystal Distributors 20953 Orleans Boulevard Alexandria, VA 22201	LCV 88496
Needlepoint footstool	Furniture Outfitters 33380 Elm Street Simi Valley, CA 92265	NPF 16000
Needlepoint pillow	Furniture Outfitters 33380 Elm Street Simi Valley, CA 92265	NPP 15600
Mohair throw	Far East Imports 88 Mountain Drive Sioux City, SD 57049	MHT 99981
Jewelry armoire	Furniture Outfitters 33380 Elm Street Simi Valley, CA 92265	JYA 16445
Mantel clock	Southside Specialties One Alpha Plaza Houston, TX 77074	MCK 01234
Noah's Ark clock	Custom Works, Inc. 168 Main Street Portland, ME 01234	NAC 01034

Description	Distributor	Product Number
French purse	TML France, Esq. 1616 Madison Avenue New York, NY 10001	FHP 85848
Mickey Mouse pocket watch	Finer Things, Inc. 8 Southside Bay Miami, FL 11101	MPW 57483

Merging Access Data with a Word Document

After updating the Access database so that it contains the data you need, you can use the data to create the thank-you letters. When you merge data from Access tables to Word documents, field names in the table are inserted into the document to tell Word where to look for the data in the Access database. The document to which you add merge fields is the *merge document* and the database table that contains the data and fields is the *merge data source file*.

TASK 3: TO MERGE DATA FROM THE
ACCESS DATABASE TO A NEW WORD DOCUMENT:

1   Close the *TopTen Selling Products* table and click the drop-down list arrow beside the OfficeLinks ▨⃁ button on the Standard toolbar.

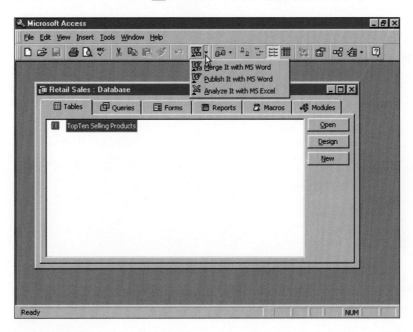

2   Select Merge It with MS Word to launch the Microsoft Word Mail Merge Wizard.

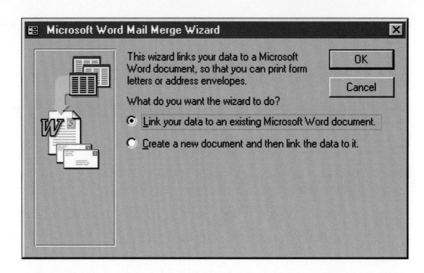

3 Select *Create a new document and then link the data to it* and press ⒠ENTER⒠.
   Word launches and displays a new document with the Merge toolbar active
   and database table fields available on the Insert Merge Field list.

4 Type the text shown in the following figure, choose the field names from
   the Insert Merge Field list, press ⒠ENTER⒠ to move to the next line, and add
   punctuation and spacing.

Current Date

«Distributor_Name»
«Distributor_Street_Address»
«Distributor_City», «Distributor_State» «Distributor_ZIP»

Ladies and Gentlemen:

It is with pleasure that we announce the success of one of your products in our retail
shops at The Willows resort. Your «Description» (Product Number «Product_Number»)
was recently listed as one of the top ten selling products at the resort.

The success of your products is a reflection of the dependability of your staff in meeting
the demands of your customers. Such service does not go unnoticed.

Best wishes for continued success in all your endeavors.

Sincerely,

Ms. Ruth Lindsey, Manager
Retail Sales

5 Save the document using the filename *TopTen Thank You Letter,* merge the database data to a new document, review the form letters and print them.

6 Close the form letters after printing without saving them and exit Word, saving changes to the merge document.

7 Close the database, saving the changes, and then exit Access.

The Conclusion

While you used an Access table as the merge data source to merge data to a document, remember that the data originated in an Excel worksheet. When you need to pull data from more than one table in an Access database, you can create a query that displays data from multiple tables and then use the query as the merge data source. In addition, you can use data from an Access report in a Word document by selecting Publish It with MS Word from the OfficeLinks button on the Access toolbar. When you choose Publish It with MS Word, Office displays your Access report as a document in Word.

If you have completed your work for the day, shut down the computer according to standard lab procedures or continue working on the summary exercise and assignment.

Summary and Exercises

Summary

- You can use the same techniques to drag and drop Excel worksheet data to an Access database that you used to drag worksheet data to a Word document.
- When you drag and drop data from a worksheet to a database, Access creates a new table in the active database.
- When you use data from an Access database as the merge file for a Word Merge document, you have the choice of selecting an existing Word file or creating a new Word document.
- Using an Access database table as a data source file automatically creates a link between the database table and the merge document.
- To use data from multiple tables in a database as a data source file, you can create a query and select the query as the file to merge to Word.
- You can also publish data from an Access report to a Word document.

Key Terms and Operations

Key Terms
import
merge data source
merge document
Merge to Word
publishing

Operations
Copy data from an Excel worksheet to create a new
  Access database table
Update an Access database table design
Merge Access database table data with a new Word
  document

Study Questions

Multiple Choice

1. To change an Access database table design,
   a. delete the table and create a new one.
   b. select the table in the database window and click the Design button.
   c. copy the data from another table and use it to create a new table.
   d. position the insertion point on a table name and press (ENTER).

2. All of the following techniques can be used to copy data from Excel to Access *except*
   a. cutting the data from the Excel worksheet and choosing Edit, Paste Special.
   b. dragging and dropping the data from Excel to Access.
   c. copying the Excel data to the Clipboard and pasting the data into Access.
   d. retyping the data from Excel into an Access table.

3. To copy data using drag and drop data from Excel to Access, press
   a. (ESC).
   b. (ENTER).
   c. (ALT).
   d. (CTRL).

4. Field names you type in the Table Design view of a table appear as
   a. inserts in the table.
   b. data entered in the fields.
   c. column headings in table datasheet view.
   d. row headings in table datasheet view.

5. As you enter data into new fields of an Access table,
   a. you have to save each field.
   b. Access saves data automatically when you move to a different record.
   c. data in existing fields changes.
   d. data automatically appears in queries.

6. When you merge Access table data to a Word document,
   a. a link is created automatically.
   b. data automatically appears in a Word table.
   c. the Access table appears in the Word document.
   d. nothing happens.

7. The toolbar that appears in Word when you merge Access table data to a Word document is the
   a. Standard toolbar.
   b. Formatting toolbar.
   c. Drawing toolbar.
   d. Merge toolbar.

8. Data from an Excel worksheet dragged into Access creates
   a. new field names.
   b. a chart.
   c. a new table.
   d. a new report.

9. Table data from multiple tables can appear together by creating a
   a. new table.
   b. query.
   c. report.
   d. new database.

10. To include summarized data from an Access database in a Word document, copy
   a. an Access report into a Word document.
   b. a query into a Word document.
   c. a form into a Word document.
   d. data to Excel and then drag it into the Word document.

Short Answer

1. To include data from multiple tables in a data source file, what database object should you merge?

2. What special toolbar appears when you merge Access data with a Word document?

3. What button do you click in Word to select a field name?

4. What special characters appear before and after a merge field in the Word document?

5. Does the table or query you use to merge with a Word document have to be open to complete the merge?

6. What does dragging Excel worksheet data create in an Access database?

7. Can you change the structure of a database table that is created from Excel worksheet data?

8. What database object do you drag to Word to include database summarized data in a Word report?

9. What Access toolbar button enables you to merge data from Access to Word automatically?

10. How do you tile applications on-screen?

For Discussion

1. How do you create a link between Access database table data and a Word document?

2. What techniques do you use to drag and drop data between an Excel worksheet and either Word or Access?

3. What happens when you drop data from an Excel worksheet into an Access database?

4. How do you merge data from multiple tables in an Access database to a Word document?

Exercise

Creating a new Access database and tables from Excel data
The board of directors of The Willows would like to see a summarization of data for sales of the three major restaurants at the resort. Figure 2.2 displays a report that Mark Taylor, manager of The Atrium Café, compiled to send to the board.

Sales Figures

	March Totals	April Totals
Atrium Cafe	$34,685.00	$32,580.00
Front Porch	$30,835.00	$32,220.00
Willow Top	$45,240.00	$42,740.00

Figure 2.2

Use the techniques explored in this project to create the report based on data contained in the *Restaurant Sales.xls* Excel worksheet you created in Excel Project 4.

1. Launch Excel, open the *Restaurant Sales.xls* worksheet, and maximize the application on-screen.

2. Launch Access, create a new blank database named *Restaurant Sales Figures,* and maximize the application on-screen.

3. Right-click the Taskbar and select Tile Vertically to tile the applications on-screen.

4. Click the Atrium Café worksheet, select the range from cells A8 through C8, drag the worksheet data into the Access database, and tell Access that the first row does NOT contain column headings.

5. Follow the same procedures to create two additional tables, one for the Willow Top and one for the Front Porch.

6. Close the worksheet and exit Excel; then maximize Access.

7. Change the field name of F1 in each table to *Restaurant Name,* F2 to *March,* and F3 to *April.*

8. Create a new query named *Sales Summary* in Access, add all three tables to the query, and design the query to contain all the fields in each table as shown here:

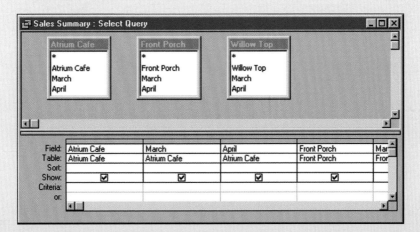

9. Create a report named *Sales Summary* based on the *Sales Summary* query and design it to appear as shown in Figure 2.2.

Assignment

Merging Access database table data with a Word document and publishing Access report data to a Word document

Before sending the report of restaurant sales to the Board of Directors, Mr. Taylor would like to have the managers of different programs and facilities at The Willows review the data. Create the document pictured in Figure 2.3 by merging name and address data from The Willows Managers table in The Willows Personnel database. Then use the OfficeLinks button in Access while previewing the report to publish the Sales Summary report in the Word document, positioning it as shown in Figure 2.3.

Current Date

«First_Name» «Middle_Name» «Last_Name»
«Street»
«City», «State» «ZIP»

Dear Friends:

Before sending the data summarized below to the members of The Willows Board of
Directors, I thought you might want to review it. Please send any comments you have
to the manager of the restaurant and voice any concerns you have to me before Friday.

Sales Figures

	March Totals	April Totals
Atrium Cafe	$34,685.00	$32,580.00
Front Porch	$30,835.00	$32,220.00
Willow Top	$45,240.00	$42,740.00

Sincerely,

Mark Taylor, Manager
The Atrium Cafe

Figure 2.3

Save the document using the filename *Preliminary Sales Report to Board* and print the
merged data form letters. Attach a copy of the main merge document to an e-mail
message to your instructor, using the Outlook Mail feature.

Presentations
Using Microsoft PowerPoint 97

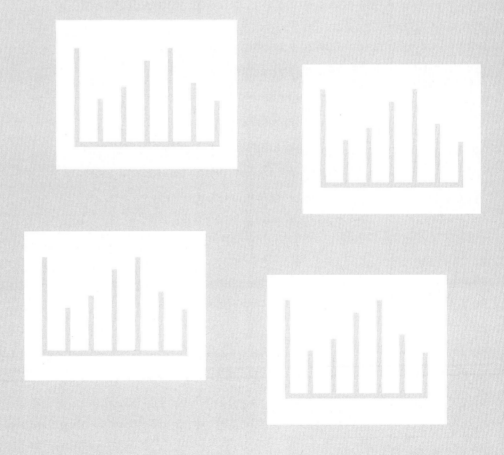

Overview

Microsoft PowerPoint 97 is a presentation graphics program that enables you to prepare slide shows and present them with style and impact. You can use PowerPoint to print handouts for the audience, speaker notes to aid presentation delivery, and overhead transparencies to use when you have no computer available. In this overview, you identify features unique to PowerPoint and see some old friends from other programs. After you get better acquainted with these basics, you'll be able to put them to use in the other projects in this module and unveil some of the power of PowerPoint.

Objectives

After completing this project, you will be able to:

➤ **Design a presentation**

➤ **Launch Microsoft PowerPoint**

➤ **Identify PowerPoint screen elements**

➤ **Create a presentation**

➤ **Display presentations in different views**

➤ **Work with menus, dialog boxes, and toolbars**

➤ **Get Microsoft PowerPoint Help**

➤ **Exit PowerPoint**

Defining PowerPoint Terminology

Presentations are collections of related slides that summarize key points of a report or act as a visual aid during an oral presentation. Whether you display slides on a computer screen, project slides onto a flat surface, or use transparencies to present slide images, PowerPoint can help you develop your presentation.

To use PowerPoint effectively, you need to become familiar with the Power-Point terminology (see Figure O.1):

Term	Description
Slide	Basic unit of a presentation, which may contain numerous slides. Each slide in a presentation is equivalent to a page of a document, workbook, or database record.
Placeholder	Predefined area outlined on a slide, containing slide text, bulleted lists, and objects such as graphs, tables, and charts.
AutoLayout	Preformatted layouts that contain object placeholders.
Masters	Layouts that contain formats for text, bullets, placeholder alignment, headers/footers, and backgrounds.
Templates	Professionally developed slide designs that you can apply to presentations to give a consistent look to all slides in a presentation.

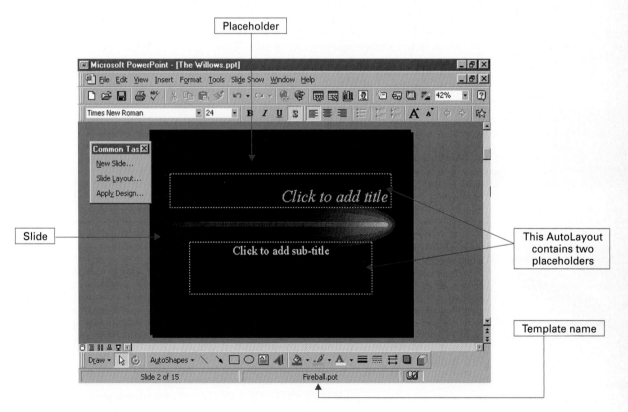

Figure O.1

Designing a Presentation

Because Microsoft PowerPoint comes with a variety of designs you can use to dress up your presentation, you can focus on the content of your presentation as you design it. Some things to consider as you plan your presentation:

- *Who* will be in your audience and how many people will attend: managers, corporate executives, salespeople, peers, and so forth.
- *What* materials do you want to use with the presentation: slides, handouts, notes, and overhead transparencies.
- *Where* is the presentation to be given: consider the size of the room, acoustics of the room, location of the speaker platform, and other factors. Remember that small printed characters are difficult to see from the back of the room, so limit lists to short statements rather than complete sentences and make the characters larger.
- *When* will the presentation occur: identify the time of day, placement of the presentation in relation to other presentations, and so on.
- *Why* are you giving the presentation: determine the message you want to communicate and the action you want the audience to take.
- *How* does the method you will use to deliver the presentation affect the presentation design: color can be used more effectively in on-screen shows than in transparencies; if no color printer is available, handouts and color transparencies might be too dark.

After you consider each of these points, you can develop a presentation targeted to your audience, design a look for the presentation that best conveys the purpose of the presentation, and jot down a brief outline of the topics you want to include in the presentation. Then you're ready to launch PowerPoint.

Launching Microsoft PowerPoint

After you have powered up your computer, logged onto required networks, and responded to messages built into your system, Windows 95 starts automatically.

TASK 1: TO LAUNCH POWERPOINT:

1 Click the Start **Start** button.

2 Point to Programs.

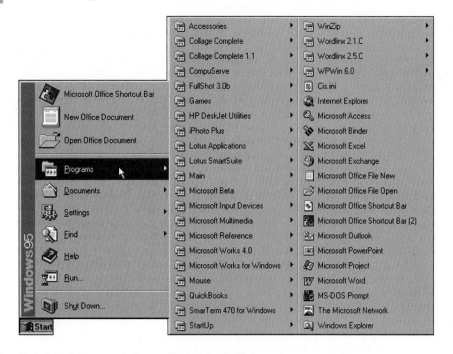

3 Point to Microsoft PowerPoint and click.

Identifying PowerPoint Screen Elements

The PowerPoint screen features a number of elements found in other application windows as well as several elements unique to PowerPoint (see Figure O.2). The first time you launch PowerPoint after it's installed on a computer, the Office Assistant pops up, introduces itself, and offers assistance. After the first time, the Office Assistant sits quietly by or hops up on the toolbar until you need it.

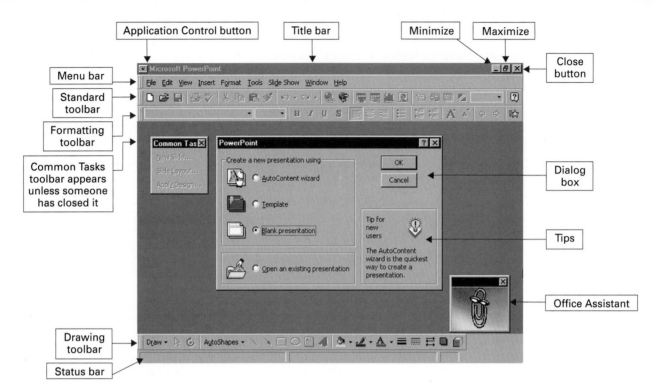

Figure O.2

Table O.1 contains a brief description of each PowerPoint screen feature.

Table O.1   PowerPoint Screen Features

Screen Feature	Description
Menu bar	Provides access to commands used to perform tasks.
Title bar	Identifies the application name and contains the application icon, Maximize/Restore, Minimize, and Close buttons. Until you save a presentation, PowerPoint names the presentations consecutively, using the generic names Presentation1, Presentation2, and so forth. After you save a presentation, the filename you assign appears in the title bar.
Standard toolbar	Contains buttons that serve as shortcuts for performing common menu commands, displaying special toolbars, or changing screen features.
Formatting toolbar	Displays buttons and list boxes to access the most frequently used formatting commands.
Common Tasks toolbar	Displays commands to accomplish the three most frequently performed tasks.
Drawing toolbar	Displays tools for creating and formatting drawn objects.
View buttons	Provides an easy way to display your presentation in a different format. These buttons do not appear in Figure O.2, but you'll see these after you create your first slide or open a presentation.
Office Assistant	Provides tips as you work and can answer some of your questions about the program.
Status bar	Displays information about the program status, instructions for performing selected tasks, active key information, functions of the toolbar buttons when you point to them, and trouble messages.

Creating a Presentation

Each time you launch PowerPoint, the PowerPoint dialog box shown in Figure O.3 presents options that enable you to create a new presentation or open an existing one.

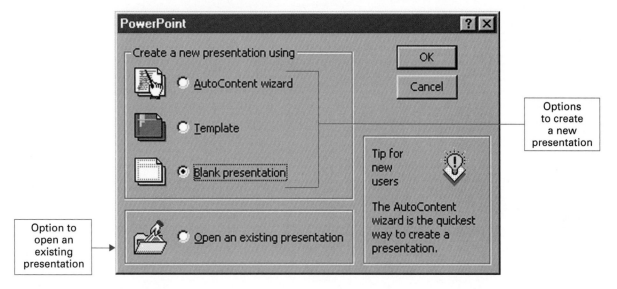

Figure O.3

Options for creating a new presentation include:

- AutoContent wizard: The wizard creates a presentation, based on the purpose of the presentation and choices you select from options the wizard presents. The wizard formats slides in the presentation to contain instructions and information about the presentation content. You then replace that instructional and informative text with the text you want to include on each slide.

- Template: Lets you choose a design for your presentation and then build the presentation from scratch by adding your own text and objects to slides you create.

- Blank presentation: Creates a plain presentation that formats slides with placeholders to contain text and objects.

When you choose to create a new presentation, PowerPoint presents a series of formats for the first slide with the title slide selected. Each placeholder on the title slide contains instructions to help you add text to the slide.

TASK 2: TO CREATE A NEW, BLANK PRESENTATION:

1 Click Blank presentation and then click OK.

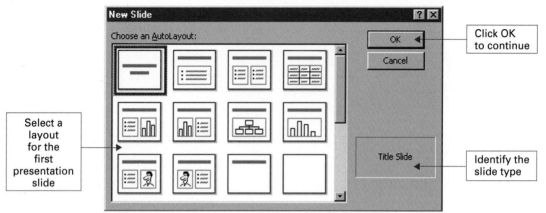

2 Click OK to accept the Title Slide AutoLayout format for the first slide in the presentation.

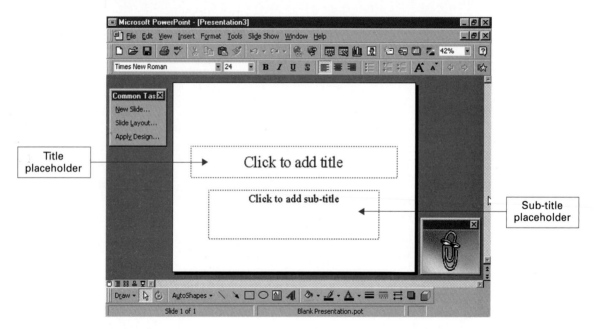

Displaying Presentations in Different Views

PowerPoint provides several views that allow you to display your presentation in different ways. Each view is designed to make working with specific features of a presentation easier:

- Slide view: Displays all slide text, formatting, graphics, charts, and other objects individually on-screen. Slide view lets you add and edit text, create new slides, create drawings, access slide objects, and change the slide format.

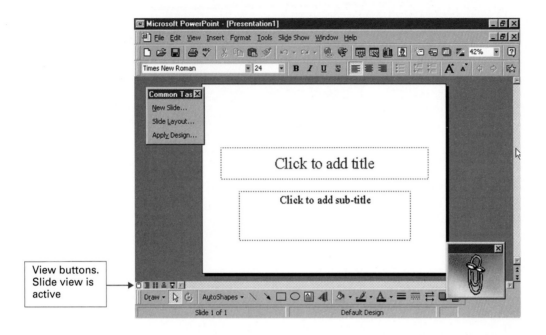

View buttons. Slide view is active

- Outline view: Displays the slide text you type into placeholders in an outline structure. Typing text in Outline view makes creating text for multiple slides more efficient. You can add and edit text, create new slides, and rearrange slides in Outline view, but you can't add other objects to slides.

Slide body text

Slide number

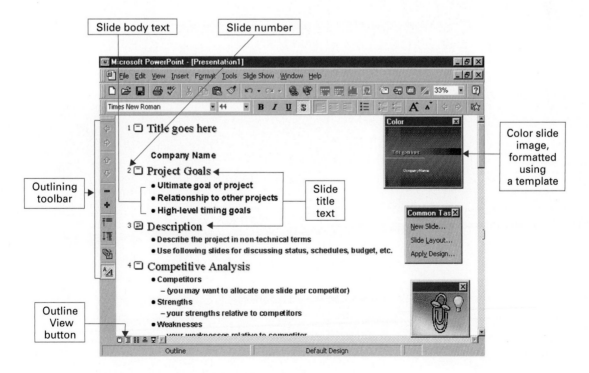

Color slide image, formatted using a template

Outlining toolbar

Slide title text

Outline View button

● Slide Sorter view: Displays thumbnail images of multiple slides on-screen at the same time. Slide Sorter view makes rearranging slides more efficient, but slides can't be edited in Slide Sorter view.

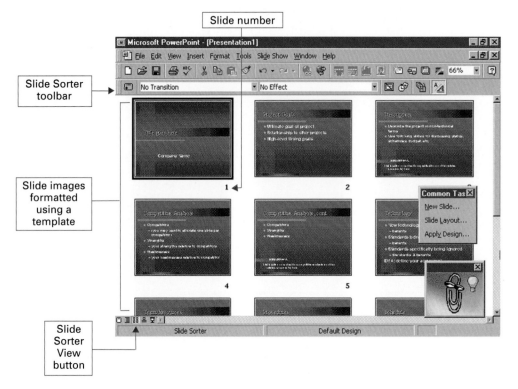

● Notes Pages view: Displays a small slide image at the top of the page and provides space below the image to type notes and supportive information about the slide contents.

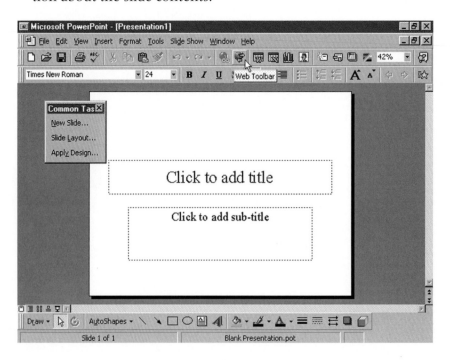

Working with Menus, Dialog Boxes, and Toolbars

Just as menus in restaurants display food items by type, menus and toolbars in PowerPoint group features and commands you use as you perform tasks in PowerPoint. Dialog boxes present options for you to choose as you create presentation files and objects, format slides and handouts, and build your presentations.

Identifying Menu Features

Menus group commands for performing tasks according to type. In Power-Point, the menu bar remains constant as you work with different presentation objects, but available menu commands change as you switch views and work with objects. To display a list of menu commands, point to the menu item and click. Figure O.4 identifies the standard features of Power-Point menus you will see:

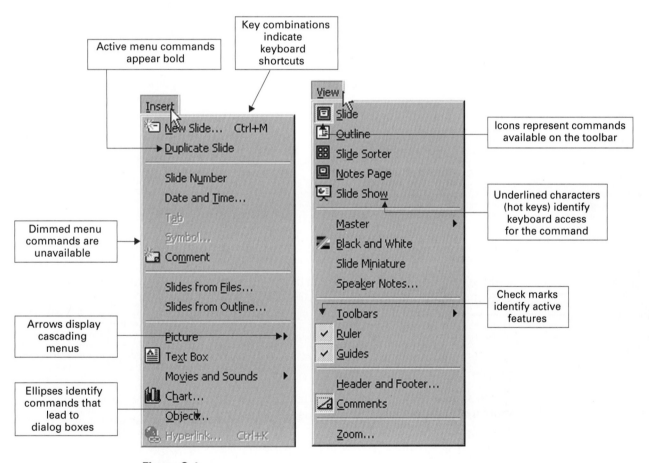

Figure O.4

Working with Toolbars

Tools on the toolbars provide easy access to many of the most frequently used menu commands and dialog boxes. To use the toolbar buttons, point to the button that represents the command you want to perform or feature you want to display, and click. *ScreenTips* identify the name of each button on the toolbar, and pop up when you point to the toolbar button.

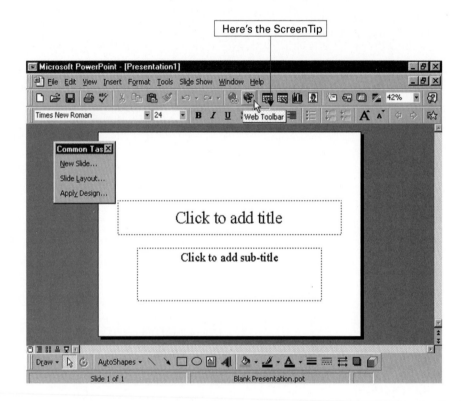

The view buttons at the bottom of the presentation window operate in much the same way as toolbar buttons. When you point to a view button, a ScreenTip identifies the view; when you click a view button, PowerPoint displays the presentation in a different format.

> **Note** The toolbars displayed in the PowerPoint window change automatically as you work with objects and perform different tasks.

Toolbars (such as the Common Tasks toolbar) that display on-screen with title bars are called *floating toolbars*; toolbars that appear on-screen with no title bar are called *docked toolbars*. You can dock a floating toolbar by dragging its title bar until the toolbar forms a narrow horizontal or vertical rectangle on any side of the PowerPoint window. You can also float toolbars by grabbing the toolbar's grip and dragging the toolbar to a new position.

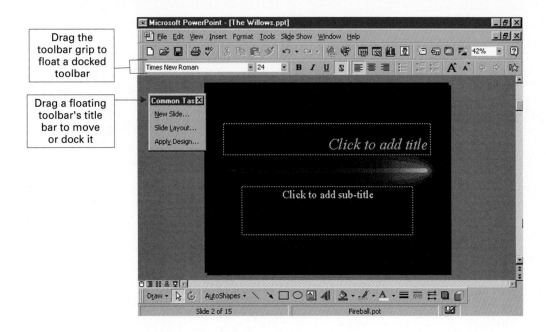

Working with Dialog Boxes

Dialog boxes appear when you select a menu command that's followed by an ellipsis and when you click certain toolbar buttons. Figure O.5 identifies features you'll see as you work with dialog boxes. Not all features will appear in every dialog box.

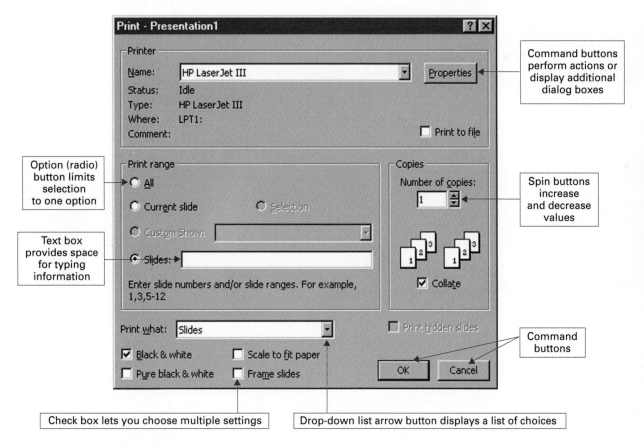

Figure O.5

TASK 3: TO DISPLAY MENUS OR
DIALOG BOXES AND USE THE TOOLBAR:

1 Point to the File menu and click.

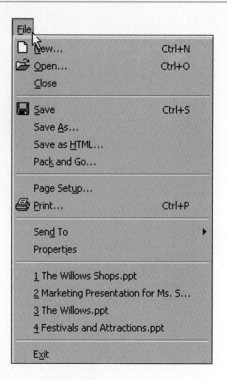

2 Choose Open.

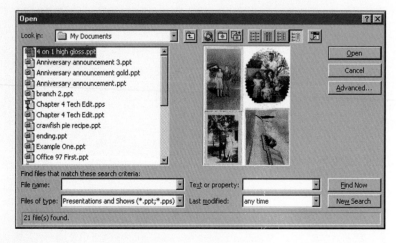

3 Click the Cancel button.
The dialog box closes and the PowerPoint presentation reappears.

4 Point to the Spelling button on the Standard toolbar and pause.

5   Click the title bar of the Common Tasks toolbar and drag it to the lower-right corner of the window.
The toolbar appears where you drop it.

6   Drag the Common Tasks title bar toward the top of the window until it becomes a flat, horizontal toolbar.

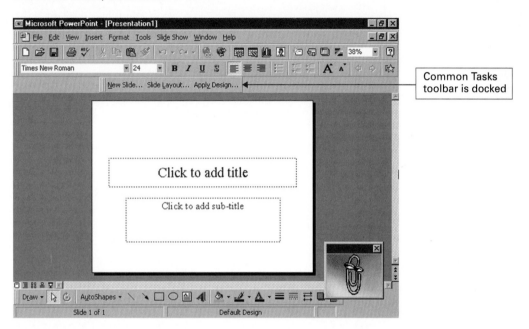

Common Tasks toolbar is docked

7   Grab the grip on the Common Tasks toolbar and drag it down until the toolbar is shaped as a square.

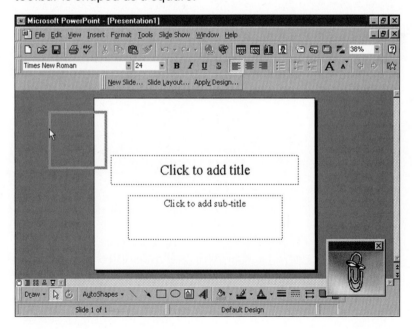

8   Release the mouse button.

9   Choose the Tools menu.

10   Press (ESC) twice to close the Tools menu and to deselect the Tools menu.

Getting Help

PowerPoint provides numerous ways for you to get online help as you work. From the PowerPoint Help menu, you can access standard features available on the Help menus of other Microsoft Office 97 applications:

- The Office Assistant, which enables you to ask questions about the task you want to perform.
- The standard three-page Windows 95 Help dialog box, which displays Contents, Index, and Find to search for information on the topic or procedure you need.
- What's This?, to obtain a brief description of a button, feature, or command.
- Microsoft on the Web to explore information about new products, obtain answers to frequently asked questions, recommend improvements to the program, and so forth.

In addition, PowerPoint provides context-sensitive help and tips as you work. You will primarily use the Office Assistant to access Help in PowerPoint.

Note Online help has proven to be a more efficient method for obtaining help than searching through voluminous manuals for tips and information about specific programs and tasks. However, "online help" doesn't refer to connecting to the Internet or a communications provider; it simply refers to the help provided by the software that's accessible from your computer.

Using the Office Assistant

The Office Assistant is a feature new to Microsoft Office 97 applications, and already the Office Assistant is growing in popularity. The Office Assistant is easy to use, is personally animated, and provides a focused list of help topics. It opens the first time you launch PowerPoint. After that, it makes eyes at you or waits on the Standard toolbar and appears as a Johnny-on-the-spot each time you call for help.

TASK 4: TO DISPLAY, USE, AND CLOSE THE OFFICE ASSISTANT:

1 Click the Office Assistant 🛈 button on the toolbar.

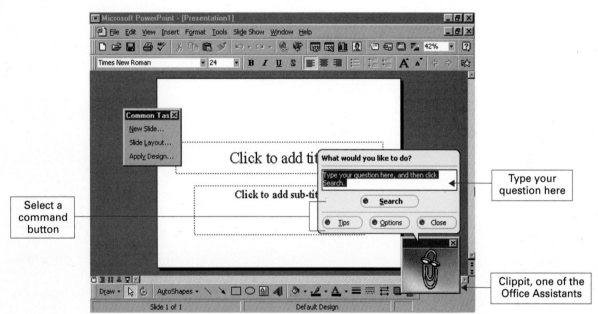

Note The Office Assistant dialog box appears in different shapes and sizes, depending on how it was last used. Results of previous Help searches may also appear, as shown on the next page.

2 Type **Add a slide** in the question textbox; then press (ENTER).

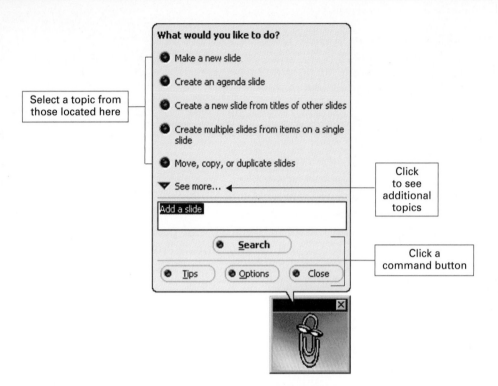

What would you like to do?

- Make a new slide
- Create an agenda slide
- Create a new slide from titles of other slides
- Create multiple slides from items on a single slide
- Move, copy, or duplicate slides
- ▼ See more...

Add a slide

[● **Search**]

[● **Tips**] [● **Options**] [● **Close**]

Select a topic from those located here

Click to see additional topics

Click a command button

3 Click the button beside Make a new slide, at the top of the related topics list.

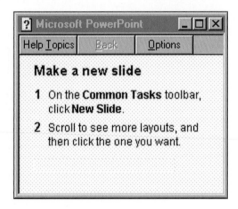

? Microsoft PowerPoint

Help **T**opics | Back | **O**ptions

Make a new slide

1 On the **Common Tasks** toolbar, click **New Slide**.

2 Scroll to see more layouts, and then click the one you want.

4 Review the information in the help dialog box and then click the Close ☒ button.
The list of related topics no longer appears on-screen; the Office Assistant remains on-screen until you close it.

5 Click ☒ on the Office Assistant window.

Getting Help from the Microsoft Web Site

If you're connected to the Internet, you can access the Microsoft Web site to obtain additional help information. The Web provides information directly from Microsoft support team members as well as information from other users.

TASK 5: TO ACCESS ONLINE SUPPORT FROM THE WEB:

1 Choose Help, Microsoft on the Web.

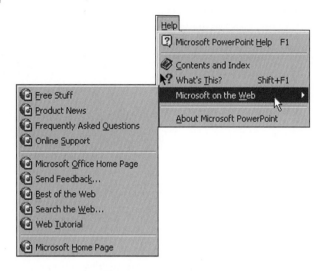

2 Choose Online Support.
Your Internet access window appears.

3 Complete the standard procedure for logging onto the Internet using your service provider.

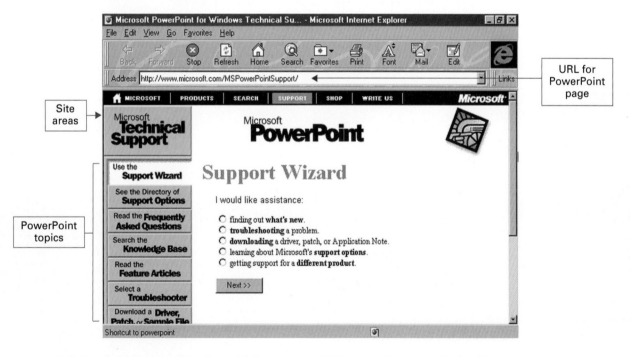

4 Select an option for which you would like assistance and click Next.
Explore several help topics when you log on and get a feel for how to navigate online support and find the information you need. Then log off the Internet.

Closing a Presentation and Exiting Microsoft PowerPoint

When you have completed your work on a presentation, you should close it. When you're finished using PowerPoint, you need to exit PowerPoint.

TASK 6: TO CLOSE A PRESENTATION AND EXIT POWERPOINT:

1 Click **X** on the presentation window.
As you close a presentation, PowerPoint examines the presentation and reminds you to save changes by displaying a message window. Click Yes to save changes to the presentation, No to discard changes, or Cancel to return to the presentation.

2 Click **X** on the application window.
If you don't save and close your presentation before exiting, PowerPoint reminds you to save changes you have made since you last saved the presentation. If no changes have been made to the presentation, the dialog box does not appear.

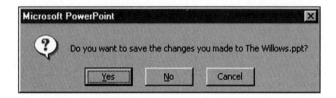

Summary and Exercises

Summary

- Microsoft PowerPoint is a presentation graphics program designed to prepare slide shows.
- Presentations may include handouts, speaker notes, slides, and outlines.
- PowerPoint displays presentations in four different views: Slide View, Outline View, Slide Sorter View, and Notes Pages View. Each view is designed to help you accomplish specific tasks.
- Each presentation may contain numerous slides, each designed to focus on a particular aspect of the broad-based presentation theme.
- Toolbars containing tools needed to accomplish specific tasks appear automatically.
- PowerPoint offers a variety of resources from which you can get online help.
- PowerPoint reminds you to save your changes before you exit the program.

Key Terms and Operations

Key Terms	Operations
AutoLayout	create a blank PowerPoint presentation
master	exit Microsoft PowerPoint
menu bar	get help with Office Assistant
Office Assistant	launch Microsoft PowerPoint
online help	retrieve help from the Web
placeholder	
ScreenTip	
status bar	
template	
title bar	
toolbar	
view	

Study Questions

Multiple Choice

1. To display the Help dialog box,
    a. choose Help, Contents, and Index.
    b. click the Office Assistant button.
    c. press (SHIFT)+(F1).
    d. choose Help, About Microsoft PowerPoint.

2. To start PowerPoint,
    a. double-click the Outlook icon on the desktop.
    b. click Start and choose Programs, Microsoft PowerPoint.
    c. start Windows 95 and then press (ALT)+W.
    d. open My Computer.

3. PowerPoint presentations can be used to generate all of the following except
   a. slides.
   b. handouts.
   c. outlines.
   d. Masters.

4. The PowerPoint view that displays a small slide image at the top of a page and provides space for speaker notes is
   a. Slide view.
   b. Outline view.
   c. Slide Sorter view.
   d. Notes Pages view.

5. When you launch Microsoft PowerPoint,
   a. a new presentation appears.
   b. the Open dialog box appears.
   c. the PowerPoint dialog box appears so that you can tell PowerPoint whether you want to create a presentation or open an existing presentation.
   d. a blank slide appears so that you can enter your title slide.

6. The PowerPoint view that displays only title and body placeholder text is
   a. Slide view.
   b. Outline view.
   c. Slide Sorter view.
   d. Notes Pages view.

7. The PowerPoint view that makes rearranging slides easier is
   a. Slide view.
   b. Outline view.
   c. Slide Sorter view.
   d. Notes Pages view.

8. The term that refers to the layout of objects on slides is
   a. AutoLayout.
   b. Master.
   c. template.
   d. slide.

9. Professional designs that contain graphics and background color schemes you can use to dress up a presentation are called
   a. AutoLayouts.
   b. Masters.
   c. templates.
   d. slides.

10. The basic unit of a presentation is a
   a. slide.
   b. placeholder.
   c. picture.
   d. template.

Short Answer

1. What are the three default toolbars displayed in the Slide view of a presentation?

2. What's the basic object of a presentation?

3. What supporting materials can you generate from a presentation?

4. How many views are available in PowerPoint?

5. Which view allows you to type text into placeholders, create drawings on a slide, and insert other objects on the slide?

6. What toolbar is displayed in Outline view that doesn't appear in Slide View?

7. What are AutoLayouts?

8. What six things should you consider as you plan your presentation?

9. What does a grayed menu command indicate?

10. What features are available on the World Wide Web to help you as you work with PowerPoint?

For Discussion

1. How does the procedure for launching Microsoft PowerPoint differ from the procedure for launching other Windows 95 applications?

2. Why is planning your presentation important?

3. What's the difference between AutoLayout formats, templates, and Masters?

4. How does the phrase "Less is more" relate to presentations?

Review Exercises

1. Designing a new presentation

The Willows Marketing department needs a presentation about the sports facilities at the resort. Marketing representatives will use the presentation during sales conferences and trade shows to provide an overview of the resort to prospective guests and convention planners. The Willows sporting facilities are listed in Table 0.2 on the next page. Use this list to develop a structure for the Marketing department presentation.

Table 0.2 The Willows Sporting Facilities

Facility	Features
Golf	Three 18-hole PGA courses Two driving ranges Five practice putting greens
Tennis	Ten asphalt courts Two clay courts Two grass courts
Exercise/Aerobic Center	Three saunas Four whirlpools Three massage beds scheduled by appointment Personal trainers Step aerobic classes twice daily Low impact aerobic classes daily
Miniature golf	Two 18-hole courses (Bye Bye Birdie and The Eagle's Nest)
Little Tree Playground	Heavy duty playground equipment for young children
Willow Pond Riding Stables	Fifteen horses One-, two-, and three-hour bridle paths Bicycle rentals
Willows Water Park	Wave pool Water slides Olympic-size swimming pool
The Willows Beach Front	Five miles of Atlantic Coast beach with lifeguards, a boardwalk, jet-ski rentals, surfing, etc.

2. Getting help

Because PowerPoint comes with professionally designed templates you can use to dress up your presentation, you need to know how to apply the templates to presentations you develop. Ask the Office Assistant to locate information about applying a template to an existing presentation.

1. Launch PowerPoint and create a blank presentation containing a title slide.

2. Click the Office Assistant button on the toolbar.

3. Type **How do I apply a template to a presentation?** in the question box of the Office Assistant window and press (ENTER).

4. Click Apply a different design to a presentation in the list of items the Office Assistant displays.

5. Review the information in the Help window.

6. Click the Show me button at the top of the Help window and watch as PowerPoint identifies the Apply Design button on the toolbar.

7. Click the Apply Design button twice to display the Apply Design dialog box.

8. Click a template name in the list of templates to display a sample of the template in the view area of the dialog box.

9. Close the dialog box.

The Solution

As the graphic artist employed by The Willows, you have been asked to put your creative talents to work designing an effective presentation. Use PowerPoint to create a new presentation, add text to the slides, and format and save your presentation by following the steps presented in the tasks that follow. Figure 1.1 shows the first five slides one of the managers sketched for the presentation.

Figure 1.1

The Setup

Just to make sure that you're on the same screen as your book, you may want to check some of the settings before you get started. This book assumes that the default settings were in place when the lab guru installed PowerPoint on the machine. However, because some students nose around where they shouldn't, some of the settings may have changed.

If you don't see the default toolbars on the screen when you open a blank presentation, choose View, Toolbars. Then click Standard, Formatting, and Common Tasks and/or Drawing to display the missing toolbar(s). If you see extra toolbars, close them. PowerPoint automatically displays appropriate toolbars as you work with different views and features in the presentation, so don't be surprised when something new pops up.

If you don't see a status bar, choose Tools, Options. When the Options dialog box displays, click the View page tab and then click the check box beside Status Bar at the top of the page. While you're in the Options dialog box, check to make sure that all options on the View page tab of the dialog box are checked except the last one—end with black slide.

If rulers appear below the toolbars and down the left side of your presentation window, you can hide them, if desired, by choosing View, Ruler. You can close the Office Assistant, or leave it active. Most of the illustrations and figures don't show the Office Assistant, but you know it's there when you need it.

Creating a Blank Presentation and a Title Slide

The Blank presentation option in the opening PowerPoint dialog box lets you create a "plain vanilla" presentation with standard text format, no color, and no graphics.

Each time you create a new presentation or add a slide to an existing presentation, PowerPoint displays the New Slide dialog box, which contains 24 AutoLayout formats. Each AutoLayout format contains placeholders that outline the areas of the slide set aside to contain text and graphic *objects* you can include on the slide. The first slide in a presentation is generally formatted with the Title AutoLayout format.

TASK 1: TO CREATE A NEW BLANK PRESENTATION WITH A TITLE SLIDE:

1 Launch PowerPoint.

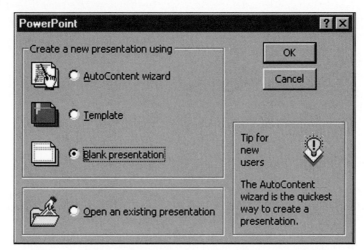

2 Click the Blank presentation option in the PowerPoint dialog box and then click OK.

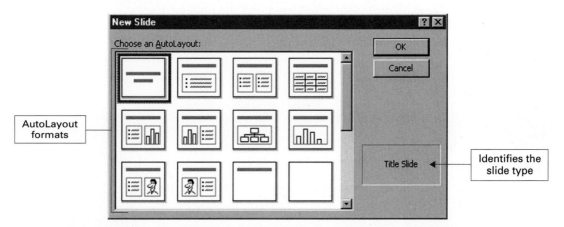

3 Click OK to accept the Title Slide AutoLayout format for the first slide.

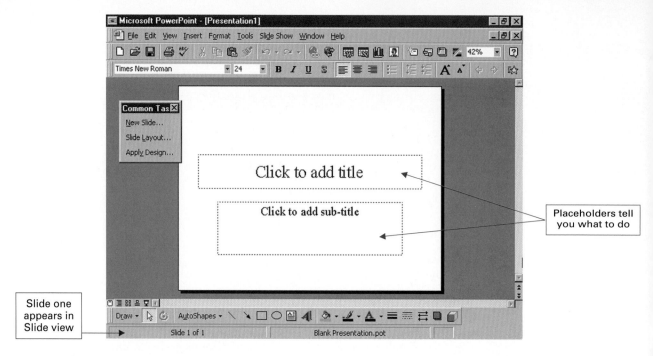

Slide one appears in Slide view

Placeholders tell you what to do

4 Click the title placeholder.
The placeholder border is selected and the insertion point appears at the center, replacing the instruction text.

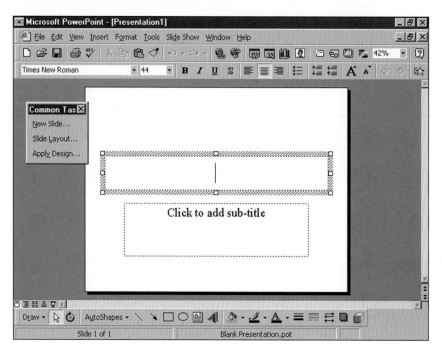

5   Type **The Willows** in the title placeholder.

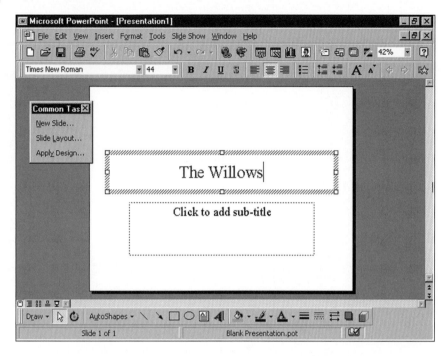

6   Press (CTRL)+(ENTER) to move to the subtitle placeholder. This area is selected and the instruction text is replaced by the insertion point.

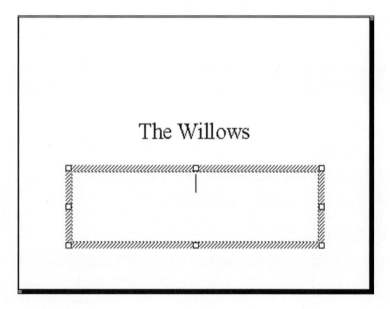

7 Type **Where Neighbors Become Friends**.

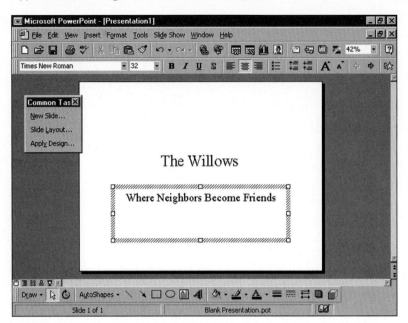

Saving and Closing a Presentation

You can use the same procedures to save a presentation in PowerPoint that you use to save files in other Windows 95 applications. All slides in the presentation are stored in one file. When you save a presentation for the first time, the Save dialog box opens the *My Documents* folder unless someone told PowerPoint to store files somewhere else. If you want to store your presentation in a different folder or on a different disk, you need to open the disk and folder before saving.

TASK 2: TO SAVE AND CLOSE A PRESENTATION:

1 Click the Save ■ button on the Standard toolbar.

2 Select a folder to store the presentation.
The folder you choose to store your document should appear in the Save in text box at the top of the Save window.

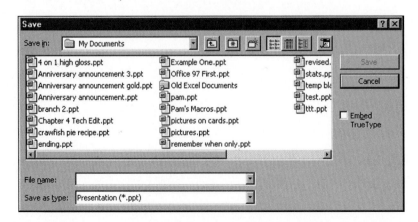

Willows power point

3 Type **The Willows** in the file name box and press ⟨ENTER⟩ or click the Save button.

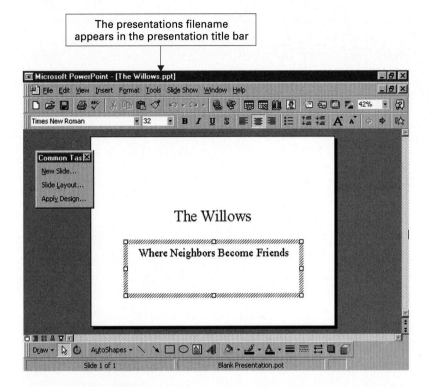

The presentations filename appears in the presentation title bar

4 Click the Close ⊠ button for the presentation window to close the presentation.

Note To create a new blank presentation after closing a presentation, click the New button on the Standard toolbar.

Opening a Presentation and Adding Slides

Most presentations consist of a series of slides, each devoted to a particular topic you want to cover in the presentation. Behind each topic slide you often need to add slides to provide explanatory information about the topic, or supporting documentation. When you want to add slides to an existing presentation, you need to open the presentation and display the slide that the new slide(s) will follow.

The procedures you use to open a presentation when PowerPoint is running are the same procedures you use to open files in most Windows 95 applications. You can also select the Open an existing presentation option from the PowerPoint dialog box when you launch PowerPoint.

TASK 3: TO OPEN A PRESENTATION AND ADD SLIDES:

1 Click the Open 📂 button.

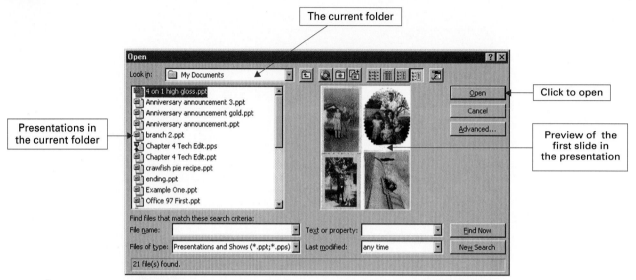

The current folder

Presentations in the current folder

Click to open

Preview of the first slide in the presentation

2 Select the folder containing your presentation from the Look in drop-down list and double-click the presentation called *The Willows*.

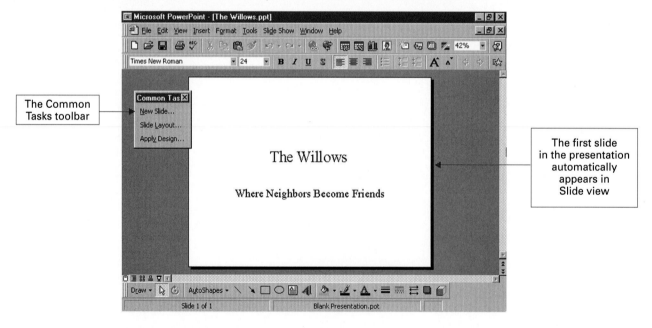

The Common Tasks toolbar

The first slide in the presentation automatically appears in Slide view

3 Click New Slide in the Common Tasks toolbar.

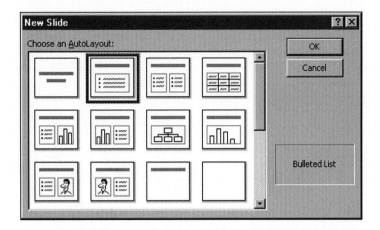

4 Click the Bulleted List AutoLayout format, if necessary, and click OK.

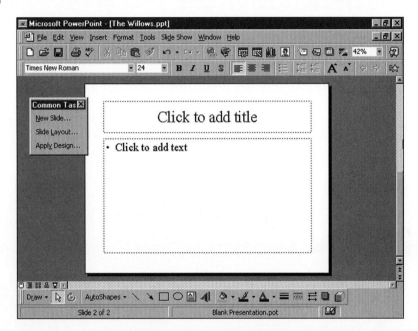

5 Click the title placeholder and type **Featuring . . .**

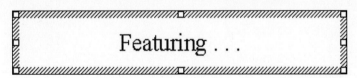

6 Click the bulleted list placeholder; then type **Lodging** and press (ENTER).

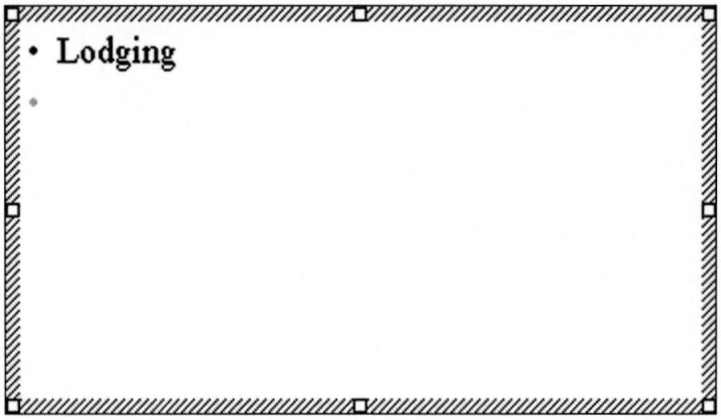

- Lodging

7 Type **Fine Dining** and press (ENTER).

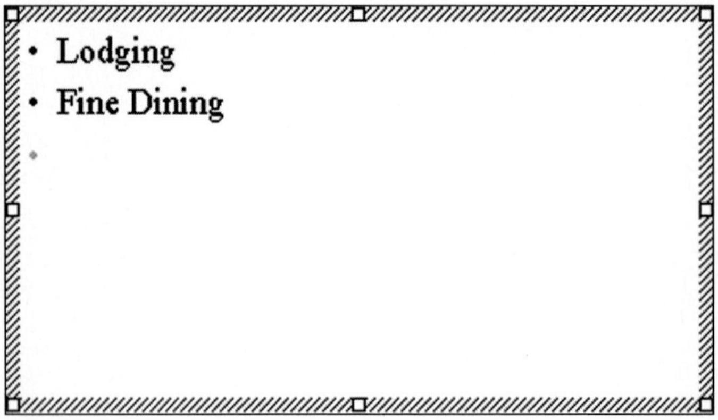

- Lodging
- Fine Dining

8 Repeat step 7, substituting the text shown below for the last two bulleted items:

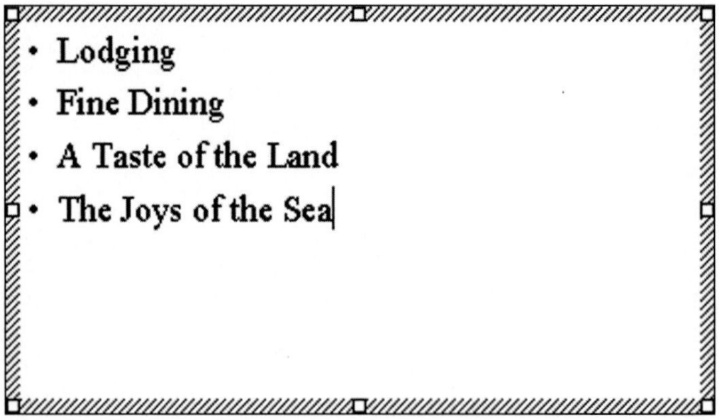

- Lodging
- Fine Dining
- A Taste of the Land
- The Joys of the Sea

9 Press (CTRL)+(ENTER) to create another new bulleted list slide.

> **Note** Pressing Ctrl+Enter from any other placeholder activates the next placeholder on the slide instead of creating a new slide.

Navigating a Presentation

As you build your presentation and your presentation begins to grow, you need to be able to navigate among the slides to display the slides you need to edit or review. You can use both the mouse and keyboard to display different slides in Slide view. Figure 1.2 identifies techniques for navigating slides using the mouse.

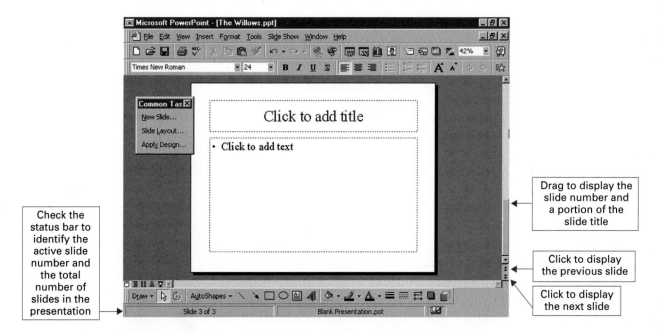

Figure 1.2

TASK 4: TO NAVIGATE SLIDES IN A PRESENTATION:

1 Press (PGUP) to display Slide 2 of the presentation *The Willows*.

2 Press (CTRL)+(HOME) to display the first slide in the presentation.

3 Press (PGDN) to display Slide 2 of the presentation.

4 Press (CTRL)+(END) to display the last slide in the presentation.

5 Click the Show Previous Slide ⬆ button to display Slide 2.

6 Click the scroll box and drag it to the top of the scroll bar to display Slide 1.

Applying a Template

PowerPoint provides a number of ***templates*** that you can use to enhance the look of your presentation. Templates provide the style, color, and pizzazz your presentation needs to attract the attention of your audience. Templates hold special font formats and text alignments, background color, and bullet formats for text contained in placeholders of the presentation. Applying a template to a presentation helps maintain consistency among the slides in your presentation.

Templates are stored in a special *Templates* folder that automatically opens when you choose a template command from the menu or toolbars. When you apply a template, all slides in the presentation are automatically formatted with the template design.

TASK 5: TO APPLY A TEMPLATE TO A PRESENTATION:

1 Click Apply Design in the Common Tasks toolbar.

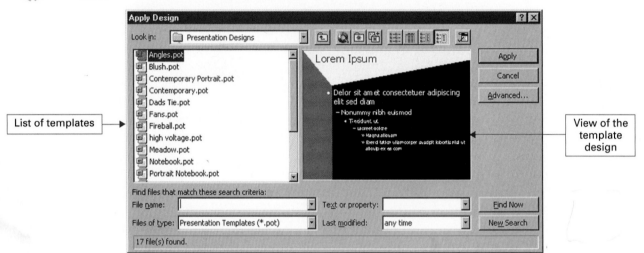

List of templates

View of the template design

2 Click Fireball.pot and view the template design.

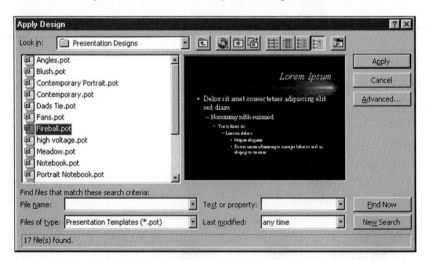

3   Click Apply to apply the template to the presentation.

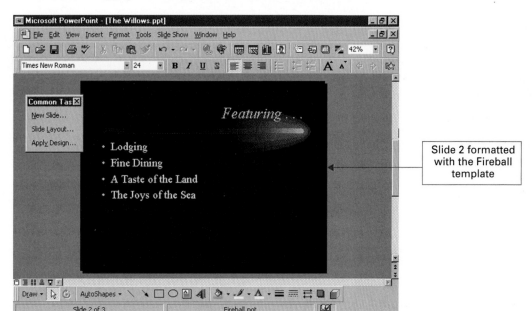

Slide 2 formatted with the Fireball template

Switching Views

When you want to review the flow of a presentation or view all slides after applying a new slide format or design, you can display your presentation using a different view. The default view, the view you have been working in, is called slide view. Slide Sorter view displays small images (often called *thumbnail images*) of each slide in the presentation so that you can review the effects of applying a template design to all the slides in the presentation. Outline view displays the title and body text you add to placeholders in a notebook-like format so you can review the content of the presentation.

TASK 6: TO SWITCH VIEWS:

1   Position the mouse pointer on the third view button at the bottom of the presentation window.

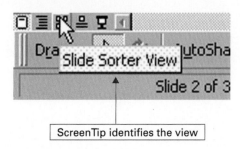

ScreenTip identifies the view

2 Click the Slide Sorter View ⊞ button.

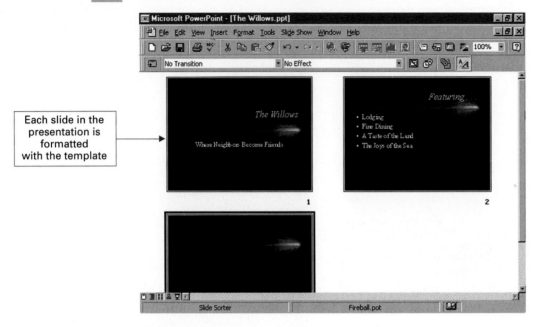

Each slide in the presentation is formatted with the template

Tip If the Common Tasks toolbar gets in your way, point to the toolbar's title bar and drag it out of the way.

3 Click Slide 3 and then click the Outline View ▤ button.
Title and body placeholder text shows the slide content.

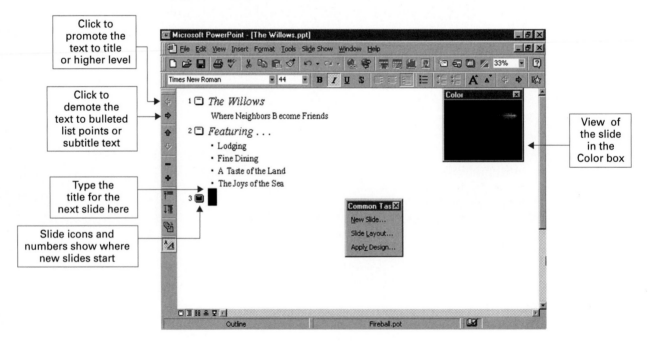

Click to promote the text to title or higher level

Click to demote the text to bulleted list points or subtitle text

Type the title for the next slide here

Slide icons and numbers show where new slides start

View of the slide in the Color box

Adding Text in Outline View

When you have developed an outline of text and information you want to include in a presentation, you'll find that Outline view enables you to type the title and body text for your slides more quickly. PowerPoint provides formatting for five levels of text plus the title text on a slide. You can move to the next text level by pressing Tab and return to a higher text level by pressing Shift+Tab. When you finish typing the outline text, you can view the slides in Slide view and add graphics and other enhancements to individual slides or apply a presentation design to all slides.

TASK 7: TO ADD TEXT IN OUTLINE VIEW:

1 Type **The Grande Hotel** as the title for Slide 3 and press (ENTER).

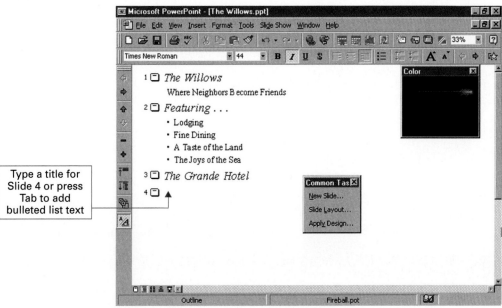

Type a title for Slide 4 or press Tab to add bulleted list text

2 Press (TAB) to add the bulleted list text and then type:

Guest Rooms
Shops
Restaurants
Meeting Rooms
Exercise Facility
Pool and Sun Deck

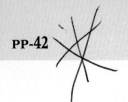

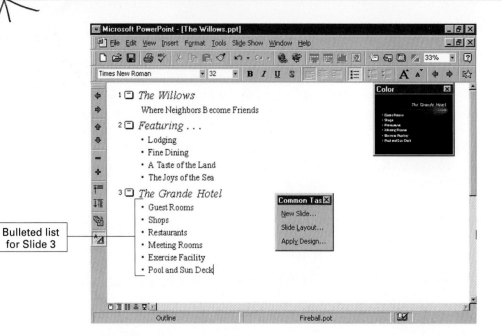

Bulleted list for Slide 3

3 Press (ENTER) after typing the last bullet point and then press (CTRL) + (ENTER) to start a new slide. Continue typing to create the following slides:

Press Tab to indent to a second level of bulleted list

4 ▢ *Willows Beach Cottages* enter
tab
• Luxury living in a cottage setting
  – Two Bedrooms in each Cottage
  – Additional Sofa Bed in Living Area
  – King and Queen Size Beds
• Fully Stocked Kitchen Facilities ◄
• Nestled Among the Links

5 ▢ *The Facilities* ◄
• Golf and Tennis
• Exercise and Aerobics
• Miniature Golf
• Playground
• Riding Stables
• Water Park

Press Shift+Tab to return to the first level of bullets

Press Ctrl+Enter to create the new slides

tab again

4 Save the changes to the presentation.

Printing Slides, Handouts, and Presentation Outlines

Because PowerPoint is primarily a graphically oriented program and can print your presentation in a variety of formats, the Print dialog box contains features and options unique to PowerPoint. For example, you can print each slide individually on a sheet of paper, print multiple slides on the same page in a format called *handouts*, or print the Outline view of your presentation. Figure 1.3 identifies additional print options that you can set to control the quality of the print for different types of printers.

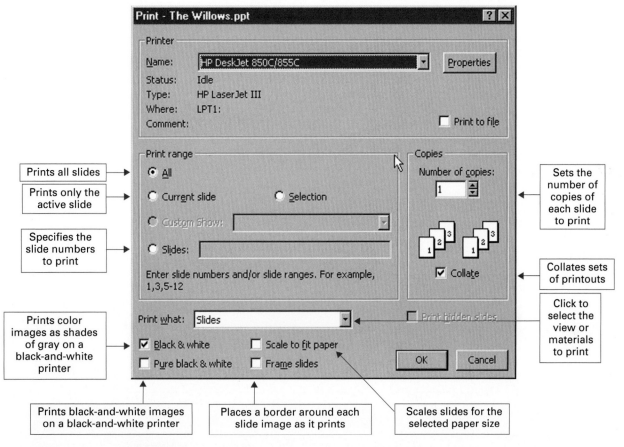

Prints all slides →

Prints only the active slide →

Specifies the slide numbers to print →

Prints color images as shades of gray on a black-and-white printer →

← Sets the number of copies of each slide to print

← Collates sets of printouts

Click to select the view or materials to print

Prints black-and-white images on a black-and-white printer

Places a border around each slide image as it prints

Scales slides for the selected paper size

Figure 1.3

TASK 8: TO PRINT SLIDES AND OUTLINES:

1 Choose File, Print to display the Print dialog box shown in Figure 1.3.

> **Tip** To bypass the Print dialog box and print the complete presentation using the print settings last set, click the Print button on the Standard toolbar. Each time you launch PowerPoint, the print settings return to the default settings.

2 Click the drop-down arrow at the end of the Print What text box.

3 Click Handouts (Six Slides per Page).

4 Click the Black & White check box, if necessary, and click OK.
PowerPoint compiles the slides, sizes them for printing together on one
page, and then prints the slides (see Figure 1.4).

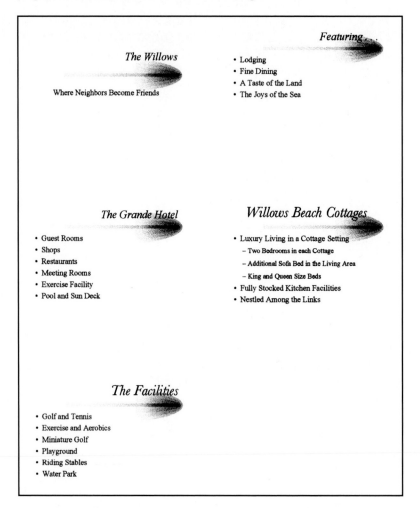

Figure 1.4

5 Choose File, Print again, select Outline View from the Print What drop-down
list, and click OK (see Figure 1.5).

1 ☐ *The Willows*
Where Neighbors Become Friends

2 ☐ *Featuring . . .*
- Lodging
- Fine Dining
- A Taste of the Land
- The Joys of the Sea

3 ☐ *The Grande Hotel*
- Guest Rooms
- Shops
- Restaurants
- Meeting Rooms
- Exercise Facility
- Pool and Sun Deck

4 ☐ *Willows Beach Cottages*
- Luxury Living in a Cottage Setting
  - Two Bedrooms in each Cottage
  - Additional Sofa Bed in the Living Area
  - King and Queen Size Beds
- Fully Stocked Kitchen Facilities
- Nestled Among the Links

5 ☐ *The Facilities*
- Golf and Tennis
- Exercise and Aerobics
- Miniature Golf
- Playground
- Riding Stables
- Water Park

Figure 1.5

The Conclusion

If time permits, practice printing different materials and setting different options in the Print dialog box to see the effects they have on the way your slides print. When you're done, save changes to the presentation and close the presentation. If you've completed your work in PowerPoint, exit the program and shut down your computer as instructed.

Summary and Exercises

Summary

- PowerPoint enables you to create blank presentations formatted with no special design as well as presentations formatted using special designs called templates. You can change the look of slides in a presentation by selecting a different template design.
- AutoLayout formats make creating slides with preformatted text easier.
- You can add, delete, format, and select presentation text using many of the same techniques used in other Windows-based programs.
- PowerPoint displays presentation slides using four different views: Slide view, Slide Sorter view, Notes Pages view, and Outline view. Each view is designed to help you accomplish specific tasks.
- Presentations normally contain numerous slides; you can add slides and move from slide to slide in a presentation using a variety of different mouse and keyboard techniques.
- You save, open, close, and print presentations using many of the same procedures used in other Windows applications; you can print a variety of different presentation materials by selecting the desired format from the Print dialog box.

Key Terms and Operations

Key Terms	Operations
AutoLayout	add slides to a presentation
handouts	create, save, open, and close a presentation
Outline view	move around a presentation
Notes Pages view	print slides and handouts
Slide Sorter view	switch presentation views
template	use templates to change the look of a presentation

Study Questions

Multiple Choice

1. To create a new, blank presentation,
   a. simply launch PowerPoint—a new presentation automatically appears.
   b. choose New Presentation from the PowerPoint dialog box.
   c. select Blank presentation from the PowerPoint dialog box and press Enter.
   d. select Template from the PowerPoint dialog box and press Enter.

2. Slides added to a presentation are formatted using
   a. an AutoLayout format.
   b. text and title boxes.
   c. blank slides that resemble blank pieces of paper.
   d. outlines.

3. New slide layouts contain
   a. fields.
   b. placeholders.
   c. tables.
   d. templates.

4. Placeholders identify
    a. slide names.
    b. slide fields.
    c. slide titles.
    d. slide objects.

5. To add a new slide to a presentation, use any of the following techniques *except*
    a. double-clicking the active slide.
    b. clicking the New Slide button on the toolbar.
    c. clicking the New Slide command on the Common Tasks toolbar.
    d. choosing Insert, New Slide from the menu.

6. Most slides contain
    a. slide tables.
    b. pictures.
    c. slide titles.
    d. slide names.

7. Outline view displays
    a. all slide objects.
    b. slide title and body text only.
    c. small slide images.
    d. slide images and notes about the slide.

8. Slide Sorter view displays
    a. all slide objects.
    b. slide title and body text only.
    c. small slide images.
    d. slide images and notes about the slide.

9. Notes Pages view displays
    a. all slide objects.
    b. slide title and body text only.
    c. small slide images.
    d. slide images and notes about the slide.

10. Slide view displays
    a. all slide objects.
    b. slide title and body text only.
    c. small slide images.
    d. slide images and notes about the slide.

Short Answer
1. How do you create a new presentation if PowerPoint is already running?

2. What's a template?

3. What are AutoLayout formats and what do they contain?

4. What are the four presentation views and when should you use each view?

5. How do you switch views?

6. How do you print handouts?

7. How can you use the vertical scroll bar to display a specific slide?

8. How do you apply a template?
9. How do you open a presentation when you launch PowerPoint?
10. How do you move from one placeholder on a slide to another without using the mouse?

For Discussion

1. What are the four options in the PowerPoint dialog box when you launch PowerPoint and what does each option enable you to do?
2. How do you identify the material you want to print, and what options should you check if you're using a black-and-white printer?
3. What are the advantages of formatting a presentation by using a template?
4. What kind of presentations could you create with PowerPoint for your other classes?

Review Exercises

1. Creating, saving, and adding slides and text to presentations

Ruth Lindsey, Manager of The Willows Shops, has been asked to display the diversity of gift items available in different shops at The Willows. She has developed the preliminary outline shown in Figure 1.6 and asks you to create a presentation using the outline.

1 The Willows Shops
  Where Exploring Becomes an Adventure
2 The Newsstand
  • Newspapers
  • Magazines
  • Recent Publications
  • The Willows Post Office
3 Sindy's Sun Closet
  • Swimsuits
  • Bathing Accessories
  • Lotions
  • Towels
  • Flippers
4 Weeping Willow Gallery
  • Paintings
  • Sculpture
  • Iron Works
  • Local Artists
5 Live Oak Gifts
6 Creative Cutlery
  • A Wide Assortment of Kitchen Wares
7 Cherry Street Market
  • Home Grown Produce
  • Natural Flora from the Carolinas
8 Victorian Tea Room
  • Victorian gifts and clothing
  • Victorian High Tea Served Daily
9 Ken's Kids
  • Children's games and toys
  • Children's clothing
10 Appalachian Crafts
  • Treasures from the Hills
  • Displays of local artists

Figure 1.6

Using PowerPoint, create a new blank presentation named *The Willows Shops*. Follow these instructions to complete the presentation:

1. Launch PowerPoint and create a new blank presentation that contains a title slide.

2. Switch to Outline view and add the text shown in Figure 1.6.

3. Save the presentation using the filename *The Willows Shops*.

4. Close the presentation and exit PowerPoint when you have completed your work.

2. Switching views, navigating presentation slides, applying a template, and printing handouts

Ms. Lindsey would like a copy of the slides in the presentation *The Willows Shops* for her assistant managers to review before she makes the presentation. She would like to have the presentation slides formatted using the template shown in Figure 1.7.

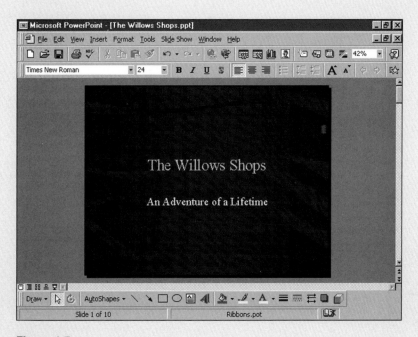

Figure 1.7

She asks you to reformat the presentation with the template and print copies for her assistant managers. Follow these instructions to meet Ms. Lindsey's request:

1. Open the presentation *The Willows Shops* and review the presentation in Outline view.

2. Display Slide 1 in Slide view and apply the Ribbons template to the presentation.

3. Review each slide on-screen using different navigation tools.

4. Save changes to the presentation and print a copy of the presentation as black-and-white handouts with six slides per page.

5. Close the presentation and exit PowerPoint when you have completed your work.

3. Creating, formatting, and printing a multi-slide presentation

1. Launch PowerPoint 97, if necessary, and create a new blank presentation that contains a title slide.

2. Create the four slides displayed in Figure 1.8.

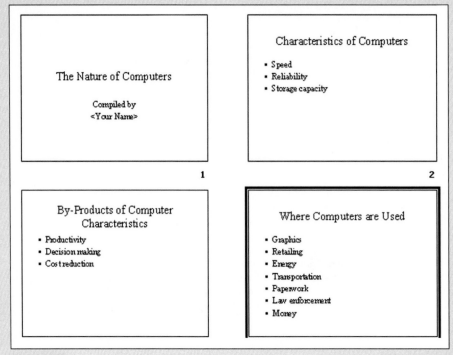

Figure 1.8

3. Save the presentation using the filename *Computers in Society xxx* (where *xxx* represents your initials).

4. Switch to Outline view and add the slides displayed in Figure 1.9.

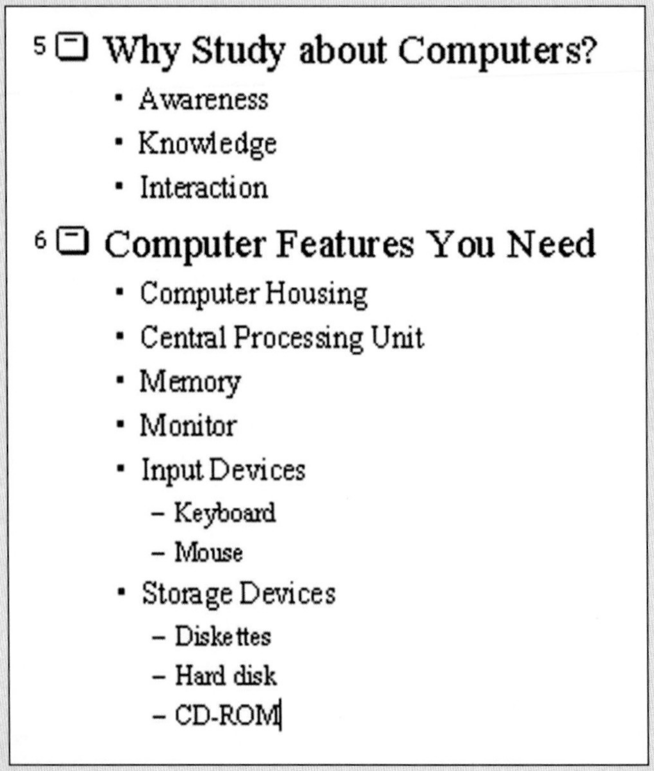

5 ☐ **Why Study about Computers?**
- Awareness
- Knowledge
- Interaction

6 ☐ **Computer Features You Need**
- Computer Housing
- Central Processing Unit
- Memory
- Monitor
- Input Devices
  - Keyboard
  - Mouse
- Storage Devices
  - Diskettes
  - Hard disk
  - CD-ROM

Figure 1.9

5. Apply a template to the presentation.

6. Redisplay Slide view and review each slide, making adjustments to slide text and format based on the template you applied.

7. Save changes to the presentation and print a copy of the presentation as black and white slides with six slides per page.

8. Print a copy of the presentation outline.

9. Close the presentation, saving changes, and exit PowerPoint.

Assignments

1. Creating, formatting, and saving a multi-slide presentation

The Willows area of South Carolina features a number of festivals and attractions. Create a presentation named *Festivals and Attractions* that contains the slides pictured in Figure 1.10.

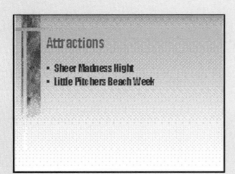

Figure 1.10

Apply the Blush template and view the presentation in all four views. Save the presentation and print a copy of the presentation as black-and-white handouts with three slides per page. Close the presentation and exit PowerPoint when you have completed your work.

2. Finding templates on the Internet

Search the PowerPoint Internet site and locate additional templates that you can use to format presentations. (Go to Microsoft's home page at WWW.Microsoft.com and then click on Products.) Download a template and apply it to the Festivals and Attractions presentation created in the preceding assignment. Save the presentation as a presentation named *Reformatted Festivals* and print a copy of the title slide. Check with your instructor or lab assistant for special instructions for storing templates.

Editing Slide Text

PowerPoint contains a variety of tools that you can use to edit text you add to slides. The techniques you use to edit text are similar to the techniques you use to edit text in other Windows 95 applications. In this project, you apply different techniques to edit and enhance text, format text placeholders, and change the setup of your slide page.

Objectives

After completing this project, you will be able to:

➤ **Select and edit placeholder text**

➤ **Change the appearance of text**

➤ **Find and replace text**

➤ **Check the style and spelling of text**

➤ **Format text placeholders**

➤ **Change the page setup**

➤ **Create a presentation using a wizard**

The Challenge

Francesca Savoy has been hired to coordinate a marketing campaign designed to promote The Willows resort. She has reviewed the presentation slides you created in Project 1 and has made changes to the slide text. In addition, she has recommended changes to the text format and text placeholder positions to improve the display of information on slides in the presentation. Slides in the presentation should appear as shown in Figure 2.1 after you complete your edits.

Figure 2.1

In addition, Ms. Savoy would like you to create the structure of a new presentation designed to be used as a marketing tool for the resort. She plans to use the presentation as a guide and will provide the text she wants to include in the new presentation from the presentation outline that you prepare. Your completed presentation outline appears in Figure 2.2.

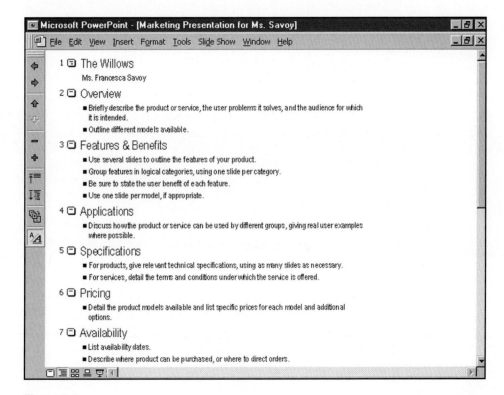

Figure 2.2

The Solution

As the graphic artist at The Willows, it's your responsibility to edit text on each slide in the presentation for The Willows, format text and text place-holders on the slides, and ensure that there are no spelling or formatting errors on the slides. Follow the steps in the tasks in this project to make the edits required by Ms. Savoy. When you complete the edits, you can create the outline for Ms. Savoy's marketing presentation using the PowerPoint AutoContent Wizard.

The Setup

Before starting this project, you may want to make sure that the following settings are active so that your presentations display in a format that matches the pictures in this book. Figures and illustrations use the default settings installed automatically with the PowerPoint program. If someone has fiddled with these settings, you may find that your screen looks different from those pictured here. Here are a few things to check:

- Do you see the four default toolbars—Standard, Formatting, Common Tasks, and Drawing? If not, choose View, Toolbars and then select the ones that are missing. Close any extra toolbars displayed.

- Display the status bar, if you don't see it, by choosing Tools, Options, and then checking the options on the View page tab. Make sure that all options on the View page tab of the dialog box are checked except the last one.

- If rulers appear, hide them by choosing View, Ruler.

- Make sure that your presentation window is maximized by clicking the Maximize button on the presentation window.

Selecting and Editing Placeholder Text

To edit text or to change the appearance of text, you must first *select* the text. PowerPoint offers a variety of techniques to select text. You can edit the text in slide placeholders using either Slide view or Outline view.

TASK 1: TO SELECT AND EDIT PLACEHOLDER TEXT:

1 Open the presentation *The Willows* and display the first slide in Slide view.

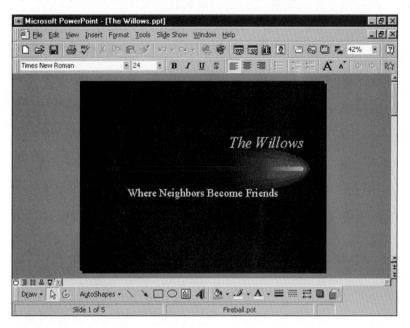

2 Double-click the word "Neighbors" and press (DELETE) to remove the word. The text appears as "Where Become Friends."

3 Position the insertion point between "Where" and "Become" and type **Guests.**

4 Display Slide 2, double-click the word "Lodging," and type **Luxury Accommodations**.

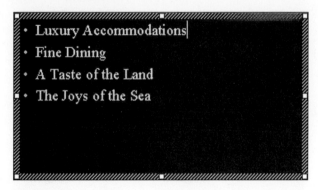

5 Select the text for the second bullet point and type **Four-Star Restaurants.**

6 Switch to Outline view and click the bullet beside the third bulleted item in Slide 2.
The mouse pointer appears as a four-headed arrow when you point to the bullet.

2 ▢ *Featuring . . .*
    • Luxury Accommodations
    • Four-Star Restaurants
    • <mark>A Taste of the Land</mark>
    • The Joys of the Sea
3 ▢ *The Grande Hotel*
    • Guest Rooms
    • Shops
    • Restaurants

7 Drag the bullet to the bottom of the Slide 2 bulleted list and drop it.

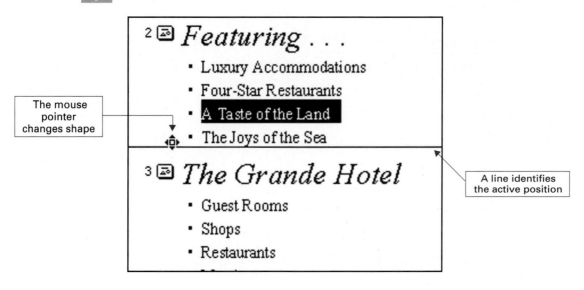

The mouse pointer changes shape

A line identifies the active position

8 Click the slide icon beside Slide 4.

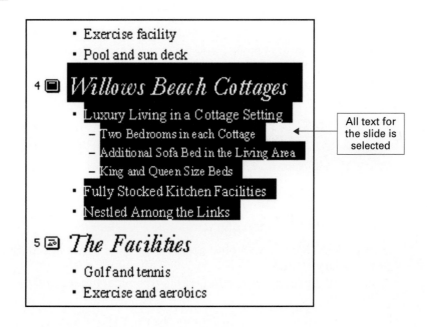

All text for the slide is selected

9 Position the mouse pointer on the selected slide icon, click, and drag the text to the bottom of the outline.

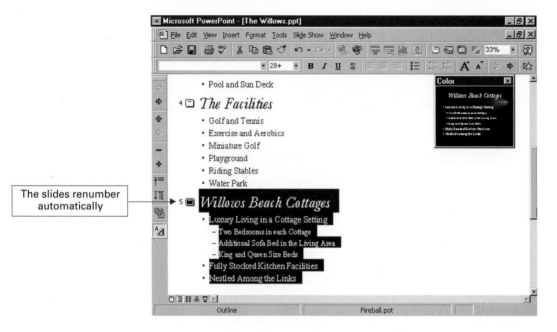

The slides renumber automatically

> **Tip** Drag the text slowly and position it carefully. If the text is "dropped" in the wrong location, use Undo to reverse the action and then try again.

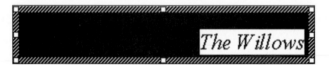

10 Return to Slide view, display Slide 1, and triple-click the title placeholder.

11 Click the Copy 🗐 button on the Standard toolbar.

12 Display Slide 5 and add a new bulleted list slide at the end of the presentation.
A new slide appears, formatted with a title placeholder and bulleted list placeholder.

13 Click the title placeholder and then click the Paste 🗐 button on the Standard toolbar.

Changing the Appearance of Text

To make the changes to the appearance of the text that Ms. Savoy requested, you need to change the font, change the font size, apply enhancements, and change the color of the text. You can apply many of these features using tools on the Formatting toolbar, as shown in Figure 2.3.

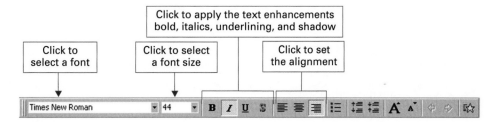

Figure 2.3

Enhancements and changes you make to slide text affect only text you select before making the change. If an enhancement you want to apply doesn't have a button on the toolbar, you can open the Font dialog box and select additional options. You can then copy the text format and apply it to text on other slides by using the Format Painter to ensure consistency.

TASK 2: TO CHANGE THE APPEARANCE OF TEXT IN A PRESENTATION:

1 Display Slide 1 of the presentation *The Willows* in Slide view and select the slide title text.

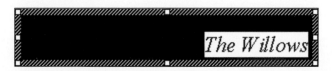

2 Click the arrow button beside the Font box on the Formatting toolbar to open the drop-down list.

3 Select Baskerville from the Font list. (If Baskerville is not available, select a font identified by your instructor or one that resembles the font shown here.)

4 Click the arrow button beside the Font Size box on the Formatting toolbar to open the drop-down list.

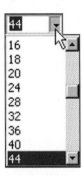

5 Scroll as necessary and select 60 from the font size list and then click the Bold **B** button on the Formatting toolbar.

6 Choose Format, Font to display the Font dialog box.

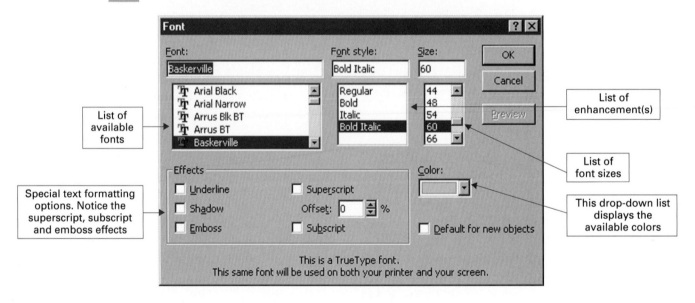

7   Click the arrow button beside the Color box, click the lighter yellow color, and press ⓔⓝⓣⓔⓡ.

8   Click **B** to remove the bold and then double-click the Format Painter ✍ button.

The mouse pointer carries a paintbrush to paint other text with the text format of the selected text

9   Display Slide 2 by clicking the next slide icon on the scroll bar and select the slide title text.
The title text appears reformatted.

10   Repeat step 9 to change the format of title text for all slides in the presentation.

11   Press ⓔⓢⓒ to drop the paintbrush.

12   Save the changes to the presentation.

> **Troubleshooting**   If you advance slides using the keyboard, the mouse drops the paint brush, so selecting text does not reformat the text. When this happens, select text containing the desired format and double-click the Format Painter again, before painting additional text.

Finding and Replacing Text

The Find feature in PowerPoint enables you to search for text contained in text placeholders on slides, in outlines, or in the notes area of notes pages. The Replace feature enables you to substitute different text for the text PowerPoint finds. Take, for example, a presentation that contains the company name that you've misspelled throughout the presentation. Using the Replace feature, you can quickly change all occurrences of the misspelled name to the correct spelling.

TASK 3: TO FIND AND REPLACE TEXT:

1 Press (CTRL)+(HOME) to display the first slide in the presentation.
You can start the Find and Replace feature from any location in the presentation; starting at the first slide in this task ensures that your screen will resemble the figures shown here.

> **Note** If a placeholder is active when you press Ctrl+Home, Power-Point places the insertion point at the top of the active placeholder. Click outside all placeholders and then press Ctrl+Home to display the first slide.

2 Choose Edit, Find.

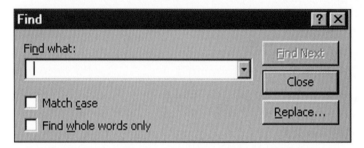

3 Type **Joys** in the Find what textbox, click the Match case check box, and press (ENTER).

First slide containing the text you want to find

Tip Drag the Find dialog box out of the way to view the text behind it.

4 Press ⌈ESC⌋ to close the Find dialog box and type **Bounty** to replace the
word *Joys*.

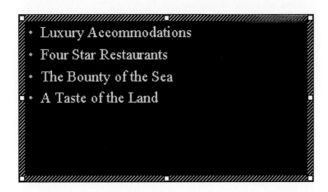

• Luxury Accommodations
• Four Star Restaurants
• The Bounty of the Sea
• A Taste of the Land

5 Choose Edit, Replace.

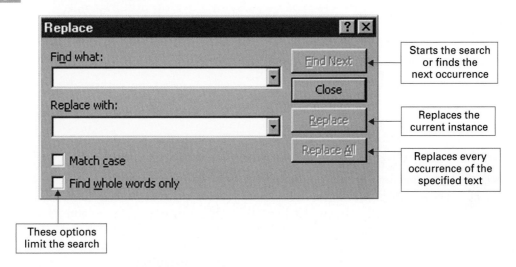

Starts the search
or finds the
next occurrence

Replaces the
current instance

Replaces every
occurrence of the
specified text

These options
limit the search

6   Type **Shops** in the Find what text box, press (TAB), type **Boutiques** in the Replace with text box, and press (ENTER).

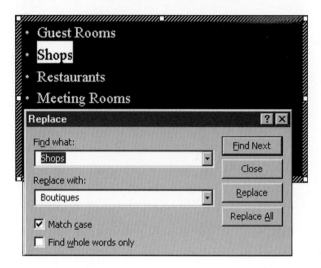

7   Click Replace.
"Shops" changes to "Boutiques."

8   Click Find Next, if necessary.

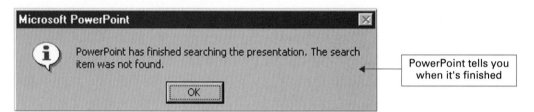

PowerPoint tells you when it's finished

9   Click OK to acknowledge the message, press (ESC) to close the Replace dialog box, and click the Save 🖫 button to save the changes to the presentation.

10   Click outside of the placeholder to deselect it.

Checking the Style and Spelling of Text

The PowerPoint Spelling feature proofs all the materials in your presentation and locates words in text placeholders that it doesn't recognize.

The PowerPoint Style Checker checks placeholder text on presentation slides for consistency in end punctuation, capitalization, and spelling. When you use the Style Checker to check capitalization, PowerPoint automatically formats all words except the first word in each bulleted item in lowercase. Checking the Spelling option in the Style Checker dialog box eliminates the need to run the Spelling feature separately.

TASK 4: TO CHECK A PRESENTATION FOR STYLE AND SPELLING:

1 Press (CTRL)+(HOME) to display the first slide in the presentation.
You can start the Style Checker from any location in the presentation;
starting at the first slide in this activity ensures that your screen will
resemble the figures shown here.

2 Choose Tools,
Style Checker.

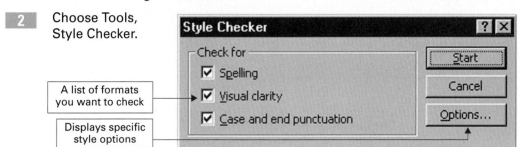

A list of formats you want to check

Displays specific style options

3 Select the check boxes for Spelling, Visual Clarity, and Case and End
Punctuation, and click Options.

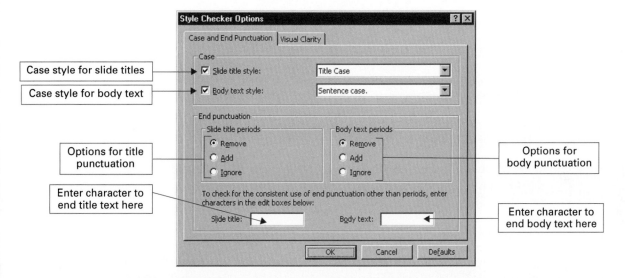

Case style for slide titles

Case style for body text

Options for title punctuation

Enter character to end title text here

Options for body punctuation

Enter character to end body text here

4 Set the options shown above on the Case and End punctuation page of the
style checker options dialog box and then click the Visual Clarity page tab.

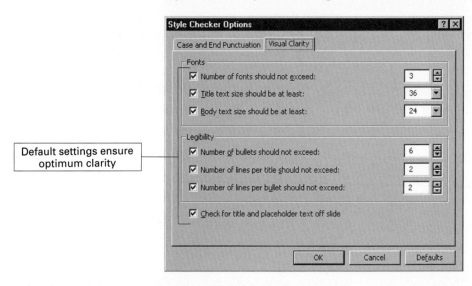

Default settings ensure optimum clarity

5 Select each option on the Visual Clarity page and change option values to those shown earlier, if necessary. Then press (ENTER) and click the Start button.

PowerPoint stops on the first style inconsistency it finds

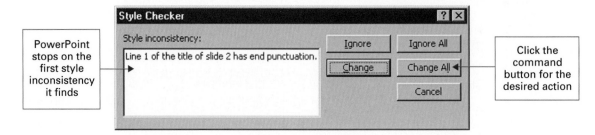

Click the command button for the desired action

Tip To see the slide text identified, drag the dialog box out of the way.

6 Click the command button for the action you want to take.
PowerPoint locates the next style error and displays a message identifying the error.

7 Repeat step 6 until you've reviewed all style errors.

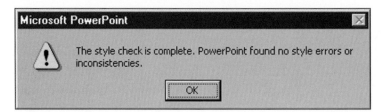

8 Click OK to close the message box and then click 🖫 to save changes to the presentation.

Formatting Text Placeholders

Placeholder objects contained on slides in your presentation can be selected, sized, and moved using the same techniques you use to size other objects. Changing the size of the text placeholder makes it possible to adjust the position of slide text and can be compared to setting margins on word processing documents. In addition, you can change the alignment and *line spacing* of all text in a placeholder by first selecting the placeholder and then adjusting the setting. Selected placeholders display *handles* on their corners and sides, as shown in Figure 2.4.

Tip Displaying the ruler helps to position and size placeholders more precisely. To display the ruler, choose View, Ruler.

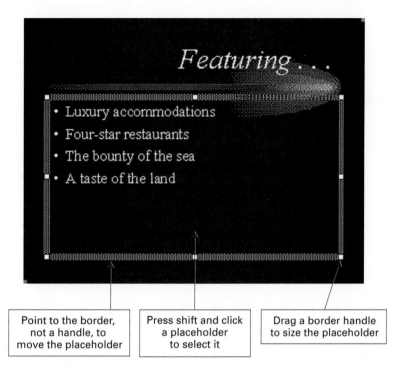

| Point to the border, not a handle, to move the placeholder | Press shift and click a placeholder to select it | Drag a border handle to size the placeholder |

Figure 2.4

TASK 5: TO FORMAT TEXT PLACEHOLDERS:

1   Display Slide 5 of the presentation *The Willows*, press (SHIFT), and click the title placeholder.

Selected title placeholder →

2   Click the Center ≣ button on the Formatting toolbar.

3   Display Slide 2 and select the bulleted list placeholder.

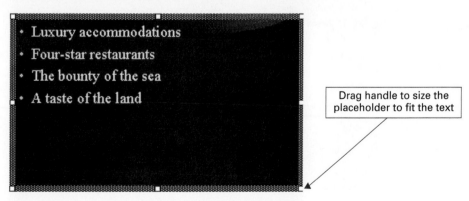

Drag handle to size the placeholder to fit the text

4 Drag the lower-right corner handle diagonally toward the placeholder text.

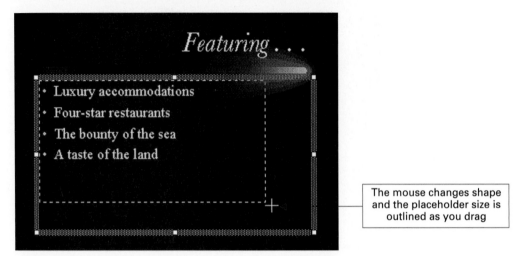

The mouse changes shape and the placeholder size is outlined as you drag

5 Position the mouse pointer on a border of the placeholder away from a handle and drag the placeholder diagonally down and right.

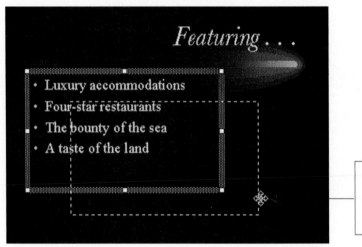

The pointer changes shape and the placeholder is outlined as you drag; when you release the mouse button, the placeholder is repositioned on the slide

6 Display Slide 5 and select the three second-level bulleted items following "Luxury living in a cottage setting."

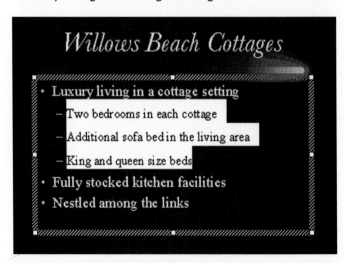

7 Choose Format, Line Spacing.

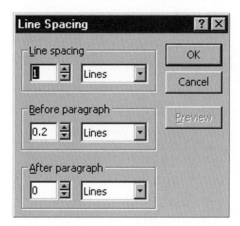

8 Click the spin buttons to increase the Line spacing to 1.5 and to decrease the Before paragraph spacing to 0; then click OK.

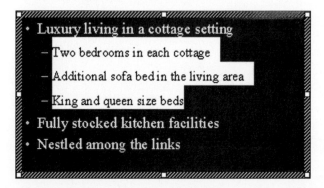

9 Save changes to the presentation.

Changing the Page Setup

To change the size and *orientation* (direction) of paper you want to use to print slides and other materials, you need to change the *page setup*. The Page Setup dialog box presents a set of options for setting the orientation of text on slides and a separate set of options for setting the page orientation for outlines, handouts, and notes pages, as shown in Figure 2.5. You can also format slides to print on different size paper by selecting the paper size from the Slides Sized For drop-down list, enter values in the Width and Height value boxes, and set the page number for the first slide in the presentation.

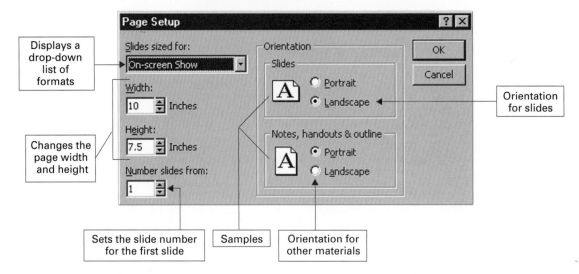

Displays a drop-down list of formats

Changes the page width and height

Orientation for slides

Sets the slide number for the first slide

Samples

Orientation for other materials

Figure 2.5

TASK 6: TO CHANGE THE PAGE SETUP FOR MATERIALS IN A PRESENTATION:

1 Choose File, Page Setup.
The dialog box in the figure below displays.

2 Change the settings in the Page Setup dialog box as in:

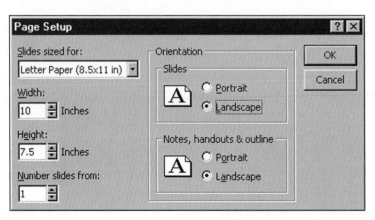

3 Click OK, save the changes to the presentation, and close the presentation.

Creating a Presentation Using a Wizard

The PowerPoint AutoContent Wizard helps you build an outline for specific types of presentations by presenting options for you to choose and enabling you to fill in specific pieces of information about the presentation. You can choose the AutoContent Wizard from the PowerPoint dialog box when you launch PowerPoint, or select the AutoContent Wizard from the New Presentation dialog box.

Using the Wizard, you can quickly and easily create the presentation outline for the marketing presentation Ms. Savoy requested.

TASK 7: TO CREATE A PRESENTATION USING THE AUTOCONTENT WIZARD:

1 Close all open presentations.
You don't have to close all presentations to use the wizard; doing so now ensures that your screen resembles those shown in this section.

2 Choose File, New, and click the Presentations tab.

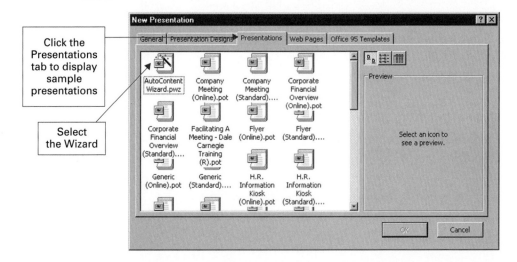

Click the Presentations tab to display sample presentations

Select the Wizard

Note: Files listed on the Presentations page that have a .pot extension are sample presentation templates. Depending on machine settings, extensions may not be displayed.

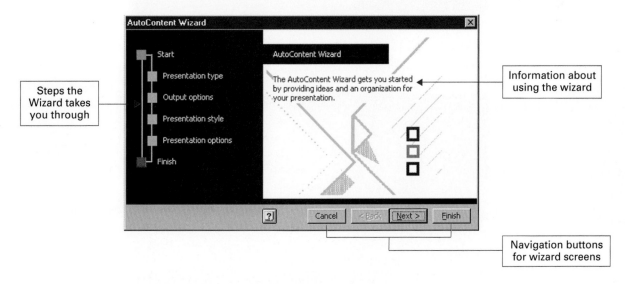

Steps the Wizard takes you through

Information about using the wizard

Navigation buttons for wizard screens

3 Doubleclick the *AutoContent Wizard.pwz.*

4 Click Next.

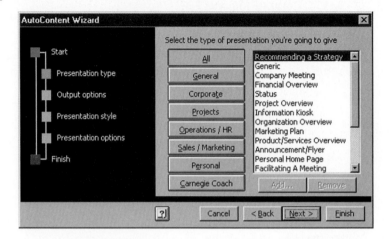

5 Click the Sales/Marketing button, select Product/Services Overview, and then click Next.

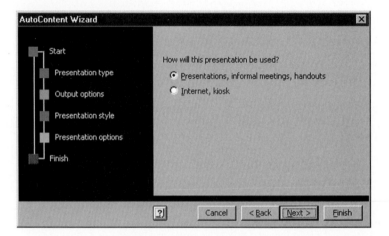

6 Select Presentations, informal meetings, handouts and then click Next.

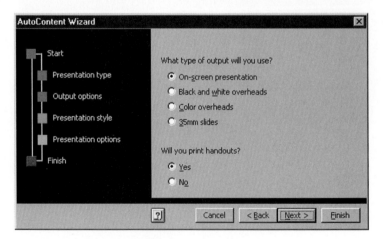

7   Click Next to accept the default presentation style options.

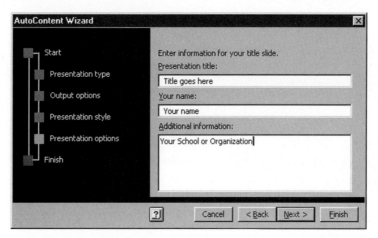

8   Type **The Willows** in the Presentation title text box, **Ms. Francesca Savoy** in the Your name text box, delete the text in the Additional information box, and then click Next.
The last screen the wizard presents instructs you to click Finish to continue. If you need to make changes to previous wizard screens, click the Back button until the screen appears, make the changes, and then click Finish from any screen.

9   Click Finish.

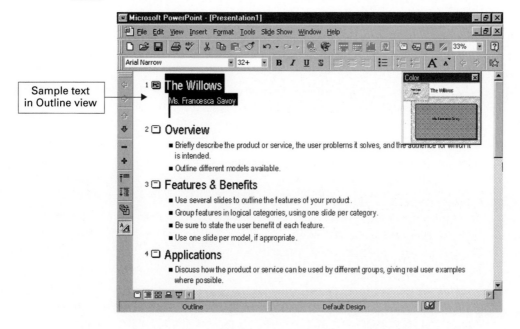

Sample text in Outline view

10   Save the presentation using the filename *Marketing Presentation for Ms. Savoy* and close the presentation.

The Conclusion

Print copies of Slides 1, 2, 4, and 5 in the presentation *The Willows* as black-and-white slides. Print a copy of the marketing presentation in Outline view for Ms. Savoy. When you're done, save changes to both presentations and close the presentations.

Summary and Exercises

Summary

- Many of the techniques used to select, insert, delete, enhance, move, and copy text used in other Windows applications can be used to work with text in Power-Point as well.
- You can use the Find and Replace commands to automatically substitute new text for existing text in a presentation.
- PowerPoint comes complete with features that enable you to check the spelling and style of slide text.
- You can change the size of object placeholders on slides by selecting the place-holder and dragging a handle; you can move the object placeholder on a slide by selecting the placeholder and dragging it to a new location.
- The Page Setup dialog box enables you to change the orientation of slides and other presentation materials and to set different dimensions for slides and pre-sentation materials.
- Wizards enable you to create a new presentation based on the purpose of a presentation, and to format the presentation using a template appropriate to the presentation type. Presentations created using wizards include sample and instructive text that you can replace with specific text to complete your pre-sentation.

Key Terms and Operations

Key Terms	Operations
AutoContent Wizard	change the size and orientation of slides and
font	presentation materials
handles	create a presentation using the AutoContent Wizard
line spacing	edit placeholder format
orientation	select and edit text
page setup	use PowerPoint tools to check a presentation

Study Questions

Multiple Choice

1. To select text,
   a. you must use the keyboard.
   b. you must use the mouse.
   c. you can use either the mouse or keyboard.
   d. position the insertion point on a word and press Enter.

2. To insert a word between existing words in a bulleted list,
   a. position the insertion point where you want the new word and type the word.
   b. delete existing text and retype all text, adding the new word where you want it.
   c. create a new blank line to contain the new word.
   d. you must use Outline view.

3. Text enhancements in PowerPoint include all the following *except*
   a. bold.
   b. strikethrough.
   c. italics.
   d. superscripts.

4. The easiest way to copy text formatting is to use
   a. copy/paste.
   b. drag and drop.
   c. menu commands.
   d. the Format Painter.

5. To copy the font for selected text in a presentation to different text, use
   a. the Format Painter.
   b. the Replace Fonts command.
   c. copy/paste commands.
   d. drag and drop techniques.

6. To ensure consistency for end punctuation among bulleted lists, use the
   a. Spell Checker.
   b. Find command.
   c. Style Checker.
   d. Format Painter.

7. To ensure that capitalization of specific terms remains consistent throughout a presentation, use the
   a. Spell Checker only.
   b. Spell Checker or Style Checker.
   c. Style Checker only.
   d. Format Painter.

8. To place extra space between bulleted list items in a placeholder,
   a. change the font.
   b. make the placeholder larger.
   c. change the line spacing for text within the placeholder.
   d. press Enter two times between list items.

9. Instead of setting margins for text on slides,
   a. click the placeholder border.
   b. use the ruler.
   c. use a dialog box.
   d. size the text placeholder.

10. The Page Setup dialog box enables you to set
   a. the orientation for slides separately from that of other presentation materials.
   b. one orientation for all materials.
   c. the size of body text placeholders.
   d. one paper size for all materials.

Short Answer

1. How do you select all text for a bulleted list item?

2. What features are copied when you use the Format Painter?

3. What's the easiest way to apply the most frequently used text enhancements?

4. What text formatting features are found on the Formatting toolbar in PowerPoint that aren't usually found on the Formatting toolbar in other Windows applications?

5. What options can you set to limit the instances of text found using the Find feature in PowerPoint?

6. How do you change the size of paper you plan to use to print a presentation?

7. What are the basic alignment settings you can apply to a placeholder?

8. How do you move a placeholder?

9. What settings can you change using the Page Setup dialog box?

10. What's the advantage of using the AutoContent Wizard to create a new presentation?

For Discussion

1. How do you choose a wizard to use for creating a presentation?

2. What's the difference between sizing a placeholder and sizing objects in other Windows applications?

3. What features does PowerPoint check when you use the Style Checker?

4. Which of PowerPoint's wizards will be most helpful to you in your area of study?

Review Exercises

1. Editing text in an existing presentation

Based on the response received from her assistant managers, Ruth Lindsey, Manager of The Willows Shops, would like you to edit text contained on some of the slides in the presentation *The Willows Shops*. Revisions to slide text appear in the outline shown in Figure 2.6.

```
 1 🖵  The Willows Shops
         Where Exploring Becomes an Adventure
 2 🖵  Sindy's Sun Closet
         • Swimsuits and Accessories
         • Sun Cosmetics
         • Beach and Pool Toys
 3 🖵  Weeping Willow Gallery
         • Paintings
         • Sculpture
         • Iron Works
         • Local Artisans
 4 🖵  Live Oak Gifts
 5 🖵  Creative Cutlery
         • A Large Assortment of Kitchen Wares
 6 🖵  Cherry Street Market
         • Home Grown Produce
         • Natural Flora from the Carolinas
 7 🖵  Victorian Tea Room
         • Victorian gifts and clothing
         • Victorian High Tea Served Daily
 8 🖵  Ken's Kids
         • Children's games and toys
         • Children's clothing
 9 🖵  Appalachian Crafts
         • Treasures from the Hills
         • Displays of local Artisans
10 🖵  The Newsstand
         • Newspapers
         • Magazines
         • Recent Publications
         • The Willows Post Office
```

Figure 2.6

Use the techniques explored in this project to edit the slides. Follow these instructions to complete the presentation:

1. Launch PowerPoint, if necessary, and open the presentation *The Willows Shops*.

2. Display the presentation in Outline view and move Slide 2 to the end of the outline.

3. Display the presentation in Outline view; select, edit, and enhance text on each slide as indicated in Figure 2.6.

4. Use the Find and Replace feature to change each occurrence of *Artists* in the presentation to *Artisans*.

5. Use the Spelling feature to check the spelling of your presentation.

6. Save changes to the presentation and print a copy of the presentation in Outline view.

7. Close the presentation and exit PowerPoint when you've completed your work.

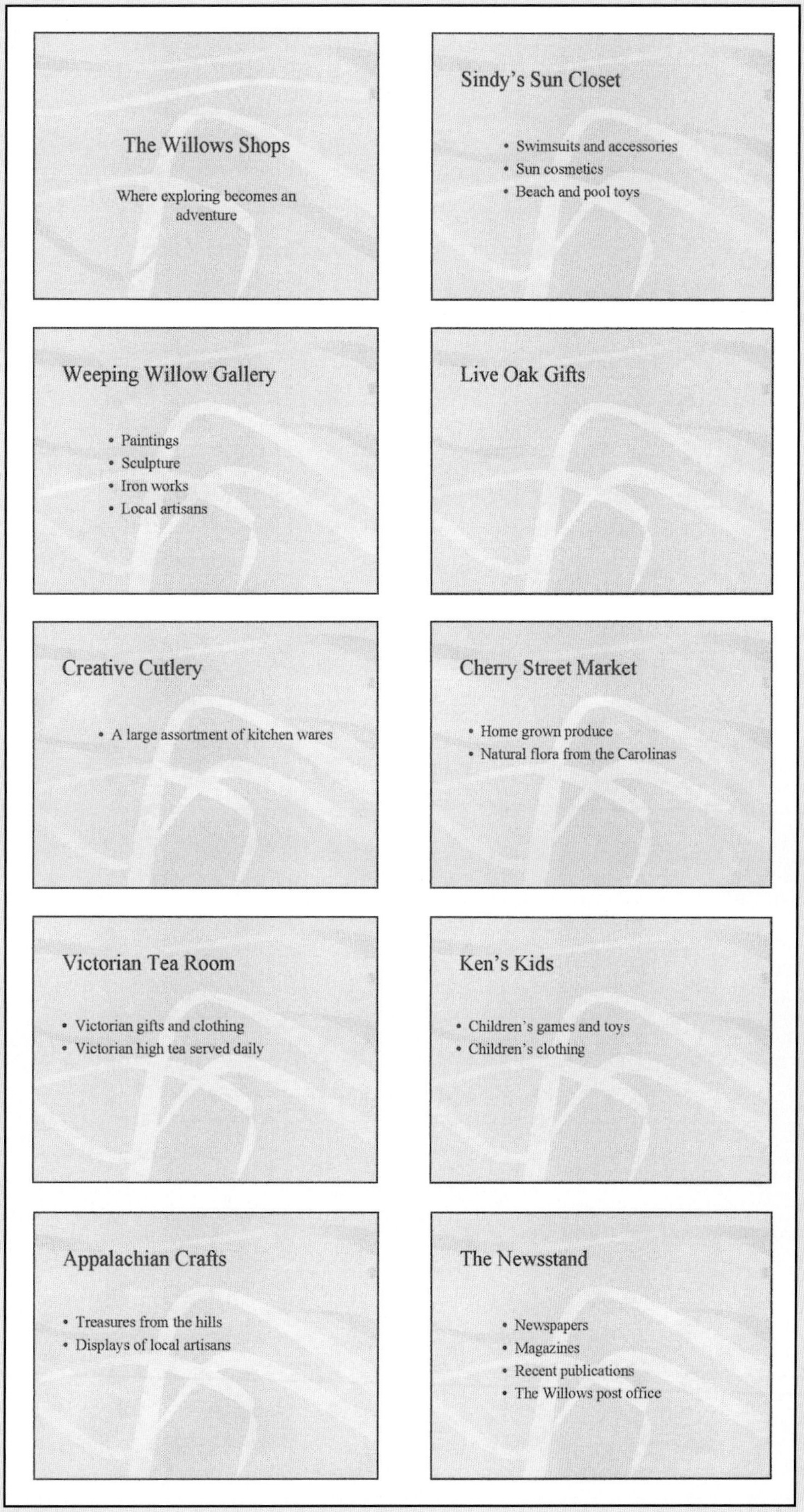

The Willows Shops

Where exploring becomes an adventure

Sindy's Sun Closet

- Swimsuits and accessories
- Sun cosmetics
- Beach and pool toys

Weeping Willow Gallery

- Paintings
- Sculpture
- Iron works
- Local artisans

Live Oak Gifts

Creative Cutlery

- A large assortment of kitchen wares

Cherry Street Market

- Home grown produce
- Natural flora from the Carolinas

Victorian Tea Room

- Victorian gifts and clothing
- Victorian high tea served daily

Ken's Kids

- Children's games and toys
- Children's clothing

Appalachian Crafts

- Treasures from the hills
- Displays of local artisans

The Newsstand

- Newspapers
- Magazines
- Recent publications
- The Willows post office

Figure 2.7

2. Formatting placeholders, changing the page setup, and checking the style of slides in a presentation

Ms. Lindsey requests the format changes shown in Figure 2.7 for slides in the presentation *The Willows Shops*.

Follow these steps to complete the formatting:

1. Launch PowerPoint, if necessary, and open the presentation *The Willows Shops*.

2. Display Slide 5 in Slide view, select the bulleted list placeholder, and set the alignment of text to center horizontally in the placeholder.

3. Size placeholders to better fit the text each bulleted list placeholder contains. Position the placeholder on Slides 2, 3, and 10 so that the left edge of the placeholder aligns at the 3″ mark on the horizontal ruler and the top of the placeholder aligns at the 1″ mark above center on the vertical ruler.

4. Position the bulleted list placeholders for Slides 5–9 so that the top edge of the placeholder aligns with the 1″ mark above center on the vertical ruler.

5. Left-align text in the title placeholder of Slide 2. Select the placeholder (not the text) and use the Format Painter to copy the alignment to title placeholders of all slides except Slide 1.

6. Use the Style Checker to check the style of text on slides in the presentation.

7. Save changes to the presentation and print slides as black-and-white handouts with six framed slides per page.

8. Close the presentation when you've completed your work.

3. Changing formatting of slides and AutoLayout of slides in a presentation

1. Launch PowerPoint and open *Computers in Society xxx.ppt* (where *xxx* represents your initials).

> **Note** If you do not have a document named *Computers in Society xxx.ppt*, ask your instructor for a copy of the file you should use to complete this exercise.

2. Make the following changes to slides in the presentation:
   - Change the font size for the title of Slide 3 so that the title fits on one text line.
   - Replace the word *reduction* on Slide 3 with *effectiveness*.
   - Search for the word *Money* and replace the word with *Finance*.
   - Italicize the title placeholder text of one slide and use the Format Painter to copy the format to all other title text.
   - Change the Line Spacing for all text on Slide 6 so that there is no space before or after the paragraphs.
   - Change the orientation for slides in the presentation to Portrait and review each slide; change the orientation for slides in the presentation back to Landscape.

3. Change the AutoLayout format of Slide 4 to 2 Column Text and add the following bullet points to the second column:

- Agriculture
- Government
- Education & training
- The home
- Health & medicine
- Robotics
- The sciences

4. Change the AutoLayout format for Slide 6 to 2 Column Text and move the *Storage Devices* bullet point and subtopics to the second column.

5. Add the following bullet point and subtopics to the second column of Slide 6:
- Printers
  - Dot matrix
  - Laser
  - Ink jet

6. Switch to Outline view and move Slide 5 so that it follows Slide 1.

7. Spell check the presentation and correct all typing and spelling errors.

8. Save the presentation using the filename *2 Computers in Society xxx* and print a copy of all slides as handouts with six slides per page.

Assignments

1. Editing and formatting slide text and placeholders

The revised *Festivals and Attractions* presentation slides appear in Figure 2.8. Use tools presented in this project to edit your presentation. Size, position, and format the text placeholders using the double-spaced, bold Modern font or the font your instructor recommends. Change the page setup of the presentation to format slides in portrait orientation. Check the spelling and style of the presentation. Because most of the features and attractions are proper names, however, don't check the presentation style for case. Save changes to the presentation and print black-and-white handouts with three framed slides per page. Close the presentation and exit PowerPoint when you've completed your work.

2. Creating a presentation using the Wizard

Ask your instructor how to obtain a presentation named *Resume.ppt*. The presentation contains an outline structure of information you should include in a résumé. Compare the sample résumé presentation to the one you designed in the Overview of PowerPoint to ensure that you've included all the necessary information. Then use the sample presentation and your own personal résumé to create a new presentation about yourself. Check the spelling and style of your presentation and format text and placeholders as desired. Apply a template to dress up the presentation. Save your presentation using your first and last names as the filename. Print a copy of your presentation as black-and-white handouts with three framed slides per page.

Close the presentation when you have completed your work.

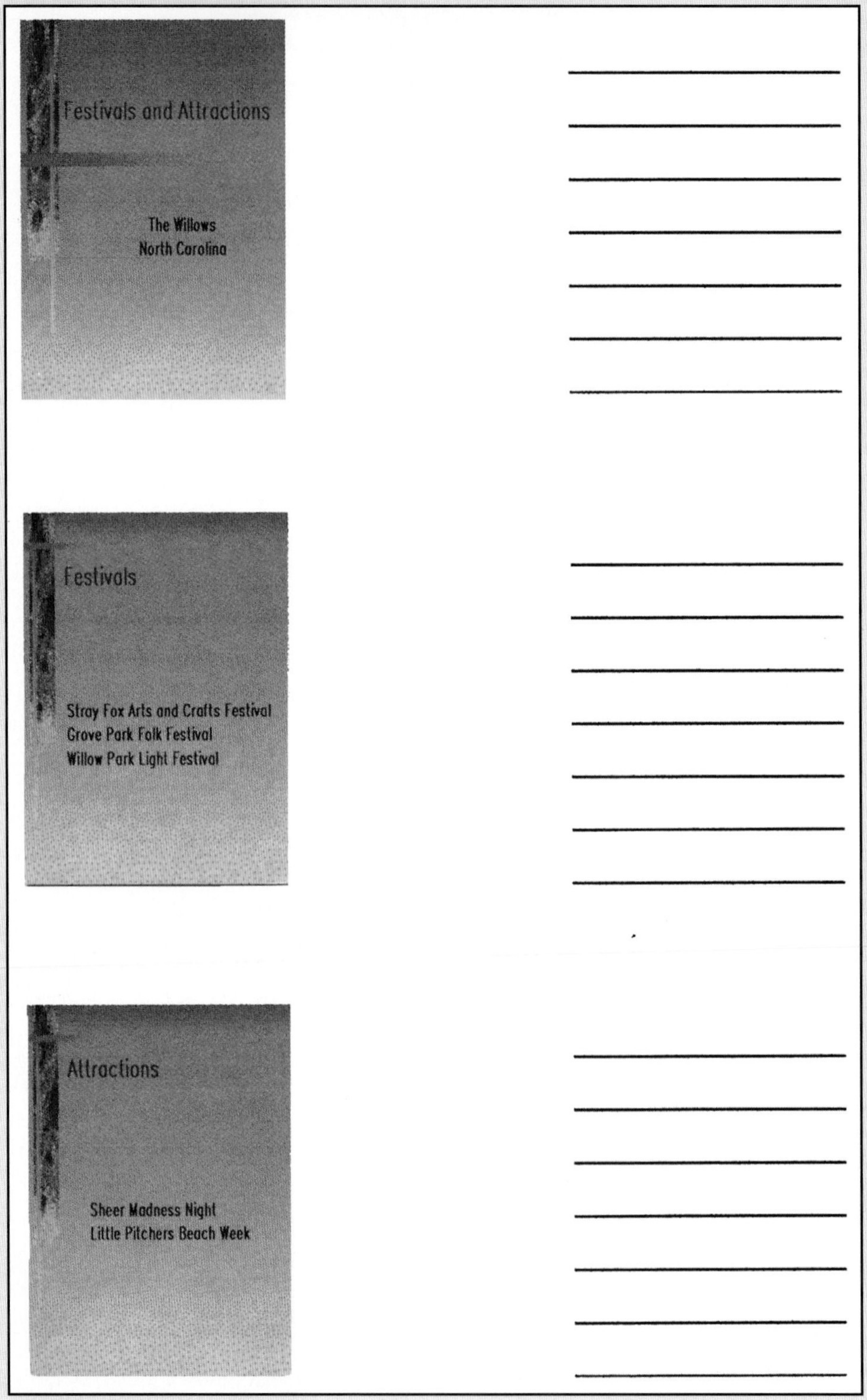
Festivals and Attractions
The Willows
North Carolina
Festivals
Stray Fox Arts and Crafts Festival
Grove Park Folk Festival
Willow Park Light Festival
Attractions
Sheer Madness Night
Little Pitchers Beach Week

Figure 2.8

Adding Art to a Presentation

PowerPoint makes dressing up your presentation with pictures quick and easy. Not only can you apply your own artistic talents to design powerful creations, but you can pull designs from the Clip Gallery or download them from the Internet. You can also use the PowerPoint WordArt module to change text into "words of art." In this project, you learn how to add graphics to your presentation slides and how to change the appearance of graphics to better fit your presentation needs.

Objectives

After completing this project, you will be able to:

➤ **Insert clip art into a slide**

➤ **Move and size clip art**

➤ **Download and insert clip art from the PowerPoint Web site**

➤ **Create WordArt**

➤ **Format WordArt**

➤ **Create drawings**

➤ **Manipulate art on a slide**

The Challenge

The template you applied to your presentations in Project 2 dressed up the design of your presentation but did nothing to fill in the blank space on presentation slides. Ms. Savoy would like for you to add appropriate graphics to slides in the presentation *The Willows*.

The Solution

As the graphics artist at The Willows, you get to add art to the slides in the presentation *The Willows*. Your dressed-up slides will appear as shown in Figure 3.1.

Figure 3.1

The Setup

So that your screen will match the illustrations shown in this project, make sure that the PowerPoint settings in the following table are selected on your computer:

Setting	Description
View menu	Choose Toolbars and then click the toolbar name for the one(s) you want to display. The four default toolbars and other toolbars that pop up automatically are displayed in this project.
Screen settings	Click the Maximize button to maximize the presentation window.
Tools menu	If you don't see the status bar, choose Options and then click the View tab. Select the check box beside Status Bar at the top of the page.

Inserting Clip Art

PowerPoint comes with a gallery of *clip art* images that you can use to enhance your presentation. You can use an AutoLayout that contains a clip art placeholder to add an image to a slide, or add an image to a slide that contains other types of placeholders. When you add a clip art image to a slide that contains a clip art placeholder, PowerPoint places the image in the placeholder and sizes it to fill the placeholder. When you add an image to a slide that doesn't contain a clip art placeholder, PowerPoint places the image in the middle of the slide and sizes it according to the default size of the clip art image.

The first time you access the Clip Gallery, PowerPoint takes a few moments to build the gallery and then presents thumbnail images of pictures.

TASK 1: TO INSERT CLIP ART IMAGES FROM THE CLIP GALLERY:

1 Open the presentation *The Willows* and display Slide 3 in Slide view.

2 Choose Insert, Picture.

3 Choose Clip Art.

Note You may see a message box telling you where you can find additional clips on the CD-ROM. Click OK to acknowledge the message.

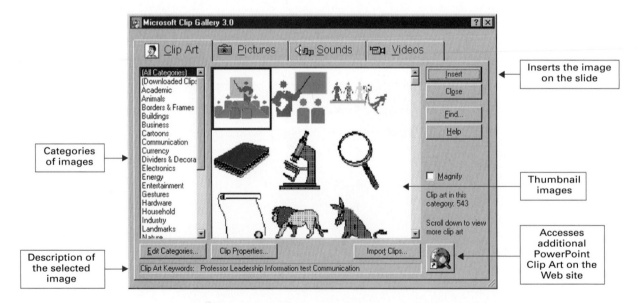

4 Click the Cartoons category and then scroll until you see the Strong Powerful Invincible Superior Human image.

Note If you don't see the image in your Clip Gallery, select a different image as directed by your instructor.

2   Click and drag the image to the lower-right corner of the slide.

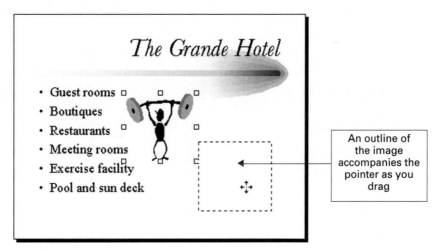

An outline of the image accompanies the pointer as you drag

3   Release the mouse button to drop the image.

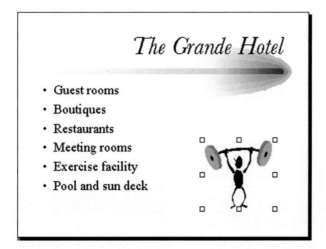

4   Position the pointer on the handle in the upper-left corner.

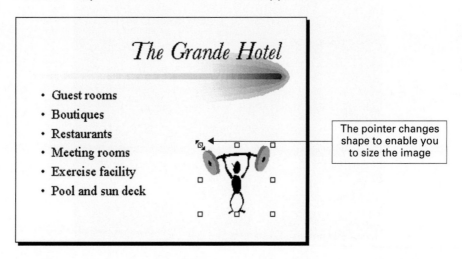

The pointer changes shape to enable you to size the image

5   Click and drag the corner handle to size the image.

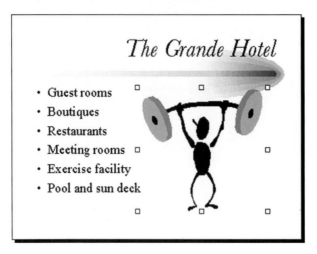

6   Save the changes to the presentation.

Downloading and Inserting Clip Art from the PowerPoint Web Site

When the Clip Gallery that comes with PowerPoint doesn't contain the pictures you need, you can search the PowerPoint Web site for additional graphics.

TASK 3: TO DOWNLOAD CLIP ART FROM THE POWERPOINT WEB SITE:

1   Log on to the Internet, using standard logon procedures, and launch the Web browser you normally use.

2   Display Slide 4 of the presentation *The Willows* in Slide view.

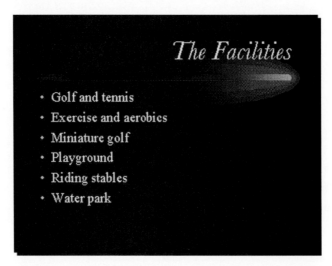

3   Choose Insert, Picture, Clip Art to open the Clip Gallery. The Clip Gallery window opens.

4   Click the globe icon representing a shortcut to the Web.

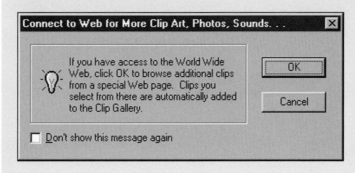

Note Depending on how your computer is set up, you may see the following message box. Simply click OK to acknowledge the message.

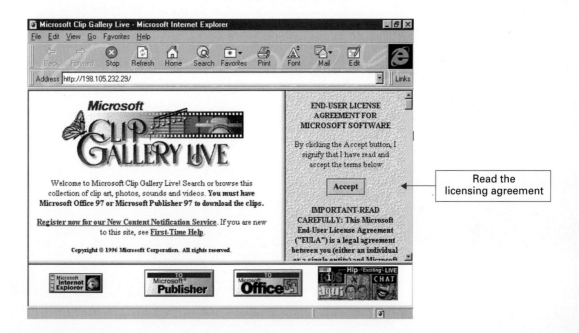

Read the licensing agreement

5 Read the license agreement and then click the Accept button.

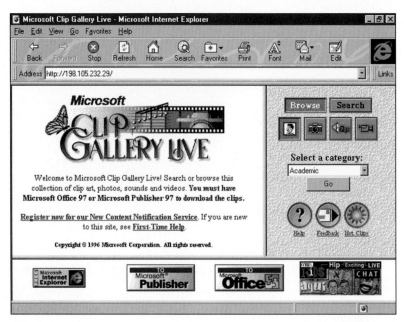

Note Because of the graphics, the Web page may be slow to load. The Web page you see may differ from the one pictured here. Microsoft changes Web pages regularly to reflect updates to software and to add new clips.

6 Click the arrow button beside the Select a category list box, select Animals, and click Go.

Total number of pictures found

Number displayed

Click the Search button to start the search

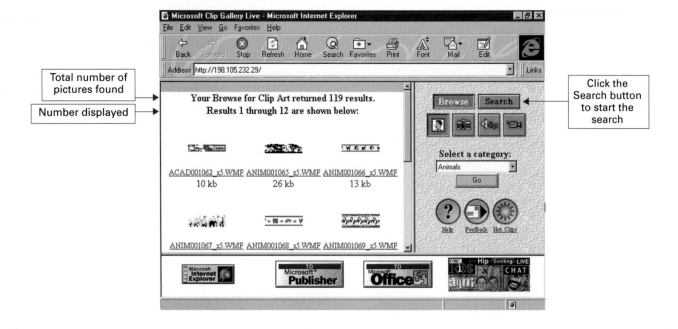

7   Click the Search button.

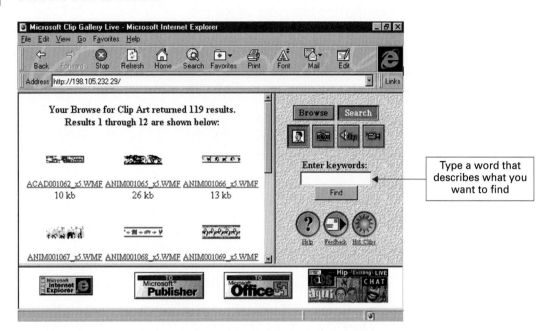

8   Type **Golf** in the Enter keywords text box and then click the Find button.

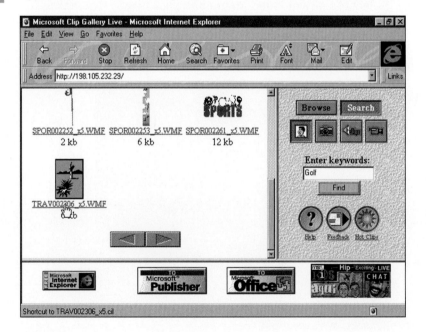

9 Scroll until you see the filename *TRAV002306_x5.wmf* and then click the filename to select the image.

Select an option to store the file →

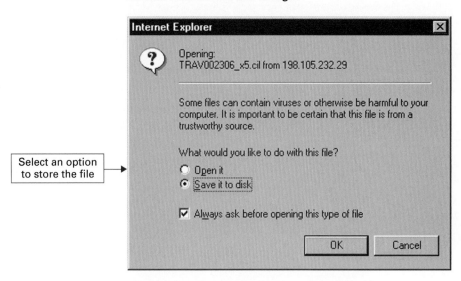

10 Click the Open it option and then click OK.
PowerPoint adds the image to the Downloaded Clips category of the Clip Gallery 3.0 window.

11 Select the downloaded image and click Insert.
PowerPoint places the image on the slide that was active when you launched the Web site.

12 Log off the Internet and display Slide 4 in PowerPoint Slide view.

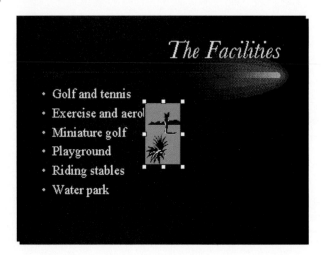

13 Size and position the graphic as shown and then save the changes to the presentation.

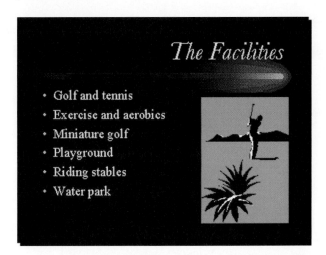

Creating WordArt

The *WordArt* module available in PowerPoint is the same module you may have used in other Microsoft applications. WordArt enables you to type text, curve, skew, or mold the text into a shape that better fits the area of the slide you want it to occupy. It's a great way to grab someone's attention.

TASK 4: TO CREATE WORDART:

1 Display Slide 6 in Slide view.

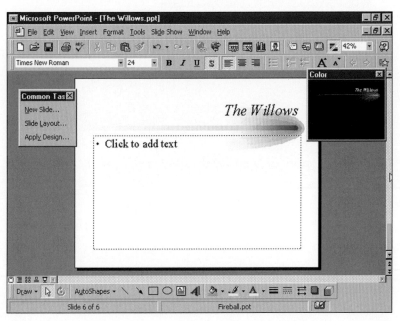

2 Press (SHIFT) and click the bulleted list placeholder; then press (DEL). The title placeholder is now the only object on the slide.

3 Choose Insert, Picture, WordArt.

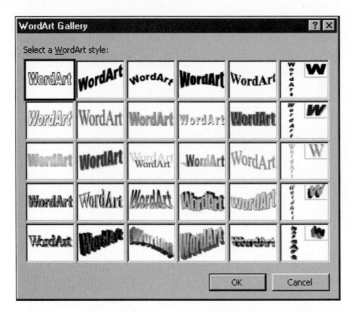

4 Select the fifth style in the top row and press (ENTER).

5 Type **A Symbol of Genteel Quality** and click OK.

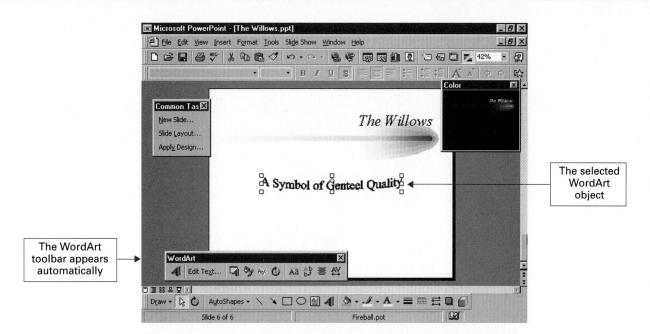

The WordArt toolbar appears automatically

The selected WordArt object

6   Drag the WordArt object to a position at the bottom of the slide.

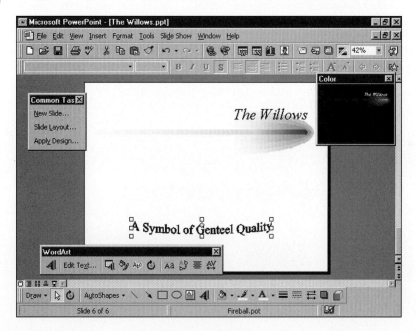

7   Save the changes to the presentation.

Formatting WordArt

After you get the WordArt object on the slide, you need to format the WordArt so that it appears the way you want it. You can use the WordArt toolbar to edit WordArt text as well as to change the shape, format, and angle of the WordArt object.

TASK 5: TO FORMAT WORDART OBJECTS:

1 Click the WordArt object on Slide 6, if necessary, to select it.
The WordArt object displays handles on the corners and sides.

2 Click the Format WordArt 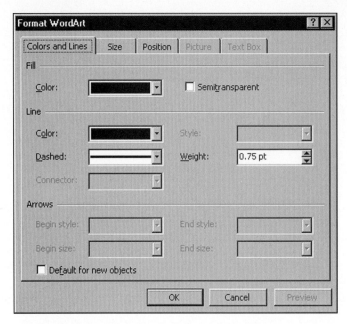 button on the WordArt toolbar.

3 Click the arrow button for the Fill Color option.

> **Note** The color you select from the Fill palette controls the color of the WordArt text.

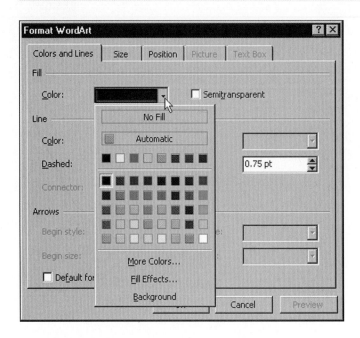

4 Click the second color box from the left on the bottom row of the color palette and then click the arrow button to open the Line Color option.

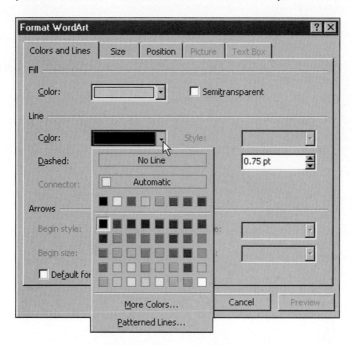

5 Click the second color box on the bottom row of the color palette and then click OK.

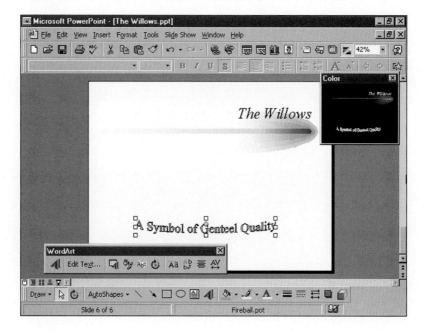

6 Click 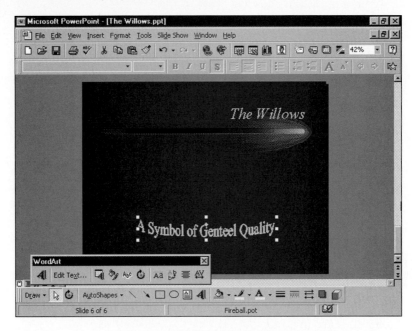 to display the slide in color.

7 Drag the top center handle of the WordArt object to expand the size of the object.

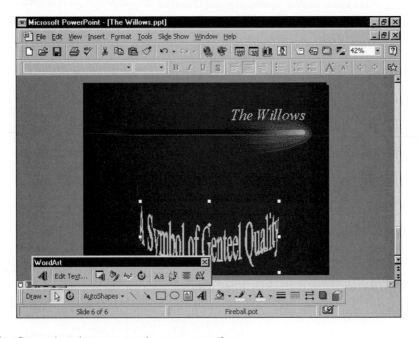

8 Save the changes to the presentation.

Creating Drawings

In addition to the special features such as WordArt, you'll also find quite a sophisticated drawing module that enables you to enhance your slides with original *freehand* creations. Even if you're no artist, you'll find the tools on the Drawing toolbar easy to use. Simply select the tool that represents the shape you want to draw, position the pointer where you want to start the drawing, click, and drag the pointer to the point where you want the shape to end.

TASK 6: TO CREATE DRAWINGS USING THE DRAWING TOOLBAR:

1   Display Slide 2 in Slide view.

> **Note** If you don't see the Drawing toolbar on your screen, position the pointer on any active toolbar, right-click, and then select the Drawing toolbar.

2   Click the AutoShapes button on the Drawing toolbar and select Stars and Banners.

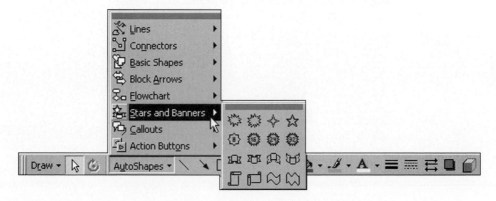

3   Click the 5-Point Star shape on the first row of the palette.
The mouse pointer changes shape and looks like a plus (+) sign.

4   Position the pointer below and to the left of the last bulleted item, click, and drag diagonally to draw the shape.

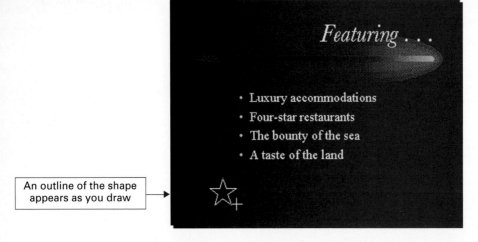

An outline of the shape
appears as you draw

5 Click the Arrow ⬉ button on the Drawing toolbar, press (SHIFT), and draw an arrow below the second bulleted item.

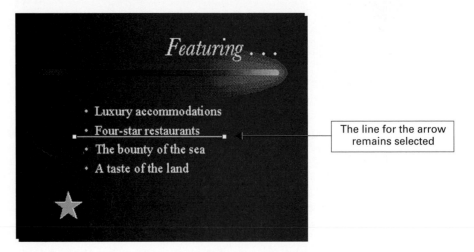

The line for the arrow
remains selected

6 Click the Arrow Style ⇄ button on the Drawing toolbar.

A ScreenTip will identify arrow
styles as you point to them

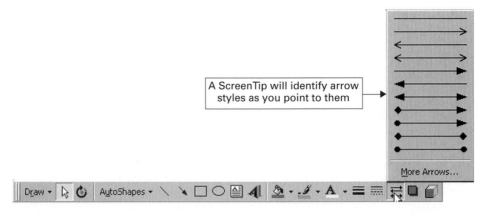

7 Select Arrow Style 10 and then double-click the line for the arrow you just drew.

8   Click the spin buttons beside the Line Weight text box to increase the weight to 2 pt, if necessary; then click OK.

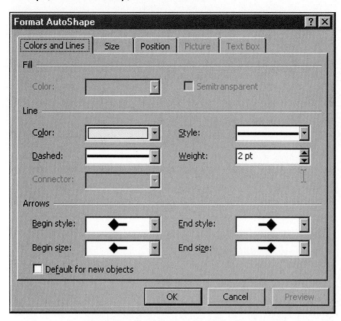

9   Click the star shape you drew earlier to select it and then click the Line Color arrow button.

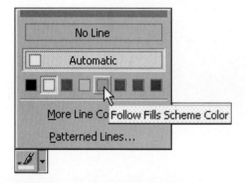

10   Click the Follow Fills Scheme Color box on the Line Color palette. Changing the line color for the star to the same color as the star fill color makes the shape a more cohesive unit by hiding the shape's outline.

11 Click the 3-D  button on the Drawing toolbar and select 3-D Style 6.

12 Press (CTRL)+**D** to duplicate the star.

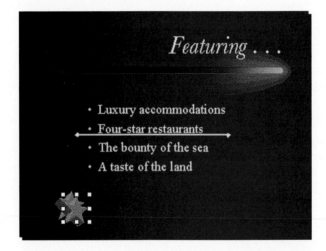

13 Drag the new star slightly up and to the right of the first star.

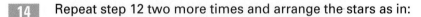

14 Repeat step 12 two more times and arrange the stars as in:

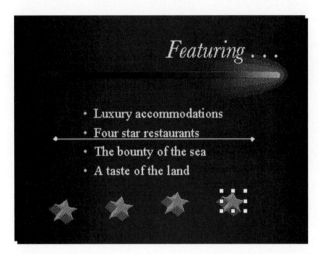

15 Save the changes to the presentation.

Manipulating Art

Clip art images that you add to slides and drawings that you create freehand often need to be adjusted so that they display appropriately on the slides. Using PowerPoint's special features, you can *flip* images to make them face the opposite direction, turn them upside down, *rotate* them to create special effects, *group* separate objects to make them stick together, and *ungroup* grouped objects to change pieces of the objects. You can also rearrange the objects so that different objects appear in front of or behind other objects.

TASK 7: TO MANIPULATE ART OBJECTS:

1 Display Slide 3 in Slide view.

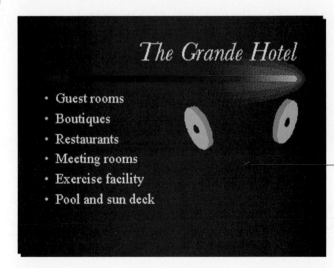

The clip art image you added is lost in the background color

2 Click the clip art image to select it and then click the Draw button on the Drawing toolbar.

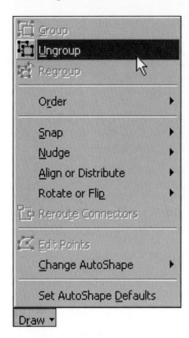

3 Click Ungroup.
A message box tells you that you are about to convert the image to a PowerPoint image. By converting the object, you can edit pieces of the object.

4 Choose Yes to convert the object to a PowerPoint image.

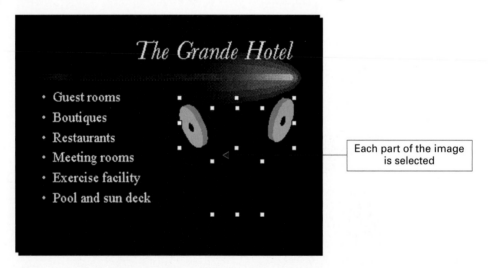

Each part of the image is selected

5 Press (SHIFT) and click the barbells to deselect them.
Only the body of the clip art image remains selected.

6 Click the Fill Color button arrow on the Drawing toolbar.

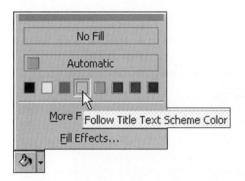

7   Click the Follow Title Text Scheme Color button on the Fill Color palette.

8   Click the barbells and ungroup the object.

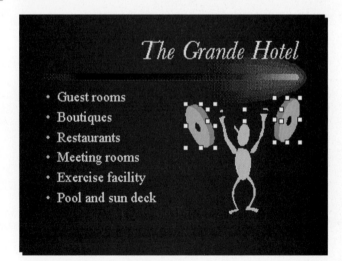

Tip If the selected object isn't made up of smaller objects, the Ungroup command on the Draw menu isn't available.

9   Press (SHIFT) and click each of the gray barbells, leaving only the bar selected.

10   Click the Fill Color button arrow 🖌▾ and click the dark gray color.

11 Click the body of the clip art image and then click the Draw button on the Drawing toolbar and select Rotate or Flip.

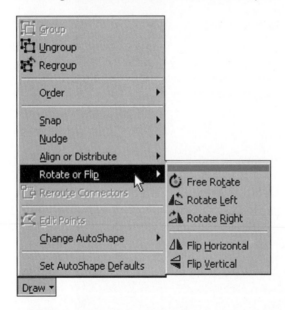

12 Click Flip Horizontal.

13 Position the pointer slightly above and to the left of the leftmost barbell; then click and drag across the clip art image.

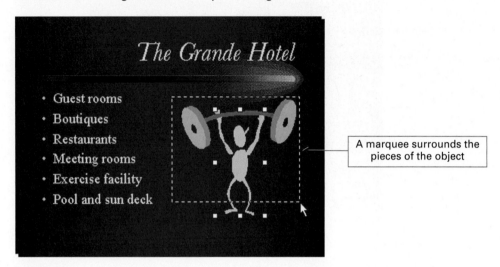

A marquee surrounds the pieces of the object

14 Release the mouse button when all pieces of the image are within the marquee.
All pieces of the original clip art image are selected.

15 Click the Draw button on the Drawing toolbar and select Group.
The image is one object again.

16 Display Slide 2, press (SHIFT), and click each of the star shapes.
All four stars are selected.

17 Click the Draw button on the Drawing toolbar and select Align or Distribute.

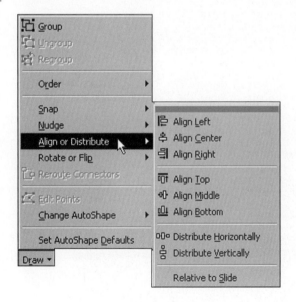

18 Select Align Top.

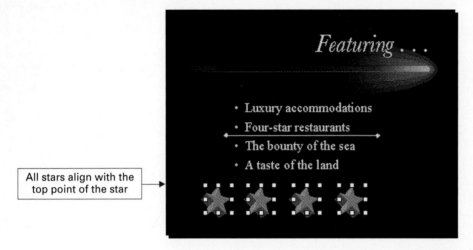

All stars align with the top point of the star

Tip If you want to position an image behind text on a slide, select the image and choose Draw, Order, and then select the Send to Back option from the cascading menu.

19 Click the Draw button on the Drawing toolbar, select Align or Distribute, and then select Distribute Vertically.
The stars are evenly spaced from each other.

20 Save the changes to the presentation.

The Conclusion

Before closing the presentation *The Willows*, print a copy of the presentation as black-and-white handouts with six framed slides per page. Then, if you've completed your work, close the presentation and exit PowerPoint. If you plan to continue with the Exercises and Assignments, close the presentation and leave PowerPoint running.

Summary and Exercises

Summary

- You can add clip art to any slide in Slide view; AutoLayout formats make accessing the Clip Gallery easy.
- WordArt lets you shape text to fit creatively on your slides. You can apply many of the techniques you use to format slide text to WordArt text.
- PowerPoint's Drawing toolbar provides tools for drawing and formatting shapes and adding special effects.
- Manipulating graphic images includes grouping, ungrouping, flipping, rotating, and aligning.

Key Terms and Operations

Key Terms	Operations
clip art	add, select, move, size, and delete presentation art
flip	create and manipulate WordArt
group	create drawings
rotate	group, ungroup, flip, and rotate art
ungroup	
WordArt	

Study Questions

Multiple Choice

1. PowerPoint comes with a number of images known as
   a. clip art.
   b. pictures.
   c. drawings.
   d. multimedia clips.

2. You can use any of the following techniques to add clip art images to your slide *except*
   a. choose an AutoLayout format that contains a clip art placeholder.
   b. choose File, Import.
   c. click the Insert Clip Art toolbar button.
   d. choose Insert, Picture, Clip Art.

3. To move a clip art image,
   a. delete the existing image, reposition the insertion point, and reinsert the image.
   b. select the image and drag a handle.
   c. select the image, position the pointer on the image away from a handle, and drag the image to a new location.
   d. outline the position you want the image to occupy and then double-click the image to make it move to the new position.

4. When you add clip art images to a document, what toolbar appears?
   a. The Formatting toolbar.
   b. The Drawing toolbar.
   c. The Insert Clip Art toolbar.
   d. The Picture toolbar.

5. To swirl title text on a slide, use PowerPoint's
   a. WordArt feature.
   b. Text Rotate command.
   c. Drawing toolbar.
   d. Clip Gallery.

6. You can edit clip art images to change the color of part of the image by first
   a. redrawing a shape on top of the part you want to change.
   b. ungrouping the image.
   c. changing the size of the image.
   d. editing the image, using Paint.

7. When you want to move two objects together and retain their current position relative to each other,
   a. delete one object, move the other, and then redraw the second object.
   b. ungroup the objects.
   c. group the objects.
   d. relayer the objects.

8. To select multiple drawn objects, WordArt, or clip art images,
   a. simply click each object.
   b. save the slide as a picture and then select the picture object.
   c. position all objects on top of each other and then outline the group of objects.
   d. press Shift and click each object.

9. When you want to display a drawn object in front of text, change the
   a. order of objects.
   b. alignment of objects.
   c. size of the objects.
   d. object grouping.

10. To size a drawn object, WordArt object, or clip art image,
    a. delete and then redraw the object.
    b. ungroup the object.
    c. select the object and then drag a handle.
    d. select the object, position the pointer in the middle of the object, and drag.

Short Answer

1. What Drawing toolbar button accesses a palette of shapes?

2. How do you copy a drawn object?

3. How do you make a clip art image face the other way?

4. How do you add WordArt to a slide?

5. How do you change the shape of a WordArt object?

6. Name the three basic ways to insert a clip art image.

7. In what shape does the pointer appear when you draw a freehand shape?

8. How does changing the order affect objects on a slide?

9. How do you change the border color and fill color of a drawn object?

10. What procedure do you use to group objects?

For Discussion
1. What additional formatting techniques can you use to enhance WordArt that are not available for formatting placeholder text?

2. How do the techniques for adding WordArt to slides differ from the techniques used to add text to placeholders?

3. How do you access additional clip art on the Internet?

4. Which of the art features presented in this project do you believe will benefit you the most?

Review Exercises

1. Adding, moving, and sizing clip art images
Ruth Lindsey, Manager of The Willows Shops, would like you to add clip art images to slides to enhance the presentation *The Willows Shops*. Suggested graphics are shown in Figure 3.2.

Figure 3.2

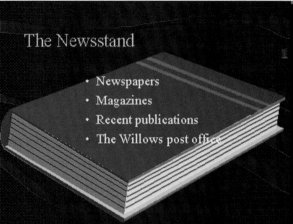

Figure 3.2 *(continued)*

If you do not have the images displayed, insert graphics of your choice or those chosen by your instructor. Use the techniques explored in this project to locate appropriate clip art to add to slides. Follow these instructions to complete the presentation:

1. Launch PowerPoint, if necessary, and open the presentation *The Willows Shops*.

2. Display the presentation in Slide view, display the slides pictured in Figure 3.2, and choose Insert, Picture, Clip Art to locate the image in the Clip Gallery.

3. Position and size the clip art images to appear as shown in Figure 3.2. Rotate and flip items as necessary to create the images displayed in the figure. Ungroup the object on Slide 3 and change the color of the character so it can be seen.

4. Save changes to the presentation and print a copy of the six slides containing clip art.

5. Close the presentation and exit PowerPoint when you've completed your work.

2. Adding WordArt and drawings to slides

Ms. Lindsey would also like to change the titles of the three slides pictured in Figure 3.3 from the presentation *The Willows Shops* to WordArt.

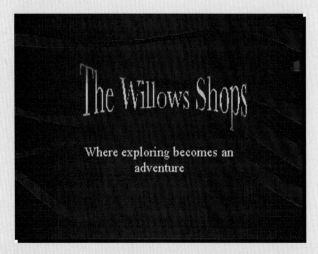

Figure 3.3

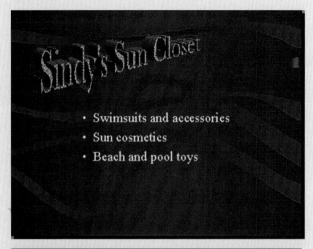

Figure 3.3   *(continued)*

Follow these steps to complete the task.

1. Launch PowerPoint, if necessary, and open the presentation *The Willows Shops*.

2. Display Slide 1 in Slide view, delete the title placeholder, add the title text as a WordArt object, and format the WordArt so that it appears as shown in Figure 3.3.

3. Repeat step 2 for Slides 2 and 4.

4. Display Slide 4 and create and format the drawn object shown in Figure 3.3, using a shadowed rectangle and a shaded four-pointed AutoShape star. Edit the colors to show gradient fill effects.

5. Save the changes to the presentation and print copies of the three slides containing WordArt titles as black-and-white handouts with three slides per page.

6. Close the presentation and exit PowerPoint when you've completed your work.

3. Adding clip art to slides in a presentation

1. Launch PowerPoint and open *2 Computers in Society xxx.ppt* (where *xxx* represents your initials).

Note If you do not have a document named *2 Computers in Society xxx.ppt*, ask your instructor for a copy of the file you should use to complete this exercise.

2. Add clip art to Slides 2, 4, and 6; flip, size, and position the art as displayed in Figure 3.4.

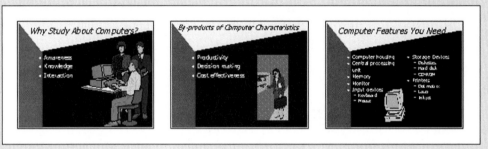

Figure 3.4

Note If you do not find the graphics displayed here, substitute appropriate graphics contained in your Clip Art Gallery for those shown.

3. Delete the title placeholder on Slide 1 and replace it with the same text formatted as WordArt, as shown in Figure 3.5.

Figure 3.5

4. Save the presentation using the filename *3 Computers in Society xxx* and print a copy of the presentation as black and white handouts with six slides per page.

Assignments

1. Adding, formatting, and manipulating clip art, WordArt, and drawings
The slides from the *Festivals and Attractions* presentation enhanced with sample graphics appear in Figure 3.6.

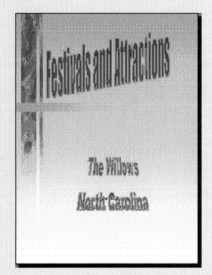

Figure 3.6

Use tools presented in this project to add clip art images, WordArt objects, and drawings of your choice to your presentation slides. Edit the clip art images by ungrouping them and changing the colors. Size and position the graphics as shown in Figure 3.6. Save changes to the presentation and print black-and-white handouts with three slides per page. Close the presentation and exit PowerPoint when you've completed your work.

2. Searching the Internet for pictures to enhance presentations
Check with your instructor on how and where to download the Willow graphic. If you have access to the Internet, click the Globe button on the Clip Gallery window to search the Internet Clip Gallery for images you can use in your résumé presentation. Otherwise, search the Clip Art Gallery that is provided in the program.

Add drawings to presentation slides, delete the slide title text (leave the title placeholder—it will not show on a slide show or print and the title placeholders are required in the next activity) and insert WordArt, formatted to create special effects. Save changes to the presentation and print a copy of your presentation as black-and-white handouts with three slides per page.

Close the presentation and exit PowerPoint when you've completed your work.

Viewing and Editing a Presentation

Most of the presentations you create are designed to provide powerful visuals to enhance oral presentations. Slides in a presentation can be formatted and shown on-screen by individuals or projected on an audiovisual screen or flat surface as you present a report to an audience.

Showing your presentations with style has a positive impact on your audience. The PowerPoint slide show feature enables you to show your presentation on a computer screen. Seeing your presentation "live" the first time can be quite satisfying—and exciting. In this project, you learn how to dress up your presentation for on-screen viewing and how to use Slide Sorter view to rearrange slides in the presentation.

Objectives

After completing this project, you will be able to:

➤ **Present a slide show**

➤ **Use the slide show shortcut menu**

➤ **Rearrange slides in a presentation**

➤ **Add slide transitions**

➤ **Animate text**

➤ **Expand slides**

➤ **Hide slides and display hidden slides**

The Challenge

Francesca Savoy has reviewed the presentation *The Willows* and has approved the design, graphics, and format of slides in the presentation. She now asks that the presentation be tweaked into its final form so that she can present it to the managers at their next meeting.

The Solution

To get the presentation *The Willows* into shape, you need to view the presentation as a slide show and then use Slide Sorter view to make final edits to the presentation. Figure 4.1 shows the final presentation in Slide Sorter view.

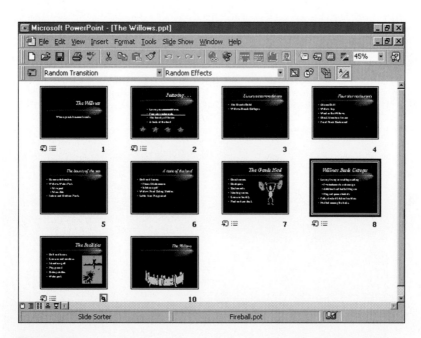

Figure 4.1

The Setup

You're switching to a different view for many of the activities in this section, and you're also going to be using the slide show feature in Power-Point. As a result, you need to select some different settings to ensure that your screen will match the illustrations shown in this project.

When you switch to Slide Sorter view, make sure that the Standard and Slide Sorter toolbars display (As shown in Task 3, Step 1 of this project). If you don't see them, choose View, Toolbars, and then select them. Close the Common Tasks toolbar if it's open.

You'll also need to work with your presentation window maximized in Slide Sorter view. Click the Maximize button on the presentation window, if necessary. Then set the Zoom control to 66%.

Presenting a Slide Show

Viewing your presentation as a slide show makes it come to life. Slide shows display slides in the presentation window without the PowerPoint toolbars, title bar, and status bar. During a slide show, each slide literally fills the screen and you can focus on slide contents to determine impact. PowerPoint offers a number of ways to launch a slide show:

- Choose View, Slide Show
- Choose Slide Show, View Show
- Click the Slide Show 🖵 button at the bottom of the presentation window

TASK 1: TO VIEW A PRESENTATION AS A SLIDE SHOW:

1 Open the presentation *The Willows* and display the first slide in Slide view. Slide 1 of the presentation appears as last shown in Project 3.

2 Click the Slide Show 🖵 button at the bottom of the presentation window.

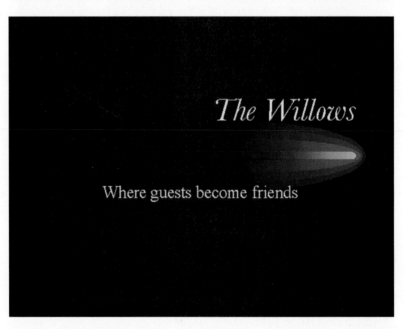

You can use both the keyboard and mouse to navigate the slides in a presentation during a slide show. Table 4.1 compares the actions for using both techniques. Practice each technique to identify the ones you like best.

Note The slide show starts with the slide displayed in Slide or Notes Pages view or the slide selected in Slide Sorter or Outline view.

Table 4.1   Mouse and Keyboard Techniques for Navigating Slides in a Slide Show

Movement	Mouse Action	Keyboard Action(s)
Advance to the next slide	Click the left mouse button	Press **N**, (ENTER), (SPACE), (PGDN), (↓), or (→)
Return to the previous slide	Right-click and choose Previous	Press **P**, (BACKSPACE), (PGUP), (←), or (↑)
Specific slide number		Type the slide number; then press (ENTER). For example, type **5** to go to slide 5 and then press (ENTER).
Stop the slide show	Right-click and choose End Show	Press (ESC)

Using the Slide Show Shortcut Menu

The *slide show shortcut menu* displays commands for accessing navigation features as well as for controlling on-screen features such as the mouse pointer and slide meter. To display the slide show shortcut menu, click the right mouse button during the slide show or press (SHIFT)+(F10).

TASK 2: TO USE THE SLIDE SHOW SHORTCUT MENU:

1   Click 🖵 to start the slide show, if necessary.
The slide that was active in Slide view appears in full-screen view.

2   Right-click anywhere on the screen.

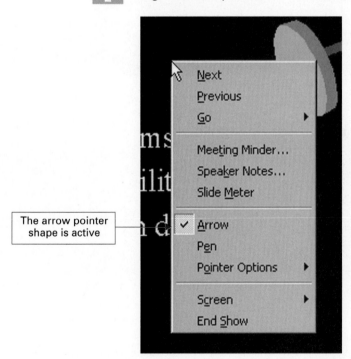

The arrow pointer shape is active

Tip You can also access the slide show shortcut menu by moving the mouse pointer on-screen until a shortcut menu button displays in the lower-left corner of the slide; then click the shortcut menu button.

3 Choose Screen, Black Screen.
The entire screen becomes black so that the audience focuses on you, the speaker, rather than on the same slide for an extended period of time.

> **Tip** You could also display a black screen while you draw or annotate.

4 Click the left mouse button to redisplay the slide.
The slide redisplays.

5 Right-click again, and then choose End Show.
The slide displayed when you chose End Show appears in Slide view.

Rearranging Slides in a Presentation

After viewing the presentation as a slide show, you may find that you need to rearrange slides so that the flow is smoother or to match changes in the oral presentation. Slide Sorter view displays miniature images (these are called *thumbnail* images, remember?) of presentation slides that you can drag to new positions. Slide Sorter view prevents slide editing; as a result, you must return to Slide view to edit slide text and graphics.

TASK 3: TO REARRANGE SLIDES USING SLIDE SORTER VIEW:

1 Click the Slide Sorter View 🔳 button at the bottom of the presentation window.

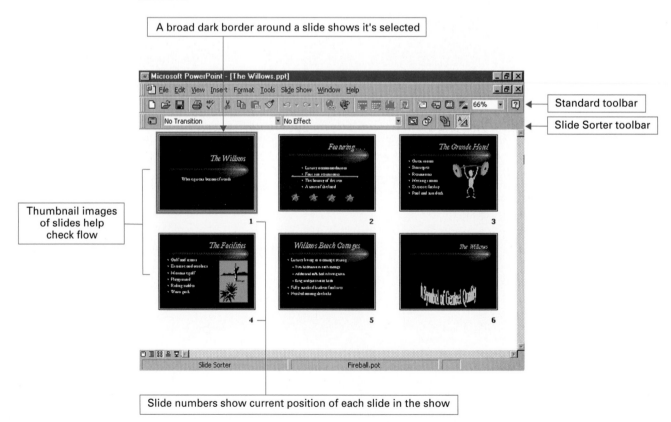

2 Click Slide 5 to select it, and then drag it to the left of Slide 4.

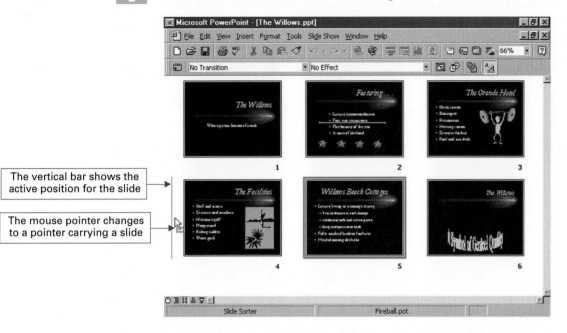

The vertical bar shows the active position for the slide

The mouse pointer changes to a pointer carrying a slide

3 Drop Slide 5 when the vertical bar appears as shown in step 2.

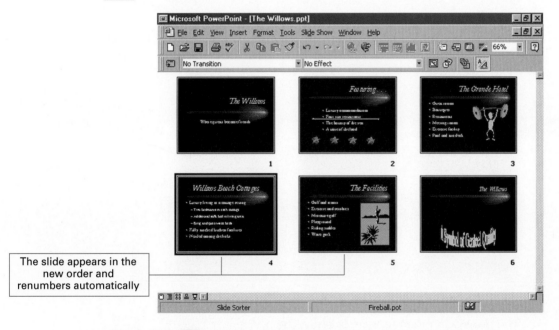

The slide appears in the new order and renumbers automatically

4 Click 🖫 to save changes to the presentation, and leave it open.

Adding Slide Transitions

Slide *transitions* create special effects as your slides go on and off the screen during a slide show. You can use the Slide Sorter toolbar to add transitions to your slides.

TASK 4: TO ADD SLIDE TRANSITIONS:

1 Display the presentation *The Willows* in Slide Sorter view, if necessary.

2 Click Slide 1 to select it and then click the arrow button beside the Slide Transition Effects list box on the Slide Sorter toolbar.

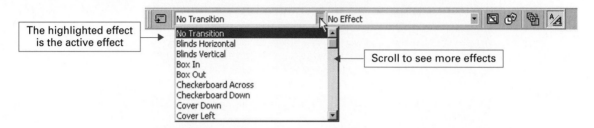

The highlighted effect is the active effect

Scroll to see more effects

3 Scroll down the effects list, if necessary, click *Dissolve,* and watch Slide 1 closely to view the effect.

The text on Slide 1 sprinkles on-screen

The selected effect appears in the toolbar

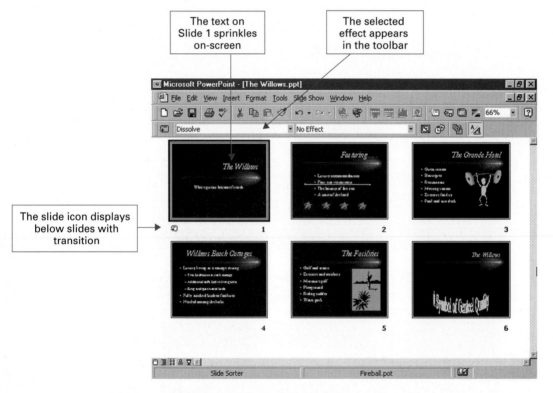

The slide icon displays below slides with transition

4 Click the slide icon below Slide 1.
The transition effect repeats to show the effect.

5 Click to select Slide 2, and then press (SHIFT) and click Slides 3, 4, and 5.
The four selected slides appear with broad dark borders.

6 Click the Slide Transition Effect arrow button, scroll down the list, and select Random Transition from the bottom of the transition effects list.
An icon appears below each selected slide.

7 Click the transition slide icon below each slide and view the transition effect.
The effect changes each time you click the icon below a slide when you use Random transition.

8 Click 🖫.

Animating Text

When you apply *text preset animations* (formerly known as *builds*) to slides, each slide title displays on-screen by itself and each bulleted list item is presented separately during a slide show. Text preset animations help focus the attention of your audience on each individual bulleted item as you discuss it and removes the distractions of presenting all bulleted points at once. Text that appears in text placeholders is affected when you apply the text preset animation effects.

TASK 5: TO ANIMATE SLIDE TEXT:

1   Click Slide 1 in Slide Sorter view.
Slide 1 is selected.

2   Click the arrow button for the Text Preset Animation list box in the Slide Sorter toolbar.

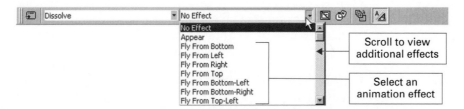

3   Scroll down the list, if necessary, and select Crawl From Right.

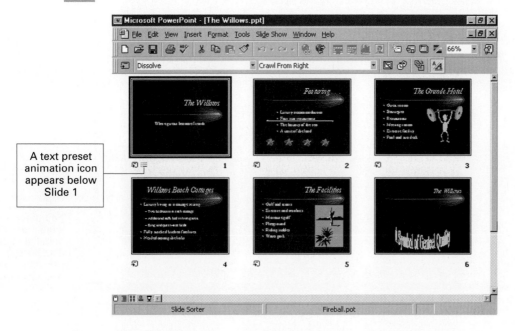

4   Select Slide 2 and select Peek From Left from the Text Preset Animations list.

5   Add text preset animations of your choice to Slides 3, 4, and 5.
Text preset animation icons appear below each slide.

6 Select Slide 1 and then click 🖳 to view the special effects applied to each slide.
Use navigation techniques to review all slides and end the slide show.

7 Click 🖫 when the slide show finishes.

Expanding Slides

When a bulleted list slide contains points that you need to expand (or expound upon), you can use the PowerPoint *expand* feature to create new slides. When you expand a slide, each bulleted list item appears as the title of a new slide. Slides you expand are often referred to as *parent slides* and new slides created from the parent slide are called *children*. When you expand a slide, the children appear in bulleted list order immediately following the parent slide.

> **Note** To expand bulleted lists, a title placeholder must appear on the slide. Slides that contain WordArt for titles will not expand if the placeholder is deleted. Empty placeholders do not print and do not appear during a slide show.

TASK 6: TO EXPAND BULLETED LISTS:

1 Select Slide 2 in Slide Sorter view.
Slide 2 appears with a broad dark border.

2 Choose Tools, Expand Slide.

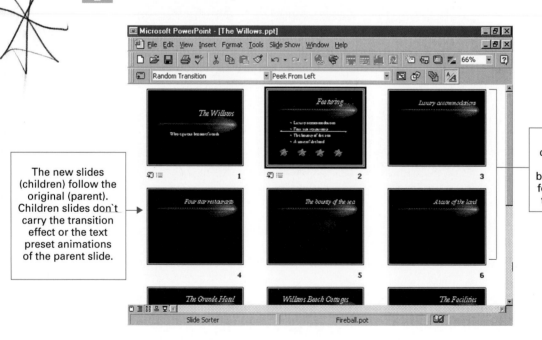

The new slides (children) follow the original (parent). Children slides don`t carry the transition effect or the text preset animations of the parent slide.

Four new slides contain titles that parallel Slide 2 bullet points. Titles follow the original template format.

3   Click ▤ to switch to Outline view.

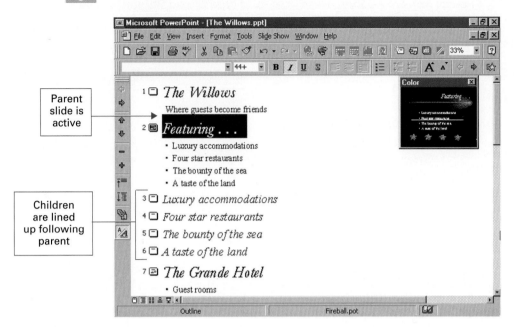

4   Position the I-beam after the word "accommodations" in Slide 3, press (ENTER) and then (TAB), and type additional text, as in:

3 ▢ Luxury accommodations
- The Grande Hotel
- Willows Beach Cottages

5 Position the I-beam after the last word in the slide titles for Slides 4, 5, and 6, press ⒠ENTER⒡, and then press ⒠TAB⒡ and type the additional text shown here as bulleted lists:

4 ▢ *Four-star restaurants*
 - Atrium Grill
 - Willow Top
 - Wind in the Willows
 - Black Mountain Tavern
 - Front Porch Restaurant

5 ▢ *The bounty of the sea*
 - Ocean beaches
 - Willows Water Park
   – Wave pool
   – Water slide
 - Indoor and outdoor pools

6 ▢ *A taste of the land*
 - Golf and tennis
   – Three 18-hole courses
   – Miniature golf
 - Willow Pond Riding Stables
 - Little Tree Playground

6 Click ⊞ to return to Slide Sorter view, click the Zoom box on the Standard toolbar, type **45**, and press ⒠ENTER⒡.

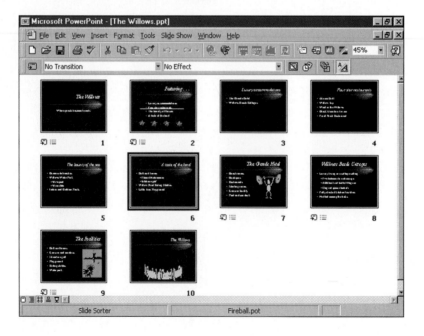

Hiding Slides and Displaying Hidden Slides

Hiding slides enables you to include slides containing detailed information or data in your presentation but display the slides during a slide show only when the audience asks questions or when you need more details about a topic. Hidden slides remain in the background during a slide show and show only when you access them.

TASK 7: TO HIDE SLIDES AND DISPLAY THEM DURING A SLIDE SHOW:

1   Select Slide 9 in Slide Sorter view.
Slide 9 appears with a broad dark border.

2   Click the Hide Slide ▧ button on the Slide Sorter toolbar.

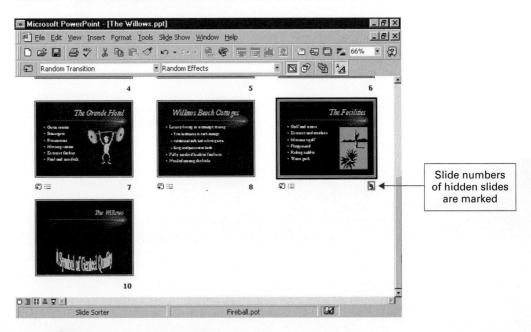

Slide numbers of hidden slides are marked

3   Select Slide 8 and then click ▆.
Slide 8 displays in the slide show window.

4   Click the left mouse button until the next slide displays.
Slide 10 now displays after Slide 8 during the slide show unless you call up Slide 9.

5   Press (ESC) to stop the slide show, select Slide 8, if necessary, and then click ▆ to start the show again.
Slide 8 displays in the slide show window.

6   Press **H** to display the hidden Slide 9.
Slide 9 title and graphic display immediately.

7   Press (ESC) to stop the slide show, select Slide 8, if necessary, and then click ▆ again.
Slide 8 displays in the slide show window.

8   Right-click on the screen and choose Go.

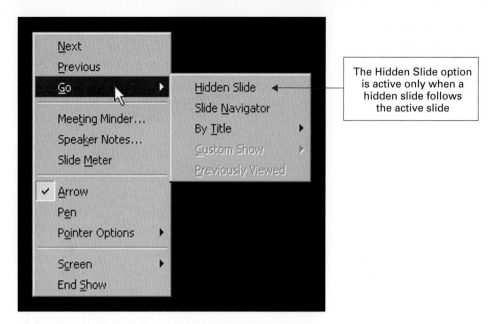

The Hidden Slide option is active only when a hidden slide follows the active slide

9 Choose Hidden Slide.
The Slide 9 title and graphic display immediately.

10 Press (ESC) to stop the slide show and then click 💾.
PowerPoint saves changes to the presentation.

The Conclusion

Before closing the presentation *The Willows*, print a copy of the presentation in Outline view. Then, if you've completed your work, close the presentation and exit PowerPoint. If you plan to continue with the Exercises and Assignments, close the presentation and leave PowerPoint running.

Summary and Exercises

Summary

- The PowerPoint slide show feature enables you to show your presentation on-screen.
- Slide shows display slides in the presentation window without the PowerPoint toolbars, title bar, and status bar.
- The easiest way to start a slide show is to click the Slide Show button at the bottom of the presentation window.
- You can use both mouse and keyboard techniques to navigate slides during a slide show.
- You can display the slide show shortcut menu during a slide show by clicking the right mouse button. The slide show shortcut menu displays commands for controlling on-screen features.
- You can also access the slide show shortcut menu by moving the mouse pointer on-screen until a shortcut menu button displays and then clicking the shortcut menu button.
- Slide Sorter view is the most efficient view to use when you need to rearrange slides or apply transitions and special effects.
- Slide transitions affect the way slides move on and off the screen during a slide show.
- Text preset animations present text on slides one bullet point at a time during a slide show. You can also set an animation to dim previously presented bullet points to enable the audience to focus on the point being discussed.
- You can use the expand slide feature to create new slides that use the bulleted list text from a parent slide. Each bulleted list item appears as the title of a new slide.
- Hiding slides enables you to include slides with supplemental information in the presentation and display the slides only when you need them.

Key Terms and Operations

Key Terms
expand
hidden slides
slide show
slide show shortcut menu
Slide Sorter view
text preset animation
transition

Operations
add transitions to slides
animate slide text using text preset animations
display different slides in a presentation
end a slide show
expand and hide slides
rearrange slides in a presentation using Slide Sorter view
start a slide show

Study Questions

Multiple Choice
1. To start a slide show,
   a. click a button on the Standard toolbar.
   b. press Enter after the last slide is completed.
   c. use the slide show shortcut menu.
   d. click the Slide Show button at the bottom of the presentation window.

2. Showing slides as a slide show displays slides
   a. all on-screen together.
   b. in Print Preview mode.
   c. one at a time, using the full screen.
   d. one at a time, as in Slide view.

3. The view that makes it easy to rearrange slides is
   a. Print Preview.
   b. Slide Sorter view.
   c. Outline view.
   d. Slide view.

4. To move a slide in Slide Sorter view,
   a. select the slide and drag it to a new location.
   b. press Delete and then press Insert.
   c. press (CTRL)+(INS).
   d. press (CTRL)+D.

5. As you move a slide in Slide Sorter view, what identifies the active location of the slide?
   a. The mouse pointer
   b. The slide outline
   c. The ruler scale
   d. A vertical bar

6. To create special effects as slides move onto the screen,
   a. use the slide show shortcut menu.
   b. press the left mouse button.
   c. add a transition.
   d. press Page Down.

7. To advance to the next slide during a slide show, use any of the following techniques *except*
   a. click the left mouse button.
   b. press E.
   c. press Page Down.
   d. press N.

8. To leave a slide in a presentation but display it only when it's needed,
   a. hide the slide.
   b. build the slide text.
   c. skip the slide.
   d. branch out to the slide.

9. One way to move to a specific slide during a slide show is to
   a. press Home and the slide number.
   b. press (CTRL) and the slide number.
   c. press (ESC).
   d. type the slide number and press Enter.

10. To stop a presentation,
   a. press (ENTER).
   b. press (CTRL)+S.
   c. press (ESC).
   d. press (HOME).

Short Answer

1. Which view enables you to select a transition from a special toolbar?

2. In what shape does the pointer appear when you move a slide in Slide Sorter view?

3. What feature do you apply to slide text so that bullet items appear one at a time?

4. When you drag and drop a slide in Slide Sorter view, how do you know where the slide will appear?

5. On what menu does the Expand Slide feature appear?

6. Name the three basic ways to launch a slide show.

7. To what view in other applications might you compare viewing slides as a slide show?

8. What's the difference between a transition and text preset animation?

9. How do you display the slide show shortcut menu?

10. What view displays the presentation when the show ends?

For Discussion

1. What design concerns should you consider when applying transitions?

2. Why do you add hidden slides to a presentation?

3. What's the advantage of applying text preset animations to slides?

4. How can you control which slide appears first during a slide show?

Review Exercises

1. Rearranging, hiding, and expanding slides and showing a presentation
The presentation *The Willows* is almost ready for Ms. Savoy to show to the managers, but it needs a bit more editing. The final presentation outline appears in Figure 4.2. Follow these steps to complete the presentation:

1. Launch PowerPoint, if necessary, and open the presentation *The Willows*.

2. Display the presentation in Slide Sorter view and move Slide 7 so that it becomes Slide 4. Then move Slide 8 so that it becomes Slide 5.

3. Select Slide 6; then click the New Slide button on the Standard toolbar and choose the Bulleted List AutoLayout. Double-click the plain new slide to display it in Slide view so that you can add slide text.

4. Type **Sandwich Shops** in the title placeholder and then add the following bulleted list to the bulleted list placeholder:
   - Willow Green on the golf course
   - The Cola Shop on the Mezzanine
   - Grey Fox Deli at The Grande Hotel
   - The 18th Hole on the golf course
   - Red Rocker at the pool
   - The Boardwalk on the beach

5. Display Slide Sorter view again, hide Slide 7, and expand Slide 9.

1 *The Willows*
Where guests become friends

2 *Featuring . . .*
- Luxury accommodations
- Four-star restaurants
- The bounty of the sea
- A taste of the land

3 *Luxury accommodations*
- The Grande Hotel
- Willows Beach Cottages

4 *The Grande Hotel*
- Guest rooms
- Boutiques
- Restaurants
- Meeting rooms
- Exercise facility
- Pool and sun deck

5 *Willows Beach Cottages*
- Luxury living in a cottage setting
  - Two bedrooms in each cottage
  - Additional sofa bed in the living area
  - King and queen size beds
- Fully stocked kitchen facilities
- Nestled among the links

6 *Four-star restaurants*
- Atrium Grill
- Willow Top
- Wind in the Willows
- Black Mountain Tavern
- Front Porch Restaurant

7 *Sandwich Shops*
- Willow Green on the golf course
- The Cola Shop on the Mezzanine
- Grey Fox Deli at The Grande Hotel
- The 18th Hole on the golf course
- Red Rocker at the pool
- The Boardwalk on the beach

8 *The bounty of the sea*
- Ocean beaches
- Willows Water Park
  - Wave pool
  - Water slide
- Indoor and outdoor pools

9 *A taste of the land*
- Golf and tennis
  - Three 18-hole courses
  - Miniature golf
- Willow Pond Riding Stables
- Little Tree Playground

10 *Golf and tennis*
- Three 18-hole courses
- Miniature golf

11 *Willow Pond Riding Stables*
- 15 Gentle rides
- Ponies for the young and young-at-heart
- One-, two-, and three-hour bridle paths
- Bike rentals

12 *Little Tree Playground*
- State-of-the-art equipment
- Sand for a soft landing
- Play counselors on-site from dawn to dusk

13 *The Facilities*
- Golf and tennis
- Exercise and aerobics
- Miniature golf
- Playground
- Riding stables
- Water park

14 *The Willows*

Figure 4.2

6. Switch to Outline view and add the text for new Slides 11 and 12 as shown in Figure 4.2.

7. View the slide show and then display the presentation in Slide Sorter view to add transitions and text preset animations you find most effective to each slide.

8. Save the changes to the presentation and print a copy of the presentation outline. Demonstrate the slide show for your instructor.

2. Editing, enhancing, and viewing a presentation as a slide show
Ms. Lindsey would also like to fine-tune the presentation *The Willows Shops* so that she can include it in her presentation to the managers. Figure 4.3 displays the finished presentation in Slide Sorter view.

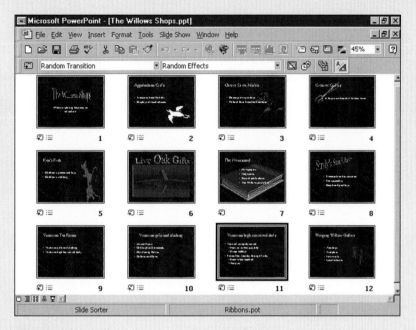

Figure 4.3

Follow these steps to complete the task:

1. Launch PowerPoint, if necessary, and open the presentation *The Willows Shops*.

2. Display Slide Sorter view and rearrange the bulleted list slides into alphabetical order by titles as follows:
   - Slide 9 becomes Slide 2
   - Slide 7 becomes Slide 3
   - Slide 7 (new) becomes Slide 4
   - Slide 9 becomes Slide 5
   - Slide 8 becomes Slide 6
   - Slide 10 becomes Slide 7
   - Slide 10 (new) becomes Slide 9

3. Expand Slide 9. Display the new Slide 10 in Slide view and add the following text to the bulleted list placeholder:
   - Ancient Lace
   - Old English Ornaments
   - Christening Gowns
   - Buttons and Bows

4. Display Slide 11 and add the following bulleted list items:
   - Tea and crumpets
     - 9:00 a.m. to 4:00 p.m. daily
     - Except holidays
   - Formal tea Monday through Friday
     - Reservations required
     - 4:00 p.m.

5. Show the presentation as a slide show and then display Slide Sorter view. Add transitions and text preset animations to the bulleted list slides and show the presentation again.

6. Make any necessary adjustments to the presentation and then save the changes to the presentation.

7. Show the presentation to your instructor and print copies of presentation slides as handouts with six framed pure black-and-white slides per page.

8. Close the presentation and exit PowerPoint when you've completed your work.

3. More editing, enhancing, and viewing a presentation as a slide show

1. Launch PowerPoint and open the presentation *3 Computers in Society xxx.ppt*.

> **Note** If you do not have a document named *3 Computers in Society xxx.ppt*, ask your instructor for a copy of the file you should use to complete this exercise.

2. Show the presentation as a Slide Show.

3. Display the presentation in Slide Sorter view and apply transitions to each slide.

4. In Slide Sorter view, move Slide 6 so that it appears after Slide 2.

5. Animate the slide text for Slides 2–6.

6. Expand the bullet text for Slides 4 and 5 to create six new slides.

7. Hide the new slides.

8. Save changes to the presentation using the filename *4 Computers in Society xxx*.

9. Print a copy of the presentation as black and white handouts with six slides per page.

10. Print a copy of the presentation outline.

11. Show the presentation to your instructor, if requested.

Assignments

1. Editing and enhancing a presentation and viewing a slide show
The slides from the *Festivals and Attractions* presentation appear in Figure 4.4.
Use the tools presented in this project to expand slides, rearrange slides, and add text to slides. Add slide transitions and text preset animations to slides in the presentation. After expanding slides, delete title placeholders on slides where WordArt is displayed. Then view the presentation as a slide show and save changes to the presentation. Present the slide show to your instructor and print pure black-and-white handouts with six framed slides per page. Close the presentation and exit PowerPoint when you've completed your work.

2. Editing and enhancing a presentation and posting it to the WWW
(Optional Assignment. Ask your instructor how to proceed.)
Edit and enhance your résumé presentation and then follow one or both of the following options, as directed by your instructor:

● Post the presentation to the Web site identified by your instructor.

● Choose File, Send To, Exchange Folder to file the presentation in Outlook. Select Microsoft Outlook from the Profile Name list and save the presentation in the Journal folder of the Personal Folders drawer or create a new personal folder with your name as the folder name (according to your instructor's directions) and store the presentation in your personal folder. Then launch Outlook, if available, and verify that the presentation name appears on the list of files in the Journal folder or in your personal folder.

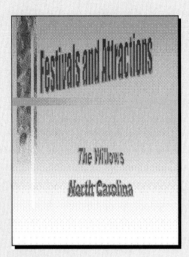

Festivals

- Stray Fox Arts and Crafts Festival
- Grove Park Folk Festival
- Willow Park Light Festival

Stray Fox Arts and Crafts Festival

- In the Spring when the blush is on the roses
- Costumes for an "Old World" fox hunt encouraged
- Treasures crafted for those who appreciate "Old World" charm
- Antiques and Hunt objects featured

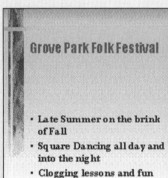

Grove Park Folk Festival

- Late Summer on the brink of Fall
- Square Dancing all day and into the night
- Clogging lessons and fun
- Outdoor cooking in the folk tradition

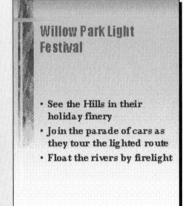

Willow Park Light Festival

- See the Hills in their holiday finery
- Join the parade of cars as they tour the lighted route
- Float the rivers by firelight

Attractions

- Sheer Madness Night
- Little Pitchers Beach Week

Sheer Madness Night

- Visit a world gone mad
- Costumes and masks required
- Kiss the pumpkin for a special treat
- Hang around the eaves with the bats

Little Pitchers Beach Week

- Midsummer fun for the young and the young-at-heart
- Activities focus on children 12 years old and under
- Teen dance Friday night

Figure 4.4

Enhancing a Presentation

Okay! You've created a fantastic presentation, edited it, and dressed it up so that you can deliver it with style, and you're ready to take the presentation on the road. A few more features are buried within PowerPoint that will help you set up your presentation to run in different environments. In this project, you learn how to fine-tune your presentations and create materials to use as you show the presentation.

Objectives

After completing this project, you will be able to:

➤ **Animate slides with sound**

➤ **Set action buttons**

➤ **Add slide timings**

➤ **Set a presentation to run continuously**

➤ **Create notes pages**

➤ **Pack a presentation to go**

The Challenge

Francesca Savoy impressed the managers when she made her presentation last week. Now the Board of Directors of The Willows wants the presentation to be set up at strategic locations throughout the resort so that guests and visitors can stop and view it. In addition, the Board has authorized Ms. Savoy, as Marketing Director, to market the resort to large organizations interested in locating resort settings for conventions. She comes to you for help.

The Solution

To get the presentation for The Willows ready for viewing throughout the resort, you need to set the presentation to run automatically. To draw the attention of guests and visitors to the presentation, you need to add some sound to your text animation. Because Ms. Savoy will be traveling with the presentation, you need to package the presentation to take on the road and develop a set of notes pages for her to use as she shows the presentation. A sample notes page appears in Figure 5.1.

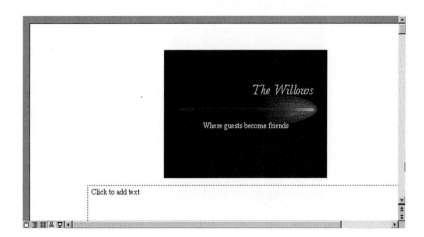

Figure 5.1

The Setup

Most of the default settings you've been using throughout this part of the book should be active as you complete the activities in this project. You'll be using Notes Pages view for part of the project, and the toolbars for Notes Pages view are the same toolbars you see in Slide view. Display the Standard, Formatting, and Drawing toolbars and close the Common Tasks toolbar so that what you see on your computer screen will match the illustrations shown here.

You'll also need to work with your presentation window maximized in Slide and Notes Pages views. Click the Maximize button on the presentation window, if necessary.

Animating Slides with Sound

In Project 4, you animated the slide text using text preset animations. The Animation Effects toolbar contains buttons that you can use to add sound to the animated text automatically or to customize the animation effect and select a sound. When you choose to add *custom animation,* you'll use the Custom Animation dialog box. The Custom Animation dialog box displays options that also enable you to dim bullet points for animated text as new bullet points display.

TASK 1: TO ANIMATE SLIDES WITH SOUND:

1 Open the presentation *The Willows* and display Slide 1 in Slide view. Slide 1 displays as last edited.

2 Click the Animation Effects ⭐ button on the Formatting toolbar.

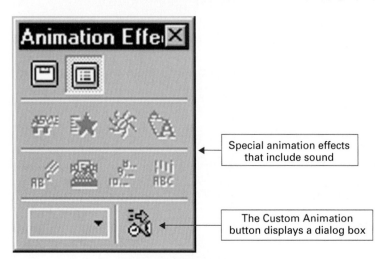

Special animation effects that include sound

The Custom Animation button displays a dialog box

3 Click the Custom Animation 🐎 button.

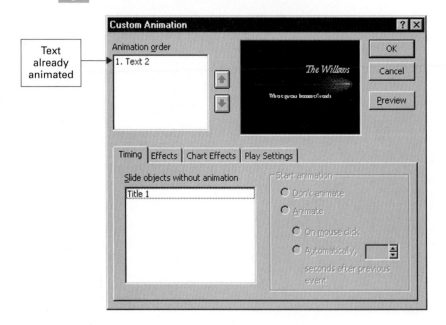

Text already animated

4 Click the Effects tab and then click "1. Text 2" in the Animation order list box.

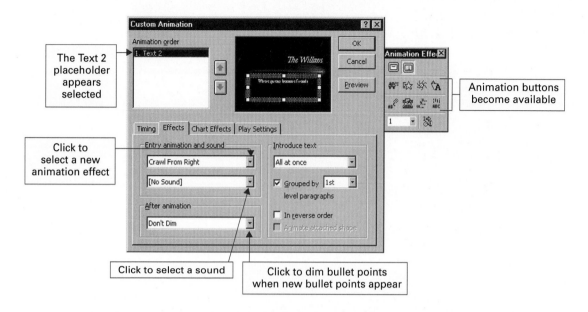

The Text 2 placeholder appears selected

Animation buttons become available

Click to select a new animation effect

Click to select a sound

Click to dim bullet points when new bullet points appear

5 Click the arrow button for the sound option and point to Whoosh.

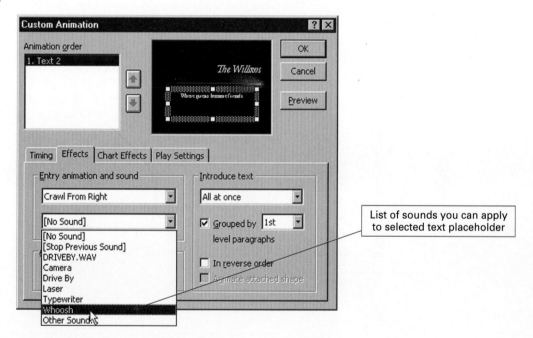

List of sounds you can apply to selected text placeholder

6 Click Whoosh to apply the sound to the animated text.
Whoosh appears in the text box.

7 Click OK to return to Slide 1 and then click the Slide Show View 🖳 button to show the slide.
Slide 1 displays in full-screen view.

8 Press (ENTER) to display the animated text and hear the sound; then press (ESC) to return to Slide view.
Slide 1 displays in Slide view.

9 Display Slide 2, select the bulleted list placeholder, and click the Typewriter Text Effect button on the Animation Effects toolbar.

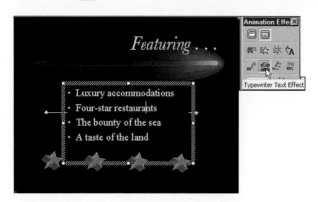

10 Click to open the Custom Animation dialog box.

Text 2 is automatically selected

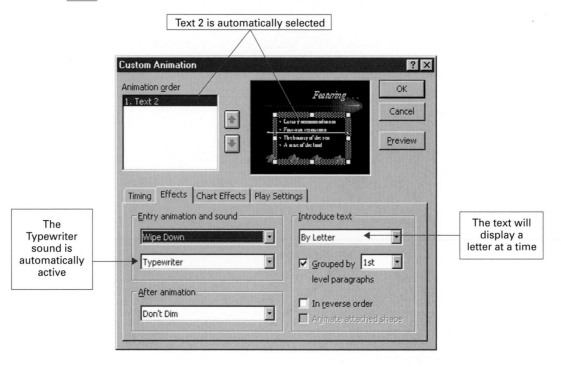

The Typewriter sound is automatically active

The text will display a letter at a time

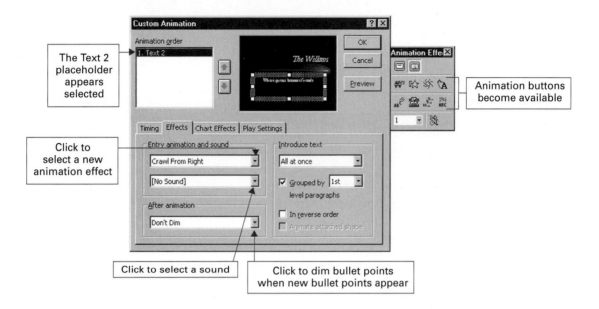

The Text 2 placeholder appears selected

Click to select a new animation effect

Click to select a sound

Click to dim bullet points when new bullet points appear

Animation buttons become available

5 Click the arrow button for the sound option and point to Whoosh.

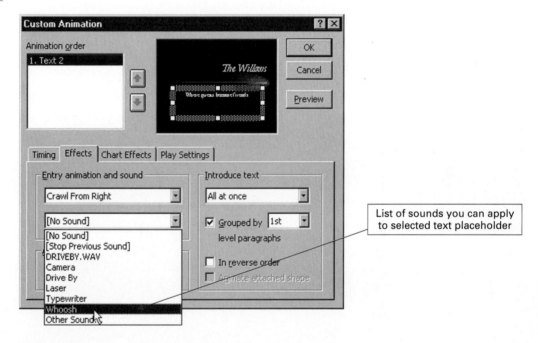

List of sounds you can apply to selected text placeholder

6 Click Whoosh to apply the sound to the animated text.
Whoosh appears in the text box.

7 Click OK to return to Slide 1 and then click the Slide Show View 🖵 button to show the slide.
Slide 1 displays in full-screen view.

8 Press (ENTER) to display the animated text and hear the sound; then press (ESC) to return to Slide view.
Slide 1 displays in Slide view.

9 Display Slide 2, select the bulleted list placeholder, and click the Typewriter Text Effect ▦ button on the Animation Effects toolbar.

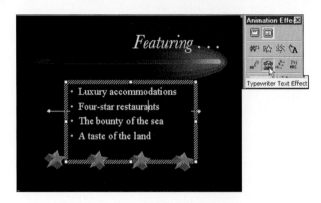

10 Click ▦ to open the Custom Animation dialog box.

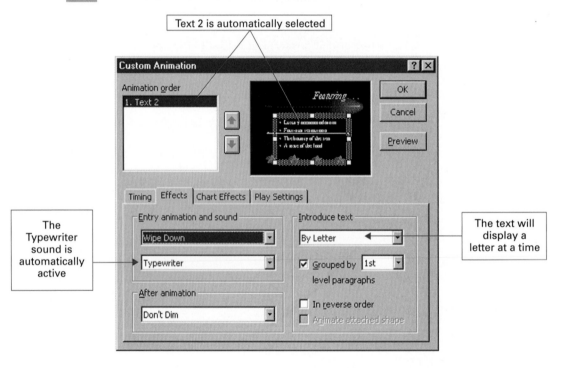

11   Click the arrow button beside the After animation option.

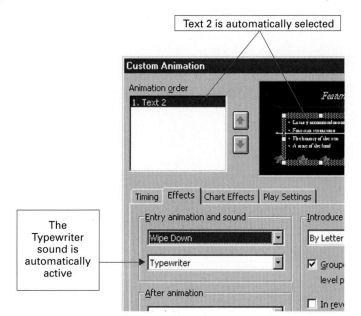

Text 2 is automatically selected

The Typewriter sound is automatically active

12   Click Hide on Next Mouse Click and then click OK to return to the slide.
Slide 2 appears in Slide view.

13   Show the slide to view the effects, press (ESC), and then save the changes to the presentation.
The text displays one character at a time and you can hear the sound of a typewriter as each character appears. Each bullet point disappears when the next bullet point displays.

Setting Action Buttons

Action buttons enable you to control the slide PowerPoint displays when you click the button during a slide show. For the presentation *The Willows,* you can add an action button to display a hidden slide that follows Slide 8. PowerPoint creates a *hyperlink* to the slide so that clicking the action button automatically displays the desired slide.

> **Tip** You can also add action buttons to enable users to choose the section of a presentation they want to view or to display documents from other applications. Explore these advanced features as you become more comfortable with PowerPoint.

TASK 2: TO CREATE AND SET AN ACTION BUTTON:

1 Display Slide 6 of the presentation *The Willows* in Slide view.

2 Choose Slide Show, Action Buttons.

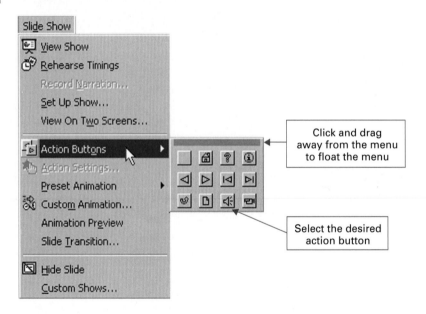

3 Click the Action Button: Forward or Next ▷ button.
The pointer changes to a plus (+).

4 Position the pointer in the lower-right corner of the slide, click, and draw a small square shape.

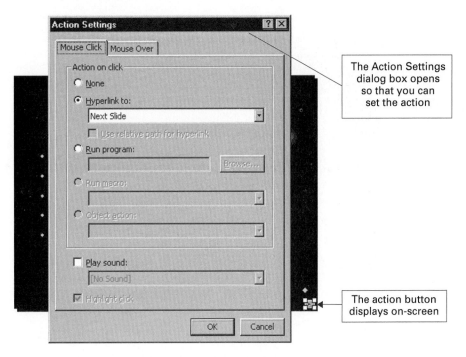

The Action Settings dialog box opens so that you can set the action

The action button displays on-screen

5 Click the arrow button beside the Hyperlink to option and select Slide.

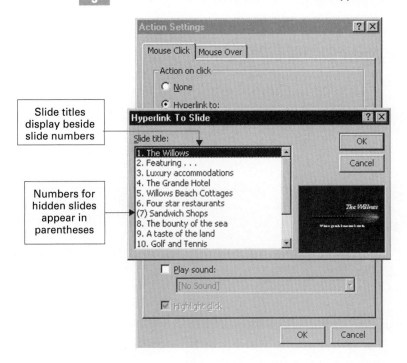

Slide titles display beside slide numbers

Numbers for hidden slides appear in parentheses

6 Select (7) Sandwich Shops and then click OK.
The slide title appears in the Hyperlink to text box.

7 Press (ENTER) to close the Action Settings dialog box and then click 🖳 to show the slide.

8 Point to the action button and click to display the hidden slide. Slide 7 displays immediately.

When you point to the action button during a show, the pointer changes to a pointing hand

9 Press (ESC) to stop the show, save the changes to the presentation, and close the Animation Effects toolbar.

Adding Slide Timings

Before you set the presentation to run automatically, you need to add slide timings so that each slide displays for a set amount of time before advancing to the next slide. After you add timings, slides move on and off the screen automatically. Of course, viewers can advance slides manually, even when timings are present.

TASK 3: TO ADD SLIDE TIMINGS:

1 Display the presentation *The Willows* in Slide Sorter view. Thumbnail images appear in Slide Sorter view.

2 Select Slide 1 and then click the Slide Transition 🖾 button on the Slide Sorter toolbar.

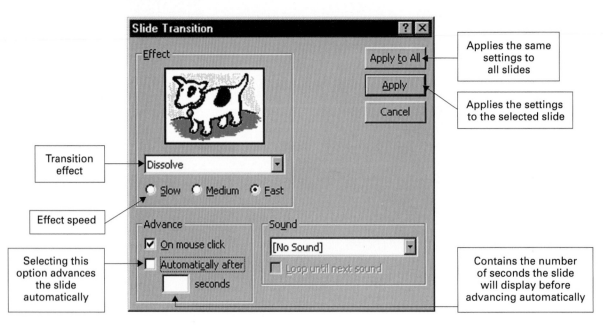

3 Click the check box beside Automatically after, type **25** in the seconds value box, and click Apply.

The slide timing appears below the slide

4 Apply the slide timings shown here to all the slides in the presentation.

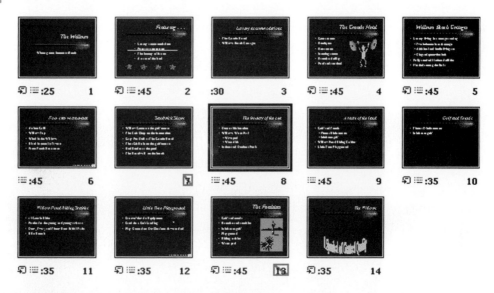

> **Note** If slide text is formatted with a text preset animation, Power-Point distributes the timing you set among the bulleted list items on the slide. As a result, a four-point bulleted list set to display for 60 seconds would display each bulleted item for 15 seconds before displaying the next bullet point.

5 Save the first few changes to the presentation and then show the presentation, letting the slides advance automatically.

Setting a Presentation to Run Continuously

You may have seen computer monitors set up in stores or at conferences or trade shows that displayed information automatically and gave you an opportunity to review the information. Now that you have the presentation set up to run automatically with timings, you can set it to start over after the last slide displays, so that it runs continuously—or *loops* back to the first slide in a never-ending circle.

TASK 4: TO SET UP A PRESENTATION TO RUN CONTINUOUSLY:

1 Choose Slide Show, Set Up Show.

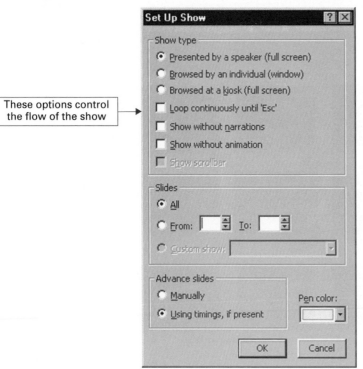

These options control the flow of the show

2 Click the Loop continuously until 'Esc' option and click OK.

> **Tip** Selecting the Browsed at a kiosk (full screen) option in the Set Up Show dialog box restricts slide advancement to timings only; manual clicking won't advance slides. Selecting Loop continuously until 'Esc' lets you advance slides manually as well as automatically.

3 Save the changes to the presentation and show the presentation, letting some slides advance automatically and advancing some slides manually.

4 Press (ESC) to stop the presentation, display Slide 6 in Slide view, and then click the Text Box 📰 button on the Drawing toolbar.

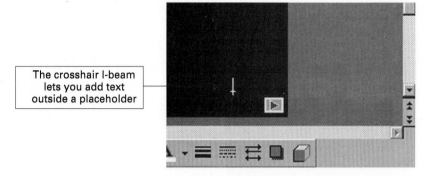

The crosshair I-beam lets you add text outside a placeholder

5 Position the I-beam to the left of the action button, click, and type **Click to see facilities summary.**
The text may appear shadowed and too large for the slide area.

6 Select the text in the text box, click the Shadow ⬛ button on the Formatting toolbar to turn off shadowing, select 14 from the Font Size list box, and position the text box if necessary.

7 Click 🖳 to view the slide and click the action button to display Slide 7.

8 Press (ESC) to stop the presentation and then save the changes to the presentation.

Creating Notes Pages

Your presentation is ready to be set up at strategic locations throughout the resort and is almost ready to take on the road. All Ms. Savoy needs now is a set of notes to take with her so she doesn't forget important points she wants to make during the presentation. The PowerPoint Notes Pages view enables you to add notes to the bottom of a page that contains an image of the slide at the top.

TASK 5: TO CREATE NOTES PAGES:

1 Display Slide 1 in Slide view and then click the Notes Pages View 🖳 button at the bottom of the presentation window.
A small image of Slide 1 appears on-screen with a Notes placeholder at the bottom. The zoom percentage makes reading difficult.

2 Change the Zoom control setting to 75%.

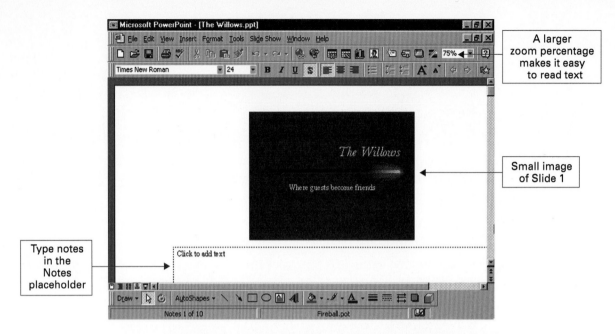

A larger zoom percentage makes it easy to read text

Small image of Slide 1

Type notes in the Notes placeholder

3 Point to the Notes placeholder, click, and type **Introduce myself and explain the purpose of the presentation. Ask audience what facilities they require for their conference.**
The text appears in the notes placeholder below the slide image.

4 Press (PGDN) to display Slide 2, click the Notes placeholder, and type **Review basic features of The Willows.**
The notes appear in the Notes placeholder of Slide 2.

5 Add the following text as notes to the following slides:

Slide 3: **Emphasize that The Grande Hotel has more than 400 rooms to accommodate large gatherings and that the cottages offer more private settings. Review specific features of The Grande Hotel and the cottages as next two slides appear.**

Slide 6: **Cite accolades of recent publications about the quality of our restaurants. Emphasize that there are less formal eateries available as well. Mention catering for special dinners. A hidden slide follows this slide and lists sandwich shops in case someone asks about them.**

Slide 8: **Ask audience what types of activities they like to explore.**

Slide 9: **Compare on-shore activities to the water sports. Stress the "something for everyone" aspect of the resort to show that families will have plenty to do while businesspeople attend meetings.**

Slide 14: **Summarize The Willows features and ask for questions.**

6 Choose File, Print.
The Print dialog box displays.

7 Select Notes Pages from the Print what drop-down list, select the Pure black & white option, click the Slides option, type **1–3,6,8,9,14** in the Slides text box, and press (ENTER).
The notes pages for the selected slides print.

Packing a Presentation to Go

Everything is set—and, as usual, just in the nick of time! Ms. Savoy is about to take off on her first marketing trip and needs the presentation on a disk to take with her. You're in luck—PowerPoint has a Pack and Go Wizard that can have her on the road in just a few minutes with disk in hand. Graphics, templates, and animation effects increase the size of presentations and make them difficult to copy to a disk. When you pack a presentation using the Pack and Go Wizard, however, PowerPoint *compresses* the presentation, making it more compact and easier to fit on one disk.

TASK 6: TO PACK A PRESENTATION TO GO:

1 Choose File, Pack and Go.

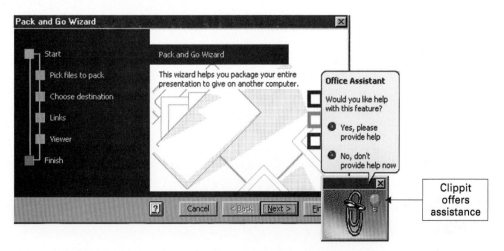

2 Click No, don't provide help now to close the Office Assistant; then click Next.

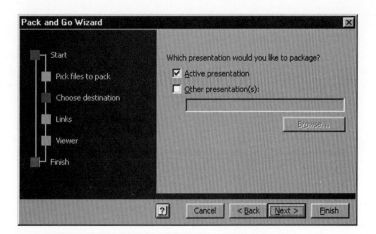

3 Ensure that Active presentation is selected and click Next.

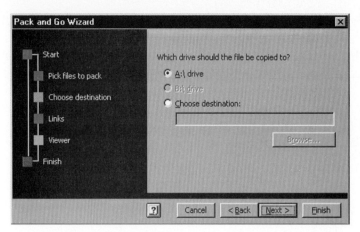

4 Ensure that the floppy drive for your computer is active, place a disk in the floppy drive, and click Next.

Note The disk you use should contain no other files, otherwise your presentation might not fit.

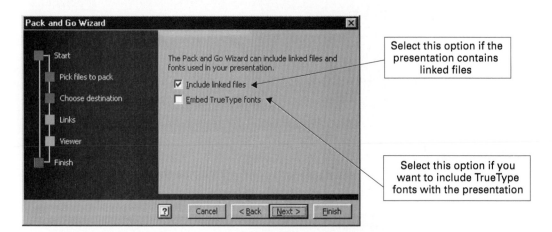

Select this option if the presentation contains linked files

Select this option if you want to include TrueType fonts with the presentation

5 For this exercise, deselect the Include linked files option because your presentation doesn't contain links, and select Embed TrueType fonts to ensure that your presentation displays properly; then click Next.

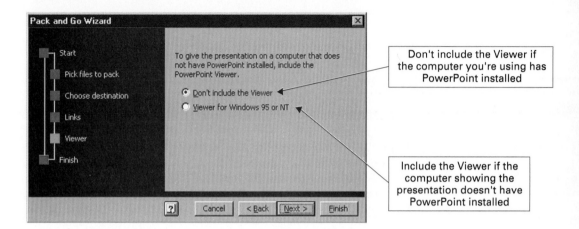

Don't include the Viewer if the computer you're using has PowerPoint installed

Include the Viewer if the computer showing the presentation doesn't have PowerPoint installed

Note If the PowerPoint Viewer isn't installed on your computer, you'll need the original PowerPoint CD to access the Viewer so that the Pack and Go Wizard can find it and pack it with the presentation(s).

6 For this example, click Don't include the Viewer and then click Next.

7 Click Finish.
PowerPoint whirs and burps a bit as it packages the presentation on the disk. When the presentation is packaged, a message window tells you that Pack and Go has successfully packed your presentation. If your presentation is too large to fit on one disk, you'll be told when to insert another disk.

8 Click OK to acknowledge the message.
Your presentation is ready to turn in to your instructor.

The Conclusion

Now that you have the presentation on disk, you can show it from any computer that has PowerPoint installed. Simply launch PowerPoint and open the presentation. If you've completed your work, close the presentation for The Willows and exit PowerPoint. If you plan to continue with the Review Exercises and Assignments, close the presentation and leave PowerPoint running.

Summary and Exercises

Summary

- PowerPoint comes equipped with animation effects that can contain sounds. You can apply these effects to slide text by using the Animation Effects toolbar.
- You can use action buttons to control the slides presented and to jump to different parts of a presentation.
- To prepare a presentation to run automatically, add slide timings to each slide to tell PowerPoint how long to leave the slide on the screen. When slide text is animated, each bullet point or animated object gets an equal share of the time allotted to the slide.
- To show a presentation at a trade show or in a location where no one is available to monitor the presentation, you can set the presentation to run continuously until someone stops the show.
- Create notes pages to type reminder notes to use during a show. Notes Pages view presents pages with slide images at the top and a notes placeholder at the bottom of the page for you to use.
- The Pack and Go Wizard prepares presentations for showing at another location. You can include a PowerPoint Viewer with the presentation if necessary.

Key Terms and Operations

Key Terms	Operations
action button	add sound to slide text animations
compress	add timings to slides so that they automatically advance
custom animation	create notes pages to accompany a presentation
dim effect	pack up a presentation using the Pack and Go Wizard
hyperlink	set action buttons to control the flow of the presentation
loop	set a presentation to run continuously
Pack and Go Wizard	
timings	
Viewer	

Study Questions

Multiple Choice

1. To jump to a different slide than the one that normally follows the active slide,
   a. create a mini-program that runs the link.
   b. add a text box to a slide.
   c. add a graphic to the slide.
   d. add an action button to the slide.

2. To select a sound for a text preset animation,
   a. record the sound using a microphone.
   b. create an action button.
   c. customize the animation.
   d. add a graphic to the slide.

3. To create a set of notes to use during a slide show, display
   a. Slide Sorter view.
   b. Notes Pages view.
   c. Outline view.
   d. Slide view.

4. You can set up a presentation to advance slides automatically by setting
   a. slide timings.
   b. a hyperlink.
   c. a loop.
   d. an action button.

5. A hyperlink attached to an action button is called
   a. an animation effect.
   b. the slide outline.
   c. slide timings.
   d. a loop.

6. When you want to set up a presentation to run without constant monitoring, set up the presentation
   a. as a slide show.
   b. with timings only.
   c. to run continuously, using a loop.
   d. to advance manually.

7. Notes Pages view displays
   a. a notes placeholder only.
   b. a notes placeholder and a slide image.
   c. a slide image only.
   d. three slides on each page.

8. To prepare a presentation to show on another computer,
   a. use the Pack and Go Wizard.
   b. copy the slide to a disk.
   c. use the Send to command.
   d. branch out to the slide.

9. Slide timings
   a. must all be set exactly the same.
   b. don't work during a regular presentation.
   c. don't let you advance slides manually.
   d. can be different for each slide.

10. When you want to disable the manual advance for a presentation,
    a. simply set slide timings.
    b. set the presentation to loop continuously.
    c. set the presentation to run at a kiosk.
    d. You can't disable the manual advance for a presentation.

Short Answer

1. How can you quickly access the Animation Effects toolbar?

2. How does the slide number for hidden slides appear in a list of slide titles?

3. What page of the Custom Animation dialog box displays sounds and animation effects?

4. What tool do you use to add text to a slide outside a text placeholder?

5. How does the Pack and Go Wizard fit a large presentation onto one floppy disk?

6. To help focus the attention of your audience on the bullet point you're discussing during a slide show, what should you do to other bullet points already presented?

7. What view makes it easy to add slide timings?

8. Where do slide timings appear on-screen?

9. How do you stop a show set to run continuously?

10. What can you change to make the text in Notes Pages view easier to read?

For Discussion

1. What does the dim feature do?

2. What advantage does applying timings to slides in a presentation provide when the time you have for a presentation is limited?

3. Where have you seen presentations set up to run unmonitored?

4. How does attaching an action button help keep track of hidden slides?

Review Exercises

1. Adding sound effects to animated text, setting action buttons to display hidden slides, adding text to a slide

The presentation *The Willows* includes numerous slides that contain animated text and a hidden slide that you need to format an action button to access. Follow these steps to complete the presentation:

1. Launch PowerPoint, if necessary, open the presentation *The Willows* in Slide view, and display the Animation Effects toolbar.

2. Display Slides 3 through 14 individually and apply an animated sound to the text preset animations already applied to the slides. Select different options to dim bullet points.

3. Display Slide 12 and add an action button to hyperlink to hidden Slide 13.

4. Display Slide 6, press (SHIFT), select the text box next to the action button, and copy the text box to the Windows Clipboard. Then display Slide 12 again and paste the text box onto the slide. Adjust the size and placement of the text box as needed.

5. Show the slide show to view your changes, and make final adjustments to the presentation.

6. Save changes to the presentation and print a copy of Slide 12 in pure black-and-white. Close the presentation.

2. Adding action buttons, animating with sound, adding slide timings, setting a presentation to run continuously, creating notes pages

Ms. Lindsey was so impressed with your work on the presentation for The Willows that she would like you to develop the presentation for The Willows Shops using the same techniques, and add a list of notes to notes pages in the presentation. A sample notes page appears in Figure 5.2.

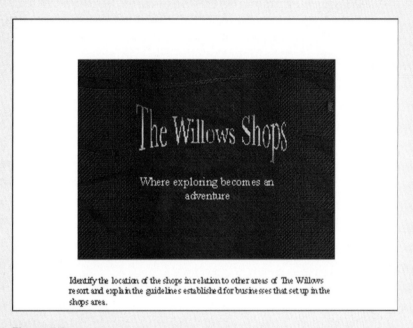

Figure 5.2

Follow these steps to format each slide in the presentation with a sound animation effect, dim bulleted list points, add timings to the all slides in the presentation, and create notes pages for the presentation.

1. Launch PowerPoint, if necessary, and open the presentation *The Willows Shops*.

2. Display Slide Sorter view and review the presentation settings. Then switch to Slide view and display the Animation Effects toolbar.

3. Display each slide in the presentation individually and apply a custom animation effect to the text already formatted with a preset animation. Apply a dim option to bulleted list text.

4. View the slide show and assess the effects. Then return to slide view and make any adjustments to slides in the presentation.

5. Display the presentation in Slide Sorter view and apply slide timings to each slide. Hide Slide 6.

6. Switch back to Slide view and add an action button to Slide 5 to access the hidden slide. Double-click the action button and change the fill and line color to make the action button blend in with the slide background.

7. View the presentation again and make certain that the action button displays the correct slide.

8. Display Notes Pages view and add the following notes to the slides:

Slide 1: **Identify the location of the shops in relation to other areas of The Willows resort and explain the guidelines established for businesses that set up in the shops area.**

Slide 2: **A series of slides about different shops starts with this slide and extends through Slide 12.**
Emphasize that the wares displayed in this craft shop are original creations of people living in the Appalachian Mountains.

Slide 3: **Stress that produce is brought to market daily.**

Slide 5: **Mention that sizes for children range from newborn to about age 12.**

Slide 7: **Mention daily delivery of all major newspapers from across the country, delivered on time, and available for room delivery.**

Slide 11: **Review operating hours and explain that special arrangements can be made for organizations holding meetings at the resort.**

9. Set the presentation to loop continuously, using the Set Up Show dialog box, and then save changes to the presentation.

10. Print a copy of all notes pages containing notes, close the presentation, and exit PowerPoint when you've completed your work.

3. More adding action buttons, animating with sound, and adding slide timings

1. Launch PowerPoint and open the presentation *4 Computers in Society xxx.ppt*.

> **Note** If you do not have a document named *4 Computers in Society xxx.ppt*, ask your instructor for a copy of the file you should use to complete this exercise.

2. Add the Typewriter Animation Effects with sound to Slide 1.

3. Set the graphic on Slide 2 to appear before the text and apply the Fly From Right effect and Camera sound to the graphic.

4. Make the following adjustments to Slide 3:

- Copy the computer graphic on Slide 3 so that it appears where the second-column text appears.
- Duplicate the computer graphic again and position the copy between the original and the first copy.
- Duplicate the computer graphic four more times, positioning the copy progressively closer to the original so that it appears to move from the first copy to the original graphic.
- Set the new graphic to appear first when the slide is presented and to dim on next mouse click.
- Set the first column placeholder to appear second.
- Arrange the duplicate computer graphics to appear third, fourth, fifth, sixth, and seventh in the animation order.

- Set the original graphic to appear eighth with the Drive By sound effect.
- Set the second column placeholder to appear last.

5. Add appropriate slide timings to each slide in the presentation and set the presentation to loop continuously.

6. Create an Action Button on Slide 4 to link to the hidden slides that follow.

7. Copy the Action Button on Slide 4 to Slide 8 to link to the hidden slides that follow it.

8. Show the presentation as a Slide Show for your instructor, if requested.

9. Create Notes Pages for three slides in the presentation and print a copy of the Notes Pages for the slides for which you created notes.

10. Save the presentation using the filename *5 Computers in Society xxx*.

11. Package your presentation to go and submit the packaged presentation on disk to your instructor.

Assignments

1. Finalizing a presentation to run continuously

The slides from the *Festivals and Attractions* presentation appear in Slide Sorter view in Figure 5.3.

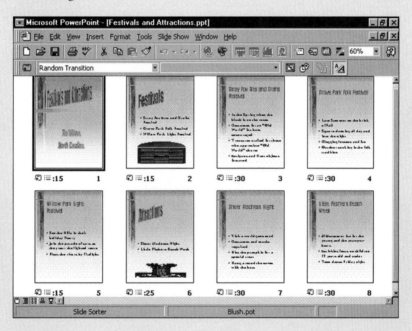

Figure 5.3

Use tools presented in this project to animate slide text with sound, add slide timings, and set the presentation to run continuously. Then view the presentation as a slide show and save changes to the presentation. Use your imagination to develop notes pages for the presentation and print copies of the notes pages that display slides in black-and-white. Set up the presentation on your computer during the next class session so that your instructor can review the special effects you've applied. Close the presentation and exit PowerPoint when you've completed your work.

2. Packing presentations to go and sending them via an e-mail message

Package the *Festivals and Attractions* and *The Willows Shops* presentations to go, using the same disk. Exit PowerPoint and launch Outlook or your school e-mail program.

Create an e-mail message to your instructor. From the floppy that contains your presentations, attach the *Pngsetup.exe* file to the mail message. Send the message to your instructor.

More PowerPoint 97

This section contains additional topics that are necessary for you to know if you want to take the Microsoft Expert exam for PowerPoint. The topics are listed in the same order as the Skill Sets outlined in the *Microsoft PowerPoint 97 Exam Preparation Guide*, which you can download from Microsoft's Web site at www.microsoft.com/office/train_cert. All other topics necessary for successful completion of the exam are covered in Projects 1 through 5 of this book.

Printing Presentations on Special Media

Exporting to Graphics Services

When you have a presentation that you would like send to a graphics service to be transformed into 35 mm slides, you can print the presentation to a file and send it to the service. To determine what file format to use to store your presentation, consult with your graphics service. Then choose File, Print, select Print to File, and then select other print options identified by your graphics service.

Printing Presentations Using a Film Recorder

If you have a graphics desktop film recorder, you can select the film recorder from the list of printers in the Print window and print the presentation to slides automatically. For information on how to use your desktop film recorder, check your film recorder instructions.

Printing Presentations on Transparencies

When printing presentations on transparencies for use on overhead projectors, be sure to choose a transparency film suitable for your computer. Set print options that work best with your printer, and then print using the same procedures you use to print on paper.

Adding Additional Objects to PowerPoint Slides

Many of the objects you want to add to PowerPoint slides are listed on the Insert menu. You will often find, however, that the most efficient way to add some of the most sophisticated and complex items to slides is by using the object AutoLayout formats.

Build a Graph

Charts graphically plot values to show data relationships to other data. The most efficient way to add a chart to a PowerPoint presentation slide when you can't import the chart from another application is to use a Chart AutoLayout format to activate Microsoft Graph. Microsoft Graph is a separate application that you can launch directly from PowerPoint. When you add a chart to a slide in PowerPoint using tools available in PowerPoint, the chart becomes part of the presentation and is not saved as a separate file.

To create a chart on a PowerPoint slide, create a new slide and format the slide using the Chart AutoLayout format. Double-click the chart object placeholder to launch Microsoft Graph. When you launch Microsoft Graph, sample data appears in a datasheet, which is a spreadsheet-like palette containing columns and rows. Data values displayed in the datasheet appear graphically plotted on the chart window behind the datasheet window. Edit the data in the datasheet by selecting the cells containing the data and then typing new data.

You can change the chart format to a different style of chart, if desired, and select chart options you want to appear on the chart. Explore menu options, and select the chart type and features you want to use. The Chart Type button on the toolbar contains a drop-down list arrow that displays a palette of different chart types to make it easy to change the chart type. The Chart menu Chart Options command opens a multi-page dialog box from which you can set chart options such as chart titles. Display the dialog box by choosing Chart, Chart Options; then click the page tab for the option you want to set. Make the appropriate changes, and choose OK.

When the chart is complete, click the PowerPoint slide to place the chart in the chart placeholder on the slide and update the presentation. Be sure to save changes to the presentation.

Add a Table

The most efficient way to add a table to a PowerPoint slide is by using the Table AutoLayout format when you create a new slide. Table placeholder appears below the title placeholder on the AutoLayout. Double-clicking the placeholder activates tools from Word that you can use to format and add text to the table. Enter the number of columns and rows the table should contain, and choose OK. Then you can type the text in the appropriate table cells using the same techniques you used to add text to spreadsheets in Excel or tables directly in Word. When you're finished, click outside the table area; the table appears on the PowerPoint slide.

After the table is placed on the slide, simply double-click the table placeholder on the slide when you need to edit table data. Select the table cell to edit and type the new text. You can format cells by selecting the cells and choosing the desired alignment or format options.

To size the table on the PowerPoint slide, select the table placeholder (but don't double-click or you'll jump to the edit mode and Word tools will appear). When you see handles on the placeholder, drag a handle to change the table size, or drag the border away from a handle to move the table on the slide.

Add an Organization Chart

Organization charts enable you to display information in a graphic layout that demonstrates a hierarchical structure. When such a format is required, you can use the Organization Chart AutoLayout format to activate tools designed for creating such a hierarchical layout.

Create a new slide using the Organization Chart AutoLayout format. Then double-click the Org Chart placeholder to launch Microsoft Organization Chart. If you start typing immediately, the text you enter appears in the box at the top of the chart. To place text in other boxes on the chart, click the box to select it and then type the text to appear in the box. Press ⌐TAB⌐ to select the next line of text in each box.

Using tools available in the Organization Chart application, you can format and change the display of boxes, and rearrange the organization of boxes when the structure of the organization changes. Buttons on the Organization Chart toolbar represent the types of boxes you may want to add. Click the toolbar button for the box you want to create, and then click the organization chart box to which you want to attach the new box. And don't forget Undo — when you make a mistake, simply undo it and try again.

The Styles menu displays a palette of layout options you can choose to arrange boxes on the organization chart. The Boxes, Lines, and Chart menus display options for formatting the look of the chart boxes. It's fun to explore options on these menus to create a special look for your organization chart.

When the organization chart you create appears as you want it, you can save the chart to use again and then update the chart on the PowerPoint slide. Choose File, Save Copy As, and type a name for the chart. Organization charts created using the Organization Chart program are saved with an .opx extension to make them easier to identify. To update the organization chart in the presentation file without closing the Organization Chart program, choose File, Update Presentation name. You can then continue to work on the organization chart until it is finished. Be sure to save additional changes before closing the Organization Chart program. Choose File, Exit and then Return to Presentation name to close Organization Chart before you return to PowerPoint.

Add Scanned Images

Additional features in PowerPoint enable you to use a scanner to acquire a picture, or *scanned image*, that you want to include in a presentation. If you have a scanner available and want to try these techniques, you must have Microsoft Photo Editor installed on your computer. PowerPoint uses Microsoft Photo Editor to work in sync with your scanner program to successfully scan an image and prepare it for inclusion in a presentation. Microsoft Photo Editor is included on the Microsoft Office 97 CD. Follow the directions on the program to install it before trying to scan an image for use in PowerPoint.

To acquire a scanned image, turn on the scanner and ensure that the scanner software is properly installed. Then Create a new slide and format the slide using the Blank AutoLayout format. Because scanned images are pictures, they can be accessed directly from the Insert menu in PowerPoint. Choose Insert, Picture, From Scanner.

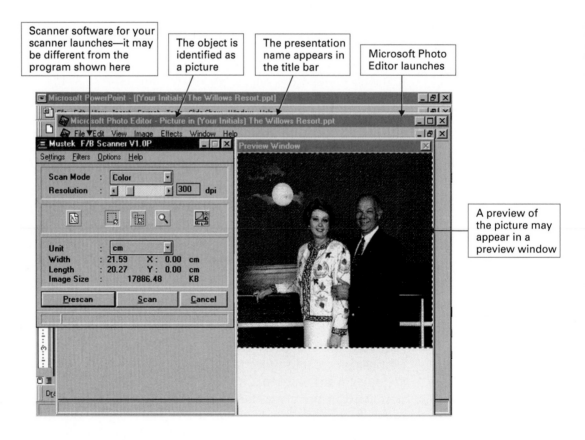

Onscreen prompts walk you through the scanning process for your scanner. Directions vary depending on your scanner type and the scanner software you have installed. When scanning is complete, choose File, Exit and Return to Presentation Name to place the image on the presentation slide. Then size and position the scanned image appropriately.

Add Sound and Movies

In addition to the built-in sounds included with PowerPoint slide transitions, you can insert music and sounds from CDs and movies onto PowerPoint slides. The techniques used to do so are similar to those used to insert pictures and other objects onto slides.

To insert music and movies, display the slide to which you want to add the music or movie. Then choose Insert, Movies and Sounds. From the cascading menu, select the object you want to add to the slide and the current location of the object (gallery, file, CD tract, and so on). When the Microsoft Clip Gallery 4.0 dialog box opens, select the page for the object you want to insert. Then select the object file you want to insert, and choose OK. If the object page in the Microsoft Clip Gallery contains no object files, you may need to import clips or download them from the Internet. Choose Import Clips to import clips stored in a folder or on a disk; click the Internet Globe button to access additional clips on the Internet. Doubleclick the video clip to play the video.

Modifying the Slide Master

Templates, as you will recall, make formatting and dressing up your presentation easy. Often you may find that the presentation templates that come with PowerPoint need a little tweaking to meet the needs for your presentation. You could change the colors and format of each and every slide in the presentation individually, but when you want the same change on every slide, it's much easier to change the Slide Master and thus change all slides at the same time. Working with the Slide Master enables you to change the background, create a custom background, or create a custom color scheme and then apply the changes to the whole presentation.

To display the Slide Master, open the presentation containing the template design you want to modify (or create a new presentation formatted with the template design you want to modify). Choose View, Master, Slide Master.

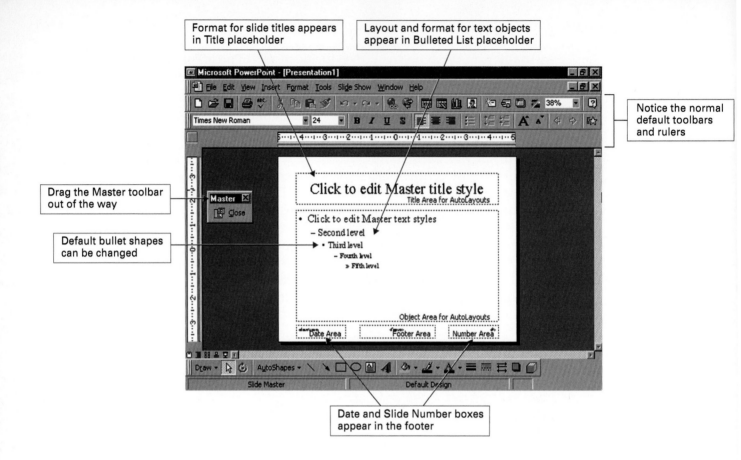

Format for slide titles appears in Title placeholder

Layout and format for text objects appear in Bulleted List placeholder

Notice the normal default toolbars and rulers

Drag the Master toolbar out of the way

Default bullet shapes can be changed

Date and Slide Number boxes appear in the footer

Create a Custom Background

The slide background provides the backdrop for all text and objects you place on the presentation slides. As a result, adding or changing the background color scheme often affects the colors of title text, bulleted list text, and colors displayed in charts and other objects you add to slides. Editing the slide background can enhance the look of the presentation.

To edit the slide background, display the Slide Master for the presentation you want to edit and choose Format, Background. From the Background dialog box, click the drop-down list for the Background fill color box, and choose Fill Effects. The Fill Effects dialog box opens and displays a variety of fill colors, shading styles, and variants. Explore the Colors and Shading styles and the Variants options until you find one you like. You can view the effects in the Sample area of the dialog box. When you're satisfied with the look, choose OK. Then choose Apply to All.

Customize a Color Scheme

Each template was designed with a specific color identified for title text, bulleted list text and lines, the background, fills, and accent colors. The combination of these colors is called a color scheme. Color schemes used in PowerPoint templates were designed by graphic artists for visual effect and for complementing other colors. When the colors displayed for different objects on your slides need to be adjusted to better fit your needs, you can edit the individual object colors by customizing the color scheme.

To do so, display the presentation containing the template you want to edit, and choose Format, Slide Color Scheme. The Color Scheme dialog box contains two tabbed pages that enable you to select a different color scheme or customize the color of an individual item. Click the color scheme on the Standard page that most closely fits the colors you want to use for the presentation. Then click the Custom page tab to display individual items and their colors, as shown in the following diagram.

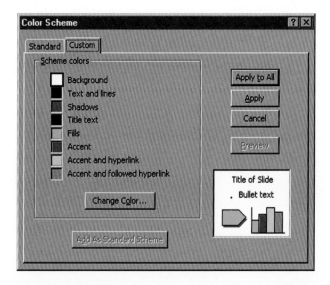

Select the object for which you want to change the color and then choose Change Color. Select the desired color for the object and choose OK. Repeat the procedure for each additional color you want to change. Choose Apply to apply the change to the active slide only, or choose Apply to All to apply the change to all slides in the presentation.

Bonus Topics

Generate Meeting Notes and Electronically Incorporate Meeting Feedback

The Meeting Minder is a PowerPoint feature that enables you to take notes as you present your presentation. These notes can be in the form of minutes to record events and discussions that occur during the presentation, or action items that identify tasks to be completed as a result of the meeting. The Meeting Minder dialog box contains separate pages for action items and meeting minutes. You can access the Meeting Minder during the presentation from the Slide Show shortcut menu or from the Tools menu in any PowerPoint view. Simply start the slide show, right-click the slide onscreen, and choose Meeting Minder.

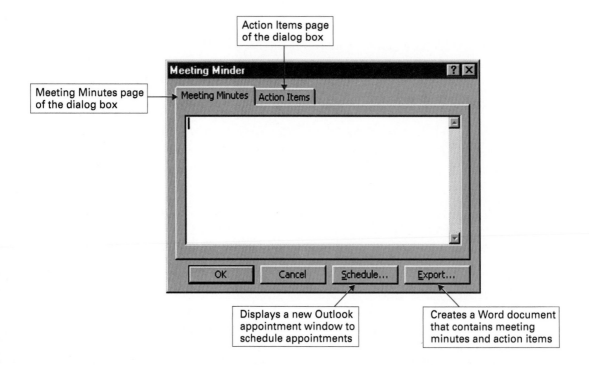

Then click the page tab for the item you want to add, type the items, and choose Add. The action item and person assigned to complete the item appear in the list box on the Action Items page. When all items have been added, choose OK. Notes and items you add to the pages of the Meeting Minder are stored as part of the presentation when you save changes to the presentation; you can recall them for review each time you open the presentation.

Present with Presentation Conferencing

To show a presentation to many people who are located at different sites but who are connected to networks, you can set up a presentation conference. As with most conferences, you must prepare for the presentation conference and invite others to attend. The Presentation Conference Wizard can help you conduct the conference after you have it set up.

To conduct a successful presentation conference, all participants must have PowerPoint 97 installed on their computers so that they can access the presentation conferencing features.

Presentation conferencing is a multi-step process. Audience participants first must set up and attempt to sign on before the presenter. Those participants connecting using the Internet must identify their Internet Protocol (IP) address and give the address to the presenter. The Presenter must log on to the conference and send the presentation to be reviewed or presented to the Audience participants.

To sign on to a presentation conference as an audience participant, log on to the Internet or local area network you plan to use to join the conference. Then launch PowerPoint 97 and choose Tools, Presentation Conference. When the Presentation Conference Wizard starts, choose Next and choose Audience, then choose Next again. Choose the appropriate connection and choose Next. Ensure that you are connected to the network, and choose Next. The IP address assigned by the network appears on the next page of the Wizard. Write down the IP address shown on the Presentation Conference Wizard page, and choose Next.

You're now ready to wait for the conference presenter to connect. Choose Finish. The Connecting to the Conference message box appears and remains active until the Presenter connects to the Conference.

To present and conduct a presentation conference, log on to the Internet or connect to the local network you want to use to present the conference. Then launch PowerPoint, open the presentation you want to present, and choose Tools, Presentation Conference. When the Wizard appears, choose Next and select Presenter. Continue to choose Next to accept the default settings for most pages and to select all slides. When the Wizard page asks for IP addresses or computer names, enter the first IP address or computer name, and choose Add. Then repeat the procedure until all conference participants are added. When you are finished, choose Finish.

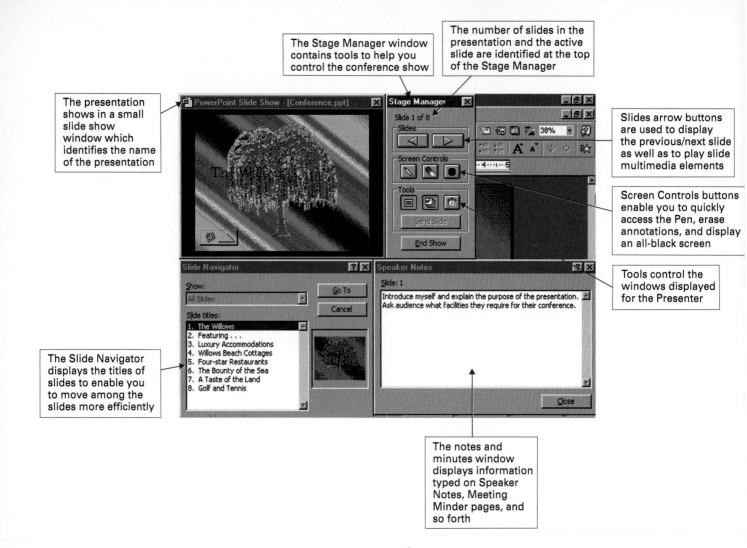

The Stage Manager window contains tools to help you control the conference show

The number of slides in the presentation and the active slide are identified at the top of the Stage Manager

The presentation shows in a small slide show window which identifies the name of the presentation

Slides arrow buttons are used to display the previous/next slide as well as to play slide multimedia elements

Screen Controls buttons enable you to quickly access the Pen, erase annotations, and display an all-black screen

Tools control the windows displayed for the Presenter

The Slide Navigator displays the titles of slides to enable you to move among the slides more efficiently

The notes and minutes window displays information typed on Speaker Notes, Meeting Minder pages, and so forth

Conducting Presentation Conferences

After connections are established between the Presenter and the Audience, each Audience participant sees the first slide onscreen in full-screen, slide-show format. Here are some tips for Audience participants:

- Use the Slide Show shortcut menu to access slide show features such as the Pen and Pen Color.
- Avoid advancing slides onscreen, and let the Presenter control the show.
- If you inadvertently advance the show, stop and wait. The Presenter will take control of the show again as long as you have not advanced the last slide and ended the show.
- If you advance the last slide so that the show ends on your screen, the Presenter cannot regain control of the show on your computer.
- When the show ends, the presentation is visible in PowerPoint. You can save the presentation locally or close the presentation without saving it.

If you are the Presenter of the conference, you will have access to controls and tools that enable you to make notes and manage the presentation. Audience participants do not see these tools. When Audience participants are annotating onscreen, your presentation may appear to freeze until they finish their annotations.

Save for the Internet

Now that you have gone beyond the basics of PowerPoint, you may want to save your presentation in a format that can be stored on the Internet. PowerPoint 97 contains special features designed to make formatting the presentation a snap.

Simply prepare the presentation and save it as you would save any presentation. Then choose File, Save as HTML (HTML stands for HyperText Markup Language, in case you're wondering). The Save as HTML Wizard launches and guides you through the process of storing your presentation in a format that can be used on the Internet. For the most part, the default options are generally the best choices unless you know precisely which choice to make. The progress bar on the left of each Wizard page shows your progress.

Accept the default options for each step. When you come to the Graphic type step on the progress bar, be sure to choose GIF, if it isn't automatically selected. GIF works well for most simple graphics. However, if you have imported photos, you may want to select another format to determine which format is best for the graphics you're using. On the Graphic size Wizard page, choose 640 by 480, if necessary, to ensure that your presentation can be viewed by most users.

Type the information you want to publish to the Internet on the Information page, and select the colors you like best on the Colors and Buttons pages. Of course, you can also accept the default colors and buttons. The last Wizard page enables you to choose a folder location to store the new folder PowerPoint creates to hold the HTML files. When you click Next after choosing a location for the new folder, PowerPoint gives you the opportunity to save the settings you've just set. Choose Don't Save the first time through the Wizard process — you aren't really certain you'll use them again.

After all the files are created, you can view the HTML files from Windows Explorer. Choose Start, Programs, Windows Explorer to launch the Explorer and open the folder PowerPoint created to store the files. When the list of files appears, you'll see quite a list of files with a .GIF extension and others with an .htm extension. Locate the file named index.htm, and double-click the filename. Internet Explorer displays the first page of the presentation that users will see if you upload the presentation to the Internet. From this index page, you can view all slides and see how the layout looks. Simply click on the slide title you want to view from the Table of Contents list, and explore the onscreen buttons to navigate through the presentation.

When you're satisfied with the way the presentation looks, ask your instructor for instructions on getting your own space on the Web and for uploading the presentation to the site.

Notes

Notes

Notes

Notes

Integrating Word, Excel, and PowerPoint

As you've already discovered, you can save valuable time by sharing data that already exists in other applications with documents and files in different applications. In this integrated project, you learn to integrate data among all Office products, learn how to share outlines between Word and PowerPoint, and how to save a file in HTML format so that you can use it on the Internet.

Objectives

After completing this project, you will be able to:

➤ **Embed a Word table on a PowerPoint slide**

➤ **Link data from Excel to a PowerPoint slide**

➤ **Create a Word document from a PowerPoint presentation outline**

➤ **Save a PowerPoint slide as a graphic and add the image to a Word document**

➤ **Create a hyperlink between a Word document and a PowerPoint presentation**

➤ **Save a presentation as an HTML file**

The Challenge

Ruth Lindsey, manager of the retail shops at The Willows resort, wants to add two slides to the The Willows presentation and create an outline using the text from slides contained in the presentation *The Willows*. In addition, Ms. Lindsey wants to include the first slide from the presentation as a graphic for the outline so that she can launch the presentation from the Word document.

The Solution

Figure 3.1 shows the two slides you will add to the presentation. Because you are comfortable with the features from all Office applications, you will use Word to add the table to a new slide in the presentation *The Willows*. The Excel worksheet contains the data shown in the second slide, so you will copy the data from Excel and link it to the slide.

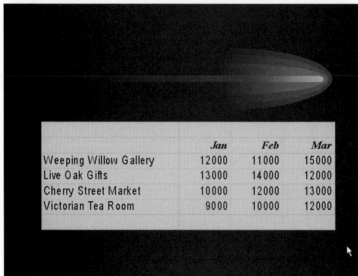

Figure 3.1

After you complete the presentation, you will use the presentation text to create the Word outline shown in Figure 3.2, capture the first slide from the presentation as a graphic, and then place the graphic in the Word outline. Finally, you create a hyperlink in Word that launches the presentation.

Figure 3.2

The Setup

To accomplish the tasks outlined in this project, you'll work with Word, Excel, and PowerPoint. You can launch applications as you need them and tile them on-screen. When you are working with only one application, maximize that application and its document window. Table 3.1 shows the settings you use.

Table 3.1   Settings

Element	Setting
Office Assistant	Close Office Assistant in all programs.
View, Toolbars	Display the Standard and Formatting toolbars in Word, Excel, and PowerPoint.
View, Toolbars	Display the Drawing toolbar in PowerPoint.
View, Ruler	Display the ruler in Word.

Embedding a Word Table on a PowerPoint Slide

When you want to include data from a Word document or an Excel work-sheet on a PowerPoint slide, you can create the data in PowerPoint using tools from Word or Excel. Objects you create in PowerPoint using tools from other applications are embedded on the slide and become a part of the presentation. They aren't saved as individual files.

> **Note** When you add an object to a presentation slide using tools from Word or Excel, you can copy the data to a Word document or to an Excel worksheet and then save them as separate files using standard procedures for saving files in the application, if desired.

TASK 1: TO EMBED A WORD TABLE ON A POWERPOINT SLIDE:

1 Open the presentation *The Willows* in Slide view.

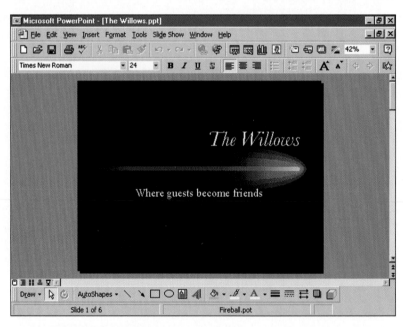

2 Click the New Slide button on the Standard toolbar and then select the Table AutoLayout format.

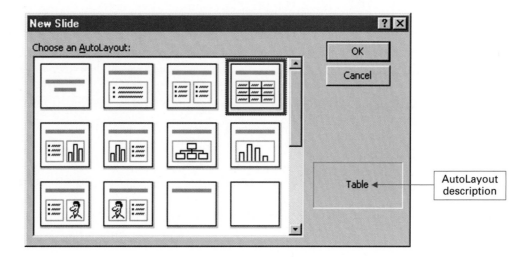

AutoLayout description

3 Click OK.

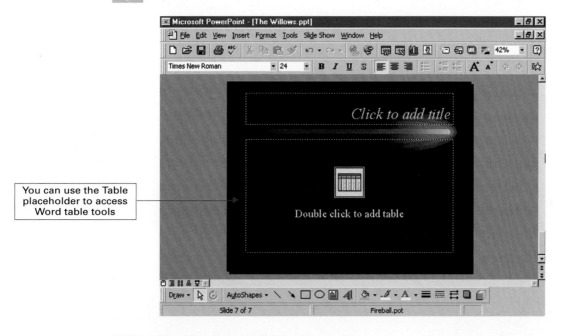

You can use the Table placeholder to access Word table tools

4 Double-click the Table placeholder.

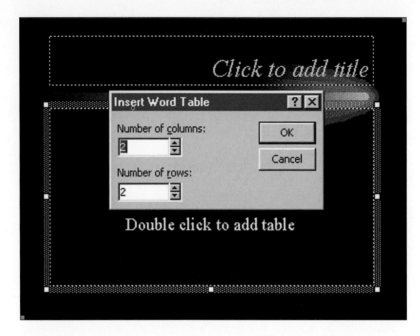

5 Type **3** in the Number of rows value box and press (ENTER).

PowerPoint stays active

Word Standard toolbar

Word Formatting toolbar

Table rulers identify columns and rows

End-of-cell markers and gridlines outline cells

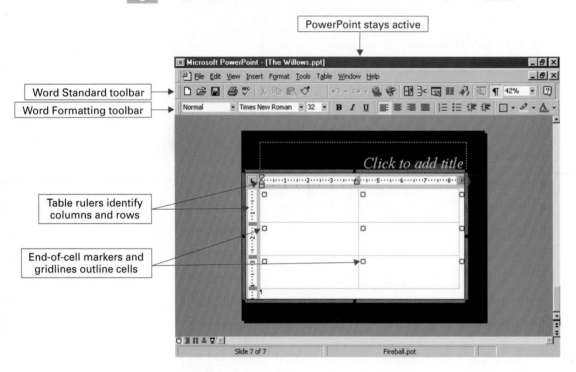

Note If you don't see gridlines, choose Table, Gridlines.

6 Type the text shown in the following illustration into cells, and change the text color to red.

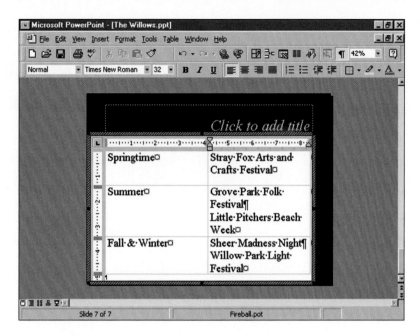

7 Press (ESC) to return to the PowerPoint slide.
PowerPoint toolbars reappear and the table text displays on the slide.

8 Double-click the table to display the Word tools again and double-click the border between the columns to adjust the width of the first column.

> **Note** If you see a dialog box when you double-click the column border, check the box beside AutoFit and then click OK.

The two-headed mouse pointer for sizing the first column

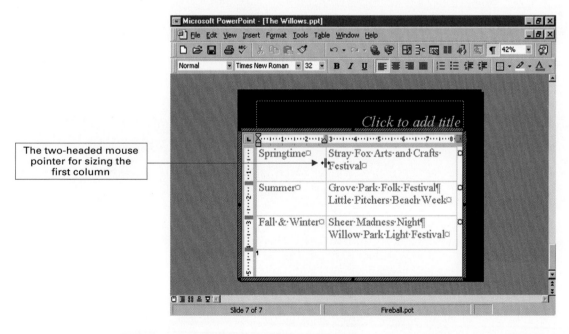

9 Press (ESC) to return to the slide and type **Willows Area Festivals** in the title placeholder for the slide.

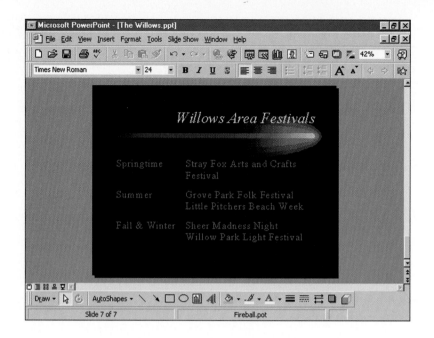

Linking Data from Excel to a PowerPoint Slide

When data you want to add to a slide exists in an Excel worksheet, you can copy the data from Excel onto the PowerPoint slide. Linking the data ensures that it can be updated in PowerPoint when the source file changes.

TASK 2: TO LINK DATA FROM EXCEL TO A POWERPOINT SLIDE:

1 Create another new slide in the presentation *The Willows,* formatting the slide with the Title Only AutoLayout.
A new slide with only a title placeholder appears on-screen.

2 Maximize Excel, open the *GiftInv.xls* workbook, and display the Sales worksheet.

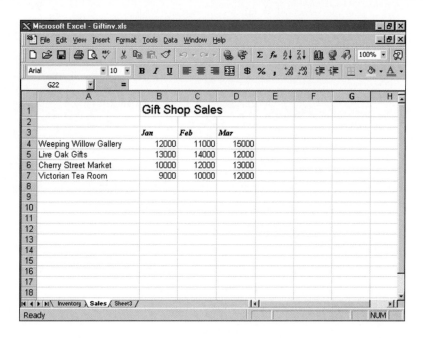

3   Tile the applications on-screen and select the cells containing text and data in the Sales worksheet.

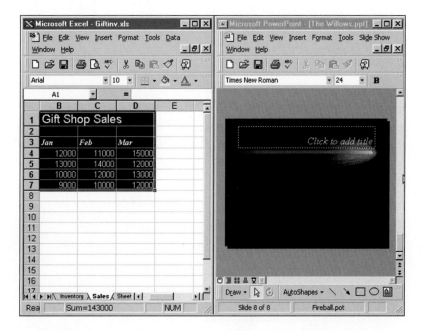

4   Click 📋.

The worksheet data is copied to the Clipboard.

5   Close Excel, maximize PowerPoint, and choose Edit, Paste Special.

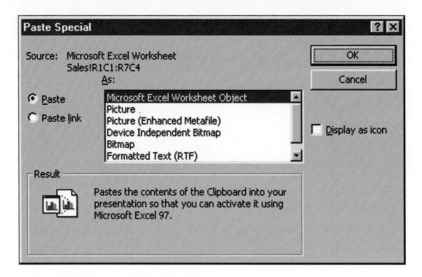

6 Choose Paste link, ensure that Microsoft Excel Worksheet Object is selected in the As list box, and click OK.

7 Right-click on the Excel worksheet object.

8   Select Format Object.

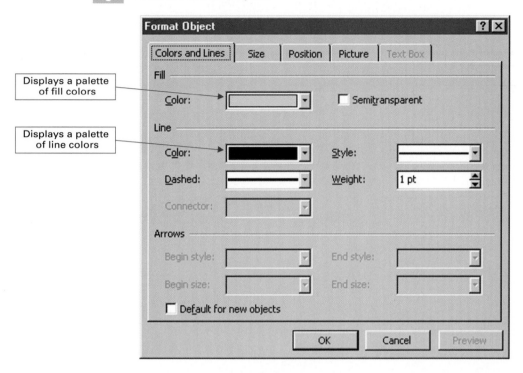

9   Click the drop-down list arrow for Fill Color and select the Follow Title Text Scheme Color; then click the drop-down list arrow for Line Color, select black, and click OK.
Text is now visible in the worksheet object.

10   Point to a corner handle on the worksheet object, click and drag the handle to size the worksheet and position it as shown in the following illustration:

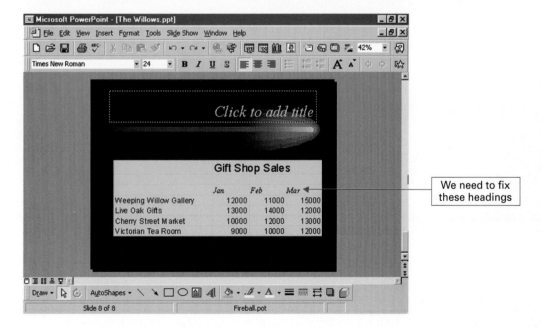

11 Double-click the Excel object.
The worksheet opens in Excel.

12 Select cells B3 through D7 and click the Right Align button.

Creating a Word Document from a PowerPoint Presentation Outline

Outlines from PowerPoint presentations often make effective guides for reports. Because the Outline view in PowerPoint prints extraneous information and slide icons, you can send the outline from PowerPoint to Word with the touch of a button and eliminate the need to retype the entire outline in Word. When you send the outline to Word, a Write-Up window opens and displays a list of formats for the Word document.

TASK 3: TO CREATE A WORD DOCUMENT FROM A POWERPOINT PRESENTATION OUTLINE:

1 Display the presentation *The Willows* in Outline view.

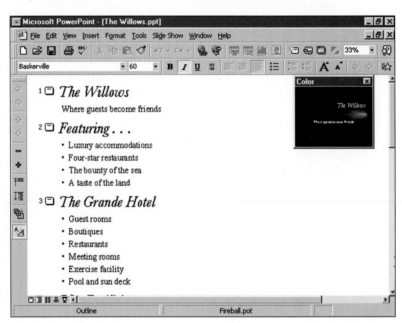

2 Choose File, Send To, Microsoft Word.

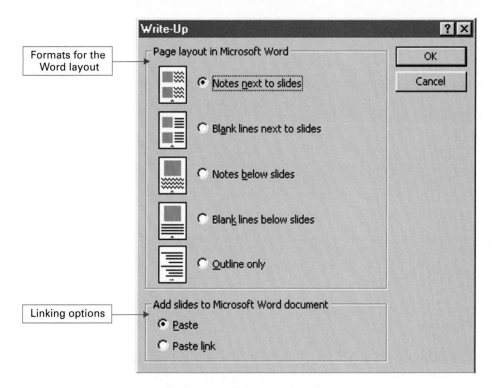

Formats for the Word layout

Linking options

3 Click the Outline only option button and then click OK.
The outline appears in a new Word document.

4 Delete the text from the last slide title, press CTRL+**A** to select all text, and left-align the text in the outline; then press CTRL+HOME to position the insertion point at the top of the outline.

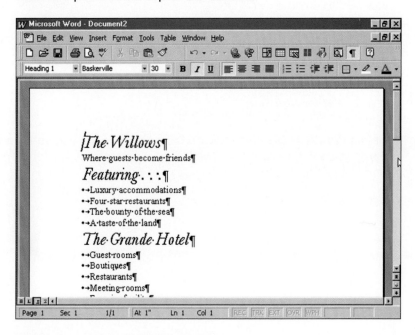

5 Delete the Slide 1 title and subtitle text.
Featuring appears at the top of the outline.

6 Save the Word document using the filename *The Willows Outline*.

Saving a PowerPoint Slide as a Graphic and Adding the Image to a Word Document

Another way to share data between Office applications is to capture information from one application as a graphic and place it into another application file. PowerPoint slides make effective graphics that not only enhance a document but also relay a message. PowerPoint includes a file option that enables you to save your slides as Windows *Metafiles,* a graphic type recognized as pictures by most Windows applications.

TASK 4: TO SAVE A POWERPOINT SLIDE AS A GRAPHIC AND ADD IT TO A WORD DOCUMENT:

1 Press (ALT)+(TAB) to access PowerPoint and display Slide 1 in Slide view. Slide 1 appears in Slide view.

2 Choose File, Save As, and click the drop-down list arrow for the Save as type text box.

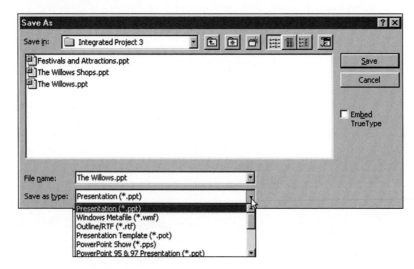

3 Select Windows Metafile (*.wmf) from the file type list, select a folder to contain the file, ensure that *The Willows* appears in the File name text box, and click Save.

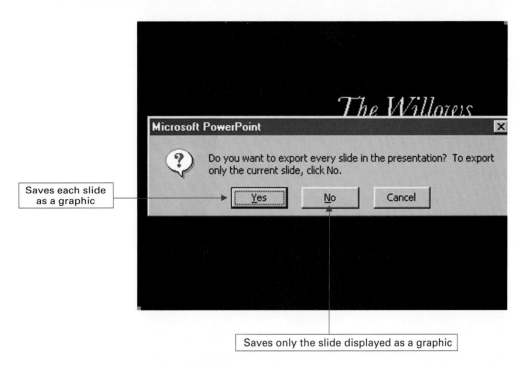

Saves each slide as a graphic

Saves only the slide displayed as a graphic

4 Click No to export only Slide 1, close the presentation, and exit PowerPoint. Word displays *The Willows Outline* document.

5 Press (CTRL)+(HOME), choose Insert, Picture, From File and then select the folder that contains *The Willows* graphic file.
The insertion point appears at the top of the Word outline, and a list of files in the folder displays in the Insert Picture dialog box.

6 Select *The Willows.wmf* file and then click the Insert button.
The slide image appears at the top of the document.

7 Click the image to select it.

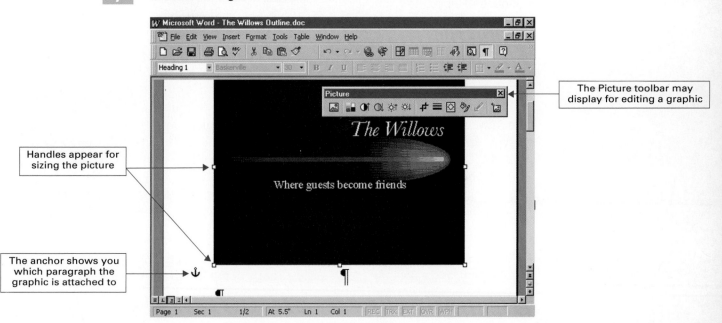

The Picture toolbar may display for editing a graphic

Handles appear for sizing the picture

The anchor shows you which paragraph the graphic is attached to

8 Close the Picture toolbar, click and drag a handle on the graphic to size the image so that it is approximately 3″ wide; then drag the image so that the left edge appears at approximately the 1.5″ mark on the horizontal ruler at the top of the document.
More of the outline appears on Page 1 of the document.

9 Select the word *Featuring* in the first line of the outline and change the font size to 20; then copy the format to other slide titles using the Format Painter. All outline text appears on one page.

10 Follow the same procedure to change all bulleted list text to 10 points; then click 🔍 to preview the document.

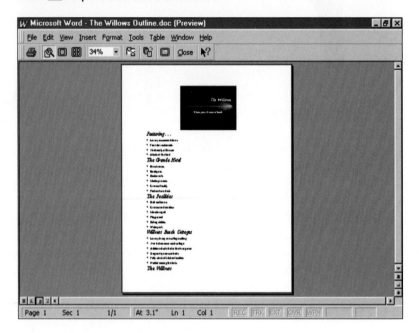

11 Save and close the document.

Creating a Hyperlink Between a Word Document and a PowerPoint Presentation

To launch the PowerPoint presentation *The Willows* from the Word document *The Willows Outline,* you can create a hyperlink between the two files. Hyperlinks in Office work the same way hyperlinks on the Internet or World Wide Web pages work—they enable you to jump from one location to another by clicking on text or graphics.

TASK 5: TO CREATE A HYPERLINK BETWEEN WORD AND POWERPOINT

1 Display the Word document *The Willows Outline* in Page Layout view, if necessary, and select the graphic slide image at the top of the document. The graphic appears with handles to show it's selected.

2 Choose Insert, Hyperlink.

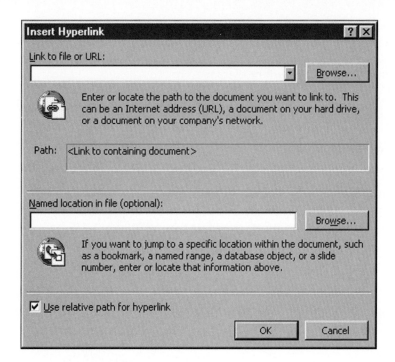

3 Click the Browse button beside the Link to file or URL text box, locate and select the presentation *The Willows*, and click OK.
The filename and location appear in the textbox.

4 Click OK.
The presentation is hyperlinked to the graphic and when you point to the graphic on the Word document, the mouse pointer changes to a pointing hand.

5 Click the graphic on the Word document.

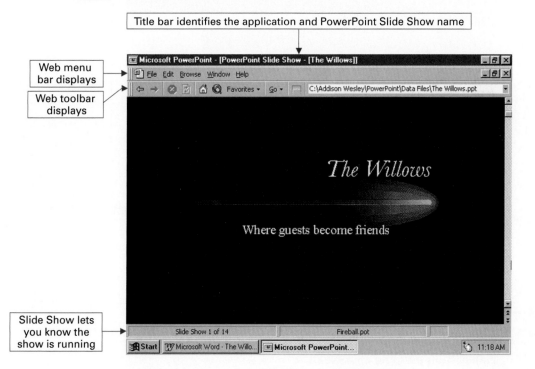

6 Press (ESC) to stop the slide show, click OK to close the show, close PowerPoint, and maximize Word.
The Word document displays with the Web toolbar active and the name of the hyperlink document displayed in the Address text box.

7 Save and close the document.

Saving a Presentation as an HTML File

You can save a file you create in any application as an HTML file so that, if you have a home page and the necessary browsers, you can send your work to a Web site. Office 97 offers Wizards to help you save your Power-Point presentations, Access database objects, and Excel workbooks in an HTML format; Word converts documents to HTML format directly.

TASK 6: TO SAVE A FILE IN AN HTML FORMAT:

1 Launch PowerPoint, if necessary, and open the presentation *The Willows,* if necessary.
Your presentation appears in the view that was active when you last saved it.

2 Choose File, Save as HTML.

> **Note** Saving files in HTML format is a special feature not automatically installed with Office 97. If saving files in HTML format does not appear or is not available on your File menu, the module of Office required to save documents in HTML format was not installed. Check with your instructor or lab assistant for installation procedures.

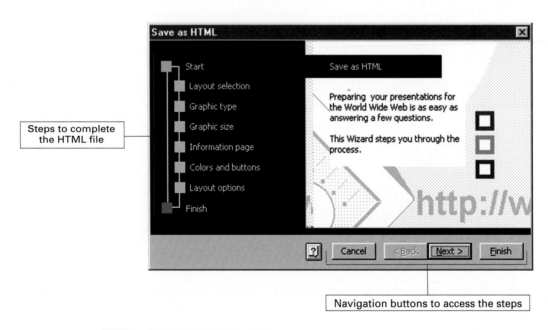

Steps to complete the HTML file

Navigation buttons to access the steps

3 Click the Next button.

4 Check New layout and click Next.

5 Select Standard and click Next.

6 Choose PowerPoint animation and click Next.

7 Choose 640 by 480 to ensure that the graphics can be viewed by most computers, select 1/2 width of screen for the graphic width, and click Next.

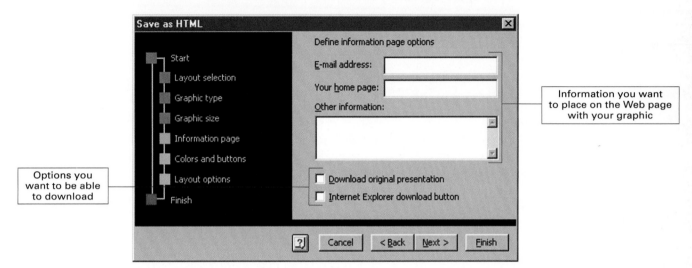

Information you want to place on the Web page with your graphic

Options you want to be able to download

8 Type your e-mail address, home page address, and other information you want displayed with the graphic on the Web and select options that enable users to download the presentation and/or the Internet Explorer; then click Next.

9 Choose Use browser colors and click Next.

10 Select the circle button style and click Next.

11 Select the button position you like best and then click Next.

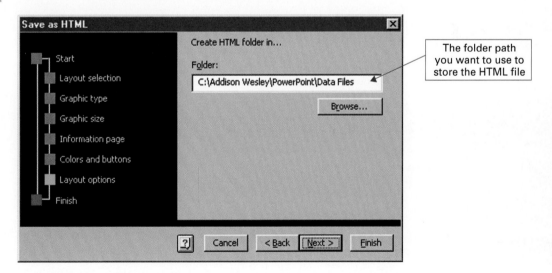

The folder path you want to use to store the HTML file

12 Click Browse, select the folder to store the HTML file, click Select, and then click Next.
The last page of the Save as HTML Wizard provides additional information and instruction for completing your HTML file.

13 Click Finish.

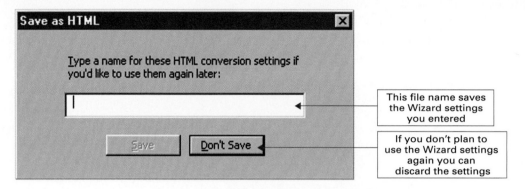

14 Type **PowerPoint Presentation** in the text box and click Save.
PowerPoint displays a message indicating that it is creating the files
required for your Web page and asks you to wait. A message window
appears when the page is complete.

15 Click OK to close the message window.
The files PowerPoint creates when you save a presentation as an HTML file
are stored in a folder named The Willows — the presentation file name. You
can send these files to a World Wide Web page using procedures defined
and available at your school.

The Conclusion

In this project, you created a new Word document using an outline of a
PowerPoint presentation. You can also create a PowerPoint presentation
by sending text from a Word document to PowerPoint using the Word
File, Send To command. When you want to include only a small portion of
data or information from a Word document in a PowerPoint presentation,
you can select, drag, and drop text from Word to a slide. You can use the
File, Save as HTML command from any Office 97 application to save a finished file in a format you can use on the World Wide Web.

If you have completed your work for the day, exit all programs and shut
down the computer according to standard lab procedures.

Summary and Exercises

Summary

- You can drag and drop Excel worksheet data to a PowerPoint slide.
- You can use the File, Send To command to share information among Office applications.
- When you want to add data using tools from other applications to create objects on slides in a PowerPoint presentation, you can select an AutoLayout format for the slide and then double-click the object placeholder to access the tools.
- You can save a PowerPoint presentation slide as a graphic file and then use it to enhance Word documents and files in other applications.
- The File, Save as HTML command saves documents, worksheets, databases, and presentations in a format you can use to upload the files to a Web site.
- Hyperlinks enable you to display files by launching them from another document.

Key Terms and Operations

Key Terms	Operations
hyperlink	Create an embedded object in PowerPoint using tools from
metafile	Word
Write Up feature	Link Excel worksheet data to a PowerPoint slide
	Send a presentation outline to Word to create a new document
	Save a presentation slide as a graphic.
	Insert a presentation slide graphic as a picture in a Word document
	Create a hyperlink

Study Questions

Multiple Choice

1. To send a PowerPoint outline to Word, use the
   a. File menu.
   b. Edit menu.
   c. Tools menu.
   d. Insert menu.

2. All the following techniques can be used to copy data from Excel to PowerPoint *except*
   a. dragging and dropping the data from Excel to PowerPoint.
   b. cutting the data from the Excel worksheet and choosing Edit, Paste Special.
   c. copying the Excel data to the Clipboard and pasting it into PowerPoint.
   d. retyping the data from Excel into PowerPoint.

3. To create a link between data from Excel and PowerPoint,
   a. press (CTRL) as you drag and drop.
   b. press (ENTER).
   c. choose Edit, Paste Special.
   d. choose File, Export.

4. When you want to create a new object and imbed it in a presentation, you can
   a. choose Insert, Table.
   b. use the drag-and-drop technique to copy it from Word.
   c. use the Clipboard.
   d. choose an AutoLayout format that contains the object placeholder you want to add.

5. When you create a new object in a PowerPoint presentation using tools from another application,
   a. the object is embedded in the presentation.
   b. the object becomes a separate file.
   c. the source application opens as a button on the toolbar.
   d. you can't create new data in a PowerPoint slide.

6. After you format a slide using an AutoLayout format that contains an object placeholder, what action do you take to access the other application tools?
   a. Press (ENTER).
   b. Double-click the object placeholder.
   c. Choose Insert, Object.
   d. Click the object placeholder and type the data.

7. When you add a Word table to a PowerPoint slide, the toolbars that appear are
   a. PowerPoint default toolbars.
   b. the Word Formatting toolbar.
   c. the Word Standard and Formatting toolbars.
   d. no toolbars.

8. To access a linked or embedded object copied from another application and added to a PowerPoint slide,
   a. close the presentation and exit PowerPoint.
   b. launch the source application and open the file.
   c. press (ENTER).
   d. double-click the object.

9. To save a slide as a graphic, choose
   a. File, Save As and select Windows Metafile from the Save as type list.
   b. Insert, Picture, From File.
   c. File, Send To.
   d. Edit, Paste Special.

10. To place a slide graphic in a Word document, choose
    a. File, Save As and select Windows Metafile from the Save as type list.
    b. Insert, Picture, From File.
    c. File, Send To.
    d. Edit, Paste Special.

Short Answer

1. What option do you choose from the Paste Special dialog box to create a link between the source and target files?

2. What application toolbars appear when you insert a Word table in a PowerPoint slide?

3. What appears on graphic objects to enable you to change the size of the graphic?

4. What dialog box appears when you send a PowerPoint presentation outline to Word?

5. How do you tell PowerPoint the type of object you plan to add to a new slide?

6. How do you access the shortcut pop-up menu for an object in a presentation slide?

7. Where does data have to be held to enable you to use the Paste Special feature?

8. How many slides in a presentation can you save as graphics at the same time?

9. How do you redisplay tools from the source application after you return an object to the slide?

10. On what menu does the hyperlink command appear?

For Discussion

1. How do you create a new document using a presentation outline?

2. What is the difference between linked files and hyperlinked files?

3. What techniques do you use to ensure that a link is created when you add data from Word or Excel to a PowerPoint slide?

4. Discuss the benefits of hyperlinking files to other files.

Exercises

Creating a PowerPoint presentation from a Word outline and saving a slide as a graphic

The Board of Directors at The Willows requests that you create a broader scope presentation to advertise The Willows on the World Wide Web. The presentation, entitled *The Most Inviting Resort,* should contain the slides pictured in Figure 3.3.

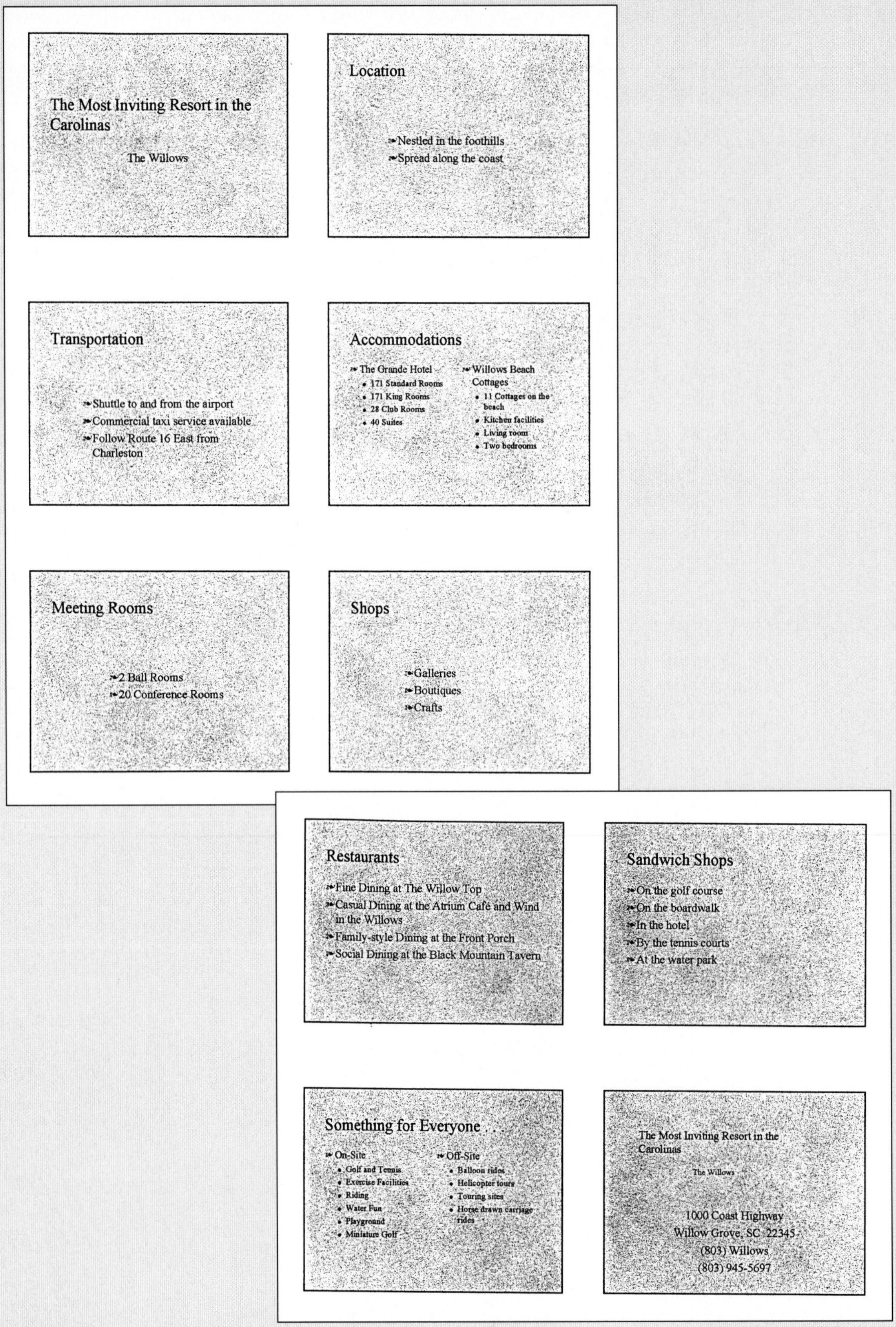

The Most Inviting Resort in the Carolinas

The Willows

Location

- Nestled in the foothills
- Spread along the coast

Transportation

- Shuttle to and from the airport
- Commercial taxi service available
- Follow Route 16 East from Charleston

Accommodations

- The Grande Hotel
  - 171 Standard Rooms
  - 171 King Rooms
  - 28 Club Rooms
  - 40 Suites
- Willows Beach Cottages
  - 11 Cottages on the beach
  - Kitchen facilities
  - Living room
  - Two bedrooms

Meeting Rooms

- 2 Ball Rooms
- 20 Conference Rooms

Shops

- Galleries
- Boutiques
- Crafts

Restaurants

- Fine Dining at The Willow Top
- Casual Dining at the Atrium Café and Wind in the Willows
- Family-style Dining at the Front Porch
- Social Dining at the Black Mountain Tavern

Sandwich Shops

- On the golf course
- On the boardwalk
- In the hotel
- By the tennis courts
- At the water park

Something for Everyone

- On-Site
  - Golf and Tennis
  - Exercise Facilities
  - Riding
  - Water Fun
  - Playground
  - Miniature Golf
- Off-Site
  - Balloon rides
  - Helicopter tours
  - Touring sites
  - Horse drawn carriage rides

The Most Inviting Resort in the Carolinas

The Willows

1000 Coast Highway
Willow Grove, SC 22345
(803) Willows
(803) 945-5697

Figure 3.3

The *Most Inviting Resort* outline is stored as a Word document on the Addison Wesley Web site (www.awl.com/is/select). You can download the outline and use it to develop the presentation. If you are unable to download this file, ask your instructor for it. Follow these steps to create the presentation:

1. Launch the Internet Explorer, access the Addison Wesley Web site, locate and download the Word document *Most Inviting Resort.*

2. Launch Word and open the Most Inviting Resort document.

3. Choose File, Send To, Microsoft PowerPoint to automatically create a presentation using information from the Word outline.

4. Position the insertion point beside Slide 2 in the PowerPoint Outline view and press ⬛TAB⬛ to make *The Willows* a subtitle for Slide 1; then display Slide 1 in Slide view.

5. Click the Slide Layout button on the Standard Toolbar and double-click the Title AutoLayout format in the Slide Layout dialog box.

6. Display each slide in the presentation to ensure that the text fits appropriately on each slide, making the following adjustments:
   - Slide 4: Format the slide using the 2 Column Text AutoLayout and then cut the information for the Willows Beach Cottages bullet point and paste it into the placeholder on the right.
   - Slide 9: Format the slide using the 2 Column Text AutoLayout and place the Off-Site information in the placeholder on the right.

7. Apply a template to the presentation. The presentation pictured in Figure 3.3 is formatted using the Serene template.

8. Add a new title slide to the end of the presentation and type the following information on the slide:

   1000 Coast Highway
   Willow Grove, SC 22345
   (803) Willows
   (803) 945–5697

9. Adjust text placeholders on each slide to display the information shown in Figure 3.3.

10. Display Slide 1 and save it as a Windows Metafile graphic; then insert it as a graphic on Slide 10, as shown in Figure 3.3.

11. Save the presentation using the filename *Most Inviting Resort* and print a copy of the presentation as handouts with six framed slides per page.

Assignments

Embedding a new object in a PowerPoint presentation, linking an Excel worksheet to a PowerPoint slide, and creating a hyperlink to display the Excel worksheet.
Mr. Gilmore wants you to add the two slides shown in Figure 3.4 to *The Willows Shops* presentation.

Figure 3.4

Create a new slide at the end of the presentation *The Willows Shops* and format it using the Object over Text AutoLayout. Select the Object placeholder and delete it. Then click the Insert Microsoft Word Table button on the toolbar and create a table with three columns and two rows. Type and format the text in the table; then add the text to the text placeholder.

Create another new slide and format it using the Blank AutoLayout. Link the Excel worksheet *TopTen* to the slide. Format, size, and change the colors of the worksheet object to match those shown in Figure 3.4.

Save the presentation and print a copy of the two new slides as handouts with two slides per page.

Create a hyperlink that opens the Excel *TopTen* worksheet when you click the Excel object on the slide. Save changes to the presentation and then save the presentation again in HTML format.

Close the presentation and exit PowerPoint.

Notes

Notes

Notes

Notes

Notes

Word 97 Function Reference Guide

Function	Mouse Action or Button	Menu	Keyboard Shortcut
Bold	Select text and click **B**	Select text, choose Format, Font, and select Bold	Select text and press (CTRL)+B
Border, create	Select object and click ▦	Select object and then choose Format, Borders and Shading, Borders tab	
Bulleted list, create	Select paragraph and click ▤	Select paragraph and choose Format, Bullets and Numbering, Bulleted tab	
Columns, create	Click ▥	Choose Format, Columns	
Document, close	Click ✖	Choose File, Close	
Document, create new	Click ▢	Choose File, New, and select template	Press (CTRL)+N
Document, open existing	Click ☞	Choose File, Open	Press (CTRL)+O
Document, preview	Click ▣	Choose File, Print Preview	
Document, print	Click ▤	Choose File, Print	Press (CTRL)+P
Document, save	Click ▤	Choose File, Save	Press (CTRL)+S
Document, select entire		Choose Edit, Select All	Press (CTRL)+A
Envelope, create		Choose Tools, Envelopes and Labels	
Footer		Choose View, Header and Footer	
Go to		Choose Edit, Go To	Press (CTRL)+G
Grammar check	Click ✓	Choose Tools, Spelling and Grammar	Press (F7)
Graphic, insert		Choose Insert, Picture	
Graphic, move	Select graphic and drag	Right-click graphic, choose Format Picture, Position tab	

Function	Mouse Action or Button	Menu	Keyboard Shortcut
Graphic, size	Select handle on graphic and drag	Right-click graphic, choose Format Picture, Size tab	Press F1
Header		Choose View, Header and Footer	
Help	Click ⍰	Choose Help, Microsoft Word Help	
Italicize	Select text and click *I*	Select text, choose Format, Font, and select Italic	Select text and press CTRL+I
Margins, set		Choose File, Page Setup, Margins tab	
Numbered list, create	Select paragraph and click ☰	Select paragraph and choose Format, Bullets and Numbering, Numbered tab	
Page break, delete		Select page break and choose Edit, Clear	Select the page break and press DEL
Page break, insert		Choose Insert, Break	Press CTRL+ENTER
Paragraph, align	Select paragraph and click ☰, ☰, ☰, or ☰	Select paragraph(s) and choose Format, Paragraph, Alignment	Press CTRL+L for left, CTRL+R for right, or CTRL+E for center
Paragraph, format		Select paragraph(s) and choose Format, Paragraph	
Paragraph, indent	☰	Select paragraph(s) and choose Format, Paragraph	
Ruler, display/hide		Choose View, Ruler	
Section break, delete		Select section break and choose Edit, Clear	Select the section break and press DEL
Section break, insert		Choose Insert, Break	
Shading, apply		Select text, paragraph(s), or cells and choose Format, Borders, Shading tab	

Function	Mouse Action or Button	Menu	Keyboard Shortcut
Special characters, insert		Choose Insert, Symbol, Special Characters	Press F7
Spelling check	Click ✓	Choose Tools, Spelling and Grammar	
Style, apply	Select text, click Style drop-down arrow, and click style	Select text and choose Format, Style	
Style, change		Choose Format, Style, select style, and click Modify	
Tab, change	Position insertion point in text and drag tab indicator to new location		
Tab, set	Click tab indicator on ruler to select tab type and click ruler where you want the tab	Choose Format, Tabs	
Table, align		Click table and choose Table, Cell Height and Width	
Table, convert text to a table		Select text and choose Table, Convert Text to Table	
Table, create		Choose Table, Insert Table	
Table, draw		Choose Table, Draw Table	
Text, copy	Select text and click 📋	Select text and choose Edit, Copy	Press CTRL+C
Text, cut	Select text and click ✂	Choose Edit, Cut	Press CTRL+X
Text, find		Choose Edit, Find	Press CTRL+F
Text, paste	Select text and click 📋	Choose Edit, Paste	Press CTRL+V
Text, replace		Choose Edit, Replace	Press CTRL+H
Text, select	Position insertion point at beginning and drag through text		Press SHIFT+any cursor movement key, such as → or END
Toolbars, display/hide	Click 🖋, ⊞ or, ✎	Choose View, Toolbars and select toolbar	

Function	Mouse Action or Button	Menu	Keyboard Shortcut
Underline	Select text and click ⊻	Select text, choose Format, Font, and select Underline	Select text and press (CTRL)+U
Undo	Click ↺ ▾	Choose Edit, Undo	Press (CTRL)+Z
View, change	Click ▤, ▤, ▤, or ▤	Choose View and select view	
Web	Click 🌐	Choose Help, Microsoft on the Web	
Zoom	Click 41% ▾ in Preview	Choose View, Zoom	

Excel 97 Function Reference Guide

Function	Mouse Action or Button	Menu	Keyboard Shortcut
AutoFormat		Select the cells and choose Format, AutoFormat	
Border, add	Select the cells(s), click the down arrow on ▣▾, and click on the desired border	Select the cell(s) and choose Format, Cells, Border	
Cell, align	Select the cell(s) and click ▤, ▤, or ▤	Select the cells(s) and choose Format, Cells, Alignment	
Cell, delete		Select the cells(s) and choose Edit, Delete	
Cell, delete data in		Select the cells(s) and choose Edit, Clear	Select the cells(s) and press (DEL)
Cell, copy	Select the cells(s) and click ▤	Select the cells(s) and choose Edit, Copy	Select the cells(s) and press (CTRL)+C
Cell, cut	Select the cells(s) and click ✂	Select the cells(s) and choose Edit, Cut	Select the cells(s) and press (CTRL)+X
Cell, format	Select the cells(s) and click appropriate formatting button (**B**, *I*, and so on)	Select the cells(s) and choose Format, Cells, and choose the desired tab	(CTRL)+1 - (one)
Cell, insert		Select the cells(s) and choose Insert, Cells	
Cell, paste	Select the cells(s) and click ▤	Select the cells(s) and choose Edit, Paste	Select the cells(s) and press (CTRL)+V
Cell, select	Drag mouse pointer through desired cells		Press (SHIFT)+any navigation key
Chart, create		Choose Insert, Object, Microsoft Graph 97 Chart	
Chart, move	Select the graph and drag	Select the chart, choose Format, Object, click on the Position tab	
Chart, size	Select a handle and drag	Select the chart, choose Format, Object, click on the Size tab	

Function	Mouse Action or Button	Menu	Keyboard Shortcut
Column, change the width	Drag the vertical border of the column in the column indicator row	Select the column and choose Format, Column, Width	
Column, delete		Select the column(s) and choose Edit, Delete	
Column, insert		Select the column(s) and choose Insert, Columns	
Comments, add		Select the cell and choose Insert, Comment	
Data, edit	Select the cell, click in the Formula bar, and edit as desired		Select the cell, press F2, and edit as desired
Data, enter			Select cell, type data, and press ENTER or any navigational key
Data, find		Choose Edit, Find	Press CTRL+F
Data, sort	Select the cells(s) and click ↕ or ↕	Select the cells(s) and choose Data, Sort	
Exit Excel 97	Click ✖ in the application window	Choose File, Exit	Press ALT+F4
Fill, add	Select the cells(s), click the down arrow on the ✎▾, and select a color	Select the cells(s) and choose Format, Cells, Patterns	
Footer, create		Choose View, Header and Footer	
Format dates		Select the cells(s) and choose Format, Cells, Number	
Format numbers	Select the cells(s) and click $, %, , , ⤒, or ⤓	Select the cells(s) and choose Format, Cells, Number	
Header, create		Choose View, Header and Footer	
Help	Click ②	Choose Help, Microsoft Help	Press F1
Page break, change		Choose View, Page Break Preview, and drag the page break line	

Function	Mouse Action or Button	Menu	Keyboard Shortcut
Page break, view		Choose View, Page Break Preview	
Preview	Click 🔍	Choose File, Print Preview	
Print	Click 🖨	Choose File, Print	Press (CTRL)+P
Row, change the height	Drag the horizontal border of the row indicator	Select the row(s) and choose Format, Row, Height	
Row, delete		Select the row(s) and choose Edit, Delete	
Row, insert		Select the number of rows you want to insert and choose Insert, Rows	
Spell check	Click ✓	Choose Tools, Spelling	Press (F7)
Start Excel 97		Choose Start, Programs, Microsoft Excel 97	
Workbook, close	Click ✕ in the workbook window	Choose File, Close	
Workbook, create	Click ▢	Choose File, New	Press (CTRL)+(END)
Workbook, open	Click 📂	Choose File, Open	Press (CTRL)+O
Workbook, save	Click 💾	Choose File, Save	Press (CTRL)+S
Worksheet, delete		Click the worksheet tab and choose Insert, Worksheet	
Worksheet, insert		Click the worksheet tab that should follow the new worksheet and choose Edit, Delete Sheet	
Worksheet, move	Drag the worksheet tab to new location	Select the worksheet tab and choose Edit, Move or Copy sheet	
Worksheet, name		Right-click the worksheet tab and choose Rename	

Access 97 Function Reference Guide

Function	Mouse Action or Button	Menu	Keyboard Shortcut
Database, close	Click ☒	Choose File, Close	
Database, create new	Click ▢	Choose File, New Database	Press CTRL+N
display page of Database window	Click page tab	Choose View, Database Objects, and then choose desired database window page	Press CTRL+TAB until the database window page appears
Database, open existing	Click 🖿	Choose File, Open	Press CTRL+O
Exit Access	Click ☒ in the application window	Choose File, Exit	
Field, delete	Display table in Design view, click field row, and click ▤	Display table in Design view, click field row, and choose Edit, Delete Rows	Display table in Design view, click field row, and press DEL
Field, insert	Display table in Design view, click field row where new field is desired, and click ▤	Display table in Design view, click field row where new field is desired, and choose Edit, Insert Row	
Field, sort	Select field and click ▤ or ▤	Select field and choose Records, Sort, Sort Order	
Form, create new	Open table or query and click ▤ ▾	Select table or query name in database window and choose Insert, Form	
Form, design	Select form name in database window and click Design OR open form and click ▤ ▾	Open form and choose View, Design View	
Form, open	Select form name in database window and click Open	Select form name in Forms page of database window and press ENTER	
Help	Click ▤	Choose Help, Microsoft Word Help	Press F1
Object, create new	Click New on object page of database window		Press ALT+N on object page of database window
Preview	Click ▤	Choose File, Print Preview	

Function	Mouse Action or Button	Menu	Keyboard Shortcut
Primary key, assign	Display table in Design view, click field, and click 🔑	Display table in Design view, select field, and choose Edit, Primary Key	
Print	Click 🖨	Choose File, Print	Press (CTRL)+P
Query, add fields	Double-click field name		
Query, add table	Click 🔳	Choose Query, Show Table	
Query, design	Select query name in database window and click Design *OR* Open query and click ▦ ▾	Open query and choose View, Design View	
Query, delete		Select the record and choose Edit, Delete Record	
Query, open	Select query name in database window and click Open		Select query name in Forms page of database window and press (ENTER)
Query, run	Click ❗	Choose Query, Run	
Query, set criteria			Select Criteria row and type operator and symbol
Record, add data		Display Datasheet or Form view and type data into fields	
Record, delete	Click record selection bar or button, click ✖	Select the record and choose Edit, Delete Record	Select record and press (DEL)
Record, insert	Display table to contain record and click ▸*	Open table to contain record and choose Insert, New Record	
Report, create	Display table or query and select AutoReport from 🔲 ▾ drop-down list arrow	Select table or query name in database window and choose Insert, Report	
Report, design	Select report name in database window and click Design *OR* Open report and click ▦ ▾	Open report and choose View, Design View	
Report, open	Select report name in database window and click Open		Select report name in Forms page of database window and press (ENTER)
Save	Click 💾	Choose File, Save	Press (CTRL)+S

Function	Mouse Action or Button	Menu	Keyboard Shortcut
Send		Choose File, Send	Press (ALT)+F, E
Spelling check	Click	Choose Tools, Spelling and Grammar	Press (F7)
Table align		Click in the table and choose Table, Cell Height and Width	
Table, convert text to a table		Select the text and choose Table, Convert Text to Table	
Table, copy structure	Click table name in database window, click , click and type new table name	Click table name in database window, choose Edit, Copy, choose Edit, Paste and type new table name	Click table name in database window, press (CTRL)+C, press (CTRL)+V and type new table name
Table, create		Choose Table, Insert Table	
Table, design	Select table name in database window and click Design *OR* Open table and click	Open table and choose View, Design View	
Table, open	Select table name in database window and click Open		Select table name in Forms page of database window and press (ENTER)
Text, copy	Select the text and click	Select the text and choose Edit, Copy	Press (CTRL)+C
Text, cut	Select the text and click	Choose Edit, Cut	Press (CTRL)+X
Text, find	Click	Choose Edit, Find	Press (CTRL)+F
Text, paste	Select the text and click	Choose Edit, Paste	Press (CTRL)+V
Text, replace		Choose Edit, Replace	Press (CTRL)+H
Text, select	Drag through text		Press (SHIFT)+any cursor movement key, such as (→) or (END)
Toolbars, display or hide	Right click on toolbar	Choose View, Toolbars and select the toolbar	
Undo	Click	Choose Edit, Undo	Press (CTRL)+Z
View, change	Click or	Choose View, Type View	
Web	Click	Choose Help, Microsoft on the Web	

PowerPoint 97 Function Reference Guide

Function	Mouse Action or Button	Menu	Keyboard Shortcut
AutoLayout, select	Click ▦ and select format	Choose Format, Slide Layout and select format	
Bold	Select text and click **B**	Select text, choose Format, Font, and select Bold	Select text and press (CTRL)+B
Bulleted list, format	Select item, right-click on screen, select Bullet, select bullet font category, and select bullet shape	Select item, choose Format, Bullet, select bullet font category, and select bullet shape	
Bulleted list or outline, set indent	Click ➡ or ⬅		Press (TAB) or (SHIFT)+(TAB)
Chart, insert	Click ▦	Choose Insert, Chart	
Clip Art, insert	Click ▦ and double-click the image to insert	Choose Insert, Picture, Clip Art, and double-click the image to insert	
Font, change size	Select text, click Font Size drop-down list, select size OR select text and click **A** or **A**	Select text, choose Format, Font, select font size	Select text and press (CTRL)+[to decrease font size or (CTRL)+] to increase font size
Help	Click ▦	Choose Help, Microsoft Word Help	Press (F1)
Italicize	Select text and click **I**	Select text, choose Format, Font, and select Italic	Select text and press (CTRL)+I
Movies, insert		Choose Insert, Movies and Sounds	
Notes Pages, create	Click ▦ and type notes in area at bottom of page	Choose View, Notes Pages, and type notes in area at bottom of page	
Object, flip		Select object, choose Draw, Rotate or Flip, and select Flip Horizontal or Flip Vertical	
Object, move	Select object, position mouse pointer on object away from handle, click and drag		Press (TAB) until object is selected and press cursor arrows until object is positioned

Function	Mouse Action or Button	Menu	Keyboard Shortcut
Object, rotate		Select object, choose Draw, Rotate or Flip, and select Rotate Left, Rotate Right, or Free Rotate	
Object, size	Select object, point to a handle and drag handle to size object		
Objects, group		Press (SHIFT) and click each object to group. Then choose Draw, Group	
Objects, ungroup		Select object and choose Draw, Ungroup	
Organization chart, insert		Choose, Insert, Object, MS Organization Chart 2.0, and OK	
Orientation		Choose File, Page Setup, select orientation	
Page Setup, modify		Choose File, Page Setup	
Placeholder, add text	Click placeholder and type text		Press (TAB) to select placeholder and type text.
Placeholder, select text	Double-click to select word; triple-click to select bulleted item or title		Press (SHIFT)+arrow keys to highlight text
Presentation, add slide	Click 🖺	Choose Insert, New Slide	Press (CTRL)+M
Presentation, create new	Click 🗋	Choose File, New	Press (CTRL)+N
Presentation, pack to go		Choose File, Pack and Go and follow screen prompts	
Presentation, run continuously		Choose Slide Show, Set Up Show, and choose Loop continuously until (ESC)	
Presentation, save as template		Choose File, Save As, Select Presentation Template from Files of type list	

Function	Mouse Action or Button	Menu	Keyboard Shortcut
Presentation, show	Click ⬚	Choose View, Slide Show *OR* choose Slide Show, View Show	
Preview	Click ⬚	There is no Print Preview in PowerPoint. Choose View, Slide Show *OR* Choose Slide Show, View Show	
Print	Click ⬚	Choose File, Print	Press (CTRL)+P
Save	Click ⬚	Choose File, Save	Press (CTRL)+S
Send		Choose File, Send	Press (ALT)+F, E
Slide, create	Click ⬚	Choose Insert, New Slide	Press (CTRL)+M
Slide, delete		Select slide and choose Edit, Delete Slide	
Slide, delete object on slide			Select object (placeholder, graphic, etc.) and press (DEL)
Slide, display next slide	Click ⬚		Press (PGDN)
Slide, display previous slide	Click ⬚		Press (PGUP)
Slide, display Master	Press (SHIFT) and click view button	Choose View, Master, and select Master	
Slide, format background		Display slide or Master, choose Format, Background, select background color or effect	
Slide, hide	In Slide Sorter view, select slide(s) to hide and click ⬚	In all views, select or display slide to hide and choose Slide Show, Hide Slide	
Slide, move in Slide Sorter view	Click slide to select it and drag it to a new position		
Slide, select in Outline or Slide Sorter view	Click slide icon or slide image		Press arrow keys until slide is selected
Select multiple slides in Outline or Slide Sorter view	Click first slide icon or slide image; press (SHIFT) and click additional slide icons or images		

Function	Mouse Action or Button	Menu	Keyboard Shortcut
Spelling check	Click ✓	Choose Tools, Spelling and Grammar	Press (F7)
Style check		Choose Tools, Style Checker	
Table, insert	Click ▦		
Text or object, copy	Select text or object and click 📋	Select text or object and choose Edit, Copy	Select text or object and press (CTRL)+C
Text or object, cut	Select text or object and click ✂	Select text or object and choose Edit, Cut	Select text or object and press (CTRL)+X
Text or object, paste	Position insertion point and click 📋	Position insertion point and choose Edit, Paste	Position insertion point and press (CTRL)+V
Template, apply	Click ▢ and select template	Choose Format, Apply Design	
Transitions, add	Display presentation in Slide Sorter view, select slide, click the transitional effect drop-down arrow, and select effect	Choose Slide Show, Slide Transition and select a transition from Effect drop-down list	
Underline	Select text and click U	Select text, choose Format, Font, and select Underline	Select text and press (CTRL)+U
Undo	Click ↶	Choose Edit, Undo	Press (CTRL)+Z
Web toolbar	Click 🌐	Choose Help, Microsoft on Web	
WordArt, insert	Click ◢ and double-click format to use	Choose Insert, Picture, WordArt, and double-click the image to insert	
Zoom	Click 41% ▾ and select zoom percentage	Choose View, Zoom, select percentage, and choose OK	

Absolute reference   In Excel, an address you use to reference a specific cell or range of cells in a worksheet; this reference, which doesn't change, is denoted with the dollar sign symbol, as in $A$1.

Action button   The button that enables you to control the slide PowerPoint displays during a slide show.

Active cell   In Excel, the cell in which you can enter data or formulas. You make the cell active by clicking in the cell or by moving to the cell with keystrokes. This cell is outlined with a black border.

Amortization   The process of paying a debt over time by making periodic payments.

Amortization schedule   A schedule of loan payments that includes a breakdown of the principal and interest portions of each periodic payment.

AND condition   A query expression using different criteria in the same criteria row of the Query Design grid. When Access uses the AND operator, only the records that meet the criteria in all the cells will be returned.

Annuity functions   A class of financial functions in Excel that involves payments or investments at regular intervals.

Application title bar   The bar at the top of the window that displays the name of the application and the Minimize, Maximize/Restore, and Close buttons.

Argument   The values an Excel function uses to perform operations or calculations.

Arithmetic operators   The operators you use to perform calculations in formulas and functions: + (addition), − (subtraction), * (multiplication), / (division), % (percent), and ^ (exponentiation).

Ascending order   A sort order in which you arrange data alphabetically from A to Z or numerically from smallest to largest.

AutoComplete   A feature that automatically completes many common words and phrases as you type.

AutoContent Wizard   A PowerPoint feature that helps you build an outline for specific types of presentations by presenting options for you to choose and enabling you to fill in specific pieces of information about the presentation.

AutoCorrect   A feature that automatically corrects many common typographical errors.

AutoCalculate   A feature in Excel that displays a calculation in the status bar when you select a range with values.

AutoFit   An Excel feature that automatically adjusts the column or row to be just wide enough to accommodate the widest or tallest entry.

AutoForm   An Excel feature that you use to create forms using the fields and information stored as part of the table or query.

AutoFormat   A Word feature that provides many different formats for a table and enables you to preview the format before you select it.

AutoLayout   A PowerPoint feature that contains object placeholders.

AutoNumber field   In Access, a field that is set to automatically enter a sequential number as each record is added to the table.

AutoReport   An Access feature you use to create simple report formats using the fields contained in a table or query.

Bold   The style you attach to text to make the font appear heavier so that it stands out.

Border   In Excel, a line that displays on any side of a cell or group of cells. You can use borders to draw rectangles around cells, to create dividers between columns, to create a total line under a column of numbers, and so on. In Word, the top, bottom, left, and right lines you add to draw attention to important text; any of these lines can be displayed or hidden.

Bound control   In Access, a control that is tied to a field in an underlying table or query.

Bulleted list   A list set off with symbols (usually black circles) that precede the text.

Calculated control   In Access, a control that uses an expression as its source of data.

Calculated field   In Access, a field in a query that contains an expression. When you display the results of a calculation in a field, the results aren't actually stored in the underlying table. Instead, Access reruns the calculation each time you run the query so that the results are always based on the most current data in the database.

Cell   The intersection of a column and a row in a worksheet or table.

Center   To align text with equal amounts of white space on each side of the text.

Center tab   A tab that distributes text equally to the left and right of the tab location.

Chart   A visual representation of data in a worksheet.

Chart sub-type   A variation on a Chart type. For example, the column type chart has these sub-types in both 2-D and 3-D: Clustered Column, Stacked Column, and 100% Stacked Column.

Chart Title   The name of the chart. You define this setting in the Chart Options dialog box.

Chart type   A chart that represents data in a specific format, such as columns, a pie, scatter points, etc.

Chart Wizard   A feature you use to create charts. When you create a chart with the Chart Wizard, the Chart Wizard decides how the chart elements will look.

Class   A category of objects used in an Access database. A specific table is an instance of an object from the table class.

Clip art   A graphic provided in a file format such as tif, wpg, bmp, and so on. Office 97 provides many clip art files and stores them in the Clip Art Gallery which is available to all Office 97 programs.

Clipboard   A memory area in which data, text, graphics, and other objects that have been cut or copied is stored.

Column   A vertical block of cells in a worksheet or a table.

Column indicators   The letters associated with the columns on a worksheet or field names in database tables.

Comment   Text that you can attach to cells in a worksheet or text in a Word document or PowerPoint slide to provide additional information.

Compress   To arrange data more tightly so that it will fit on a disk; for example, the Pack and Go Wizard compresses presentations.

Constant   A value that remains unchanged.

Context-sensitive help   Help on the task you're performing provided by the Office Assistant. If the Office Assistant doesn't display the help you want, you can type a question to obtain the desired help.

Control   A specific object, such as a text box, that is added to a form or report in Access.

Controls   Objects on a form or report that display data, perform actions, or decorate the form or report in Access.

ControlTip   A helpful tip that pops up over a control when you move the mouse pointer over the control.

Criteria   In Access, conditions you set in a grid to limit the information displayed in the datasheet.

Currency   A data type that is useful for calculations involving money and for fixed-point calculations in which accuracy is particularly important.

Custom animation   In PowerPoint, the special effects you add to animation settings using the Custom Animation dialog box. The Custom Animation dialog box displays options that also enable you to dim bullet points for animated text as new bullet points display.

Database   A collection of information related to a particular subject or purpose.

Database management system (DBMS)   A computer application used to create and maintain databases.

Database object   The tables, queries, forms, reports, macros, or modules that comprise an Access database.

Data labels   The names you attach to different types of data in a chart. You define this setting in the Chart Options dialog box.

Data range   A block of cells used to create an element in a chart.

Data Source document   In Word, a document that contains the variable information that will be used to "fill in the blanks" in a mail merge document.

Data table   A table containing the data that is used to create a chart.

Datasheet view   In Access, the view in which you can see multiple records on-screen at the same time; this view makes data entry more efficient.

Data type   In Access, the characteristic of a field or a variable that determines what kind of data it holds.

Data validation   In Access, methods for controlling how data is entered into your database. Validation rules and input masks are two useful methods for data validation.

Date/time   A data type that contains date and time values for the years 100 through 9999.

Decimal tab   A type of tab that aligns text on a decimal.

Descending order   A sort order in which you arrange data alphabetically from Z to A or numerically from largest to smallest.

Design modifications   Any enhancements you make to your database objects.

Design view   In Access, the view of a table, query, form, or report object in which you can modify the object's properties.

Detail section   In Access, the part of a form or report that holds the field data controls and pulls information from database tables.

Dim effect   The setting that causes animated text to lighten or dim as new bullet points display on a slide during a slide show.

Document Map   A new Word 97 tool that lists all the document headings, similar to an outline, in a pane on the left. The headings are linked to the document so that you can click a heading and go directly to the text in the document.

Document title bar   The bar at the top of the document window that displays the document title and the Minimize, Maximize/Restore, and Close buttons. If the window is maximized, no document title bar displays and the document buttons display in the menu bar.

Edit   To change the field information contained in a record.

Edit mode   In Excel, the mode in which you edit the contents of a cell.

Endnotes   In Word, notes (comments or references) grouped together at the end of the document. The reference in the text to which the endnote applies is generally numbered, and the endnote displays the same number.

Enter mode   In Excel, the mode in which you enter data in a worksheet.

Error mode   The mode Excel switches to if you make an error when entering data in a cell.

Expand   To create new slides in PowerPoint, using bullet list text from another slide. When you expand a slide, each bulleted list item appears as the title of a new slide.

Expression   A combination of symbols—identifiers, operators, and values—that produces a result.

Expression Builder   A graphical workspace for designing expressions for a specific control object or control.

Field   A field object that represents a column of data with a common data type and a common set of properties.

Field data box   The part of the field control that connects data from a table to a form or report in Access.

Field label   The part of the field control that identifies data in a form or report in Access.

Field properties   A property is an attribute of a field that defines one of its characteristics; an example is the size property of a text field.

Fill   A color or a shade of gray that you apply to the background of a cell or data. Also called *shading* or *patterns*.

Filter   In Access, to select only those records in a table that contain the same value in the selected field.

Find   A feature available using the Find dialog box to locate one or more records displayed in a table or form.

Flip   To turn images so they face the opposite direction vertically or horizontally.

Floating palette   A palette of toolbar buttons that "floats" in the window instead of being displayed as a bar that spans the width of the window.

Font   The type and style of text.

Footer   Text that prints at the bottom of every page.

Footnotes   Comments or references that appear at the bottom of the page. The reference in the text to which the footnote applies is generally numbered, and the footnote displays the same number.

Form   In Access, a database object used to display data from tables or queries in an aesthetically-pleasing format.

Form Header/Footer   In Access, the area of a form in which you supply information such as the form title that you want to display on each screen or printed page.

Form view   In Access, the view which displays records on-screen one at a time in an aesthetically pleasing format.

Formatting toolbar   Contains buttons and controls for formatting. To use the toolbar, click a button to perform a command or view a dialog box.

Formula   A mathematical statement that performs calculations. You create and enter formulas to perform the specific calculations needed.

Formula bar   The area at the top of the window in Excel that displays the cell address and the contents of the active cell. You can use it to enter and edit data and formulas.

Function   A type of formula included in Office 97 that is designed to perform a special calculation.

Graphic   A piece of art that adds interest to a document, slide, report, etc.

Gridlines   In Access, cell borders in Datasheet view used to separate fields of data and records. Also, lines displayed in Form Design View and Report Design View to mark sections of the form or report to help align fields. In Excel, the vertical and horizontal lines in a chart that mark the values.

Grid points   Dots displayed on-screen in Form Design or Report Design view that help you align field controls.

Group   To combine separate graphic or drawn objects into one.

Handles   The squares on the corners and sides of selected placeholders, graphics, drawn objects, or charts that enable you to size the object.

Handouts   Printed versions of your PowerPoint presentation. You can display two, three, or six slides on each printed handout page.

Hard page break   A user-defined page break.

Header   Text that prints at the top of every page.

Hidden slides   Slides that remain part of a presentation but don't display unless you specifically access them.

Hyperlink   Underlined text or a graphic that you use to jump to a location on the Internet or on an intranet, to an object in your database or in another database, or to a document on your computer or on another computer connected by a network.

Image control   A control that is used to display pictures in an object such as a form or report.

Indent   To move lines of text in from the left or right.

Information   Data that is meaningful within a specific context.

Input mask   In Access, a property of a control that you use to make data entry easier and to control the values users can enter into the database.

Insertion point   The blinking, vertical line that marks the current typing position.

IPMT function   An Excel function that returns the interest payment for a given period for an investment based on periodic, constant payments and a continuous interest rate.

Italic   The style you apply to text to make the font appear slanted so that it stands out.

Justify   To change the alignment of text so that it is spread evenly between the margins.

Key field   In Access, a field that contains different (unique) data for each record and that you can use to organize records. You can assign only one key field to each table.

Kiosk   A booth at a convention or shopping mall where you can set up a presentation to run continuously.

Label control   An unbound control used to display descriptive text such as titles, captions, or brief instructions on a form or report.

Layout Preview   The view in which Access displays data from only a few records so that you can check the layout and then make adjustments before printing.

Leader   Characters, such as periods, that appear before the tab. Any type of tab can have a leader.

Left-align   To change the alignment of text so it is on the left margin of the document, cell, placeholder, etc.

Left tab   A tab type that causes text to align on the left.

Legend   The description of elements in a chart. You define this setting in the Chart Options dialog box.

Line spacing   The amount of space between lines of text.

Loan scenario   The principal, interest, and term values used to calculate a loan payment.

Loop   To play back continuously in a slide show or to go back to the first slide after the last slide has played in a never-ending circle.

Macro   A set of one or more actions that each perform a particular operation, such as opening a form or printing a report. Macros can help you automate common tasks.

Mail merging   A process in which you insert text from a file containing a list of information into a form file such as a form letter. The process involves three steps: creating the file that contains the list of information, creating the form, and merging the two files.

Main document   The document, usually a letter, with which you merge the list of names in the Data Source document when you use the mail merge feature.

Margin   The white space around text. The default margins in Word are 1 inch for the top and bottom and 1.25 inches for the left and right.

Master   In PowerPoint, a layout that contains formats for text, bullets, placeholder alignment, headers and footers, and backgrounds.

Memo   A data type used to store random entries exceeding 255 characters.

Menu bar   The bar at the top of the window that provides access to commands used to perform tasks. The menu bar may change, depending on the task you're performing and the program you're using.

Mode indicator   In Excel, a feature displayed on the far left side of the status bar. It shows a word that describes the current working condition of the program.

Module   A collection of Visual Basic programming procedures stored together to customize the Access environment.

Navigate   To move from one record to another in a table or form.

New document   A new blank Word document. Document 1 is automatically opened for you when you open Word.

Newspaper columns   The style of columns in which text flows from one column to the next as columns fill up. Word can create multiple newspaper columns of equal or unequal widths.

Normal view   In Word, the view you use to examine text. Normal view doesn't show the white space for margins or the area on a page that hasn't been used.

Notes Pages view   The PowerPoint view that displays a small slide image at the top of the page and provides space below the image so that you can type notes about the slide contents.

Numbered list   A list set off with numbers, often to indicate a sequence of steps.

Numeric (number)   Data type used to hold numeric data used in mathematical calculations.

Numeric constant   In Excel, numeric data that is entered into a cell of an electronic spreadsheet.

Object   A table, query, form, report, macro, or module in a database.

OLE   Object Linking and Embedding, a way of automating how information is shared among applications.

Office Assistant   The new, on-the-spot Help feature that pops up frequently to offer help on the task you're performing. The Office Assistant enables you to ask questions about the task you want to perform.

Online help   The help provided by the software that is accessible from the computer.

Order of precedence   The sequence in which each operation should be performed when a formula has more than one operation. The order of precedence is as follows: exponentiation, then multiplication or division (from left to right), and finally addition or subtraction (from left to right). If the formula has parentheses, the operation(s) in the parentheses are performed first.

Orientation   The direction in which text prints on a page. Orientation can be Portrait or Landscape.

Outline view   The PowerPoint view that displays the title and body text you add to placeholders in a notebook-like format so that you can review the content of the presentation.

Pack and Go Wizard   A PowerPoint feature that prepares presentations for showing at another location. The Pack and Go Wizard compresses the presentation, making it easier to fit on one disk.

Page break   A break that separates pages of text.

Page Break Preview   In Excel, the view in which you can see where the pages will break when the worksheet prints.

Page Footer   The section of a form that contains any information you want to appear at the bottom of every printed page of a form.

Page Header   The section of a form that contains any information you want to appear at the top of every printed page of a form.

Page Layout view   In Word, the view you use to see margins and unused space as well as a visual page break between pages.

Page setup   Options for margins, orientation, and size of paper used.

Paper size   The size of the paper on which you will print.

Pattern   A color or a shade of gray that you apply to the background of a cell or data. Also called *fill* or *shading*.

Placeholder   A predefined area outlined on a slide for placing text, bulleted lists, and objects such as graphs, tables, and charts.

PMT function   An Excel function that returns the payment on the principal for a given period for an investment based on periodic, constant payments and a constant interest rate.

Point mode   In Excel, the mode in which you're pointing to cells to build a formula or function in a worksheet.

Present value   The total amount that a series of future payments is worth now, calculated using the PV function.

Principal   The amount of money borrowed through a loan.

Print Preview mode   The mode that shows the full page view of the current page of the current worksheet. In this mode you can view additional pages of the worksheet, or you can zoom in on the page so that you can actually read the data, if necessary.

Property   An attribute of an object that defines one of the object's characteristics, such as size, color, or screen location, or an aspect of its behavior, such as whether it is enabled or visible. To change the characteristics of an object, you change the values of its properties.

PV function   An Excel function that returns the present value of an investment. The present value is the total amount that a series of future payments is worth now.

Query   Used to view, change, and analyze data in different ways. You can also use them as the source of records for forms and reports. Query objects contain information that determines how underlying table data is displayed on the screen.

Query datasheet   A window that displays the results of a query in a row and column format.

Query design grid   The lower pane displayed in the query design window containing columns where you define the fields of data the query will display.

Query Design View   A view for queries where you create or modify a query.

Range In Excel, a block of cells selected as a group.

Rate The periodic interest rate used to calculate a loan payment.

Ready mode In Excel, the mode in which the worksheet is ready to receive data or execute a command.

Record A collection of related field data stored in a table, such as a person's name and address.

Record source A table or query that contains records the form displays.

Relational database A database that enables you to store data using a variety of different objects all related to the central theme of the database.

Relational database management system (RDBMS) A database management system (DBMS) specifically designed to utilize the relational database model.

Relationships Connections between fields of tables contained in a database to identify common field data.

Relative reference A worksheet address that Excel automatically changes when a formula is copied to another location.

Replace An option available in the Find dialog box to replace field values.

Report An organized format for summarizing and grouping database data to provide meaningful information in a printed format.

Report Design window A graphical workspace displaying the report's bound and unbound controls.

Report Footer A report section for specifying the information that you want to appear at the end of an Access report.

Report Header A report section for specifying the information that you want to appear at the beginning of an Access report.

Right-align To change the alignment of text so it aligns on the right of the margin, cell, placeholder, etc.

Right tab A tab type that causes text to align on the right.

Rotate To turn or spin objects to create special effects.

Row A horizontal block of cells in a worksheet or table.

Row indicators The numbers associated with the rows on a worksheet.

Ruler The scale that displays the settings for the margins, tabs, and indents. The ruler also can be used to make these settings.

Run In Excel, the procedure used to play back a macro that has been recorded. In Access, the action of applying query specifications to a table to display field information and records.

Scientific notation A number format used for very large numbers and very small decimal numbers. For example, the scientific notation for 1,000,000,000 is 1E+09 which means 1 times 10 to the ninth power.

ScreenTips Short explanations that pop up when you point to any toolbar button, identifying the tasks the buttons perform.

Scroll bars The bars on the side or the bottom of the window that enable you to scroll the screen vertically and horizontally.

Section break In Word, a break that defines a new section in a document. You need to create a new section in a document if you want to use different formats, such as paper size and orientation, or if you want to create different headers and footers for each section.

Select Browse Object button In Word, a button you use to change the navigation buttons.

Select query A query that returns record information in a query datasheet without changing the underlying data.

Selection bar In Word, the white space in the left margin of the document window where you can click to select text.

Shading A color or a shade of gray that you apply to the background of a cell or data. Also called *fill* or *pattern*.

Slide show The display of slides in the presentation window without the PowerPoint toolbars, title bar, and status bar. During a slide show, each slide fills the screen, and you can focus on slide contents.

Slide show shortcut menu A list that displays commands for accessing navigation features as well as for controlling on-screen features such as the mouse pointer and slide meter. To display the slide show shortcut menu, click the right mouse button during the slide show.

Slide Sorter view The PowerPoint view that displays small images (often called *thumbnail images*) of each slide in the presentation so that you can apply and review special and template designs.

Soft page break A break automatically inserted by Word 97 when a page fills up with text.

Sort The action of displaying records in ascending or descending order.

Sort criteria Criteria added to a query or report specifying how the records shall be ordered.

SpellIt The automatic spell-checking feature. When you type a word that isn't in the dictionary, a wavy red line appears. Instead of erasing the word with the Backspace key, you can correct it by selecting the correct spelling from a shortcut menu.

Standard toolbar Contains buttons and controls used to the most common perform commands. To use the toolbar, click a button to perform a command or view a dialog box.

Status bar The bar at the bottom of the program window that displays information about the program and the current file. Instructions for performing selected tasks, active key information, and trouble messages.

Style A collection of format settings that are grouped together and given a name. When you apply a style, the text takes on all the formatting stored in the style.

Syntax A set of rules, like grammar rules, that dictate the structure or order of the elements in a formula.

Tab Preset stop points set on the ruler or with a dialog box used to align text.

Tab key The key on the keyboard you use to indent paragraphs.

Table In Access, the primary object of a database that stores field names, field descriptions, and field data. Tables display multiple records in a row/ column format similar to a spreadsheet layout. In Word, a grouping of columns and rows (like a spreadsheet).

Table Design view The view used to create or modify a table's structure.

Table Design window A window displaying the table design grid.

Tables and Borders toolbar In Word, the tools for drawing a table. When you draw a table, the Tables and Borders toolbar displays automatically. It may appear as a palette.

Table structure The field names, data types, and properties defining the physical arrangement of a table.

Template A professionally developed slide design that you can apply to presentations to give a consistent look to all slides in a presentation. In Word, a predesigned document you can use to create a new document.

Term The amount of time over which a loan is repaid.

Text Text or combinations of text and numbers, as well as numbers that don't require calculations, such as phone numbers. Text fields may contain up to 255 characters of information.

Textbox control A bound control that is used primarily on a form to modify or add field data to an underlying field.

Text preset animation A slide presentation (formerly known as a *build*) in which each slide title displays on-screen by itself and each bulleted list item is presented separately during a slide show. Text preset animations help focus the attention of your audience on each individual bulleted item as you discuss it and removes the distractions of presenting all bulleted points at once.

Timing The set amount of time a slide appears before automatically advancing to the next slide.

Title bar The bar at the top of the program window document or object window that identifies the application name and contains the application icon, Maximize/Restore, Minimize, and Close buttons.

Toolbar A bar that contains buttons for performing commands. To use the toolbar, click a button to perform a command or view a dialog box.

Toolbar grip The vertical lines on the left side of a toolbar that can be used to drag the toolbar to a new location.

Transitions Special effects that appear as your slides go on and off the screen during a slide show.

Unbound control A control on a form or report that is not bound to a specific field.

Underline The rule added under text so that it stands out.

Ungroup To separate a grouped object into its individual pieces so that individual pieces of the object can be changed.

Update In Access, to change the field data contained in a record.

Validation rule A property used to specify requirements for data entered into a record, field, or control.

Validation text A property used to specify the message to be displayed to the user when a validation rule is violated.

Variable A symbol, such as the letter x, that represents an item of data. A variable may change its value within a function or formula.

View The way in which Office 97 programs display presentations, documents, worksheets, and database objects on screen.

Viewer A software program with which you view slide shows.

Visual Basic Visual Basic is the programming language, by Microsoft, that is used in Excel and throughout the Office environment for recording and editing macros.

Wait mode   In Excel, the mode in effect when the worksheet is busy and cannot accept data or commands.

Web toolbar   The toolbar containing buttons for Internet use. To display the Web toolbar, click the Web Toolbar button in the Standard toolbar. To hide the Web toolbar, click the Web Toolbar button again.

Word processing program   A program used to create documents such as memos, letters, envelopes, reports, manuals, and so on.

WordArt   A feature you use to change text into words of art. WordArt enables you to curve, skew, or mold the text into a shape.

Workbook   A file that contains Excel worksheets. By default, a new workbook file has three worksheets.

Worksheet   A page in a workbook file.

Worksheet scroll buttons   The buttons you use on the scroll bar to scroll the tabs for the worksheets.

Worksheet tab   A part of the window that displays the names of worksheets in the current workbook. Clicking a tab displays the worksheet.

X axis   The horizontal axis in a chart. You define this setting in the Chart Options dialog box.

Y axis   The vertical axis in a chart. You define this setting in the Chart Options dialog box.

Yes/no   Yes and No values and fields that contain only one of two values (Yes/No, True/False, or On/Off).

Index

Internet Explorer 4.0 (IE)

Word 97 (WORD)

Excel 97 (EX)

Access 97 (ACC)

PowerPoint 97 (PP)